Designing
Commercial
Interiors

Designing
Commercial
Interiors

SECOND EDITION

Christine M. Piotrowski, ASID, IIDA

Elizabeth A. Rogers, IIDA

BICENTENNIAL
1807
WILEY
2007
BICENTENNIAL

John Wiley & Sons, Inc.

DISCLAIMER

The information and statements herein are believed to be reliable, but are not to be construed as a warranty or representation for which the authors or publishers assume legal responsibility. The advice and strategies contained herein may not be suitable for your situation. This book is sold with the understanding that the publisher and the author are not engaged in rendering professional services. Users should consult with a professional where appropriate. They should undertake sufficient verification and testing and obtain updated information as needed to determine the suitability for their particular purpose of any information or products referred to herein. No warrant of fitness for a particular purpose is made.

All photographs, documents, forms, and other items marked "Figure" are owned by the organization, association, design firm, designer, or author. None of the figures in this book may be reproduced without the expressed written permission of the appropriate copyright holder. A few manufacturers and products are mentioned in this book. Such mention is not intended to imply an endorsement by the authors or the publisher of the mentioned manufacturer or product.

This book is printed on acid-free paper. ♾

Copyright © 2007 by John Wiley & Sons. All rights reserved

Published by John Wiley & Sons, Inc., Hoboken, New Jersey
Published simultaneously in Canada

No part of this publication may be reproduced, stored in a retrieval system, or transmitted in any form or by any means, electronic, mechanical, photocopying, recording, scanning, or otherwise, except as permitted under Section 107 or 108 of the 1976 United States Copyright Act, without either the prior written permission of the Publisher, or authorization through payment of the appropriate per-copy fee to the Copyright Clearance Center, 222 Rosewood Drive, Danvers, MA 01923, (978) 750-8400, fax (978) 646-8600, or on the web at www.copyright.com. Requests to the Publisher for permission should be addressed to the Permissions Department, John Wiley & Sons, Inc., 111 River Street, Hoboken, NJ 07030, (201) 748-6011, fax (201) 748-6008, or online at www.wiley.com/go/permissions.

Limit of Liability/Disclaimer of Warranty: While the Publisher and the author have used their best efforts in preparing this book, they make no representations or warranties with respect to the accuracy or completeness of the contents of this book and specifically disclaim any implied warranties of merchantability or fitness for a particular purpose. No warranty may be created or extended by sales representatives or written sales materials. The advice and strategies contained herein may not be suitable for your situation. You should consult with a professional where appropriate. Neither the Publisher nor the author shall be liable for any loss of profit or any other commercial damages, including but not limited to special, incidental, consequential, or other damages.

For general information about our other products and services, please contact our Customer Care Department within the United States at (800) 762-2974, outside the United States at (317) 572-3993 or fax (317) 572-4002.

Wiley also publishes its books in a variety of electronic formats. Some content that appears in print may not be available in electronic books. For more information about Wiley products, visit our web site at www.wiley.com.

Library of Congress Cataloging-in-Publication Data:
Piotrowski, Christine M., 1947–
Designing commercial interiors / Christine Piotrowski, Elizabeth Rogers. — 2nd ed.
    p.   cm.
Includes bibliographical references and index.
ISBN-13: 978-0-471-72349-3 (cloth)
1. Commercial buildings — Decoration — United States. I. Rogers, Elizabeth A., 1939– II. Title.

NK2195.C65P56   2007
747'.852—dc22

2006102171

Printed in the United States of America
10 9 8 7 6 5 4 3

To my parents, Casmier and Martha,
for watching over me while this was written.
Christine M. Piotrowski

To the Max and Maxine Rogers family.
Elizabeth Rogers

Contents

Preface

It has been gratifying that this book has been so warmly received by students, educators, and professional interior designers. This new edition of *Designing Commercial Interiors* has allowed us to make many changes, adding material and images to enhance its content. The commercial interior design industry has changed, and thus our look at commercial interiors has necessarily been influenced by these changes. Sustainable design continues to grow as a critical issue in commercial interiors, whether that means specifying low-VOC paints or helping a client achieve a high level of LEED certification. Accessibility for an aging population is an ongoing concern that is an absolute necessity in planning any of the facilities covered in this book. Security has become even more important since the tragic events of 2001. These issues are only a few of the changes to the book.

Interior design is still problem solving. Practitioners and students are requested to plan and specify interiors that are aesthetically pleasing, yet with an increasing emphasis on functionality. No designer can solve the client's problems without appreciating the purpose and functions of the business. Understanding the business concerns of the specific commercial facility is essential to help the interior designer make more informed design decisions. Doing research about a facility before beginning to design and plan a project may not be fun, but research and learning the "business of the business" is an indispensable part of successful interior design practice. And herein lays the basic purpose and premise of this book.

The second edition remains a practical reference for many of the design issues related to planning a wide variety of commercial interior facilities. Many new images and graphics have been added to enhance the text. The book now includes information on additional types of commercial interior spaces and thus offers an even broader overview of commercial interior design practice. It retains its focus on the types of commercial design spaces most commonly assigned as studio projects and those typically encountered by the professional interior designer who has limited experience with commercial interior design.

The book is organized similarly to the first edition so that the subject matter can be used by professors in whatever sequences are required for their specific class. Professionals seeking information about specific types of facilities can turn easily to the relevant chapters.

An introductory chapter has been added to provide an overview of the commercial interior design profession. It gives the student a glimpse of what it is like to work in the field and where the jobs are. An important part of this chapter is a discussion of critical issues in commercial interior design today. Topics on sustainable design, designing for security and safety, accessibility, licensing, and ethical behavior are among the topics included in this new chapter.

The three chapters on offices have been completely revised and consolidated into two. The first deals with the functional and operational issues of designing offices, including new material on corporate culture. The second describes the planning and design elements in the design of conventional and open office systems projects. This revision makes these chapters much more user friendly.

The next seven chapters focus on the functions and design concepts of the most common categories of commercial facilities. Each chapter begins with a brief historical overview followed by an explanation of the functional business concerns of the facility. Next is a discussion of the planning and design elements critical for the successful design of such facilities. Detailed design applications are provided to clarify important characteristics in designing these facilities. New design applications discussions in this second edition include hotel spas and recreational facilities, as well as the design of bed and breakfast inns, the design of coffee shops, gift stores and salons, courthouses and courtrooms, and golf clubhouses.

In addition to these new design applications sections is one new chapter on senior living facilities. We have also separated the institutional spaces into two chapters to make the material more manageable. One chapter deals with institutional spaces such as courthouses, libraries, and educational facilities, and the second covers institutional spaces with a more cultural focus such as museums and theaters.

There are several other changes to the second edition. The popular glossary has been expanded to include many new terms. Relevant new references have been added at the end of each chapter in addition to the general references in the Appendix. Along with the books and articles at the end of each chapter are lists of Web sites of organizations and trade magazines that relate to each chapter. An extensive list of trade associations affiliated with the design industry is listed in the Appendix. With these references, students, professionals, and professors can obtain more detailed and specific information about the many different commercial interiors discussed. This combination will make this book an important reference for all readers.

We hope you will find that the additions of text and visuals to the second edition will help make this book an even more valuable resource as you undertake the interior design of commercial facilities. Whether you are a student or a professional, we hope that it will help you enjoy this very exciting and challenging way to make a living!

CHRISTINE M. PIOTROWSKI
ELIZABETH A. ROGERS
2006

Companion Web Site

There are additional discussions related to the overall subject matter of this book on the John Wiley & Sons Web site. A revised discussion of Project Management and new discussions on Restoration and Adaptive Use of commercial facilities can be found at:

www.wiley.com/go/commercialinteriors

We invite you to go to the site for this valuable and interesting companion information.

Acknowledgments

There is never enough opportunity to thank all the people who have contributed their time, expertise, and support to make this second edition a reality. First, we want to thank all those design practitioners and educators who provided suggestions on content and direction over the years that contributed to this second edition.

Many new images and graphics have been incorporated into this book to make it a more visual experience. We especially want to thank all those practitioners, design firms, photographers, publications, public relations directors, and companies that allowed us to reprint photos or other graphics. Space does not allow us to name them individually here, but their names are gratefully provided in captions throughout the book.

Christine would especially like to thank Linda Sorrento, ASID, IIDA, and Andrea Pusey at the USGBC, for reviewing and suggesting material on sustainability. Thank you to Robin Wagner, ASID, who lent her expertise on the design process, and to Corkey Binlinger, ASID, for reviewing the chapter on food and beverage facilities. Christine would also like to thank William Murtagh for offering suggestions on the restoration material. As always, my old-time colleague David Petroff, IIDA, gave me great suggestions on the chapters concerned with office design. And once again, thanks to Bob Krikac, IIDA, Greta Guelich, ASID, and Beth-Harmon Vaughn, FIIDA, for their suggestions.

Although they are not mentioned specifically, Christine also wants to thank all those individuals and companies that provided information and guidance as we prepared the first edition. Thanks again to the folks at Haworth, Inc., Herman Miller, Inc., and Steelcase, Inc., for so much assistance. Christine would also like to thank again those former students at Northern Arizona University who helped instigate this book in the first place, and all those students across the country who every day find out how exciting and challenging commercial interior design practice really is. She also wants to thank her past clients for their challenges in commercial design, which gave inspiration to many years of teaching.

Christine would also like to extend her thanks once again to her family and many friends for understanding the writing process and helping to get her through the final stages.

Elizabeth would like to thank the Lied Public Library for all their help, the Iowa Western Community College computer lab, and the Nodaway Valley Historical Museum for the use of their facilities in researching information for the book.

For their expertise and suggestions regarding information included in the book, Elizabeth would like to thank Dr. John Brady, DVM, Kenneth Caldwell, Dennis Cole, computer specialist, Thompson & Rogers, attorneys-at-law, Denny Sharp, president of FEH, Sunshine Terrace Foundation, and the Marie Eccles Caine Foundation. In addition, she would like to thank once again all the people mentioned in the first edition from Utah State University and others who provided assistance with that edition.

Thanks from Elizabeth to her brother, John Rogers, for his encouragement and professional contributions to the material on the design of courthouses and golf facilities. Thanks to all family members and friends for their continuing support. And a special thanks to Elizabeth's commercial clients, who provided the design experience and background to participate in this project.

Finally, we would both like to give special acknowledgment and thanks to Paul Drougas, Raheli Millman, Lauren La France, and Amanda Miller at John Wiley & Sons for having so much patience, understanding, and encouragement in bringing the second edition to completion.

CHAPTER
1

Introduction

You interact with commercial interiors every day, stopping at a fast-food restaurant for a quick lunch or studying for a test at the library. Perhaps you visit a textile showroom to pick up samples for a project or join a friend at an athletic club to work out. Maybe you pick up your child at a day-care center. All these facilities and many others represent the kinds of interior spaces created by the division of the interior design profession commonly called *commercial interior design*.

Designing *commercial interiors* involves designing the interior of any facility that serves business purposes. Facilities that fall under the category of commercial interior design include businesses that invite the public in, such as those mentioned above. Others restrict public access but are business enterprises such as corporate offices or manufacturing facilities. Commercial interiors are also part of publicly owned facilities such as libraries, courthouses, government offices, and airport terminals, to name a few. Table 1-1 provides additional examples.

TABLE 1-1 Common Specialties and Career Options in Commercial Interior Design

Corporate and Executive Offices

- Professional offices
- Financial institutions
- Law firms
- Stockbrokerage and investment brokerage companies
- Accounting firms
- Real estate firms
- Travel agencies
- Many other types of business offices
- Restoration and renovation of office spaces

Healthcare Facilities

- Hospitals
- Surgery centers
- Psychiatric facilities
- Special care facilities
- Medical and dental office suites
- Assisted and senior living facilities
- Rehabilitation facilities
- Medical labs
- Veterinary clinics

Hospitality and Entertainment Facilities

- Hotels, motels, and resorts
- Restaurants
- Recreational facilities
- Health clubs and spas
- Sports complexes
- Convention centers
- Amusement parks and other parks
- Theaters
- Museums
- Historic sites (restoration)

Retail/Merchandising Facilities

- Department stores
- Malls and shopping centers
- Specialized retail stores
- Showrooms
- Galleries

Institutional Facilities

- Government offices and facilities
- Schools—all levels
- Day-care centers
- Religious facilities
- Prisons

Industrial Facilities

- Manufacturing areas
- Training areas in industrial buildings
- Research and development laboratories

Transportation Facilities/Methods

- Airports
- Bus and train terminals
- Tour ships
- Yachts
- Custom airplanes—corporate
- Recreational vehicles

Other Career Options

- Residential interior design specialties
- Retail sales associate
- Sales representative for manufacturer
- Interior design manager
- Project manager
- Public relations
- Teaching
- Facility planner for corporations
- Computer-aided design (CAD) specialist
- Renderer and model builder
- Product designer
- Specification writer
- Magazine writer
- Marketing specialist
- Museum curator
- Merchandising and exhibit designer
- Graphic designer
- Wayfinding designer
- Lighting designer
- Commercial kitchen designer
- Art consultant
- LEEDs certified designer
- Codes specialist
- Textile designer
- Color consultant
- Set design

There are many other ways to specialize or work in interior design and the built environment industry. Be careful not to create too narrow a specialty, as there may not be sufficient business to support the firm.

These interiors can be as exciting as a restaurant in a resort hotel or as elegant as a jewelry store on Rodeo Drive in Beverly Hills (Figure 1-1). A commercial interior can be purely functional, such as the offices of a major corporation or a small-town travel agency. It may need to provide a comfortable background, as in a healthcare facility. It can also be a place to learn.

Figure 1-1 A fine dining restaurant in a resort. The Inn at Palmetto Bluff, Bluffton, South Carolina. (Interior design by Wilson & Associates, Dallas, TX. Photographer Michael Wilson.)

Commercial interior design was once referred to as *contract design*. In fact, many interior designers still use this term, which developed from interior designers' use of a contract to outline services, fees, and responsibilities related to the project. Until approximately 30 years ago, contracts of this type were used primarily by interior designers working on business facilities. Today, most residential interior designers also use contracts, so the designation is less applicable.

This challenging and exciting profession has had a huge impact on the interior design and construction industry in the United States and throughout the world. *Interior Design* Magazine's reports on the industry's 100 largest design firms stated in January 2006 that approximately $1,610,000,000 was generated by these firms in commercial projects alone in 2005.[1] That's right—1.61 billion dollars. Of course, this represents only a portion of the total commercial interior design industry.

We begin with a brief historical overview of the profession, followed by a discussion of why it is important for the commercial interior designer to understand the business of the client. We then describe what it is like to work in this area of the interior design profession. We conclude with a discussion of important issues concerning the design of commercial interiors—sustainable design, security and safety, licensing, professional competency examination, ethics in the profession, and professional growth. Subsequent chapters provide a detailed look at many functional and design concept issues for the most common categories of commercial facilities.

Table 1-2 presents vocabulary used throughout the chapter.

---

[1]*Interior Design* magazine, January 2006, p. 95.

TABLE 1-2 Chapter Vocabulary

- BUSINESS OF THE BUSINESS: Gaining an understanding of the business goals and purpose of a commercial interior design client before or during execution of the design.
- COMMERCIAL INTERIOR DESIGN: In the interior design profession, the design of any facility that serves business purposes.
- DESIGN-BUILD: One contract is given to a single entity for both the design and construction of the facility (see Box 1-1, p. 10).
- FAST TRACK: Rapid development of projects from conception to completion. Often plans for one part of the project are completed while other parts are under construction.
- FURNITURE, FIXTURES, AND EQUIPMENT (FF&E): All the movable products and other fixtures, finishes, and equipment specified for an interior. Some designers and architects define FF&E as furniture, furnishings, and equipment.

- LEED: Leadership in Energy and Environmental Design. A voluntary certification program of the U.S. Green Building Council (USGBC) that rates buildings that are healthier, profitable, and environmentally responsible.
- "SPEC": Building a building before it has any specific tenants. Developers of commercial property are "speculating" that someone will lease the space before or after construction is completed.
- STAKEHOLDERS: Individuals who have a vested interest in the project, such as members of the design team, the client, the architect, and the vendors.
- SUSTAINABLE DESIGN: Design that is done to meet the present needs of the project while considering the needs of future users. The most widely accepted definition of sustainable design is provided on page 15.

Historical Overview

In this section, we provide a very brief overview of the roots of commercial interior design. Each chapter concerning the design of facilities also includes a brief historical perspective. An in-depth discussion of the history of commercial design is beyond the scope of this book.

One could argue that commercial interior design began when the first trade and food stalls opened somewhere in Mesopotamia or another ancient country. Certainly buildings that housed many commercial transactions or that would be considered commercial facilities today have existed since early human history. For example, business was conducted in the great rooms of the Egyptian pharaohs and the palaces of kings; administrative spaces existed within great cathedrals, and in portions of residences of craftsmen and tradesmen.

The lodging industry dates back many centuries, beginning with simple inns and taverns. Historically, hospitals were first associated with religious groups. During the Crusades of the Middle Ages, the *hospitia*, which provided food, lodging, and medical care to the ill, were located adjacent to monasteries.

In earlier centuries, interior spaces created for the wealthy and powerful were designed by architects. Business places such as inns and shops for the lower classes were most likely "designed" by tradesmen and craftsmen or whoever owned them. Craftsmen and tradesmen influenced early interior design as they created the furniture and architectural treatments of the palaces and other great structures, as well as the dwelliings and other facilities for the lower classes.

As commerce grew, buildings specific to business enterprises such as stores, restaurants, inns, and offices were gradually created or became more common. Consider the monasteries (which also served as places of education) of the 12th century, as well as the mosques and temples of the Middle East and the Orient; the amphitheaters of ancient Greece and Rome; and the Globe Theatre in London built in the 16th century. From the 17th century on, the design of commercial building interiors became increasingly important.[2] For example, offices began to move from the home to a separate location in a business area in the 17th century, numerous bank buildings were constructed in the 18th century, and hotels began taking on their grand size and opulence in the 19th century (Figure 1-2).

---

[2]Tate and Smith, 1986, p. 227.

Figure 1-2 The 19th-century Hotel Kenyon is typical of the period, although not opulent. (Photograph used by permission, Utah State Historical Society. All rights reserved.)

Furniture items and business machines such as typewriters and telephones, as well as other specialized items, were also being designed in the 19th century. Other examples of the emergence of commercial interiors will be presented in other chapters.

The profession of interior decoration—later interior design—is said by many historians to have its roots in the late 19th century. When it began, interior decoration was more closely aligned to the work of various society decorators engaged in residential projects. Elsie de Wolfe (1865–1950) is commonly considered the first professional independent interior decorator. A recent publication on de Wolfe called her "the mother of modern interior decoration."[3] De Wolfe supervised the work required for the interiors she was hired to design. She also was among the first designers, if not the first, to charge for her services.[4] In addition, she was one of the earliest women to be involved in commercial interior design. She designed spaces for the Colony Club in New York City in the early 1900s[5] (Figure 1-3).

Although most of the early commercial interior work was done by architects and their staff members, decorators and designers focusing on commercial interiors emerged in the early 20th century. One woman designer most commonly associated with the beginning of commercial interior design was Dorothy Draper (1889–1969).[6] She started a firm in New York City and, starting in the 1920s, was responsible for the design of hotels, apartment houses, restaurants, and offices. Her namesake firm still exists.

In the 20th century, reinforced concrete, modular construction technologies, and numerous other advances in the building industry changed the appearance of commercial facilities. The early commercial buildings of architects such as Frank Lloyd Wright, Bauhaus architects such as Walter Gropius, and International Style architects such as Le Corbusier, to name just a few, advanced commercial architecture and interior design with contemporary aesthetics. Technology also changed the interior finishing of structures. New products such as bent tubular steel for furniture designed by Mies van der Rohe and Marcel Breuer, molded plywood used by Alvar Aalto and Charles Eames, and the fiberglass designs of Eero Saarinen also

---

[3]Sparke and Owens, 2005, p. 9.
[4]Campbell and Seebohm, 1992, p. 70
[5]Campbell and Seebohm, 1992, p. 17.
[6]Tate and Smith, 1986, p. 322.

Figure 1-3 The Trellis Room at the Colony Club, New York City, designed by Elsie de Wolfe. (Photograph from Elsie de Wolfe, *The House in Good Taste,* New York: The Century Co., 1913.)

changed the interior design of commercial facilities. These are only a few of the achievements and advances in furniture design and interior design made in the early 20th century.

The sweeping open spaces of the Johnson Wax Building in Racine, Wisconsin, designed by Frank Lloyd Wright, were precursors of the open plan designs that emerged in office spaces. Open planning or open landscape, began in 1958 in Germany.[7] That planning concept gradually gained acceptance and caused major rethinking of office planning. New furniture items focusing on the use of panels and individualized components were introduced in the late 1960s, changing office planning and design dramatically (Figure 1-4). Additional discussion of these changes can be found in Chapters 2 and 3.

Commercial interiors changed for many reasons in the second half of the 20th century. Technological changes in construction and mechanical systems, code requirements for safety, and electronic business equipment of every kind have impacted the way business is conducted throughout the world. Consumers of business and institutional services expect and demand better environments as part of the experience of visiting stores, hotels, restaurants, doctors' offices, and schools—everywhere they go to shop or conduct business. Interior design and architecture must keep up with these changes and demands. This is one of the key reasons that an interior designer must be educated in a wide range of subjects and understand the business operations of clients.

The interior design profession also grew in stature in the 20th century with the development of professional associations, professional education, and competency testing. The decorators' clubs that existed in major cities in the 1920s and 1930s were the precursors of the two largest interior design professional associations in the United States. The American Society of Interior Designers (ASID) has over 38,000 members involved in residential and commercial interior design, with chapters located in 48 states and/or cities. The International Interior Design Association (IIDA) has over 10,000 members also involved in residential and commercial interior design, with 30 chapters in the United States and internationally. In Canada, the national association is the Interior Designers of Canada (IDC). It provides a unified voice for the seven provincial associations in Canada to promote educa-

---

[7]Pile, 1978, p. 18.

Figure 1-4 Action Office workstation from the 1960s with the use of panels and individualized components. (Photograph courtesy of Herman Miller, Inc., Zeeland, MI.)

tion and practice in the profession. Members of the IDC must be professional members of their provincial association. There are many smaller specialized professional associations as well. Contact information on several professional associations is presented in the Appendix.

In professional education and testing, the most significant advances occurred in the second half of the 20th century. Many schools have had interior design programs with varying content and quality since the early 20th century. In 1963 the Interior Design Educators Council (IDEC) was organized to advance education in interior design and meet the needs of faculty members in interior design programs. The growth of the profession encouraged many other programs, and in 1970 the Foundation for Interior Design Education Research (FIDER) was incorporated to serve as the primary academic accrediting agency for interior design education. In 2005, the Foundation changed the name of the organization to the Council for Interior Design Accreditation. The National Council for Interior Design Qualification (NCIDQ) was incorporated in 1974 to meet the need for an independent organization to test for competency in the profession.[8] Table 1-3 lists other milestones in the development of professional associations. Contact information and Web site addresses of the organizations mentioned in the preceding discussion are listed in the Appendix.

This overview of the history of commercial interiors is by necessity very brief. The reader who would like more information about the history of commercial interior design can consult one of the references at the end of the chapter.

Understanding the Client's Business

The design of a commercial interior begins with an understanding of the *business of the business*, which refers to understanding the goals and purposes of a business. In fact, it is important to understand the business specialty even before seeking projects in that specialty. When the interior designer and team understand the client's business in general and the client's goals for the project from a business point of view as well as from a design standpoint, solutions are more functional for the client and lead to more creative design concepts.

For example, space planning and product specifications are different for a pediatrician's suite than for the offices of a cardiologist. Planning decisions are different for a

---

[8]The NCIDQ examination is also used as the competency examination in all the provinces of Canada.

TABLE 1-3 Key Milestones for Interior Design Associations

1931	American Institute of Interior Decorators (AIID). The first national professional association for interior decorators.
1936	The American Institute of Interior Decorators changed its name to the American Institute of Decorators (AID).
1957	National Society for Interior Designers (NSID) became the second national professional interior design association.
1961	American Institute of Decorators changed its name to the American Institute of Interior Designers (AID).
1963	Interior Design Educators Council (IDEC) organized to advance the needs of interior design educators.
1969	Institute of Business Designers (IBD) formed primarily for commercial interior designers.
1970	Foundation for Interior Design Education Research (FIDER) organized to advance the academic accreditation of interior design curriculums.
1974	National Council for Interior Design Qualification (NCIDQ) incorporated. It is primarily responsible for development and administration of a qualification examination in interior design.
1975	AID and NSID merged to form the American Society of Interior Designers (ASID).
1982	Alabama became the first state to pass title registration legislation for interior design practice.
1993	United States Green Building Council (USGBC) founded. Promotes research and design of environmentally responsible buildings and interiors.
1994	International Interior Design Association (IIDA) formed by the merger of IBD, the International Society of Interior Designers, and the Institute of Store Planners.

Source: Excerpted from Christine Piotrowski, *Professional Practice for Interior Designers,* Wiley, 2002, p. 13. (Reprinted with permission of John Wiley & Sons, Inc.)

small gift shop in a strip shopping center than for one in a resort hotel. Understanding this from the onset is critical for the design firm.

An obvious advantage of understanding the client's business is that the interior design will be more functional. Businesses seek interior design firms that are not "learning on the job" with the client's project. Of course, creative solutions that are aesthetically pleasing are important to many clients. However, a creative and attractive office that does not work or is not safe is not helpful to the client. Creativity alone does not mean success in commercial interior design.

One issue that influences the interior design of a commercial space is the type of facility: is it a doctor's office suite with exam rooms or a hospital acute care unit? Is it a coffee shop or a high-end, full-service restaurant? Is the project an elementary school or the business college at a university? Is it a bed and breakfast or a convention hotel? Each type of facility has many different requirements. Space planning, furniture specification, materials that can be used, codes that must be adhered to, and the functions and goals of the business are just some of the many factors that influence the interior design based on the type of facility (Figure 1-5).

Location is another issue. Is the project in a small town or an urban area? Will the accounting office be located in a strip shopping center or an office building? Is the restaurant in a stand-alone building or incorporated into a hotel? The impact of the location of the business will relate to the client base the business wants to attract. The dollars spent on the interior may very well be different based on the project's location. Customer expectations will be greater when the business is located in a high-end area.

Another issue is the expected customers of the business. Different design decisions will be made if a restaurant's customers are neighborhood residents, tourists, or business executives. Obvious differences in design and amenities will be made for a hotel along an interstate highway than for a resort hotel in the mountains. Retail stores catering to Gen-

Figure 1-5 Radiology department reception area. Scottsdale Healthcare–Shea, Scottsdale, Arizona. (Interior design by Greta Guelich, ASID, Perceptions Interior Design Group, LLC, Scottsdale, AZ; architecture and engineering by Martin P. Flood, AIA, Architecture + Engineering Solutions, LLC, Phoenix, AZ. Photographer: Mark Boiscliar.)

eration Y will have different detailing and color choices from stores located in retirement communities.

The type of work conducted in a business also varies with the nature of the business. The work done in a coffee shop that only sells coffee products and bakery goods is very different from that of a full-service, high-end restaurant. The display fixtures and ambiance of a jewelry store are significantly different from those of a sporting goods store. Acceptable accommodations for a traveler at a motel along the highway are entirely different from those of the individual who has traveled across the country to attend a professional conference.

Your client is another influencing factor. He or she may be the owner of an accounting office or the neighborhood restaurant or bed and breakfast, or developer, creating office space for anyone or any type of office function. Then again, the owner might be the board of directors and the facility manager for a major corporation's new headquarters or the local jurisdictional governing body, retaining an interior designer for the design of a new county courthouse. Maybe your client is a charitable foundation adding a new wing to a museum. Each client has different goals for the business, and the interior designer is challenged to satisfy all their unique demands.

Obviously, understanding the business of the business and its characteristics is important to understanding how to go about designing the interior. The more you know about the hospitality industry, for example, the more effective your solutions will be for a lodging or food service facility. Gaining experience and knowledge about retailing will be an advantage for you in designing any kind of retail space. In fact, the more you know about any of the specialty areas of commercial interior design, the greater your success in working with those clients.

Subsequent chapters provide an overview of the business of many kinds of commercial interior design specialties. They will help you begin to appreciate the critical issues that a business client will expect you to understand as you become engaged in the project. These chapters will also provide references for many of the design issues related to planning and designing commercial interiors, as well as indicating areas for additional research.

Working in Commercial Interior Design

The design of commercial interiors is complex and challenging. It requires attention to detail, comfort with working effectively as part of a team, and the ability to work with numerous *stakeholders*—individuals who have a vested interest in the project, such as members of the design team, the client, the architect, and vendors. Often the interior designer works with employees of the business rather than the owner. However, design decisions must also please the owner. Regulations must be met that can influence certain decisions and choices about the interior design. The architect, interior designer, contractor, and other stakeholders involved in the design, construction, and installation of products must be sure that the design decisions meet the aesthetic goals of the client and adhere to building, life safety, and accessibility standards and codes that apply to the particular type of facility.

Commercial interior design projects must follow all phases of the design process closely. Missing steps or halfheartedly doing any of the tasks in programming, schematic design, or design development; incomplete preparation of construction documentation; or faulty contract administration can be disastrous. Thus, interior designers working in one of the commercial specialties must be very detail oriented to ensure that all tasks are performed completely and correctly. Margins for error are often nonexistent, as many projects are

BOX 1-1	WHAT IS DESIGN-BUILD?

Most projects in commercial interior design are created in a sequence in which the project is designed by the architect, interior designer, and others. The design is then put out to bid to obtain pricing for the construction and FF&E from other companies, and then it is built. Some projects are built on a fast-track schedule. In a simple example, the layout drawings and specifications for furnishings are completed for a hospital while the hospital is under construction.

In recent years, a new method of constructing commercial buildings and their interiors called *design-build* has emerged and become more popular. In design-build, one contract is given to a single entity for both the design and construction of the building. The single-source contract company has both design and construction staff. It may also be a company with one service offering, such as architecture, that forms a joint venture with firms offering other services.

The Design-Build Institute of America (DBIA), founded in 1993, "predicts that by the year 2010, half of all nonresidential construction in America will be by the design-build method."* Design-build means greater integration of services right from the beginning. Clients see options for the design. After they choose the design, a fixed price can be established at the beginning, reducing the added cost of change orders. Design-build also means greater savings for the client since construction costs and design can be more tightly controlled as the design is developed. Fast-track construction is also more effective since the construction and design are going on in a more coordinated fashion, with responsibility under one roof.

From a business standpoint, design-build is more risky since the design-build firm must assume liability and responsibilities that would otherwise be passed on to separate companies. For example, many architectural and interior design firms that employ an architect may not be able to do design-build projects because they do not have a contractor's license.

Although the risks of design-build are greater from a business standpoint, so are the potential revenue benefits. Clients also like the idea of having only one company responsible since it makes communication easier.

*Beard et al., 2001, p. 24.

Programming

Activities involving researching the client's needs, site restrictions, code regulations, environmental issues, security issues, and economic impacts, among others. This activity often culminates in written design concepts or program statements, reports, and generalized sketched graphic drawings.

Schematic Design

Programming information is synthesized and then converted to preliminary floor plans, elevations, and other orthographic and sketched drawings that seek to explore and explain the design concepts. Codes, building systems, sustainability issues, security issues, mechanical systems, and movable furniture and furnishings are explored and tentatively specified and budgeted.

Design Development

Upon the client's approval of the schematic design plans, the necessary orthographic drawings, furniture layouts, systems plans, and other finalized drawings to assure compliance with applicable building, life safety, and accessibility codes and regulations are developed. FF&E specifications are finalized and budgets are completed. These documents apply applicable/desired sustainability criteria.

Contract Documents

With the client's approval of the design development drawings and documents, interior construction drawings and specifications for all interior non-load-bearing partitions are prepared that are in compliance with applicable building, life safety, and accessibility codes and regulations. Mechanical, electrical, lighting, and security systems are planned in accordance with the designer's legal capacity or coordinated with consultants. If required by the design contract, bid documents and equipment installation drawings are prepared; coordination with potential vendor requirements is assured where special installation may be needed. FF&E specifications are also completed.

Contract Administration

Depending on the jurisdiction, the interior designer can act as an agent for the client in issuing bid documents, qualifying bidders, and administering the bid process. In some areas, the interior designer may be required to hold a contractor's license to supervise installation or provide on-site supervision or coordination of work by vendors. In any case, the interior designer will consult with contractors and vendors and assure that FF&E installation is completed in accordance with plans, specifications, and requirements. Ongoing project management and administration is provided to ensure satisfactory completion of the project through client move-in and postoccupancy assessment.

fast-tracked, where design plans for one phase of the project are created as construction is proceeding on another phase to ensure early occupancy. It is far easier to take care of the details as they arise than to solve problems later on.

Programming is of particular importance and the information obtained at the beginning of the project must be carefully gathered. Information about the client's space and aesthetic preferences is only the beginning. Of course, it is important to understand what codes or other standards may apply to the project. Regardless of the type of facility, the client's business goals and plans are very important in the successful functional design of the interior. Knowing where the business wants to go is as important to the designer as where it is on the day that programming information is obtained. Many large interior design firms offer assistance with strategic planning for businesses that do not already engage in this type of planning. An overview of the stages in the design process is presented in Box 1-2.

Teamwork is also a vital part of commercial projects. Since the projects can be very large, it is difficult for one or two people to handle all the work. Project managers and senior design staff will be in charge of several interior designers and support personnel.

Entry-level and junior members of the staff are often delegated smaller, targeted tasks. However, all the tasks needed to complete these projects are important. Willingness to be part of the team, effectively doing one's job, and offering to be involved are not only important in completing the project but bode well for advancement in the firm.

A critical skill for commercial interior designers is effective communication. Whether one is referring to verbal, written, or design graphics, communicating the designer's concepts and justifications for design ideas is critical. General correspondence and notes that must be forwarded to the client and peers, as well as accurate specifications of the products, are a few examples of written communications that must be accomplished in a professional manner. Interior designers must make numerous verbal presentations to clients, team members, clients, supervisors, and others. Making such presentations effectively and professionally is a crucial skill for interior designers to master. Of course, graphic communications have become easier with the computer. As long as the correct information is inputted, the drawings will be accurate. Skill in computer-aided drafting (CAD) is mandatory in commercial interior design. Accuracy is important to meet codes and regulations.

The interior designer must satisfy several users of the interiors. First is the owner of the property itself. This might be a developer building an office building on *spec* with no particular tenant in mind. The owner of the property might be a corporation building a new corporate headquarters or branch facility or a hotel chain building or remodeling a property. For publicly owned buildings like government offices and schools, the first user to be satisfied is the jurisdictional governmental agency that will actually own the property (Figure 1-6).

A second group of users of a commercial facility is the employees working for the tenants or businesses. Study after study has shown that productivity in offices is related to the design of the office itself. Research shows that if the facility has been designed with a pleasing and safe atmosphere as well as a functional environment, the employees will work more effectively. An exciting interior for a restaurant that brings in large crowds willing to spend on food and drink will bring better-quality wait staff to serve the customers. Unfortunately, the employees don't usually get to "vote" on the design decisions, but they may vote unofficially through their willingness to stay with the company and serve its clients effectively.

Figure 1-6 Government facilities as represented by this county courthouse courtroom interior. (Photograph courtesy of 3D/International.)

A third user is the customer who comes to the facility. In some instances, the ambiance of a restaurant or the beauty of the setting of a resort influences whether a customer returns. In other circumstances, ambiance plays a minimal role in this decision. The relationship of a doctor to a patient is more important than the doctor's exquisitely designed office. If your local city government offices had marble on the walls and floors and gold faucets in the restrooms, as a citizen, you might think that your tax dollars had been overspent. Designing for these various users is challenging, to say the least.

Adherence to building, life safety, and accessibility codes is another critical part of the work of commercial interior designers. The health, life safety, and welfare of the client and the various users of the facility affects many design decisions, including space planning, architectural materials, lighting, furniture and fabric specification, and even the color palette in some situations. There can be no margin for error or fudging of the codes in a commercial project. The user of the facility trusts that the design and specification of the facility are safe in all the ways the jurisdiction requires.

Finally, as mentioned before, the interior designer should know something about the client's business before seeking a commercial interiors project. Understanding the business of the business is crucial to solving the problems and achieving the functional and aesthetic goals of the client. No designer can solve the client's problems without understanding the problems as thoroughly as possible.

Where the Jobs Are

Commercial interior design is a very challenging way to work in the design profession. It is exciting to be part of a team that is responsible for the interior design of any kind of commercial facility. Being involved in the project from its inception and seeing it come together as it is constructed and the various components are installed can be thrilling. Like any career it is also hard work, sometimes involving long hours, certainly working effectively with team members, and perhaps dealing with irate clients. However, few interior designers who have worked in commercial interior design for many years would do anything else.

There are important issues to consider when working in commercial interior design whether you are a student considering entering this part of the profession or a professional considering moving from residential to commercial interior design. This section will cover some key concepts about working in the field.

All but the smallest commercial interior design projects require a team of designers and related professionals. An independent interior designer can design the interior of a medical office suite or a bed and breakfast, a small retail store or other smaller-scale projects. Large projects like building a resort hotel, remodeling a high school, or designing a new county government building require teamwork. In some respects, every project, regardless of its size, is accomplished by the efforts of a team.

Led by a project manager and a senior project designer, the project team may include interior designers at many skill and experience levels. The team may involve architects, lighting designers, engineers, and consultants—perhaps a commercial kitchen designer for a restaurant, for example. Entry-level and mid-level interior designers will assist more senior members of the team in drafting, product and materials research, codes research, and other tasks.

Let us not forget the client and his or her team of decision makers. The project manager and team members must be able to work with the client to reach decisions about many issues as the project moves through its design phases. The project may have several layers of client decision makers. For example, for a hotel, the facility manager, housekeeping manager, security office, banquet manager, food and beverage group, hotel general manager, and the owners or developers will all have a say in the design decisions.

The interior designer and client are only part of the design team. A general contractor and many subcontractors will be hired to do the actual construction work. Vendors who will supply the *furniture, fixtures, and equipment (FF&E)*[9] and materials are selected

---

[9]FF&E can also be defined as furniture, furnishings, and equipment; a designation based on a specific contract document widely used by architects. The authors will use *furniture, fixtures, and equipment* in this text.

through competitive bidding. The design project manager must be prepared to work with these various stakeholders to ensure that the project is completed as designed and specified, on time and on budget.

Exactly what your role will be in the team will depend on what kind of firm you decide to work for. Whether you choose to work for a small interior design firm or seek employment in a large multifaceted firm or an office furnishings dealership is up to you. Each has positives and negatives. A small firm gives entry-level and less experienced interior designers an opportunity to become involved in projects sooner. Perhaps inventorying existing furniture to be used in the remodeling of a law office doesn't seem like design, but it is a way for the entry-level interior designer to gain an understanding of the design considerations for that professional office and become closely involved in the reality of office furniture and equipment.

Small firms rarely have the opportunity to work on glamorous projects like casinos, large resort hotels, flashy new restaurants, or corporate headquarters. The experience gained in the small firm, however, provides the entry-level interior designer with valuable training and skills that can be taken to the firm that gets the glamorous projects—assuming that is a goal.

Another consideration in working for a small firm is that it is healthy and strong as long as the owner keeps up the efforts to market the firms services and obtain new clients. Small firm owners are constantly changing hats from project manager to marketing director, general manager, and interior designer. If new projects stop coming because the owner is busy with design work, then the less experienced professional staff may need to look for other jobs. Constant marketing for new work is a reality of any firm. Even a large firm can lose its focus or be caught in an economic downturn.

If you wish to work for a larger firm, you will definitely need to work well with others and willingly take orders and directions from more senior interior designers. You may also find yourself spending time doing what may seem to be drudge work—taking care of the library, endlessly drafting small project details, and keeping files organized. This is part of the apprenticeship common in larger firms.

Working for a larger firm may bring prestige and more opportunity for internal mentoring. Project managers in larger firms are expected to do more supervision and training of newer staff than the owner of a small firm. This is a great opportunity to learn skills and techniques in such areas as how to deal with clients and other stakeholders, shortcuts in developing schematic and construction drawings, and many other aspects of the profession (Figure 1-7). Larger firms may also be more responsive to your involvement in a professional association and professional educational updating.

For most entry-level designers, the greatest disadvantage of working for a large firm is that they will not be given their own clients for some time. The firm must know what you can do and feel confident about your capabilities in working with clients before you are allowed to manage your own projects. Unless you have worked somewhere else, it may take you two or three years to move up to project responsibility in a large multifaceted interior design or architecture firm.

A third place to work in commercial interior design is an office furnishings dealership. Companies that specialize in offices and feature systems furniture are great places to begin and maintain a career in commercial interior design. The interior designers in such companies focus on large corporate and many kinds of professional offices. The learning and training received here prepare many interior designers to move to an interior design firm that might specialize in hospitality, healthcare, or government facilities.

The opportunities mentioned in this chapter only scratch the surface. There are all types of firms combined with design specialties that create many opportunities for those interested in commercial interior design. Sometimes it is not as glamorous as the work done by colleagues doing private residences. Sometimes the publicity is less frequent. But there is great satisfaction in being a part of the profession making an impact on how consumers of every kind and economic level keep the wheels of industry rolling along!

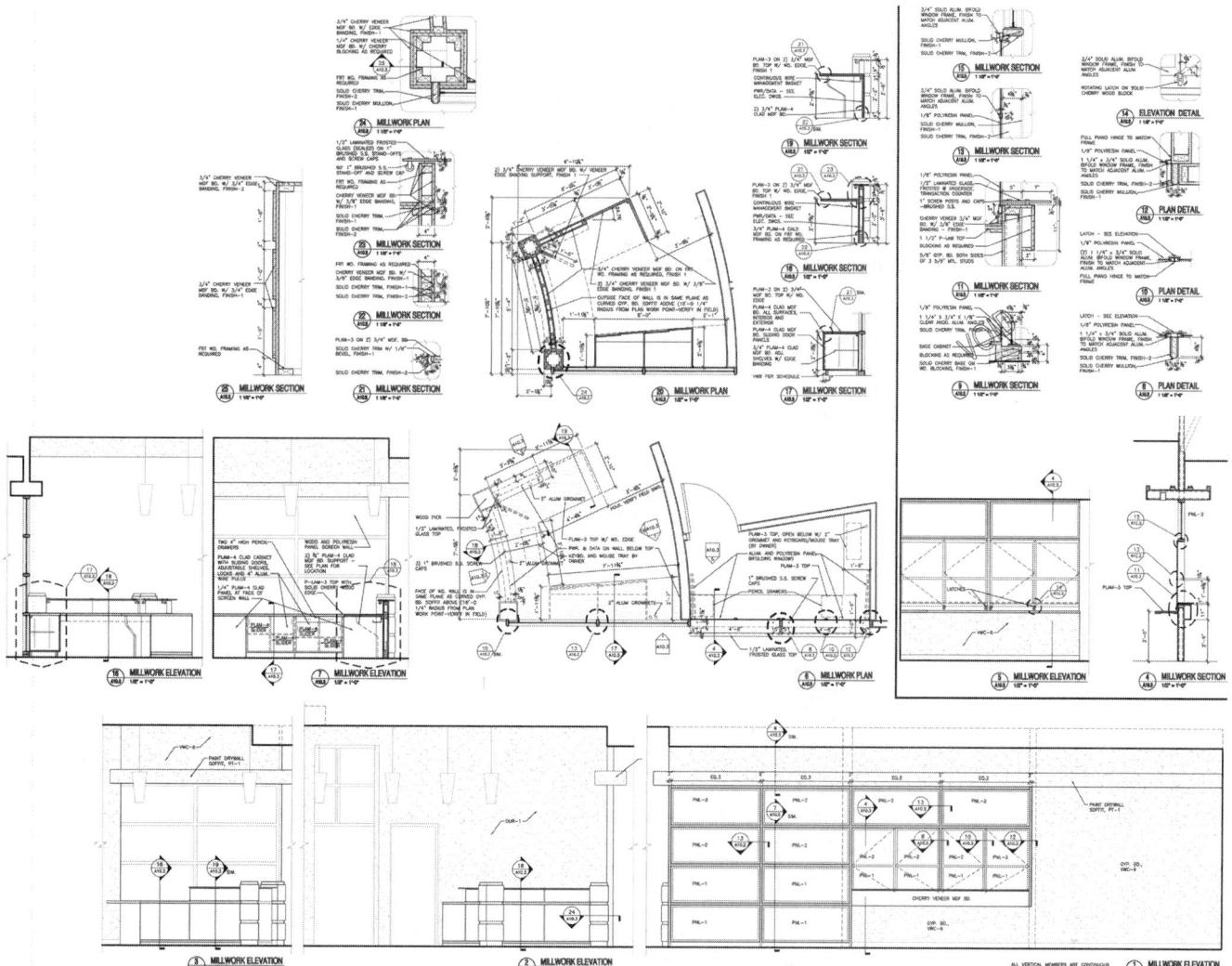

Figure 1-7 These millwork drawings are an example of one of the design documents commonly created by interior designers. (Drawing courtesy of Bialosky + Partners Architectures.)

Critical Issues

This last section looks at several issues that are important, even arguably critical, to what is occurring in the commercial interior design profession in the 21st century. The authors acknowledge that each of the following sections on sustainable design, security and safety, accessibility licensing, professional examination, ethics, and professional development could take up a separate chapter. However, they offer a context to issues that the student or professional seeking employment in commercial interior design should have. Books and articles in the end-of-chapter References section point the reader to further information on these topics.

Sustainable Design

A very important issue facing commercial interior designers in the 21st century is sustainable, environmentally safe design, also commonly called green design. According to the World Commission on Environment and Development, *sustainable design* seeks to "meet the needs of the present without compromising the ability of future generations to

TABLE 1-4 Common Green Terms

- **Cradle-to-cradle:** products that can be reused or recycled, or that will decompose when sent to a landfill.
- **Cradle-to-grave:** products that have not been reused or recycled, or that will be otherwise discarded before their useful life is complete.
- **Energy efficient:** products that use less energy and perform as well as products that are not energy efficient.
- **Graywater:** water from sinks, showers, and laundry that is collected and lightly treated for reuse for watering lawns and other places where potable water is not required.
- **Life cycle assessment (LCA):** analysis of materials, products, and buildings to evaluate their environmental and health impacts over their life.

- **Life cycle costing (LCC):** a method of combining the initial cost of products with the cost of their maintenance, periodic replacement, and residual value.
- **Potable:** water than can be used for drinking and cooking.
- **Renewable energy:** energy sources that are not depleted when used, such as solar energy.
- **Volatile organic compounds (VOCs):** toxic fumes emitted from carpeting, paints, the glues to make the composite woods in furniture, and other common materials or products.

meet their needs."[10] It involves finding a balance between meeting users' immediate needs in constructing a building and finishing its interior while creating as little harm as possible to the environment for future generations. Being sure that the veneer you choose for a desk or cabinet comes from a certifiably sustainable source is a way of utilizing green design. Sustainable design means finding methods and processes of design that consume fewer nonrenewable resources and are more energy efficient. The designer chooses to use materials and products for the interior that are also less damaging to the environment in both their manufacture and their use as finished products. Table 1-4 provides some additional terms interior designers should be familiar with in relation to sustainable design.

Constructing buildings and completing their interiors consumes vast quantities of materials—only some of which are renewable. According to the U.S. Department of Energy in 2003, all buildings in the United States (residential and commercial) consume 40 percent of raw materials and generate more than one-third of municipal solid waste.[11] Other sources report that construction waste accounts for 40 percent of what goes into landfills. In addition, the Environmental Protection Agency (EPA) reports that indoor air quality is on average 2 to 10 times more polluted than outside air. *Volatile organic compounds* (VOCs) are toxic fumes emitted from carpeting, paints, the glues used to make the composite woods in furniture, and many other common materials and products used in commercial and residential interiors. Some are carcinogens; all can cause irritation and allergic reactions in many people. The sealed environment of many office buildings and other types of commercial spaces with poor ventilation means that indoor air can be very harmful due to the products that are specified.

Too often architects, interior designers, clients, and users of buildings and interiors continue to deplete our natural resources in every way imaginable. We continue to add nonrecyclable waste to landfills whenever we demolish and throw away building materials. We specify products that off-gas toxic pollutants, overspecify the lighting in interiors, and design with materials like exotic woods that are not known to come from certified forests. Why? Because too many persons believe that it is easier and cheaper to continue to use nongreen products and construction methods. Comments such as "It costs more to renovate a building than to tear it down and rebuild a new structure" and "Materials from sustainable sources are more generally expensive than those from nonsustainable sources" are used by detractors to downplay sustainable design.

---

[10]World Commission on Environment and Development, 1987, p. 43.
[11]USGBC, 2003, p. 3.

Increased demand on resources by the economies of emerging countries and wasteful practices make sustainability and thinking green critical issues for those in the built environment industry and for consumers. As responsible professionals, we need to think beyond recycling plastics and paper in the office.

Sustainable building design became a prominent part of the architecture and interior design professions in the 1970s. The oil embargo of 1973 forced everyone in the built environment industry and consumers to consider energy usage and efficiency in the design of their projects. Designers began examining solar energy potential in earnest as one way to cut down on our dependency on fossil fuels. In 1977 a cabinet-level Department of Energy was created to deal with energy conservation and usage in the United States. The 1970s also saw the beginning of recycling efforts as a way to deal with overfilled landfills. Earth Day programs help to bring additional attention to the need for sustainable design and energy and resource conservation in many ways.

Environmental concerns continued to impact the attention of those in the built environment industry. In the 1980s, it became more widely known and reported that our buildings were making us sick, so more attention was paid to the interior environment and the products used there. The 1980s and 1990s saw continued and growing research and conferences on environmental issues. The United Nations World Commission on Environment and Development defined sustainable development and provided a major boost to the growing concern for sustainable buildings and green design.

Sustainable building and design have continued to grow through the efforts and support of the architecture and interior design professional associations and the government, along with business and industry. One of the most successful nonprofit organizations is the U.S. Green Building Council (USGBC). Founded in 1993, this organization brings together professionals in architecture and construction, real estate developers, interior designers, product manufacturers, government agencies, and others in or interested in the design-build industry. Today the USGBC works to "promote buildings that are environmentally responsible, profitable and healthy places to live and work."[12]

A very important part of the work of the USGBC is the *LEED® Certification* program. LEED—Leadership in Energy and Environmental Design—is a voluntary green rating system that helps define buildings that are healthy, profitable, and environmentally responsible. LEED Certification validates a building owner's efforts to create a green building. LEED Certification can be obtained for New Construction, Existing Buildings, and Commercial Interiors. LEED Certification will also include certification of Homes, Neighborhood Developments, and Core and Shell projects. Essentially all the types of commercial interiors that are discussed in this book fall under the LEED for Commercial Interiors (LEED-CI) Rating System. Table 1-5 provides a summary of this rating system.

From a business standpoint, the designer may wish to point out the following points from the USGBC to a client related to pursuing LEED-CI ratings:

- "Reduces operating and maintenance costs
- Improves property value
- Enhances occupant health and productivity
- May reduce liabilities related to air quality and other indoor environmental issues"[13]

When a project is reviewed for LEED Certification, it must meet all prerequisites and is awarded points based on five categories of achievement: Sustainable Sites, Water Efficiency, Energy and Atmosphere, Materials and Resources, and Indoor Environmental Quality, with additional points awarded for Innovation and Design Process. Let us look at these categories as they relate to a generic commercial structure, with emphasis on the interior.

The categories of Sustainable Sites, Water Efficiency, and Energy and Atmosphere are not areas of responsibility for most interior design firms. But a few words related to these areas are warranted. The category of Sustainable Sites looks at where the building is built. For example, points are awarded if tenants select a building located in developed areas with existing infrastructure, such as an urban area, rather than farmland or undisturbed

---

[12]USGBC Mission Statement from web page, May 2005.
[13]USGBC, 2004, LEED-CI brochure.

TABLE 1-5　LEED-CI Green Building Rating System

Sustainable Sites

Goals

- Develop only appropriate sites
- Reuse existing buildings and/or sites
- Protect natural and agricultural areas
- Support alternative transportation
- Protect and/or restore natural sites

Water Efficiency

Goals

- Reduce the quantity of water needed for the building
- Reduce municipal water supply and treatment burden

Energy & Atmosphere

Goals

- Establish energy efficiency and system performance
- Optimize energy efficiency
- Encourage renewable and alternative energy sources
- Support ozone protection protocols

Materials & Resources

Goals

- Use materials with less environmental impact
- Reduce and manage waste
- Reduce the amount of materials needed

Indoor Environmental Quality

Goals

- Establish good indoor air quality
- Eliminate, reduce, and manage the sources of indoor pollutants
- Ensure thermal comfort and system controllability
- Provide for occupant connection to the outdoor environment

Innovation & Design Process

Goals

- Recognize projects for innovative building strategies and sustainable building knowledge

Note that there are additional subcriteria to the above.

Source: LEED-CI (brochure), 2004. © U.S. Green Building Council.

greenfields. Points are also awarded if the building site provides priority parking for car pools or van pools, alternate fuel vehicles, or underground parking rather than on-grade parking lots. In the category of Water Efficiency, points are awarded for highly efficient fixtures and equipment such as low-flow faucets and toilets. And in the category of Energy and Atmosphere, the building owner or tenant must meet specific and stringent code requirements related to refrigerants for HVAC systems. These are only a few examples of the ways tenants can be awarded points toward LEED-CI Certification levels.

Of more concern to the interior designer is the rating category Materials and Resources. It is important to use materials that are salvaged, refurbished, or reused. Examples include wood for flooring that might come from a demolished building or using existing furniture moved from a previous location. The project receives points when the design maintains interior nonstructural components such as walls, flooring, and ceiling systems that help to conserve resources and reduce waste. Projects also receive points for diverting construction waste from landfills using strategies such as recycling. As much as possible, interior designers should specify carpets, wall finish materials, and ceiling treatments that are made from low-toxicity or nontoxic materials. The specification of materials that contain recycled content, such as carpet made from recycled plastic bottles, is another way to receive LEED points. Specifying products made from rapidly renewable material such as wool carpet will also earn LEED points. All these things and many others are examples of what can be done in the specification of interior products to help keep a space green.

Indoor Environmental Quality is another important category that is reviewed for LEED Certification. The interior designer can have a significant impact on the space and ensure a healthy, productive environment for the tenant. As much as possible, the designer should specify carpets, wall finish materials, and ceiling treatments that are made from low-emitting materials. Low-VOC paints compliant with LEED standards should be used for painted surfaces. In addition, the interior designer should look for low-toxicity fabrics and foams for upholstered goods.

If smoking is not prohibited (such as in a restaurant), the smoking area must be designed in such a way that the smoke is vented out of the building, not circulated into nonsmoking areas. Rooms within a building designated as smoking areas should be enclosed with impermeable full-height walls and doors, not just with a partition that is open at the top (as is the case in many restaurants and bars), and operated at negative pressure compared to surrounding areas.

Here are a few more important ways for the project to earn LEED points. The interior designer can make sure that sealants and adhesives for the installation of carpeting and wall treatments do not exceed VOC limits. The designer can also avoid specification of furniture items that have used formaldehyde in adhesives. Providing occupants with control over lighting, temperature, and ventilation contributes to LEED points. To varying degrees, this can be done with raised floor systems. Designers who maximize occupants' access to daylight will achieve more points for the project.

The last category is Innovation and Design Process. A project obtains a point for utilizing the services of a LEED Accredited Professional. Projects are also awarded points if the project implements a new technology or strategy that is not covered in the rating system.

Obviously, when the interior designer is involved from the beginning of the project, incorporating LEED guidelines is easier. The designer understands the goals of the project and makes specification and space-planning decisions that are in line with certification guidelines. Ideally, the architect and interior designer are LEED Accredited Professionals. Interior designers who wish to know more about the qualifications and process for becoming LEED accredited should contact the USGBC at the Web site address at the end of the chapter.

Another factor in designing and selling green buildings to clients is economics. Most complaints from clients who do not want to go green focus on this issue. They have heard about the extra expense of using low-VOC paint or building a section of the restaurant for smoking with a separate ventilation system and move away from green design. However, recent projects have proven that green design and sustainable building do not have to be more expensive. While some projects have a slight increase in up-front costs, green buildings provide significant cost savings in the long term due to increased energy and water efficiency and improved employee performance. Efficient and thoughtful design from the very beginning of a project can guide the design team to many cost-effective decisions that add to LEED Certification.

One economic technique that can be incorporated into planning for a green or sustainable project is *life cycle assessment* (LCA), which analyzes materials, finished products, and buildings to evaluate their environmental and health impacts over their life. This environmental assessment can begin at the time raw materials for a specific product are obtained and continue through its manufacture into a final product, its installation in a building, and its eventual disposal. For a client who is committed to having a truly green facility, LCA of the products and materials is critical. LCA measures overall "environmental performance of a product over its full life cycle, often referred to as 'cradle-to-grave' or 'cradle-to-cradle analysis.'"[14]

Products that can be reused or recycled or that will decompose when sent to a landfill are considered *cradle-to-cradle* products. An example would be solid wood flooring that can be reused in another project, packaging used to ship recycled goods, and any kind of material that is completely biodegradable. A product that is used and is not reused, recycled, or otherwise discarded before its useful life is complete is considered a *cradle-to-grave* product in green design terms. Carpeting that is removed because of an aesthetic change to the interior and is taken to the landfill is a common example. Another example is the shipping cardboard that goes to a landfill rather than a recycling plant. Clearly, cradle-to-cradle products are considered greener than cradle-to-grave products.

Another economic technique that is used in relation to sustainable design is *life cycle costing* (LCC), which combines the actual cost of the product with the cost of its maintenance,

---

[14]Kibert, 2005, p. 285.

periodic replacement, and residual value. Everything, of course, has an initial cost. If carpet tiles are specified rather than broadloom carpet, for example, damaged tiles can easily be replaced. By contrast, if broadloom carpet is damaged, the entire room might have to be recarpeted. Of course, the economic benefits of LCC will affect long-term owners of the building rather than tenants.

According to green design experts, a project that has utilized sustainable design methodologies and products can also be more valuable to an owner. Maintenance costs will be lower; safer indoor air quality will result in fewer employee absences; and the natural quality of many products used in a green building is often more pleasing and attractive, creating an environment that both employees and guests will appreciate.

Energy conservation impacts the work of the interior designer, regardless of the type of commercial space that is being designed. According to the Department of Energy, buildings consume 68 percent of all electricity.[15] One of the largest energy users in commercial spaces is lighting. Many states have mandated low-watt lamps and lighting specification with maximum watts per square foot to help reduce electrical energy use. A few considerations in lighting design that can be applied to many types of commercial spaces are offered here. Other lighting design techniques are provided in each chapter's sections on Planning and Interior Design Elements and Design Applications.

Low-watt, high-output fluorescent lamps used in place of incandescent lamps also produce energy savings. A larger portion of the energy used by incandescent lamps is released as heat, adding to the burden of the HVAC system. Designs that utilize as much daylighting as possible reduce the amount of energy consumed by artificial lighting. Of course, in some areas, extensive use of windows for daylighting can cause energy loss due to heat gain through the windows. In those cases, the design team should specify low-E, high-performance window glazing. In many commercial projects, sensors that turn lights on and off when someone enters or exits a space such as a conference room or classroom can help reduce energy consumption. Designs that combine ambient and task lighting can also enhance energy efficiency, regardless of the use of most spaces. "By providing a variety of independent task lights in interiors, the designer can achieve the most important goal: good illumination where it is needed and no waste of energy where it is unnecessary."[16]

The interior designer can also increase energy efficiency by specifying energy-efficient equipment. Appliances like refrigerators and stoves in employee cafeterias and electronic equipment like computers and printers that have received the Energy Star designation save energy. Low-flow faucets in showers and toilet rooms in hotels save energy by reducing the hot water used.

These are just a few ways that the interior designer can help to bring energy efficiency to commercial interiors. As part of the design team, the interior designer should encourage the architect and client to utilize as many energy-efficient and sustainable design products and construction methods as possible.

As the reader can see, sustainable design can be incorporated into all types of commercial projects using thoughtful space planning and careful specification of products. Consider these examples: the odor of new carpet does not exist in the new medical office suite; wood table tops in a restaurant substitute for the off-gassing of plastic laminates and composite wood tops; offices move full-height walls to the center of the space, allowing daylight to penetrate into the office footprint[17]; and low-water-usage water closets are specified in sports arenas.

This brief overview of sustainable design has been provided to raise awareness of the importance of green design in commercial interiors. There are several works in the References that you may wish to read to gain further information on this important planning and designing practice for the 21st century. The works listed in the References are only a few of the materials available on sustainable design.

---

[15]USGBC, 2003, p. 3.
[16]Pilatowicz, 1995, p. 58.
[17]The *footprint* is the perimeter of the building or project space plus any core partitions.

Security and Safety

Owners, developers, and tenants of every type of commercial facility are concerned about the security and safety of their employees, clients, and visitors. The tragic events of September 11, 2001, heightened the importance and awareness of making buildings safe. Stories about workplace shootings, harm to customers and employees in retail settings, school violence, and theft of personal information are regularly reported. Customers and employees expect to be safe in public and business environments. Clients are asking design teams to plan for better security and safety in all types of commercial facilities.

Common security and safety issues include protection of employees and customers, life safety, burglary, employee pilferage, vandalism, theft of company records, and protection of company property such as intellectual property. The threats can come from many sources, and the issues vary with the type of business. In a retail store, theft of merchandise is a big security issue. In hospitals and medical office suites, theft of controlled substances creates design challenges. In offices, unauthorized visitors can cause a variety of security problems. Guests at hotels want to feel safe in their rooms and while walking the grounds. Individuals want to feel safe exiting auditoriums and theaters. Many professional offices have huge amounts of personal customer information stored on computers, the theft of which can cause enormous harm for the business and customers. Government buildings face threats of terrorism.

The easiest way for interior designers to meet their responsibilities related to security and safety in the commercial projects they design is to adhere strictly to applicable building and life safety codes. Model building codes, notably the International Building Code (IBC) in the United States and the National Building Code (NBC) in Canada[18] standardize construction standards and provide limited mechanical systems, accessibility, and interior finishing standards. In addition to the building codes are the Life Safety Code published by the National Fire Protection Association (NFPA), which provides standards for fire and life safety but not building construction. Separate mechanical codes such as the National Electrical Code and the National Plumbing Code provide regulations for these systems. The local jurisdiction may have additional regulations. For example, some jurisdictions have stronger design standards for earthquake protection in all types of facilities. Food service facilities and hospitals, to name just two, have various health department regulations that can impact the interior design of a facility.

However, there is no model code for security planning and design. Issues of security can be found in building codes and local jurisdictional codes. Yet, most security plans and solutions are derived from discussions with the business owner, security experts, and vendors who supply products like card-access entry locks, security cameras, and blastproof glass.

When it comes to safety issues for the protection of those whom S. C. Reznikoff calls the "captive consumer"[19]—workers and users of a commercial facility—planning and specification decisions based on strict adherence to building and life safety and fire safety codes are critical. Arrangement of exits, sizes of exit access corridors, planning for places of refuge, specifying architectural materials with low smoke propagation or flame resistance, and many other life safety issues are mandatory design fundamentals.

Interior designers must become aware of security options for their clients' facilities. "Good security involves physical as well as electronic barriers. The physical layout and construction of a space can have a profound effect on fundamental security as well as on how easy or difficult it is to plan and install monitoring and access devices."[20] Many businesses want a security system that protects but is not visible but transparent. Visible layers of security can create unnecessary anxiety in employees, customers, or other users of the facilities. Security can be transparent by providing clear sight lines to entrances from reception counters or other areas in lobbies and waiting rooms. Bullet-resistant glass in windows in some types of medical facilities and financial institutions is another way to add

---

[18]British Columbia has its own model code.
[19]Reznikoff, 1989, p. 14.
[20]Ballast, 2002, p. 312.

subtle but effective security in design. When the project is more complex, requiring an extensive security program, the interior designer will work with the architect and a security consulting firm along with the client to make security plans.

Security issues need to be addressed in programming so that the interior designer knows what level of security is needed for the facility and can make necessary adjustments in space planning and specifications to address security needs. Many projects will need solutions such as card access to hotel rooms, electronic security devices at entrances to retail stores, and buzzer access from a doctor's waiting room to the exam rooms, to mention a few. Security cameras are used to monitor not only the entrances of many buildings, but also stores, banks, schools, and many other facilities that may be considered high risk.

Lighting is a major way to increase occupants' feelings of security and safety. Appropriate lighting design eliminates dark or hazardous areas in interiors. Good lighting means that occupants feel safe since they can see where they are and where they are going—as well as who might also be in the area.

A thorough discussion of security design concepts is beyond the scope of this book. This information is provided to make the student aware that security issues can impact the interior design of many commercial facilities. Remember that each type of commercial facility has distinctive safety and security issues. Interior designers must become knowledgeable about how to best provide safety and security for their clients and the clients' customers. These systems are no longer a choice. They have become, unfortunately in our free society, mandatory.

Accessibility

By now the reader is no doubt familiar with the Americans with Disabilities Act (ADA) and the guidelines that were established in the 1990s to make public buildings more easily accessible for individuals with many disabilities. As of this writing, revised guidelines are being reviewed by various agencies and enforcement is expected to begin—well, whenever numerous government agencies have completed their review and the new guidelines find their way into state and local codes. These guidelines have been modernized to reflect changes in technology, building codes, and users' needs.

As the baby boom generation ages, becoming 60 years old as of 2006, the need to continue to keep buildings accessible for all people has become critical. Interior designers and others in the design-build industry should not consider the design guidelines as impediments to good and creative design. The guidelines should always be viewed as a means to ensure that everyone can enjoy using those creatively designed buildings and interiors.

The new guidelines are expected to simplify many of the compliance requirements. This simplification will help designers do a better job of making commercial public buildings more accessible. It will also help determine whether spaces are not accessible when they should be. Spaces that were very restrictive in their design or lacked easy-to-apply standards will now be simpler to design.

In the meantime, this book provides numerous comments in sections of the chapters concerning accessibility guidelines in public commercial interiors. Although references and comments are primarily based on the ADA guidelines, the term *accessibility* has been used rather than *ADA* in most cases, since a jurisdiction may have design guidelines in place of or in addition to those of the ADA.

Every time you as a healthy individual use the ramp instead of the stairs, sneak into the larger accessible toilet stall, or use the "star" to recognize the lobby button on an elevator, think of the person with a disability who cries for joy when these simple accommodations are available. Then be sure that you have checked and rechecked your floor plans and specifications to ensure complete compliance in providing accessible and simple accommodations for your commercial interiors projects.

Licensing and Registration

The licensing of interior design professionals remains an important though sometimes contentious issue. Interior designers have sought to be licensed since the 1950s. The first state

TABLE 1-6 Interior Design Licensing Terminology

- **Building permitting privileges:** A jurisdiction's granting a design professional the right to submit his or her construction drawings to a building code official to obtain a building permit for the project.
- **Grandfather clause:** A provision in the legislation that allows individuals working in the profession or using a protected title (*interior designer,* for example) prior to enactment of the legislation to meet standards that are now higher than those they previously required. For example, a jurisdiction may require the person to pass the NCIDQ examination. The grandfather clause may allow those who have been practicing but have never taken this exam to continue to use the title *interior designer* without taking the exam.

- **Sunset:** Legislation written to include automatic termination of the program or law unless it is reauthorized by the jurisdiction's legislature.
- **Title act:** Legislation that limits the use of a specific title, such as *interior designer, certified interior designer,* or *registered interior designer,* to those who meet the requirements established by the jurisdiction. Title acts do not require the designer to become licensed to practice interior design and do not prohibit nonregistered individuals from providing interior design services.
- **Practice act:** Acts that limit who may engage in or practice a profession; legislation that strictly limits who may provide interior design services in any manner as those services are defined by the jurisdiction.

to pass legislation to license or register interior design professionals was Alabama in 1982. As of 2006, more than half of the states have some form of licensing, certification, or registration legislation that defines who may practice interior design or use the title *interior designer.* Other states continue to seek regulation of the work of the interior design profession. Table 1-6 provides terminology related to licensing or registration of interior design professionals.

Why is this important? The profession has become increasingly complicated, and responsibility for what is done to a commercial or residential interior to meet standards of safety is more complex than it was even 30 years ago. Interior designers are held responsible for providing safe environments for their clients and the users of commercial (and residential) interiors. Technology in the construction of interiors continues to evolve and become more complex. Building and life safety codes demand critical decisions concerning space planning and product specification to ensure the safety and health of occupants of commercial interiors. Sustainable design knowledge and criteria are necessary to reduce the harm to our environment and to avoid harming continuous users of commercial spaces. Security issues will continue to impact the interior design of all types of commercial facilities. These are critical issues for any interior designer who requires greater accountability.

Licensing or registration ensures consumers that the interior designers they hire for their commercial projects have the education, experience, and competence to provide interior design services. Jurisdictions that have legislation concerning the practice of interior design require intensive educational preparation related to the knowledge base and skill sets required during the phases of a design project. They also require passage of a competency examination whose minimum requirements to sit for the examination focus on education in interior design and work experience.

Licensing or registration legislation in a jurisdiction may also require the designer to keep up-to-date in the profession by mandating a specific number of hours and types of continuing education seminars, workshops, or classes. Continuing education offerings are commonly developed based on a specific number of clock hours, not semester-long classes, as in a formal academic setting. In many jurisdictions, the majority of the hours of continuing education must focus on topics concerning the health, life safety, and welfare of the consumer.

Professional Competency Examination

Competency examination of interior designers has been discussed by professional associations and educators since at least the 1950s. An examination was developed in the 1960s by the professional association that later became ASID. Today, the examination that is required in all jurisdictions that have any type of legislation is the National Council for Interior Design Qualification (NCIDQ) examination. Passing the NCIDQ exam is also a requirement of ASID, IIDA, IDC, IDEC, and Canadian provincial associations for members to be recognized at the highest professional level of their association.

All professions require an examination to test minimum competency related to any type of licensure or registration. In fact, an examination of competency is a criterion of any profession. Interior designers should place the goal of passing the NCIDQ exam at the top of their list, whether or not their jurisdiction requires it or whether or not they wish to be professional members of an association. Passage of the NCIDQ examination shows clients that the interior designer has the education, experience, knowledge, and skills sets required by the profession today. It is a personal achievement that interior designers should willingly pursue.

The NCIDQ examination tests the general knowledge and skills of the minimally competent interior designer who has achieved educational preparation and work experience over approximately six years.[21] The six-part examination, given over two days, tests through multiple-choice questions and various design practicum tasks the full range of knowledge and skills that a minimally competent interior designer should have.

Passing the NCIDQ examination provides the interior designer a certificate indicating successful completion of the examination. NCIDQ is not a member organization like ASID or IDC, and "NCIDQ" cannot be used as an appellation. The NCIDQ certificate is a practice credential indicating an individual's demonstrated competence in the knowledge and skills required of today's professional interior designer.

Information about the exam and the other services that the NCIDQ offers is available on their Web site or by calling their office. The Web site for NCIDQ is listed at the end of this chapter.

Ethical Behavior

Ethical behavior and ethical standards have been common themes in the news media in recent years. Corporate executives, government employees, and the media have come under scrutiny regarding how they do their jobs, what they say, or how they interact with their constituencies. Perhaps you might feel that ethics does not apply to the work of an interior designer. However, you would be mistaken.

Ethical standards and a code of ethics are part of one's application to a professional association. *Ethical behavior* in interior design means conducting oneself in a manner that is considered right by and for those practicing the interior design profession. Ethical standards have been established by the professional associations and serve as a guide to those who choose to affiliate with an association. Ethical standards might also be in some way a part of licensing/registration qualifications.

How an interior designer interacts with clients, vendors, contractors, and other designers is affected by adherence to ethical standards. For example, if a client comes to you with a set of drawings for a gift shop and then asks you to redesign the shop and sell the products to the client, interior design ethical standards require you to ask questions and conduct yourself in certain ways. Is the client still under contract to the other design firm? That is the important question in this example. Suppose that you have agreed to design and procure products for a medical office suite for a specific contracted price. However, when you come back with your drawings and specifications, your price is now far above that original budget and your design has ignored goals stated by the client. In this case, you have not met the ethical obligation to work in the best interest of the client.

If you join a professional association, you will be expected to conduct yourself and your business in accordance with the ethical standards of the association.[22] Conversely, the fact that an interior designer is not a member of an association does not give him or

---

[21]The current specific hours of education and work experience requirements can be obtained from NCIDQ.
[22]A code of ethics can be obtained from any of the professional associations by contacting their headquarters or chapter offices.

her free rein to behave unethically. Unethical behavior and business conduct of one designer can tarnish the reputation of everyone in the profession. Clients become leery of working with interior designers.

Ethical behavior is not hard, it is not overly time-consuming, and it is not inconvenient. Conducting oneself in an ethical manner is simply one more standard for judging oneself as a professional and allowing the consumer to see the value the interior designer places on his or her obligations to clients and the profession. We expect the professionals in law, accountancy, medicine, and real estate, for example, to behave ethically when we deal with them as clients and patients. They too should expect ethical behavior from the interior designers they hire to design their offices, medical suites, hotel rooms, stores, and myriad other commercial spaces. Ethical behavior is a responsibility of all interior designers as just one more way to improve the professional image and standing of interior design.

Professional Growth

Obtaining an education in interior design, taking the professional competency examination, and completing other requirements toward licensure or registration are all important milestones in the professional growth of a commercial interior designer. Many designers also become members of a professional association such as ASID, IIDA, or IDC.

Professional associations provide many benefits to members that enhance professional growth. Networking opportunities at local chapter meetings help to broaden an interior designer's contacts in the industry. Attendance at national meetings moves that networking opportunity to a national and even an international level. However, the old saying that you get back what you put in is important.

Certainly join a professional association for its newsletters, member meetings, benefits such as insurance programs, and many other reasons. But also join to become active by volunteering for a committee. Here the young interior designer in particular gains greater insights into group dynamics and leadership characteristics. Interior designers at any level gain valuable experience and have fun while helping to organize chapter events and programs. Later on, election to a chapter's board or office enlarges a designer's skills and knowledge through the training that is offered for board members. Officers expand their network of contacts and friends through training conducted for chapter officers by association national offices. Active participation in an association is a great way to gain confidence in speaking and writing—important communication skills for any interior designer.

Another way to gain professional growth is through continuing education. Education does not stop when one receives a diploma at the end of an interior design program. Professionals should seek additional information at seminars, workshops, and training programs that offer *continuing education unit (CEU)* credit. In fact, many jurisdictions with licensing or registration legislation require CEU credits to maintain the license or registration. Professional associations may also require, but in any case highly recommend continuing education for their members.

Continuing education seminars provide up-to-date information on a wide variety of topics in the profession. These seminars and workshops are short, most taking one day or less. Some are even available online or by correspondence so that the busy professional can obtain continuing education even with a busy work schedule.

Successful professionals find numerous ways to continue to grow and add value to the work they produce. That added value will come back to the interior designer in a variety of positive ways!

Summary

Working in commercial interior design—regardless of the specialty—is exciting. The opportunity to design highly creative interiors may not come often to everyone; however, the possibility is always on the horizon. The opportunity to help client firms become more effective businesses is also satisfying. Think of how wonderful it would feel to be involved in the design of corporate offices for a major corporation in Manhattan or a new pediatrics wing for a hospital. One day, maybe you will be the project manager for a new mega resort/casino or a bed and breakfast that continually wins hospitality industry awards. Of course, your design for a small accounting office or a neighborhood restaurant is also important. The opportunities in commercial interior design are endless.

This chapter has provided a snapshot of what it is like to work in commercial interior design. A brief historical overview revealed the roots of this branch of the profession. The chapter then discussed the importance of understanding a client's business, which is critical to the successful interior designer in a commercial specialty. The work environments of commercial interior design and the challenges of the field were also considered. The chapter concluded with a brief examination of some issues critical to the profession in the 21st century.

Chapters 2 through 10 provide information on important functional and design criteria for key types of commercial interior design specialties. Each chapter will help you understand the nature of the business of the business, as well as provide a foundation for design decisions.

REFERENCES

Abercrombie, Stanley. December 1999. "Design Revolution: 100 Years That Changed Our World." *Interior Design Magazine*, pp. 140–199.

Allen, Edward and Joseph Iano. 2004. *Fundamentals of Building Construction*, 4th ed. Hoboken, NJ: Wiley.

American Society of Interior Designers (ASID). 2003. "Green Design." *ASID ICON*. May. Several articles in this issue.

Applebaum, David and Sarah Verone Lawton, eds. 1990. *Ethics and the Professions*. Englewood Cliffs, NJ: Prentice-Hall.

Ballast, David Kent. 2002. *Interior Construction and Detailing*, 2nd ed. Belmont, CA: Professional Publications.

Baraban, Regina and Joseph F. Durocher. 2001. *Successful Restaurant Design*, 2nd ed. New York: Wiley.

Beard, Jeffrey L., Michael C. Loulakis, and Edward C. Wundram. 2001. *Design-build: Planning through Development*. New York: McGraw-Hill.

Berger, C. Jaye. 1994. *Interior Design Law & Business Practices*. New York: Wiley.

Blakemore, Robbie G. 1997. *History of Interior Design & Furniture: From Ancient Egypt to Nineteenth-Century Europe*. New York: Wiley.

Campbell, Nina and Caroline Seebohm. 1992. *Elsie de Wolfe: A Decorative Life*. New York: Clarkson N. Potter.

Cassidy, Robert. 2003. "White Paper on Sustainability." *Building Design & Construction Magazine*. November. Supplement.

Clay, Rebecca A. 2003. "Softening the Fear Factor." *ASID ICON*. August, pp. 10–12.

———. Spring 2005. "Integrating Security & Design." *ASID ICON*, 36–41.

Coleman, Cindy and Frankel + Coleman, eds. 2000. *Design Ecology. The Project: Assessing the Future of Green Design.* A brochure published by the International Interior Design Association, Chicago.

Demkin, Joseph A., ed., and the American Institute of Architects. 2003. *Security Planning and Design: A Guide for Architects and Building Design Professionals*. New York: Wiley.

Earth Pledge. 2000. *Sustainable Architecture White Papers*. New York: Earth Pledge (various authors, no individual editor listed).

Farren, Carol E. 1999. *Planning and Managing Interior Projects*, 2nd ed. Kingston, MA: R. S. Means.

Flynn, Kevin. "LEED and the Design Professional." *Implications*. InformeDesign. Vol. 02, Issue 09.

Gueft, Olga. 1980. "The Past as Prologue: The First 50 Years. 1931–1981: An Overview." *American Society of Interior Designers Annual Report 1980*. New York: ASID.

Gura, Judith B. Fall 1999. "Timeline to the Millennium." *Echoes Magazine* (special edition).

Herman Miller, Inc. 1996. "Herman Miller Is Built on Its People, Values, Research, and Designs." News Release. December 15. Zeeland, MI: Herman Miller, Inc.

———. 2001. "Companies Go Green." Brochure. Zeeland, MI: Herman Miller, Inc.

Interior Design. 2006. "The Top 100 Giants." January, pp. 95+.

Jones, Carol. 1999. "Defining a Profession: Some Things Never Change." *Interiors & Sources Magazine*. September.

Kibert, Charles J. 2005. *Sustainable Construction*. Hoboken, NJ: Wiley.

Klein, Judy Graf. 1982. *The Office Book*. New York: Facts on File.

Long, Deborah H. 2000. *Ethics and the Design Professions*. Monograph. Washington, DC: NCIDQ.

Malkin, Jain. 2002. *Medical and Dental Space Planning*, 3rd ed. New York: Wiley.

McDonough, William and Michael Braungart. 2003. "Redefining Green." *Perspective*. Spring, pp. 20–25.

———. 2005. "Making Sustainabilty Work." *EnvironDesign Journal*. Spring, pp. 34–38.

Mendler, Sandra F. and William Odell. 2000. *The HOK Guidebook to Sustainable Design*. New York: Wiley.

Nadel, Barbara A. 2004. *Building Security: Handbook for Architectural Planning and Design*. New York: McGraw-Hill.

National Park Service. 1994. "Guiding Principals of Sustainable Design." Available at www.nps.gov/dsc/dsgncnstr/gpsd/ch1.html

Null, Roberta with Kenneth F. Cherry. 1998. *Universal Design*. Belmont, CA: Professional Publications.

Pilatowicz, Grazyna. 1995. *Econ-Interiors*. New York: Wiley.

Pile, John. 1978. *Open Office Planning*. New York: Watson-Guptill.

———. 2003. *Interior Design*, 3rd ed. Upper Saddle River, NJ: Pearsen/Prentice-Hall.

———. 2005. *A History of Interior Design*. New York: Wiley.

Piotrowski, Christine. 2002. *Professional Practice for Interior Designers*, 3rd ed. New York: Wiley.

———2003. *Becoming an Interior Designer*. New York: Wiley.

Ranallo, Anne Brooks. 2005. "Cradle to Cradle." *Perspective*. Spring, pp. 17–22.

Reznikoff, S.C. 1989. *Specifications for Commercial Interiors*. New York: Watson-Guptill.

Rutes, Walter A., Richard H. Penner, and Lawrence Adams. 2001. *Hotel Design, Planning, and Development*. New York: W.W. Norton.

Scott, Susan. 2002. *Fierce Conversations*. New York: Berkley Books.

Sewell, Bill. 2006. *Building Security Technology*. New York: McGraw-Hill.

Solomon, Nancy B. June 2005. "How Is LEED Faring After Five Years in Use?" *Architectural Record*, pp. 135–142.

Sparke, Penny and Mitchell Owens. 2005. *Elsie de Wolfe: The Birth of Modern Interior Decoration*. New York: Acanthus Press.

Stitt, Fred A., ed. 1999. *Ecological Design Handbook*. New York: McGraw-Hill.

Tate, Allen and C. Ray Smith. 1986. *Interior Design in the 20th Century*. New York: Harper & Row.

Thompson, Jo Anne Asher, ed. 1992. *ASID Professional Practice Manual*. New York: Watson-Guptill.

U.S. Green Building Council. February, 2003. *Building Momentum: National Trends and Prospects for High Performance Green Buildings*. Washington, DC: U.S. Green Building Council.

———. 2004. "LEED-CI." Brochure. Washington, DC: U.S. Green Building Council.

U.S. Green Building Council. No date. "Making the Business Case for High Performance Green Buildings." Brochure. Washington, DC: U.S. Green Building Council.

Watson, Stephanie. "Learning from Nature." *Implications*. InformeDesign. Vol. 02, Issue 04.

Whiton, Sherrill and Stanley Abercrombie. 2002. *Interior Design & Decoration*, 5th ed. Upper Saddle River, NJ: Prentice-Hall.

Williams, Shaila. 2006. "The New Rules." *Perspective*. Winter, pp. 42–46.

World Commission on Environment and Development. 1987. *The Brundtland Report: Our Common Future*. Oxford: Oxford University Press.

WEB SITES

American Society of Interior Designers (ASID) www.asid.org

Careers in interior design site www.careersininteriordesign.com

Council for Interior Design Accreditation (formerly the Foundation for Interior Design Education Research). www.accredit-id.org.

Design-Build Institute of America (DBIA) www.dbia.org

Interior Design Educators Council (IDEC) www.idec.org

Interior Designers of Canada (IDC) www.interiordesign-canada.org

International Interior Design Association (IIDA) www.iida.org

National Council for Interior Design Qualification (NCIDQ) www.ncidq.org

U.S. Green Building Council (USGBC) www.usgbc.org

Architectural Record www.architecturalrecord.com

Building Design & Construction magazine www.bdcmag.com

Canadian Interiors www.canadianinteriors.com

Contract magazine www.contractmagazine.com

Design-Build Dateline magazine www.dbia.org

Eco-Structure magazine www.eco-structure.com

EnvironDesign® Journal (a supplement to *Interiors & Sources* magazine)

InformeDesign newsletter www.informedesign.umn.edu

Interior Design magazine www.interiordesign.net

Interiors & Sources magazine www.isdesignet.com

Journal of Interior Design www.idec.org

The Office

It can be argued that the design of offices is the backbone of commercial interior design. Almost all interior design firms design office facilities because most commercial interiors include some sort of office space. Here are a few examples: the manager of a retail store needs office space to place and check orders; a hotel provides office space for managers; industrial manufacturers need office spaces for the leader of the company; banks provide private or semiprivate offices for loan officers; doctors need an office for consultations with patients; and let's not forget the principal's office in schools. Name the facility and at least one space somewhere in the business is considered an office.

The goal of office work is, of course, to provide specific task accomplishment by individuals and groups that assists in achieving the overall goals of the business. However, all office work is not the same. The work of an administrative assistant to a corporate executive is very different from that of a support secretary in the firm. The office work of the principal is quite different from that of a doctor or accountant. It is therefore

Figure 2-1a The reception room of this office space is creative and innovative in approach. (Photograph courtesy of Randy Brown Architect.)

Figure 2-1b Commercial headquarters: typical workstations. (Interior design by Robert Wright, FASID, with Kellie McCormick, ASID, Bast/Wright Interiors, San Diego, CA. Photographer: Brady Architectural Photography.)

important that the layout and design of an office support the functional needs of the jobs within the specific business activity. Factors such as the size of the company and the geographic location are just two of the many other elements that impact the design of office spaces (Figure 2-1a, 2-1b).

Today's business leaders must cope with many challenges, and these challenges can impact the work of the interior designer on an office project. Organizational changes can come quickly, as a business must be prepared to alter direction to meet the changes that constantly affect the economy and the businesses' markets. Financially, businesses must be managed with care, since competition can easily impact the success of a business. And businesses today must operate in an ethically responsible manner toward employees, customers, competitors, and the business community.

Personal exposure to offices does not usually provide the student with an understanding of the organizational workings of an office or the kinds of equipment required for different jobs. The design of offices likely introduces the student to lists of job names, furniture names, and space requirements with which he or she is less familiar. Understanding the functional responsibilities and goals of the business is important in order to best develop working adjacencies into space plans and make design specification decisions for the office areas.

This chapter provides an explanation of the functional distinctions of office work. Understanding these distinctions in job responsibilities is important for space planning and product specification decisions. Interior designers must understand the nature of the business in general and the businesses of the firms for which they do design work because design decisions can have a direct effect on the business. How so? An office that is poorly planned or has the wrong furniture products can contribute to the office workers' inability to do their jobs, negatively impacting the bottom line of the client company. On the other hand, effective functional design and planning, along with sensitive specification of products and materials, can lead to an increase in employee productivity, effectiveness, and satisfaction.

The chapter begins with an historical overview of office environments, followed by a discussion of office operations. This discussion is first based on a traditional organizational structure, which is still utilized by many businesses. It is followed by a look at the office organizational structure that is developing in the 21st century. Facility management and planning are considered as part of the overview of office operations. Next, the functional requirements of numerous kinds of specialized offices, both traditional and those used in open office planning, are described. Information on image, status, and organizational culture concludes the chapter. Planning and design concepts are presented in the next chapter.

Table 2-1 presents vocabulary used throughout the chapter.

TABLE 2-1 Chapter Vocabulary

- CLOSED OFFICE PLAN: Planning of offices around the private office—with full-height walls—for use by one individual. Sometimes this is referred to as *conventional office planning.*

- DELAYERING: A reduction in management and supervisory layers, resulting in enlargement of the responsibilities of the individual worker and work teams.

- DOWNSIZING: A reduction in the number of employees within a company to make operations cost-effective and to be more responsive to customers' demands.

- MODIFIED OPEN PLAN: A plan combining open office workstations and a number of private closed offices.

- EMPOWERMENT: Allowing employees to make certain decisions themselves rather than going through many layers of management and perhaps waiting for days for decisions to be made.

- OFFICE LANDSCAPE: Translation of *Bürlandschaft,* a planning method using plants and desks rather than wall partitions or free-standing panels.

- OPEN PLAN: Planning methodology using movable wall panels and/or furniture items to divide the office footprint and create the work areas.

- STICK FURNITURE: A slang term for wood furniture.

- WORKSTATION: The space that represents an office of an open plan project.

Historical Overview

An office provides the environment for individuals to do the administrative work of the business. Office work is central to the activities of many businesses and professions, both large and small. How that work is done has changed over millennia and continues to evolve today. The environment of the office changes with the needs of business, technology, the market, and the wishes of the business owners.

Offices have always existed. In ancient times, an office may have been the space two people occupied as they shook hands on a deal for, say, a carpenter to make a table for a neighbor. As economies and industries grew, offices became more formalized. Specialized office work grew as a way of recording the transactions of a business and as professions developed. As industry and trade became more sophisticated, the need for offices and office furniture and equipment expanded. Historically, the first major change in the growth of specialized office functions and offices occurred during the Industrial Revolution. The change from an agricultural to an industrial economy required additional office functions as new businesses were created and more specialized tasks were needed (Figure 2-2).

During the second half of the 19th century, the closed plan was the predominant way of arranging office spaces. This involved a private space for the boss or owner, with clerks and secretaries occupying separate spaces. Recall the private office of Ebenezer Scrooge and his clerk, Bob Cratchit, in the front office at a tall desk lit by a single candle in Charles Dickens' *A Christmas Carol*. Larger businesses would place the clerks in a large open space called a *bull pen*. The offices of the owners and managers were always larger and often more decorative than the sparse desk, chair, and lamp on the workers' desks (Figure 2-3).

The 20th century saw the real growth in offices resulting from a growing list of business functional specialties and office equipment. Women in the workforce also had an impact as business owners and architects realized that female workers had a different view of their environment. The emergence of commercial interior design as a specialty also started in the early 20th century, although few thought of it as such.

As industries absorbed production workers, the offices of companies increased in size. Closed plans in offices continued into the early 20th century until designers such as Frank Lloyd Wright, with the Larkin Administration Building (1904), started to open up office

Figure 2-2 A small real estate office circa 1900 depicting the use of office space and furnishings popular at the time. (Photograph used by permission, Utah State Historical Society. All rights reserved.)

Figure 2-3 Office space circa 1900 with an open bull pen shared by various employees. (Photograph used by permission, Utah State Historical Society. All rights reserved.)

space plans. Specialized pieces of furniture and office equipment like the typewriter, dictaphone, and telephone all impacted the design of offices in the early 20th century.

Significant changes in the office environment occurred during and right after World War II. Many office workers were needed to support the war effort. As corporations grew during the war, the numbers of office workers increased enormously. Social scientists started researching organizational structures and employee productivity. Other researchers theorized on the changes to come in the office environment as technology impacted how work was done in the office. In addition, the better-educated professional in the office environment was increasingly dissatisfied with the way offices were planned—with the bosses on the perimeter and other workers in open bull pens.

Office interior design—and commercial interior design itself—saw significant changes after World War II. Unlike previous office architecture, where more than one company was located in a building, corporate headquarters were created for a single tenant. This gave the building owner much more control over the architecture, interior space planning, interior finishes, and furniture specification. As corporations' strength and business grew, they added branch headquarters offices in large cities. These branch headquarters spaces often had to be designed following corporate standards in terms of space allowances and even the finishes of furniture items and architectural surfaces.

Office workers continued to grow in number as corporations expanded in the postwar economy of the 1950s. This growth challenged designers and architects to develop new ways to handle the increasing number of employees without requiring the corporation to continually build new office space. A German management consulting group called the *Quickborner Team für Planung und Organisation*, headed by Eberhard and Wolfgang Schnelle, wanted to find a way to improve performance and productivity in the office. With the help of a planning expert, they developed the concept of an open landscape by laying out the "offices" to increase communication between workers. The Quickborner Team coined the term *Bürolandschaft*, which means *office landscape*,[1] to define their planning idea (Figure 2-4). Although some point to the open office planning begun by Frank Lloyd Wright, historically this trend began in Germany in the 1950s.[2]

---

[1]*Office landscape* is a planning method using plants and desks rather than wall partitions or free-standing panels. It was first used in Germany in the 1950s.
[2]Pile, 1978, p. 18.

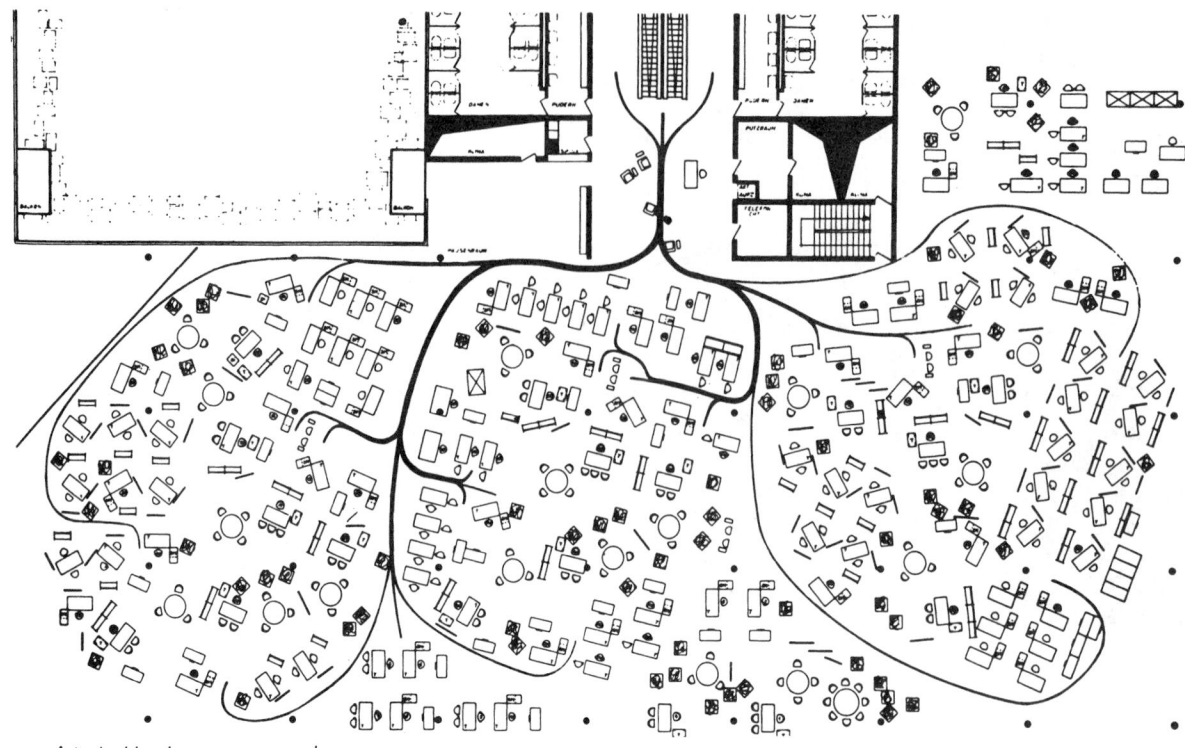

A typical landscape or open plan.

Figure 2-4 Quickborner office landscape depicting the laying out of the "offices" to increase communication between workers.

The original open landscape concept did away with all private offices and placed both managers and staff members in an open plan. The rather irregular arrangement of the furniture was not based on any specific type of plan. This made designers and office managers who did not understand the new ideas believe that these early plans were created by accident and did not represent good planning. However, the planning was actually based on work relationships between individuals and work groups and founded on very sound principles. The office workers who worked together or in close relationships were grouped to-

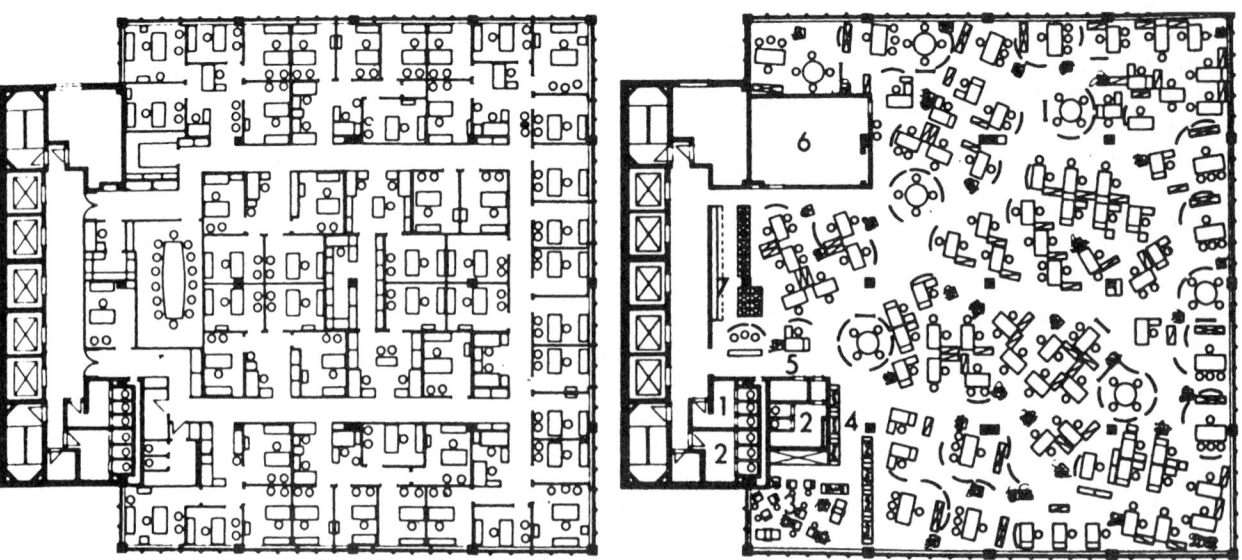

Figure 2-5 First office landscape in the United States for the DuPont Corporation. The plan on the left is for the conventionally designed floor, while the one on the right is for the experimentally designed floor.

gether to improve productivity. In 1967, the first project utilizing the open landscape in the United States was a department within the DuPont Corporation in Delaware (Figure 2-5). Although designers and business owners had used the open plan concept for some time, this was the first time in modern office design that the whole facility utilized an open plan.

Open plan (earlier called *open landscape*) is a planning methodology that uses movable wall panels and/or furniture to divide the office footprint and create the work areas with few full-height partition walls. Later development of furniture specifically for this type of planning affected how businesses were managed, because it placed greater emphasis on work groups or teams rather than on the individual workers. Office design in the 1960s and 1970s actually became more humanistic, with greater concern for the ability of the individual worker to have some freedom in the design and specification of his or her work area.

New furniture products helped change the way the office environment was designed. In the 1960s, Robert Probst, a designer working for Herman Miller, Inc., designed a furniture product called Action Office® (see Figure 1-4). Action Office was originally designed to fit into the conventional private office, but since its introduction coincided with acceptance of the open landscape, it began to be used in open landscape projects. It was redesigned in 1968, incorporating vertical divider panels and the hanging components with which we are familiar today. Although Action Office in a sense violated the rules of the Quickborner group, it seemed to be clearly acceptable in furnishing the open landscape project. The panels and vertical stacking components helped create privacy while still maintaining essential openness. As open office planning caught on, other furniture manufacturers created products that could be used for this planning concept.

A major improvement in providing for a healthier office environment was the emphasis on ergonomically designed seating starting in the late 1970s. This form of seating reduces back and leg pain for workers who must sit at a computer terminal eight hours a day. Fortunately, designers have not stopped with ergonomic seating, but have incorporated the concepts of ergonomics into many products used in office and home environments.

Numerous new product designs since the 1990s have given office areas a more open look. These newer products resulted from the demands of companies and employees when corporations started to decentralize control. As greater responsibility was given to employees working in teams rather than individually to complete work assignments, new ideas for office layout and furniture products became necessary (Figure 2-6).

Figure 2-6 The Redwood Trust Offices workstations are designed to provide a team system. (Huntsman Architectural Group. Photography by ©David Wakely.)

Office planning and design today combine the approaches that have evolved over the history of office design. Traditional case goods or *stick furniture,* systems furniture, the open plan, and the closed plan all can be applicable to the needs of the client. Enhanced environmental planning has also become important in today's offices. An increasing number of clients want their projects to be LEED certified to create a better environment for their employees and show their own clients their concern for the global environment. In addition, the challenge of incorporating technological changes into office furniture arrangements that do not harm employees adds to the interior designer's responsibility to design excellent interiors. Personal computers are on every desk; laptop computers and cell phones allow for mobile offices; telecommuting permits workers and clients to be on different continents and still conduct business "one-on-one."

Even in the 21st century, with all the changes that have occurred in work organization and management, furniture, and office equipment products, one thing remains relatively unchanged in most companies: The boss still gets the biggest office with the most furniture and furnishings, while the staff and production workers get spaces and furniture adequate to do the job.

An Overview of Office Operations

Twenty-first-century work is changing and so too must offices where that work is accomplished. Downsizing,[3] telecommuting, globalization of the marketplace, and many other forces have changed the structure of businesses in the 21st century. Information and knowledge are now the keys to office work, and the ability to work with and transfer that information is critical. Technological changes have affected all businesses. Even the smallest businesses can have a global reach due to technology. Teams and the ability of the office environment to meet their needs are very important to this change in the organizational structure. Scarcer human resources in some industries and professions means that 21st-century workers have more say about their work environment.

Technology now allows work that was traditionally done in an office to be accomplished remotely. Laptop computers, personal digital assistants (PDAs), cell phones, and wireless Internet links all potentially make large office buildings to house all employees a thing of the past. In some ways, this eases the pressure on the business to provide all the space and furniture for employees in a single location. Still, decisions about space, office equipment, and aesthetics continue to impact the work of the commercial designer creating any kind of office environment.

A business enterprise—whether housed in an office or a retail store—must have the ability to alter itself with the flow of change created both within and from outside forces. If a business changes its organization, this generally impacts the planning of its offices. During the economic downturn of 2001–2002 many businesses vanished, unable to cope with the changes that affected them. Flexibility in office design and product specification can help a business as it reorganizes its purpose, goals, and strategic plan (Figure 2-7).

Although many workers can work at home—assuming that their bosses let them—many still choose to come to the office. Much of the reason for this is the camaraderie and the chance to socialize with one's peers. For many, the purpose of socializing is to bounce ideas off each other as problems are worked out. So, while the number of companies that allow employees to work away from the office grows, many workers choose to spend some time in the office at least a few days a week.

Owners, managers, and supervisors perform the work necessary to plan, manage, and control the activities required to maintain the business. Each job within a department or division has specific responsibilities that enhance the likelihood of the business achieving its goals. The interior designer must understand each of these different job functions, since they may require variations in office spaces and the furniture provided to execute job responsibilities.

---

[3]*Downsizing* is a reduction of the number of employees within a company to bring about cost-effective operations and to be and being more responsive to customer demands.

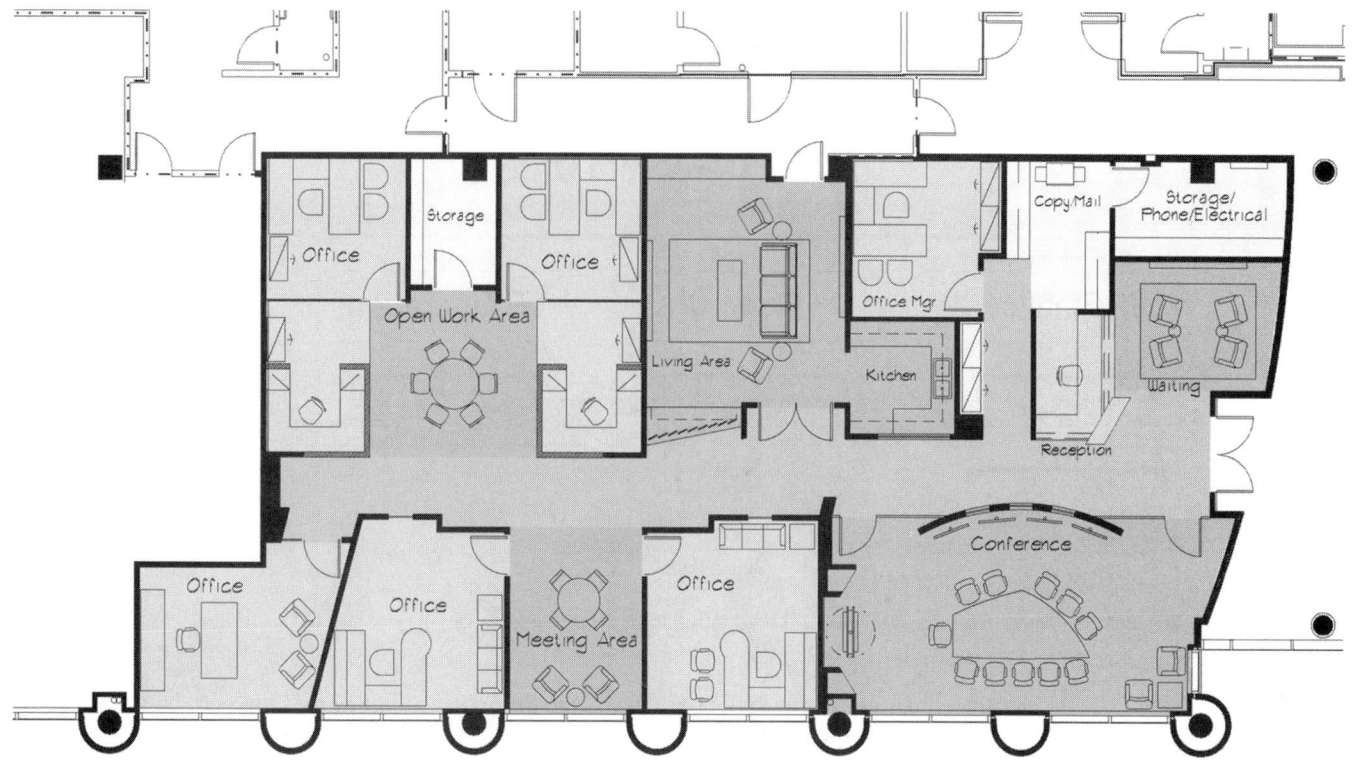

Figure 2-7 Floor plan indicating flexibility in office design. (Drawing courtesy of Burke, Hogue & Mills Architects.)

Traditional Organizational Structure

Although the world of office work has changed in many ways, a basic organizational structure still must exist. Traditionally organized businesses have the most clearly defined organizational structures. The larger the organization, the more defined this structure becomes. Structure helps define responsibilities so that each department meets its goals, which in turn meet the goals of the enterprise as a whole. When the business has a formal reporting authority, it is said to have centralized control whereby the boss makes the decisions with or without input from the employees. In part, these relationships are explained by the corporation's *organizational chart* (Figure 2-8). Yet the formal chart is often merely that—a formal description of organizational structure. However, it is not surprising to find that the day-to-day work relationships that keep the enterprise going do not strictly adhere to this chart. Interior designers find out about these informal channels of communication by using common programming methods, such as one-on-one interviews and on-site inspections. Formal and informal reporting structures are also acknowledged by the use of employee questionnaires completed during programming.

Although these traditional hierarchical descriptions and terms are changing in many corporations, they remain the backbone of organizational structure. Technology has had a dramatic impact on the office hierarchy since so many members of the traditional chain of command can comfortably do their jobs remotely via teleconferencing, e-mail, and so on. Of course, modification of the organizational structure from the traditional chain of command to a decentralized organization works only for some companies. Changes in organizational structure make the programming phase of the project critically important. The interior designer must understand what each department does, how departments relate to each other, what individuals within the department do, and how these individuals relate to each other. These factors will impact the space planning and adjacency planning of an office facility of any size.

Using a large corporation as an example, the following text describes where job functions fall within the operations of a business. Keep in mind that these same areas or divisions exist in many smaller business, though not as formally as those described here. Large business enterprises are commonly broken down into several departments. Our

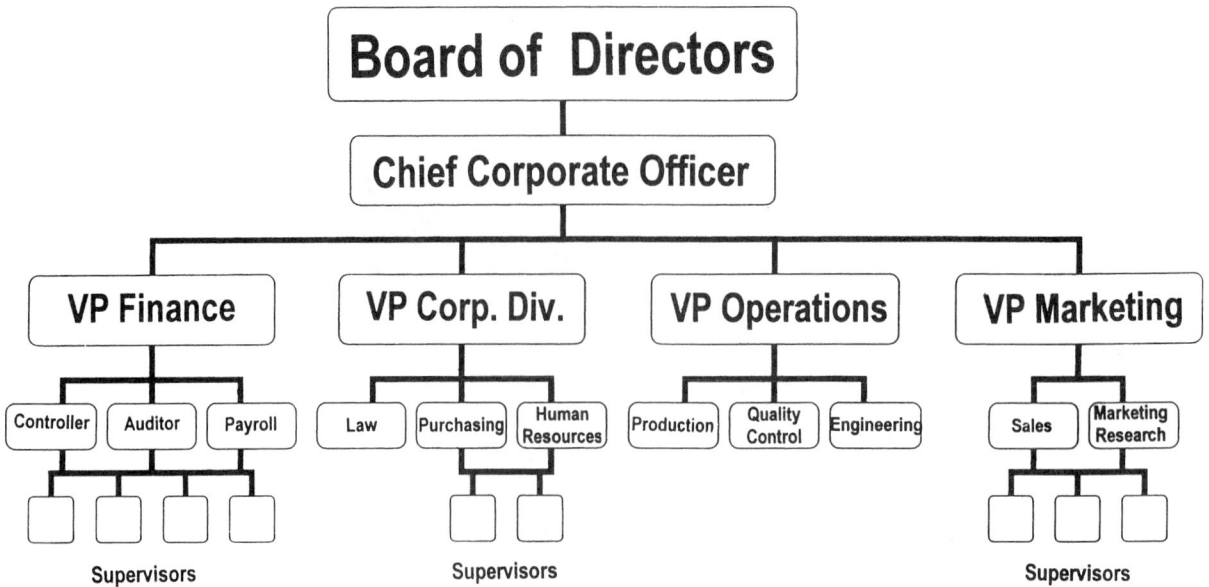

Figure 2-8 Corporation's organizational chart. (Illustration by Alisha Newman.)

sample business is broken down into the following departments: Executive, Corporate/Legal, Finance, Operations (or Manufacturing), Marketing, and Administration.

The *Executive Department* includes the CEO or president, along with the executive staff. The CEO, along with departmental vice presidents, determines overall policies and implements the policies of the board of directors.[4] The Executive Department is responsible for financial planning and overall general administration (Table 2-2).

The *Corporate* or *Legal Department* consists of the many departments related to the overall operation of the whole corporation. Departments with responsibility for legal, tax, and insurance issues, as well as purchasing, are commonly included in the Corporate Department.

The *Finance Department* is responsible for financial planning, analysis, accounting, and the preparation of financial reports. All of the other financial aspects of the company, such as processing of receivables and payables, payroll, and other matters dealing with finances, are also the Finance Department's responsibilities.

The *Operations Department* is in charge of producing the goods or services of the company. Operations include such things as design and engineering of new products, materials management, purchasing, quality control of production, and distribution of goods to buyers. In a service-oriented company, this department is responsible for the production of services such as construction drawings by an architectural firm.

The *Marketing Department* has multiple responsibilities for the marketing, advertising, and sales of its total product line. The marketing department determines how best to convey the information about products or services to the consumer.

The *Administration Department* includes those departments that are responsible for providing services to the other departments. The personnel department is one example.

Each of the above departmental or divisional areas has slightly different space requirements and furniture needs based on job function and type of business. For example, even today, when everyone in an office has a computer, attorneys still use legal-size paper and require larger file cabinets to house records than other departments, which use letter-size paper. Individuals working in communication departments may be reviewing storyboards, which are used to lay out proposed advertising campaigns.

Each business has spaces and functional requirements similar to those described above. It is all rather relative, in a way. For a doctor's suite, one could describe the spaces that

---

[4]The *board of directors* consists of individuals elected by the shareholders of a corporation. They are legally responsible for setting overall corporate policy, delegating operational power, and selecting the president and other chief officers.

TABLE 2-2 Common Job Titles in a Corporate Office

Job titles and responsibilities vary based on the size of the company and the business conducted. The terms presented here are the most common terms for individuals in a traditional hierarchy as represented in the organizational chart in Figure 2-8.

- **Chief executive officer (CEO):** The highest-ranking individual in the business. In smaller companies, he or she may have the title *president* or *principal* rather than CEO.
- **Vice presidents:** The second highest layer of management. Vice presidents work primarily with the CEO and are responsible for specific departments or divisions of the business.
- **Department managers:** Individuals who supervise a group of employees responsible for a specific area of the business, such as the accounting department.

- **Supervisors:** Generally below the department managers. They supervise individuals who perform specific functions, such as the bookkeeper in an accounting department.
- **Manager:** An individual whose responsibilities are to plan, control, organize, provide leadership, and make decisions.
- **Line manager:** An individual who is responsible for activities that directly relate to revenue production of the company.
- **Staff manager:** An individual who provides support, advice, and expertise to line managers. Managers of the personnel office and the accounting department are examples.
- **Employee titles:** There can be dozens of titles for employees doing the work in a firm—for example, project manager, senior designer, designer, and technician in an interior design firm.

the doctors themselves use as the executive division. The officer manager of a doctor's suite performs many jobs of the corporate division. The area where patients check in and pay for services, as well as the spaces occupied by office workers responsible for providing these services, can be thought of as the finance division. The patient exam rooms, perhaps a small surgery, laboratory, and other medical-specific spaces are the operations divisions of a medical suite. Marketing is not generally an issue with physicians, but that function would be part of the doctor's or office manager's responsibilities. And one could argue that all areas except the medical treatment areas are similar to the administration division.

The New Office Organizational Structure

Many businesses, from the largest corporations to the smallest firms, have redefined how work is accomplished and how the environment to accommodate that work is organized. Advances in technology, reengineering of work processes, downsizing of businesses, and globalization of the marketplace are just a few of the many changes associated with the challenge of business in the 21st century. For the student and the design professional who must creatively solve the design problems of the new office environment, it is vital to understand this new work structure. Indeed, students will find themselves working in design firms that embrace many of these concepts. This section briefly discusses how the structure of work has changed and will continue to change.

In response to the challenges of a rapidly changing economy and a business market, most companies today have had to reorganize their operations and organization. Many of the largest corporations have reengineered their organizations. According to Hammer and Champy, *reengineering* is "the fundamental rethinking and radical redesign of business processes to achieve dramatic improvement in critical, contemporary measures of performance, such as cost, quality, service, and speed."[5] In the 1990s and again around 2001, many companies went through another change process in response to a slumping economy. The term often applied to this process is *downsizing*. Downsizing results in the reduction in the number of employees within a company to make operations cost-effective and be more responsive to customers' demands. Many businesses go through massive reorganization when downsizing is instituted, often leading to the elimination of thousands of jobs.

---

[5]Hammer and Champy, 1993, p. 32.

Figure 2-9 Freestanding systems furniture where vertical panels are not used or are not essential to the components' configuration. (Photograph courtesy of Haworth, Inc.)

Let us not assume that job titles and divisional groupings like those described in the section on traditional office organization do not exist in the new restructured organization. In many situations, they still remain. The working relationships, however, are less formal due to the greater empowerment given to teams to get work done. *Empowerment* means that employees are allowed to make certain decisions themselves, rather than going through many layers of managers and perhaps waiting for days for decisions to be made. This reduced formality has a tremendous impact on the way offices are planned and the equipment provided each layer of worker in the organization (Figure 2-9).

Downsizing and reengineering have impacted the formal reporting structure of many businesses. For many companies, the formal pyramidal structure shown in Figure 2-8 has been changed to a flatter structure, with more interdisciplinary work groups functioning as teams. This change in structure, often called *delayering,* means there are fewer management and supervisory layers, resulting in enlargement of the responsibilities of the individual worker and work teams. This added responsibility, or empowerment, makes many employees feel that they are more a part of the business. Empowerment gives the employees access to information to make decisions. This is very important, as many employees are now working outside the confines of a corporate building, either in a home office, while waiting at the airport for their next flight, or on the plane.

Advances in technology have had a large impact on modifying organizational structures. Technology allows many kinds of work to be done faster, more accurately, and from almost any location. Telecommuting allows an individual to work away from the main office at home, on the road, or at a satellite office. This takes appropriate workers to the customer, solving problems, taking orders, and generally satisfying the customer faster. Groups can reorganize their work environment quickly because technology has improved office furniture and equipment to the point where a worker might only have to move his or her files and laptop to some other location (Figure 2-10). Downtime for the relocation of electrical, telephone, and other data links becomes minimal in the new office environment.

Organizational restructuring and employee empowerment change how work is done. A company with a nontraditional work structure and environment makes an individual or team responsible for all parts of the project from beginning to end. In a traditional com-

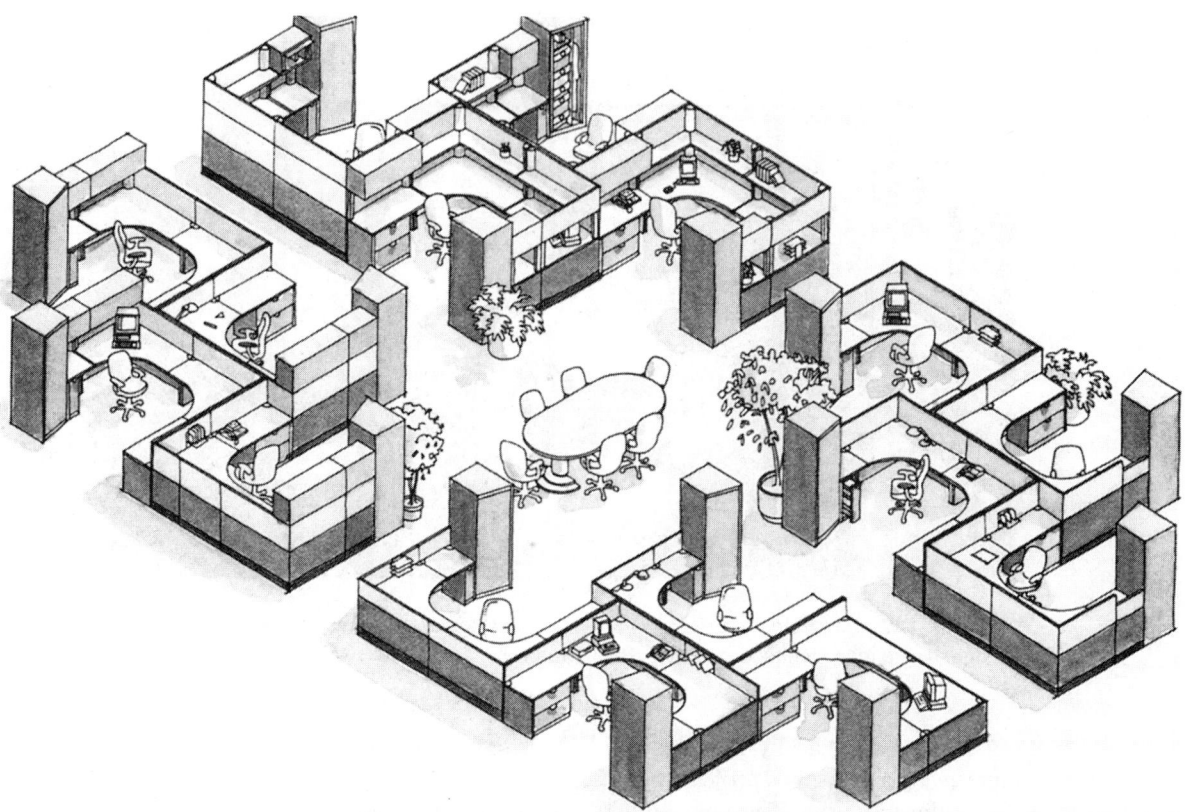

Figure 2-10 Drawing indicating a small conference area for use by the surrounding work areas. Versatility of the work space allows flexibility in use. (Copyright Steelcase, Inc.; used with permission.)

pany, an end product is broken down into parts; each part is the responsibility of an individual or a small group who, after accomplishing some goal, will pass the part to the next individual or group, as on an assembly line. This team approach helps a company develop new products faster and hit the market with the new products ahead of its competitors. Thus, teams today are flexible, changing size and personnel, depending on the scope of the problem facing the team. Some individuals are members of more than one team at a time. The team will function effectively only if free-flowing interaction between the team members exists (Figures 2-11a, 2-11b).

Teams can be defined in many ways, but they generally fall into three types: linear, parallel, and circular. A *linear* team is the simplest form; each member performs part of the task needed to complete the total job. The work is passed from one person to another until the task is complete. The second kind of work team is called a *parallel team*. In this case, a team is assembled for a specific project based on the specialized skills of team members. Often the team members come from different departments and work together while handling other duties in their regular departments. A team assembled to do a design project is an example of a parallel team (Figure 2-12). This team could stay together after the project is done, but since team members are also working on other projects, their main responsibility can shift to another project when one project is completed. The third kind of team is a brainstorming or *circular team*. In this case, a team is organized to do creative and innovative work. Members can come and go throughout the course of the project, and the team disbands when the project is completed.[6]

Where work is done is also a major difference in the 21st-century office. Some jobs in the new office require space and planning for team interaction and work to occur. Flexible work spaces must be designed to accommodate the needs of teams that might work

[6]Herman Miller, Inc. 2001b, p. 3.

Figure 2-11a View from the exterior with the team placement of furnishings indicating flexibility in design. (Huntsman Architectural Group. Photography by ©David Wakely.)

on a project for a few days to over a year. Then the space could be reconfigured for a new team and a new project. Other jobs are handled by individuals via telecommuting. With the modern office environment becoming more fluid than its traditional predecessor, it is important for the designer to discover during programming the variety of space requirements the business will need. The designer must place more emphasis on understanding the corporate organization and culture as well as the company's furniture needs.

Even with the changes in organizational structure, many companies still require designers to plan private offices along the perimeter of the building. However, the employees originally assigned to these spaces more frequently find themselves working with team members in other parts of the building or even at another company location. Thus, these private offices often stand empty or are used as conference rooms. Many executives placed in private

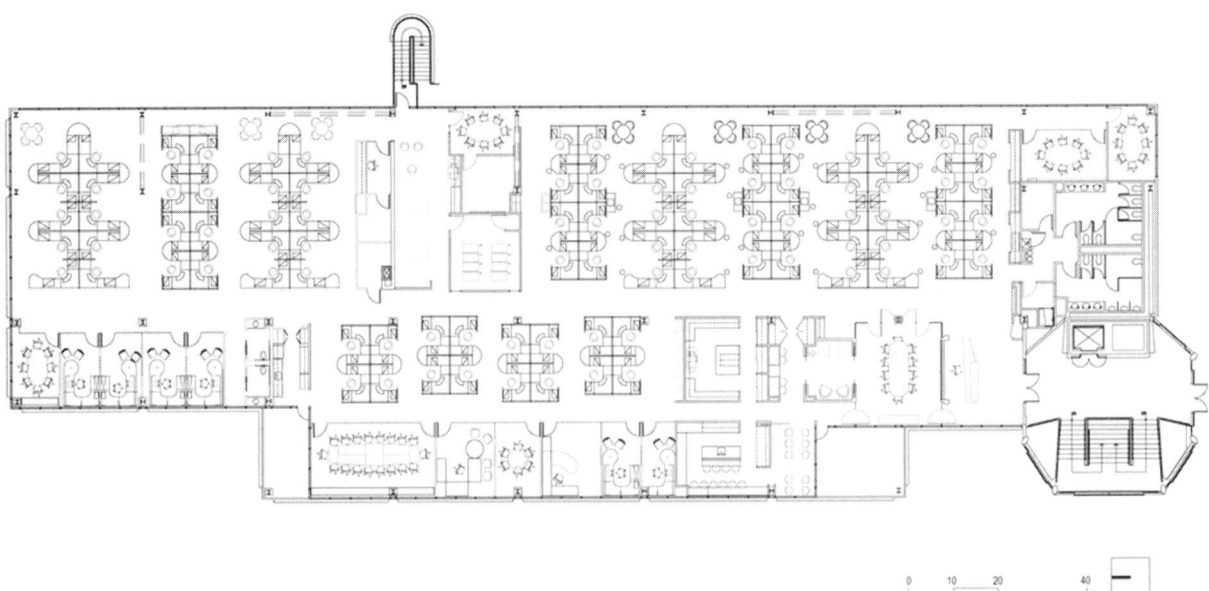

Figure 2-11b Floor plan showing the placement of systems furniture within the space. (Drawing courtesy Huntsman Architectural Group.)

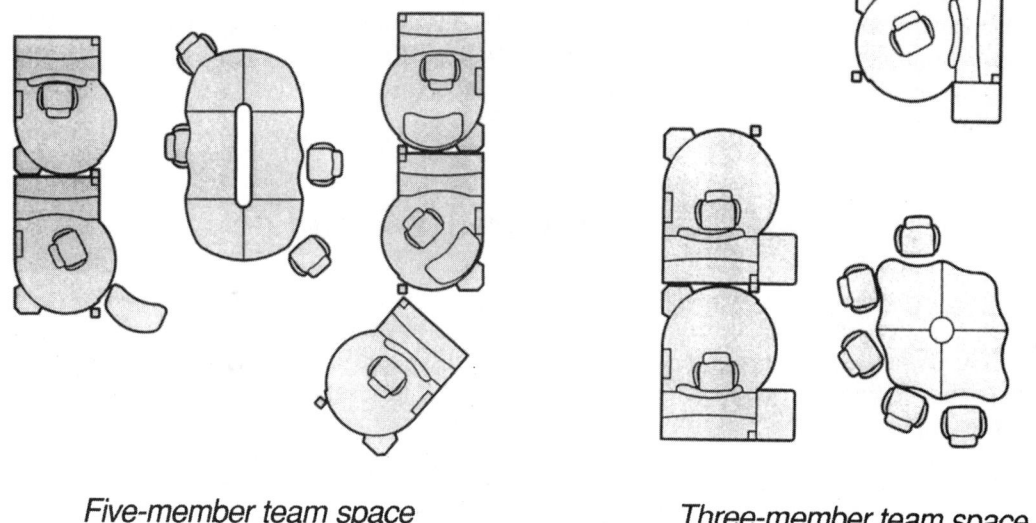

Five-member team space   *Three-member team space*

Figure 2-12 Three- and five-member team spaces with individual workstations flanking the common areas are an example of flexibility in team spaces. (Copyright Steelcase, Inc.; used with permission.)

offices feel cut off from the employees. Moving into an open office space allows them to get back in touch with their staff. Opening up the walls of offices also means more useful communication between employers and levels of workers. In other situations, companies ask designers to plan an area of the facility with no full-height enclosed offices or conference rooms on the perimeter but instead to place these—if they are planned at all—in the interior of the area. This gives more employees access to windows, daylighting, and the view.

TABLE 2-3 Alternate Office Terminology

- **Alternative officing:** A term that describes the many different impacts on the design of office space and the workplace.

- **Employee churn:** Turnover in the office staff.

- **Free address:** Unassigned work spaces that are available to anyone on a first-come, first-served basis. No reservations are needed to use them.

- **Guesting:** An assigned or unassigned work area provided to a visitor from another company.

- **Hoteling:** A system of unassigned work spaces that are available to workers by reservation—as in a hotel.

- **Hot desk:** The same as the free-address station. Its name is derived from the reality that the desk may be "hot" from the previous user.

- **Just-in-time:** Another type of unassigned workstation or space. An open, flexible work area that individuals or groups can use for various periods of time.

- **Landing sites:** Unassigned workstations that cannot be reserved. As with a hot desk, the employee "lands" in an unoccu-pied work area when he or she arrives at the main or satellite office building.

- **Satellite offices:** Work centers established away from the main office but convenient to the territory of the outside workers. These are generally not branch offices with complete full-time staff and assigned workstations.

- **Shared assigned work areas:** Stations that are shared by two or more individuals, such as a secretarial station where two or more workers working part-time use the same work space.

- **Telecommunication center:** An executive office center where the main office has leased space. More than one corporation may have offices there.

- **Unassigned office space:** Space that is not designated for an individual worker. It can be used by any number of people on any given day. Unassigned offices may need to be reserved at a reservation desk.

- **Virtual office:** Everything the individual needs to work can be carried theoretically in a briefcase or car—cell phone, modem, portable laptop computer, fax, and printer. Thus, the virtual office can be anywhere.

Office workers today are doing their jobs in ways that rarely exist in the traditional office environment. The reengineering of corporations and work strategies has created new ways for employees to work, requiring changes in the office environment. Technology and mobility have also moved many office workers out of the main office's four walls and into the outside world or into their homes (Table 2-3).

Facility Management and Facility Planning

All businesses consist of the facility and the people who work there. For example, the facility in a store is the space and the fixtures used to display the merchandise. In a hotel, the facility is the guest rooms, restaurants, and other features. For a corporation's offices, the facility is the building housing the offices and all the equipment provided for the work of the employees to be performed.

The responsibility for making sure that the facility is planned appropriately and for providing what employees need to do their jobs falls to the facility management department. *Facility manager* is a position formerly often called *plant manager, director of physical plant,* or even *office manager.* When it comes time to decide if a new facility should be built or leased, the facility manager will be part of the team to arrange for that new space. And when interior design work is scheduled, the interior designer will no doubt work with the client's facility manager. Facility managers are responsible for making sure that the working environment is as optimal as possible considering corporate goals, policies, and budget. *Facility management* involves the total nonfinancial asset management of a business. According to the International Facility Management Association (IFMA), "facility management is a profession that encompasses multiple disciplines to ensure functionality of the built environment by integrating people, place, process and technology."[7]

The facility manager is usually the prime contact with the interior designer on a project since the facility manager often functions as the in-house project manager for any construction and installation. The facility manager is also involved in long-range facility planning, management of the FF&E, the manufacturing equipment, real estate acquisition, and interior space utilization. In other words, this individual is in charge of managing the enterprise's capital assets.[8]

The facility management department manages the facility planning department. *Facility planning* involves the programming and space planning of offices and other areas of commercial businesses. Facility planners, sometimes called *space planners,* are most often involved with the layout of the spaces and generally have little responsibility for the aesthetics of the interiors. They are concerned with space planning and layout of office areas, support operation areas such as training rooms, and space needed for other business functions. Many retail chains use facility planners to determine the best layouts for merchandise display to encourage sales. Hospitality enterprises—especially hotel chains—use facility planning to maximize guest services and convenience. Government agencies also use facility planners to determine office layouts. Individuals in the planning department will work with the facility manager and outside architects, interior designers, contractors, and others in planning and constructing the facility.

Types of Office Spaces

Office facilities generally contain very similar types of spaces. These typical spaces may exist whether the interior designer is responsible for a project involving a major corporation or a small professional office. Of course, not all businesses will have all the types of spaces discussed in this section.

---

[7]IFMA Web site, "What Is FM?," accessed April 26, 2005.
[8]*Capital assets* is an accounting term that generally means any property, buildings, and equipment required to conduct business.

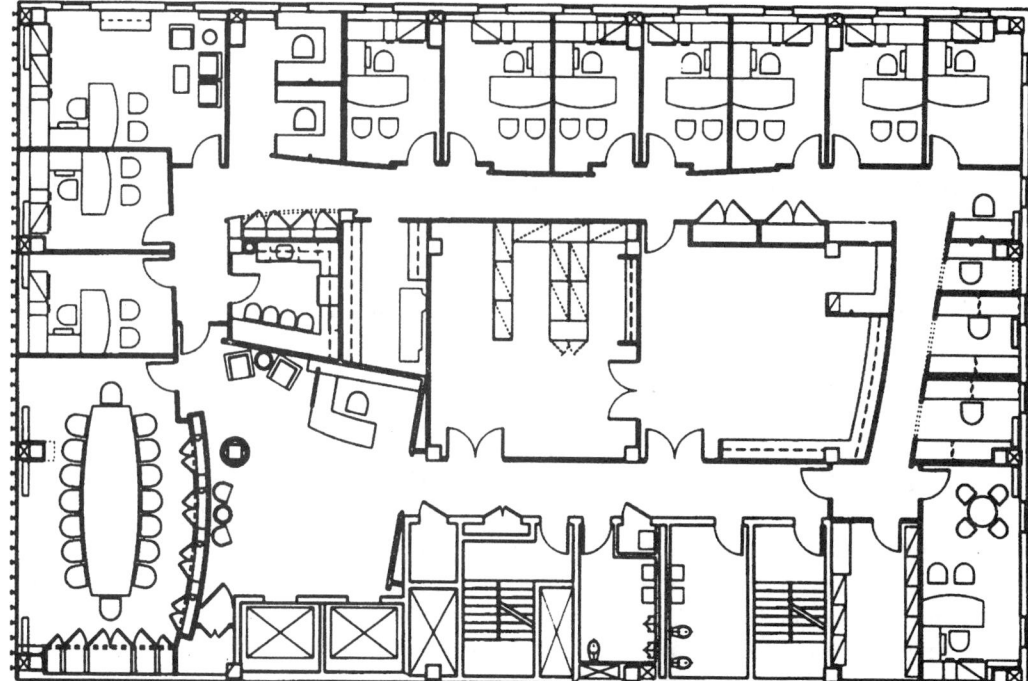

Figure 2-13 Floor plan of a corporate office showing a closed floor plan. (Plan courtesy of RTKL Associates, Inc.)

Today's office design involves three basic planning methodologies. One of them uses a *closed office plan,* in which the office is planned around the private office—with full-height walls—for use by one individual (Figure 2-13). Sometimes this is referred to as *conventional office planning.* Today, few businesses other than some professional offices, offices for high-ranking employees, or small businesses are entirely planned around private one-user office spaces.

On the other end of the planning spectrum is the *open plan* methodology, which does not use full-height walls to create office spaces. In fact, in its purest form, no employee has an office with full-height walls and a door for privacy. This planning methodology uses movable wall panels and/or furniture items to divide the office footprint and create the work areas. The term *workstation* is often applied to the "offices" of an open plan project. Space allowance and equipment specification are based on functional needs rather than status. Offices are often provided less filing and storage space and infrequently provided space for visitors compared to offices in a closed plan. This open plan may be the ubiquitous cubicle portrayed in the Dilbert™ cartoons made famous by Scott Adams or some other configuration of space. As we saw in the discussion of the new office, team-oriented clusters of workstations replaced the cubicle in the office landscape. Team areas must be designed to accommodate the many different types of work styles that may occur. Today, individual work areas often surround a commons where team members can come together to work on problems or discuss issues. Individual workstations need to be flexible for future change. Some teams need to retain a conference or work area for the duration of the project.

Many companies today are more likely to use a *modified open plan,* which combines a number of private closed offices. These are still commonly placed along the perimeter walls of the office footprint or located adjacent to the central core. Most other employees are housed in open work stations that are created using systems furniture.

Why do closed offices still exist? In many cases, it is a matter of status. People who have worked many years for a company, moving up the corporate ladder, take great satisfaction from achieving the status of a closed private office. Many workers feel that they are more productive in a closed office or cubicle. But many researchers have shown that this is not the case. The closed office will still find a place in office environments. Whether for privacy, status, or security, some individuals will want, even demand, a closed office or at least a "closed" cubicle.

This discussion of typical office spaces is based on a traditional office hierarchy. However, the types of office spaces described also apply to the changing office hierarchy of the 21st century.

Executive offices and suites: These include offices for the highest-ranking individuals, generally in closed plan private offices. The executive office area is often located on the top floor or premium location in the facility. A separate reception area and a receptionist to greet visitors to the executive office suite are also common. A large boardroom or conference room is important in this area. The owners or managers of smaller businesses have their own versions of the executive suite, being given more space in premium locations.

Staff office spaces: These office spaces are reserved for managers and some supervisors. Depending on the organization, staff offices are planned within the general work area for each department. Staff offices for managers are smaller and have less impressive furniture than that is used in the executive suite. Supervisors rarely have a private office. They are positioned in the area where their employees are located.

General office spaces: These office spaces—commonly called workstations—are frequently designed using one of the many open office systems of furniture. General office spaces are workstations for production employees such as accountants, sales representatives, and computer programmers and represent the largest number of office spaces. Their specific furniture and equipment needs can vary a great deal according to the primary job in each department (Figure 2-14).

Ancillary or support spaces: These are various types of spaces that are required to support basic office work. With the exception of the primary reception room, ancillary spaces are designed and specified with utility rather than aesthetics in mind. A list of common ancillary spaces with their square footage allowances is provided in Table 3-2 in the next chapter.

Figure 2-14 Florida Business Interiors depicting general office spaces. (Photograph courtesy of Burke, Hogue & Mills Architects.)

Image and Status

Look at Figures 2-1b and 2-16. Both of these photos are of office facilities. Each conveys a different image of the company to its employees and customers. An interior designer not only plans the space, but also designs the interior envelope to reflect the firm's attitudes toward its employees, customers, visitors, and vendors, as well as the client's budget, goals, and plans. All of these reflect the image of the company. An important part of the designer's job is to interpret what the company wants its design image to be (Figure 2-15).

A company reveals something about itself by the interior design decisions it makes and the image its interiors portray. In today's economy, with competition rampant in almost every industry, projecting an image or brand that helps convey clarity and positive values is critical to the continued success and growth of firms of all sizes whose business is conducted in office facilities. Not all companies can afford the highest-quality furniture and finish products. For a small firm like a small law office, high-priced furnishings and

Figure 2-15 Reception area for Steelcase Worklife, New York City, reflects the image of the company and the design image. (Photograph courtesy of Steelcase, Inc.)

Figure 2-16 Executive office featuring a desk, conference area, and soft seating (Photograph by Peter Paige.)

finishes will frighten potential clients away. By contrast, clients of a top legal firm will expect an expensive interior.

Image is not just the quality of the furniture and accessories used. It is an expression of the company itself and starts with programming decisions that lead to the planning and interior specification decisions needed to complete the project. The interior designer must attempt to express that image when selecting the products, colors, textures, and styles that create the final interior design of the facilities. For example, no matter how up-to-date it may be, a financial institution with traditional values and organizational structure designed with glass and chrome furniture does not reflect the conservative image desired by conservative clients.

Design solutions today must create a background that reflects the culture and goals of the company. Planning must produce functional arrangements of employees who can easily do their jobs. Clients require interior designers to handle all the details while the project is being designed and to ensure that the work is done without error. The interior designer must use colors and textures that enhance the function of the space and make a statement about the business while creating an environment in which the client is happy (Figure 2-16).

With the delayering of the office hierarchy, the concern for status has taken on new meanings. In these flattened corporations, rank seems to have less privilege. Yet, employees want to retain at least some semblance of status. For a firm with a traditional hierarchy, providing elements of status is relatively easy. The corner office with the larger desk and finer upholstery is the easy solution. Let's look quickly at ways to provide status in offices today.

Status in an office environment is generally provided by one or more of these three features: size of the office, location of the office in the building, and quality and quantity of furniture. Even in an organization with only a few employees, it is obvious who is in charge—the person in the largest office. The large corner office with windows on both sides is a prime location in many companies and is another way of providing status to the occupant. However, in companies that use more open plans, the status office may be located closer to the core or within the team area.

The last status criterion relates to the quantity and quality of furniture and treatments in an office. The higher one's position in an organization, the better the quality of the furniture. Often the size of the furniture is the key to status. A larger desk or a higher-backed posture chair can be the status symbol signifying rank in the office. Even with systems furniture, a company can designate status by the finishes on the panels and surfaces of the open plan stations. Managers' workstations can be specified with premium fabrics or veneers on the panels, while those of general employees often have simple finishes.

The interior designer must be sure that he or she understands what privileges each employee rank includes. It may be more important to the company to impress clients by providing elegant reception areas and conference rooms than by using expensive fabric on the chairs in managers' offices. Managers may claim that they need a closed office to hold confidential meetings with subordinates or to maintain client confidentiality, but it may be decided to hold all conferences in separate areas. It is the interior designer's responsibility to research the needs of each employee or group of employees and combine them with the requirements of the company in terms of budget and privilege. This is not always an easy task for the interior designer, but it is a challenge that must be met in today's competitive climate for both the interior designer and the client.

Corporate Culture

An important part of office planning is the ability of the business, and thus of the interior designer, to understand the corporate culture of the organization and how this affects the office environment. By *corporate culture*, we mean policies, employee behavior, company values, image of the company, and assumptions about the world of work. The culture of the company has a definite impact on the success of any office redesign project. It becomes particularly important when the company is making a change in the interior design of the facility. If a company has been traditionally organized, with a strong chain of command, a move to an open plan with leaders in nonprivate offices will be difficult unless the company informs and involves the employees in the decisions and direction of the changes to come. Redesign of the offices from a hierarchical closed plan to some version of an open plan may be necessary to create a cultural change that will make the company more competitive.

The interior design and planning of office areas and product specification can enhance or harm the culture of the office. A strong corporate culture keeps everyone working for jointly held beliefs and goals. When interior design, planning, and product specification are handled correctly, the right employees are in the right locations. Their best efforts improve customer satisfaction and the company's image, and they are encouraged to use their best judgments for the good of the company.

To prevent the expensive mistake of designing an office facility that is not compatible with its corporate culture, interior design firms offer a service called a *cultural audit* as a predesign service. "The cultural audit helps define the activities that need to be built into the change process for it to have a chance to succeed."[9] It might be done in conjunction with or following the company's strategic planning process. This is important, as the mission, vision, and goals of the company are related to the corporate culture. A cultural audit of the company before space planning is undertaken helps to improve planning—especially for companies in transition from a traditional to nontraditional office plan.

A cultural audit often involves interviewing key personnel along with a random sample of other persons who will be working in the project area. If a very large number of employees will be housed in the project space, questionnaires might be used to gather information about how space is used, what is needed, and how communication takes place. Interior designers can also learn quite a bit about the use of space and offices by visually surveying the existing offices. For example, offices filled with extra file cabinets could mean

[9]Becker, 2004., p. 115.

that an employee is not turning files over to a central file area, is simply a "pack rat" unable to let go of any piece of paper, or actually needs to retain a large number of files.

The information from the cultural audit helps the interior designer make better recommendations on space allocation, space planning, and product specifications. Plans are better when developed around actual functional needs rather than rank or status. Furniture products are specified that match employee needs, i.e., flexible workstations for team areas and private or semiprivate offices for managers and other executives who really need privacy. Technology and mechanical interface issues become easier to manage with better product specification.

When changes take place that dramatically affect the workplace environment and how employees are expected to function in the new environment, the changes will usually succeed if the employees have been involved to some degree. "Workplace design is a powerful catalyst for organizational change, and a great tool for improving organizational effectiveness.[10] When employees are part of the process and are informed about how these changes will improve the overall effectiveness of the company as well as the individual's work responsibilities, the change will occur more smoothly.

Summary

In commercial interior design, most money is spent on the design of offices. As the United States and most other developed countries continue to change to service economies, this will remain true. Technology is changing the way offices function and the manner in which they are designed, but offices will always exist. Even office workers who telecommute or work from a home office will likely have a "head office" to report to—assuming that they are not entrepreneurs.

As a student in a commercial interior design class, you should consider taking a general business or management class to understand how office management and operations are changing in the 21st century. In addition, you should be constantly observing and learning about offices every time you have an opportunity to enter one. Observe how the spaces have been planned, what kinds and styles of furniture are used, and the size of each item. Examine the treatment of floors, walls, windows, and fabrics. And, if you have the opportunity, use a journal to sketch ideas that are interesting to you. These sketches might provide valuable ideas for solutions in the future. It is also important to read the trade magazines that feature office projects. These are full of great design ideas for a variety of offices and commercial spaces. *Contract*, *Interiors and Sources*, and *Interior Design* all feature commercial facilities in each issue.

This chapter has focused on the functional and organizational influences on the office environment. It has briefly discussed the typical work responsibilities of a generic corporation, as well as providing planning and design fundamentals relevant to the different levels and job functions of an office facility. Chapter 3 presents a detailed discussion of furniture specification for conventional and open systems projects, as well as an overview of aesthetic elements, mechanical systems interface, and code issues affecting the office environment.

---

[10]Tobin, 2004, p. 3.

REFERENCES

Addi, Gretchen. 1996. "The Impact of Technology on the Workplace," a paper presented at the ASID National Conference.

Albrecht, Donald and Chrysanthe B. Broikos. 2000. *On the Job: Design and the American Office*. New York: Princeton Architectural Press, and Washington, DC: American Building Museum.

American Society of Interior Designers. 1998. *Productive Workplaces: How Design Increases Productivity*. Brochure. Washington, DC: ASID.

———. 2001a. *Futurework 2020. Phase Two*. Washington, DC: ASID.

————. 2001b. *Futurework 2020. Phase One.* Washington, DC: ASID.

————. 2001c. "Cultural Influences." *ASID ICON.* September, pp. 18–21.

————. 2001. *Workplace Values: How Employees Want to Work.* Washington, DC: ASIID.

Barber, Christine and Roger Yee. n.d. "Brave New Workplace." Available at www.knoll.com

Becker, Franklin. 1981. *Workspace. Creating Environments in Organizations.* New York: Praeger.

————. 1982. *The Successful Office.* Reading, MA: Addison-Wesley.

————. 2004. *Offices at Work.* San Francisco: Jossey-Bass.

————. 2005. "New Ways of Working." *ASID ICON.* Summer, pp. 28–30ff.

Becker, Franklin and Fritz Steele. 1995. *Workplace by Design.* San Francisco: Jossey-Bass.

BOSTI Associates. 2005. "Economic Benefits." Available at www.bosti.com

Boyett, Joseph H. and Henry P. Conn. 1992. *Workplace 2000.* New York: Plume.

Brandt, Peter B. 1992. *Office Design.* New York: Watson-Guptill.

Brill, Michael and the Buffalo Organization for Social and Technological Innovation (BOSTI). 1984, 1985. *Using Office Design to Increase Productivity,* 2 vols. Buffalo: Workplace Design and Productivity.

Business Week. 1996. "The New Workplace." April 29, pp. 107–113ff.

Cornell, Paul and Mark Baloga. 1994. "Work Evolution and the New 'Office'." Grand Rapids, MI: Steelcase, Inc.

Cotts, David G. and Michael Lee. 1992. *The Facility Management Handbook.* New York: American Management Association.

Cutler, Lorri. 1993. "Changing the Paradigm: Is It Workplace or Work Environment of the Future?" Zeeland, MI: Herman Miller, Inc.

De Chiara, Joseph, Julius Panero, and Martin Zelnik. 1991. *Time Saver Standards for Interior Design and Space Planning.* New York: McGraw-Hill.

DeVito, Michael D. 1996. "Blueprint for Office 2000: The Adventure Continues." *Managing Office Technology,* December, pp. 16ff.

DYG, Inc. May 2001. The *New Workplace: Attitudes and Expectations of a New Generation at Work.* Research Study. East Greenville, PA: Knoll, Inc.

Farren, Carol E. 1999. *Planning and Managing Interiors Projects,* 2nd ed. Kingston, MA: R. S. Means.

Firlik, Mike. 2005. "The Next Evolution of the Personal Workspace." Brochure. Grand Rapids, MI: Steelcase, Inc.

Friday, Stormy and David G. Cotts. 1995. *Quality Facility Management.* New York: Wiley.

Gitman, Lawrence J. and Carl McDaniel. 2003. *The Best of the Future of Business.* Mason, OH: South-Western/Thomson-Learning.

Gomez-Mejia, Luis R., David B. Balkin, and Robert L. Cardy. 2005. *Management,* 2nd ed. New York: McGraw-Hill.

Gould, Bryant Putnam. 1983. *Planning the New Corporate Headquarters.* New York: Wiley.

Hammer, Michael and James Champy. 1993. *Reengineering the Corporation.* New York: HarperCollins Business.

Harrigan, J. E. 1987. *Human Factors Research.* New York: Elsevier Dutton.

Harris, David A. (ed.), Byron W. Engen, and William E. Fitch. 1991. *Planning and Designing the Office Environment,* 2nd ed. New York: Van Nostrand Reinhold.

Haworth, Inc. and International Facilities Management Association. 1995. *Alternative Officing Research and Workplace Strategies.* Holland, MI: Haworth, Inc.

————. 1995. *Work Trends and Alternative Work Environments.* Holland, MI: Haworth, Inc.

Herman Miller, Inc. 1996. *Issues Essentials: Talking to Customers About Change.* Zeeland, MI: Herman Miller, Inc.

————. 2001a. *Telecommuting: Working Off-Site.* Zeeland, MI: Herman Miller, Inc.

————. 2001b. *Office Alternatives: Working Off-Site.* Zeeland, MI: Herman Miller, Inc.

————. 2002. *Making Teamwork Work.* Zeeland, MI: Herman Miller, Inc.

————. 2003. *The Impact of Churn.* Zeeland, MI: Herman Miller, Inc.

————. 2004. *Demystifying Corporate Culture.* Zeeland, MI: Herman Miller, Inc.

International Code Council. 2000. *International Building Code.* Leesburg, VA: International Code Council.

International Facility Management Association. n.d. "Official Statement on Facility Management." Brochure. Houston: International Facility Management Association.

————. 2004. "Facilities Industry Study." Research Study. Houston: International Facility Management Association.

————. 2005. April 26. "What Is FM?" Available at www.ifma.org.

Kaiser, Harvey H. 1989. *The Facilities Manager's Reference.* Kingston, MA: R. S. Means.

Kearney, Deborah. 1993. *The New ADA: Compliance and Costs.* Kingston, MA: R. S. Means.

Klein, Judy Graf. 1982. *The Office Book.* New York: Facts on File.

Knobel, Lance. 1987. *Office Furniture: Twentieth-Century Design.* New York: E. P. Dutton.

Kohn, A. Eugene and Paul Katz. 2002. *Building Type Basics for Office Buildings.* New York: Wiley.

Lundy, James L. 1994. *Teams.* Chicago: Dartnell.

Marberry, Sara O. 1994. *Color in the Office.* New York: Van Nostrand Reinhold.

Myerson, Jeremy and Philip Ross. 2003. *The 21st Century Office.* New York: Rizzoli.

Pelegrin-Genel, Elisabeth. 1996. *The Office.* Paris and New York: Flammario.

Pile, John. 1976. *Interiors Third Book of Offices.* New York: Watson-Guptill.

———. 1978. *Open Office Planning*. New York: Watson-Guptill.

Propst, Robert. 1968. *The Office: A Facility Based on Change*. Grand Rapids, MI: Herman Miller, Inc.

Ragan, Sandra. 1995. *Interior Color by Design: Commercial Edition*. Rockport, MA: Rockport.

Random House Unabridged Dictionary, 2nd ed. 1993. New York: Random House.

Rappoport, James E., Robert F. Cushman, and Daren Daroff. 1992. *Office Planning and Design Desk Reference*. New York: Wiley.

Rayfield, Julie K. 1994. *The Office Interior Design Guide*. New York: Wiley.

Raymond, Santa and Roger Cunliffe. 1997. *Tomorrow's Office*. London: E & FN SPON.

Shoshkes, Lila. 1976. *Space Planning: Designing the Office Environment*. New York: Architectural Record.

Shumake, M. Glynn. 1992. *Increasing Productivity and Profit in the Workplace*. New York: Wiley.

Steelcase, Inc. 1987. *The First 75 Years*. Grand Rapids, MI: Steelcase, Inc.

———. 1991. *The Healthy Office: Lighting in the Healthy Office*. Grand Rapids, MI: Steelcase, Inc.

———. 1991. *The Healthy Office: Ergonomics in the Healthy Office*. Grand Rapids, MI: Steelcase, Inc.

———. 2004. "Demise of the Corner Office." Available at www.steelcase.com.

———. 2005. "Understanding Work Process to Help People Work More Effectively." Available at www.steelcase.com.

Tate, Allen and C. Ray Smith. 1986. *Interior Design in the 20th Century*. New York: Harper & Row.

Tetlow, Karin. 1996. *The New Office*. Glen Cove, NY: PBC International.

Thiele, Jennifer. 1993. "Go Team Go!" *Contract Design*. March, pp. 29–31.

Tillman, Peggy and Barry Tillman. 1991. *Human Factors Essentials: An Ergonomics Guide for Designers, Engineers, Scientists, and Managers*. New York: McGraw-Hill.

Tobin, Robert. 2004. "Adopting Change." Available at www.steelcase.com

Vischer, Jacqueline C. 1996. *Workspace Strategies*. New York: Chapman and Hall.

Voss, Judy. 1996. "White Paper on the Recent History of the Open Office." February 26. Holland, MI: Haworth, Inc.

———. 2000. "Revisiting Office Space Standards." Available at www.haworth.com

———. 2004. "Team Workspace." Available at www.haworth.com.

Wolf, Michael. 1992. "Furniture: A New Breed of 'Knowledge Worker' Requires Office Environments of the Future." *I.D. Magazine*. October, pp. 40ff.

Yee, Roger and Karen Gustafson. 1983. *Corporate Design*. New York: Van Nostrand Reinhold.

Zelinsky, Marilyn. 1998. *New Workplaces for New Workstyles*. New York: McGraw-Hill.

WEB SITES

Buffalo Organization for Social and Technological Innovation (BOSTI Associates) www.bosti.com

Building Owners and Managers Association www.boma.org

International Facility Management Association www.ifma.org

Buildings www.buildings.com

Contract magazine www.contractmagazine.com

Fast Company magazine www.fastcompany.com

Interior Design magazine www.interiordesign.net

Interiors & Sources magazine www.isdesignet.com

Metropolis magazine www.metropolismag.com

Note: Additional references related to material in this chapter are listed in the Appendix.

3

Office Interior Design Elements

Thorough programming research to define the client's requirements in terms of types of offices and supporting facilities is needed before the designer begins preliminary space planning. The overall layout and design must meet specific functional needs for employees to do their work effectively. Specific needs and design decisions will depend on the type of business or service, the size of the company, the firm's clients, the term of the lease, and even the geographic location of the company. Design decisions will also be affected by the organizational structure of the firm. It is important for the designer to know if the company is managed by a traditional hierarchy or uses a less traditional hierarchy.

Interior designers must understand the work methods and organizational structures of client firms in order to produce functional office environments. Planning and products ideas must respond to organizational initiatives regardless of the company's organizational structure. Appropriate furniture products, innovative space planning, designs that accommodate a diverse workforce, and responsive mechanical interface are all part of the work environment in the 21st century.

This chapter introduces the student and the professional to the interior design elements that are used in the design of office facilities. It begins with an overview of office design followed by explanations of furniture products—both conventional and office systems—and various architectural finishes commonly used in office facilities. The chief concerns in designing mechanical systems, with an emphasis on lighting and computer workstations are presented, along with a discussion of code issues.

The chapter concludes by outlining specific design guidelines for a small office specified with case goods and a predominantly closed planning system, a project utilizing office systems products, and a brief discussion of important criteria for the design of a home office.

Overview of Office Design

In the previous chapter, we discussed a few of the differences between closed and open office floor plans. We also mentioned that the company's organizational structure will have an impact on the space planning and interior design of the facility. The design of the office facility plays an important part in how well the company's work is done. Probably the most famous study showing this connection is the one done by the Buffalo Organization for Social and Technological Innovation (BOSTI), published in 1984 and 1985. Researchers showed that factors such as layout, design, and appearance affected job satisfaction and job performance. Ongoing research by this group has shown continued economic benefit to firms with a well-designed workplace.[1] Good workplaces with distraction-free environments bring positive results for companies.

A successful office project involves many design activities and challenges. Office design, which for some does not seem to be very difficult, involves numerous design components that must be brought together in a plan that facilitates employee productivity. Since many employees in an office work together on assignments, space planning is critical to the success of the project. There may be hundreds of employees in an office facility, requiring careful attention to information gathering during programming.

Regardless of whether a project will have a closed plan utilizing partitioned offices and case goods furniture, a totally open plan specified with office systems furniture, or a combination of these concepts, the planning and design elements involved will be very similar. Preplanning activities will start the project. Gathering information on the space and equipment needs of each employee, as well as the space and equipment needs of all other support areas is very important in the preplanning phase, more commonly called the *programming phase*. Then the interior designer will prepare documents and plans on space allocation, furniture specification, and architectural and furniture finish selections. Other important planning elements for an office project, as well as any type of commercial project, include mechanical interface, lighting design, accessibility requirements, and attention to codes.

Table 3-1 presents vocabulary used throughout the chapter.

Preplanning

Clients often ask interior design firms to help them determine if the space to be leased or built is sufficient for their needs. This is a service the design firm and client consider particularly important for new construction or if extensive tenant improvements appear to be called for in a significant space to be leased. Of course, even a small project could benefit from a complete review of its benefits before design drawings are begun. One way of establishing this without preparing drawings is by the use of a feasibility study.

Feasibility studies are "in-depth research into the costs of planning and providing specifications"[2] for a project. In very large projects, the study will also look at the financial

---

[1]Bosti Associates, "Economic Benefits." Available at www.bosti.com/benefits
[2]Piotrowski, 2002, p. 410.

TABLE 3-1 Chapter Vocabulary

- AISLE: An unenclosed path of travel that occupies space between furniture and equipment.
- CASE GOODS: Furniture items made of "cases" such as desks, credenzas, and bookcases.
- CORRIDOR: A path of travel defined by full-height walls and any partitions more than 69 inches high.
- DEMISING WALL: Any partition used to separate one tenant space from another. Each tenant is responsible for one-half of the thickness of all demising walls.
- DEMOUNTABLE WALL: A type of interior partition that is built at a factory and held in place by tension with a gripper on the floor and special attachment at the ceiling.
- GENERAL USE FURNITURE: Standard office furniture such as desks, credenzas, and file cabinets.

- NET AREA REQUIRED: The space determined to accommodate all offices and support spaces.
- PREMISES: The space described to be rented.
- RENTABLE AREA: The total amount of square footage required for office and support spaces. It includes allowances for demising walls, columns, mechanical closets, and even a portion of the exterior walls.
- SYSTEMS CREEP: Every time a panel run using systems furniture makes a turn, an allowance must be made in the drawings for the thickness of the panel and the connecting hardware.
- SYSTEMS FURNITURE: Furniture composed of free-standing panels and components.
- WORKSTATION: The space that represents an office of an open plan project.

and economic impacts of construction, of moving the staff, and many other factors that can impact the project. Feasibility studies are conducted in many kinds of commercial interiors projects, not just office projects. The reader will find additional information about these studies in other chapters of this book.

During programming, the interior designer must obtain information about the employees' work relationships and job adjacencies, communication patterns, furniture requirements, privacy needs, and technology usage such as corporate networks and teleconferencing. Keen observation, asking the client thoughtful questions, and/or utilizing predesigned questionnaires completed by employees can be used to help the interior designer learn about the business of the client and specific planning and product needs for all offices, storage needs and areas, and support spaces. If questionnaires are not used, interviews are necessary to be sure that the interior designer understands the working relationships in order to plan the adjacencies correctly. This background information is vital for effective planning and design decisions, regardless of the type of business and the specific type of office facility.

Understanding the work relationships and job adjacencies helps the designer to locate each department and each office space in each department. *Adjacency matrixes* developed from questionnaires, interviews, or observations are key aids that help the designer understand how to develop the floor plan. Adjacency matrixes help the interior designer plan locations for individuals and departments that must work together. Individuals who need to communicate frequently must be located near each other. Programming information will also help the interior designer ensure that work teams are located so that group communication can take place in a comfortable, efficient environment. Furniture needs are also determined during the programming process.

These programming research methods are applicable to both closed and open plans. If the interior designer and client have considered using systems furniture, the design must decide which components will be needed in the workstations. Remember that open office planning uses freestanding, less-than-full-height movable divider panels, and individual components to create functional work stations (Figure 3-1). The panels are not fixed to the floor or ceiling. The configuration of the panels and components is stable because of the panel layout. Programming data and matrixes developed to clarify adjacencies are then applied to the schematic floor plans that will show preliminary space allocations, partition layouts, and traffic paths.

Figure 3-1 Freestanding panels in an open office plan showing functional work environments called *workstations*. (Photograph courtesy of Kimball Office Group.)

Of course, several other kinds of information are researched during programming, including code, safety, and security requirements. Other tasks are described in Chapter 1.

Space Allocation

How much space is enough for departments as a whole or for the various offices and support spaces needed for an office facilities project? This question is researched and the answer is determined during the programming phase of a project. Central to determining space allocation allowances will be the decisions regarding a closed versus an open or modified open plan, the numbers of employees in each job function, and the types of support spaces required. Building and accessibility codes need to be researched to make sure that the interior designer does not violate any code restrictions when determining space allocations. The type of furniture that is likely to be used will also impact space allowances.

Large businesses will have predetermined allowances for many levels of job functions based on corporate policy. For example, typical corporate standards are 250 square feet for vice presidents, 200 square feet for senior managers, 150 square feet for managers, 100 square feet for supervisors, and 48 to 64 square feet for secretarial and clerical staff. The designer is normally required to plan the facility using corporate standards when they exist or to develop them when they do not exist.

When square foot allowances are not controlled by corporate policy, the designer can determine them by developing typical plan sketches of the offices and areas. Once the designer understands the job functions, he or she can determine what kinds and sizes of furniture are expected in each space. The designer should know whether certain individuals are to be given additional space for either functional or status reasons. The manager of the real estate division may be given a larger office to accommodate the review of large sets of drawings. A senior vice president may be allocated a larger office than the other vice presidents. Accessibility codes will also require additional square footage for some

Figure 3-2 Typical floor plans for office spaces based on hierarchical level or specific job responsibility. (a) Secretarial and clerical staff: 48 to 64 square feet. (b) Supervisor: 168 square feet. (c) Mid-level manager: 200 square feet. (d) Senior manager: 250 square feet. (e) Executive office: 330 to 360 square feet. (Plans courtesy of Interior Design, Utah State University.)

TABLE 3-2 Square Foot Ranges for Support Spaces

Support Space	Sq. Foot Range (30,000 SF Office or Less)	Sq. Foot Range (30,000–100,000 SF Office)	Sq. Foot Range (100,000+ SF Office)
Reception	250 SF/300 SF	300 SF/400 SF	1000 SF
Conference Room	250 SF/300 SF	300 SF/500 SF	750 SF
Workroom	250 SF	250 SF	300 SF
Training Room	—	750 SF	1500 SF
Computer Room	400 SF	1000 SF	2500 SF
Equipment Rooms	120 SF	250 SF	250 SF
File Room	120 SF/200 SF	200 SF/400 SF	1200 SF
Copy Room	200 SF	300 SF/400 SF	1000 SF
Mail Room	200 SF	300 SF/400 SF	1000 SF
Library	200 SF/300 SF	400 SF/600 SF	1200 SF
Pantry	200 SF	300 SF	300 SF
Day Care Center			8000 SF
Fitness Center			4000 SF/6000 SF
Cafeteria			10000 SF/12000 SF
Conference Center			12000 SF
Auditorium			5000 SF

Source: Rayfield, *The Office Interior Design Guide.* Copyright © 1994. Reprinted with permission by John Wiley & Sons.

employees. When planning is completed, prototypical floor plans of furniture layouts for the offices can be sketched. Experienced designers often have a "library" of typical office layouts on the computer that can be used in the early programming discussions with the client. Figure 3-2 shows several typical floor plans for closed office spaces based on a hierarchical level or specific job responsibility.

When an open plan product and planning concept are used, the typical space allowances are determined in a similar manner. However, the square footage allowed for each job function is generally less than that of a closed plan. The organization and configuration of the components on panels will factor into the amount of square footage needed for the station of each employee. Even in an open plan project, status may be a factor in some companies. In addition, work methodologies, such as use of teaming versus individual work assignments, affect square footage requirements. All these factors must be considered in determining the layouts.

In addition to the typical offices are a variety of support spaces. Conference rooms or areas, places for storing files, copy machine locations, coffee areas, and other spaces are commonly part of an office plan. When a project is located in a high-rise building, these support spaces are placed adjacent to the central core. When there is a large footprint, some smaller "neighborhood" support spaces may also be part of the plan. Table 3-2 gives the square foot ranges for support spaces common to office facilities.

Circulation paths move people through the office facility and connect the departments together. A major circulation path is provided to move people into and out of the general office space. This may be a major fire-rated corridor from the elevator around the building core providing access to the one or more office suites on the floor. Alternatively, the major circulation path may only be the path from the front exterior door through corridors and aisle ways in a small office on the ground floor. When the plan is a closed one, the circulation paths are considered corridors. If an open or modified open plan is used, at least some of the circulation paths will be pathways through the open plan areas (Figure 3-3).

Figure 3-3 In a modified open plan, some of the circulation paths will be pathways through the open plan areas. (Interior Design/Architecture: IA Interior Architects.)

The designer must ensure that major circulation paths are designed to adhere to all applicable building codes. Circulation paths defined as *corridors*—that is, paths of travel defined by full-height walls and any partitions over 69 inches high—are required by code to be a minimum of 44 inches wide unless the occupant load is less than 49.[3] Circulation paths defined as aisles must also be sized for the occupant load and generally are required to be a minimum of 36 inches wide. An *aisle* is defined as an unenclosed path of travel that occupies space between furniture and/or equipment. If systems divider panels are the "furniture items" creating the passageway, the divider panels must be less than 69 inches high; otherwise, the passageway might be considered a corridor. The actual width of major circulation paths and exit corridors may need to be larger, based on the number of occupants in the suite and on the floor of the building. Circulation paths also need to meet the Americans with Disabilities Act (ADA) or other accessibility guidelines in effect. Special design elements, such as areas of refuge, wheelchair turnaround space, and maneuvering alcoves, may also be required. The appropriate code book should be referenced when planning space allocations and when actual space planning begins.

Circulation paths and space require 20 to 50 percent additional floor space. This does not include space for the major traffic paths that are considered exit paths from suites into core exit access. The exact amount of space will be influenced by whether the project is a closed plan with primarily private offices versus an open plan, the requirement or desire for generous circulation paths, the number of spaces required in the project, and the footprint of the space. Open office projects generally take up more space than projects with full-height walls and often need 40 to 60 percent more circulation space. That requirement, however, will vary based on the type of systems furniture used and whether the circulation paths are designed with twists and turns (some sort of maze), another open

---

[3]Dimensions related to building, fire safety, and accessibility codes used throughout this book were based on the 2000 International Building Code and the ADA. Local regulations may be different from those provided. The reader is responsible for verifying actual current codes.

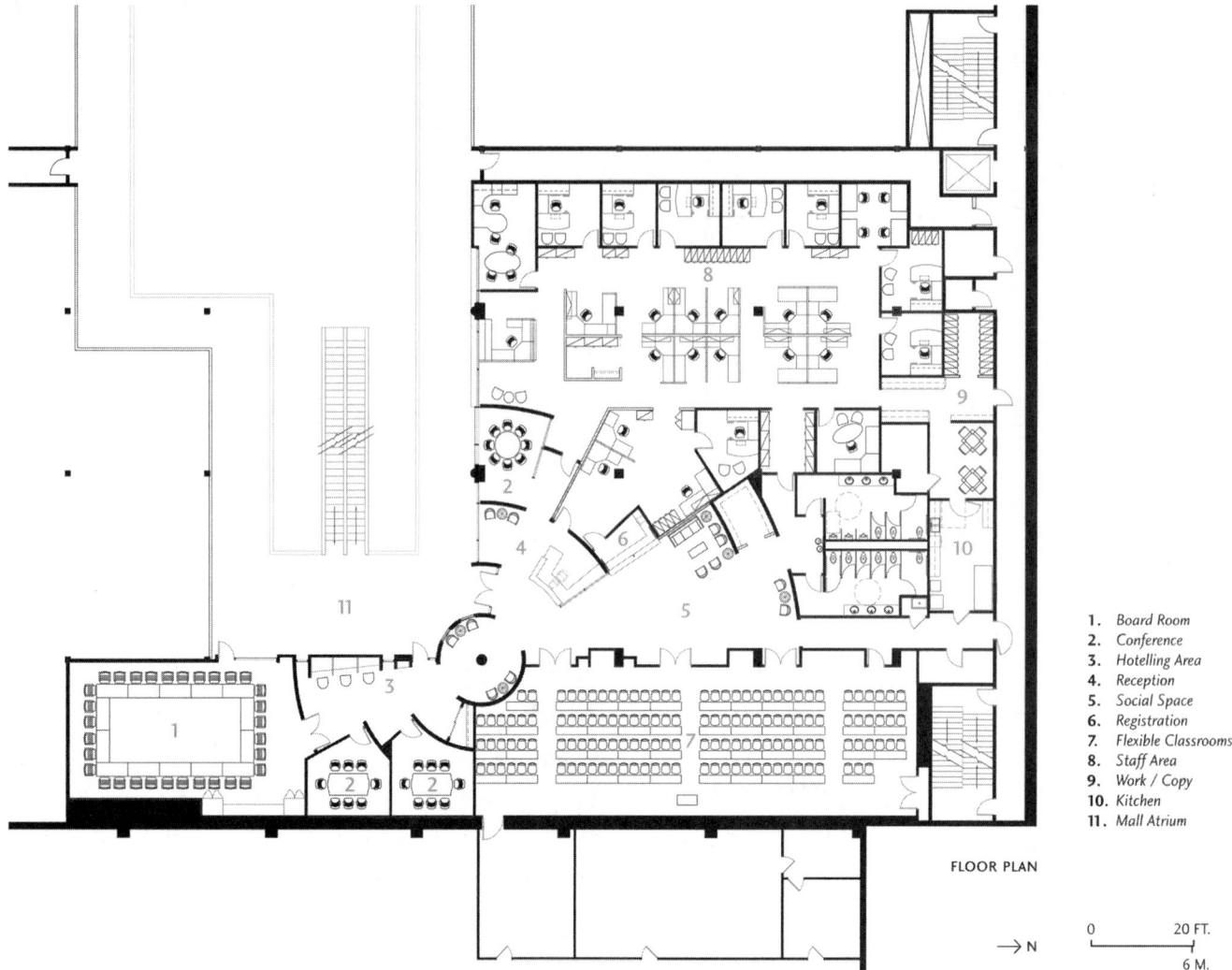

1. Board Room
2. Conference
3. Hotelling Area
4. Reception
5. Social Space
6. Registration
7. Flexible Classrooms
8. Staff Area
9. Work / Copy
10. Kitchen
11. Mall Atrium

FLOOR PLAN

→ N

0   20 FT.
                6 M.

Figure 3-4 Floor plan indicating open and closed areas and circulation paths. (Plan courtesy of Bialosky + Partners Architects.)

arrangement, or a more cubicle-oriented plan (Figure 3-4). Straight paths are more efficient but can be boring in a large layout. Mazes take up a lot of space, as do floor plans on angles. Although there is no sure way to determine how much space should be allowed, the guideline above will help the reader estimate how much total space is needed to plan office facilities (Figures 3-5a and 3-5b).

These space allowances for all workers and support spaces comprise the *net area required* to plan the facility—in other words, the space needs for offices, support spaces like conference rooms and file rooms, and internal circulation space. But this net area does not allow for architectural features and spaces that are considered part of the required office facility. These additional areas include general circulation space, columns, wall thicknesses, electrical closets, and other similar spaces. The terms in Table 3-3 provide additional information when a client intends to lease office space rather than own it.

Once space allocations for the various office facilities are determined and the functional adjacencies of each job function and department are clarified, the designer is ready to begin schematic planning of the floor plan. Schematic plans will be developed to test the information obtained in the programming phase and to begin to show the client potential layouts for the project.

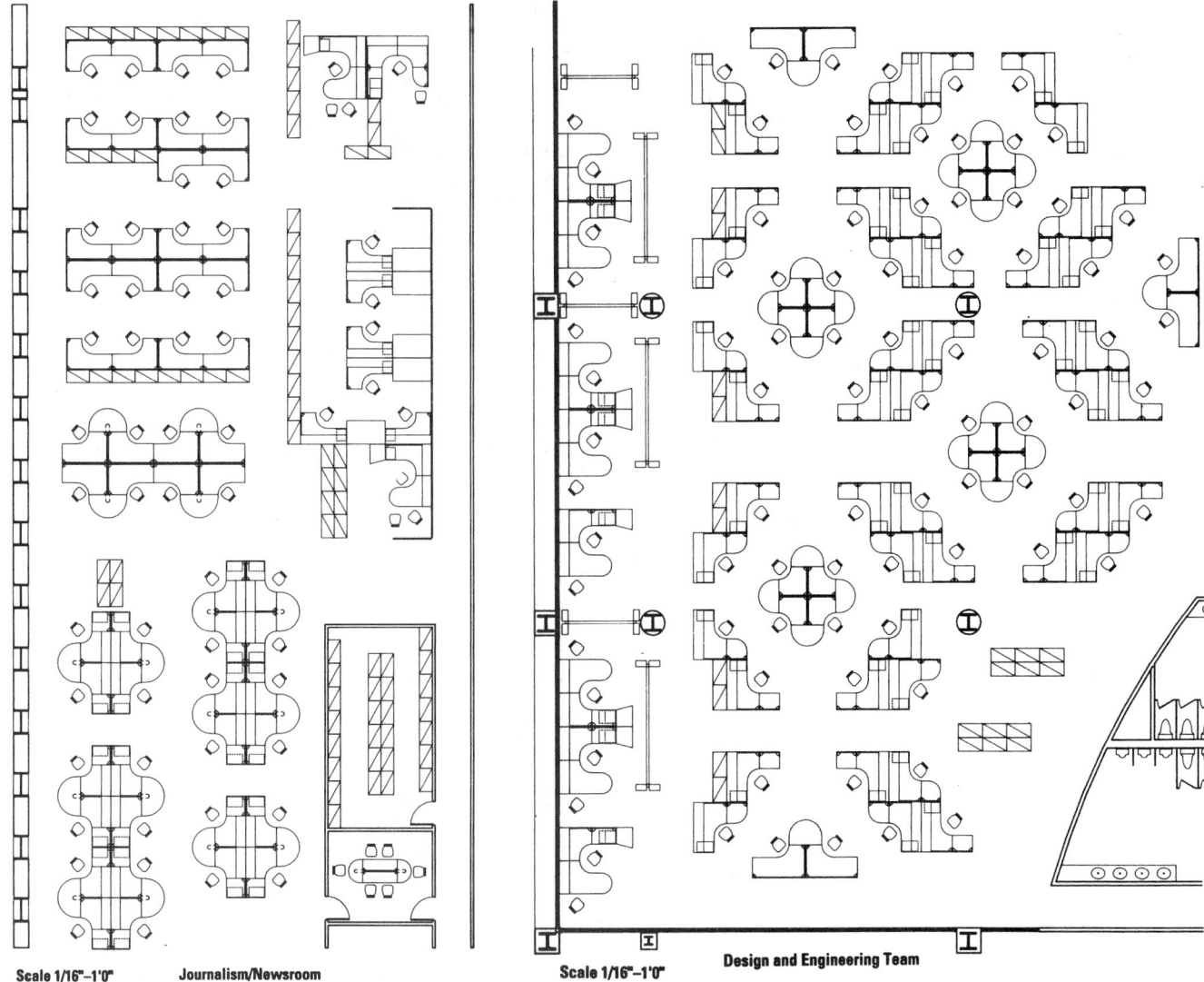

Scale 1/16"–1'0"   **Journalism/Newsroom**

Scale 1/16"–1'0"   **Design and Engineering Team**

Figure 3-5a Systems furniture layout indicating straight circulation paths. (Copyright Steelcase, Inc.; used with permission.)

Figure 3-5b Systems furniture layout indicating angled circulation paths. (Copyright Steelcase, Inc.; used with permission.)

Office Furniture

The furniture specification decisions that are made after the programming research is completed should focus on the functional needs of the client, the employees, and the project in general. If the products selected do not help the employees to do their jobs, the client will not care how beautifully or creatively the interior was designed. The item, be it a desk, seating unit, or file cabinet, must first satisfy performance criteria. A desk that is too small or a file cabinet that will not hold the client's file folders is not a correctly specified product.

Office furniture is also selected based on cost. It ranges from inexpensive items to high-end stock pieces to semicustom and custom furniture items with very high prices. Most clients and interior designers think of the initial cost of the goods as the only cost. However, there is a long-term cost, the life cycle cost, that factors in maintenance and replacement (see the discussion in Chapter 1). Budget-priced furniture may have a low initial cost, but it will likely have to be replaced sooner than a more expensive item. More expensive items will be better built and made of higher-quality materials that will take wear and tear far better, resulting in less frequent replacement. Higher-quality furniture has better warranties, providing an additional economic benefit to the client. Higher-quality furniture items

TABLE 3-3 Selected Leasing Terminology

- **"As is"**: The space is rented by the tenant without any changes to the interior. The tenant may request changes, but the landlord is not obligated to provide them.
- **Building standards**: Predetermined architectural finishes and other details the tenant can use with no extra charge.
- **Build-out allowance**: An amount per square foot representing the cost of building partitions, basic plumbing and lighting fixtures, and architectural finishes.
- **Build to suit**: The landlord will build the interior of the commercial space to suit the needs of the tenant.
- **Capital improvements**: Permanent changes to the building's interior that cannot be removed without damaging the structure, such as wood floors. They increase the value of the space and are paid for either by the landlord or by the tenant without compensation.
- **Demising wall**: Any partition used to separate one tenant space from another. When calculating allowances for needed square footage, each tenant is responsible for one-half of the thickness of all demising walls. Partition walls separating the tenant's space from the public corridors are not demising walls, and the tenant does not pay for that thickness.
- **Lease-hold or tenant improvements**: Upgrades or other improvements to the

rented space paid for by the tenant. If they are physically attached to the building, they belong to the landlord if the tenant moves out.
- **Premises**: The space described to be rented. The description should include the usable square footage and other details of the space.
- **Rentable area**: The total amount of square footage required for office and support spaces. It includes allowances for demising walls, columns, mechanical closets, and even a portion of the exterior walls.
- **Tenant work letter**: A contract used to supplement the lease describing the specific interior construction and finishing of a leased space. It specifies what the landlord will provide and what the tenant is responsible for.
- **Trade fixtures**: Materials or equipment attached to the building paid for by the tenant. These must be easily removed from the building without damaging the structure and are not integral to the structure; otherwise, they are not considered trade fixtures.
- **Usable square footage**: The amount of space that can actually be used for the office or other facility. It excludes demising walls, exterior walls, structural columns, chases, and electrical closets within the space.

have superior design characteristics, making them a better fit with the client's aesthetic goals for the office. Many projects will be designed with mid-priced products. Fortunately, the performance and aesthetic quality in this price range are quite high.

Without question, aesthetics are important. Choosing furniture styles and a color scheme to create a pleasing interior contributes to employee satisfaction with the workplace. However, the majority of clients are more concerned with product performance and price than with aesthetics. That is always unfortunate from the designer's point of view.

The most traditional category of furniture is called *general use furniture*, also known as *conventional furniture* or *freestanding furniture*. The other category of office furniture is called *systems furniture* or *open office furniture*. General use furniture includes desks, credenzas, bookcases, file cabinets, and seating, while systems furniture includes items created from less than full-height movable panels with components that become freestanding units or cubicles. General use furniture is further categorized into case goods and seating. *Case goods* are items made of "cases," like desks, credenzas, bookcases, file cabinets, and the like. Some designers also think of tables as case goods, but many just refer to them as tables. Let us begin to describe typical office furniture by discussing items of general furniture commonly specified in many sizes and categories of offices. Later in this section we describe common characteristics of systems furniture (Table 3-4).

A typical middle manager's office with general office furniture will have several pieces of case goods and seating units. A desk is the common denominator in offices. Few office jobs can be performed without some kind of desk. Desks come in a variety of sizes and types, as shown in Figure 3-6. The size and arrangement of pedestals and possibly returns match the functional needs of each job and, at times, the job status of the employee. Designers need to be careful about choosing a return for a desk. Many returns are

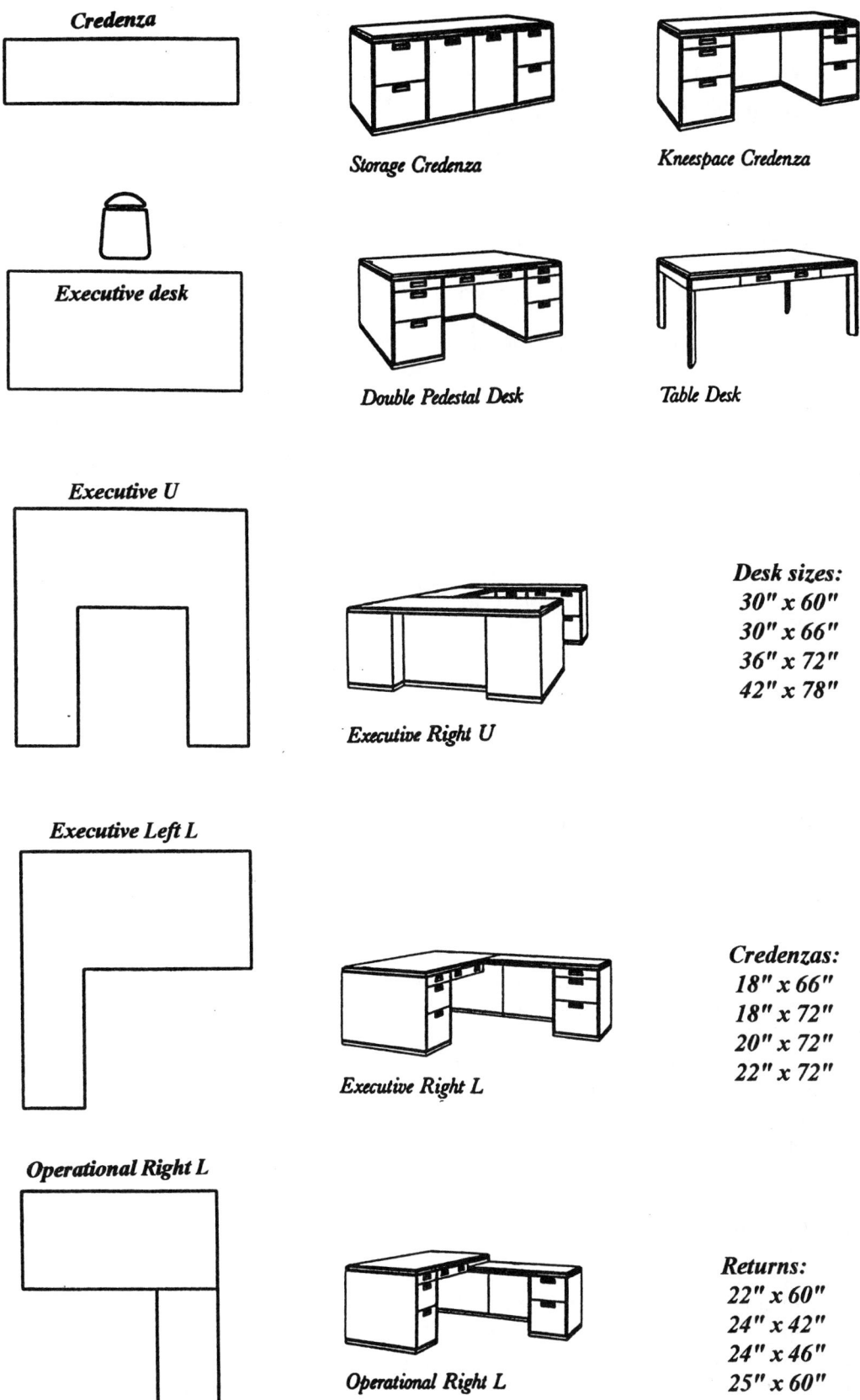

Credenza

Storage Credenza

Kneespace Credenza

Executive desk

Double Pedestal Desk

Table Desk

Executive U

Executive Right U

Desk sizes:
30" x 60"
30" x 66"
36" x 72"
42" x 78"

Executive Left L

Executive Right L

Credenzas:
18" x 66"
18" x 72"
20" x 72"
22" x 72"

Operational Right L

Operational Right L

Returns:
22" x 60"
24" x 42"
24" x 46"
25" x 60"

Figure 3-6 Desks are manufactured in a variety of shapes and sizes. Credenzas are used for storage as well as for computer use. These examples are typical sizes and configurations for case goods. (Line drawings courtesy of Kimball Office Group.)

TABLE 3-4 Case Goods and Office Seating Terms

Furniture Items

- **Case goods:** Furniture items made of "cases" like desks, credenzas, bookcases, file cabinets, and so on.
- **Conventional furniture:** Desks, credenzas, file cabinets, and bookcases.
- **Credenza:** A storage unit with pedestals or cabinets for extra storage.
- **Double pedestal desk:** A desk with two drawer units.
- **Executive return:** An additional desk unit at the same height as the desk.
- **Lateral file cabinet:** A space-efficient file that is generally 18 inches deep with a variety of widths.
- **Pedestal:** A configuration of drawers 15 to 18 inches wide.
- **Return:** An additional desk unit only 25 inches high that creates an L- or U-shaped desk.
- **Single pedestal desk:** A desk with only one drawer unit.
- **Table desk:** A desk unit without pedestals.

- **Vertical file cabinet:** The traditional filing unit that is usually 15 to 18 inches wide by 28 inches deep.

Seating

- **Ergonomic chair:** A wide variety of desk chairs in many styles designed for increased user comfort.
- **Executive chair:** A desk chair that is wider and has a higher back than most desk chairs. Usually designed with arms that are fully upholstered.
- **Guest chair:** Any chair—usually small—that is used at or near the desk by visitors.
- **Posture chair:** A desk chair designed to improve posture and comfort.
- **Sled base chair:** A guest chair with a piece of metal or wood extending from the front to the back legs. This makes it easier to move than a chair on legs.
- **Task chair:** Also referred to as a *secretarial* or *operational chair.* It is a smaller-scale chair with or without arms (that are recessed) for employees doing repetitive tasks like typing.

not sized properly for computers and keyboards. Refer to Box 3-1 for more information concerning computer workstations.

There are a few other common furniture items in management and executive offices. The first is the credenza. It serves primarily as an extra storage unit and is specified to have the same basic width as the desk. A credenza is almost always positioned behind the desk and often accommodates some kinds of office equipment, like an adding machine or even a computer—though this is not a good place for a heavily used computer. A second common item is a file cabinet. While the advent of the computer promised the "paperless office" in the 1970s, in reality many businesses must keep paper files and records for several years. Files that must be referred to frequently are kept in desk or credenza pedestals. Other files needed by specific workers are kept in a file cabinet in the office or moved to a central filing area when they are no longer needed but must be retained. File cabinets vary in size to accommodate letter- and legal-size paper. Because vertical file cabinets take up so much floor space, many designers prefer to use lateral files (Figure 3-7). These are not as deep as vertical files, but they are wider. Not only are they more efficient in using floor space, but more filing inches are available compared to the drawers of a vertical file. When a company has to store large numbers of files, the standard lateral and vertical file cabinet is not cost effective. Open-shelf filing units provide storage for large quantities of file folders (Figures 3-8 and 3-9).

Central filing areas are rooms filled with file cabinets or filing systems. The location of these filing areas—and the location of library stacks in an office or other heavy equipment—must consider the load on the floor. A building structure has two kinds of loads. The *live load* includes the weight of people, furniture, and equipment added to the building. The *dead load* refers to permanent structural elements of the building. Consider a few examples, a four-drawer, 42-inch-wide lateral file cabinet filled with paper can weigh 720 pounds.[4] For a library area such as a law library, the weight of books is harder to determine since books vary so much in size; 25 to 30 pounds per cubic foot of space is

---

[4]De Chiara et al., 1991, p. 287.

Figure 3-7 Typical filing units: a lateral drawer file on the left and a vertical drawer file on the right. (Illustration courtesy of SOI Interior Design.)

Figure 3-8 Mobile open-shelf filing units provide storage for extensive amounts of information. (Photograph courtesy of Jim Franck, Franck & Associates, Inc.)

Figure 3-9 Open unit provides high-density, high-access filing in a modular structure. (Photograph courtesy of TAB, Palo Alto, CA 94304, 1-800-672-3109.)

a common estimating factor.[5] When these units are massed together in one area, it is very easy for their combined weights to exceed the load limits of the floor. The interior designer, with the advice of an architect or engineer, must estimate the total load of these massed storage units. The designer can obtain the live load limits of the floor from the facilities managers, the leasing agents, or the architect to ensure that the floor will not sag or even fail. If the estimated load of the massed units exceeds the safe load limits, it will be necessary to either reinforce the floor or move the storage units to more than one location.

The office will also be provided with seating. The seating piece behind the desk used by the office worker is called *desk seating,* a *posture chair,* a desk chair, or a variety of other names created by manufacturers (Figure 3-10). Side, guest, and conference chairs are items used by office guests and in conference rooms. Other office chairs include secretarial, operational, management, stools, high-back executive, stacking, sled base, and others. Soft seating is another type of seating unit. This group includes lounge chairs, love seats, settees, modular seating, and sofas—generally fully upholstered.

Comfortable, supportive chairs are a requirement, not an option, in office design. An office worker should have a comfortable chair that is functional and supports the body properly. Since the introduction of ergonomic seating for office workers in the 1970s, desk seating has become more comfortable and healthful. Ergonomic chairs are designed not only for greater comfort but also to be more functionally useful. Manufacturers and chair designers have created a variety of ergonomically designed seating to meet the job functions and the status requirements of different levels of employees (Figure 3-11).

There are several functional options related to office chairs. Units used behind a desk and in conference rooms are almost always specified with casters to allow them to move more freely. A single wheel caster is used for hard surface floors and double wheel casters for carpet. Chairs for offices and conference rooms can also be specified to swivel and

---

[5]De Chiara et al., 1991, p. 190.

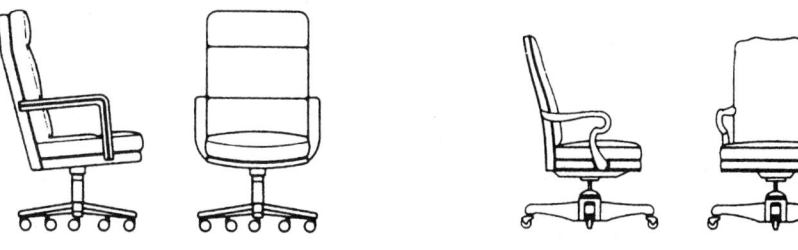

Contemporary executive chair   **Traditional executive chair**

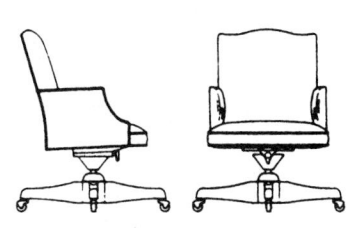

Traditional client chair   **Conference chair**

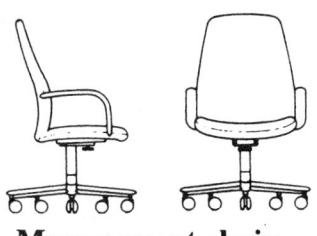

Management chair   **Task chair**

Figure 3-10 Seating units used in offices. (Drawing courtesy of Gunlocke.)

Figure 3-11 Conference room using ergonomically designed Herman Miller Aeron chairs. (Photograph courtesy of 3D/International.)

tilt. These options are appreciated by the office worker, regardless of job or rank, for their comfort. Guest chairs used in offices, often in reception areas of small businesses, and in small conference rooms come in many styles, providing various functional and aesthetic options. It is common for manufacturers to have several versions of the same style chair so that a single source can be used for seating.

Upholstery should also be selected with maintenance as well as aesthetics in mind. Office chairs and other seating, whether behind the desk or as a soft seating unit in an office or the reception area, takes a lot of wear and tear. Manufacturers provide many options for upholstery to suit the interior designer's and company's aesthetic goals. The upholstery fabrics available from the factory are guaranteed to look right and stand up to the hard use of office seating. Interior designers can also use *customer's own materials* (COMs), selecting goods from a source other than the chair manufacturer. However, some seating companies cannot use COM fabric because the shape of the chair or fabric is not flexible enough. Even if the fabric is accepted, the manufacturer may not guarantee the performance of a COM. Seating units are always more costly when COM is specified.

The alternative to using case goods or conventional office furniture when a company decides to use an open or modified open plan for its office layouts is some type of systems furniture. Terms that are useful in understanding systems furniture are presented in Table 3-5. Systems furniture combines vertical panels that are less than full height with components like shelves and worksurfaces that are hung from the divider panels to create the offices—which are commonly called *workstations*. A major advantage of using systems furniture is potential space savings. By utilizing more vertical space via the divider panels, stations can be functionally designed to meet the individual job requirements while saving many square feet of floor space. For example, a small manager's office using conventional furniture requires a minimum of 120 to 140 square feet. This same workstation could be accommodated in 80 to 100 square feet with a systems furniture design. Assuming that the stations are planned based on true functional needs, the total space savings could reduce the amount of square footage the company needs to rent or build, thus reducing rental or construction expenses significantly (Figure 3-12). Table 3-6 highlights some key advantages and disadvantages of using systems furniture.

There are hundreds of options in the styles of systems furniture, providing the interior designer with many choices to meet the functional needs, aesthetic desires, and price

TABLE 3-5 Systems Furniture and Planning Terms

- **Components:** The individual items, such as shelves, worksurfaces, and drawer units, that are attached to or hung from the divider panels.

- **Counter caps** (also called transaction surfaces): Used on low panels (34 to 48 inches high) in reception areas to create a more private across-the-counter transaction area.

- **Divider panels:** The vertical support units that form the workstations and from which components are hung. Width and height dimensions of panels are given in nominal dimensions. The most typical nominal panel widths are 12, 18, 24, 30, 36, 45, and 48 inches. The most typical panel heights are 30, 36, 39, 45, 47, 53, 63, 72, and 85 inches.

- **Office landscape:** A design methodology developed in the 1950s using conventional furniture and plants, but few if any wall partitions.

- **Pedestal:** A combination of drawers that can be suspended from the worksurface. It is mobile or freestanding and functions like a pedestal on a case goods desk.

- **Peninsula worksurface:** A worksurface that attaches at one end to another worksurface and juts out into the workstation to create a desk-like appearance.

- **Storage shelves:** Components that come in various heights and widths; they are open or closable.

- **Systems furniture** (also called modular furniture): A furniture product that consists of divider panels and components used to provide station functionality.

- **Task lights** (also called shelf lights): Luminaries that fit under shelf units.

- **Workstation:** An individual work area or "office" created by the use of vertical divider panels and components

- **Worksurface:** The product that serves as the desktop. It may be rectangular, curved, corner, split top, or curvilinear in shape.

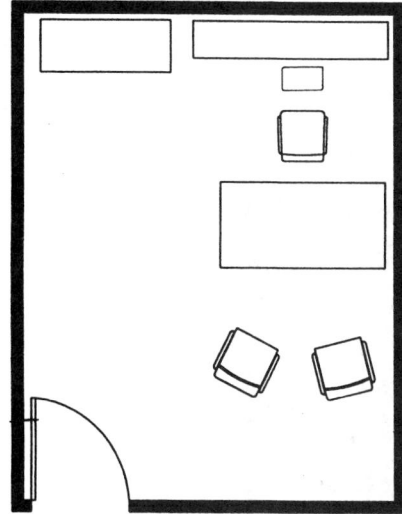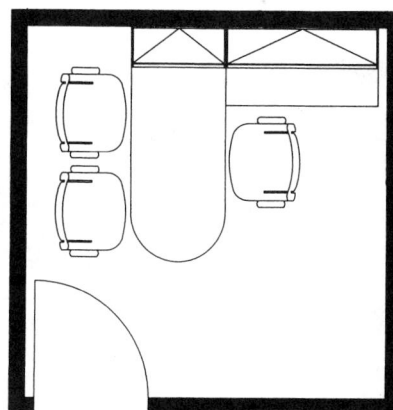

Figure 3-12 Plans of two managers' offices showing savings in square footage with the use of systems furniture, on the right, as opposed to the conventional office, on the left. (System plan courtesy of Herman Miller, Inc., Zeeland, MI.)

point of systems furniture for office projects. Not only are the styles and finishes different, but the way the products are configured varies. However, when all the differences are noted by the manufacturers' representatives, there are really only six categories of systems products that have been developed over the years.

- *Vertical divider panels.* This is the simplest and generally least expensive way of using systems furniture and the open plan. Divider panels—possibly with the use of overhead shelves—are combined with freestanding desks. Power and technology cannot be run through the base of the panels. Panels have low acoustic ratings.
- *Case goods product.* Generally, components are attached to and supported from the sides of panels. The furniture has the look of conventional furniture using the open plan (Figure 3-13).

TABLE 3-6 Advantages and Disadvantages of Using Open Plan and Systems Furniture

Advantages

- *Lower build-out and construction costs.* Fewer full-height partitions are needed. Some permanent mechanical systems construction is reduced as well.
- *Less down time.* Less time is needed to tear down workstations and reconfigure the spaces for new uses than for demolition and new construction of hard walls.
- *Flexible.* Reconfiguration of workstations can be done quickly and can easily meet individual employees' needs.
- *Energy savings.* Open plans generally reduce costs for building and operating the HVAC system. Less ductwork, wiring, and other kinds of hard equipment at the time of initial installation are required.
- *Potential tax savings.* Panels are considered furniture and as such are subject to a different depreciation calculation than full-height walls.

Disadvantages

- *Lack of privacy.* Loss of the private office remains an issue in many projects.
- *Noise.* Open plans can be noisy if acoustical issues are not addressed.
- *Lack of status.* A workstation has less status than an office. However, the styles of furniture and finishes available today make it easy for the designer to provide for distinctions in status.
- *Initial higher furniture costs.* Panels and components are initially more expensive than movable furniture and constructing walls. Systems becomes cheaper when the client needs to reconfigure space often.

Figure 3-13 Use of open plan systems furniture with a case goods appearance. (Photograph courtesy of Kimball Office Group.)

- *Modular component systems* (also called *panel based*). These products consist of monolithic vertical panels that support a wide variety of components anywhere along their height. Components are cantilevered from the back panels, not the side, and are generally adjustable in 1-inch increments (Figure 3-14).
- *Frame and tile.* A steel frame is the basis of the layout of stations. Horizontal tiles and components create the station and finish the exterior surface, giving a more architectural look to the systems furniture (Figure 3-15).
- *Raceway system.* The freestanding units have an integrated raceway that, depending on the manufacturer, can be located at any height to carry the necessary electrical, computer, and telephone cabling.
- *Pole-based system.* Vertical poles are configured with horizontal screens to define workstations and support components. Fast and easy to reconfigure, these systems work well for noncubical work stations (Figure 3-16).

Systems furniture is very flexible to accommodate changes in workstation configurations. It is very adaptable to changes in office technology. L- and U-shaped configurations

Figure 3-14 Modular component system showing vertical panels supporting components. Action Office system. (Photograph courtesy of Herman Miller, Inc., and Hedrick Business Photography.)

Figure 3-15 Horizontal tiles and components add a more architectural look to the systems furniture. (Photograph courtesy of Herman Miller, Inc., Zeeland, MI. Photographer: James Terkeurst.)

Figure 3-16 A pole-based system has boomerangs positioned outbound, which gives each worker more square footage and accessibility. (Resolve system. Courtesy of Herman Miller, Inc., Zeeland, MI.)

provide plenty of surface space for equipment and regular paperwork. Overhead shelves and many other types of components provide all the functional equipment equivalences of a case goods–style office in less space.

Open office projects are planned around a skeleton of divider panels. The panels create workstations, form aisles, and provide varying amounts of privacy. Depending on the product, components such as shelves, worksurfaces, and files can be suspended from the panels. Panels also provide a certain amount of acoustical control and allow for the distribution of electrical, telephone, and data transmission throughout the space. Panels are freestanding or self-supporting, meaning that they are not attached to the floor. Care must be taken in the design of the station and the way components are used so that the panels are designed safely. It is essential to follow the manufacturer's directions on how to design with any open plan panel system and components.

Panels are available in several different widths and heights to meet the needs of employees and support their functions. These vary with the manufacturer and the type of product but generally have nominal widths ranging from 12 to 60 inches and heights ranging from 34 to 96 inches. Most workstations consist of panels that are 53 to 85 inches high. Panels of this height provide what is called *sit-down privacy*, meaning that the individual within the station, when seated, generally cannot be seen by individuals passing by (see Figure 3-14). Seventy-two to 85-inch-high panels provide what is commonly called *stand-up privacy*. This means that the individual in the station, even when standing, generally cannot be seen by someone passing by. Panels of this height are often used for the workstations of upper-level personnel and for conference spaces. Lower heights are used for counters such as a receptionist station (Figure 3-17).

The interior designer must remember that panels also have thickness. His or her detailed floor plans should consider the thickness of panels and any systems creep that might be involved. *Systems creep* means that every time the panel run makes a turn, the designer must allow for the thickness of the panel and any connection hardware. Designers who forget to plan systems projects with the proper panel thicknesses and systems creep find that their floor plans often do not fit the space. Not all panels have the same thickness, so the interior designer must be sure that panel thickness is considered when planning (Figure 3-18).

Figure 3-17 Vertical panels, at varying heights, can support a wide variety of components. (Photograph courtesy of Kimball Office Group.)

Systems workstations are completed with the specification of various components. Horizontal surfaces called *worksurfaces* in place of desktops and table tops, open or closed shelving, file units, drawer configurations, and numerous miscellaneous pieces provide the total work environment of the stations. Depending on the system and the design of the product, components can be hung in many locations on the panel, providing numerous

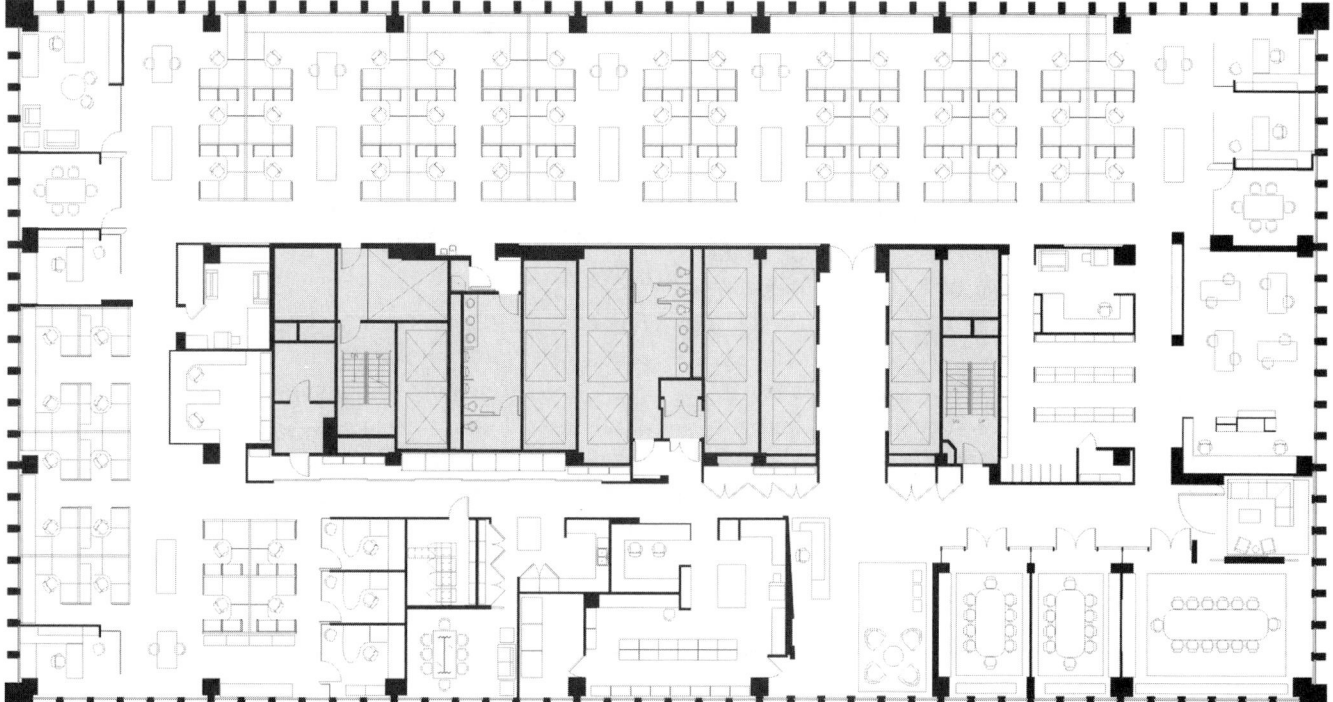

Figure 3-18 Floor plan example of systems office planning. (Floor plan courtesy of Huntsman Architectural Group.)

BOX 3-1   DESIGNING COMPUTER WORKSTATIONS

Many employees work in an office or workstation that has not been designed to effectively incorporate a computer. Computer workstations require planning and careful specification of furniture to help prevent unnecessary physical trauma to employees. A huge medical cost to businesses is carpel tunnel syndrome. It is usually associated with disorders affecting the arms, wrists, and fingers because of repetitive tasks at a keyboard. Constant repetitive movements resulting in potential injury to hands, fingers, and arms can be the result of poorly designed work areas or the employee's work habits.

There is no perfect solution to the problem of creating a healthy, responsive computer workstation. People have varying body dimensions, different vision characteristics, and different ways of working. However, there are some standards that help create a responsive computer workstation. The research on these standards has been performed primarily by systems furniture and computer hardware manufacturers. This section discusses important planning considerations for computers in office environments.

An effective and healthy computer workstation requires specification of an appropriate desk, seating, and lighting. There are many furniture items today that can be used to accommodate computer equipment and provide a measure of comfort. Case goods products are less flexible than systems furniture. The designer needs to select case goods with care so that as much flexibility as possible is achieved with the cabinet to be used for the computer. Systems furniture provides many options since there is greater adjustability and a variety of components to design a workstation.

Proper positioning of the monitor and keyboard is essential in the specification and design of a computer workstation. Monitors should be located within a maximum 40 degree field of view. This means that the top of the monitor should be level with the worker's eyes and the user's chin should have a slight downward slant. For many workers, the standard desk height of 29 to 30 inches locates the monitor at the wrong height for proper vision. Adjustments in the height of the monitor should not have to be done haphazardly but rather by proper specification of furniture or components. There is no consensus as to how far the monitor should be from the worker's eyes; however, a range of 18 to 22 inches is common. Keyboards should be positioned so that the wrists are not sharply bent, resting on the desktop, or resting on the edge of the keyboard. Keyboard trays below the desk surface allow this position with most furniture products.

Comfortable seating is needed as well. Ergonomically designed seating that allows the worker to sit comfortably at the computer reduces back, leg, and arm problems. Chair seats and backs should be adjustable. The backrest should have lumbar support, and its position should be adjustable so that the lumbar support area fits the user's back comfortably. Ideally, the seat pan is a *waterfall front*, which is a rounded soft edge at the knee edge of the chair. This feature promotes comfort and helps prevent stress against the back of the legs. The edge of the seat pan should not be in contact with the back of the employee's knees. If the chair has armrests, they should be recessed from the front edge of the chair so that the chair can be pulled up to the keyboard, providing proper seating distance. When the worker is seated, his or her feet should rest flat on the floor or be supported by a small footrest. This means that the seat height should also be adjustable.

Eyestrain, fatigue, and blurred vision are some of the problems that are caused by poor lighting design in computer areas. The best solution to the lighting problem for computer work areas is a combination of properly designed ambient or low-level general lighting with task lighting at the workstation. The computer monitor should be positioned at a 90 degree angle to adjacent windows rather than facing windows or having the windows behind the screen to prevent glare.

This brief discussion has concentrated on office applications. However, the design principles and guidelines apply to all computer stations, regardless of the type of business. Interior designers need to work with the client, lighting designer, and computer hardware supplier to ensure that the workstations and offices supplied with computers are designed to prevent health problems caused by poorly designed work areas as much as possible.

configurations to meet the functional job needs of employees. Exactly how many components may be put on one or both sides of the panels, and what kind of support is required, are dictated by the manufacturer. The interior designer must check with the manufacturer of the furniture product being used to make sure that it is being designed to be stable and safe.

Materials and Finishes

Improvements to the interior of an office building increase the value of the building for the owner. The greater the value of the architectural finishes utilized, the more value is added to the asset. For example, marble floors in the corridors of the executive area will add more value to the building than carpet. If the client owns the building, he or she may see the use of high-end materials for walls and floors as a contribution to the company's assets.

On the other hand, when a client rents a portion of a building, improvements to the building made by the tenant belong to the landlord, not the tenant. That is why many clients are reluctant to spend a great deal of money on special architectural finishes when they rent office space. The costs for those materials come primarily out of the pocket of the tenant, but the value goes to the landlord.

Tenants receive an allowance from the landlord to pay for certain improvements to the space. The allowance is usually for a group of materials that are considered building standards, as well as for the cost of building and supplying certain non-load-bearing structural elements such as partitions, plumbing, and architectural lighting fixtures. This is done to maintain some continuity of design in exterior and interior public spaces. Some of these standards, like window treatments and door styles, must be used. If the interior designer cannot utilize the building standards or wishes to specify materials that are priced beyond the built-out allowance, then the client may approve of upgrading the materials. The client pays the difference between the allowance and the upgrade. As noted in Table 3-3, these upgrades are called lease-hold improvements; an upgrade from vinyl tile in the entry to marble is an example. The landlord is generally in favor of these improvements, since they increase the value of the property. Some improvements, however, may be discouraged, as they make renting the space to another tenant in the future difficult.

Materials used on the floors, walls, and ceiling, as well as window treatments, must meet the applicable building and accessibility codes. Architectural finishes must be commercial-grade products to stand up to heavy wear and maintenance. Let us look at flooring materials first.

Carpeting is the most common material for flooring in most areas of the office. Resilient and hard surface materials are also used in some areas, especially utilitarian areas like mail rooms and storage rooms. Carpeting provides acoustical control and is more comfortable. Commercial-grade carpets with a tightly tufted or woven short-level looped surface function best for heavy foot traffic, movement of chairs, and overall ease of maintenance. Care must be taken in the specification of carpet since dry conditions and carpet fibers can create static electricity, which can damage computer data or hardware. Carpet with static-inhibiting fibers is the best solution to this problem. Topical treatments can also be used; however, they are not as reliable. Cut pile surfaces will show traffic patterns faster unless they are extremely dense carpets with a short nap. It will also be much harder to move office chairs on a plush surface than on a looped surface. On the other hand, executive areas that receive less wear can be specified with cut pile surfaces and more luxurious materials. Code requirements will also vary for carpets, depending on the space where the carpet is used. In general, carpet must consist of National Fire Protection Association (NFPA)-101® Class I or Class II materials. Interior designers must check with the applicable jurisdiction for specific code requirements for the facility. ADA requirements limit the height of the pile with backing to 0.5 inch.

Interesting custom designs can be created with carpet tiles that might not be possible with broadloom carpet. When the project is primarily an open plan project, carpet tiles are particularly advantageous. They can provide access to floor outlets and raised floor mechanical chases without damaging the flooring. In fact, carpet tiles are required when carpeting is used over a raised floor. Carpet tiles are manufactured and installed in sections 18 to 24 inches square. Depending on the manufacturer's instructions, carpet tiles might be installed with self-releasing or minimal adhesives so that they can easily be replaced if damaged or if they show heavy wear. The initial cost of the tiles is greater than that of broadloom carpet of equivalent quality. The ADA requirements cited above also apply to carpet tiles.

Resilient and hard surface materials are noisier than carpet and are used sparingly in office environments. The heaviest traffic areas, like entrance lobbies, public corridors, and restrooms, are commonly specified to have resilient and hard surface flooring. Some areas of the office that require higher-end design specification, such as portions of executive suites, might also see the use of woods, ceramic tiles, or stones for flooring materials. Interior designers need to choose resilient and hard surface materials carefully to ensure that office users do not slip on slick surfaces. Some of these materials also require more maintenance to keep them looking good. This factor alone can influence the selection of flooring materials.

The specification of materials for use on full-height partition walls will be regulated by the location of the walls within the project space. An exit access corridor wall will have higher code restrictions and thus more limitations on material types compared to the walls creating a private office or conference room. If a wallcovering is to be used in corridors and exit ways, only commercial-grade materials should be specified. A wide variety of patterns and colors of commercial wallcoverings is available to create the right backdrop for corridors and other partition walls in the interior spaces. Depending on local codes, the designer may have the option of using residential-grade materials in private offices and conference rooms. If the designer wishes to use textile wallcoverings, he or she must check with the local jurisdiction concerning any code restrictions. In some jurisdictions, textiles on walls are allowed only if a sprinkler system is in the facility or the textile is treated with a fire-resistant chemical. Unfortunately, this will change the color of the textile to some degree. Architectural surfaces in office occupancies that will qualify for classification as businesses must be Class I when used in enclosed stairways, Class II when used in other corridors, and Class III in other areas.

TABLE 3-7 Selected Construction Terminology

- **Base building:** The shell of the building, including building core structures such as elevators and restrooms.

- **Bearing walls:** Walls that support the loads of floors and/or ceilings from above.

- **Curtain wall:** An exterior wall that supports no weight except its own and is attached to structural members of the building.

- **Dead load:** The permanent structural elements of the building.

- **Demountable wall:** An interior partition that is built at a factory and held in place by tension.

- **Floor slab:** Commonly reinforced concrete made as an on-site poured floor or of precast units. Floor slabs can be made in other ways and of other materials as well.

- **Live load:** The weight of people, furniture, and equipment added to the building.

- **Metal studs:** Preformed steel units used in place of wood studs in commercial buildings. Other structural units that mirror many wood structural pieces can also be made of steel.

- **On grade:** Structural flooring placed directly in contact with the ground.

- **Plenum:** The space between acoustical tiles and the floor above in a commercial building. Mechanical systems such as lighting, electrical, and plumbing systems can be located in the plenum.

- **Stick built:** A slang term for construction of partitions and other parts of a building constructed on site.

- **Suspended acoustical ceiling:** Acoustical tiles are suspended on T-shaped runners. These runners are attached by wires to the floor deck above and the perimeter walls. Light fixtures can be placed within the grid resting on or attached to the T-runner.

Most office partitions are stick built on site and, depending on the building classification and local codes, are constructed of metal or wood studs covered with drywall. Some clients use demountable walls for the office partitions. A *demountable wall* is an interior partition built at a factory in specific sizes. These walls are then held in place by tension via a gripper system on the bottom of the wall and attached to the T-bar in suspended ceilings at the top. They can be relocated when the needs of the office require a new space plan. Demountable walls require less down time for demolition and new construction. They can be finished with drywall and painted, but are most commonly finished with a vinyl or fabric wallcovering that meets Class A fire code requirements. Demountable walls can also accommodate windows and doors so that fully private offices of almost any size or configuration can be created. Electrical and communications cables fit within cavities in the wall sections. Plumbing, however, is not generally accommodated in demountable walls since they are not thick enough to handle waste pipes (see Table 3-7).

The primary materials used for ceilings in commercial offices facilities are ceiling tiles made primarily of fiberglass. In most large spaces, the predominant type of ceiling tile specified is 2 by 4 feet. In smaller rooms, a 2 by 2 foot tile might be used. Ceilings have various qualities of sound absorption and finishes.

The tiles are installed in a metal ceiling grid suspended from the structural ceiling above. Mechanical systems like HVAC ducts, electrical wiring, plumbing for fire sprinklers, and telephone and data cables are installed in the space between the acoustical tiles and the structural ceiling above. This space is called the *plenum*. Lighting fixtures can be easily dropped into the grid or holes can be cut to install various kinds of spot and can lighting.

Some clients want to eliminate the suspended ceiling in certain areas and keep the appearance of the mechanical systems as part of the design. Eliminating a suspended ceiling means that the space will be noisier. Generally, the ceiling will control 60 to 65 percent of sound; 25 to 30 percent relates to furniture and 5 to 10 percent to flooring. Other factors that can improve acoustical control in the space should be investigated and specified to maintain a pleasant work environment.

Window treatments are quite simple in commercial office interiors to present a uniform look from the outside. The most common treatments used to achieve this effect are either vertical or horizontal blinds. When an area such as an executive office is being designed, the interior designer might specify fabric drapery over the blinds. However, local fire codes may prohibit the use of textile window coverings in commercial offices unless the material meets a high flame resistance standard or the fabric is treated with a flame-resistant chemical. Like textile wall coverings, flame-resistant treatments of window coverings almost always change the color of the fabric and the hand of the material.

Color is important in the office interior—as in any commercial interior—because it "contributes to the productivity and to the psychological satisfaction of the occupants in a space."[6] Interior designers can do a wide variety of exciting designs or create calming backgrounds by the use of color in office interiors. The Color Marketing Group (CMG) annually forecasts the colors that will predominate in fashion, interior design, and other products and services related to consumer and commercial industries. Interior designers look to these forecasts to determine what might happen to the products they will get from manufacturers, as well as what they can suggest to clients as cutting-edge design.

Color preferences are incredibly varied in office facilities. Interior designers generally have many choices on color schemes. Some businesses may have color standards for their offices, and these standards as well as general color preferences expressed by the client must be honored. A workable and pleasing color scheme, in conjunction with proper lighting, can increase productivity and worker comfort; thus, color schemes should be selected carefully.

Interior designers should remember light reflectance factors related to color choices. Light values will reflect a high percentage of light, while dark values will reflect very little light. Office areas with few or no windows should not be specified with dark colors.

---

[6]Ragan, 1995, p. 33.

Almost any color combination can work in today's office facility if it is planned carefully and if it meets the wishes of the client.

Mechanical Systems

As with most types of commercial spaces, the interior designer has a support role in the design and specification of the mechanical systems for an office project. The designer may provide lighting design services or a specialty lighting designer may be retained to plan the lighting from the floor plans and equipment drawings. When specifying any systems projects, the interior designer will be involved in the planning of electrical, data, and telecommunications service, as these are integral to most divider panels. Acoustic treatment is another "mechanical system" the interior designer must understand, as it is integral to the planning of systems furniture products. The fact that the interior designer may be less involved in the design of mechanical systems does not negate his or her responsibility to understand how these systems work and are a part of the overall office design.

This section provides information on the design of the mechanical systems of an office project. We will discuss lighting design, electrical interface especially as it impacts open plan systems products, data and telecommunications, and acoustics.

Lighting

The latter half of the 20th century saw lighting design for offices emphasize a uniform quantity of light throughout the space, generally providing substantially more light on the desk surfaces and surrounding space than was actually needed. This uniform quantity of light—created by the use of fluorescent fixtures incorporated into the acoustical ceiling tile grid—did not consider the visual comfort or quality of the lighting or the aesthetics of the light in the interior. The late 1970s began an era of change in the design of office lighting. An energy crisis brought on by an oil embargo and skyrocketing energy costs encouraged building owners, architects, interior designers, and manufacturers to seek out more efficient ways to light the office environment. Today there are many more options to provide energy-efficient lighting to meet functional requirements.

Interior designers face the greatest challenge in lighting designs when the client is leasing office space. Most often, the building owner has dictated the types of lighting fixtures, the sizes of fixtures, and even the colors of the lamps in the fixtures. Replacing building standard fixtures adds substantially to the build-out cost for the tenant, who has financial responsibility for the upgrades. When a client cannot afford to make changes, the interior designer will need to do more careful planning and specification of colors, materials, and textures to design a space that is functional and attractive.

Lighting specification begins with identifying the tasks to be performed in each area and room of the office facility. This information is used in conjunction with standard lighting level guidelines provided by the Illuminating Engineering Society to calculate the required lighting for the different tasks and areas of the facility. The types of fixtures and the placement of fixtures to achieve the required lighting levels must be carefully researched and specified (Table 3-8).

In an office, lighting specification is complicated because of computer monitors. Light from windows as well as from ceiling fixtures can easily cause glare, leading to eye fatigue. *Glare* is uncomfortably bright or reflected light that makes it difficult for an individual to see properly. It occurs when the light is brighter than that to which the individual is accustomed. The light from a window reflecting on a computer screen makes it nearly impossible to see the screen. Light reflecting down from direct ceiling fixtures also creates great difficulty for the office worker. This indicates how important it is for the designer to specify general and task lighting with great care beyond the specification of the fixture.

Like nearly all kinds of commercial interiors, offices utilize three types of lighting to meet the needs of the client and the interior designer. *Ambient lighting* (sometimes called

TABLE 3-8 Office Lighting Levels

	Footcandle Guideline
Auditoriums and assembly spaces	30–100
Lobbies	50
Corridors	10–20
Conference rooms	30
Routine work with task lighting as needed	50–100
Moderate computer work with some task lighting	20–60
Drafting	100–200

general lighting) provides a uniform level of illumination sufficient for individuals in the space to move around safely. The most common method to accomplish this is direct ambient lighting using fluorescent fixtures surface mounted or recess mounted on the ceiling. Ambient lighting can also be achieved by an indirect method whereby light is bounced off the ceiling from fixtures that are standing on the floor, placed on top of shelves, or suspended from the ceiling rather than directed down from the ceiling. This indirect method is a common lighting solution when the open plan and systems furniture are used.

Ambient lighting often does not provide adequate-quality light for many tasks. Small movable fixtures such as desk lamps or undershelf fixtures deliver light to a specific location, creating *task lighting*. Task lighting provides each office worker with the additional light needed to work comfortably. Tungsten-halogen lamps are commonly found in task fixtures. They are very efficient and compact, producing good color rendition and essentially white light. The high temperatures that these lamps operate at can be dangerous unless the lamp itself is shielded and not placed so that combustible materials come in contact with the lamp or the area of the fixtures where the lamp is housed.

In large office spaces, accent lighting may be used. Track lighting, lighting in soffits, and spotlights provide design interest to the interior. Artwork may be highlighted in the reception area and conference room, soffit lights may be specified in the employee lunchroom, and track lights may even be used as supplemental or primary ambient fixtures instead of fluorescent tube fixtures. The designer must factor accent lights into the overall light levels since these fixtures will contribute to the overall ambient light level.

Daylighting has become a more critical form of office lighting with the new interest in energy conservation and sustainable design. Daylight is natural light produced by the sun that enters a building through windows, skylights, or reflections off surfaces. Interior design planning that removes the traditional full-height-wall private office from the perimeter of the building allows more daylight to enter the entire office space. Factoring daylighting into the lighting load may allow companies to reduce or modify the number of artificial light fixtures and the types of lamps used. However, daylighting also has a down side. Increased glare, heat from the sun through uncovered windows, veiling reflections, and sun damage to furniture and finishes all must be considered as part of the trade-off when using daylight as a functional lighting source. And, of course, daylighting provides no functional light if the offices must be available to workers at night.

Electrical, Telephone, and Data Communications

The greatest challenge in providing electrical, telephone, and data communications services to offices occurs when the program calls for the use of any type of open office systems furniture. If the project is predominantly a closed plan with conventional furniture, providing electrical services (as well as the other systems) is much less complicated. The interior designer is most concerned with the wiring system within the building. The National Electrical Code (NEC), part of the National Fire Protection Association (NFPA), continues to provide the standards for planning the electrical systems in commercial interiors. The reader is urged to check the NEC and local code interpretations to properly plan the office electrical service. Table 3-9 provides terms important to the discussion on electrical, data, and communications systems.

In designing an office facility, the interior designer must locate on his or her equipment plans all office equipment and lighting fixtures that will be specified. In addition, the reflected ceiling plans must indicate the ambient and accent fixtures planned for all

TABLE 3-9 Selected Mechanical Systems Terminology

Lighting

- **Ambient lighting**: Provides a uniform level of illumination sufficient so that individuals in the space can safely move about the area. Also referred to as general lighting.
- **Fixture**: The housing of the luminaire without the lamp.
- **Glare**: Uncomfortably bright or reflected light that makes it difficult to see properly.
- **High Intensity Discharge (HID)**: A type of lamp that produces a high level of light and is very energy efficient. It is used in large spaces as indirect ambient lighting.
- **Lamp**: The glass bulb or tube that, with its inner workings, creates light. In lay terms, it is the floor or table lighting device.
- **Luminaire**: The lighting product comprising the cord, fixture, and lamp. It is commonly called a *lamp* and is generally portable.
- **Task lighting**: Lighting provided to a specific location.

Electrical Systems

- **Access floors**: A raised floor added over a floor slab. The space houses electrical, telephone, and data cabling and HVAC ducts.
- **Amperage**: The amount of electrical current required to operate appliances or equipment.
- **Armored or BX cable**: Two or more insulated wires and a ground wire covered by a flexible wound mental wrapping. It is sometimes called *flexible cable*.
- **Dedicated circuit**: A separate circuit with its own hot, neutral, and ground wires, none of which are shared with any other circuit.
- **Flat cable**: Electrical wiring that has been flattened within a plastic material and then shielded between thin galvanized steel plates. Receptacle boxes can be attached along the flat cable strip. Data and communications flat cable is also available. Flat cable cannot be used under broadloom carpet.
- **Power entry**: A generic term for the point where the building's electrical serv-

ice is wired to a divider panel that feeds power to a series of panels.
- **Rigid conduit**: A heavy steel tube in which insulted wires are fed through to carry electrical wiring.
- **Nonmetallic sheath or Romex cable**: Two or more insulated wires covered by a nonmetallic, moisture-resistant sheath to carry electricity.

Data Systems

- **Coaxial cable**: A data cable with a central core conductor surrounded by insulation material covered by a metal sheath that acts as a second insulator and then finished with an outer coating.
- **Fiberoptic cable**: A data cable utilizing a thin glass filament wire for the transmission of signals.
- **Four-pair cable**: Four sets of two copper wires twisted together and covered by an insulating material.
- **Local Area Network (LAN)**: A telecommunications network designed to eliminate the possibility of signals that would interrupt the network.
- **Twisted-pair cable**: Two copper wires twisted together, shielded by an insulator. It is a basic type of phone/data cable.
- **WLAN**: A wireless version of LAN.

Acoustics

- **Decibel (dB)**: The scale of measurement of sound. The higher the number, the louder the sound. Normal conversation has a rating of 65 dB at a distance of 3 feet.
- **Noise Reduction Coefficient (NRC)**: A numerical value between 0 and 1 representing the fraction or percentage of energy (striking the material) that is absorbed. A rating of 0 means that no sound is absorbed. A rating of 1 means that all the sound is absorbed.
- **Sound Transmission Class (STC)**: A one-number rating that describes the ability of an object to block the transmission of sound. An STC of 0 means that there is no drop in sound level through the object; an STC of 50 means that very little sound goes through.

areas. Interior designers also specify locations for outlets and switches (as well as the types of these items) to ensure that office equipment that will be specified can be accommodated. At minimum, these specifications must adhere to local electrical codes for the occupancy and building type. The actual responsibility for designing the electrical system and meeting the electrical code requirements rests with the architect and the consulting electrical engineer. The interior designer's electrical plans will also provide locations for data and telecommunications equipment. These plans will be reviewed and finalized by the company providing telephone, Internet, and data service.

Commercial buildings have either single-phase or three-phase electrical service. The difference is significant when the client wishes to use primarily an open plan and predominantly or exclusively office systems furniture. *Single-phase service* is called 240/120 V service. It is the former standard for electrical service still found in older commercial buildings. It is designed to support two sets of 120 volt circuits. *Three-phase electrical service* is the present standard in newer commercial buildings. It is called 208 Y/120 V service and is designed to support three sets of 120 volt circuits. This will take care of standard needs in the office space and is necessary to fully utilize all the circuits of a multiple-circuit open office system. In addition, 480 Y/277 V systems are needed for major equipment like the air conditioning system. Older buildings may require new wiring to properly utilize systems furniture products.

Electrical and communications services can be provided to the interior in several ways. Obviously, all these methods are much simpler to achieve and interface electrical and communications service to required locations in new construction and remodeling projects. When the designer must fit the project to the existing structure, more careful planning and coordination are needed. Any of the methods can be connected to the electrical components integrated into systems furniture or case goods products.

The most common method is through partition walls and on the surface of columns. This method is shown in Figure 3-19(c). The interior designer can specify the locations for outlets on the walls as long as these specifications at minimum adhere to local electrical codes. With systems furniture, if the existing outlets are in the right place or can be planned appropriately, this is an inexpensive way to connect panels to the building's electrical system.

Increasingly popular in new commercial office structures is the use of raised floors—also called *access floors*—for electrical and data service (Figure 3-19(b)). The raised floor creates a second floor over the slab. The space between the slab and the raised floor allows the introduction of electrical, telephone, and data cabling. Even HVAC supply flows can be installed within the raised floor, giving flexibility to this system and cost savings in construction through energy savings. The raised floor provides unlimited access to electrical and data systems when the project specifies the use of systems furniture. Carpet tiles are installed over the raised floor system to provide a finished appearance. Broadloom carpet is not allowed with the use of a raised floor.

If the building has used a floor grid for these mechanical services, the floor will have recessed troughs which contain the conduits for electrical, data processing, and telephone service (see Figure 3-19(e)). This is an expensive initial installation and creates problems for the designer whether the project is a closed plan or an open plan. Not all installations are on a grid that will work with the panel system and stations sizes. Most commonly, the grid is not lined up with the panels since the grid was done before the furniture arrangement was designed.

Another common and relatively inexpensive method for remodeling projects is through drops called *power poles* from the ceiling plenum (see Figure 3-19(a)). In commercial buildings with plenums, it is possible to provide power drops exactly where they are required by incorporating power poles to carry the cables and wires from the ceiling grid to the floor. Outlets in the power pole allow for plug-in capability or a panel system product is hard-wired to the power pole.

Electrical and data connections can also be made using a poke through system. In this case, wiring is brought up by drilling holes through the floor deck from the plenum below. The wiring is finalized through surface-mounted or recessed floor monuments, connections to the systems panels, or sometimes power poles. Drilling holes in the floor,

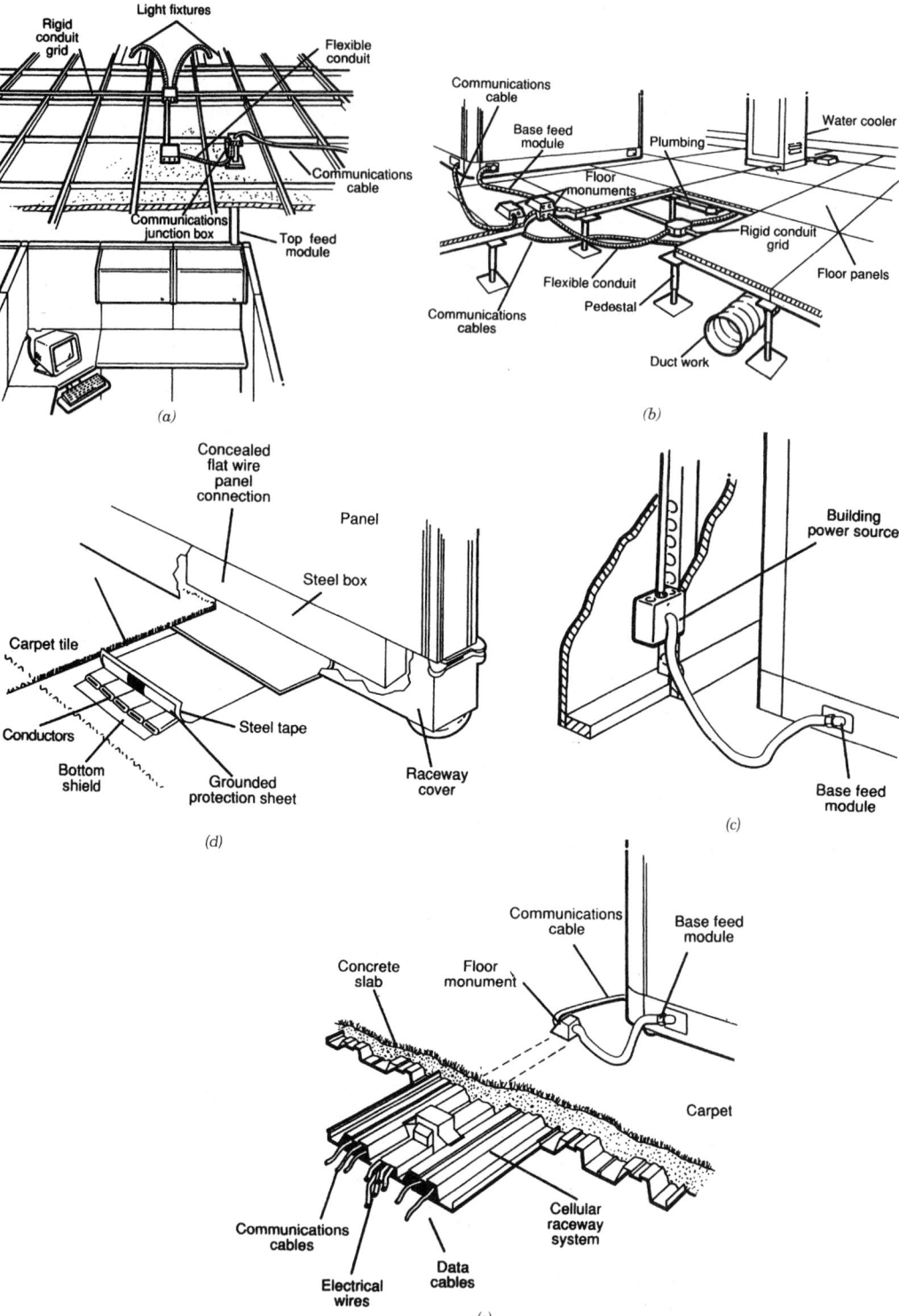

Figure 3-19a–e Electrical service to the panels. (a) Topped with power pole, (b) raised floor, (c) base feed from wall, (d) from flat-wire cable, (e) floor raceway. (Drawing courtesy of Haworth, Inc.)

called *core drilling*, can be done only if the number and locations of the holes do not destroy the structural integrity of the floor system.

A final method is flat cabling. Wiring is flattened, encased in plastic, and attached to the rough floor using special installation techniques to guarantee safety (see Figure 3-19(d)). The flat cable is connected to the wall or a column and runs to the place where the con-

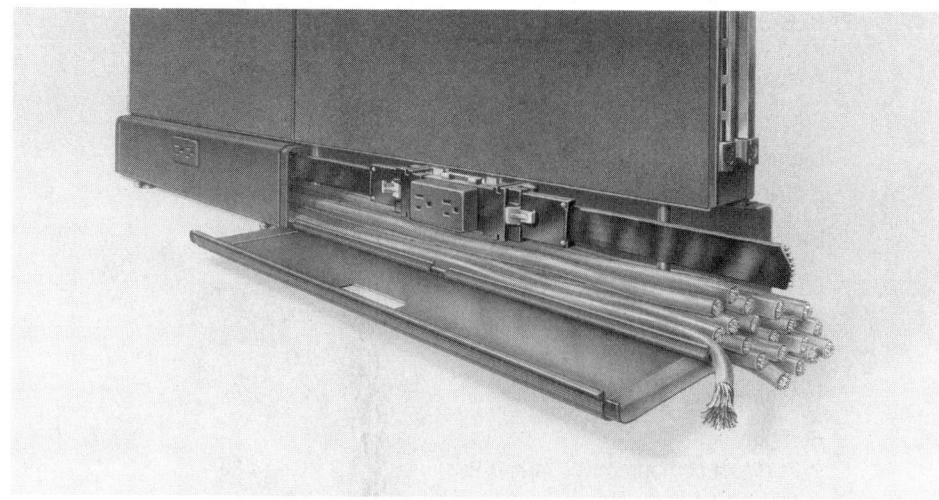

Figure 3-20 Base feed system. Action Office energy distribution system. (Photograph courtesy of Herman Miller, Inc., Zeeland, MI. Photographer: David Jackson.)

nections to panels, power poles, or floor monuments are located. With the popularity of raised floor systems, flat cabling is now used less frequently.

Specification and planning with systems furniture involves understanding the methodology the manufacturer has used to integrate electrical and data communications service with the panels. The most common is the *base feed* system (Figure 3-20). A trough runs along the base of each panel and contains separate channels for electrical conduit and telecommunications cables. By code, these communications cables must be separated from electrical wiring. A second common method of distributing these services in panels is called a *belt line* system. In this case, the outlets and channels are approximately 30 inches above the base of the panel. That height allows for plug-in above the work surface. A vertical channel along one side of the panel brings the service from floor entries or base feeds up to the belt-line feed unit. This is connected to the building's system by any of the methods discussed above.

The integrated electrical components in systems furniture today have two circuits, and others have up to six circuits and space for numerous bundles of telephone and data cables. Multiple circuit systems are important so that the electrical load of the office layout is distributed without overloading the service. With multiple circuits, one circuit is dedicated for use by computer equipment. This "clean" circuit—called a *dedicated circuit*—with its own ground helps prevent the loss of data due to in-house power surges. To properly plan the electrical system for panels and determine the type of electrical service needed, the designer must know the amperage of common office equipment that will be placed in the stations. Table 3-10 lists the amperage for many common pieces of office equipment.

A final design consideration concerning electrical and telecommunications services is wire management. The appliances commonly used in an office today all have wires that must be plugged into outlets or cables that connect one piece of computer equipment to another. These wires and cables can produce a very unsightly and even dangerous mess of "spaghetti" under desks, worksurfaces, and many other places. Systems furniture provides for good wire management by the use of troughs placed just below the worksurface or integrated into the panels. This capability is not always a part of the design of case goods furniture. The interior designer should consider wire management and specify products to help manage these wires and cables to prevent injury, violate codes, and even constitute a fire hazard.

Acoustics

An office can be a noisy environment unless everyone is in a private office and has the door closed. That is rarely the case in today's offices. Although computer equipment—

TABLE 3-10 Amperage of Common Office Equipment

Answering machine	.08
Adding machine	.05
Large electronic calculator	.2
Pencil sharpener	.25
Electric eraser	.25
Radio	.05
Clock	.03
Fan	1.0
Typewriter	1.5
Computer equipment	
Personal computers (VDTs and PCs)	0.08–4.80
Stand-alone printers	3.0–11.0
Processor/disk drive unit	0.08–12.0
Modems	.15
Copiers	
Stand-alone	15.0
Desktop	7.0–10.0
Coffee brewer	10.0
Microwave	8.0–12.0

Source: Steelcase, Inc., used with permission.

especially printers—is much quieter than it was 10 or 15 years ago, noise from equipment, telephone conversations, and business or casual conversations can add significantly to the noise that disturbs work. When the office has primarily an open plan, acoustics becomes an even greater challenge for the interior designer to plan and handle.

The mere existence of noise is not the issue. What is a concern is noise that distracts people from their work. Loud or repetitive noises in particular can interfere with concentration. However, it seems that hearing conversations beyond one's immediate work area is especially disruptive. Generally, it is not the actual noise that is a problem but whether the conversations are intelligible.

Intelligibility refers to the ability to gather information from available sounds. As little as 15 percent of the words in a sentence may make the meaning of the entire sentence clear to the listener. If this drops to less than 10 percent, intelligibility almost vanishes. Sounds may be audible—stimulate the ear—without carrying any intelligibility or without being annoying. In an open plan office, the designer must limit the intelligibility to specified zones while reducing other sounds to tolerable levels.

Sound is measured in terms of *decibel levels* or *dB*. All sounds have different decibel levels, as shown in the examples in Table 3-11. Normal speech between two persons takes place at a distance of about 3 to 3½ feet and produces a decibel level of about 65 dB at the listener's ear. This is such a common level that people tend to adjust their voice level or physical separation to establish to. Have you noticed that restaurants are sometimes exceptionally noisy because of added cell phone conversations? Levels below 30 dB are considered very quiet; levels about 85 dB are very loud, and speech is almost impossible.[7]

Interior designers, acousticians, and architects do not try to make an office as quiet as possible. Some ambient noise will always be present. In fact, when a room is very quiet (no ambient sounds), any sound can be distracting. The idea is to create an environment that is free of distraction, not free of noise. Acoustical control can be achieved by con-

[7]Harris et al., 1991, p. 49.

TABLE 3-11 Decibel Ratings

Deafening	Thunder	dBA of 140
Very loud	Loud street noise	dBA of 100
Loud	Noisy office	dBA of 60
Moderate	Average office	dBA of 50
Faint	Quiet conversation	dBA of 20
Very faint	Normal breathing	dBA of 10

Source: Harris et al. *Planning and Designing the Office Environment,* 2nd ed. Copyright © 1991. Reprinted by permission of John Wiley & Sons, Inc.

trolling the source, the path, and the listener. Careful zoning of work groups—especially those that will be noisy—is important in an open plan project. Utilizing divider panels that have a high acoustical value around persons who can't seem to lower their voices when on the phone is another option. In an open plan project, when people do not need to be in direct communication with each other, the designer should face them away from each other. Noisy work teams should be kept away from those that need quiet.

Thoughtful specification of flooring, wall treatments, and ceiling materials also helps control noise. Carpeting obviously has more acoustic properties than hard surfaces and resilient materials. Specify carpets that provide an NRC of about .40. In areas where constructed full-height partitions are used, sound between offices or areas can be reduced by insulating the walls. In spaces that need very strict reduction of sound transference, the partition walls need to be built up to the next floor deck, not just to the dropped ceiling, so that sound cannot transfer through the ceiling plenum. It may not seem significant, but a vinyl wall covering has better acoustic properties than painted walls. If possible, cover the wall surface at least from the floor to 6 feet above the floor with acoustical materials. Lighting fixtures, for example, that replace absorptive ceiling tiles seriously add to acoustical problems. Using parabolic or egg crate diffusers rather than a flat lens will also help. Windows are commonly a serious contributor to noise unless they are covered with fabric drapes and the drapes are kept closed—an unlikely occurrence. Try to use window walls as traffic aisle walls rather than as part of the workstations.

Masking noise can also help reduce its intelligibility. Masking does not eliminate or reduce noise; rather, it increases the sound level in the space. Sound masking can be achieved by using simply a music system that plays nondistracting music. In more difficult situations or where music cannot be used, an electronic noise-generating system may be needed to produce a background sound. It should be used when the existing background is too quiet to mask annoying sounds or to cover up speech sounds that should not be overheard. The sound produced by electronic masking systems generally sounds like a hiss but is thought of as white noise. It can be adjusted throughout a large space so that sound levels are higher or lower, as needed by nearby occupants. Masking systems should be planned with the aid of an acoustician.

Security

In offices and office buildings, security focuses first on the safety of the employees in the facility. After ensuring their security, almost all offices must secure company and client information. Any of the security issues discussed in Chapter 1 could be a challenge for the office facility, regardless of its size. The reader may wish to refer back to this brief introduction.

The interior designer needs to discuss security issues with the client during programming. Many companies will need minimal security beyond fireproof safes or file cabinets to store paper and computer records. Others will want the design team to include a security consultant in the design of sophisticated monitoring and access systems. The design team must understand what level of security is needed so that the design will protect the employees and property without causing undue cost or even anxiety.

How many and what kinds of security mechanisms are needed depend on the nature of the business. A research and development company must protect data and prototypes of new products. Banks have to guard funds, negotiable securities, and other documents. The theft of computers from an accounting office gives the thief extensive information on businesses and personal financial information that can lead to identity theft of the accounting firm's clients. Workers in government offices may feel particularly vulnerable to intrusions of unauthorized individuals.

Many office buildings have security guards on the street level by the elevators. Security guards often are used to provide security passes to visitors. The desk or counter for the security guards is a custom-designed millwork item that must accommodate telephone equipment, perhaps monitors displaying security cameras, storage cabinets, computers and printers to print out visitors' badges, and other needs specific to the corporation. Visitors are not generally allowed to wander through office facilities. They are accompanied by an employee to conference rooms or employee offices for meetings. The security system in an office building may also be linked to the fire safety system.

As with many kinds of commercial facilities, clear sightlines in reception rooms and lobbies with observant employees is often the first line of defense in an office facility. Passing traffic from reception areas to the work areas that are secured with buzzers or at least a closable door prevents visitors from wandering into the facility unescorted. Placement of a receptionist across from the elevators makes security easier on each floor of a high-rise office building.

Employees may also need to show identification cards or use card access passes to move from the entrance to the upper floors of the building. Card access or keypad hardware is often required for access to secure rooms like computer rooms and areas where financial records are kept. More sophisticated access systems like retinal scanning devices may be required of the most secure areas in government buildings and corporate research areas.

If the project requires secure rooms, the interior designer should understand that standard partitions do not provide more security. Wallboard can be easily penetrated to break into a room unless special provisions are made. The partition must go to the ceiling deck above, not the dropped ceiling. It may even be necessary to reinforce some walls with steel or masonry. A lower level of acoustical security for a conference room can be achieved by specifying batt insulation in the walls. However, this is not enough for highly sensitive secure rooms.

Security and safety of the employees and visitors to office facilities can take many forms. The interior designer must work with the client, architect, and security consultant to do all that is possible to meet the security needs of the particular business.

Code Requirements

Offices as well as all other commercial facilities are subject to building, life safety, and accessibility codes and regulations. The interior designer's responsibility in this area begins with understanding which codes actually affect the project. Today most jurisdictions in the United States have adapted all or parts of the International Building Code (IBC) along with the companion fire, plumbing, electrical, mechanical, and other codes. However, a jurisdiction may still use one of the other model codes. The model codes for life safety (or fire) are generally those written by the NFPA, which includes the Life Safety Code (NFPA 100). In the United States, accessibility regulations are governed by the ADA. The primary code used in Canada is the National Building Code of Canada (NBC). In Canada, each province may have specific code variations that affect elements of the design and specification of structures. Canada and its provinces have their own accessibility regulations and do not use the ADA guidelines. A jurisdiction can also modify one of the model codes or write its own codes to suit its needs and laws. Remember that the codes in effect in the location of the design firm's office may not be those existing at the location of the project. It is the designer's responsibility to know what codes are applicable to the project's location.

Office buildings and professional service offices such as accounting, law, medical (not housed within a hospital), and other offices are considered business occupancies. This classification will direct many of the interior designer's decisions concerning space planning and architectural finish specification. In addition to the occupancy type, the occupancy load will affect planning decisions. For example, a small office having up to 50 occupants can generally be designed with only one exit door. An office with 51 or more occupants will require two exits. As the number of occupants increases, additional exits must be provided. Offices on the second story or above may be required to have additional exits, even with occupancy under 50. Naturally, these general requirements may not be true in all cases and in all jurisdictions. The designer must check applicable codes. The building codes will affect design choices in areas such as the size, number, and locations of egress doors; the size of corridors and aisles; specification of architectural finishes; and permissible lengths of corridors. Of course, there are many other code issues that will influence the design of individual projects.

In the United States, office facilities are generally considered public buildings or at least the business occupancy is open to the general public. When this is the case (some office facilities may not meet this criteria), the office plan must meet the ADA's accessibility design guidelines in every respect. The ADA guidelines affect the size of corridors and aisles; the location of areas of refuge in multistory and very large one-story buildings; design and location of signage; heights of reception counters and drinking fountains; flooring specifications; and, of course, the design of public toilet facilities. Interior designers should provide circulation paths at least 44 inches wide, to provide turnaround areas at intersections of paths, and should design entrances into workstations that are at least 36 inches wide to facilitate accessibility in all plans. Remember that corridors in closed plan projects may need to be larger than 44 or 36 inches, depending on the size of the total space and the number of occupants in any one complex. The reader should refer to the accessibility design guidelines for specific accessibility requirements. Chapter 9 includes a discussion of the design specification of accessible public restrooms.

Most jurisdictions adopt the Life Safety Code published by the NFPA for detailed regulations on finish materials. However, the building codes also have chapters that deal with finish materials. In office facilities, the finishes applied to the walls, floor, ceiling, and window treatments will have restrictions. Materials in exits and exit access corridors will be required to be Class A or B for walls and ceiling and Class I or II for floor finishes. Materials in private offices or other spaces within the office can be Class A, B, or C and Class II.

Depending on the jurisdiction and building type where the office is located, the fabric, the fillings, and even the upholstered furniture items must pass one or more tests. Smolder resistance tests such as the Cigarette Ignition Test determine the smolder resistance of a textile or a seating mock. The ASTM E1537 Test Method for Fire Testing of Real-Scale Upholstered Furniture Item, also know as the *CAL 133* or *TB 133 test,* is a very strict smolder test; all components of the seating item—fabric, stuffing, and frame—must pass the test.

Manufacturers who produce commercial-grade upholstery, wall coverings, and flooring test their products and certify that they have passed certain tests. These test results are identified on hang tags and catalogs. Fire marshals or other code officials may require that testing information be provided before the client can occupy a space. The interior designer should be sure to give this information to the client for his or her records.

In states that require the whole furniture item to pass the CAL 133 test, manufacturers test the seating item and certify that it passes the test; otherwise, the unit cannot be used in many types of occupancies. If any one item in the unit fails the test, the unit cannot be used. This test is applicable to occupancies that contain 10 or more seating units, especially in places of assembly and institutional occupancies. Some jurisdictions may require that seating pass this test in large office environments as well. This fire safety code has been adopted by many states in addition to California. The reader should verify whether TB 133 is applicable to his or her jurisdiction.

Office projects utilizing an open plan and systems furniture must also be designed to meet specific code requirements even though open office products are furniture. The products as delivered by the manufacturer will meet minimum code standards since manufacturers produce panels and screens to meet Class A fire safety standards when specified with the standard vertical surface fabrics or materials. If the designer wishes to substitute COM fabrics for any panel or component item, the fabrics selected must be considered Class A or must be treated to conform to this standard. Neglecting to do this will leave the interior designer liable for bringing the noncompliant materials up to code.

Designing commercial projects to meet applicable codes and regulations is a critical concern for interior designers involved in any type of commercial specialty. An in-depth discussion of the code requirements for each type of commercial facility is beyond the scope of this book. Interior designers unfamiliar with the codes should consider taking a course at a university or college or attend appropriate continuing education workshops and seminars. In addition, designers should have copies of the model codes in effect in their jurisdictions in their personal libraries and perhaps some of the books mentioned in the References at the end of this chapter as well.

Design Applications

This section presents information on planning and design concepts applied to office facilities. It will help the reader understand the basic space and functional equipment needs of private offices using casework furniture and several support spaces in a generic office-based business.

This is followed by a brief discussion applying office systems to a group of employees. Recognize that it is not possible to discuss each type of business or specific job function in this chapter. This section also considers the design of home offices since many entrepreneurs conduct their service-oriented businesses from home.

Closed Office Plans

Closed office plans are designed to provide private offices with full-height partition walls. These walls may be constructed on site or specified using full-height demountable wall systems. Closed office plans are common in many small professional offices such as those of accountants and consultants, as well as the executive areas of large corporations. The closed office plan provides security for individual employees of many businesses.

Reception and Waiting Areas

Business offices use a reception or waiting area as the place where clients and guests are received. A reception area can take many forms. Most often it is a space that the visitor must pass through to gain access to employees. Its size is dictated by the number of visitors who are commonly expected to wait for brief periods. A comparison familiar to most readers is the large size of the reception and waiting areas of many medical office suites versus the usually modest size of a small professional office.

A reception area is designed and specified to create the right image and introduce visitors to the business. The larger the business, the more elaborate this reception area becomes. Smaller businesses may merely have a few chairs located near the entrance door. Interior designers are challenged to create a reception area that introduces the company while keeping the functional needs of the reception area in mind.

For security, the receptionist must be able to monitor incoming and outgoing traffic. Thus, the receptionist's desk must be planned to have visual control of the entrance to the office suite from outside as well as into the back office areas. The receptionist often has other responsibilities involving the need for a telephone and computer, perhaps security monitors, and space for other paperwork or sorting. The furniture specified for the receptionist must be selected or designed to accommodate these various job functions. The receptionist will be given a custom-designed counter or, in a small office, a desk. Depending on the nature of the business of the organization, this counter may have to be designed to meet accessibility guidelines. Receptionists as well as almost all secretaries have small armless chairs so that the chair can be easily pulled up close to the desk or return.

Visitor traffic from the reception area often requires visitors to pass through doors into the general office space for security. Some businesses, such as medical office suites, require the visitor to approach a window within the reception area and sign in. The receptionist is thus in a separate room, not in the reception and waiting room. Large firms may locate personnel offices, training rooms, and some conference areas adjacent to the reception area so that visitors are restricted in how far they may enter the facility. Major corridors move visitors from the reception room to the different areas of the office facility.

Higher-quality furniture and materials are common to set the tone and image the company wishes to convey to its visitors. For a small business, the products specified for the reception area may be similar to those used in other office areas rather than upgraded. The seating units in a reception area are frequently chairs rather than sofas. Many styles of seating can be used in the reception area, from the small chairs discussed earlier in this chapter to larger chairs that fit the design concept of the office complex. Image and price impact the actual specification. A few end tables for magazines may be needed, and some companies may have display cabinets of their products in the reception area.

Executive and Private Offices

The larger the business, the more likely an executive office suite will be planned for the CEO and vice presidents. The owner of a small professional business and the upper management of many kinds of office-based businesses will also have private offices. In general, it is the boss's or owner's office that is designed to impress guests and even employees who have business with the firm. This section focuses on private offices but includes comments cncerning an executive office suite.

An executive office suite is almost always a closed plan due to the privacy these individuals need. Obviously, a closed plan in this area also provides appropriate status and image-focused design that is important to impress visitors. The executive office suite is often placed on the perimeter of the top floor or in another prime location in the building (Figure 3-21). In large corporations, it is a "world of its own" with private elevators to the executive floor, a separate reception area, and perhaps a private dining room, lounge, and other amenities. In smaller facilities, business owners locate their office where they feel the prime location might be. For some, that could be the rear of the suite, even if this means that they do not have many windows. The interior designer will advise the client of the best location to meet the client's needs and overall project goals.

An executive office suite will contain a reception area. This area may not be very large, but its functions are similar to those of any reception area in any business. It is a place to greet visitors to the suite, provide a comfortable place for the visitors to wait, and convey a certain image. A receptionist or administrative assistant will greet visitors and likely have various administrative duties. Furnishings in this area are similar to those in the main reception area, although their style and quality generally are higher. Beautiful fabrics, wall coverings, and accessories are also specified to give the reception area the look of importance required.

The executive suite commonly has a boardroom. Boardrooms of large businesses project the image and status of the company to the visitors invited to this space (Figure 3-22). This spacious, well-appointed conference room is designed as much to impress as it is to hold meetings. It is not uncommon to have the conference table custom designed in beautiful woods and surrounded by large, comfortable chairs. Designers also provide projection screens, marker boards, and cabinets that can house a beverage service and other accouterments for high-level business meetings. In some cases, a projection room behind the boardroom is provided to house the necessary audiovisual equipment and setups for projection into the conference space.

Visitors will move down corridors to the appropriate executive office, to be greeted by the private secretary many upper-level executives are assigned. Executive offices are large, sometimes hundreds of square feet in size. There is really no standard for the offices of top executives other than what company policy and/or individual interests dictate. For a

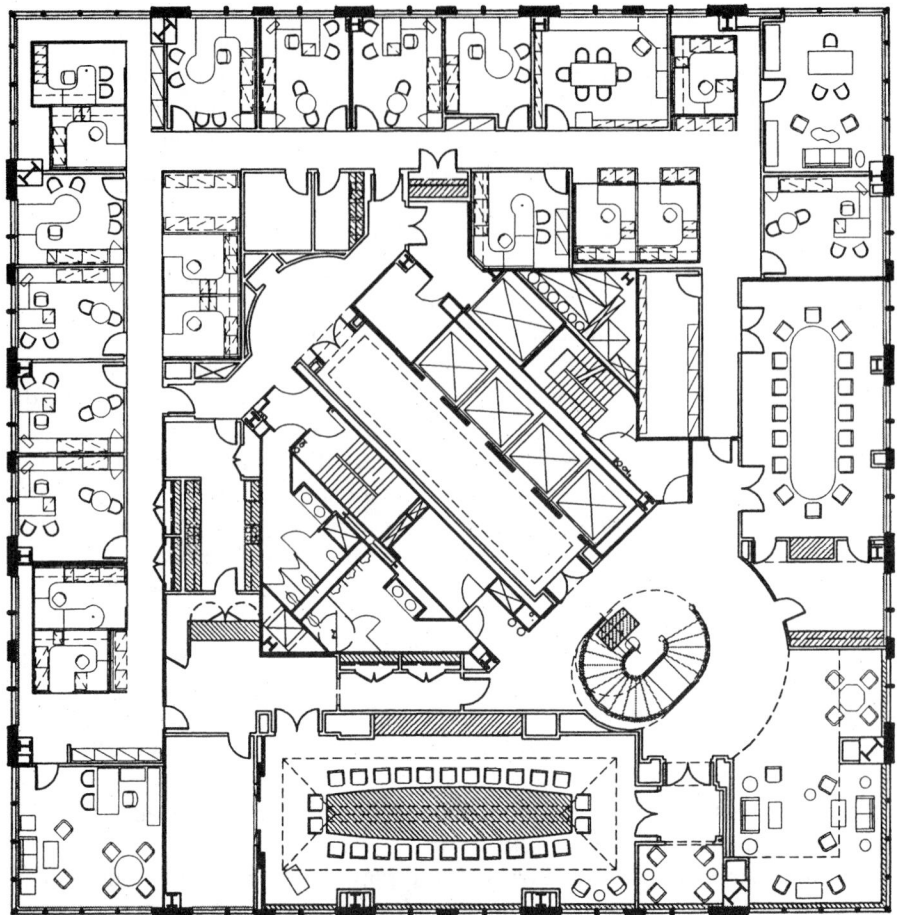

Figure 3-21 Floor plan of a corporate office in a multistory office building. Note that the executive offices are positioned flanking two major conference rooms. (Plan courtesy of Fox & Fowle Architects.)

small business, the owner's office might be approximately 250 square feet; larger companies will likely provide over 400 square feet—or more—for the CEO.

Executive offices provide not only work space, but sometimes a conference area and almost always a soft seating group. A large desk and matching credenza unit; a large posture chair for the executive; two or more guest chairs at the desk; a soft seating group consisting of club chairs, love seats, settees, or sofa and club chair arrangements; and perhaps additional storage units such as bookcases, file cabinets, or display cabinets are all common in executive offices. Colors and styles of furniture are also tailored to individual tastes in the executive suite.

Furniture arrangements are also important in executive and other private offices. A desk placed to face the door, with guest seating placed in front of the desk, makes a more powerful statement than a desk facing away from the door or placed against the wall. Another nonpower arrangement finds the desk placed perpendicular to the door. Soft seating groupings in L- or U-shaped configurations are more conducive to casual conversation, while seating placed across from a coffee table is more formal.

Color schemes are commonly neutral for the architectural finishes, with stronger colors and patterns used in upholstery. Of course, this can vary widely with the executive. However, the interior designer must recognize that executive offices are not hospitality facilities, so strong colors and large patterns are generally not appropriate. There are many excellent works that discuss the specifics of hierarchy and design to project power in executive offices. One such book is *The Office* by Élisabeth Pélegrin-Genel.

Let us now consider key points concerning other private offices. Mid-level management staff could also be placed in private offices with full-height walls. In a small com-

Figure 3-22 Boardrooms project the image and status of the company. Florida Business Interiors conference room. (Photograph courtesy of Burke, Hogue & Mills Architects.)

pany, most work areas for job functions above staff positions could also be located in small private offices. These offices are primarily furnished with a smaller desk and credenza than those given to upper-level management. They also contain smaller guest chairs and are unlikely to have conference or soft seating groupings. Mid-level managers who have more frequent meetings might be given extra guest chairs positioned approximately where a soft seating arrangement would be placed in a larger office. Figure 3-2 provides common furniture layouts for a middle management private office. In larger firms, mid-level personnel in private offices generally all have the same style of furniture. Many companies provide some variation by changing the color of fabrics on seating or the color of wall covering. Specifying many styles and colors of products throughout the facility is not practical, as costs for each individualized space can become prohibitive in large numbers.

The size of other private offices can range from approximately 250 square to 144 square feet. The size differences are based on job title and company standards. Figure 3-2 illustrates private offices of various sizes. Furniture specification for a private office would include a desk and credenza, posture chair, and guest chairs at minimum. A conference table or soft seating group or unit is an option at upper management levels.

Upper-level executives almost always have an administrative assistant located right outside their office. He or she will have a large desk or cabinet to accommodate a computer terminal similar to that of the other clerical staff. File cabinets to hold records for his or her boss are also common.

The partitions of the executive office suite may be constructed of metal studs covered in wallboard. Insulation in these walls provides more acoustical control, considering the sensitive nature of the conversations in these spaces. Walls could also be built using demountable wall units. Businesses that have decided to use systems furniture products for the executive offices may choose this option, since it provides flexibility in space planning and may also accommodate the systems components on the walls. Lighting is often softer in executive offices, although recessed fluorescent fixtures are still common. The use of spotlights or track lighting is more common here, as well as task lights for the desk and a soft seating area.

Ancillary and Support Spaces

Many kinds of support or ancillary spaces may be needed for an office. These spaces provide workrooms or backup spaces to the main office functions. Table 3-2 lists the square footage of common support spaces. Of course, not every office will have all of these functional spaces as rooms. For example, a small office is unlikely to have an employee lunchroom. However, a counter would be located to provide space for a coffee maker, small refrigerator, and other items. Although these areas are discussed in this section on the closed plan, the designer will also plan and specify similar spaces for the open plan.

The first support area is the *conference room*. Even the owner of a sole practitioner professional office prefers to have certain meetings or presentations in the comfort of a conference room rather than over a desk in an office. Although a conference room can be a very formal setting, it is more relaxed than an office. In larger companies, conference rooms provide space for employee meetings, training, and presentations to clients. Conference rooms are generally enclosed in full-height walls for privacy. In an open plan project, a conference space or team area might be in the open, with no panels or walls surrounding the seating and table. This provides flexibility for the team as it expands and contracts in size.

Conference room sizes vary with use. A conference room or area can be as small as 120 to 150 square feet and comfortably accommodate four people and a small table approximately 36 to 48 inches in diameter or 60 inches long. The designer can plan approximately 30 square feet minimum per person for conference rooms that do not include cabinets or credenzas for storage. The space should not feel cramped, providing sufficient room for the table, chairs, and circulation space. If presentations are made with a leader standing at a podium—or at least at the front of the room—allow three or more feet of extra space at the front of the room. Even if a podium is not used, be sure that sufficient circulation space has been provided so that someone can write on a chalkboard or point at a screen (Figure 3-23).

Conference rooms are furnished with a table and chairs. Round tables are very good for small groups, though rectangular tables are also used. In a large conference room, a boat-shaped table is used. This table looks like the plan view of a boat with its ends flattened. This shape makes it easier for everyone at the table to see everyone else. A common size for a rectangular table for eight people is 8 feet in length, allowing approximately 36 inches of table length per person on one side of the table. Remember that someone will be seated at both ends as well. The size of the table is proportional to the size of the chairs; the larger the chairs, the larger the table (Figure 3-24).

Chairs are often specified with casters or sometimes a sled base for ease of movement. In the more important conference rooms, they may also be specified as swivel/tilt chairs.

Figure 3-23 Three standard conference rooms. The one on the left has four tables banked together, which allows versatility in placement. The one in the middle shows a small conference table. The one on the right shows a typical boat-shaped conference table, which provides good sightlines for communication. (Drawing courtesy of Cody D. Beal.)

Figure 3-24 Traditional conference table in a conference room with a media wall housing a rear projection screen. (Photograph courtesy Architectural Design West Architects. Scott Theobald, project architect. Copyright photograph © USU Photography Services.)

These features help to make sitting in the meeting more comfortable. Small staff meeting rooms may have smaller chairs with fewer features than chairs specified for conference rooms where presentations to clients will take place.

The interior designer needs to verify the need for specialized conference equipment for these areas. Conference rooms may need chalkboards, liquid writing surfaces, tack boards, screens for showing films or slides, and televisions and VCR, DVD, and teleconferencing equipment. In larger conference rooms, a small counter area and even a small sink and refrigerator unit might be needed when refreshments are served. Conference rooms used by clients are often designed with higher grades of furniture and furnishings than those used only by the employees.

Multiple lighting systems, such as recessed or surface-mounted fixtures for normal lighting and spotlights on dimmers when audiovisual equipment is used, are common lighting solutions in enclosed conference rooms. Fixtures should be on multiple switches and dimmers to adjust the lighting to suit occupants' needs. Plan the furniture locations and lighting fixtures so that sufficient light is provided on the table surface, not behind guests. Appropriate spotlights might then be needed for the podium or front of the room.

The globalization of many large businesses has increased the demand for alternative conferencing solutions and possibly *teleconferencing*. The high cost of travel has decreased the number of business trips to visit clients. In addition, with the increasing amount of telecommuting, satellite offices, and alternative office solutions for growing businesses, teleconferencing has grown in importance. Conference rooms are equipped with television monitors and plasma screens, along with cameras and conferencing sound systems, to accommodate meetings with individuals in remote locations. Some manufacturers have developed specialized conference tables with data ports, pop-up screens at the table, and other options to deliver teleconferencing capabilities. And with the mini cameras that can be provided at the work station, teleconferencing can also occur easily in any workstation or office. Special attention must be paid to acoustics, lighting, and sight lines in conference rooms where teleconferencing will take place.

Acoustic control is very important. Sounds within the room can reverberate and make it difficult for the remote group member to hear the proceedings. Ambient noise from outside the conference room can also make it difficult to hear for those in the conference room. As much as possible, these rooms should be treated as mini sound studios, with sound-absorbent materials on the walls and high-quality acoustical ceilings.

The interior designer needs to consider data and telephone connections and microphones or tabletop conferencing speakers. These are connected to the building's systems through access ports built into the table from the floor. The designer must also carefully consider the size and shape of the table and seating layout for camera locations and proper viewing angles of projection screens.

Other audiovisual presentations may also take place in conference rooms. Digital projectors, also known as *LCD projectors,* are used with a PC for many presentations. A screen or white board provides the projection surface. Rear projection screens and rear projection cameras might be installed in large conference rooms. Training rooms and large conference rooms might require a speaker's podium with controls for audiovisual equipment. Some clients will also ask for a conference room with an audiovisual projection room at the back of the room. Obviously, the needs of specialized equipment, lighting, sound control, and furnishings in conference rooms are varied and must be carefully determined by the interior designer.

A small or medium-sized office will likely locate a *copy area* in a storage room or along a corridor of sufficient size to accommodate the machine and traffic. In a large facility, there may be copy stations strategically located throughout the space, with a centralized copy center in the services core. Space must be provided for the machine and for storage of supplies. The space allowance needs to include the equipment, adjacent counters or tables required as work areas, and space to service the equipment. Floor space for the machine operator and circulation space past the copy machine must also be allowed. The designer needs to check with the client and the copy machine company about size, weight, and mechanical systems specifications. Copy machines other than desktop models may require a 220 electrical line and a separate circuit. This must be noted on drawings and in specifications.

Some types of business offices have extensive resource materials. Often these materials are kept centralized in a *resource materials area* rather than scattered throughout the facility. Examples are the law library in a law office, sample catalogs needed by interior designers, and advertising brochures for the marketing department. Reference items require shelving to house the specific goods. A shelf designed to hold law books is different from that needed to store an interior designer's samples. The designer must know exactly what is being stored and any special environmental or security requirements concerning the goods when deciding on the exact locations of these areas and products to be specified.

Open Office Plans

This design application section on open office plans and systems furniture will not refer to any specific manufacturer's product line. There are too many differences among the products available from any one company, let alone from the dozens of manufacturers of products for open plan projects. This discussion is generic, focusing on staff-level employees.

Open office systems furniture was accepted by most office facilities from the late 1970s and into the 1980s. The space saving provided a great incentive for companies to switch to systems furniture. Flexibility and adaptability to changing employee needs cemented the use of these products for most jobs in many types of office-based businesses.

The project's interior designer will help the client determine exactly which product line should be specified. However, a major corporate client may have standardized on one or two product lines or may have existing agreements with certain manufacturers. Naturally, the interior designer must honor the client's commitments and design the project using these products. Conceptually, planning of office and support spaces using office systems furniture is the same regardless of the product line. However, each product has distinct differences in sizes of panels, widths of components, and various other factors that affect safe, logical planning. Thus, the interior designer will need a certain amount of information and guidance from manufacturers' representatives on the best way to plan using the product.

In an open office, circulation space differentiates traffic aisles from traffic corridors. In some jurisdictions, a corridor may exist if divider panels over 69 inches in height are used on one side and a full-height partition is used on the other side of the corridor. In this case, the corridor must be a minimum of 44 inches if it is in a space with an occupant load of over 50. Remember that aisles are circulation spaces between furniture items, and between furniture items and partitions, as long as those partitions or divider panels are less than 69 inches high. An aisle can be less than 44 inches unless it serves a large number of occupants or must meet Americans ADA or other accessibility regulations.

An allowance of 25 to 40 percent for circulation space is common in systems projects. The more generous allowance will be common in projects that are more open and provide for flexible working areas, which are common today. The tighter allowance will be more common when a plan is based on a cubicle approach with a majority of individual workstations. Wider circulation spaces give a more open, spacious feeling. Main traffic spaces should be sized according to occupant load and local code requirements.

Workstations rather than offices are designed to meet strict functional needs rather than the status needs of those in private offices. Thus, workstations are smaller than private offices and are often farther away from the prime areas in the facility. Depending on the planning and teaming philosophy of the company, department supervisors or team leaders may have their workstations located along the window walls or mixed in with those of their departmental teams.

Workstations are formed with panels. The height of the panels will be determined by equipment needs and job function. The size of the workstation in square feet will also be based on function. A workstation for staff members can be 64 to 120 square feet. Naturally, some are larger and others smaller based on needs and job rank. The station is then completed with the appropriate configuration of components for worksurfaces, storage, and filing. One or two guest chairs might also be included in the workstation, depending on the employee's job function. Specific component needs will vary considerably, depending on the job responsibilities. Information gathered during programming, as well as company standards and the interior designer's experience, will be applied in determining the proper component needs of employees.

Open and partially enclosed L- and U-shaped (or even triangular) workstations are common today. These configurations are advantageous for locating a computer in the corner and preserving space on one or both sides of the computer for other work areas. With today's more compact computer monitors and flat screens, worksurfaces at least 24 inches deep are appropriate to create the station. Special corner worksurfaces with a keyboard tray option are available. A file cabinet or panel-hung file component and bookshelves for storage of additional reference materials can be specified, depending on employee job needs. Specific job requirements may necessitate additional furniture or components. For example, architects and interior designers need surfaces to spread out large sheets of drawings (Figure 3-25), and attorneys need more filing and storage equipment.

Desk chairs in staff work stations are often some type of posture or ergonomic chair. It is specified without arms or arms that are recessed from the front edge of the seat pan. This allows the worker to pull the chair up to the proper distance to make working on the computer more comfortable. Box 3-1 has additional information on seating in relation to computer workstations.

Divider panels can be fabric covered, providing the opportunity to inject color and patterns into the office. Divider panels might also be finished in wood laminates, selected melamine finishes, or other finishes. Color and pattern can also be introduced in the workstation via tack boards, shelf covers, and seating. In other situations, panels are kept neutral, whether fabric covered or hard surface, with color introduced by the material on seating and accessory items like the fronts of storage shelves. Recognition of status can involve specifying worksurface finishes in wood veneer or wood laminates for managers and neutral tones for lower-level employees.

In an open plan project, a secretary often has a counter similar to the one described for the receptionist. However, the size of the station will involve an appropriate configuration of

Figure 3-25 Architects and interior designers need surfaces to spread out large sheets of drawings. (Photograph courtesy of 3D/International.)

33- to 42-inch-high panels. These counters may need to be designed to conform to accessibility regulations. Interior components provide worksurfaces for paperwork, the computer, and any needed filing and storage cabinets. Secretaries also have file cabinets and storage cabinets for office supplies unless there are storage rooms in their departments. As a group, secretaries rarely have a guest chair or other seating near their desks.

In designing an area for a team, a key concept in planning and specifying is flexibility. Today all the major manufacturers of system furniture offer many options that are designed to be flexible and meet the needs of clients whose work teams demand the ability to customize their work areas. The interior designer should be sure that he or she understands the system to be used for the team area—or any area—of the facility before beginning the schematic design.

These team areas are likely to be designed using divider panels that can accommodate worksurfaces, shelves, and other components to create the work area. Team areas are more open than many other work areas. Screens or short panels might be used to define an individual's work space while still maintaining an open plan. Depending on the needs of the group or even parts of the team, small movable conference tables might also be specified in a workstation. Team conference space may be necessary, along with the appropriate number of workstations.

Today's office environment also likely requires space for telecommuters and other off-site workers to land and use space at a headquarters location. Free-address individual stations—those not assigned to a particular individual—can be planned for the office facility so that telecommuters can reserve an on-site workstation for a period of time. Depending on the number of employees in this situation, teleconferencing and videoconferencing facilities need to be designed and planned as well. Refer to Table 2-3 for alternative office terms.

Home Offices

The dramatic explosion in technology has made working at home possible at low cost. Hundreds of thousands of entrepreneurs start businesses from their homes, setting up an office space in a spare bedroom, a remodeled garage, or a corner of the dining room.

High-end residential projects today almost always include a home office, and midpriced houses in the 21st century have a den or home office as an option. Whether it is a place for a telecommuter or entrepreneur to work full time or to continue work not finished at the office, the home office should be designed with thought and good planning principles. Interior designers have found this niche an interesting specialty. It is, of course, more closely related to residential than commercial interior design, but it is considered in this book due to the large number of entrepreneurs operating businesses from home and the number of businesses that allow employees to work at home. This section will not differentiate the space or equipment needs for home offices of entrepreneurs from those of employees working at home.

The flexibility of working at home is very attractive and, for an entrepreneur, an inexpensive way to start many service businesses. A home office has always been an option for interior designers and architects who want to get their own practices off the ground. Consultants of many kinds, accountants, and some attorneys, among others, find working from home advantageous. However, not everyone is suited to this option. It takes discipline to work from home, whether one works for a company or oneself. The location of the home office, its layout, and its furnishings can help at least to some degree.

The design of a home office starts with determining its location in the residence and the equipment needs related to job function. The interior designer must also clearly understand the extent of the client's interaction with family issues during the work day. Space in the family room with the children nearby may be the only option for some home office workers, but it is not the best situation for serious work activity. Ideally, the home office is located in a separate bedroom or another private space. This separation is needed to separate work responsibilities from home and family responsibilities. When the office has to be located in another space like the family room, the designer should make it seem different from the family space. Divider panels or tall bookcases that create a "room" within a room can help.

The home office should be furnished with desks, chairs, and filing and storage cabinets that meet the client's functional needs and cost limitations. Standard programming techniques are used to analyze the kind of work being done and what types of office equipment are being used. The furniture and equipment needs of a home-based investment broker will be quite different from those of an architect. A computer and keyboard, printer, copying machine, and fax machine fill up desk space very quickly in a home office. File storage, reference materials, catalogs, and other needed support materials must also be considered.

A key consideration in the price point of furnishings is whether clients will visit the home office. If the entrepreneur holds meetings away from home, then he or she may be inclined to use budget-priced furniture. Image is as important in the home office as in any commercial office location, so when clients come to call, the interior designer should encourage the client to use higher-quality products. Proper desks, adjustable chairs, lighting for office work, and electrical/cabling needs are all important parts of design for the home office.

One option is to simulate the corporate office, with a desk, a credenza, and guest seating. The closet becomes the location for files and reference materials storage. Some clients might substitute a work counter for the credenza, since it will provide greater surface and storage space. Another common option is custom cabinets or furniture that creates a work area facing the wall, generally utilizing a corner for the computer, with a table desk or conference table in the middle of the room. A third option is to use open office systems products to create the work area. Depending on the product, components can be attached to the wall or hung from panels placed against the wall. This arrangement is sometimes used when the corporation provides furniture for the employee. The reader may wish to refer to Box 3-1 for design tips concerning the computer workstation. The floor plan should make it easy for the home office worker to access files and reference materials. Sufficient space must be planned so that the desk chair does not hit other pieces of furniture or make it difficult to get around the desk (Figure 3-26).

When working with a home-based office client, the designer needs to discuss the importance of using quality furniture products. Many home-based entrepreneurs start on a shoestring and have a hard time seeing the necessity of purchasing quality furniture items. Buying quality furniture is especially important, as already mentioned, for entrepreneurs

Figure 3-26 A work space in a designer's office located in his residence. (Photograph courtesy of Craig A. Roeder, designer.)

who bring clients to their home office. Budget solutions work for a while, but the cost of replacing budget items will increase the long-term cost of the business. Many commercial office and systems furniture manufacturers have modified and designed products specifically for the home office.

Let us consider a few other pieces of furniture for the office. Good desk seating is important. Many an entrepreneur has found that the dining room chair—a nice budget item—leads to backaches and leg problems. Adjustable chairs that provide proper seated posture for long hours of work are just as important in the home office as they are in the standard office. One of the many ergonomically designed chairs available in various prices is the correct solution. The interior designer should specify at least mid-priced filing cabinets and bookcases to give the worker furniture that will last until he or she is ready to move to a freestanding office site. Budget equipment will not last, given the home office worker's heavy use. In selecting furniture for the home office, the axiom "You get what you pay for" is certainly true.

Light and neutral colors work best in a home office since they make the typically small rooms, crowded with furniture and equipment, seem less confining. However, the opportunity to design the office as the client sees fit versus duplicating the corporate environment can lead to exciting color, wall finish, and furniture choices—especially in larger spaces. The environment of the home office has to be pleasing for the worker who must now spend 8 hours there versus the corporate environment. The designer needs to help the home office owner choose colors and materials that will enhance the office space but not create uncomfortable surroundings. Bright splashes of color should be provided in artwork rather than in strong wall colors when the office space is small (Figure 3-27).

Homes built before the late 1990s generally do not have the built-in electrical and telephone service needed by today's home office. A home office may need multiline phones so that the business and home phones can be answered. High-speed Internet service is a must for most home businesses. A separate line for the fax machine is another. Phone companies and Internet providers can retrofit most locations. The homeowner must coordinate that work with the service companies.

Figure 3-27 High-quality furnishings in a home office. (Photograph courtesy of Craig A. Roeder, designer.)

Older homes might also experience power surges or spikes when a converted bedroom is filled with a computer, printers, fax machine, and copying machine. The designer and homeowner should check with an electrician about the opportunity to add another circuit to the home office space to safely operate office equipment. If possible, a dedicated circuit for the computer will ensure safety from power surges—except when the power goes out due to a storm. Many of these issues are not a problem in newer homes or can be easily dealt with in new construction.

A low, even amount of ambient light with task lights at the desk or work surface is appropriate for lighting in the home office. This will also help reduce eye fatigue from glare on the computer screen and provide appropriate lighting for other work. Few homes today have ceiling fixtures in bedrooms. Task fixtures, undercounter cabinet fixtures, and floor lamps must be carefully selected to provide proper nonglare light. Daylight is also an option, but elimination of glare on computer screens must be considered in the relationship between the location of the computer monitor and windows.

Building codes generally will not affect the conversion of an interior room to an office in existing homes. New construction or the conversion of garages into living space will involve code restrictions. Homeowners' associations and local laws may also restrict the location of a business in a home. These are issues the home owner should research before hiring an interior designer. A designer engaged to do this kind of project must investigate the zoning restrictions for these situations first and then proceed with the actual design work.

Summary

The designer specializing in the interior design of office spaces may be involved in designing spaces as grand and complex as a corporate headquarters for an international manufacturer, an office for a local real estate agency, or a humble home office. Regardless of the size of the project, the interior designer is challenged to meet the functional needs of the occupants, meet the budget needs of the owners, and provide the aesthetic elements that the business's clients may expect.

The commercial interior designer specializing in corporate design must be constantly learning about the way business works. With that knowledge, the designer must analyze product standards for a wide range of workers, realizing that while both a stockbroker and a graphic designer need a desk, each requires many other items that are different from each other. Furniture products in an office also are a mix of conventional and systems furniture. Planning an office using conventional furniture is different from planning the same office using systems furniture. The sometimes hundreds of pieces that make up a particular systems product line can be easily described (and have been by many) as a giant erector set of parts. Mastering these parts in order to properly plan an office environment is a challenge for many interior designers. But designing an office involves more than furniture. It also means choosing materials, colors, textiles, accessories, and adequate lighting, interfacing with the mechanical systems of the building, and meeting code requirements. Options are limited by the client's wishes, budget, and imagination.

This chapter has presented an overview of the elements in the design of office spaces, providing the foundation of understanding what must be considered in the planning, design, and specification of offices, big and small. The design applications sections have provided detailed information on the planning of a closed plan, an open plan, and a home office.

If you are interested in office interior design as your design specialty, you may want to consider attending NeoCon, the national contract furniture show held each June in Chicago. There you will join over 30,000 individuals involved in various aspects of the commercial design industry to view what is new in office furniture and products used in commercial interiors of all kinds. Much product information on systems furniture and conventional furniture products is available from manufacturers' Web sites as well.

REFERENCES

Allie, Paul. 1993. "Creating a Quality Work Environment in the Home Office." *Interiors and Sources*. September/October, pp. 128ff.

ASID Report. 1993. "The Home Office: A Design Revolution." November/December.

————. n.d. *Sound Solutions: Increasing Office Productivity Through Integrated Acoustic Planning and Noise Reduction Strategies.* Washington, DC: American Society of Interior Designers.

Becker, Franklin. 1981. *Workspace: Creating Environments in Organizations.* New York: Praeger Scientific.

————. 2004. *Offices at Work.* San Francisco: Jossey-Bass.

Becker, Franklin and Fritz Steele. 1995. *Workplace by Design.* San Francisco: Jossey-Bass.

Berens, Michael. 2005. "Better Lighting & Daylighting." *ASID ICON.* Summer, pp. 49–50ff.

Blake, Peter. 1991, "Something Amiss in Offices." *Interior Design.* May, pp. 208–209.

Brandt, Peter B. 1992. *Office Design.* New York: Watson-Guptill.

Brill, Michael and the Buffalo Organization for Social and Technological Innovation (BOSTI). 1984, 1985. *Using Office Design to Increase Productivity,* 2 vols. Buffalo, NY: Workplace Design and Productivity.

Dana, Amy. 1992. "Glare and VDT." *Interiors.* March, p. 81.

De Chiara, Joseph, Julius Panero, and Martin Zelnik. 1991. *Time Saver Standards for Interior Design and Space Planning.* New York: McGraw-Hill.

Farren, Carol E. 1999. *Planning and Managing Interiors Projects,* 2nd ed. Kingston, MA: R. S. Means.

Gissen, Jay. 1982. "Furnishing the Office of the Future." *Forbes.* November 8, p. 78.

Harmon, Sharon Koomen and Katherine E. Kennon. 2005. *The Codes Guidebook for Interiors,* 3rd ed. New York: Wiley.

Harris, David A. (ed.), Byron W. Engen, and William E. Fitch. 1991. *Planning and Designing the Office Environment,* 2nd ed. New York: Van Nostrand Reinhold.

Hastings, Judith and Tony Waller. 1996. "Stay at Home and Go to Work," *Interiors and Sources.* January/February, p. 92.

Haworth, Inc. 1986. *Designing with Haworth.* Grand Rapids, MI: Haworth, Inc.

————. 1993. *Ergonomics and Office Design.* Holland, MI: Haworth, Inc.

————. 1995a. *Work Trends and Alternative Work Environments.* Holland, MI: Haworth, Inc.

————. n.d. *The ADA and the Workplace.* Grand Rapids, MI: Haworth, Inc.

————. n.d. *Complying with Electrical Standards.* Grand Rapids, MI: Haworth, Inc.

Haworth, Inc. and the International Facilities Management Association. 1995b. *Alternative Officing Research and Workplace Strategies.* Holland, MI: Haworth, Inc.

Herman Miller, Inc. 1991. *Cumulative Trauma Disorders.* Zeeland, MI: Herman Miller, Inc.

———. 1993. "Effectively Managing the Office of the 90s." Zeeland, MI: Herman Miller, Inc.

———. 1994. *Input and Pointing Devices.* Zeeland, MI: Herman Miller, Inc.

———. 1994. "Office Environments: The North American Perspective." Research summary. Zeeland, MI: Herman Miller, Inc.

———. 1996. *Evolutionary Workplaces.* "Office Alternatives: Working On-Site." Zeeland, MI: Herman Miller, Inc.

———. 1996. "Herman Miller Is Built on Its People, Values, Research, and Designs." News Release. December 15.

———. 1996. *Issues Essentials: Talking to Customers About Change.* Zeeland, MI: Herman Miller, Inc.

———. 2001. *Office Alternatives: Working Off-Site.* Report. Zeeland, MI: Herman Miller, Inc.

———. 2001. *Telecommuting: Working Off-Site.* Report. Zeeland, MI: Herman Miller, Inc.

———. 2002. *Body Support in the Office: Sitting, Seating, and Low Back Pain.* Research report. Zeeland, MI: Herman Miller, Inc.

———. 2002. *Long and Winding Road: Getting Electricity, Voice and Data to the Desktop.* Research report. Zeeland, MI: Herman Miller, Inc.

———. 2002. *Making Teamwork Work.* Research report. Zeeland, MI: Herman Miller, Inc.

———. 2003. *New Executive Officescapes.* Research report. Zeeland, MI: Herman Miller, Inc.

———. 2003. *The Impact of Churn.* Research report. Zeeland, MI: Herman Miller, Inc.

———. 2003. *Three-Dimensional Branding.* Research report. Zeeland, MI: Herman Miller, Inc.

———. 2004. *Demystifying Corporate Culture.* Zeeland, MI: Herman Miller, Inc.

———. n.d. *Keeping Your Options Open.* Zeeland, MI: Herman Miller, Inc.

Hohne, Jennifer. n.d. "Prevention of Mouse-Related Pain." Available at www.haworth.com.

International Code Council. 2000. *International Building Code.* Leesburg, VA: International Code Council.

International Furnishings and Design Association. 2000. "Technology Revolutionizes Future Homes." Press release, November 4.

Kearney, Deborah. 1993. *The New ADA: Compliance and Costs.* Kingston, MA: R. S. Means.

Klein, Judy Graf. 1982. *The Office Book.* New York: Facts on File.

Knobel, Lance. 1987. *Office Furniture: Twentieth-Century Design.* New York: E. P. Dutton.

Kohn, A. Eugene and Paul Katz. 2002. *Building Type Basics for Office Buildings.* New York: Wiley.

Kruk, Leonard B. 1996. "Facilities Planning Supports Changing Office Technologies." *Managing Office Technology.* December, pp. 26–27.

Lueder, Rani, ed. 1986. *The Ergonomics Payoff: Designing the Electronic Office.* New York: Nichols.

Maassen, Lois. 1989. "The State of the Office: 1990." *Herman Miller Magazine.* Grand Rapids, MI: Herman Miller, Inc.

Marberry, Sara O. 1994. *Color in the Office.* New York: Van Nostrand Reinhold.

McGowan, Maryrose, ed. 2004. *Interior Graphic Standards*: Student Edition. New York: Wiley.

Myerson, Jeremy and Philip Ross. 2003. *The 21st Century Office.* New York: Rizzoli.

Nadel, Barbara A. 2004. *Building Security: Handbook for Architectural Planning and Design.* New York: McGraw-Hill.

Parikh, Anoop. 1995. *The Book of Home Design.* New York: Harper/Collins.

Pélegrin-Genel, Élisabeth. 1996. *The Office.* Paris and New York: Flammario.

Pile, John. 1976. *Interiors Third Book of Offices.* New York: Watson-Guptill.

———. 1977. "The Open Office: Does It Work?" *Progressive Architecture.* June.

———. 1978. *Open Office Planning.* New York: Watson-Guptill.

———. 1984. *Open Office Space.* New York: Facts on File.

Piotrowski, Christine. 2002. *Professional Practice for Interior Designers*, 3rd ed. New York: Wiley.

Pulgram, William L. and Richard E. Stonis. 1984. *Designing the Automated Office.* New York: Watson-Guptill.

Ragan, Sandra. 1995. *Interior Color by Design: Commercial Edition.* Rockport, MA: Rockport.

Random House Unabridged Dictionary, 2nd ed. 1993. New York: Random House.

Rappoport, James E., Robert F. Cushman, and Karen Daroff. 1992. *Office Planning and Design Desk Reference.* New York: Wiley.

Rayfield, Julie K. 1994. *The Office Interior Design Guide.* New York: Wiley.

Raymond, Santa and Roger Cunliffe. 1997. *Tomorrow's Office.* London: E & FN SPON.

Rewi, Adrienne J. 2005. "Live Wired." *Perspective.* Spring, pp. 9–14.

The Seabrook Journal. 1996. "Designing Around Technology: The Home Office." Fall.

Sunset Books, eds. 1995. *Ideas for Great Home Offices.* Menlo Park, CA: Sunset.

———. "Demise of the Corner Office." 2004. www.steelcase.com

"Workers Cry Over Lighting" Workplace Surveys. 2004. www.steelcase.com

———. 2005. "Understanding Work Process to Help People Work More Effectively." www.steelcase.com

———. 2000. *Musculoskeletal Disorders.* Report. Grand Rapids, MI: Steelcase, Inc.

———. 1991a. *The Healthy Office: Lighting in the Healthy Office.* Grand Rapids, MI: Steelcase, Inc.

———. 1991b. *The Healthy Office: Ergonomics in the Healthy Office.* Grand Rapids, MI: Steelcase, Inc.

Steelcase, Inc. 1986. *Wiring and Cabling: Understanding the Office Environment.* 1986. Grand Rapids, MI: Steelcase, Inc.

Steffy, Gary. 2002. *Architectural Lighting Design*, 2nd ed. New York: Wiley.

Steiner, Sheldon. 1991. "Power to the People." *Contract.* June, pp. 83–84.

Tetlow, Karin. 1996. *The New Office.* New York: PBC International.

Thiele, Jennifer. 1993. "Go Team Go!" *Contract Design.* March, pp. 29–31.

Tillman, Peggy and Barry Tillman. 1991. *Human Factors Essentials: An Ergonomics Guide for Designers, Engineers, Scientists, and Managers.* New York: McGraw-Hill.

Tobin, Robert. 2004. "Adopting Change," Article 360. Available at www.steelcase.com

Vischer, Jacqueline C. 1996. *Workspace Strategies: Environment as a Tool for Work.* New York: Chapman & Hall.

Voss, Judy. 2000. "Revisiting Office Space Standards." Grand Rapids, MI: Haworth, Inc.

Yee, Roger and Karen Gustafson. 1983. *Corporate Design.* New York: Van Nostrand Reinhold.

Zelinsky, Marilyn. 1998. *New Workplaces for New Workstyles.* New York: McGraw-Hill.

Zimmerman, Neal. 1996. *Home Office Design.* New York: Wiley.

WEB SITES

American Institute of Architects www.aiaonline.com

American National Standards Institute www.ansi.org

Associated General Contractors of America www.agc.org

BOSTI Associates www.bosti.com

Building Owners and Managers Association www.boma.org

Business and Institutional Furniture Manufacturers Association www.bifma.com

Canadian Construction Association www.cca-acc.com

Construction Specifications Canada www.csc-dcc.ca

Construction Specifications Institute www.csinet.org

Illuminating Engineering Society of North America www.iesna.org

International Association of Lighting Designers www.iald.org

International Code Council www.intlcode.org

International Facility Management Association www.ifma.org

National Council of Acoustical Consultants www.ncac.com

National Fire Protection Association www.nfpa.org

Buildings www.buildings.com

Contract magazine www.contractmagazine.com

Interior Design magazine www.interiordesign.net

Interiors & Sources magazine www.isdesignet.com

Articles, books, and manufacturers' publications are continually being published on the topics discussed in this chapter. It is impossible for the authors to provide all these references. Students and professionals should seek additional information from suppliers or through literature and Internet searches.

Additional references related to material in this chapter are listed in the Appendix.

CHAPTER

4

Lodging Facilities

We have always traveled. To trade, buy or sell goods, find a better place to live, for politics and security. For most of recorded history, our needs and expectations were simple—a roof over our heads that kept us dry and maybe the availability of a meal nearby. Now we travel for business, to attend professional conferences, take a vacation, try to win our fortune at a casino, or just to relax and get away from home for a few days. In each of these situations, we expect more than a roof and a meal.

Today, rooms at lodging facilities need to be large, clean, and secure, with amenities in line with higher and higher price points. On-property restaurants, gift shops, room service, and Internet service are standard demands. And that is just the beginning. Guests no longer want a small shop to get a newspaper, but a store with tourist T-shirts and other clothes, newspapers and snacks, souvenirs, and even nice gifts to take home. They want not just a coffee shop, but a gourmet restaurant, a spa, and two pools—one for the kids and one for adults. Thus, the lodging industry must continually reinvent its properties,

TABLE 4-1 Chapter Vocabulary

- AMENITIES. Services or items that are provided to make the guest's stay more convenient or pleasant. Examples include soap, hair dryers, bathrobes, high-speed Internet access, and in-room mini bars.
- BACK OF THE HOUSE. Those areas where employees have minimal contact with guests, such as the business office, laundry, and kitchen.
- GUESTROOM BAY. The amount of space required to house a single standard guest room.
- FRONT OF THE HOUSE. Those areas where employees have the most contact with guests, such as the registration desk, guest rooms, and food and beverage areas.
- FUNCTION SPACES. Spaces utilized for meetings, banquets, and other specialized functions.
- GUEST SERVICES. Services provided to enhance the guest's stay at the facility, such as room service, valet service, bell service, health club, and dining room.
- HOTEL MANAGEMENT COMPANY. The individual or corporation that has made an agreement with the hotel owner to operate the hotel facility.
- KEY. A guest room that is considered a rentable unit.
- LODGING FACILITY. A facility that provides sleeping accommodations for individuals away from their permanent homes. Most also provide food and beverage services. Sometimes called a *lodging property* or a *transient living facility*.
- PROPERTY. The lodging facility, including the building and all the land owned by the facility.

services, and amenities to meet the demands of today's business, recreation, and family traveler.

Lodging facilities are one part of the hospitality industry. "The word hospitality has ancient roots, dating from the earliest days of Roman civilization. It is derived from the Latin word *hospitare*, meaning 'to receive as a guest.'"[1] The hospitality industry also includes food service facilities of many kinds and beverage facilities such as bars and lounges. Design discussions concerning these sections of the industry are presented in the next chapter.

This chapter begins with a brief history of the lodging industry, followed by an overview of the responsibility areas and management structure of a generic hotel. To be successful in this highly competitive specialty in commercial interior design, the designer must understand the functional concerns of a hotel or other lodging facility. A survey of the different types of lodging facilities is included. The chapter then discusses specific criteria that affect the planning and design of lodging facilities. The interior design criteria for a generic hotel are then considered, covering areas commonly assigned as projects to students: the lobby, guest rooms, function areas, and recreational areas. A brief explanation of the design goals for food and beverage facilities within lodging properties and bed and breakfast facilities concludes the chapter.

Table 4-1 presents vocabulary used throughout the chapter.

Historical Overview

Lodging, or more appropriately the hospitality industry, has ancient roots. Early travelers moved from location to location for commerce, to avoid persecution, provide information to rulers about their lands, and many other reasons. Travelers were welcomed by others at religious facilities and private homes. Accommodations were meager at best, providing shelter from the weather and perhaps a meal. Taverns and inns evolved during the Roman Empire. Travelers were allowed to stay at monasteries during the Middle Ages.

Inns and taverns continued to improve and offer better accommodations and meals to travelers from the sixteenth century on. Most were located along roads connecting villages and cities. Inns and taverns also were found in city centers. As time went by, these

---

[1]Dittmer and Griffin, 1993, p. 4.

facilities also provided local politicians and leaders places to gather. The first inn built specifically as a hotel in the United States was the City Hotel, which opened in 1794 in New York City.[2] According to Gray and Liguori, the first first-class hotel in the United States was the Tremont House built in 1829 in Boston. "The Tremont innovates such features as private rooms with locks, soap and water for each room, bellboys, and French cuisine."[3]

The cities saw tremendous growth in hotel construction during the nineteenth century as businesses flourished and people began to move from rural areas to cities during the Industrial Revolution. Many wonderful "modern" hotels were built in the 1800s throughout the United States. Comfortable places were demanded by the wealthy, and clean, safe lodging was sought by the lower classes. Small hotels and inns were built along the railroad tracks that began to take eastern residents to the opening of the West. The 19th century saw the development of grand hotels in the large cities, like the first Waldorf Astoria in New York City (first built in 1896; relocated and rebuilt in 1931), the Palace Hotel in San Francisco (1875), and the Palmer House in Chicago (1870s). Even luxurious tourist facilities such as the Grand Hotel on Mackinac Island, Michigan, and the Hotel del Coronado in San Diego, California, both opened in the 1880s, were demanded by the wealthy. The national parks also offered great hotels for early travelers who wanted a chance to experience the Wild West with accommodations that were only mildly "wild." A few examples are the El Tovar Hotel at the Grand Canyon, Old Faithful Inn in Yellowstone National Park, and the Wawona Hotel in Yosemite National Park—all built in the late 1800s (Figures 4-1a, 4-1b, and 4-2).

At the turn of the 20th century, hotels were often the most elaborately designed buildings in cities and towns. The Conrad Hilton in Chicago (1920s) was the largest hotel in the world for many years, with 3000 rooms. The Beverly Hills Hotel in California (early 1900s) and the Arizona Biltmore in Phoenix (1929) are other early examples of these grand hotels.

There were many smaller hotels in the smaller cities and along the roads. Elsworth M. Statler is often credited with starting the concept of the hotel chain by building Statler Hotels in numerous cities beginning at the turn of the 20th century.[4] His hotels offered many design concepts that set a new standard for guest comfort. The Depression of the 1930s resulted in the closing of many hotels throughout the country. There was little travel, as most people could not afford the expense. Occupancy at hotels hit an all-time low.

With the conclusion of World War II came the end of gas rationing and the limited production of private automobiles. Americans suddenly took to the road in their new cars. People who had never ventured very far from home suddenly had wanderlust and wanted to see their country from one coast to the other. Small hotels, cottages, and tourist cabins had been springing up since the turn of the century. This immense interest in travel, along with the expansion of the interstate highway system, provided the opportunity for entrepreneurs to begin the design and construction of newer varieties of lodging for travelers.

Before the motels came tourist cabins. These were mostly small, independently built units containing a bedroom and no bathroom, though this was added later. Clustered around a picnic area, and perhaps a small swimming pool, motels offered clean accommodations to the traveler away from the big cities. Over time, motels added restaurants and larger cabins and began connecting the units together rather than making them separate.

Early motels and smaller hotels along the highway were often small structures on one floor. Many "motor inns" were small cabins providing privacy from neighbors but little space. Motels are usually much smaller than hotels, and have fewer services and amenities. Kemmons Wilson, a building contractor from Tennessee, improved the design of early motels when he conceived the Holiday Inn Motel in 1952. His concept provided larger, nicer rooms in his roadside hotels, marking an important transition in highway lodging from tourist cabins. He also included a restaurant on the property, creating a more

---

[2]Gray and Liguori, 1994, p. 4.
[3]Gray and Liguori, 1994, p. 5.
[4]American Hotel & Lodging Association, 2005, "History of Lodging," available at www.ahla.com

Figure 4-1a The Grand Hotel on Mackinac Island, Michigan. (Photograph courtesy of the Grand Hotel, Mackinac Island, MI.)

Figure 4-1b Hotel del Coronado in San Diego, California. (Photograph courtesy of Hotel del Coronado.)

service-oriented facility. That first Holiday Inn led to the corporation that today represents the largest lodging business in the world.[5]

As business continued to boom, new urban hotels, resorts, and lodging facilities catering to business travelers and the increasing number of wealthy travelers were built. Hotels began providing amenities and services previously available only at the very expensive hotels in urban areas. For example, air conditioning became common in the 1940s, along with radios and television sets in the guest rooms.

---

[5]Dittmer and Griffin, 1993, p. 105.

Figure 4-2 Interior of Old Faithful Lodge lobby, Yellowstone National Park. (Photo courtesy of Finley-Holiday Films.)

Hotel construction continued to boom as travel became easier, business travelers created more and more competition, and guests in general demanded more amenities and finer design in lodging facilities. Extensive resort development added other options to the traveling public. Walt Disney World in Orlando, casino hotels in Las Vegas, and innumerable other resorts, hotels, and specialty lodging facilities have led to unprecedented options in price, design, size, and type. According to the American Hotel & Lodging Association, there were fewer than 10,000 hotels throughout the United States in 1900. In 2004, there were over 47,000 properties with over 4 million guest rooms.[6] This dynamic industry provides a large range of services and exciting entertainment venues, as well as design challenges to interior designers and architects. These will be described briefly in the next section.

Overview of Lodging Business Operations

According to the latest statistics from the American Hotel & Lodging Association, the lodging industry in 2003 had over $113.7 billion dollars in sales.[7] This industry has a huge impact on the U.S. economy and on local economies as well. Travelers stay for business, leisure, family vacations, and many other reasons. At the very least, guests expect comfort and safety at their hotel, motel, or bed and breakfast. The level of comfort expected varies greatly with the price the guest is willing to pay and the type of facility chosen.

This leads us to the overall goal of the design of lodging facilities: to provide an atmosphere congruent with the type of facility and guest target market. The interior designer must create an atmosphere and design specification that will appeal to guests and make

[6]American Hotel & Lodging Association, 2006, "History of Lodging," and "2004 Lodging Industry Profile," available at www.ahla.com

[7]"2005 Lodging Industry Profile," 2006, American Hotel & Lodging Association, available at www.ahla.com

them feel that the hotel they choose is the kind of place where they wish to spend one or more nights.

Like many industries, the lodging industry has worked hard to overcome the harmful effects on tourism after the 9/11 terrorist attacks. Lodging is affected by the ups and downs of the economy, since much of the industry depends upon consumer confidence in traveling for vacations and business. Delivering well-designed guest services goes beyond aesthetic values. It is important for the designer to understand the lodging business in order to better appreciate the operational goals that will affect the interior design of the facility's spaces. Hotel managers and developers are constantly researching and redefining the services that are offered. These services impact the interior specifications as well as the overall space planning needed to meet the functional requirements. Thus, an important part of the designer's programming efforts will involve understanding what the lodging facility is really selling to the public.

Management and Responsibility Areas

The management and responsibility areas of lodging facilities have many variations based on the actual ownership (whether it is part of a chain or independently owned), size, and type of facility, to name the most important factors. Management priorities will also differ from one type of facility to another. For example, far more personal service and privacy will be provided in a superluxury hotel than in any kind of smaller suburban hotel. The recreational focus of a hotel such as a casino may require a separate manager at the executive level, whereas this responsibility will be part of the assistant manager's responsibilities in a smaller facility. However, there are some standards that apply regardless of the type of lodging facility.

Some differences are very logical. Small facilities like independently owned hotels, motels, and inns will be managed by only a few people, while the management of larger facilities will involve several levels of personnel. Owners or top-level management for hotels that are part of major chains are often located at a corporate headquarters, where the chairman of the board, president, and other top managers set directions and goals for the on-site managers. For smaller facilities like a bed and breakfast, the owner is more likely to be on site.

The overall management or administration of the facility begins with the administrative team. The general manager and assistant general manager have responsibility for overall operations. The food and beverage manager is commonly an executive-level manager in all but the smaller facilities, and is responsible for the operation of restaurants and other food services, including banquet service and room service. Depending on the type of hotel, administration will also focus on the management of conferences and specialized services such as a casino area. Marketing directors manage the marketing campaigns for the property and may also be involved in conference, banquet, and special programs management. The administrative services section of the administrative group also includes accounting and human resource management (see Table 4-2).

In many respects, the most important responsibility areas are the departments or groups of workers providing services related to the front office, guest rooms, and guests. This group of responsibility areas, often called the *rooms department,* also includes housekeeping, security, and other services for guests. Front office responsibilities include registration and checkout, reservations, concierge, doorman, and bellmen services. From a service point of view, these areas provide the guest's first impression of the facility. From an interior designer's point of view, the lobby's design and signage make an important first impression in welcoming the guest.

The housekeeping department, which is part of the rooms task group, is responsible for the daily care of guest rooms and all other areas of the facility. Guests do not so much see these activities as experience them. Lodging facilities managers in the highly competitive market of the 21st century know that poor housekeeping services will likely result in guests failing to return on their next visit. The housekeeping department, along with the property operations department, will also work with interior designers on minor refurbishing and other issues related to the planning and design of the facility. The director of

TABLE 4-2 Common Lodging Responsibility Areas

- **Administration**: overall management of the property Includes

  The general manager, department managers, accounting, and human resources functions

  Specialty areas such as casinos, health clubs/spas, and business center

  Banquet planning and management

- **Rooms** (may be called *guest services*): primary services for guest use of property

  Front desk and office—for registration, checkout, and reservations

  Guest rooms and suites—housekeeping and basic maintenance

  Other guest services—bellmen and specialty areas like hotel clubs or executive floors

  Concierge—information services to guests such as for entertainment options, restaurants, and event tickets

  Security—protecting property and guests from harm or hazards

  Owned or franchised gift shops, clothing stores, or other retail options

- **Food and beverage**: any type of food services provided by the hotel

  Restaurants, including food preparation areas

  Beverage service

  Room service

  Banquets

- **Property operations**: engineering and maintenance of the physical plant of the property

  Building systems and grounds

  Renovation management

  Repairs and maintenance

housekeeping is responsible for the upkeep of guest rooms and the entire facility. He or she will interface with the designer on design and remodeling assignments.

The responsibility of the food and beverages department is to provide quality food service. This service can be another important reason that guests choose the hotel for their stay or event. Even smaller hotels along the highway have seen the benefit of providing quality food and beverage services. Some types of facilities provide elaborate gourmet restaurants, and uniquely designed bed and breakfast facilities provide a special breakfast. Food service represents an important segment of the revenue of the hotel, and in some cases a restaurant can become a signature feature of the property. Banquet services for business conferences and meetings are other important functions of this department. Businesses bring conferences and meetings, families come for special occasions such as weddings and other special events book hotel ballrooms and meeting rooms. The food and beverage department provides the food services required for such events.

Other guest services have become very important to the success of a hotel. For example, business centers are becoming a standard service in all sizes and types of hotels. Health clubs or workout areas have joined the ubiquitous swimming pool found in even the smallest facilities. In-house game rooms for children, tennis courts, and affiliation with a golf course are just a few of the entertainment options that might be available. Personal services such as laundry service and dry cleaning, hair salons, newsstands, and gift shops are other optional guest services.

The reason for providing any or all of these additional services is to make a guest's stay as pleasant, stress-free, and enjoyable as possible. Whether these services are provided or not will impact the scope of the project for the interior designer and will influence the design and specification of the different areas affected by the accommodation of these extra services.

Security of the property and the guests is another important aspect of lodging operations. It might fall under the category of rooms or the property operations department. The security group is charged with making the lodging facility and its property safe for guests and employees. Security staff attend to guest complaints about noise or suspicious activities, monitor safety equipment, and otherwise ensure the safety of guests, employees, and the property. The property operations group focuses on maintenance, building systems, and grounds. These individuals are responsible for the maintenance of all aspects of the hotel property including the updating of guest rooms. The plant engineer is responsible for the supervision of all areas related to the building itself—mechanical systems such as heating, ventilation, and air conditioning, plumbing systems, and general repairs needed in guest rooms or other areas of the facility.

Types of Lodging Facilities

Travelers and other users of lodging facilities today have a wide variety of facilities from which to choose. These differing facilities cater to the diverse needs of the public and have grown in reaction to the demands of the market. Types of lodging are based on the services offered, as well as location and special services. The industry caters to a wide variety of guests from business travelers and conventioneers to families on vacation. A guest might be looking for a place to stay for the night as the family drives across country on vacation. Perhaps the guest needs a convention hotel or a place to hold a meeting. Then again, the guest may choose a bed and breakfast inn to spend a few days luxuriating away from home. All these types of lodging facilities are available to serve the diverse market of guests in this country and throughout the world.

Hotels are generally large facilities offering a variety of rooms, from standard guest rooms to luxurious suites, along with a choice of restaurant and beverage services and other services and amenities. As can be seen in Table 4-3, there is a great variety of hotels in today's hospitality marketplace. A hotel may be planned as a superluxury facility, providing superior interior design and impeccable personalized services. Some hotels are considered resort hotels, catering to specialized guest interests such as tennis or golf. In the 1990s, the spa resort gained favor with many guests looking for the relaxation and pampering of a health spa. A hotel may also be a low-cost lodging facility near the interstate highway, catering to the auto traveler. Hotels can also be classified by location.

TABLE 4-3 Primary Types of Lodging Facilities

Hotels	Motels	Others
Downtown or city center	Budget	Bed and breakfast
Suburban	Suburban	Lodge
Convention	Airport	Inn
Conference	Highway	Hostel
Commercial	Motor inn	Extended stay
Residential and condominium		Tourist home
Boutique		Boarding house
Superluxury		Executive training and conference center
Mega hotel		University conference center
Casino		
Airport		
Highway		
Resorts		
Golf, tennis, beach		
Ski		
Spa resorts		
Vacation ownership resorts		
Theme park resorts		
Cruise ships		
All-suite		
Shopping mall hotel		

Figure 4-3 Interior lobby of a conference center hotel. (Photograph courtesy of The Houstonian Hotel, Club & Spa in Houston, TX.)

Many famous hotels are located in urban centers or downtown areas. A hotel can also be located in a suburban area, away from the central downtown district, and in rural areas providing locations for many resort hotels. Obviously, a hotel has many faces.

Let us now define some of these specialized hotels. *Convention hotels* cater to large business, professional, or other organizational groups, where the emphasis during the stay is on meetings or related activities. *Conference centers* are hotels specially designed and organized for smaller meetings and conferences than those held at convention hotels. They offer many of the same facilities as the convention hotel, but for meetings on a smaller scale (Figure 4-3). Hotels that cater to business travelers are commonly located in urban centers or near central business districts and are called *commercial hotels. Boutique hotels* are usually smaller than the other types of hotels. They are trendy, emphasizing high fashion in their design and amenities. Boutique hotels are commonly located in downtown areas, but can be found in many locations. The *superluxury hotel* provides impeccable service, amenities, and design. The staff places an emphasis on the privacy of guests, discretion, and security. *Casino hotels* combine various price points of interior design with the casino experience. Casino hotels often are combinations of theater, entertainment, great food, and beverage facilities and, of course, places to spend the night when gambling is concluded for the day.

Resort hotels are lodging facilities that have as part of their services extensive recreational facilities or activities. Resorts hotels come in many varieties, including those catering to guests interested in high-quality golf experiences, ski lodges, luxurious beach resorts, or mixed-use theme park resorts (Figure 4-4). *Residential hotels* are those in which

Figure 4-4 Lobby and reception area at the Le Telfair Golf and Spa Resort, Mauritius. (Interiors by Wilson & Associates, Dallas, TX; photograph by Peter Mealin.)

the majority of guests are accommodated for long-term stays, perhaps months or even years at a time. *All-suite hotels* are lodging facilities where all the guest rooms are suites consisting of a separate bedroom and living area. Many all-suite hotels also offer kitchen facilities within the suite.

In the early 20th century, the automobile created the opportunity and desire to travel and see the world. Tourist cabins and motels served the traveling public in those early years. *Motels* are lodging facilities that generally offer limited services and cater primarily to the traveler using an automobile. They were originally located in suburban and rural areas. Arthur Hineman is credited with opening the first motel in California in 1925.[8] He is also credited with coining the term *motel*.[9] Motels today are located in many areas, including downtown areas or near airports. They are usually in the middle to budget price range. Motel parking is commonly at or near the guest rooms, making it convenient for guests to unload luggage from their cars. Some motels have food and beverage services and many provide swimming pools, but there are usually few other services since most guests do not stay for more than one or two days. If you would like a glimpse at the wonderful design of early motor inns and motels, take a look at John Margolies' book *Home Away from Home*.

Here are brief descriptions of a few other types of lodging establishments:

- *Bed and breakfast inn.* These facilities originated from early inns. There are many types, ranging from converted private residences to redesigned historic structures. They are more individualized than standard hotels and are primarily owned by an entrepreneur.
- *Extended-stay or all-suite facility.* Generally classified as hotels, these facilities provide a private bedroom and a separate living room space that often includes a kitchenette. They are a residential solution for families and business travelers who are away from home for an extended period of time.

[8]Walker, 1996, p. 56.
[9]Rutes, Penner, and Adams, 2001, p. 44.

- *Lodge.* Facilities commonly associated with a recreational activity such as skiing or fishing. They are usually small and are located in basically rural areas or areas close to the recreational activity.
- *Hostel.* Economy lodging facilities that often cater to students and budget-minded travelers. Hostels have very simple rooms and often lack in-room bathrooms. Some even require guests to bring their own linens.
- *Inn.* Small to medium-sized facilities designed to give guests the feeling of a small, comfortable home. They may be located in a rural area or a big city, one story or multi-storied, offering a full range of guest services including food and beverage services.

The modern traveler is faced with multiple decisions when planning a stay at a lodging facility. The type of lodging facility, the kinds of amenities expected, necessary guest services, and the price for the stay are decisions the guest must contemplate. Although these decisions affect every guest, they also affect the design program and concept with which the interior designer, architect, and owner must contend in the development of the lodging facility.

Planning and Interior Design Elements

Lodging properties undergo remodeling to refresh the interiors of guest rooms and public spaces in order to remain competitive. The hospitality industry in general has learned that design is integral to the success of a hotel. Guests will pay higher prices at many types of hotels for premium design, amenities, and, of course, services. Even the budget-priced hotels and motels understand that in today's competitive arena, a plain, simple room is not enough. In a more expensive property such as a luxury or resort property, beautiful textiles, soft comfortable beds, plasma televisions, and in-room whirlpool baths or even fireplaces are common.

The variations in type of hotel, its market, and its concept are always critical to the decisions that the interior designer must make concerning materials, products, and styles of FF&E for all the interior spaces. A convention hotel in New York City will be designed with different criteria than an all-suites hotel in a smaller city in a western state. However, there are also similarities in the design of lodging facilities. For example, guest rooms have minimum standard sizes and furniture configurations, regardless of the type of facility. All lodging facilities need a lobby with a place for guests to register and pay their bills. And the basic operational functions discussed above must be considered as well. In this section, we discuss the planning and design concepts of a generic type of hotel, since hotels will provide the greatest challenge to the design team.

Regardless of the type, size, and location of a lodging property, it has three basic products to sell to potential guests. The key product is guest accommodations or guest rooms. The interior design of guest rooms can range from the simple, basic designs found in numerous facilities to exquisite antiques found in superluxury hotels. Additional guest services comprise the second product. These services can include the amenities in the guest rooms, gift shops and newsstands, food and beverage services offered through restaurants and room service, and recreational activities such as a spa or swimming pool. The third product used to set the theme and design of the hotel is ambience. As the reader knows, ambience gives the facility its look and personality. Interior architectural finishes, lighting design and fixtures, style of furniture, accessories, fabrics, and many other elements create the desired ambience. However, ambience is not only the effect of the interior. The exterior design and landscaping should work together with the interior to create an overall theme.

The planning and interior design elements that will be the focus of this section are presented first in a brief discussion concerning feasibility studies and design concept statements. This is followed by an overview of space allocation and traffic patterns, furniture and finishes, lighting and mechanical interface, and code considerations. These brief discussions relate to a generic hotel property, focusing on the interior designer's responsibility for these areas.

BOX 4-1   EXTERIOR DESIGN CONCEPTS

The exterior design of the hotel property sets expectations and impressions for guests and visitors to the property. Perhaps it is the startling recreation of the New York City skyline in a Las Vegas mega casino hotel. Then again, it might be the grandeur of the sweeping colonnade and porch along the front of the Grand Hotel on Mackinac Island, Michigan (see Figure 4-1a). Whatever the architecture of the lodging facility, a guest's impression is confirmed or refuted with the exterior design.

The exterior design is defined by the concept and theme, geographic location, number of guest rooms and guest services, and target guest. It might look like a Native American pueblo in the rolling hills of New Mexico or a sleek contemporary conference center hotel in an urban area. A property may have a grand landscaped driveway that entices the guest from the main highway to the front entrance, or it may be a log cabin tucked away under the pine trees in the mountains. Whatever the exterior design, it must draw the guest and visitor to the main entrance of the facility smoothly and without confusion (Figure 4B-1).

The main entrance serves to draw the guest to the lobby. The main entrance doors are usually located under a canopy or *porte cochere* located over the driveway at the main entrance. This canopy also protects guests from bad weather. Here guests will arrive for check-in or valet service or queue for tour buses, shuttles, and taxicabs. A vestibule between the exterior and the lobby prevents cold air, rain, or snow from blowing into the lobby as the doors are opened. Multiple doors at the front entrance are almost always a must unless the lobby space and type of hotel are small enough to utilize only a 6-foot-wide entrance door. Sizes of doors, types of doors, floor finishes, and the kind of glass required in doors and in windows surrounding doors are all regulated by building codes. Should the interior designer have any responsibility for these details, he or she must carefully review local codes and conditions to ensure proper specification.

Depending on the size and type of hotel, there may be several "main entrances." The main entrance to a casino hotel is often directly into the casino space. The casino entrance is always prominent and

Figure 4B-1 The Bellagio Spa Tower and fountain, Las Vegas, Nevada. (Photo courtesy of MGM Mirage.)

exciting, but it may not be the most convenient entrance to the registration desk. Hotels with large function and conference spaces often have a second main entrance directly into the ballroom prefunction space. Resorts that have day use spas frequently have a secondary entrance directly to the spa so that day use visitors have the option of entering the spa directly or entering through the main lobby.

Exterior signage must identify the hotel and provide way-finding for guests around the hotel. Exterior signage commonly incorporates the hotel's logo (also called a *mark*) with the name of the hotel and may include the logo of a management group such as Best Western, Inc. Exterior identity signage might be as extravagant as that used by casino hotels or subdued—sometimes almost nonexistent—in most luxury and superluxury hotels. *Way-finding* uses signs, graphics, and directional arrows to help individuals find their way around complex properties and building interiors. Directional signs are needed to help guests get to the main entrance from parking areas, locate restaurants, find entrances to conference centers or convention displays, and locate elevators, guest rooms, and recreational facilities on the property.

The exterior design sets the stage for what the guest will experience in the lobby and the rest of the interior of the facility. The interior designer must be sure that whatever he or she plans and specifies for the interior spaces retains the feeling developed for the exterior and expands the successful execution of the total design concept.

Feasibility Studies and Concept Statements

Owners, developers, and property managers of a lodging facility take the decision to develop a new facility or undergo a major renovation very seriously. The complexity and expense involved require careful consideration of the market potential and financial investment for the project. The conceptualization and design of lodging projects usually begin, then, with a feasibility study. All major commercial design projects involve feasibility studies. They are discussed here due to their importance in the design of a hotel property.

It is critical to the success of a lodging property to determine the goals and objectives of the project along with economic factors, demographic analysis, and other criteria deemed important to the design and development of the new facility. This analysis, called the *feasibility study,* is necessary to help determine if the project will succeed before construction begins. It is an objective report on the possible success (or lack of success) of the hotel concept. It is reviewed carefully by the owner, developer, and property management team to determine where, if any, changes to the concept need to be made before architectural programming and design begin.

For a hotel project, the feasibility study is generally prepared by a consultant who specializes in this type of work. It may take the consultant months to prepare the study and will cost the project owner thousands, perhaps hundreds of thousands, of dollars. The time and money spent on the feasibility study could save the developer many times the study's cost by avoiding poor decisions concerning the proposed property.

The consultant will study any impact of the geographic location and points of interest to tourists concerning the project. This is done as part of good business planning to prevent building a hotel that is only minimally different from the existing facilities in a crowded market. The feasibility study will also look at the number of guest rooms and the mix of types of rooms, if banquet facilities are needed, as well as the projected demand for conference spaces and other services such as a health club. To determine these factors, the consultant will study competition, lodging demands, future growth of the location, and the surrounding business or recreational impact.

Financial factors are very important in the feasibility study analysis. Estimated operational costs for staffing the hotel, running the mechanical systems, and operating full-service kitchens for the food and beverage operations are considered. Other operational costs such as for providing laundry and housekeeping services, maintaining security systems, providing parking services, and even watering interior and exterior plants are all considered in the feasibility study. All these costs of doing business cannot exceed reasonably attainable revenues or the project will not be profitable. Costs for generating the design documents, site development, actual construction, and finishing costs are only part of what will be required to build a hotel. Revenue projections are also developed in order to prepare a pro forma income statement of expected revenue and expenses. These revenue projections are based on industry standards adjusted for the local market. They are based on the desired types of guest rooms and other services that will bring in revenues to the hotel.

Feasibility studies and concept statements go hand in hand in the predesign of a lodging property. The *concept* is an overall idea that unifies all parts of the facility and provides a specific direction for the design. It is usually prepared after the feasibility study since that information will direct portions of the concept statement. The concept statement focuses the planning and design of all the interior spaces, as well as the design of every other detail of the hotel's operation such as uniforms, graphics, and even the colors of linens for guest rooms.

The concept statement will examine characteristics of the feasibility study such as the guest target market, the service offerings, the mix of accommodation offerings, and the ambience. Different specification decisions will need to be made based on the type of hotel and the expected guest market. Service offerings impact the conceptual design in terms of space allocation and budgetary factors. A resort will have many more recreational facilities and options for guest accommodations than a small suburban hotel along the highway. Designers need to understand the projected mix of guest accommodations in order to plan appropriately for the interior treatment of each different type of guest room. For the interior designer, the ambience is especially important. Ambience involves many elements ranging from wallcoverings and the style of furniture to the colors of guest linens, decorative elements in guest rooms and public spaces, and the many other items that make the interior, general concept, and operations all come together in an unified whole.

Space Allocation and Circulation

The stakeholders with primary control over the space allocation of a hotel will be the owner, the architect, and, to a lesser degree, the interior designer. This team will determine how much of the total space will be devoted to guest rooms and how much to other service areas. The key to earning revenue for the hotel is guest room spaces. Thus, the allocation of space to guest rooms versus all other function and support spaces is a critical issue. As can be seen in Table 4-4, the amount of guest space can vary from around 90 percent for motels to around 55 percent for mega resorts. Space allocation for the actual guest rooms typically ranges from 350 square feet for a standard room with two double

TABLE 4-4 Guest Space for Different Types of Lodging Properties

Lodging Type	No. of Rooms	Service Level	% of Total Hotel Space Devoted to Guest Rooms[a]
Motel	100	Economy to mid-price	85–95
Motor Inn	100–200	Mid-price	75–85
Commercial Hotel	200–400	Mid-price to luxury	75–85
All-Suite Hotel	150–300	Mid-price to first class	75–85
Suburban Hotel	150–300	Mid-price to first class	75–85
Convention Hotel	200–2000	First class	65–75
Resort	varies	Mid-price to luxury	65–75
Mega-resort	>1000	First class	55–65
Conference Center	100–300	Mid-price to first class	55–65

[a]Includes guest room corridors, stairs, elevators, and linen storage.

Source: Stipanuk and Roffmann, *Hospitality Facilities Management and Design*, 1992, p. 365. East Lansing, MI: Educational Institute of the American Hotel & Motel Association.

TABLE 4-5 Typical Guest Room Space Allowances

King bed	312 to 450 square feet
Double-double	375 to 475 square feet
One bedroom suite	950 square feet
Resort room	465 square feet
Luxury room	450 to 650 square feet
Budget room	275 to 325 square feet
Accessible king	351 to 416 square feet
Standard two bedroom suite	1200 square feet
Luxury two bedroom suite	1480 square feet
Conference suite	725 to 950 square feet

Note that these allowances are approximate and will vary with the hotel management. Data obtained from: McGowan, Kruse, 2004, p. 378–379 and DeChiara, Panero and Zelnik, 1991, p. 374–379.

beds to 1400 square feet and up for deluxe presidential suites. In some types of hotels, larger portions of the total structure will be devoted to such things as food and beverage facilities, banquet or meeting rooms, and recreational spaces. It is easy to see that a bed and breakfast inn will have only a small amount of space for non–guest rooms, while a casino hotel will have a significant amount of space devoted to non–guest room facilities. Table 4-5 represents a variety of typical guestroom space allowances. Allowance includes space for the bathroom.

It is important for the management stakeholders and design team to work together to determine estimated space needs for all the functions of the hotel property. Allocations must be categorized into the amounts of space needed for front-of-the-house and back-of-the-house activities using standards that might be available from the property developer or overall industry standards. The interior designer assists in this process by applying his or her knowledge of the space standards needed for layouts of furniture for different functions. Refer to Table 4-6 for guidelines on total space allocation for the various areas of a lodging facility.

TABLE 4-6 Total Space Allocation

	Motor Inns	Commercial	Convention	All-Suite
Number of guest rooms	150	300	600	250
Number of bays[a]	150	315	630	250
Net guest room area (sf)[b]	310	330	350	450
Gross guest room area (sf)[c]	420	480	500	675
Total guest room area (sf)	63,000	151,200	315,000	168,750
Total public area	9,000	27,000	67,500	22,250
Total back-of-the-house area	6,750	23,400	67,500	20,000
Total hotel area (sf)	78,750	201,600	450,000	211,000
Total hotel area/room (sf)[d]	525	672	750	844

[a]A bay is the space equivalent to a standard guest room; many suites are two (or more) bays, or the equivalent of two (or more) typical guest rooms.
[b] sf = square feet
[c] Gross guest room area includes an allowance for corridors, stairs, elevators, walls, etc.
[d]Total hotel area per room includes a portion of all public and back-of-the-house space.

Source: Stipanuk and Roffmann, *Hospitality Facilities Management and Design,* 1992, p. 365. East Lansing, MI: Educational Institute of the American Hotel & Motel Association.

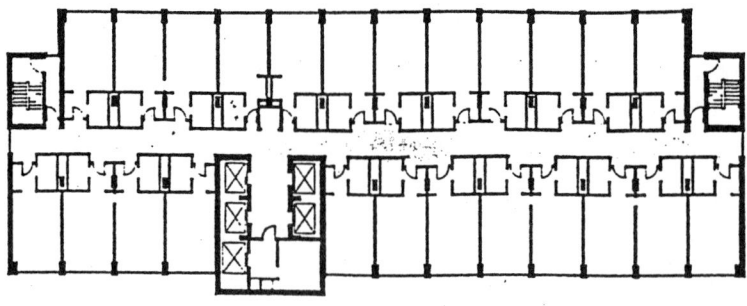

Double-Loaded Slab

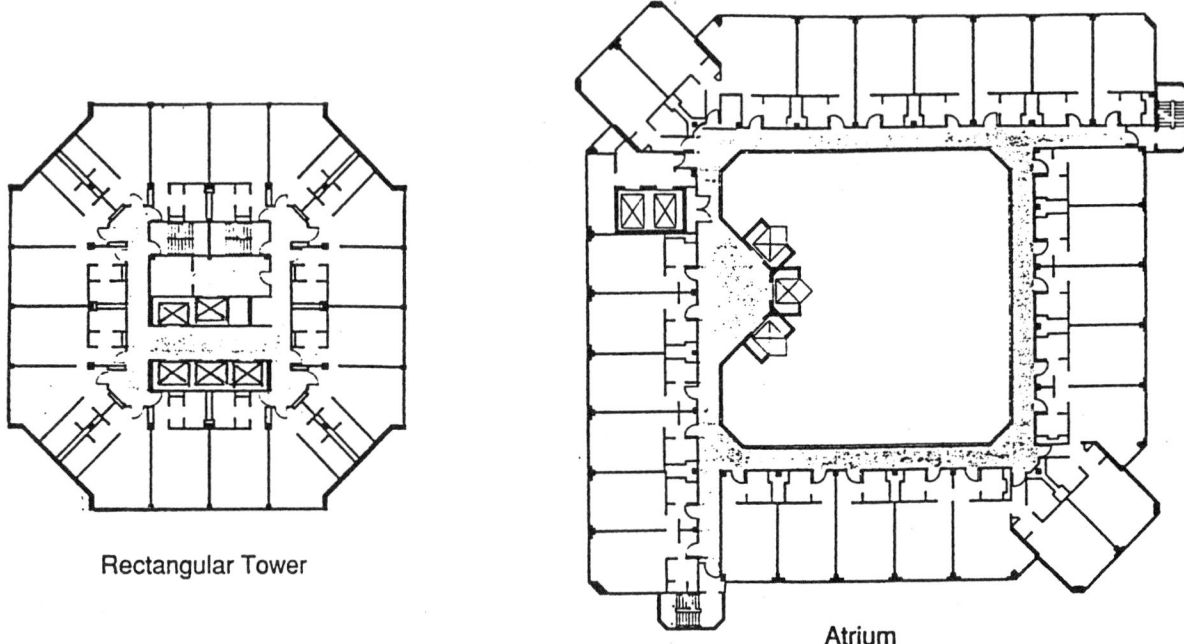

Rectangular Tower

Atrium

Figure 4-5 Layouts of guest room configurations. (From Stipanuk and Roffman, *Hospitality Facilities Management Design*, 1992. East Lansing, MI: Educational Institute of the American Hotel and Motel Association.)

Moving guests, visitors, and staff smoothly through the hotel is important for safety, guest enjoyment, and overall functional effectiveness. These traffic patterns are the responsibility of the architect through his or her organization of all hotel spaces. The footprint layout of guest accommodations influences the traffic patterns of the entire facility. Figure 4-5 provides sample layouts of typical guest room floor configurations.

The interior designer will be more concerned with the second set of traffic patterns. This involves space planning within specific functional spaces such as the lobby and various function rooms. Traffic aisles in function spaces and around furniture items must adhere to codes as well as provide sufficient space for occupants to flow through the spaces. The number of occupants of the various spaces will determine criteria for the layout of furnishings and needed traffic aisles and corridors within the different types of functional spaces in a hotel. Since a hotel is a public space, the interior designer will also have to ensure that the traffic paths around furniture in public spaces meet applicable accessibility standards.

Furniture and Finishes

Furniture and finishes define the concept and character of a lodging facility. The products and colors used throughout the public spaces and guest rooms are as varied as the types of facilities. Return to Figure 4-2 and note how the interior treatment is congruent with the concept of a hotel in a recreational area. It would be hard to imagine this interior in a hotel in New York City.

Generally, the highest-quality furnishings and materials will be reserved for the lobby and the guest rooms. These spaces are the primary places that influence the guest and therefore must be given the most careful consideration. As Figure 4-4 shows, the lobby sets the mood for the entire facility and must be specified to strike the right impression. Use of beautifully designed custom millwork on the registration desk, high-quality finish products for architectural surfaces and upholstery, and quality accessories are some of the ways the interior designer creates the appropriate ambiance. Lobby furniture must withstand the abuse of numerous users, guests bumping suitcases into and placed on the furniture, and regular maintenance.

There are many factors to consider in the design of guest rooms. Interior finishes in guest rooms must be easy to maintain and stand up to abuse. Carpeting is usually tightly tufted carpeting over padding in the bed area, with various other materials such as ceramic tile in the bathroom and dressing area. High-end hotels utilize finer-quality finish materials and furniture products. Interior designers must be careful in their specification of items for the guest rooms. Putting significant dollars into guest rooms can break the budget, since adding even one more accessory item to a guest room might involve thousands of dollars as the item is potentially added to perhaps hundreds of guest rooms.

Thus, selecting FF&E that creates the mood and concept without increasing the cost for each space and guest room is a delicate balancing act. The challenge to the interior designer is to specify products that will be aesthetically appropriate for the concept and allow easy maintenance while standing up to the abuse of heavy use. Just as the fabrics selected for a guest room will require more frequent cleaning than those in the lobby, the fabric selected for lobby seating at a rough-and-tumble dude ranch resort will need to be quite different from that for a convention hotel, such as one in Boston or Manhattan.

Mechanical Systems

Lighting design and the fixtures selected to carry out the lighting design play a very important part in creating the excitement and ambiance of the interior spaces in a lodging facility. Think of the exciting lighting that is provided in the gaming areas of casino hotels. Think also of the functional and aesthetic lighting needed in lobbies, meeting rooms, and all other public areas as well as the guest rooms. Creative details in wall treatments, materials, and furniture products will be lost or ignored if the lighting is poor. On the other hand, the selection of decorative light fixtures in keeping with the design concept can make the specification of needed light levels more difficult. The interior designer and lighting designer must work together avoid overlighting in their desire to create a dramatic space or underlighting an area by forgetting the tasks and functions of the space. Mandated or requested energy conservation may limit the designer in specifying the number of watts per square foot in any public spaces. Designers must be aware of any jurisdictional restrictions as well as the client's wishes in specifying fixtures for the hotel. The heavy use of incandescent lamps in any kind of fixture in public spaces, and especially in guest room, will creates an energy conservation dilemma since these lamps generate more heat.

As with many kinds of commercial interiors, three kinds of lighting effects are used in a lodging facility. General lighting is needed for general traffic movement and safety within any interior space. Accent lighting is used to call attention to specific areas or elements of the space—for example, the lobby bar in a large hotel (Figure 4-6). In some areas, a third type of lighting called *sparkle lighting* is used to create special effects and give atmosphere to a room. Food and beverage facilities frequently use sparkle lighting to add excitement to the space. An example of sparkle lighting in a lobby is the use of very low wattage strip lighting along the underside of the nose of stair treads.

Certain areas in a hotel, as well as hotel restaurants, often require a fourth type of lighting called *performance lighting*. Meeting rooms, ballrooms, and other function rooms, as well as large restaurants that have live entertainment, require lighting systems that can spotlight a speaker or performer. "Performance lighting systems are often simple, employing

Figure 4-6 Accent lighting is used to call attention to specific areas or elements of the space. (Photograph courtesy of 3D/International and dMd Design.)

track lighting and separate dimming channels to permit dramatic illumination of a solo performer, small group, or keynote speakers."[10]

Meeting rooms, ballrooms, and other public spaces also require lighting solutions that are adaptable to accommodate varied activities that can go on in these spaces. General lighting should be flexible so that light levels can be lowered for meals or if slides or movies are presented as part of a conference. Ballrooms frequently use chandeliers to provide general lighting as well as serve as a design accent. Sconces to create accent lighting can only be used on the hard walls in function spaces. Full-height movable partitions are used to divide large spaces like a ballroom into smaller meeting rooms. An on-site restaurant, for example, will require bright lighting for breakfast and lunch service and more subdued lighting in the evening for dinner service.

Guest room lighting design must also be planned for a variety of activities. Like the specification of the furniture and finish items, the lighting design of the guest room has a strong relationship to residential design. Task lighting at the bedside for reading is often provided by small fixtures on bedside tables or wall sconces. High-quality task lighting is necessary for shaving and applying makeup in the bathroom and dressing area. Switches that control general lighting—usually via a floor lamp in the guest room or a ceiling fixture at the door—provides safe lighting when the guest enters the room. Additional lighting for reading or working is necessary at a desk or table area.

Computerized registration and operations systems as well as sophisticated telecommunications systems are common in all types of lodging facilities. Specialized systems for registration have been developed for the lodging industry. Integrated computer systems for other operational areas of the facility will likely be part of the planning. In the registration and lobby areas, the design of custom cabinets, or specification of other furniture and seating for these functions, will be part of the interior designer's responsibilities. Telecommunications design will include the phone systems in guest rooms, including fire safety information and voice messaging for guests.

Nearly all types of lodging facilities today include options for telecommunications and Internet service in guest rooms. In addition, the interior designer may have to design business areas for guests on guest room floors or in specialized business areas somewhere in the public function areas of the hotel. The designer will work with telephone, data, and computer consultants for this service planning. Guest rooms commonly are provided with a phone at the bedside as well as on the desk. The desk phone is also the location for Internet access.

Point-of-sale (POS) computers will be located in the gift shops, restaurant, bars, and anywhere else where sales might occur. *Point-of-sale* refers to the cash register or sales area of any kind of business where the purchase is made by a customer or entered on behalf of a customer. The POS units also help maintain inventory in gift shops and speed up ordering in food and beverage facilities. In a hotel, the POS computers automatically charge the guest's room for meals or other purchases, assuming the guest signs the charge slip, making checkout bills more accurate.

The interior designer will be required to consult with the architect, various engineers, and contractors when special treatments such as fountains and live plant displays are planned for any area of the facility. A wide variety of consultant work on specialized mechanical needs will be required in the design of food and beverage facilities and their commercial kitchens. Should recreational facilities be included in the program, the designer

---

[10]Karlen and Benya, 2004, p. 104.

may coordinate and consult with the architect and others on specialized needs related to these activities.

Security

Guests expect to be safe and secure while staying at the hotel. Yet, guests do not want to feel that they are in a guarded fortress. Many security measures are transparent, meaning that they exist but are not visible. Luxury hotels and resorts will have extensive security plans and devices to ensure the safety of the property and guests. However, even a small bed and breakfast must provide a safe, secure environment for its guests.

Clear sightlines for the registration staff is an easy first security measure. In hotels where the registration desk is set back from the entry points, security or hotel staff may be stationed near the doors to direct guests and observe them for threats. Location of the cash register for the gift shop is another important factor in preventing shoplifting since staff is usually minimal in a hotel gift shop.

Card access entry to guest rooms and to the pool or other recreational facilities is so common that we think of it as transparent. Security bolts, when thrown, make it extremely difficult for a burglar to enter a guest's room. The reader may have noticed a layer of privacy in a high-rise hotel when riding the elevator. Certain floors can be accessed from the elevator only with the guest's room card. Card access systems can also be programmed to record each time a card is used to further monitor access to guest rooms as well as back-of-house areas.

Hotels use many hidden security cameras or closed circuit television systems in the public areas and the grounds that are monitored in a security office at a large hotel or from the front desk in a smaller property. Closed circuit television monitoring can be set up to operate continuously or when triggered by motion or a door opening.

It is also easy to miss seeing the well-designed smoke detectors and fire sprinklers. In-room safes have been installed in many mid-priced and more expensive guest rooms. Of course, guests can always leave valuables at the hotel front desk's safe deposit boxes or safe. Security personnel regularly walk the property to watch for potential break-ins or physical harm to guests. Many hotels in downtown urban areas have security guards at the hotel elevators in the evening and only allow guests to use the elevators.

All of these security systems will be discussed by the interior designer and the hotel management during programming so that the designer understands what will be necessary. A security consultant might then be hired by the interior designer or the client to help with the overall plans for the security system.

Code Requirements

There are numerous dangers and serious consequences when building and life safety codes are not strictly applied to a lodging facility. Accessibility codes will impact design decisions in many spaces of this type of facility. To begin with, hotels are considered to be a type of residential occupancy in the building codes. However, all but the smallest lodging facilities are actually mixed occupancies. A lodging property can include a combination of residential, assembly, business, and mercantile occupancies. Code requirements for this mixed-use space must be carefully reviewed in order to properly plan the interiors of the different spaces.

A combination of the applicable building, fire, and life safety codes will also impact the design decisions related to the materials and, in some cases, the products specified for a lodging facility. As always, the applicable codes are those for the location of the property and may vary from location to location even within the same urban area, state, or province.

Let's look at a few factors concerning traffic paths. Corridors that are considered exit access corridors will have more stringent requirements related to their width as well as their architectural finishes. Some aisles between furniture might also have width restrictions since they may be considered exit access aisles. Widths of corridors and aisles are based largely on the occupancy load in the specific areas and on uses of spaces. Because of accessibility requirements, corridors and aisles are generally required to be a minimum of 36 inches wide. There are limited exceptions to this standard, and the appropriate code should be reviewed for potential applications.

Code requirements also vary, depending on the use of specific spaces within the facility. For example, carpet specified for exit access corridors needs a higher fire safety classification than carpet in guest rooms and hotel offices. This is also the case for other architectural finishes. Although most jurisdictions regulate the architectural finishes only in hotels, some jurisdictions have specific restrictions on furniture items and fabrics used in this type of facility. California Technical Bulletins CAL 117 and CAL 133 apply to upholstered furniture used in spaces where more than 10 seating units are located. The designer must determine if this code requirement or other local code requirements affect the specification of furniture items—especially seating—or design furnishings elements for the project. Additional information on code requirements in specific areas of a lodging property is presented in the Design Applications section of this chapter.

Meeting accessibility requirements is another facet of design that the interior designer must address. In the United States, the ADA affects lodging facility design in many ways. All public and common use areas must be designed to comply with the basic design guidelines of the act. This includes such things as the paths of travel, counters in the lobby and

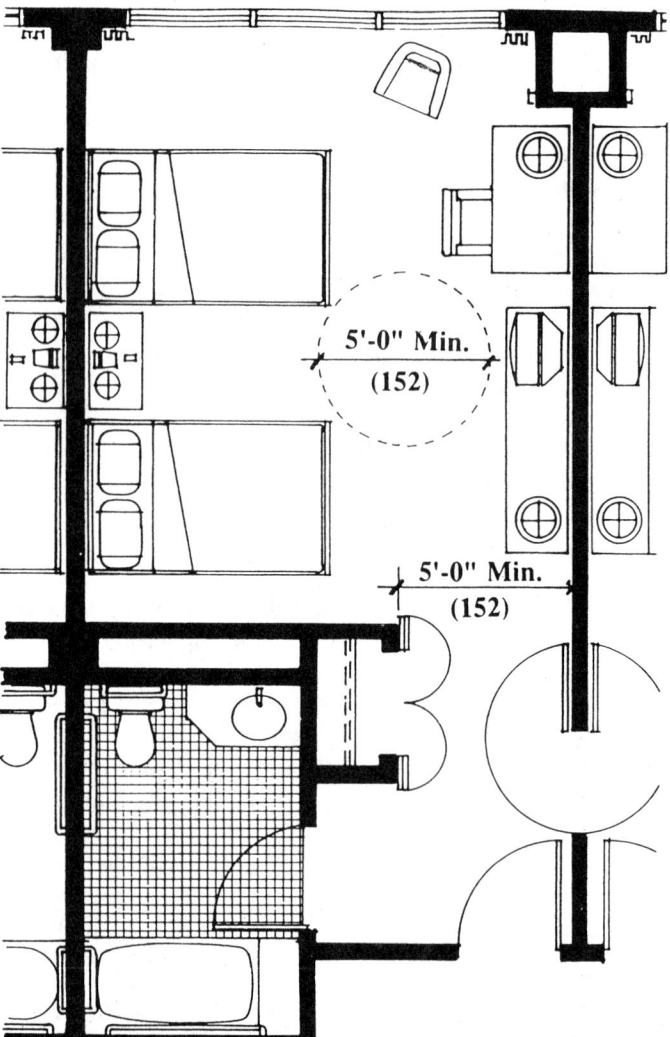

Figure 4-7 Double-double room that is accessible, as noted by the five-foot turnaround dimension. (From DeChiara et al., *Time Saver Standards for Interior Design and Space Planning.* 1991. Reproduced with permission of the McGraw-Hill Companies.)

restaurants, public toilet facilities, and access to meeting rooms, gift shops or other retail areas, and recreational facilities. A portion of each different guest room configuration (queen, king, double-double, and suites), not just one type of room, must be designed to meet accessibility standards. Hotels with 50 or more sleeping rooms are required to have a percentage of those rooms designed with roll-in showers. Figure 4-7 shows a typical double-double room that is accessible. Visual and auditory emergency signals are also required in guest rooms and other areas. Please be aware that the revised ADA guidelines in review at the time of this writing may be different than facts stated in the chapter.

In public areas such as the registration desk and the cash desk in retail stores, an accessibility accommodation to meet design guidelines for sales areas is needed. The designer can meet this requirement by either designing a section of the counter no higher than 36 inches above the floor, providing an auxiliary counter nearby, or designing a folding shelf into the counter to facilitate registration and business transactions.

The larger the lodging property, the greater the responsibility of the interior designer and design team for meeting all types of codes. If the interior designer will be involved in remodeling an older structure, he or she must be sure that any design recommendations made to the client meet the current codes. A renovation can have a significant impact on the design in order to meet codes. What the client considers a simple refurbishing code officials may determine is a major renovation requiring multiple code modifications in the design. As always, it is the interior designer's responsibility to know how the law affects the project.

Design Applications

The design of a lodging facility is a fascinating and exciting area of commercial interior design. As the reader has already seen, involvement in this type of facility is complex and carries with it many responsibilities. Lodging properties come in many sizes and price points. The type of property will impact the interior design of all the public spaces and guest rooms. A guest room in a luxury hotel will be larger than that commonly found in a convention hotel. The design and specification of seating for the "lobby" of a bed and breakfast will be significantly different from those in a resort hotel. Conference spaces will be larger in business and conference hotels than in suburban facilities.

Lodging facilities have many specific functional needs that must be addressed. General ambiance and concepts must attract and, occasionally, positively astonish guests so that they will want to return. Guest comfort and safety are aspects of the interior design that impact every project, whether it is a bed and breakfast in a small town or a mega casino hotel with a big budget. The interior design for function spaces, recreational facilities, and food and beverage spaces is also critical to the overall satisfaction of guests that brings them back again and again.

This chapter focuses on specific design and planning issues for the lobby, guest rooms, function spaces, spas, and recreation spaces in a generic hotel. These are spaces that would most likely be the responsibility of an interior designer and are often presented to challenge students in design studio projects. This section also includes a brief discussion of the planning of food and beverage facilities as part of a lodging property. Chapter 5 deals with other types of food and beverage facilities and presents a more in-depth discussion of design elements. There is a great deal of variation in the interior design and specification of these similar spaces based on the type, size, and location of the property; thus, the information provided in this section is generic in nature. An excellent reference on these differences can be found in the book *Hotel Design: Planning and Development*, by Rutes, Penner, and Adams.

The Lobby

The lobby provides the first critical impression the guest or visitor will have of the hotel. It might be intimate and well appointed in a boutique hotel or large, bustling, and dramatic to handle the crowds for a convention. Whatever its size and design, it not only

Figure 4-8 Lobby of the Inter-Continental Hotel in New York City. (Design by Kenneth E. Hurd and Associates.)

creates a visual impression, but has many important functions to perform for the guests. The planning of both the functional elements and the design aesthetics requires careful attention to detail and concern for the hotel's operational and thematic goals (Figure 4-8).

The design of hotel lobbies have undergone many changes over the years. Hotels generally did not have lobbies until the 19th century. In those early years, only the luxury hotels had lobbies large enough to be statement-producing gathering places. That situation gradually changed as more and more travelers took to the roads after World War II. The first atrium lobby at the Hyatt Regency Atlanta (designed by John Portman in the 1960s) showed that a lobby could be a prominent feature of a hotel property. Large and multistory lobbies became popular as the number of guest rooms grew. This was especially true of the hotels that served convention and business guests. The smaller, intimate lobby remained the norm for many types of hotels and suite hotels that sought to create the intimacy of the older grand hotels. Today, while many types of hotels require a large, dramatic lobby, interior designers try to plan for a friendly and even homey feeling by creating smaller seating groupings or using other design devices to create an intimate feeling in a large space.

The lobby is a busy place with guests and visitors coming and going, sometimes at a frantic pace and in great numbers. Not only does it serve for check-in and check-out, it is the main circulation space moving guests to the guest rooms and to public spaces such as restaurants, recreation areas, and conference spaces. The lobby serves as a place for guests to meet other guests and visitors, and perhaps to relax away from guest rooms, thus becoming a gathering place (Figure 4-9).

Attention to the planning of circulation space and traffic patterns is very important. New guests checking in with luggage will want to find the registration desk easily and locate the elevators to get to their rooms. Sometimes the amount of this traffic alone can cause congestion in the lobby when several large groups check in at the same time. This important primary traffic pattern must adequately handle expected peak volumes of traffic. Secondary traffic paths must smoothly move guests and visitors from the lobby to restaurants, retail outlets, and gift shops, as well as function rooms. Secondary traffic paths also move guests to seating provided in the lobby.

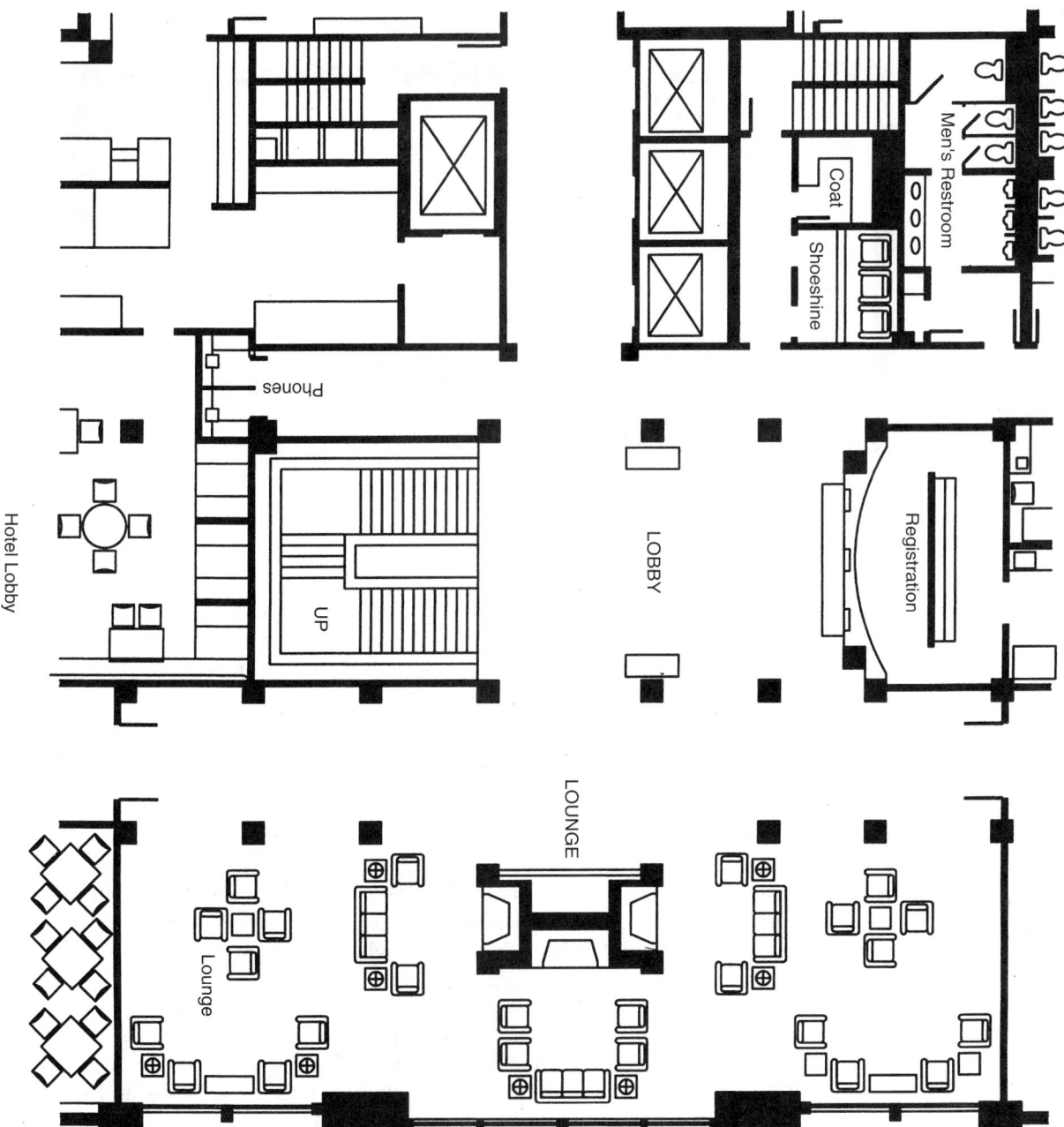

Figure 4-9   Registration area and lounge in a hotel lobby. (Designed by and courtesy of Cody D. Beal.)

The main functional component of the lobby is the registration area, sometimes called the *front desk*, although a desk per se is rarely used today. Space must be planned for guests to register, check out, and obtain general guest information. Queuing space for those waiting to speak to staff is needed, along with the actual space for the front desk. Of course, the larger the hotel, the more space will be needed for these functions. It is suggested that a minimum desk space of 6 feet each be allowed for registration, check-out, and cashier stations; that two stations be allowed for the first 150 rooms; and that one additional station be planned for each 100 additional rooms.[11] Calculations must be

---

[11]Rutes, Penner and Adams, 2001, p. 284.

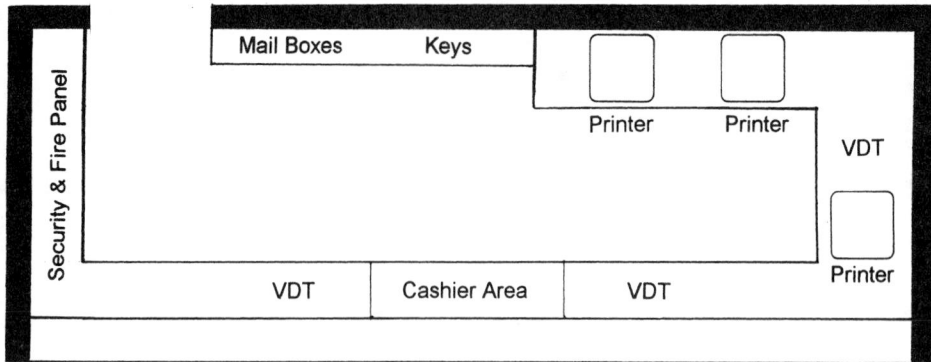

Figure 4-10 Small registration desk indicating space for various functions in the front desk/lobby area. (Illustration courtesy of SOI Interior Design.)

made about how many guests will be arriving at peak times to determine the amount of circulation space needed for queuing (Figure 4-10).

In a small facility, it is especially important that the front desk staff have visual control over the entrance and lobby area. The desk clerk must be able to see and greet arriving guests quickly to help create that all-important good first impression. In larger hotels, bell staff or even a host or hostess can guide an arriving guest to the front desk. It is also common to locate some seating near the front desk. This seating is provided for those accompanying the person registering or checking out.

There are several other functions that take place at the front desk or that are included in this area. Table 4-7 lists these other functions. One function deserving attention is concierge services. In larger hotels, a concierge is a staff member who provides information about the local area, helps with reservations for dinner at local off-site restaurants, sells tickets for plays or sporting events, and provides other aid to make the guest's stay more enjoyable and trouble-free. Depending on the size and type of hotel, public restrooms, house telephones, and public telephones might also be located near the front desk (Figure 4-11).

The overall size of the lobby and seating in the lobby are determined by the type of facility. For a small facility such as a bed and breakfast or suburban hotel, the lobby will be small, providing a minimal amount of soft seating to perhaps watch TV. A large convention hotel's lobby needs to be quite large and will have numerous sofas and soft seating units arranged in conversation groups. Some hotels also provide a few desks or tables where guests can write letters or postcards in the lobby. Resort hotels often have large lobby seating areas so that guests have a gathering place or a place to enjoy a view. Luxury and superluxury hotel lobbies are commonly small, private, and very elegant.

The concept and theme of the hotel will establish the design treatments and ambience of the lobby and hotel in general. Styles of furniture and fabric choices, architectural millwork and architectural treatments and finishes, accessories, and, of course, the color scheme

TABLE 4-7 Typical Front Desk Functions

■ Guest registration stations	■ Reservations
■ Guest check-out and cashier stations	■ House and pay phones
■ Guest mail and messages	■ Events directory
■ Key boxes	■ Bellman station (nearby)
■ Guest information (concierge)	■ Bellman carts storage (nearby)
■ Space for assistant manager	■ Luggage storage (nearby)

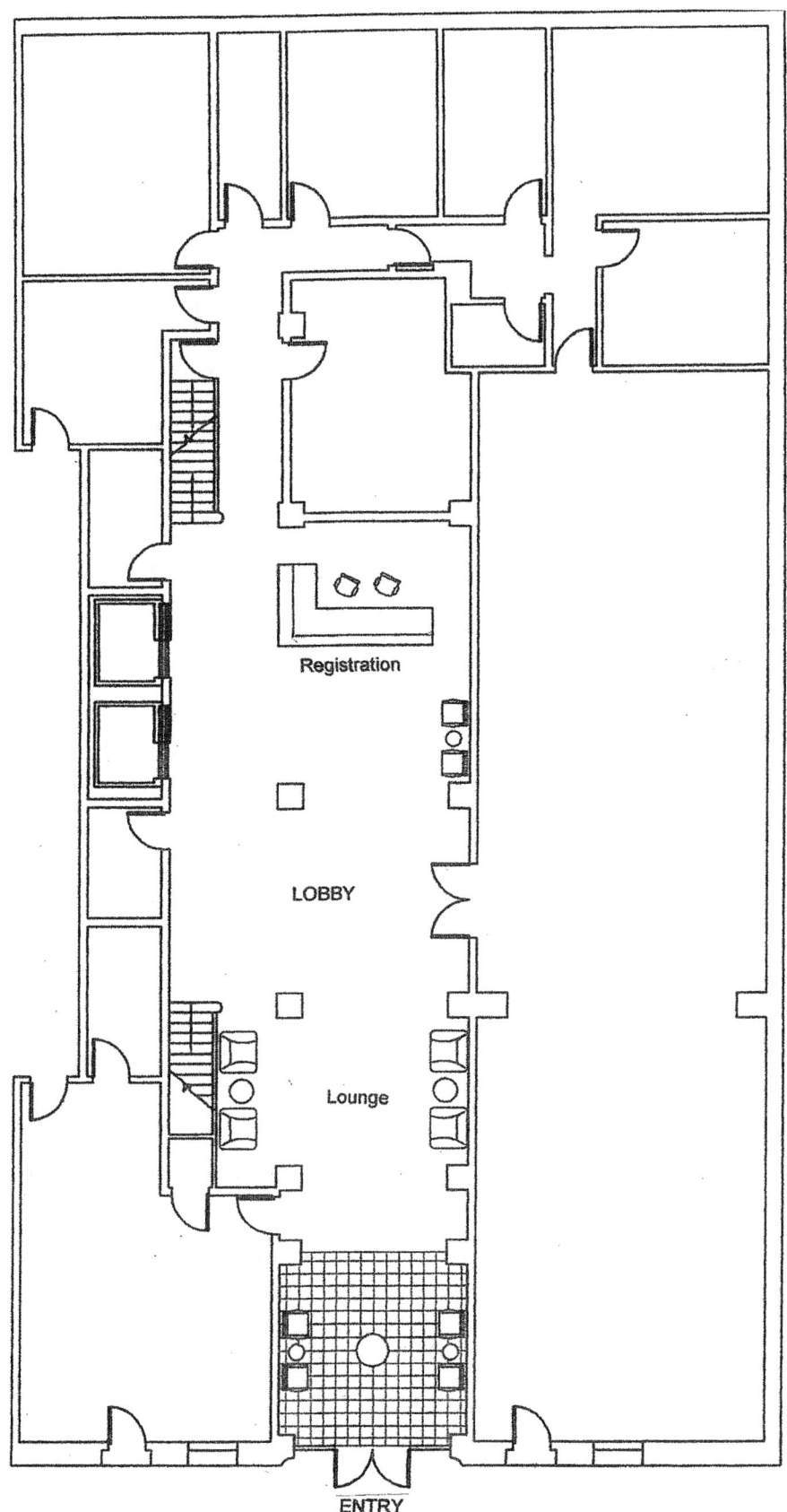

Figure 4-11 Floor plan of a lobby in a small hotel. (Designed by and courtesy of Stephen Howard.)

will be driven by the concept developed in the early planning of the facility. Materials on architectural surfaces and upholstery must be durable and easy to maintain, as well as meet local fire safety codes. It is common for major traffic paths to be defined by some type of hard surface flooring, while carpeting is used in seating areas. When carpeting is used, most designers use patterned carpet in large areas to help hide traffic paths and spills. Walls can be treated with many materials that will meet appropriate codes. Upholstery fabrics must also be durable and easy to clean. Colors and patterns of fabrics should be selected to help hide spills and dirt, or the fabrics should be treated with a high-quality stain repellent.

Most of the lighting design decisions for the lobby involve determining general lighting. Of course, accent, task, and even sparkle lighting is also used to help accentuate the design concept and provide needed lighting solutions for the particular space. Ten foot-candles of general lighting is sufficient for guests and staff to move safely through the spaces. Task lighting for reading and writing letters might be needed in some areas of the lobby. Tabletop fixtures might also be utilized in small seating groups to help create a residential feeling and provide additional general lighting. Accent lighting to call attention to artwork, signage, and display features is often required. Visual punch and interest can be added, depending on the concept, by the use of sparkle lighting.

Computer workstations for registration and checkout of guests are an absolute necessity in today's lodging industry. Computers perform these functions as well as provide necessary information for the owners and management of the property. Most hotels have stand-up stations for registration, though some resorts, bed and breakfast inns, and boutique facilities handle these functions at a sit-down desk. Accessibility standards may require a sit-down registration station when most registration is handled at a stand-up counter. The design of the registration desk must be carefully coordinated with the data systems consultant, since extensive cabling will be required for the front desk and auxiliary functions that require computers and other telecommunications equipment.

The last element to consider in the design of the lobby is signage. Prominent signage will be used to identify the registration desk, concierge station, bell desk, and cashier. Other signage will be needed to direct guests to the elevators, restaurants and cocktail lounges, stores, function spaces, and recreational areas. Very large properties will often include a site map to help guests find their way around. Other signage will be used to meet the specific needs of the type of hotel and locate the services provided for guests and visitors.

Guest Rooms

From a functional point of view, the planning and design of guest rooms involves providing the greatest number of rooms at the lowest expense relative to the type of lodging facility and the target market of expected guests. From an interior design point of view, the aesthetics involves the important attempt to make uninteresting rectangles interesting and exciting. Guests are often hoping for or expecting a space that is more luxurious and aesthetically interesting than what they have at home. The interior designer and all of the stakeholders in the project strive to fulfill this expectation in the planning and design of guest rooms. The portion of this section devoted to the interior design elements of the guest room focuses on a typical guest room with two double beds or a queen/king-sized bed.

It is obvious that hotels gain the largest percentage of their income from renting guest rooms. At the same time, the design of the guest rooms and the products and finishes for these spaces is the greatest expense. Adding one item to a room may not seem like much, but that item could be multiplied by hundreds, as it will likely be repeated in each room. Each item and each finish specified for the guest rooms must be done with careful consideration for expense, aesthetics, and function. Each additional foot of floor space planned for typical guest rooms and suites also reduces the total number of rooms. The design team's planning goals in this area will be to provide as many of the different sized rooms considered essential, based on the type of hotel being developed, without providing too much extra space. With 55 to 85 percent of all the space in a hotel devoted to guest

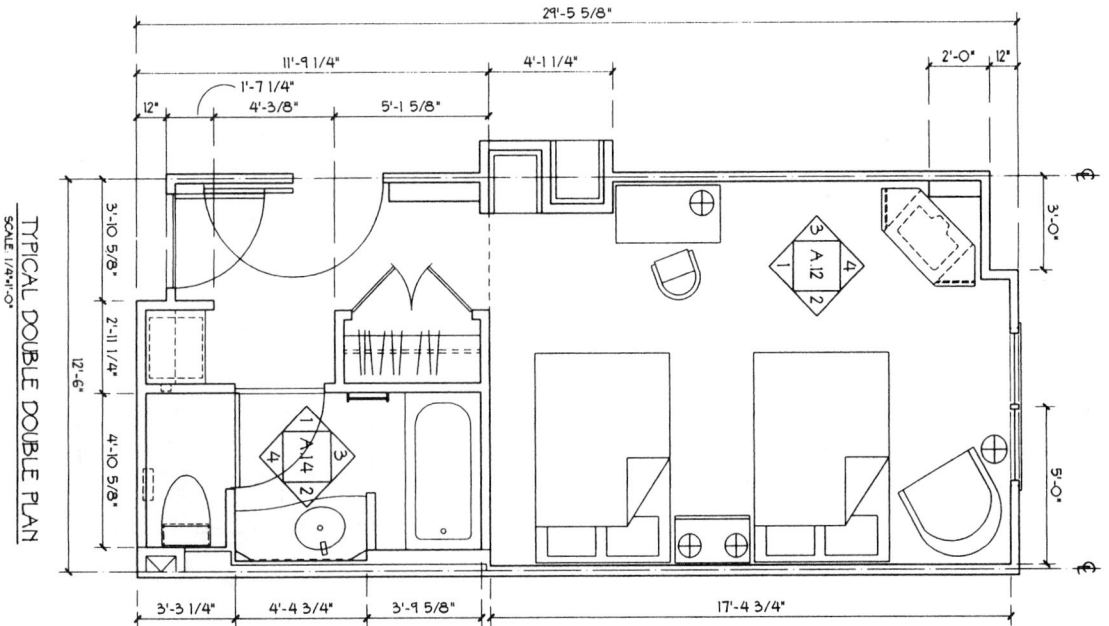

Figure 4-12 A typical double-double floor plan in a hotel. (Plan courtesy of Holiday Inns.)

rooms,[12] the actual cost of floor space as well as the specification of FF&E in guest rooms can become quite high if this consideration is ignored by the designer.

The first consideration in planning the guest room areas is the overall guest room floor configuration. Guest room floor planning involves determining the greatest number of rooms and suites on each floor, as well as providing space for guest and service elevators, stairs, and service areas such as linen rooms, vending areas, and circulation space. Depending on the type of hotel, other areas may be planned for each floor. For example, premium suite floors may include a small lounge where afternoon beverages are available for guests only on that floor. Conference hotels may provide a business communications area on certain guest floors in addition to a general business center on the main level.

The three most common configurations are shown in Figure 4-5. Most hotels are a variation of one of them. The greatest number of rooms in the smallest gross square footage is achieved with the double loaded slab. As can be seen in the figure, a central corridor provides for a large number of rooms on either side. A second common configuration is the tower plan. In this case, a central core with elevators and other service spaces is surrounded by the guest rooms. The tower plan can take the shape of a circle, triangle, or square. In atrium plans, the central core becomes an open atrium expanding the interior space. Guest rooms are arranged on the perimeter, with room entrances along the corridors that overlook the lobby atrium. Glass elevators in atrium plans take advantage of the view that allows guests to see the atrium space from ground level to some upper floor level. Service functions for atrium hotels are placed away from the atrium itself.

Planning for guest room locations involves careful application of the room mix determined during the feasibility study and concept development. The *room mix* is the configuration of different types of rooms required based primarily on the size and number of beds in the room. Two other terms that are used in discussions about the number of guest rooms are *key*, which refers to a rentable unit, and *guest room bay*, which is the space equivalent to a guest room.[13]

Any one floor of the hotel will likely have a variety of room sizes. Some rooms will have a queen- or king-size bed, while others will have two double beds (called a *double-double*). Figures 4-12 and 4-13 illustrate common guest room layouts. Others might be

---

[12]Stipanuk and Roffman, 1992, p. 365 (hardcover edition).
[13]Rutes, Penner, and Adams, 2001, p. 263.

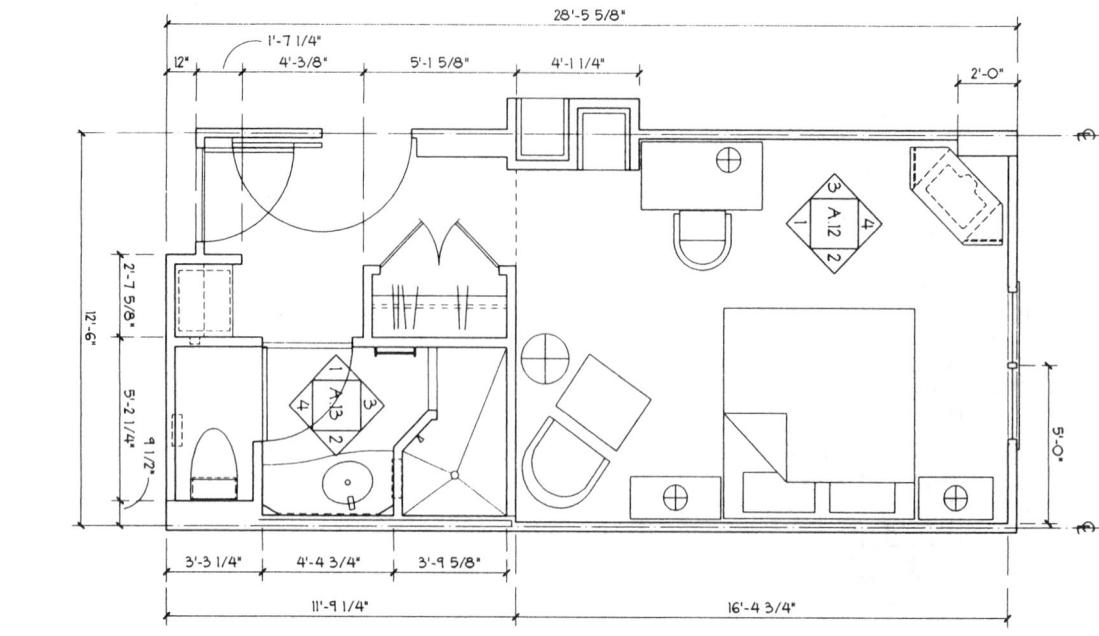

Figure 4-13 Guest room layout with the option of an adjoining room. (Plan courtesy of Holiday Inns.)

small suites with a sleeping area separate from a sitting room and so on. The room mix will also be affected by the number of connecting rooms required, the size of the bathrooms, and the overall size of the rooms.

Many readers have no doubt been in a hotel where the room has a king-sized bed and barely enough room between the edge of the bed and the dresser to open the dresser drawers. Yet, another hotel provides generous space with essentially the same pieces of furniture. Today, guests have high expectations concerning the interior design of their hotel guest rooms. Thus, hotels compete for guests by offering larger guest rooms, exciting guest room décor, interesting art and accessories, comfortable desk chairs, and, oh yes, feather beds! Of course, the design of the room and the quality of the products used will vary with the type of the hotel and price point of the room charges (Figures 4-14a and 4-14b).

To begin with, the interior plan and design of the guest rooms are influenced by the architectural decisions related to the slab design, along with decisions concerning the location of the bathroom, doors, and windows. The interior designer's primary responsibility is to provide the appropriate amount of furniture and accessories to achieve the goals of the hotel and the target market of expected guests.

Guest rooms are compact spaces; in a sense, they are mini homes with distinct functional zones whose space needs to be planned. These zones include sleeping, lounging, working, and bathroom/dressing. These zones are easily clarified in the floor plans of Figures 4-12 and 4-13. Key points in the planning of zones other than the dressing and bathroom zones are highlighted in Table 4-8 on page 132.

The bathroom/dressing zone is most commonly located adjacent to the entrance to the guest room, with the closet located in that same area. In high-priced hotels and those that cater to the business and convention guest, guest room bath areas are designed with greater attention. Guest demands for more space, nice fixtures, and enhanced overall design challenge the interior designer to create pleasing bathrooms that are more than utilitarian spaces with three fixtures.

One common ploy is to separate the lavatories from the tub and water closet space. Resorts and luxury properties add a shower to the bathroom and perhaps a whirlpool tub rather than a standard bathtub (Figure 4-15). Larger spaces, elegantly designed fixtures, quality materials, and extra amenities are used to compete for the discerning guest. The hotel's target market will have a great influence on the space allowances and materials specifications in these zones.

Figure 4-14a Luxurious guest room at the Monte Carlo Resort and Casino. (Design by and photograph courtesy of Anita Brooks/Charles Gruwell Interior Design International, Las Vegas, NV.)

Figure 4-14b Interior design of a guest room reflecting the tropical ambiance of the Westin Rio Mar. (Design by and photograph courtesy of Hirsch Bedner Associates.)

TABLE 4-8 Tips for the Design of Guest Rooms

- Provide sufficient space on all sides of all beds for housekeeping services.
- Provide a minimum of one bedside table with a lamp and space for a small clock radio as well as a light fixture. Many hotels provide a bedside table and lamp on both sides of queen- and king-sized beds.
- Soft seating, either a comfortable club chair or love seat positioned for easy viewing of the television. Floor or table lamps are also required in this location.
- Love seats and sofas, if specified, are often sleeper units to provide room for extra sleeping accommodations.
- An armoire or custom cabinet that will accommodate a television as well as dresser drawers.
- A table desk or dresser/desk combination, along with a chair such as a dining room–style chair, make up the work area. Business class and higher-priced hotels use office desk chairs in the work area.
- The work area will also require an extra telephone, Internet connection, and a task light.
- A small eating zone might be part of the concept, with a small refrigerator with a chargeable bar and snack service, as well as a coffee maker.
- A suite hotel provides a small kitchen—which could be as simple as a sink and a microwave oven or a true small kitchen with full-size appliances—plus a small dining table and chairs.
- Appropriate accessories such as wall mirrors and framed graphics selected to enhance the design concept of the rooms.

Considered part of the dressing zone but generally located across from the beds are the armoires or dressers. Dressing areas require a dresser, closet, mirror, and space to accommodate luggage. How much room is allowed for these areas will vary with the type of hotel. Hotels where guest will be staying for several days or possibly even a few weeks will have more dresser space, larger closets, and storage space for luggage.

Competition and guest demands also mean that the hotel property owner has to increase the quality of the furniture items and materials on the seating pieces in the room while carefully considering price economies. Headboards, mattresses, chairs, dressers,

Figure 4-15 Presidental suite bathroom at the Gaylord Texan Resort and Convention Center, Grapevine, Texas. (Interior design by Wilson & Associates, Dallas, TX. Photographer: Michael Wilson.)

desks, and other furniture and millwork must be commercial-grade products to take abuse but look like something the guest may have at home. Plastic laminate finishes on furniture items are most commonly selected for tables, dressers, and headboards. Luxury and higher-value properties utilize wood-veneered case goods. Fabrics for bedspreads and soft seating should be selected with maintenance and fire safety in mind, even though the building and fire codes generally do not regulate those materials.

Architectural finishes must be easy to maintain while taking a lot of abuse and use. Commercial-grade carpeting and hard surface flooring are a must, as are commercial-grade wall coverings. Luxury hotels are one of the few types of facilities that can effectively use a limited amount of non-commercial-grade materials for wallcoverings in guest rooms. For the flooring, carpeting over padding in solids, tone-on-tone patterns, or small patterns is most common in guest rooms with slip-resistant floor materials in the baths. Textured vinyl wallcoverings, grasscloth, and even painted surfaces serve as wall treatment options. Faux finishes are used sparingly and only in some luxury properties due to their high cost. Larger patterns are more often reserved for bedspreads and draperies. Window treatments should include both an overdrape of some decorative fabric or pattern and a blackout drape to provide privacy and light control.

Artwork and other accessories are necessary to complete the design concept, but they must be chosen with economy as well as appearance in mind. Reproduction paintings, prints, and photographs for the walls are most common, with small bookshelves and books supplied in many resort and vacation hotels. Theft is an issue in a hotel. It is common to have wall accessories physically attached by screws rather than being hung, as in a home. Small accessories on dressers and tables are seen only in luxury properties—if at all. In many hotels, even lighting fixtures are fixed to the walls or tables to make it difficult for them to be stolen.

A television, VCR, or DVD player and a video game controller have become expected accessories in guest rooms. Many resorts and urban hotels have also placed CD players in the rooms in addition to the ubiquitous bedside radio. The placement of the TV must be planned for viewing from the bed as well as the lounge area. The TV is most often located in an armoire in combination with the dresser. However, lower-priced facilities may still place the TV on top of a low dresser or cabinet. Luxury resorts have specified wall-hung plasma televisions to save space and offer one more luxury appointment to the guest room.

General and safety lighting via a ceiling fixture at the entrance door or a floor lamp on a switch at the entrance door is a must. Sconces or bedside table fixtures provide additional general lighting and serve as task lights for reading in bed. Task lights are also needed at the desk and soft seating locations. If the room is large, coved lighting may be employed for general lighting. High-quality lighting is needed in the bathroom and the dressing area. Most hotels have changed to fixtures using longer-burning fluorescent lamps to provide better energy economy.

Hotels have always included a number of suites to accommodate guests with particular needs. All-suites hotels became popular with business travelers and families in the last quarter of the 20th century. Suites are also popular in upscale and luxury hotels. They provide all the function areas discussed above in a more residential setting, separating the sleeping area from the living room and eating areas. Larger suites have multiple bedrooms, conference rooms or dining rooms, and separate lounge areas (Figures 4-16a, 4-16b, 4-17a, and 4-17b).

Suite rooms are commonly located on the upper floors of the hotel, providing better views, quiet, and privacy. Some hotels place suites at the corners of the floors, where it is sometimes difficult to create regular-sized rooms. Suites may have private balconies or patios whenever the hotel has feature views of the city or area. The designer also will upgrade the quality of materials, furniture, and accessories in the suites, making these rooms worth their higher prices. A portion of suite accommodations will also have to be designed to meet the ADA requirements.

Club floors and lounges have become popular at upscale, convention, luxury, casino, and other types of hotels. Club floors have access restricted to guests on those floors and provide small lounges where special amenities or extra services are offered. A club lounge

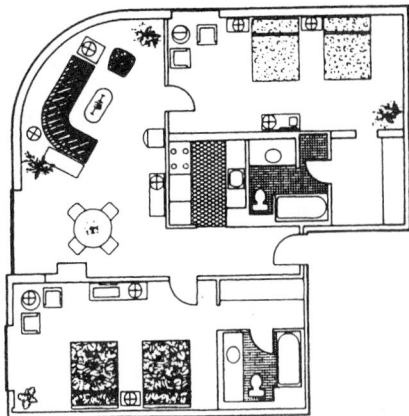

Two Bedroom Suite - 1280 sq. ft.

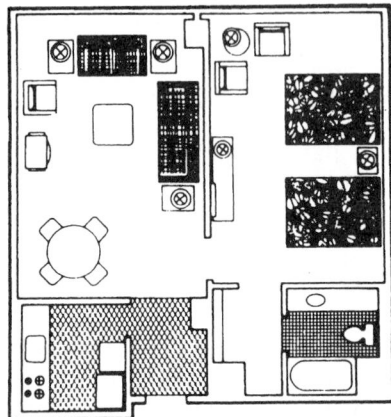

One Bedroom Suite - 840 sq. ft.

Figure 4-16a Floor plan of a Double Tree guest suite, Houston, Texas. (Courtesy of Double Tree Guest Suites.)

Figure 4-16b Parlor suite at the Double Tree Mission Valley. (Photograph courtesy of Planning, Design, & Application, Inc./P.D.&A.)

Figure 4-17a Larger suites have dining rooms and separate lounge areas. Valencia Hotel. (Photograph courtesy of 3D/International, and dMd Design.)

Figure 4-17b Guest suite at the Valencia Hotel. (Photograph courtesy of 3D/International and dMd Design.)

might include continental breakfast, and beverages may be offered in the afternoon. A concierge and other personalized services for guests willing to pay premium prices are common in club lounges.

Club lounge space planning and furniture specification will vary based on the services offered. However, club lounges often provide soft seating groups, two-top and four-top tables and chairs, a service bar for food and beverages, and wide-screen televisions. A business area might be off the main lounge, and in family-oriented hotels a small game room might also be included. The materials and products in the club lounge will be similar to the more expensive products specified for the guest rooms on these floors.

Code requirements for guest rooms need to be verified with local jurisdictions. Depending on the jurisdiction and the size of the facility, architectural finishes for walls within guest rooms could be required to meet Class A, B, or C standards. Flooring materials must meet Class II standards as a minimum. Draperies and other vertical textile hangings are required to pass the vertical flame test. Mattresses must meet local code restrictions, which might exceed the standard U.S. federal DOC FF4-72 test requirement.

A portion of guest rooms and bathroom facilities must be designed and specified to meet accessibility standards. These standards were discussed in the general section on interior design code requirements earlier in this chapter. Figure 4-7 shows a typical ADA guest room layout. Note that projects located outside the United States may have different accessibility requirements than the ADA guidelines. Design decisions made in this space must satisfy today's discerning guest.

Fire sprinklers and visual and auditory warning systems are also necessary in all new and remodeled lodging facilities. Regulations for all these materials, products, and systems reflecting the greater concern for guest safety has also meant more concern for the materials used on the floors, tub, and shower floors, and the addition of safety grab bars even in rooms not designated to be accessible.

Function Spaces

An important component in the design of most types of lodging facilities today is the planning of specialized spaces for meetings and banquets. These spaces are referred to as *function spaces*. Hotels began adding function spaces to their properties in the late 19th century to accommodate civic meetings.[14] Function spaces help produce additional revenue via the room rental as well as additional food service, guest rooms for exhibitors, and extra money spent at the hotel by participants. Even small lodging facilities make space available for special functions of outside groups.

Hotels generally have a mixture of function room sizes to accommodate the varying needs of users. A large ballroom, variously sized meeting rooms, and smaller breakout rooms generally make up the function spaces. They are generally multipurpose rooms that can house meetings, seminars, wedding receptions, trade shows and conferences, and many other activities requiring space for large numbers of guests in a single room or multiple spaces. Flexibility of these spaces is very important. It might be necessary to set up a space with individual chairs in either a classroom style using narrow tables or a theater style, using all chairs for a business meeting or presentation one morning, then convert the space for a luncheon the next day and set up for a trade show display over a weekend. For example, a conference hotel may require a ballroom that can be used for a large keynote presentation or for exhibitions, or that can be broken into smaller meeting rooms by partitioning the ballroom with full-height movable walls. A small hotel may only have a ballroom that can accommodate wedding receptions or be divided into small conference rooms. A large resort hotel will have multiple ballrooms and breakout rooms to accommodate several groups at one time.

Large hotels that target conventions and business travelers might have a special wing for the meeting rooms and banquet room. In most other cases, function spaces are located near the lobby for easy access by guests and outside visitors. Larger hotels commonly provide exterior access to the section of the hotel dedicated to function spaces. This is done because many of the individuals using the function spaces are not hotel guests. It is also common for larger hotels to have secondary lobbies off these exterior entrances. These secondary lobbies, also called *prefunction spaces,* provide a gathering space and room to set up registration desks or even required food service. It is important to have restrooms, public phones, and coat rooms nearby.

Planning the actual amount of square footage for the function spaces is rarely the responsibility of the interior designer. This discussion is provided to give context to the de-

---

[14]Rutes, Penner, and Adams, 2001, p. 296.

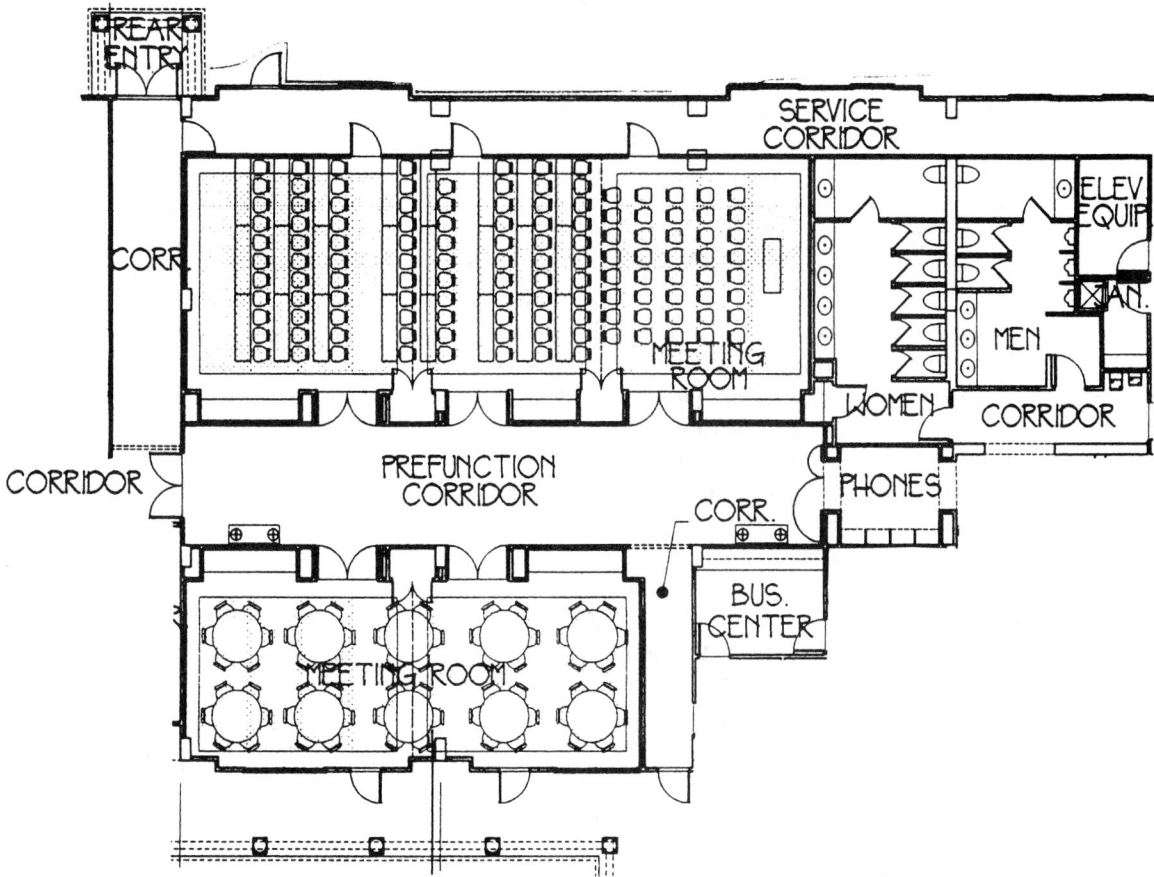

Figure 4-18 Floor plan showing the prefunction corridor and service corridor flanking the various meeting rooms. The lobby is in close proximity. (Plan courtesy of Holiday Inns.)

sign responsibilities of the interior designer in this area of the hotel. The space allotted to the function areas will depend upon the type of hotel and the guest target market. Space allowances are related to the number of guest rooms. For example, a convention will plan the ballroom to be two to four times the number of guest rooms, while a resort hotel's ballroom may be only one times the number of guest rooms. In other words, a large hotel will allow 60 to 100 square feet per guest room for function areas, while a small hotel might allow only 10 to 20 square feet per guest room.[15] Direct access from the kitchen for food service is also necessary. Moving of food from the kitchen is often done on wheeled carts through back-of-house corridors behind the ballroom and other function rooms, and then the plates are carried on trays to the function space by wait staff (Figure 4-18).

Furniture arrangements in the function spaces fall into three basic categories. For meetings and seminars the room can be set up in theater—also called *auditorium*—style with individual chairs. An alternative to this arrangement, called *classroom* seating, uses small tables and chairs that can be arranged in numerous configurations. The third arrangement is banquet seating using round tables 54 to 72 inches in diameter that accommodate 6 to 10 diners. To handle the flexible use of the spaces, back-of-house hallways and storage areas are planned to store extra chairs and tables.

Furniture and furnishings in function spaces must be specified to sustain the heavy traffic, spills, and movement of furniture. Chairs are small, usually only 18 inches wide by 24 inched deep, and must be stackable. Upholstery fabrics are textured vinyl, commercial-grade nylon fabrics, and other textiles that can take considerable wear and tear. These simple armless chairs can be dressed up with slipcovers when the event is a

---

[15]Stipanuk and Roffmann, 1992, p. 378 (hardcover edition).

wedding or formal banquet. Patterns and colors of materials will be selected in keeping with the overall themes or concept of the hotel. Tables must be foldable and chairs must be stackable so that hotel staff can move them easily from one function space to storage space to another function space.

Architectural finishes and treatments must be selected to meet code requirements and be easily maintained by the housekeeping staff. They should also be selected to serve as backgrounds, not statements. Patterned carpets are often specified to help disguise spills and traffic patterns. Carpet layouts are often done to facilitate the placement of furniture in the large open spaces. Wall finishes need to be very durable. In some spaces, chair rails are used to decrease the possibility of chairs scuffing the walls. It is also suggested that fabric wall panels be used to control acoustics. Should one or more walls in a function room include windows, the designer must specify full blackout drapes or blinds.

Another design component of the function spaces is lighting design. Since the rooms must be designed with flexible use in mind, so should the lighting specification and fixture selection. All the variously sized function rooms should utilize fixtures that can provide adjustable lighting levels. When a room is used for a meeting or a speaker, lighting needs to be dimmed so that PowerPoint presentations, movies, slides, or any other audiovisual methodology used can be seen while the audience can still see to take notes. Usually lower light levels are appropriate for meals, especially in the ballroom for a formal dinner. If the space is used for exhibition displays, a higher light level will be needed.

Much thought is given to the design of the ceiling surfaces, selection of fixtures, and lighting design possibilities in these spaces. Fixtures for general, accent, functional lighting, and spotlighting might be required in any one functional space. Large ballrooms may have chandeliers as well as elaborate built-in ceiling lighting systems. The design of the ceiling and the incorporation of the lighting fixtures into the ceiling often make the most dramatic design statement in function spaces. These large spaces require high ceilings, which can range from 12 to over 30 feet. Ceiling design will also include selection and spacing of smoke detectors, sprinkler heads, emergency lighting, speakers, and mechanical grills for heating/air conditioning. The ceiling is a complex design element in a function room of any size.

Function spaces are assembly occupancies in the mixed occupancy of a hotel. As such, the interior designer must carefully space plan initial room sizes and furniture layouts to ensure that traffic aisles and pathways will meet exit access requirements. Almost all rooms will require two exits, and some will require additional exits. Carpet and flooring materials should be specified to meet local fire codes as well as accessibility standards. Exit signage, sprinklers, and emergency warning systems are also important components of function spaces. Electrical and communication services must be planned so that extension cords that might be needed to use the speaker's projector do not interfere with safe access from the space.

Well-thought-out signage to move guests and visitors to function spaces is another challenge. Guests must be able to find their way easily from the entrance or lobby to prefunction spaces and these special-use rooms themselves. Each room will have signage at the entrance doors. Floor-standing signs are used to supplement individual room signs to help direct visitors to the appropriate meeting room. Often the rooms have names in common with the theme or location of the hotel. For example, function rooms in many hotels in the Phoenix, Arizona, area have rooms with names such as Grand Canyon, Camelback, and Sedona in keeping with the Arizona landscape and localities.

Spas and Recreational Facilities

Few types of lodging facilities can exist without some recreational facilities. At a bed and breakfast, it might be an outdoor jacuzzi or a sauna. Numerous kinds of lodging properties provide a swimming pool in a landscaped courtyard. Hotels that cater to families have added game rooms with video games for the children. Other facilities provide on-site tennis courts and perhaps volleyball courts. If the hotel is not adjacent to a golf course, arrangements are made for guests to golf at nearby courses. Health clubs are also becoming a common component of lodging facilities today as guests demand a way to keep up with their exercise programs when away from home. Resort hotels often include spa services with quiet, relaxing areas for a massage, steam bath, saunas, and other specialized services. The list of recreational facilities available to guests is varied.

It is very important for the recreational facilities to provide easy access by guests. Many guests do not like walking through the lobby to get to the swimming pool, spa, or health club areas. In golf and tennis resorts, separate clubhouses are common so that guests can change their clothes, take a shower, and visit a pro shop away from the main hotel. Hotels in smaller markets and even many luxury resorts often make some of their recreational facilities available to local residents. When this is the case, one entrance to the recreation area or spa is provided from the parking lot. Let us focus on spa and health club areas. This brief discussion will take the reader from the entry of a generic spa and health club through the various spaces common in this section of the hotel.

The term *spa* is associated with luxury and good health, and this facility is commonly considered a health resort offering a variety of services such as massages, hydrotherapy, health education, and various treatments. The interior designer must produce a design solution which meets the guest's expectations of specialized treatment in a calm, luxurious surrounding and simultaneously meets the guest's need for safety, security, and practicalities associated with the operation of the spa.

A reception counter with a small waiting area is provided in the entrance. Storage is needed here for locker keys and perhaps robes and towels. The space plan and traffic paths will move guests from the reception area to separate areas for men and women. Workout rooms are commonly coed, while spa treatment areas are usually gender separated. Some hotels, however, provide areas where couples can obtain treatments together, use coed pools, and obtain coed food service.

From the reception area in larger hotels, guests will walk back to a locker room or dressing area. If lockers are provided, an allowance of 16 to 20 square feet per person is common. Lockers 36 inches high are stacked to accommodate sufficient locker space. This size locker can accommodate personal items as well as street cloths if folded. Some hotels with large spa areas may provide full-length lockers so that the guest's clothing does not have to be folded. Lockers require plastic laminate interiors with wood or laminate exteriors. Dressing areas including showers, toilet facilities, and counters for hair dryers are needed. Storage for clean and dirty towels is an important planning issue in the locker room and dressing area.

In either the reception area or an internal relaxing area, space is provided for water or other refreshments. Larger facilities will include a juice bar or even a spa restaurant attached to the spa and health club. Larger spas and those that also cater to nonguest use of the spa might have small shops selling soaps, lotions, clothing, and other items located off the reception area so that visitors and guests can make purchases at the gift shop without entering the spa area.

If the guest is using workout areas, he or she will enter the workout room or go to other recreational facilities after changing in the locker room. Depending on the hotel, guests may have access to the pool area from the spa and health club or even a private pool. Space allowance for the workout room is obviously tied to the combination and number of exercise machines placed in the room. Space is needed for the various types of equipment plus a traffic path in front of and perhaps behind the equipment. Of course, space is needed between each item as well. Some pieces of equipment will require more space than others. The designer should check with the manufacturer of each piece of workout equipment to ensure that safe spacing has been provided.

Guests utilizing spa services are often asked to relax in an internal rest area after changing while waiting for the therapist. Guests often return to this area to relax again before changing or going to another part of the health club or spa to relax after treatment. Chaise lounges or lounging chairs are most common here, upholstered in materials that can withstand moisture. Soft lighting, views to the outdoors, or walled patios helps create a soothing place to relax before and after a treatment or workout.

Individualized rooms for massage and spa treatments require certain equipment. The massage table is the focal point. It is usually 24 inches wide by 72 inches long. The height of the table must be sufficient for the massage therapist to operate without severely bending

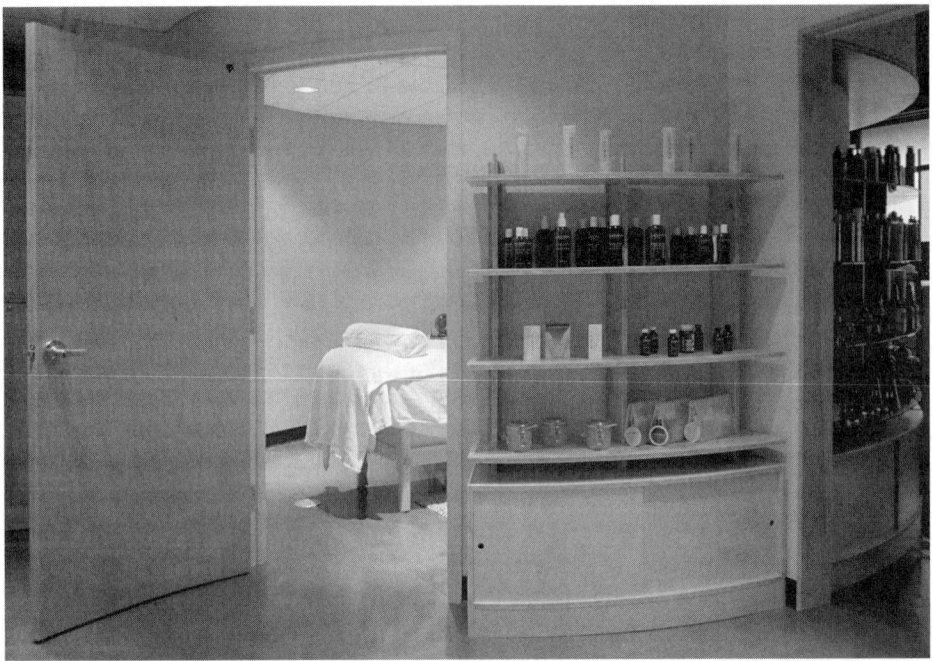

Figure 4-19 Spa with a view into the massage room. (Courtesy of Jim Postell, architect and designer. Photographer: Scott Hisey Photography, www.hiseyphotography.com)

over. Sufficient space surrounding the table is needed so that the therapist has access to all four sides. Cabinetry or shelves are needed for storage of products and possibly for towels, wash cloths, and sheets used during the treatments. Depending on the use of the specific treatment room, a sink cabinet might be needed. Although water is always available in the relaxation area, a water cooler could provide spring water for the guest in the treatment room. Heating units, such as heated towel bars, are used to keep towels and sheets warm for guest comfort. Aromatherapy might be used to promote relaxation (Figure 4-19).

Architectural materials and any upholstery must be able to withstand higher humidity levels, more constant cleaning, and maintenance for health concerns. Textured vinyl upholstery material provides a more upscale appearance on chairs or lounges than smooth vinyl upholstery. The workout area is generally carpeted, and the walls are covered with large expanses of mirrors. Spa treatment rooms are also carpeted to enhance acoustics. Slip-resistant ceramic tile is critical for flooring except in lounges, where softer flooring materials might be allowed. Ceilings are often finished in ceramic tile or other finishes that will resist high humidity.

Natural light with use of skylights and large areas of glass facing contained garden areas are key points of spa and health club areas. This is augmented by track and ceiling lighting, as well as appropriate accent lighting to provide comfortable light levels in the most relaxing areas such as massage and treatment rooms and the higher light levels needed in workout rooms. Soft lighting is a must in the spa treatment rooms. Specialized task lights might be needed in some treatment rooms.

Important building code issues will also affect the design and specification of spa and workout areas. Stringent code requirements concerning locations of outlets, lighting fixtures, and switches are very important considerations in the design of spa and health club rooms. Remember that a spa or health club area will also have to meet accessibility guidelines.

Food and Beverage Facilities

The opportunity to enjoy great food is a common experience for hotel guests as well as local residents who go to hotels for special occasions. Many local residents visit resorts and hotels for Sunday and holiday brunches and buffets. The breakfast served at many inns is a special treat for guests. Smaller hotels located near a highway might lease space to a chain restaurant providing convenient food service for guests weary from travel. Almost all lodging facilities provide some food service.

A *food service facility*—most commonly thought of as a restaurant—is any retail establishment that provides cooked or prepared foods to consumers. *Beverage facilities* are defined as those providing alcoholic beverage service. Of course, there are some kinds of restaurants that do not serve alcoholic beverages—notably fast food restaurants—and most establishments that serve alcoholic beverages also offer some food service. However, the two definitions are common in the industry. In this section we discuss general considerations and business distinctions for these facilities. Specific design concepts and applications for generic food and beverage facilities are presented in the next chapter.

Food and beverage services in hotels and other lodging facilities have been part of the mix of service since the inns centuries ago provided food for the weary traveler. Except for luxury hotels, food service in hotels was generally not known for high quality until the early 20th century. Most hotel restaurants only served breakfast, as travelers did not have a reason to stay for lunch or dinner. Thus, there was no challenge to create a good kitchen. Competition from freestanding restaurants where good-quality food was served reduced guest visits to hotel restaurants. In the second half of the 20th century, fast food and chain restaurants changed the eating habits of many persons. This competition forced hotels to consider food and beverage service as an additional marketing tactic and a revenue stream resulting in a dramatic increase in the quality and types of food and beverage service found in lodging facilities today.

Dedicating space to any kind of food service must be carefully thought out because of the high cost of developing and maintaining that space. It must produce a profitable level of revenue, which can be a challenge in some lodging locations. In an urban area, for example, hotel guests have many choices for all their meals beyond what is available in the hotel. Thus, good food and the use of a distinctive theme in the restaurant's design, type of service, and attention to the guest's attitude toward food service needs are all parts of the decision package for food and beverage facilities located in hotels. For example, in a suburban hotel, breakfast is the main meal, while lunch has a minimal customer demand. Luxury hotels and urban resorts will also attract local residents for special occasion dinners or business lunches. Franchise outlets for coffee service in the morning, ice cream shops, delis, snack bars and brand name facilities like McDonalds within the hotel complex have been added to properties to attract guests to stay "inside" rather than going off the property.

Design and business concepts for the restaurants and other food service locations will be developed along with the concept for the whole property. Multiple service options may have different themes and design concepts or share an overall theme. Themes may be based on the overall theme of the hotel or driven by marketing concepts for the nonhotel guest diners the hotel wishes to attract. Design themes will also be impacted by the type of service, such as full service with a maitre d' versus casual dining. All of these considerations—and these are only the primary issues—will impact the interior designer's responsibilities for the layouts and for aesthetics and product specifications.

Depending on the size of the overall property, the restaurant will be located off or very near the lobby area. Large properties with several restaurants generally locate them in relation to views, accessibility to parking lots, in a place where they can be seen from the street, or near the pool/recreational areas. Locating at least one facility for the convenience of guests who might use the restaurant only for breakfast is a common space planning criterion. In many hotels, at least one hotel food service facility is planned with an exterior entrance to attract local customers. In downtown areas, hotels may have rooftop restaurants themed to attract the local weekend visitor as well as the hotel guests (Figure 4-20).

Most restaurants in hotels will also provide alcoholic beverage service. In addition, a separate beverage area commonly called a *lounge*—also referred to as a *cocktail lounge* or bar—is also included at most hotel properties. Since lounges are often located adjacent to the lobby, it is common for them to be in enclosed spaces to reduce noise filtering into the lobby or nearby restaurants. The theme may follow the adjacent restaurant or may be individualized. For example, in a downtown hotel near a sports facility, the lounge may

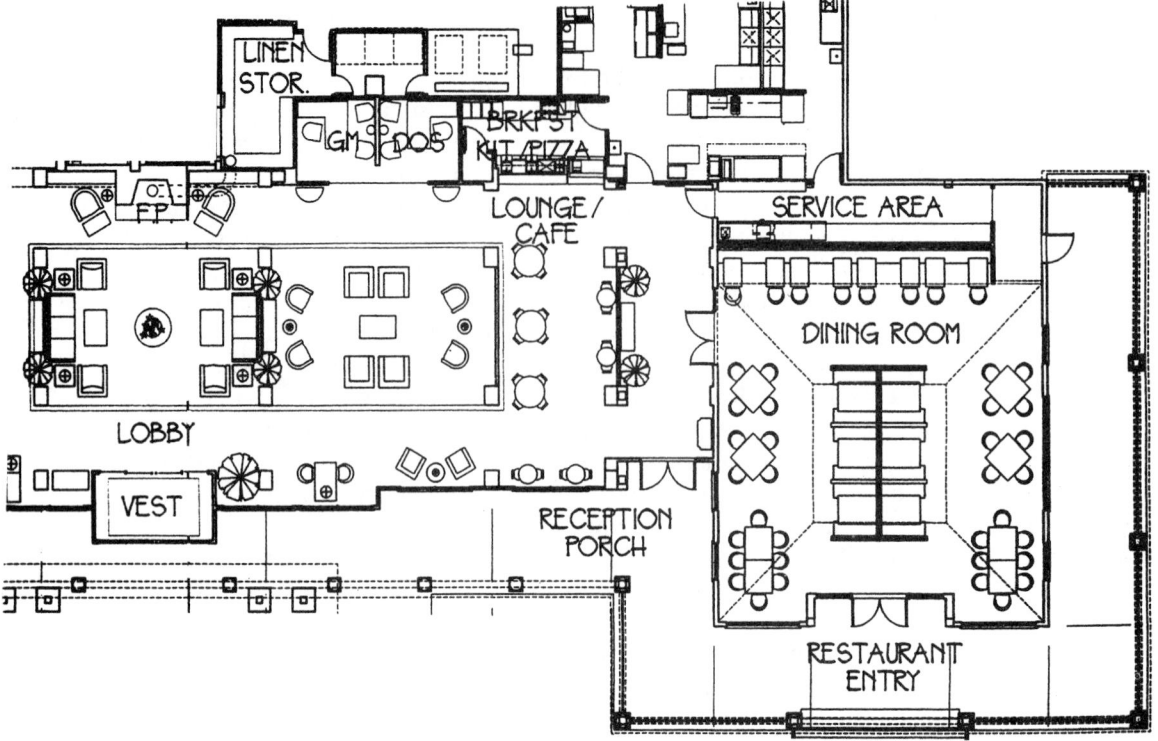

Figure 4-20 Floor plan of a restaurant in a hotel showing its relationship to the lobby. (Plan courtesy of Holiday Inns.)

have a sports theme; in a luxury hotel, there may be a cigar lounge where guests who wish to smoke are welcomed.

Of course, there will be the bar area itself. The design of the bar is a great creative challenge for the interior designer, as the bar is a focal point in the room. There must be easy access for staff since food service space for appetizers is essential. Hotel lounges are specified with small tables with a height of 25 to 27 inches rather than the normal restaurant table height of 29 inches. Chairs at these tables are usually smaller-scale lounge chairs on casters. Seating is also provided using sofas, love seats, and club chairs arranged in small groupings. The seating units selected in a hotel lounge are generally movable, since guests will invariably rearrange furniture to bring larger groups together than are normally accommodated in the furniture plan.

Evening entertainment can be as simple as a television set, live music, or a dance floor. Lower light levels are provided since it is a place for relaxing. With television watching—especially for sporting events—being very popular in lounges, space planning of the seating arrangements should take this factor into consideration. Depending on how active the entertainment component is for the lounge, nearly 70 percent of the total square footage should be devoted to lounge seating or a combination of lounge seating and the entertainment area. Because of the entertainment factor in the hotel cocktail lounge, lighting specification and design is very important and must be flexible to accommodate a variety of entertainment modes. The sound system must also be considered so that individuals on the dance floor clearly hear the music, while other areas, for guests who are less interested in the music, remain quieter.

Newer large hotels locate bars within the lobby area that are referred to as *lobby bars*. Lobby bars were created to give guests and visitors something interesting to do in the atrium lobbies designed in the 1960s and 1970s. Large properties have embraced the lobby bar because it is a great revenue generator, as guests and visitors use the area to meet before or after dinner or meetings. A slight physical barrier to separate the lobby bar from the hotel lobby is often created to prevent underage individuals from using the space. Comfortable seating with sofas and soft seating around small tables are the primary furniture items along with the bar. Easy access to the kitchen by staff is necessary

Figure 4-21 Hotel lobby bar at the Valencia Hotel Riverwalk. (Photograph courtesy of 3D/International and dMd/Dodd Mitchell Design.)

since appetizers, snacks, and even light meals are available in most lobby bars. In the morning, this area is where departing guests might find coffee service available as they wait for a shuttle bus or taxi (Figure 4-21).

The design of food and beverage facilities in hotels is an exciting specialty that often gives the interior designer more creative license than the design of other areas of the hotel. Designers should become familiar with all aspects of food and beverage operations and have some knowledge of hotel operations as well. The reader who wishes to become involved in the design of a food and beverage space in a hotel is urged to begin by reading the next chapter.

Bed and Breakfast Inns

In cities and towns big and small, individuals have converted part or all of private residences into a lodging facility most commonly referred to as a *bed and breakfast inn*. These smaller and more intimate lodging facilities welcome travelers to stay in a homier environment than is found in hotels and motels. They are known by many names such as country inns, cottages, B&Bs, and host homes. Others are designed from the ground up, created to provide a specialized theme.

Bed and breakfast inns are commonly owned by independent hospitality entrepreneurs. Interior design budgets for their facilities are smaller than those for a hotel. Yet, there are also luxury bed and breakfast inns boasting room rates as high as those of any luxury resort. Most bed and breakfast establishments combine high-quality interior design and personalized service with guest amenities for the guest's comfort. An in-room jacuzzi, perhaps a front porch, and a fireplace in the room are all welcome amenities. Bed and breakfast inns offer the full breakfast or a substantial continental breakfast as part of the room rate, but few have full food and beverage facilities for other meals.

This type of facility will have a lobby and a reception desk. However, the lobby often functions as a living room rather than as a formal lobby, as in hotels. Comfortable furniture in keeping with the theme of the facility is provided, along with possibly a television and a place to write cards and notes or play table games. A cozy fireplace is also

Figure 4-22 Lobby area of a bed and breakfast inn. (Courtesy of the Old Rock Church and Providence Inn; 1-800-480-4943 www.providenceinn.com)

common in the lobby. Although the "B" in B&B does not stand for beverage, these facilities often offer evening cocktails or wine service to guests. Some have small bars as well, either as part of the lobby or in a separate room, depending on the size of the overall facility. The reception desk might be a window into the office or a small counter or table desk. Of course, even the bed and breakfast inn uses computerized reservation and management systems today (Figure 4-22).

Bed and breakfast inns are often established in historic districts or older residential areas that have been rezoned for commercial businesses. For this reason, the interior designer and client must pay special attention to the costs and expectations of bringing the building up to local codes for a residential R1 classification. Much structural work is often required, as guest rooms require private bathrooms in many concepts where a bathroom did not exist. Adequately planning a commercial kitchen in a residential kitchen or building that had an entirely different use, such as an old fire station or a bank building, can also be a challenge for the designers.

Guest rooms require the same basic furniture items specified for any hotel guest room. The rooms are often designed around themes, with each room having a different theme. In smaller facilities, no two rooms will be alike. This variety challenges the interior designer to find fabrics, furniture items, and accessories for the many different themes. For example, for an inn in a mountainous small town near a lake, one room might have fishing as a theme, another skiing, and so on (Figure 4-23).

Materials and products are varied, yet architectural finishes and textiles will have to adhere to current local codes. Properties that have been established in historic structures may have some leeway with codes, but guest and property safety should always be ensured by the interior designer. The designer does have to remember that a bed and breakfast inn is still a commercial property and that the products selected should meet the maintenance and wear criteria that would be applied to any other lodging property. Accessibility requirements must also be met. The local jurisdiction is likely to require that at least one unit be designed to accommodate the ADA or other applicable regulations in line with the "reasonable accommodation" guideline.

Most bed and breakfast inns only serve one meal—breakfast. Others that are larger inns might also offer dinner service. Meals are served in appealingly designed dining rooms often providing tables and chairs set for two or four guests. Guests are also directed to nearby restaurants to suit the guest's desire for other meals. If the property is made up of individ-

Figure 4-23 Guest room in a bed and breakfast inn. The theme of the room is a pioneer home, referring to the exposed beams in the room, which were hewn by the early pioneers. (Photograph courtesy of the Old Rock Church and Providence Inn, 1-800-480-4943 www.providenceinn.com)

ual cabins, guests may also have small kitchens. In this case, guests may have the option of preparing their own meals or having meals served in the room as part of the room rate.

Depending on the size of the facility and its location, the bed and breakfast inn might provide limited recreational amenities. There may be common area amenities such as a sauna, spa, or pool. Guests might choose to hike, horseback ride, play golf, ski, or pursue any number of other activities available either on the property or in conjunction with nearby facilities. Some inns also cater to small conferences, providing the dining room or other spaces for meetings.

A bed and breakfast inn has many variations, and interior design opportunities are as unlimited as the owner's wishes. The interior designer, however, must remember to design with budget, concept, the target market, and applicable codes in mind, just as he or she would in designing a mega hotel.

Summary

In 2005, it was widely reported in the media that the Wynn Las Vegas hotel in Las Vegas, Nevada, cost a whopping $2.7 billion! This is a testimonial to this exciting and challenging specialty in commercial interior design. It is rare even in the hospitality and lodging industry for an architectural and interior design firm to be given this type of budget. The designer wishing to enter this specialty should never forget that big budgets with wide open concepts are the exception. In fact, most projects have far more limited budgets.

The interior designer's work must support the concepts and goals of the owner and must coordinate with the architect and other stakeholders. Attention to detail, thoughtful budget deliberations, and careful working habits are necessary for the designer engaged in lodging interior design. This is also an area of design in which the ability to work with a team is of the utmost importance.

The purpose, goals, and operational objectives of lodging facilities have been discussed in this chapter. Interior design elements and concepts focusing on a generic hotel property with special emphasis on the lobby, guest rooms, function spaces, and recreational spaces such as spas have been provided to explain basic design planning issues in these areas. The chapter has also provided a very brief overview of the history of lodging, as well as basic explanations of the different types of facilities. The reader may wish to investigate material in the References list below for more details on the operations and design of lodging facilities.

REFERENCES

American Hotel & Lodging Association. 2005. "History of Lodging." www.ahla.com

———. 2005. "2004 Lodging Industry Profile." www.ahla.com

Architectural Record Book. 1960. *Motels, Hotels, Restaurants and Bars*, 2nd ed. New York: McGraw-Hill.

Arthur, Paul and Romedi Passini. 1992. *Wayfinding*. New York: McGraw-Hill.

Asensio, Paco, ed. 2002. *Sap and Wellness Hotels*. Barcelona: Artes Graficas/Viking.

Bardi, James A. 1990. *Hotel Front Office Management*. New York: Van Nostrand Reinhold.

Baucom, Alfred H. 1996. *Hospitality Design for the Graying Generation*. New York: Wiley.

Berens, Carol. 1996. *Hotel Bars and Lobbies*. New York: McGraw-Hill.

Curtis, Eleanor. 2001. *Hotel Interior Structures*. West Sussex, England: Wiley-Academy.

Davies, Thomas D., Jr. and Kim A. Beasley. 1994. *Accessible Design for Hospitality*, 2nd ed. New York: McGraw-Hill.

Dittmer, Paul R. and Gerald G. Griffin. 1993. *The Dimensions of the Hospitality Industry*. New York: Van Nostrand Reinhold.

Donzel, Catherine, Alexis Gregory, and Marc Walter. 1989. *Grand American Hotels*. New York: Vendome.

Fellows, Jane and Richard Fellows. 1990. *Buildings for Hospitality*. London: Pitman.

Gray, William S. and Salvatore C. Liguori. 1994. *Hotel and Motel Management and Operations*, 3rd ed. Englewood Cliffs, NJ: Prentice Hall.

Hardy, Hugh. 1997. "What Is Hospitality Design?" *Hospitality Design*. January/February, pp. 66–68.

Harmon, Sharon Koomen and Katerine E. Kennon. 2005. *The Codes Guidebook for Interiors*, 3rd ed. New York: Wiley.

Hayes, David K. and Jack D. Ninemeier. 2004. *Hotel Operations Management*. Upper Saddle River, NJ: Pearson/Prentice Hall.

Huffadine, Margaret. 2000. *Resort Design*. New York: McGraw-Hill.

Karlen, Mark and James Benya. 2004. *Lighting Design Basics*. New York: Wiley.

Kliczkowski, H. 2002. *Cafés: Designers and Design*. Barcelona: Loft Publications.

Kliment, Stephen A., ed. 2001. *Building Type Basics for Hospitality Facilities*. New York: Wiley.

Knapp, Frederic. 1995. *Hotel Renovation Planning and Design*. New York: McGraw-Hill.

Lawson, Fred. 1995. *Hotels and Resorts: Planning, Design and Refurbishment*. Jordan Hill, Oxford, England: Butterworth-Architecture, Linacre House.

Margolies, John. 1995. *Home Away from Home*. New York: Bulfinch Press/Little, Brown.

National Park Service. 1994. "Guiding Principals of Sustainable Design." National Park Service web site: www.nps.gov/dsc/dsgncnstr/gpsd/ch1.html

Radulski, John P. 1991. "Specifying for the Bath." *Restaurant/Hotel Design International*. January, pp. 22ff.

Riewoldt, Otto. 2002. *New Hotel Design*. New York: Watson-Guptill.

Robson, Stephani and Madeleine Pullman. "Hotels: Differentiating with Design." *Implications*. InformeDesign, Vol. 3, Issue 6.

Rutes, Walter A., Richard H. Penner, and Lawrence Adams. 2001. *Hotel Design: Planning and Development*. New York: W.W. Norton.

Rutherford, Denney G., ed. 1995. *Hotel Management and Operations*, 2nd ed. New York: Van Nostrand Reinhold.

Sawinski, Diane M., ed. 1995. *U.S. Industries Profiles*. "Hotels and Motels." New York: Gale Research, Inc.

Standard and Poors. 1996. *Standard and Poor's Industry Surveys A–L*, Vol. 1. New York: McGraw-Hill.

Stipanuk, David M. and Harold Roffmann. 1992. *Hospitality Facilities Management and Design*. East Lansing, MI: Educational Institute of the American Hotel and Motel Association.

Walker, John R. 1996. *Introduction to Hospitality*. Englewood Cliffs, NJ: Prentice Hall.

Wilson, Trisha. 2004. *Spectacular Hotels*. Dallas: Signature Publishing Group.

WEB SITES

American Hotel & Lodging Association. www.ahla.com

International Hotel & Restaurant Association www.ihra.com

Professional Association of Innkeepers International www.paii.org

Hospitality Design magazine. www.hdmag.com

Hotel Business magazine www.hotelbusiness.com

InformeDesign newsletter www.informedesign.umn.edu

Lodging magazine www.lodgingmagazine.com

Note: Additional references related to material in this chapter are listed in the Appendix.

Food and Beverage Facilities

When you are involved in the design of a food and/or beverage facility, remember that customers do not go there just to eat or drink. They go for socializing, celebrating, conducting business, romance, and even to give the primary meal preparer a break. From the simplest neighborhood restaurant to the most prestigious gourmet facility, interior design plays an important part in the facility's success. The atmosphere desired by the owners is also undeniably important:

> Restaurant design has become as compelling an element as menu, food, wine and staffing in determining a restaurant's success. . . . To be effective, restaurant design must strike a nearly impossible balance between three competing agendas: that of the guest, who must feel welcome, aroused and transported; that of the staff, which must be able to complete its tasks in a smooth, stress-free flow that allows for maximum hospitality; and that of the restaurant's owner, for in providing all this comfort for guests and staff, there must still remain the proper ratio of selling area to manufacturing space to allow for maximum profit.[1]

[1]Danny Meyer, guest forward. Reprinted with permission of PBC International from *The New Restaurant: Dining Design 2* by Charles Morris Mount, p. 9, © 1995.

TABLE 5-1 Chapter Vocabulary

- BACK OF THE HOUSE: Those areas of the facility that are generally not visited and/or used by guests, such as the kitchen.
- BANQUETTE: Booth-type seating built along a wall, configured with a freestanding table and chairs.
- BEVERAGE FACILITIES: Those sections of a restaurant or freestanding facility that primarily serve alcoholic beverages.
- CONCEPT: The ideas brought together by the owner that serve as basis of all planning and design decisions for the facility.
- DEUCES: Term for tables that seat two guests, also called *two tops*.
- FOUR TOPS: Term for tables that seat four guests.
- FRANCHISE RESTAURANT: A restaurant operated under the guidance and requirements of the company that holds the rights to the original concept.
- FRONT OF THE HOUSE: Those areas of the facility that are regularly visited and/or used by guests, such as the dining room and bar.
- INDEPENDENT RESTAURANTS: Those owned and managed by an individual or investment group and created by the owners' imagination and creativity.
- MAITRE D': The head waiter in a restaurant.
- SEAT TURNOVER RATE: The estimated number of times a table will be used in any one day. This will vary greatly based on the type of restaurant and the type of service offered.
- SINGLE-UNIT RESTAURANT: A restaurant that exists in only one location.

Food service facilities provide prepared foods for immediate consumption, either on or off the premises. The beverage portion of the industry provides alcoholic beverages for on-site consumption. Of course, beverage service can also apply to nonalcoholic beverages. This chapter focuses on the establishment that offers both food and beverage service.

We begin with a historical overview of the food and beverage industry, followed by an overview of the business operations of restaurants. We take a brief look at various kinds of food service facilities, followed by a discussion of the planning and design of a generic restaurant. The design concept section further describes the design of a full-service restaurant and provides information on kitchen and bar design. Coffee shops have become a big part of this industry, and a section on their design has been included.

Table 5-1 presents vocabulary used throughout the chapter.

Historical Overview

In the movie *Shakespeare in Love* (1996), set in the 16th century, one scene found the actors in what we would now call a tavern. One of the many spoofs in the film was the board with the special of the day. Until the 18th century, citizens who sought food and beverage service went to inns, taverns, and roadhouses like the one portrayed in the movie. Food quality at these early establishments was poor. In the 16th century bouillon—a simple soup—was one of the foods considered to be a restorative or *restaurant*. This French word gradually became associated with establishments that provided food service. In Paris in the 1760s, a man named Boulanger opened a shop to sell food to city dwellers. One of the popular items he sold was bouillon, thus becoming an early restaurateur[2] (Figure 5-1).

According to Martin E. Dorf, cafés, which predated restaurants, first only sold coffee from coffee stalls, then small shops sprung up in the late 16th century.[3] Europeans enjoyed the camaraderie of the cafés, and they became fashionable places to meet friends. Today's coffee shops meet this same consumer demand. The bistro was also a French

---

[2]Dorf, 1992, p. 12.
[3]Dorf, 1992, p. 13.

Figure 5-1 Drawing of the interior of an 18th-century inn depicting the bar area. (From Edwin Tunis *Colonial Living,* 1957. Copyright © 1965 by Edwin Tunis. Copyright renewed 1993 by David Hutton. Originally published by World Publishing Company, reprinted 1976 by Thomas Y. Crowell. Reprinted by permission of Curtis Brown, Ltd.)

invention—a place for working men and struggling artists in the late 19th century to gather. From these humble beginnings, all the various types of food and beverage facilities have developed, from quick, slick fast-food eateries to elegant restaurants offering carefully prepared gourmet food in beautiful surroundings.

Many centuries ago, abbeys and monasteries operated breweries for their own use. Gradually, the monasteries provided resting places for travelers, offering their beverages to their guests. Later, taverns provided beverage service, with food also being served. The serving of alcoholic beverages in inns, hotels, and restaurants spread over time. In the 1920s in the United States, federal Prohibition laws forbade the consumption of alcohol. However, secret clubs, called *speakeasies,* were established so that customers could still purchase their now illegal alcoholic beverages. After Prohibition ended in the 1930s, the beverage portion of the hospitality industry expanded as people increasingly went out to eat. Beverage service continues to be part of the hospitality industry as more and more consumers go out for meals, entertainment, and socializing (Figure 5-2).

Inns and taverns where travelers and locals could find prepared food were common in the American colonies and the young United States. Food service in urban areas gradually found its way into hotels as the population centered in the cities in the 19th century. It was the move from rural areas to the cities that created the demand for increased numbers and kinds of food service facilities during the Industrial Revolution.

In the cities, different types and styles of food service developed. City workers required quick meals, and speed of service often took precedence over the quality of food. Horse-drawn carts or pushcarts referred to as *lunch wagons* were the first attempt to appeal to this market. In the 1880s, these carts—often called *diners*—became large enough to provide indoor sit-down service of sandwiches, soups, and beverages. Soda shops where ice cream creations were sold (Figure 5-3), lunchrooms (Figure 5-4), and cafeterias with the focus on efficiency of production and service were other restaurant ideas created to meet demands in the later years of the 19th century and into the early 20th century.

One solution designed to meet the demands of consumers for fast food during the early 20th century was the automat, invented by Joseph Horn and Frank Hardart of

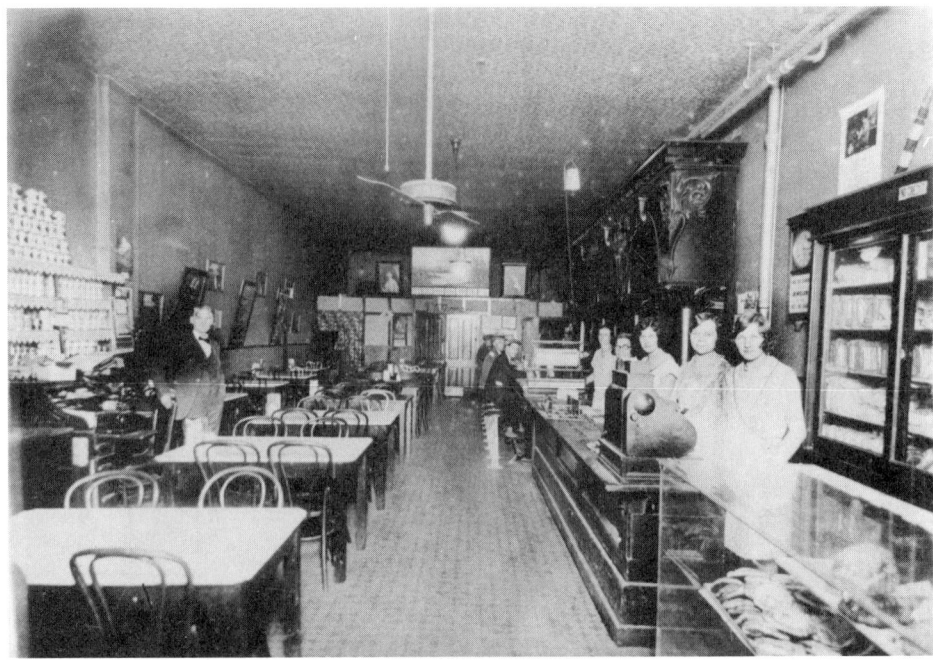

Figure 5-2 Restaurant and home bakery first constructed in the late 1800s and used as a restaurant until the 1940s. (Photograph courtesy of the Nodaway Valley Historical Museum.)

Philadelphia. The automat restaurant displayed precooked food behind small glass windows. Patrons would walk up to the service line where the food was displayed, insert the proper change into slots, and instantly receive their food choice. In the early 20th century, Horn and Hardart opened an automat in Times Square in New York City. It was ornately designed and offered fast service to busy New York businesspeople, shoppers, and tourists for decades. About the only place one can see an automat today is in the

Figure 5-3 Soda fountains were popular food service facilities. (Photograph used by permission, Utah State Historical Society. All rights reserved.)

Museum of American History in Washington, DC. Unfortunately, it is not in operation.[4]

The upper classes, however, demanded higher-quality food and an elegant atmosphere. At the fancier restaurants, evening dinners were formal affairs with gloved waiters serving multiple courses. An evening meal at one of these restaurants, like Delmonico's in New York City or the Willard Room within the Willard Hotel in Washington, DC, might take hours to enjoy. Although fine dining was available in the larger cities of the United States, this was rarely true in smaller towns until the mid-20th century.

For the rail traveler, obtaining a decent meal on the road was a real adventure until Fred Harvey opened a series of Harvey House restaurants along the Atchison, Topeka, and Santa Fe Railroad. The Harvey Girls, waitresses at the restaurants, provided good service and decent food in the minimum time the railroad allowed for meal stops.

As automobile travel became more popular, roadside restaurants opened to meet the demands of these travelers. "Home-cooked" meals of varying quality led some entrepreneurs to open early chain restaurants like those of Howard Johnson. Their turquoise and orange color scheme was easy to remember, along with food quality that could be counted on at any location. Many other specialized types of restaurants developed especially after World War II, all trying to entice customers through their doors. Competition for the travelers' dollars led to roadside restaurants with every kind of food and many styles of architectural design. The expansion of restaurant choices and quality matched the booming economy in the cities and the demand of the public for better food services.

Other restaurant types developed as the economy, demographics, and demands of the growing baby boomers influenced the industry. Drive-in restaurants, fast food chains, and franchise restaurants became very popular in the 1950s and remain so today. Chains and franchises were created to meet the demand of guests who ate away from home and wanted to count on a specific quality in the food and atmosphere of the restaurant (Figure 5-5). Patrons knew that no matter where they were, their expectations would be met at the chain restaurants. According to Dittmer and Griffin, the first fast food chain was not McDonald's (which started in the 1950s) (Figure 5-6), but White Castle Hamburgers, which opened in Kansas in 1921.[5] Howard Johnson's was one of the first chain restaurants.

The popularity of the French style of preparing foods gave way to the lighter fare of nouvelle and California cuisine. These changes brought on an emphasis on lighter foods and natural foods in restaurants that also influenced changes in the look of restaurants—exterior design, interior design, and interior concepts. Today, every conceivable type of food, service style, and design atmosphere exists to satisfy the preferences of the public. If you are interested in obtaining more information about the history of the food service industry, you may want to read the books mentioned in the References at the end of this chapter and any books that provide an introduction to the food and beverage or hospitality industry. A few are mentioned in the chapter references. A photograph of the interior of Windows on the World, which was located in the North Tower of the World Trade Center (1976–2001) in New York City, is presented, and dedicated to those who lost their lives on September 11, 2001 (Figure 5-7).

Figure 5-4 Although increased dining facilities were offered, luncheonettes remained popular for their quick service and versatility. (Photograph of JoAnn's "B" Street Café courtesy of Hayashida Architects, Sady S. Hayashida, principal. Photographer: Dennis Anders, Dennis Anders Photography.)

---

[4]The movie *That Touch of Mink*, starring Doris Day and Rock Hudson, features scenes in a New York automat.
[5]Dittmer and Griffin, 1993, p. 99.

Figure 5-5 Franchises and chain restaurants proved convenient for travelers. (Village Inn photograph courtesy of VICORP Restaurants, Inc., Denver, CO.)

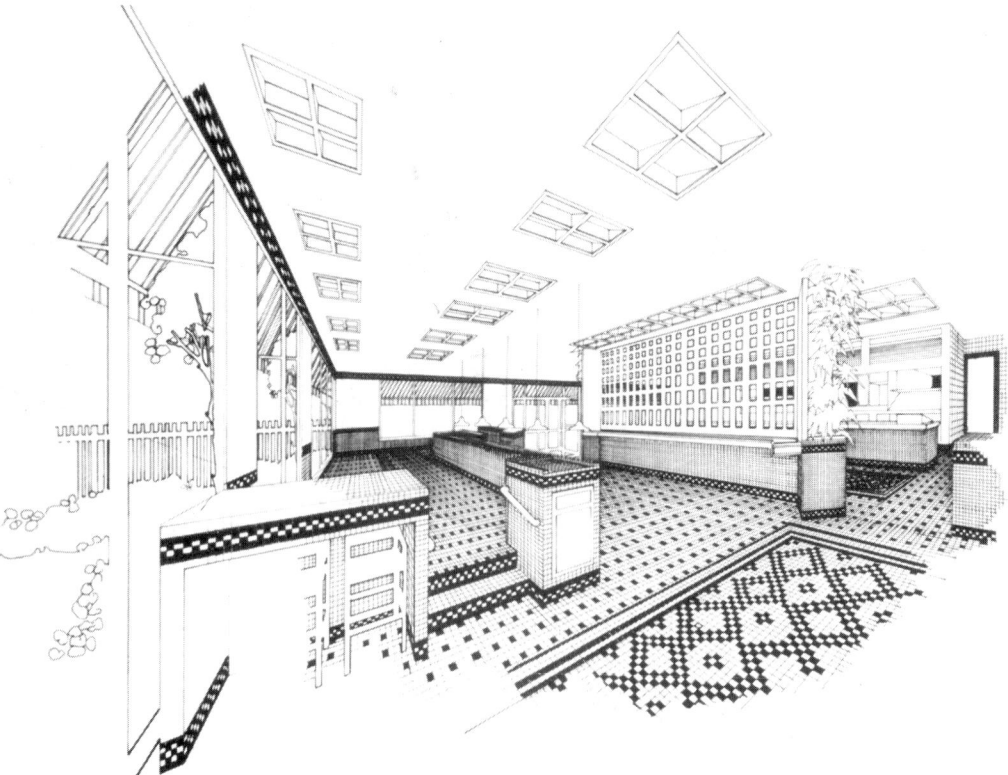

Figure 5-6 Rendering of a McDonald's franchise fast food restaurant. (Drawing courtesy of Janet Schirn Design Group 2005.)

Figure 5-7 The Windows on the World Restaurant (1976–2001) was located at the World Trade Center in New York City until 2001. (Photograph courtesy of Windows on the World.)

Overview of Food and Beverage Business Operations

According to the National Restaurant Association, there are over 900,000 restaurants in the United States, which did approximately $476 billion worth of business in 2005.[6] We have all seen restaurants come and go in our neighborhoods or work locations. Popular ones are full at lunch and dinner, demonstrating the highly competitive nature of this industry. A restaurant is also a challenging specialty in commercial design. Restaurants provide some of the most interesting and exciting design work for interior designers. The interior design can be just as important to guests as the name or reputation of the chef. But, of course, the quality of the food is essential to the success of a restaurant.

The principal goal of a restaurant or beverage facility is to provide food and a certain level of service in an atmosphere that satisfies the guests and encourages them to come back. The owner must decide what level of food, service, and atmosphere he or she desires. The goals for the restaurant are based largely on the guest target market he or she hopes to attract. Concept development and good planning are essential. The interior designer must understand these goals in order to design an atmosphere that supports the intended concept (Figure 5-8). "Today's dining designs focus on making a space comfortable, inviting, and entertaining, with a consistent theme throughout the experience."[7]

Achieving an effective design comes from understanding the operations of such a facility. If there is a management group, they will set the policies and make overall operational decisions for the restaurant. The manager is responsible for carrying out those policies and ensuring that the employees are trained and motivated. He or she will also work with the chef and kitchen staff to ensure that the proper amount of food is available each day. The manager is also responsible for hiring and training the wait staff and kitchen staff.

A host, sometimes called a *maître d'*—defined as a head waiter—greets the guests and shows them to their table. The host is also responsible for taking reservations and maintaining the appearance of the dining room. Servers or wait staff work directly with the customer, taking orders and serving meals. They frequently are also responsible for preparation of some

---

[6]National Restaurant Association, Industry Research Page, March 2005, available at www.restaurant.org
[7]Katsigris and Thomas, 2005, p. 27.

Figure 5-8 View of the Ceiba Restaurant, Washington, D.C., showing tables set for service. (Photograph courtesy of Interior Architect: IA Interior Architects. Interior designer: Walter Gagliano, ASID. Photographer Ron Solomon © 2004 ron@ronsolomonphoto.com)

food items such as salads, beverages, and perhaps desserts. As we all understand, the quality of the servers is an important factor in whether a guest returns. Some restaurants also have busing staff to clean and reset tables. In a beverage facility, there will also be a bartender and cocktail servers, who will have direct contact with the customer. All of these employees are also considered front-of-the-house staff.

The section of the restaurant that the customer generally does not enter is considered the back of the house. Employees who are primarily back-of-the-house staff are the kitchen staff and the manager. The kitchen staff includes the chef, specialty chefs, and cooks. There are also support employees who prep cook, wash dishes and, in larger restaurants, pantry workers who assist in pulling foods from storage areas.

The stakeholders in the design of a new facility—or a major remodeling—can be a large group of individuals. The owner has ultimate decision-making and financial responsibility for the resulting planning and design. Some restaurant owners are entrepreneurs who are very involved in the project from beginning to opening. Other owners are investors rather than day-to-day workers. The restaurant will also have an on-duty manager who is also part of the design team, providing insights on operational issues during the planning. The chef is another important stakeholder. Although the chef is generally more concerned with the kitchen layout, the menu planned by the chef can directly affect the interior design. An architect will be involved in the structure and exterior design and may provide interior design services. The interior designer involved in the project may work for the architect or may be a specialty designer independent of the project architect. And finally, a food service consultant or commercial kitchen designer will likely be involved to plan the kitchen and other back-of-the-house areas in conjunction with the architect and interior designer. Consulting engineers who provide design guidance to the architect in terms of electrical, plumbing, and other functional elements are also part of the group of stakeholders.

Concept and Menu Development

This highly competitive industry requires owners to look carefully at the potential market and costs of developing and operating a new food service facility. A thorough feasibility study of the market, competition, financial issues, menu, pricing of menu items, style of service, concept, and other factors is part of a food service feasibility study.

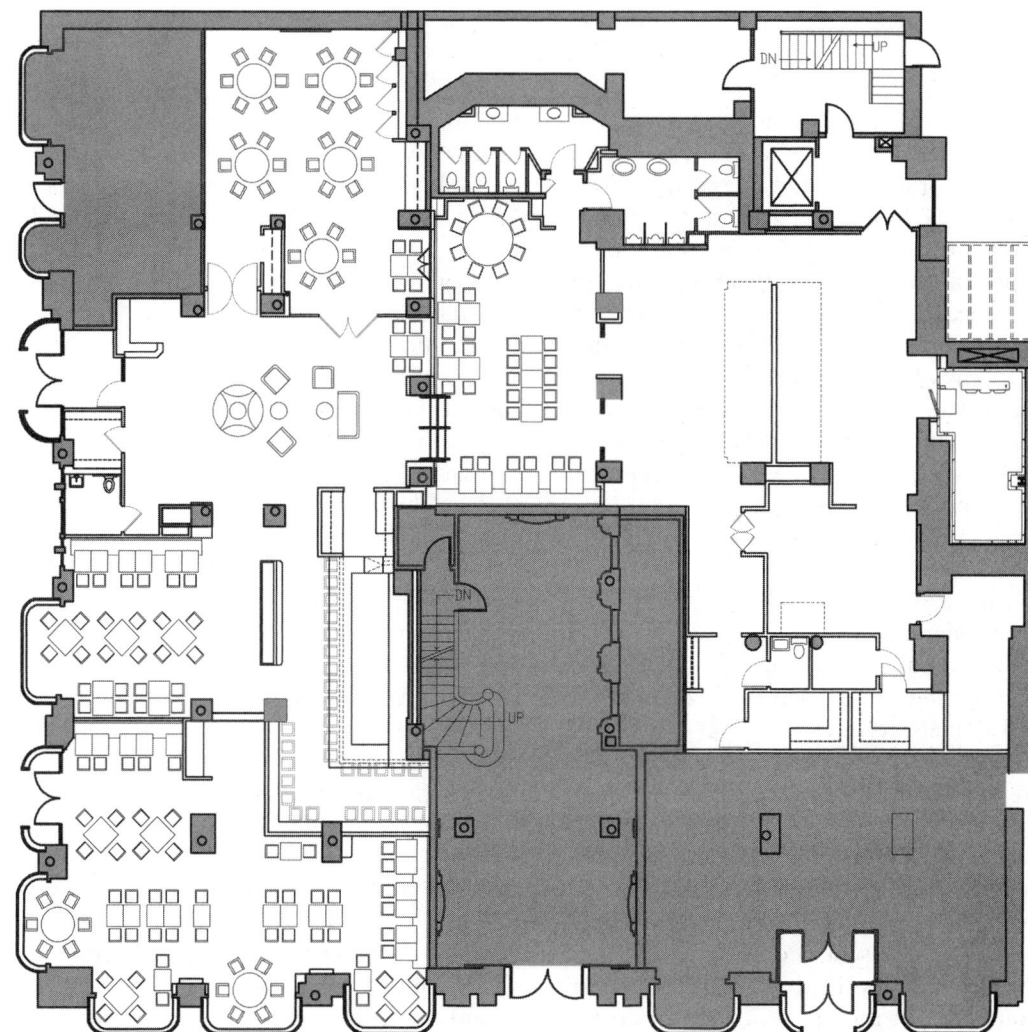

Figure 5-9 Floor plan of the Ceiba Restaurant, Washington, D.C. (Drawing courtesy of Interior Architect: IA Interior Architects. Interior designer: Walter Gagliano, ASID.)

Significant parts in the development of a feasibility study are the business concept and the menu. "The concept for a foodservice operation is the overall plan for how it will meet the needs and expectations of its intended market."[8] The design concept is prepared in conjunction with the business concept or detailed after the business concept has been prepared. The concept is important regardless of the size and complexity of the facility. Obviously, the more complex the restaurant, the more important the concept becomes. The design portion of the concept must describe what the total impression or idea for the facility will be to help the owner attract the target market. The overall concept must look at all the factors that will impact the operations of the restaurant, including the location, architectural design, menu, style of service, pricing, mood (formal or informal), basic ideas on interior design, colors, uniforms, and many other factors.

The inspiration for the interior and exterior designs might come from several sources. A common starting point is a theme, such as a nautical theme for a seafood restaurant or a rock and roll theme for the Hard Rock Café chain. The concept might reflect a particular region or be inspired by a particular ethnic cuisine. It might be a gourmet restaurant to cater to the luxury dinner guest or a hot dog vendor on a city street. Whatever the design concept, it must be developed carefully and must be based on a clear idea of what the owner wishes to achieve and the kinds of guests the restaurant will most likely attract (Figure 5-9).

[8]Birchfield and Sparrowe, 2003, p. 4.

The market analysis is a very important part of overall concept development. A restaurant idea without a market of potential guests willing to patronize the facility might mean that a great design or menu goes unnoticed, resulting in failure. A thorough market analysis will look at the demographic and descriptive makeup of targeted customers. Demographic factors like age and income level in the vicinity of the target market are particularly important to research as part of the concept and feasibility study. Another important part of the market analysis is the competition. This research will also tell the owner if there are too many restaurants of a similar kind in the vicinity to support one more. An experienced interior designer may also provide an opinion on the location.

Location, location, location is important in establishing any new business. The area demographics will help the owner understand if the type of restaurant he or she wishes to open will be supported by the local population or if patrons must travel to reach it. Is the restaurant going to be located in a suburban area, downtown business district, adjacent to entertainment areas, or in a small town near shopping? A restaurant that can be highly successful in one location can be a dismal failure in another.

Food and service style will also be impacted by the location of the facility. Restaurants in the business district and in shopping areas of urban places, for example, find that much of their business will be generated during the lunch period. Shopping malls have eating facilities at many price points, from fast food outlets to full-service lunch and dinner restaurants. Restaurants located next to or near entertainment venues will vary, based on the venue. Restaurants could provide breakfast, lunch, and dinner service if the market around the entertainment venue demands all-day service or might focus only on lunch and dinner service.

The menu and style of service, plus a pleasant atmosphere related to the menu, are keys in developing the concept. "Food may not be what brings people to a restaurant the first time. . . . However, food is, in large measure, what keeps people coming back. . . ."[9] The well-thought-out and superbly designed restaurant of today must keep up with the changing tastes and demands of customers in terms of food and decor. "Many experts feel that restaurants have a lifespan, of sorts, of five to seven years."[10] Concepts become stale as new ones emerge, with a common remodeling threshold occurring at about five years. In this highly competitive industry, today's hot concept could be a vacant space in the future if owners do not constantly refine the concept and offerings to stay current and to keep customers coming back. This obviously creates repeat business for the interior designer specializing in food and beverage facilities.

The menu helps provide the direction of the interior design. For example, a menu of Asian food will often suggest design concepts with an oriental focus in the interior specifications. A seafood restaurant could utilize design concepts ranging from sailing to fishing to the ocean. "The menu tends to reflect the character and mood of the establishment, not only by which items are being presented but also how those items are represented, the typeface used, the layout of the menu itself, and the colors employed."[11]

The concept also involves the style of service. A fine restaurant will have the most intense service, as the guests take a long time to enjoy their meal. Any table service facility will mean slower turnover of the guests, and this will impact the revenue of the restaurant. It will also have many impacts on the interior design and on space planning of the facility. Quick or fast food facilities have the greatest turnover, which likewise impacts the design decisions to be made by the architect and interior designer.

These factors are not all that must be researched and considered by the owner of a new food and beverage facility or before a major remodeling of an existing one. However, they are the issues most important to the overall design of the facility. The interior designer and the rest of the design team must be sure that they understand the business concept as the design and ambiance of the facility are planned and specified.

---

[9]Baraban and Durocher, 2001, p. 10.
[10]Katsigris and Thomas, 2005, p. 49.
[11]Lundberg, 1985, p. 55.

TABLE 5-2 Types of Food and Beverage Facilities

■ Independently owned	■ Within another structure
■ Single-unit restaurant	■ Fine dining
■ Chain or franchise	■ Casual dining
■ Specialty	■ Family restaurants
■ Theme	■ Cafeterias
■ Ethnic restaurants	■ Food courts
■ Full-service	■ Buffet restaurants
■ Fast food or quick service	■ Bars or taverns
■ Freestanding	■ Lounges

Types of Food and Beverage Facilities

Restaurants are not as easy to classify into distinct types as lodging facilities since the food and beverage industry is constantly evolving. Many in the hospitality business disagree on how to classify the different types of food and beverage facilities. Another factor that makes it difficult to classify these facilities is that some fall into more than one category. However, there are several classifications of food and beverage facilities that stand out (see Table 5-2).

A starting point in classifying restaurants is ownership. An *independent facility* is owned and managed by an individual or a partnership that creates the facility on their own. Most often it exists at a single location and is sometimes referred to as a *single-unit restaurant.* The owner or partners generally play an integral part in the operations and activities of the facility. When the independently owned facility becomes successful, the owner may open a similar facility in another location.

Another type of ownership that classifies restaurants is the chain restaurant. A *chain* involves multiple locations of one restaurant concept.[12] It might remain under the control of a small group of owners, like the independent facility, with the original creator and ownership group running each remote location. A multilocation facility can also be a franchise. In a *franchise,* the owners purchase a license to operate the facility under the guidance and requirements of the company that holds the rights to the original concept. The person who buys the franchise—the franchisee—benefits by owning a restaurant that has an established reputation.

The other way of classifying food and beverage facilities is by the type of service they provide. For our purposes, we classify restaurants into fast food, full service, and specialty service. Any of these might fit into any of the ownership categories.

The *fast food* or quick service restaurant is one with which we are all familiar. Fast food restaurants began as food carts on streetcorners. Most readers, however, associate fast food with restaurants like McDonald's, Kentucky Fried Chicken (KFC), Taco Bell, and scores of others. The interior designer of a fast food restaurant recognizes that the customer will eat quickly and leave after a short time. It must be well organized and, with the chains, the design concept has strong similarities from one location to another. Food courts at shopping malls offer a variety of fast food items, providing shoppers with many options for a quick meal while spending time at the mall. These are technically a combination of a fast food restaurant and cafeteria-style service. However, guests take all of their food and beverages to the table themselves.

Full-service restaurants make up a huge number of food service facilities. A *full-service restaurant* has a large selection of menu items served by wait staff. This type of restaurant started in the 19th century when restaurants began offering meals served by waiters. Full-service restaurants have many themes, which might affect the service style. For example, a restaurant may offer a salad bar as an option to plated salads served by wait

---

[12]Many other kinds of commercial facilities can be chains as well.

staff. However, in the most common situation, a waiter takes a customer's order and serves the meal. A full-service restaurant can be at any menu price, providing table service to suit anyone's taste and budget (Figures 5-10a and 5-10b).

A subcategory of the full-service restaurant is the high-end restaurant. High-end, full-service restaurants have an increased level of service, superb food, and higher prices. The

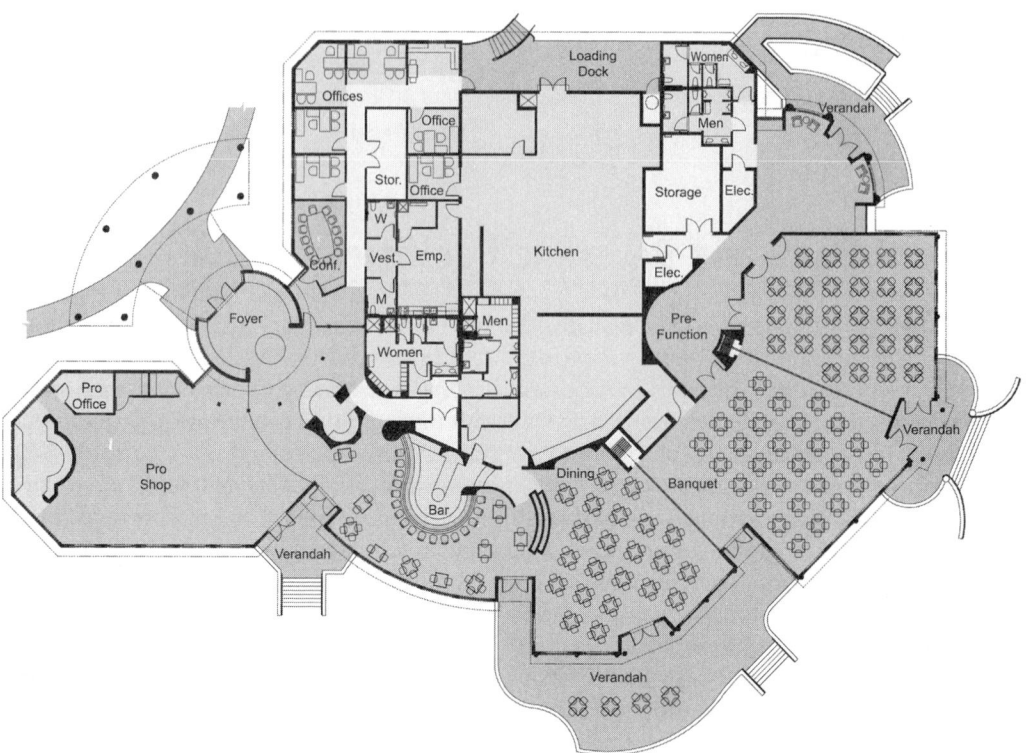

Figure 5-10a Floor plan of the Mystic Dunes Restaurant and food facilities. (Plan courtesy of Burke, Hogue & Mills Architects.)

Figure 5-10b Interior of the Mystic Dunes Restaurant. (Photograph courtesy of Burke, Hogue & Mills Architects.)

ambiance of these restaurants also usually reflects higher design or is in some way special compared to many other restaurants. These restaurants have a maître d' to greet guests, captains, and perhaps two levels of wait staff to take customers' orders and serve meals, bus people to clean tables, and perhaps even a sommelier (a wine waiter). Gourmet or haute cuisine (meaning "high food") brings customers back. Restaurants such as the Four Seasons in New York City, Spago in Los Angeles, Morton's in Chicago, and T. Cook's at the Royal Palms Resort in Phoenix are examples of this type of restaurant.

Between fast food and full-service restaurants are those that combine some aspects of both types of specialty service. Cafeterias, buffet restaurants, and family-style restaurants fall into this category. Cafeterias are generally those facilities where guests walk along a service line viewing and choosing from a variety of food items displayed in premeasured portions. They take their tray to a table and might be served beverages by a wait staff employee. At a buffet-style restaurant, guests serve themselves unlimited portions from the display of food items featured for the day. Again, a wait staff employee will bring beverages to the guest's table. The third version of this combination service is the family-style restaurant. In this situation, guests serve themselves from platters and bowls of selected items brought to the table by wait staff.

Other specialty restaurants focus on a certain type of food, a theme, or a style of service. A seafood restaurant, an ethnic food restaurant, and a restaurant with a specialized theme such as a sports-oriented facility are examples. Another type of specialty restaurant is the family or casual dining restaurant. They feature casual interior design and good, wholesome, "home-cooked" food. Many are independently owned, but some are chain restaurants.

Planning and Interior Design Elements

As we saw in the earlier discussion of concept development, the owners or developers of a restaurant must consider the business concept and design concept together. Achieving both is critical. The interior design of those areas that the guests will utilize—the entry, waiting area, dining room, restrooms and bar area—the front of the house, must mesh with the design of the back of the house utilized by the staff—kitchen, food storage area, office, and other service areas.

Not all interior designers are qualified to plan the back of the house of a restaurant—especially the complex space planning and equipment specification of the kitchen. Commercial kitchen design consultants are generally brought into the project as part of the planning team. According to many experts, that creates a problem, as the two consultants do not always communicate carefully enough for the front of the house and back of the house to work well together. "If the front of the house is not designed to support the back of the house, or the back of the house is not designed to carry out the concept expressed in the front of the house, then the operation suffers."[13] It is easy to see how important it is that the interior designer and the kitchen designer coordinate space planning, design concepts, and general communication right from the beginning of the project. If the restaurant calls for a display kitchen, this coordination is critical.

This overview of interior design elements focuses on the entry/waiting area and dining room. Additional information on each of these factors, as well as on these elements in relation to the kitchen and the beverage space in a restaurant, is presented in the Design Application section later in the chapter.

Space Allocation and Circulation

Is your client's project a neighborhood family-style ethnic restaurant with a small lounge as well as a dining room? Perhaps you have been hired to design the interior of a coffee shop offering small bakery items. Or does your restaurant project, located near an upscale

---

[13]Baraban and Durocher, 2001, p. 1.

BOX 5-1	RESTAURANT EXTERIOR DESIGN

Whether the restaurant is located in a strip shopping center, a mall, or a freestanding building, the exterior façade is always designed with the total concept in mind. In some situations, the owner and designer may not be able to fully design the façade. However, inviting signage and window treatments may help set the mood for what is to come inside.

Vernacular architecture and symbols have been used to call attention to restaurants. Over time, giant root beer barrels, teapots, igloos, and castles helped owners create an identity for their restaurant and helped the customer find a particular place among the competition. In more recent decades, neon lighting and signage have beckoned the guest to the restaurant. The design of the exterior must attract customers and draw their attention away from competing facilities in the same vicinity.

The exterior design, signage, and entrance façade can bring instant recognition. The use of signage and a logo in the exterior design can help the guest identify the establishment. The golden arches of McDonald's, the iconic oversized guitar at Hard Rock Café restaurants, and the simple black, yellow, and white exterior of California Pizza Kitchen bring instant recognition and an expectation of food quality and service. Even the price of the food can be conveyed with the signage; it seems that the more expensive the restaurant, the smaller the sign!

The exterior design has a direct relationship to customer perception and to ultimate success from the customers' point of view. Restaurants along highways will need larger signs than those located along streets with pedestrian traffic. In an urban area, a choice location is on the corner of any building or intersection. Being on the corner provides immediate visibility by pedestrians and motorists from two directions.

Exterior lighting helps set the mood for what will be found inside. Bright neon lighting or colored spotlights usually indicate a casual atmosphere. Accent lighting, used for example as small white lights in trees at Tavern on the Green in New York City and many other restaurants, adds interest and sparkle to the exterior.

The entrance façade and door can be key design elements. Canopies call attention to the entrance, providing the needed focal point. The entrance area and door design must help identify the restaurant, distinguishing it from all the others. Door specification should also be done in keeping with applicable accessibility and building codes. The doors need to swing out into the exterior and have a weight that does not exceed any applicable limits in the jurisdiction. Because of building code requirements, revolving doors should not be used unless an additional leafed door or doors are provided. Once guests have gone through the entrance doors, they are ready to enjoy the interior design and the food within!

resort, have the potential to be a four-star gourmet full-service restaurant featuring an elegant interior with a cigar lounge? The type of restaurant, style of service, menu, and location will all have an impact on the space allocation of the facility. That is because each situation will require different amounts of space for the functional areas in a restaurant.

The revenue-producing areas of the restaurant are, of course, the dining room and the beverage facility. The space allocation of these areas and the impact of the related codes are critical for revenue success. The bottom line is not solely a terrific concept or theme with a well-planned service structure and menu in the ideal location. The bottom line relates to filling the restaurant, and that means providing sufficient table seating in the dining room and lounge to generate revenue.

Restaurants essentially have the same space needs, regardless of their type. An entry and possibly a waiting area, the dining space with wait stations, the kitchen, and other back-of-house spaces are needed whether the facility is a fast food outlet or a gourmet restaurant. Additional spaces such as a lounge where alcoholic beverages are served, guest restrooms, room for a salad bar or display kitchen, and possibly other spaces to meet the business concept of a specific facility are also generally needed.

The space allocation for entry and waiting areas varies widely. Depending on the climate, a vestibule is needed and must be planned to meet accessibility standards. The host

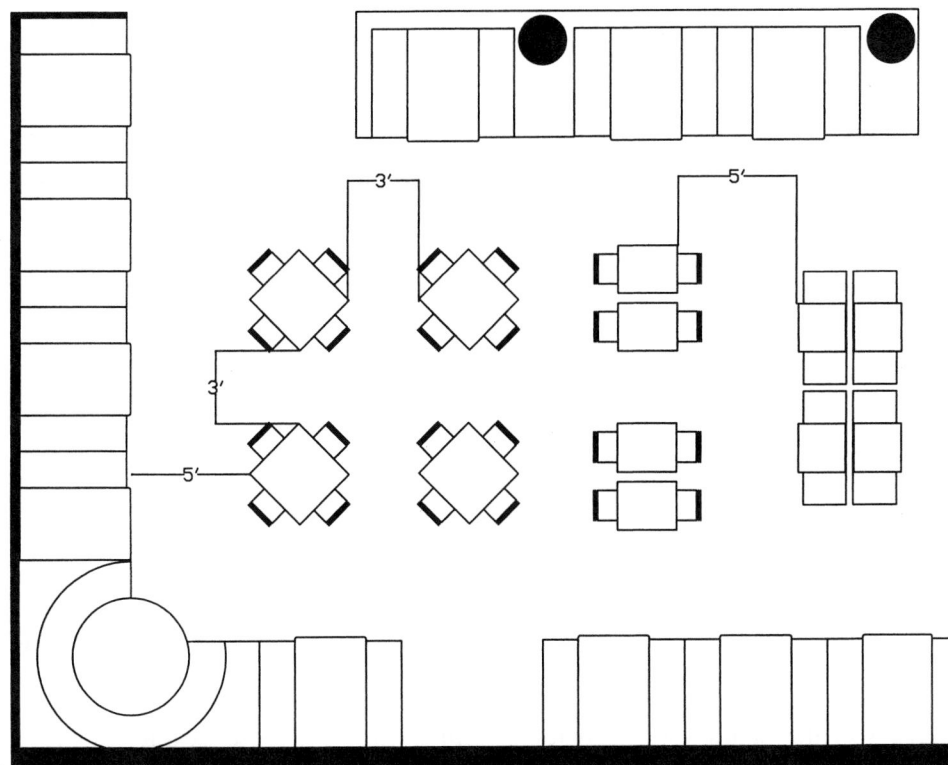

Figure 5-11 Dining room layout indicating traffic aisles and spacing between tables and booths. (Drawing courtesy of LeAnn Wilson.)

or maître d' podium must be easy to find, and designers often use it to create a focal point in the entry/waiting area. Some restaurants do not provide an actual waiting area in order to use as much space as possible for dining room seating. In a chain restaurant, there is commonly a waiting area with chairs or benches for guests waiting for a table. An upscale restaurant will rarely provide seats for waiting guests, expecting them to wait in the bar. A fast service facility will have no actual waiting area. Instead, it will provide queuing space for the lines to form before the cash registers. Thus, it is difficult to provide a rule of thumb on space allowances for this area. However, approximately 8 to 10 square feet are allocated for each wait seating space.

The dining room space allowance is defined by the business concept and is planned based on the combination of table sizes, shapes, and even the chairs themselves. Additional space will be needed for wait stations and traffic paths. The allowance for the bar and lounge seating area obviously impacts the dining room space. However, since bars generate more revenue per square foot than dining space, the trade-off is an important consideration. All these factors will impact the number of seats, which impacts potential revenue (Figures 5-11 and 5-12). "You can often assume that in terms of square feet per seat, you will need 16 to 18 for a cafeteria, 18 to 20 for counter service, 15 to 18 for table service at a hotel club restaurant, 11 to 14 for fast-food table service, 10 to 11 for banquets, and 17 to 22 for specialty formal dining. Waiting areas, coatrooms and storage areas are not included in these figures."[14]

Depending on the type, service style, and concept of the restaurant, the main circulation space should be 3 to 5 feet wide. As a rule of thumb, 15 square feet per seat is common in full-service high-end restaurants, though the allowances can vary from 10 to 20 square feet, depending on the type of facility and codes. As always, the interior designer must space plan the dining room to meet the specific jurisdiction's code requirements. Circulation space between tables will vary, depending on the arrangement of the tables. In

---

[14]Dorf, 1992, p. 41.

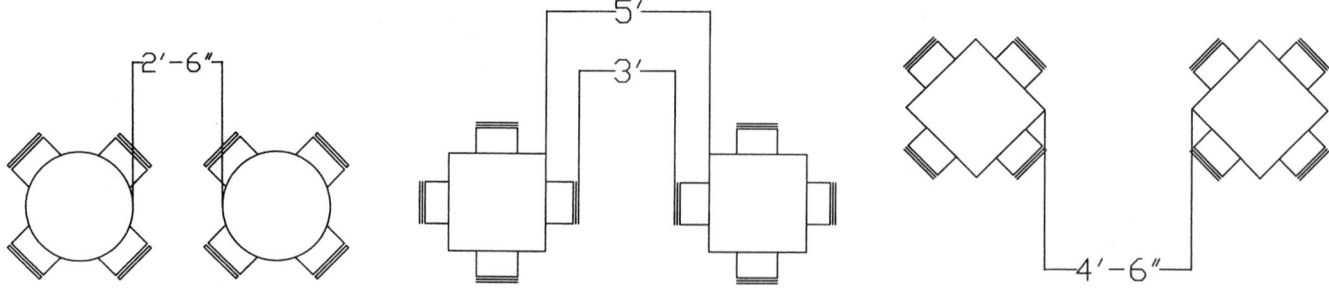

Figure 5-12 Circulation space between tables will vary, depending on the size, shape, and placement of the tables. (Drawing courtesy of LeAnn Wilson.)

addition to circulation space, the designer must plan for activity space—that is, space that allows the wait person to stand at a table and not in the circulation space. The allowance for this space is between 18 and 30 inches. Mid-priced table service and upscale restaurants in particular place tables and other seating arrangements with more generous spacing between them to give the feeling of privacy. The space allowance for booth seating is shown in Figure 5-13, and that for banquette seating is shown in Figure 5-14. Approximately 1 foot is a comfortable distance between tables at a *banquette*—a continuous bench along a wall with tables and chairs across from it.

The layout of the tables and the type of seating will also impact seating capacity. Square tables placed diagonally offer more efficient arrangements than tables placed at right angles. Tables that seat four persons—called four tops—waste seating capacity when only one or two people are seated there. Tables that seat two guests, called deuces or two tops, are often included in the table mix since more single diners patronize restaurants today. Some restaurants use large round tables for big groups or purchase tables with a foldup section that converts a square table to a round one. Table and chair seating in the dining room takes up more room than banquette seating. It should be remembered that banquette seating is less private and is more appropriate for conversation and people watching (Figure 5-15).

Another seating solution that impacts seating capacity and space allocation is booths. Many customers prefer booths because of their "psychological" privacy. Booths are usually designed to seat four or more persons and, from a business standpoint, are economically inefficient when used by only one or two people. Building codes restrict minimum

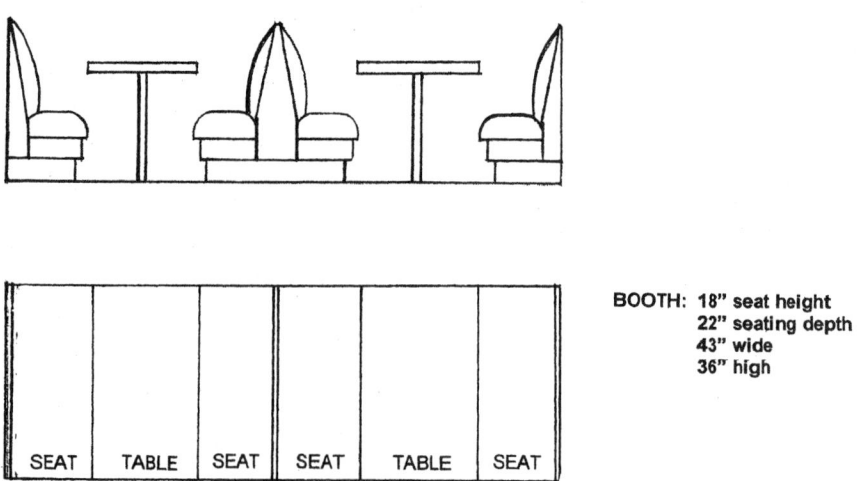

BOOTH: 18" seat height
22" seating depth
43" wide
36" high

Figure 5-13 Drawing of booth seating with dimensions. (Illustration by SOI Interior Design.)

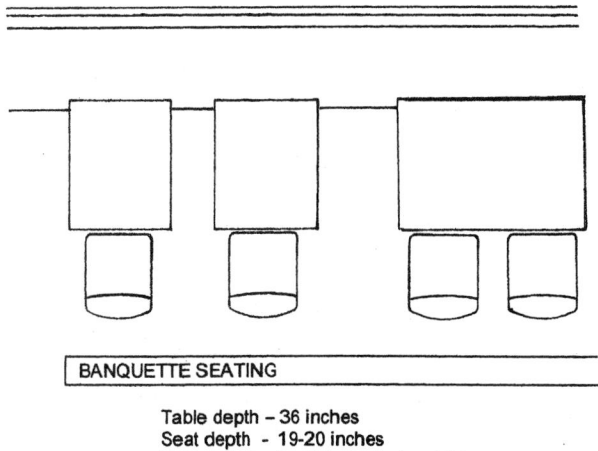

BANQUETTE SEATING

Table depth – 36 inches
Seat depth - 19-20 inches
Banquette back – 36 plus inches high

Figure 5-14 Drawing of banquette seating with dimensions. (Illustration by SOI Interior Design.)

square footage allowances on fixed seating units that include fixed tables in food and beverage facilities. The interior designer needs to check the applicable codes when planning to utilize any kind of fixed seating.

Another space allocation consideration in the dining room is for wait stations. *Wait stations,* also called service stations, is the term for the area required for storing clean and dirty dishes, glasses, coffee service, and other items dependent on the restaurant. On average, one small wait station of approximately 2 by 2 feet is recommended for every 20 seats and one large station of approximately 8 feet by 30 inches for every 50 seats. Point-of-sale (POS) computers can be added to the wait stations or will need to be planned in other dining room locations.

If the restaurant has a bar or lounge, different space allocation criteria will be necessary. Beverage areas include the bar itself, the back bar, possibly room for seating at

Figure 5-15 The far wall in this space contains banquette seating. (Photograph courtesy of 3D/International and dMd/Dodd Mitchell Design.)

TABLE 5-3 Estimates of Space for the Kitchen Functional Areas

Functional Areas	Space Allowed (%)
Receiving	5
Food storage	20
Preparation	14
Cooking	8
Baking	10
Warewashing	5
Traffic aisles	16
Trash storage	5
Employee facilities	15
Miscellaneous	2

Source: Reprinted with permission. Edward A. Kazarian. 1989. P. 734. *Foodservice Facilities Planning.* 3rd ed. John Wiley & Sons.

the bar, and any other seating or activity space such as a dance floor in the beverage area. Beverage areas usually require 8 to 10 square feet per person, plus the space for the bar and back bar, plus traffic space along bar stools. The standard allowance for seating at the bar is 28 inches per stool horizontally along the bar. There is no rule of thumb for the bar and back bar since these can be designed in so many ways. According to McGowan, the front bar can be 28 to 38 inches deep, the work activity zone between the front and back bars can be 30 to 36 inches, and the back bar can be 24 to 30 inches deep.[15] The designer must work with the owner and bar manager to determine the kind and size of equipment, amount of bar seating, and amount of storage at the bar to determine the estimated space allowance for this part of the beverage facility. Finally, an allowance of approximately 10 to 15 square feet per person for lounge seating will be needed, depending on the size of the table and the style and size of chairs.

Because of the variations in the type of service and the complexity of any establishment's menu, there is no standard rule for the size of the kitchen as a percentage of the overall size of the facility. The amount of space required for the kitchen areas also depends on the type of facility, the menu, the number of seats desired, and the expected number of meals in a day. One rule of thumb is that the kitchen area should be about one third the size of the dining room.[16] Other experts say that the rule is 40 percent kitchen to 60 percent dining room.[17] When the menu items are primarily fresh food—meaning that the restaurant is receiving each day's food in the morning—more space will be needed for the kitchen. Restaurants using more processed foods may be planned with smaller kitchens. Table 5-3 provides space estimates for the kitchen's functional areas. Additional information on planning all of these areas in a food and beverage facility is provided in the Design Application section later in the chapter.

Furniture

If a facility has decided to provide seating in the waiting area, a common solution will be benches. Benches are more common than chairs, as they provide more seating in the same space. They also can't be moved, cutting down on the labor necessary to keep the wait-

---

[15]McGowan, 2004, p. 388.
[16]Baraban and Durocher, 2001, p. 55.
[17]Birchfield and Sparrowe, 2003, p. 91.

ing area neat. As the price point of the restaurant goes up, the likelihood of the benches being upholstered also increases. If chairs are used, they will be the same or very similar to those used in the dining room. A counter or podium for the host or maître d' is also required in the waiting area. This is often a custom-designed unit large enough to accommodate the seating chart of the dining room and lounge, a telephone, and space for the wait list or reservations book.

Guests like to have a choice in their seating in the dining room. Combinations of tables, chairs, booths, and/or banquettes are used to provide these options and still meet the seating goals established by the business and design concepts. There are many choices available to the interior designer in the specification of furniture items to meet the design concept. Interior designers also have the option of designing custom tabletops with the use of resin coatings. Common table sizes are shown in Table 5-4.

Tables are square, rectangular, and round and seat anywhere from 2 people to groups of 8 to 10. As discussed earlier, table sizes, commonly referred to as *tops,* refer to the number of people who can be accommodated at the table. Tables should also be sturdy, with bases that are easy to keep in balance and sufficient leg room for the diners. Tables are typically 30 inches high, whether at a freestanding table setup, a banquette, or a booth. Squares and rectangles are best; they can be arranged to accommodate a large group that wants to sit together.

Seating in a restaurant is planned with the comfort level and ambience defined in the concept. It is also a major investment, and only good to high-quality commercial-grade seating should be specified. Chairs can range from simple fixed or movable hard-surface pieces in a fast food restaurant to fully upholstered armchairs in a high-end full-service facility. Armchairs are quite common in full-service facilities since they provide more comfort. However, an armchair takes up more space, and this factor needs to be considered in relation to the size of the tables, the concept, and the space allowances. Chairs should have a height from the floor to the top of the back of no more than 34 inches and a seat height of 18 inches.

Some seating may be provided by banquettes and booth. This seating usually involves a custom design. The seat and often the back of the banquette are upholstered. Tables in the banquette area can be combined to create seating for larger groups. Booths take up less space than the same number of seats at a table but are more difficult to maintain. They were once used primarily in lower-priced restaurants, but they have become quite popular in upscale facilities since they seem to provide more privacy. Much can be done with the design of the booth, giving the interior designer additional options.

Custom millwork and cabinets are designed for screens or dividers, wall treatments, wait stations in the dining room, and the bar in the beverage space. Other custom cabinetry may be required, depending on the concept and theme. For example, counters and cabinets to hold displays of food are used in some restaurants. Cabinets may also be needed for the display of souvenir T-shirts or other souvenir items.

TABLE 5-4 Common Restaurant Table Sizes

For One or Two Guests	■ 30-by-48-inch rectangular table
■ 24-by-30-inch rectangular table	■ 36-by-48-inch rectangular table
■ 24-by-36-inch rectangular table	■ 42- to 48-inch round table
■ 42-by-48-inch rectangular table	
■ 30- to 36-inch round table	**For Five or More Guests**
	■ Most restaurants will combine smaller tables to accommodate larger groups rather than using large tables. Cafeterias and some ethnic themed restaurants may have larger rectangular or round tables.
For Three or Four Guests	
■ 36-by-36-inch square table	
■ 40-by-40-inch square table	

Depending on the design concept, type, and size of the restaurant, other furniture and equipment items may need to be obtained or designed. These might include a wine display, cabinets and finishes for a display kitchen, and cabinets to accommodate salad bars or buffet lines.

Most restaurants today utilize point-of-sale computers or hand-held wireless terminals for order entry. The POS computers require a counter space of approximately 24 by 24 inches and should be placed at a stand-up height. A touch screen rather than a keyboard is part of the special design of these computer terminals. They can be programmed to provide not only ordering information to the kitchen, but also useful data for the manager and owners. Computer ordering allows precise inventory control as well as reports on the types of food most commonly ordered by customers.

Materials and Finishes

Materials and finishes in the front-of-the-house areas will naturally express and complement the design concept. Let us first look at some design considerations for furniture items and then architectural finishes. Wood tabletops that remain uncovered by cloths are warmer than those finished in plastic laminates. However, wood is harder to maintain and subject to damage by wet glassware and food spills. Plastic laminate tops are easy to maintain and take a lot of abuse. Resin-coated tops are one way to have a wood table finish without the problems of abuse and high maintenance. Resin tops can also be manufactured to include logos or other graphics, and this treatment provides a way for the interior designer to add an interesting design feature. Table bases can have wood or metal legs, a pronged pedestal, or a bell pedestal. Interior designers combine tabletop choices with the bases, providing custom design to the facility's tables.

There are numerous choices for the specification of seating in a food and beverage facility. Chair frames can be obtained in wood, metal, or even plastic and can be finished in many colors and finishes. Fabrics for seating units also vary with the style and type of restaurant. Easy-to-maintain vinyl and hard-surface materials are common in fast food and lower-priced full-service restaurants. Whatever textile is used on seating, the designer must keep in mind soiling, food spillage, ease of maintenance, abrasion resistance, snagging, and pilling. Seating takes a lot of use and abuse (so the owner hopes), so the type of material used on the seating unit must not only work aesthetically but be able to handle the expected upkeep. Fabrics with loose or floating threads may appear elegant but are easy to snag and should be avoided. Tightly woven fabrics come in many textures and patterns to meet the needs of the design concept. In addition, the interior designer must be sure that the fabrics specified for seating units meet local fire safety codes (Figure 5-16).

Architectural finishes provide almost unlimited options for the interior designer. The combination of paints, wall treatments, flooring materials, and other architectural finishes and accessories is huge. The limiting factors are obvious—initial cost, meeting code requirements, and ease of maintenance. The designer will need to decide if the wall treatments are to be a focal point of the interior design or a backdrop. For example, paneling with traditional molding, cornices, and chair rails establishes the traditional interior that would accept many traditional-style chairs in a formal dining room. Chair rails also help to protect the walls from the backs of chairs. Textile wallcoverings should be selected with care, as they will require a higher standard for fire safety. Painted surfaces should be semigloss or high gloss for easier cleaning. Wallpapers and other wall finishes should be commercial-grade materials that will resist the abrasion of chairs banging and rubbing against the surface. Whatever material or type of finish is applied to the walls, ease of cleaning and resistance to damage are important factors in their specification. All of these hard-surface materials for the walls increase the sound level of the restaurant, so other surfaces or treatments might be needed to cut down on the noise.

There are many options for flooring materials in the dining room. Materials will be specified to meet the overall concept as well as provide easy maintenance. Interesting flooring treatments can be quite exciting in a restaurant. Changes in flooring surfaces can help

Figure 5-16 Elegant restaurant located in the Country Club of Orlando, Florida. (Photography courtesy of Burke, Hogue & Mills Architects.)

the traffic flow and direction in large restaurants. The main traffic aisles might be finished in a patterned carpet while the areas where tables will be set up will take a nonpatterned carpet, or vice versa. In a high-end restaurant, terrazzo or marble may be used for the traffic aisles, but carpet might be used where tables and booths are arranged. When a carpet is specified, medium-sized or multicolored patterns are used to add interest but also to hide traffic paths. Carpets need to be tightly tufted with a short pile to allow easy movement of chairs and possibly carts. Nylon and nylon-wool blends are especially good for restaurant carpets, since they allow frequent cleaning. Hard-surface and resilient materials will be noisier than carpets but involve few code restriction and regulations. Wood flooring can be scratched by chair legs, requiring extra maintenance. If used, stone and ceramic tile floors must be made slip resistant for the safety of customers and staff. In lower-priced facilities, commercial-grade vinyl and composite tiles are appropriate.

Color specification and lighting design go hand in hand in a restaurant. Color is an easy way to convey themes and concepts in a restaurant's design. Lighting specification can make a great color scheme a success or failure, as the variations in lamps and fixtures will affect the perception of colors. Since colors are seen because of the lighting introduced, and the lighting selections affect the true or apparent colors, the successful restaurant must be designed with these two in unison.

What are the "best" colors to use? Baraban and Durocher report that "color cycles literally move around the color wheel, gradually shifting from the cool colors to the warm colors and back again, with each trend enjoying a lifespan of about eight years."[18] Sometimes unexpected color choices can be very exciting for some restaurants and provide a more formal feeling in others. For example, consider mauve, gold, and walnuts in a Chinese restaurant. This interior creates a more formal feeling, which may bring a different client to the restaurant. However, bright primary colors in a formal restaurant will seem out of place since they encourage fast turnover—something not expected in this type of

[18]Baraban and Durocher, 2001, p. 77.

restaurant. "Color influences the length of stay along the lines of contrast, particularly value: the higher the contrast, the shorter the average length of stay."[19]

Lighting Design and Acoustics

Consider how you might react in the following facilities: a brightly lit fast-food restaurant versus a formal restaurant with reduced light levels via wall sconces and low-watt spotlights where you have had a special dinner. Two different restaurants with two different lighting treatments create environments that put you as a guest in a different mood and may even change your behavior. Appropriate lighting is a very important part of the overall design of any type of food service facility. In fact, many experts consider lighting to be the single most important element in the interior design of a successful food and beverage facility.

Lighting design plays many important roles in a restaurant. It must provide sufficient light for safety while at the same time helping to set the appropriate mood. Guests should be able to read the menu without needing a flashlight, and although this may seem facetious, it sometimes seems literally true for older diners. Lighting design also affects the appearance of food. Finally, good lighting enhances the appearance of the guests.

It is common for a designer who has specialized in lighting design to be part of the design team for many restaurant projects. Lighting in a restaurant can be complex, and most interior designers do not have the in-depth knowledge of lighting technology to plan the lighting design. The lighting designer might work for the architectural or interior design firm or might be an outside consultant specializing in this highly technical area. Of course, interior designers who may be retained to design a food and beverage facility should have some understanding of the importance of lighting design in this application.

Three types of lighting are commonly used in the design of dining areas: indirect ambient, accent, and sparkle lighting. Overall lighting is provided by indirect ambient lighting to allow comfortable movement and functioning in the space. Cove lighting, direct and indirect fixtures, and spotlights can all be used together to achieve the overall lighting required by a specific design concept. Accent lighting, such as provided by wall sconces, can highlight accessories and add interest to the space. Sparkle lighting is produced by a variety of light sources that create special effects both in providing true lighting and in setting the general mood. Pinpoint lights, light reflected off mirrors and glass, and low-watt fiberoptic lights can produce sparkle. As in a hotel, a few types of restaurants will also need some type of performance lighting. Refer back to Chapter 4 for comments on performance lighting.

Lighting levels will be based on the activity in any area of the restaurant. Five to 15 foot-candles is the minimum recommended light level in the dining area of high-end, intimate-dining, full-service restaurants. This would increase to 75 to 100 foot-candles in a fast food restaurant. Table 5-5 indicates the lighting levels in other areas of the restaurant. The dining room, entry, and bar should be on a dimming system to allow changes in lighting levels throughout the day.

Numerous types of lighting fixtures can be used in this type of facility. Care should be used by designers in specifying pendent fixtures over tables that can be moved. Tables may have to be rearranged for large groups, and then pendent fixtures may end up in awkward places. In many full-service and intimate-dining restaurants, fixtures that use various kinds of incandescent lamps remain popular. Incandescent lamps are very flattering to people and food. The problem with this type of lamp is the high heat output for the number of watts produced, which increases the HVAC costs. Energy-saving lamps provide more light at lower energy costs, but they should be "limited to spaces with high ceilings and more theatrical, dramatic environments, because they tend to create harsh, bright spots of light when used too close to objects."[20]

A new type of lighting option today is the *light-emitting diode* (LED). This low-voltage light uses technology to focus light in a specific direction. It comes in many col-

---

[19]Kopacz, 2004, p. 236.
[20]Dorf, 1992, p. 51.

TABLE 5-5 Restaurant Lighting Levels in Foot-Candles by Area

Restaurant Area	Minimum Foot-candles
Receiving	25–45
Storage	15–20
Prepreparation	20–30
Preparation/production	30–50
Warewashing	70–100
POS/cashier	35–50
Intimate dining	5–15
Fast food dining	75–100

Source: Baraban and Durocher, p. 119. (Reprinted with permission of John Wiley & Sons, Inc.)

ors, gives off more light than an incandescent lamp, and costs less to operate. Another new type of lamp is the E-lamp, which "uses a high-frequency radio signal instead of a filament to produce light. Inside the sealed globe, the rapidly oscillating radio waves excite a gas mixture, which, in turn, gives off light. The light hits a phosphorus coating on the inside of the globe and glows."[21] There are many other new types of lighting fixtures that can be used to provide functional and aesthetic lighting of a food service establishment. Information on these solutions is provided in the references.

Energy efficiency is also an issue in the design and specification of lighting. In some jurisdictions, the restaurant may be limited in the number of watts per square foot that the fixtures produce. This may call for some extra planning and specification to meet the design concept needs. Energy efficiency may also be affected by the need to limit the use of incandescent lighting—which is warmer in color—due to the fact that it is also warmer in temperature and uses more power than compact fluorescent lamps. The incandescent lamp produces more heat than fluorescent lamps, which, as mentioned above, could mean an increase in HVAC needs. However, fluorescent lamps are not particularly attractive light sources in restaurants that have a subdued atmosphere. These are the factors that influence the lighting designer in the specification of lighting for a food and beverage facility.

Restaurants can be very noisy places. A lot of noise is expected in fast food restaurants, but many other types of full-service facilities are also noisy. Almost everything that goes on in a restaurant adds to the noise level of the facility. Guest traffic, chairs moving, servers taking orders and delivering food to the guests, kitchen noise, and even the background music or entertainment provided all add to the acoustical potpourri of the environment. Ceiling treatments that absorb sound and carpet on the floor provide the most acoustical control. Space planning that divides the dining room into smaller sections with the use of partitions can reduce the noise to some degree. However, to be most effective as an acoustical treatment, the dividers must reach the ceiling. Choosing upholstery rather than hard surfaces for seating units and using tablecloths to reduce the sounds of dishware and utensils are other techniques that will help reduce overall noise levels.

Other design elements that can also reduce noise from the large expanses of wall surfaces include acoustical panels and baffles made of sound-absorbing acoustical materials covered with fabrics. High-quality acoustical ceiling treatments and low-volume sound systems are also useful in masking the unpleasant noises that can occur in a restaurant. Careful consideration of where the service islands are located, where dirty dishes are stacked, the location and baffling of kitchen doors, and even the use of electronic ordering systems rather than wait staff shouting orders all will help reduce noise.

---

[21]Katsigris and Thomas, 2005, p. 191.

Security

Security and safety planning in a food and beverage facility relies upon adherence to the building and life safety code requirements. The biggest place for potential dangers in the restaurant is the kitchen. Employee injuries from the equipment and tools used to prepare foods are one issue. Proper flooring is needed so that staff members do not slip on slick floors. Rubber floor mats or commercial-grade, slip-resistant, hard-surface flooring materials are necessary in the kitchen.

Guest safety is also an issue with flooring selected at the entry doors, in restrooms, and along traffic paths. Marble is a beautiful material for the entry of a restaurant, but it also represents an accident waiting to happen when water from snow and rain is tracked inside. Decorative textile and wood treatments on walls need to be treated with fire-retardant chemicals. Special care should be given to wall and ceiling treatments near or next to lighting fixtures.

Here are a few other design points the interior designer can easily include to increase security. The manager's office will require a safe so that cash and credit card slips can be transferred to the manager's office. The storerooms for alcoholic beverages and foodstuffs should not have windows to avoid a break-in. Storage areas should also be away from the employee locker rooms, where pilfered foodstuffs can be easily hidden in lockers.

Code Requirements

The interior designer should know which codes apply to the facility to be designed so that the right codes are used. The International Building Code classifies food and beverage facilities as Assembly occupancies (A-2). Applicable code books must be checked to see how these restrictions will affect design planning and specification decisions. For example, a fast food restaurant or a cafeteria that has fixed seating will have code restrictions that are different from those for restaurants with booths and table and chair seating. It is the interior designer's responsibility to understand which model codes are in effect for the specific location and type of facility, and make planning and specification decisions in accordance with those codes. Some aspects of the project that will be affected by the code classification are the overall number of seats and subsequent space planning of the dining areas, what materials can be used on architectural surfaces, and what types of textiles can be used on seating. A restaurant in a hotel or office building may have different requirements than a freestanding restaurant.

Codes will also affect the amount of square footage required. Most codes allow an occupant load factor of 15 square feet per person for seating areas or less, depending on the exact application and use of the space. This provides space for aisles and small wait stations, but not for restrooms, beverage areas, the entry, and the waiting area. This seating allowance may be satisfactory for a small restaurant with casual service, but it may be very low for a high-end facility. Restaurants with fixed seating will have other requirements. Commercial kitchens require a minimum of 200 square feet per kitchen staff member. Remember that these allowances are used to calculate load factors for the number of occupants, not the actual square footage required for the dining room or kitchen.

The building and life safety codes affecting assembly occupancies will vary with the total occupancy, the type of building that houses the facility, whether the facility is new construction or a renovation of an existing building, and whether it is a single occupancy or considered part of a mixed occupancy. Flooring materials, wall finishes—especially in exit access corridors or other exit areas—and window treatments must meet local code requirements. Restaurants also must be designed with health department regulations in mind. The majority of these regulations affect the kitchen and food preparation areas but may impact the specification of materials in the dining room as well. Restaurants with display kitchens, salad bars, or buffet bars in the dining room will all impact other design decisions in the dining room.

Upholstery fabrics on seating units are regulated by local codes, and specific fire-resistant materials may have to be used on seating units in dining and beverage areas. Some states require the whole seating unit to meet CAL 133 or similar fire safety regulations. Wall finishes will also be required to meet Class A, B, or C standards based on the location of the wall areas and the building classification. As always, textile wallcoverings must meet Class A standards if the jurisdiction will allow them at all.

Several accessibility regulations will also potentially impact the design of the restaurant and beverage facility. A portion of the tables or other seating, generally 5 percent, must be made accessible. The traffic paths to the restrooms must also be readily accessible. Sometimes the tables are packed too closely, making it difficult, if not impossible, for someone in a wheelchair to move through the dining room.

Codes require that restroom facilities be provided in all food service and beverage facilities. The size of these spaces will be determined by the occupant load based on building codes and the version of the building code that regulates the facility. The building codes will also determine the number of fixtures in toilet facilities for the public and employees. This too will vary based on the jurisdiction and the version of the building code that impacts the facility. For example, if a facility with an occupant load of 75 must meet the International Building Code, it will require a minimum of two water closets and one lavatory for the public women's facility and one water closet, one urinal, and one lavatory for the men's.[22] Of course, the interior designer should recommend a larger number of water closets and lavatories in busy facilities. Additional toilet facilities for employees may also be required. The building code and ADA guidelines will determine how many stalls and lavatories will have to meet accessibility standards. Additional information on toilet facilities is provided later in this chapter and in Chapter 9.

Design Applications

The most successful restaurants have a complete concept package. That is, the exterior design is eye-catching, the interior is inviting and pleasant for the type of restaurant and style of service, and the menu offers a delicious variety of food. The establishment is also located to attract guests, and the price of the food is in line with the qualities already mentioned. The interior obviously plays a key role in the success of the restaurant. However, a great interior with terrible service and disappointing food will not bring a guest back. The design concept establishes the elements that will be used and sets up a progression from the exterior through the interior. The design concept elements must coordinate with the exterior design and flow from the front entry through all the public areas of the facility. Design concept information will now be presented for a full-service restaurant. There will also be a brief discussion of design concepts for a coffee shop, which today is one of the most popular food and beverage facilities.

Full-Service Restaurant

Interior design concepts and issues vary widely with the type of facility and style of service. These important planning concepts will be discussed in the context of a generic full-service restaurant with a separate beverage area that caters to the adult dining guest.

This section takes the reader from the entrance through the spaces of the establishment as if walking in the front door and being allowed back into the kitchen. Interior design elements of furniture specifications, colors and materials, mechanical interface, and codes are all discussed.

Entry and Waiting Areas

As stated earlier in the chapter, the exterior design and appearance can be important in attracting a guest to the restaurant. Walking through the doors and experiencing the design of the entry and waiting areas is a true test of the guest's impressions and expectations of the facility. The design of this space is thus very important in the development of the facility.

---

[22]International Building Code, 2000, p. 547.

The entry also provides an important transition from the outside to the interior environment. When guests visit a restaurant for the first time, they often pause in the entry area to get their bearings. Entries often include a vestibule to create a transition from outside to inside. Depending on the location of the restaurant, the entry vestibule may need to be large to accommodate emergency egress and accessibility issues. The type and service style of the facility will create different needs in the entry. For a full-service restaurant, the entry serves as a transition space for customers moving into the dining area. The ceiling in the entry is often lower than that in the dining areas to facilitate this transition. Fast food restaurants use the "entry" as queuing space for guests waiting to place orders.

There are many activities that commonly occur in the entry. Of course, there is the entering and exiting of guests. The entry must also accommodate the host or maître d' station and the arriving guests. An allowance must be made for traffic to restrooms that might be positioned off the entry. Seating is often provided for waiting guests. If waiting space is not provided, guests will be directed to the bar or lounge. In full-service restaurants, the host podium is placed away from the door to draw customers into the ambience of the restaurant and maybe even allow them to savor some of the odors of the food to come.

There are some other functions that might be housed in the entry and waiting area. Many restaurants have turned waiting areas into incremental sales areas. The sale of T-shirts and other restaurant souvenirs is popular at many theme restaurants. Upscale restaurants may make a wine display part of the waiting area design. Coatrooms might be included in high-end, full-service facilities. Public telephones and toilet facilities for guests are often located off the entry, though many newer concepts place these areas in the back of the facility to prevent guests from leaving without paying.

Materials and colors selected for the entry set the stage for what the patron will experience in the dining room and beverage area. Architectural surfaces are selected with maintenance in mind, as well as the aesthetic statement for which the designer and owner strive. Slip-resistant flooring or walk-off mats are needed at the entry doors and hard-surface materials are generally used in the other parts of the entry and waiting area. The materials and finishes used in the entry must meet the same code requirements as those in the dining room and beverage area.

Restaurant designers commonly state that restaurant lighting is similar to theater lighting. The lighting specification and design in the entry set the stage for what is to come. Thus, the lighting in the entry will add to the first impression of the design of the dining room. Ambient lighting will provide the overall lighting needed in the entry. Spotlights or task lights are added at the host podium.

Dining Areas

The planning and design of the dining room is an exciting challenge for hospitality designers. The design concept and business concept will drive the final design, but the design options are numerous regardless of the necessary limitations. The interior designer will likely start the schematic design process with the space plan of the dining room and adjacent activity areas. The number of seats required by the owner is the starting point for this planning.

The number of seats, including the projected sizes, shapes, and combination of tables and booths, is directly related to the income of the facility. The greater the number of seats, the greater the potential income. Yet, the maximum number of seats will be impacted by codes based on the square footage and footprint of the restaurant. The space plan of the dining room will impact the number of seats as well.

Creating smaller dining areas within the whole dining space with the use of partition walls and screens creates a more intimate dining room and some acoustic control in a large facility. It can, however, reduce the total number of seats. Interior designers often use full-height or partial-height walls to create these smaller "dining rooms in a dining room." Curving walls can be used by incorporating banquettes along the curves. This design strategy also creates secluded spaces for guests in some restaurant concepts, providing semiprivate dining spaces that are not really private dining rooms (Figure 5-17).

Raised or sunken areas are another way to subdivide the space. However, accessibility regulations such as those of the ADA require that all portions of dining areas be accessible. Should the designer plan raised or sunken areas, even second-floor areas, seating areas must be made accessible. Ramps take up a lot of room, and designing the space with fewer than three steps can cause tripping. Rather than using sunken areas, the designer might decide to change ceiling heights to create intimacy. When there are smoking and nonsmoking areas in the restaurant, the ADA also requires that accessible seating be provided in each section.

In space planning the dining room, the designer must be concerned with traffic flow from the entry and waiting area and throughout the dining room. Plans must also consider wait staff traffic into and out of the kitchen as heavy trays of food are carried to the tables and dirty dishes are returned. Maneuvering trays through a maze of passageways from the kitchen to the farthest dining areas can be cumbersome as well as dangerous.

Sometimes the design of the restaurant may create prime locations by accident, although few interior designers admit to that! Prime tables are the best tables in the house, requested by good customers and VIPs (at very exclusive restaurants). The designer's plan and overall design should attempt to make all tables seem like the prime table. Not all tables can be at the window with an unobstructed view of the ocean. Dining room plans should consider the location of tables in relation to sightlines from the seating areas into the kitchen or wait areas and avoid that location if at all possible. If necessary, partial walls can be used to hide wait stations and the entry to the kitchen (Figure 5-18).

Wait stations are another functional area needed in the dining room. From a design standpoint, these areas are hardly ever attractive and always seem to be noisy. However, they are necessary to provide efficient service. The larger the facility, the more service stations will be required where dining areas can be remote from the kitchen.

Figure 5-17 Example of private area secluded for dining. Also refer to Figure 5-9 for examples of a dining room within a dining room. (Photograph courtesy of 3D/International and dMd/Dodd Mitchell Design.)

Wait stations can be designed to blend into the dining room and should be screened to prevent guests from seeing the mess in the service areas. They require space for some glassware and coffee service, water, iced tea and coffee, a small ice bin, and backup flatware and napkins. Other items needed by guests are often stored here as well, such as bottled or packaged condiments and perhaps take-home containers. Depending on the philosophy of the owner, the POS computer for ordering guest food may also be located in or near the service stations.

From a design standpoint, surfaces for the wait stations must resist moisture and be easy to clean. Flooring must be slip-resistant, and lighting should be glare-free. If the wait stations are located in the dining room, the design of the cabinetry and finishes should match with the overall design concept of the dining room. When located more privately so that they are essentially unseen by the guest, they can be more utilitarian in finish and design.

Once the design concept and table layout are determined, the interior designer begins to make *furniture and finish specifications*. Naturally, the sizes and shapes of tables are an important part of that specification, as they will impact the number of seats that will be accommodated by the space plan. Square and rectangular tables can easily be joined together for larger groups. The warmth of a wood tabletop provides a different feeling to the guest than a laminate or other hard-surface top. Tablecloths give a feeling of elegance, whether for lunch or dinner service, and reduce noise. Linen tablecloths and napkins bring

BOX 5-2   DESIGNING PRIVATE DINING ROOMS

When a special occasion arises, we gravitate toward special places. Going to a favorite or very special restaurant is certainly one way to celebrate. A large group, though welcomed by any restaurant, can sometimes be disruptive. Many upscale restaurants—and even some fast food facilities—have included private dining rooms or areas that can be closed off for large groups.

Private dining rooms give the guests and the host control over the atmosphere and food offerings, just as at home, without the need to clean up

Figure 5B-1 Wine room at the Old Hickory Restaurant, Gaylord Texan Resort & Convention Center, Grapevine, Texas. (Interior design by Wilson & Associates, Dallas, TX. Photographer Michael Wilson.)

when everyone leaves. The private dining room encourages large-group dining and is a great source of extra revenue. Some restaurants even charge an extra fee for the use of the private dining room in addition to the food and service charges.

A private dining room doesn't have to be closed off by doors, but it certainly can be. It might be a more private section of the restaurant with nearly full-height partitions to give it privacy. Most private dining rooms are designed to be closed off from other areas with a wall or doors of glass so that other diners can see the group and the group can see into the dining room. Glass walls help provide a feeling of spaciousness to the private dining space and might encourage other diners to reserve it in the future (Figure 5B-1).

Private dining rooms can be any size but are designed to seat a minimum of six guests. Of course, an intimate dinner for two can also be served in the space. Groups can also be bigger, based on the kinds of events the restaurant owner feels can be accommodated. The size and location of the dining room need to be carefully weighed against the location of the

kitchen. A large private dining room can prevent regular guests from being served promptly. (Have you ever been frustrated by the large busload of tourists that arrived minutes after you sat down for your one-hour lunch?) Should the business concept call for multiple private dining rooms, including a very large one, the owners and designer may need to consider a separate kitchen for these extra spaces.

Businesses have found the private dining room a great place to hold special business meetings. Restaurants for the business guest have audiovisual capabilities like plasma projection screens, conference room marker boards behind custom cabinets, and microphones (for larger spaces) in the design for the space.

The interior design generally mirrors that of the main dining room. However, if the space is private, the finishes and seating can be varied to make the room even more special. Elaborate custom millwork as a wall treatment, using a portion of the wine cellar as a backdrop, and special accessories in cabinets or on the walls are all possible in the private dining room.

Figure 5-18 Interior of Ferraro's Restaurant. Note the partial wall that helps divide the space. (Photograph courtesy of Realm Designs, Inc., Sandra F. Lambert, ASID, Warren, NJ. 908-753-3939.)

a measure of elegance to any upscale facility and even to a somewhat informal theme restaurant such as a dinner-only sports-theme restaurant. Yet, the uncovered tabletop might be just what is needed in more casual full-service facilities. Chain theme restaurants often forgo formalities like linen tablecloths to help remind guests of the diners of the 1960s.

The type of seating specified for the dining area conveys a lot to the customer about the kind of dining experience to expect. The size and style of the chair add much to the interior design and will have an impact on space allowances as well. The larger the chair, the more space seating will require and potentially will reduce the number of tables that can be used. Fully upholstered chairs indicate to the customer that the dining experience will be formal, with a leisurely pace throughout the meal. However, fully upholstered chairs are more difficult to maintain. Armchairs or armless chairs with an upholstered seat and back or just an upholstered seat are very common in most medium- to high-priced restaurants. Chairs also need to have sturdy frames and leg structure. Commercial-quality furniture is a must for dining chairs in restaurants.

Chairs on casters are specified in many restaurants. These chairs can be moved more easily by customers, especially on the carpeted floors. As in an office, if a caster is specified for carpet, it is best to use a double-wheel caster and also specify tight, short-tufted carpet. If a hard-surface flooring material is used, the chairs should be specified with nylon foot pads to make it easier to move the chairs. However, these foot pads can scratch wood floors. Dining chairs must be matched to the height of the tables, with seat heights at 18 inches above the floor when the table height is 27 to 30 inches above the floor.

Booths and banquettes have become popular in upscale restaurants. Booths can be designed with screens or other dividers that rise 4 feet or more above the seat, providing mini private dining rooms for diners who want privacy. Banquettes appeal to those who wish to be seen. Since booths or banquettes are commonly custom designed, care must be taken so that the seat is not too soft, which would make the table too high as well as

Figure 5-19 Fully upholstered chairs indicate that the dining experience will be formal, as in the Oak Room Restaurant, Castle at Tarrytown, New York. (Design by and photograph courtesy of Peter Gisolfi Assoc., Architects.)

make it difficult for guests to get in and out of the booth. Although older guests often prefer booths, this common design flaw makes it very difficult for older patrons to use booth or banquette seating satisfactorily.

Fabrics for chairs and seating units can provide a further background to an interesting arrangement of wall accessories or other thematic devices or enhance a restaurant where the walls are a background to interesting fabrics. Seating at upscale restaurants uses natural fabrics or other quality textiles to add to the ambience. Delicate fabrics in an upscale restaurant could be used on chair backs rather than the seats, which will get harder use. Fabrics should be commercial-grade materials that have inherent stain resistance or have been treated to repel most stains (Figure 5-19).

Patterned upholstery fabrics should be specified carefully so that the pattern is in scale with the chair or seating piece. Booths and banquettes should not be button tufted or otherwise deep tufted, since tufts are places for crumbs to accumulate. Vinyl is a good material for booth seats since it is easier to slide into a booth with a vinyl-covered rather than a fabric-covered cushion. Suede-style vinyl gives the look of leather at a lower cost.

Architectural finishes for floors and walls are important design elements in a restaurant since these surfaces are so large and visible. They can be treated as subtle backgrounds for interesting upholstery fabrics on seating, provide exciting accents in themselves through the patterns and treatments utilized, and pull the interior of a large space together into a cohesive whole. Ceiling and window treatments must be selected for ease of maintenance while helping to set an aesthetic backdrop. The treatment of these large surfaces must be carefully considered by the interior designer.

A medium-sized patterned carpet used throughout the dining room will call attention to the traffic path but hide wear caused by the traffic. This covering might be chosen over hard-surface materials for acoustical reasons. A tightly tufted carpet with a short pile of a nylon-wool blend will be especially good for maintenance, to hide traffic patterns, and to allow for easier movement of chairs. A smaller pattern can then be used to define the areas for tables and under booth tables. Resilient materials are appropriate at the wait stations and along the salad bar line. This variation of flooring materials will help differentiate functional areas, and the choices will considerably ease cleanup and maintenance.

Wall surfaces are huge "canvases" for enhancing the design concept or serving as a simple backdrop. Curved walls or walls with angles direct the flow of the dining room and can be an exciting way to divide the dining room into smaller, more intimate dining spaces. Pierced or closed screens, stained glass, upholstered panels, various kinds of wood trim pieces, and numerous other kinds of materials can be used above the divider walls to enhance the design concept. These walls can also help reduce noise.

Wall treatments that are more intricate, such as paneling with moldings at the ceiling and chair rails, are more expensive initially and to maintain over the long run. Maintenance is an important factor in the selection of wall treatments. In some situations, murals or large paintings help to "finish" the walls. Paint, the most economical wall material, should not be used in areas where chairs will scratch the wall surface. Paint applied above booth tops and chair rails can create interesting changes in wall materials. In other areas, fabric wallcoverings over acoustic panels that meet code requirements should be considered rather than painted walls. These acoustical panels will also help reduce noise. Hard-surface materials like mirrors, metals, paneling, and large expanses of glass are good utilitarian materials in the right situation but will be noisy.

Ceiling treatments can provide an interesting finishing touch to the interior or be ignored in the design. Ceilings are a challenge since they contain many necessary mechanical items. Light fixtures, HVAC vents, fire sprinkler heads, and perhaps music speakers can all interrupt the ceiling surface.

The most common treatment for the ceiling is painted drywall—a natural way to hide all these mechanical features. However, drywall is another hard surface that will add to the noise in the dining room. Acoustic ceiling tiles can be used instead to reduce levels and provides easier access to ceiling mechanical systems than drywall ceilings. Specially treated fabrics over acoustic fiberglass panels suspended from the ceiling might also be appropriate, depending on the codes in the jurisdiction. Suspended or dropped ceiling sections, fabric panels stretched above the dining area, and many other kinds of treatments or even accessories must be carefully planned with the lighting designer, the HVAC engineer, and the fire sprinkler engineer. These ceiling treatments cannot interfere with this important environmental and safety system.

Window treatments—if used at all—will also be selected to complement the theme and style of service. Window treatments must also be specified with the potential view and the environmental impact on the interior in mind. A table by the window facing the parking lot might be acceptable for a mid-priced restaurant located along the highway but totally unacceptable at an upscale establishment. It is also wonderful to watch the setting sun at a restaurant along the ocean; however, the setting sun in Las Vegas might be less pleasant to view if the architect has not specified energy-efficient windows. Materials used for the windows must meet the applicable codes in the jurisdiction. Strict code restrictions will affect the use of any fabrics for window treatments.

Color in the dining room can and should follow color psychology recommendations. The selection of colors not only creates an agreeable interior but also increases the guest's appetite. Colors that have strong appetite appeal are most of the colors in the warm section of the color wheel as well as true greens. The purples, yellow-greens, and mustard tones, as well as gray, have little appeal. Blues, seldom used in foods, are good colors for backgrounds. "To be more specific, a peak of appetite and agreeable sensations exists in the red-orange, and orange regions. Pleasure decreases at yellow-orange, increases again at yellow, reaches a low at yellow-green, and is restored at clear green."[23]

The lighting design in the dining area can be as functional as that of a fast food restaurant, mood enhancing in a high-end gourmet facility, and everything in between. Experts agree that interior lighting is very important for achieving a successful interior in a food and beverage facility. "Correct lighting enhances the mood of a dining area, the appeal of

---

[23]Mahnke and Mahnke, 1993, p. 102.

the food, and the efficiency of a kitchen. And yet, in each of these situations, 'correct' means an entirely different thing."[24] In the dining room and bar areas, lighting levels must be carefully calculated so that the proper selection of fixtures will provide the appropriate levels of light required for the design goals. All lighting should be on a dimmer system so that lighting levels can be changed to suit the time of day. The specification of general and accent lighting fixtures and light levels should enhance the concept of the total interior design.

Much of our psychological response to places, things, and events is based on our visual impressions. Lighting plays a significant part in promoting the comfort of the guest and providing a successful restaurant experience. Poorly designed lighting can hinder, if not destroy, that experience.

Only a few guests in certain hip restaurants enjoy being at a table with strong lighting that makes them the center of attention. Down lights should provide nonglare lighting on the table so that the guests are comfortable, and can easily read the menu and see their companion across the table. Having the fixtures on dimmer switches allows for changes in lighting levels to suit the time of day. Brighter light for the lunch crowd and softer lighting in the evening during dinnertime will be appropriate. When the interior designer wishes to use fixtures over a table, it is best to position these over fixed tables so that rearranging the tables does not cause overlighted or underlighted tables.

Many restaurants include outdoor dining in their concepts. Seating in these areas must be controlled by the host and provide easy access for the wait staff. Furniture items must be selected that can withstand changing weather conditions. A brief discussion on this subject has been included in the section on golf clubhouses in Chapter 10.

The Kitchen and Back of the House

The efficient and effective planning of the kitchen and the back-of-house area for a food service facility is critical to the financial success of the enterprise. Regardless of the type of facility, the space planning and equipment layout of the kitchen areas must include a careful functional analysis of the whole restaurant concept. Obviously, there are differences in the equipment needs and layout of different types and styles of food service. However, there are many common principles as well.

Commercial kitchen planning is done primarily by certified commercial kitchen planners or engineers. It is discussed in this section to provide functional information and an appreciation of the complexities and design decisions in the overall facility plan. We will consider the planning issues of the kitchen from receiving and storage through the food preparation. This is because kitchen planners are concerned about the flow of the food products into the facility and the plating of foods for service in the dining areas. In addition to the food preparation areas of the kitchen, depending on the size of the facility, additional back-of-the-house space will be allowed for the office and employee areas. These areas are discussed in this section as well. Table 5-3 in the Planning and Interior Design section provides planning estimates of space for the many production areas.

The receiving area should be located near the receiving door for stand-alone facilities or those in strip shopping centers. For the largest food service facilities or those in hotels and high-rise mixed-use buildings, the receiving area needs to be near a loading dock. Space is needed in this area for checkin and short-term storage until the food or other items can be moved to their proper storage area after inspection. Good lighting is needed here to aid in the inspection.

Local health department regulations usually do not allow trash and garbage to be removed through the receiving area to prevent contamination of fresh foods by garbage. The architect, kitchen designer, and/or interior designer will plan a second door near the ware washing area as an exit to the dumpsters and grease dumpsters.

Adjacent to the receiving area will be the various storage rooms or equipment for foodstuffs and dry goods. The square footage requirements for each of these areas will depend on the menu offered, the number of seats in the dining area, and the turnover at the facility. Storage space is needed for three types of goods: dry, refrigerated, and frozen. Bot-

---

[24]Katsigris, and Thomas, 2005, p. 185.

tles, cans, and boxes of food and beverage items that can be stored at room temperature are stored in a dry storage room or space. Dry storage also is needed for paper supplies, such as napkins, toilet paper, paper towels, takeout containers, and cloth items like tablecloths, napkins, and uniforms. Even though the dry storage room or rooms might be located on an outside wall, they should not be planned with windows to prevent theft. It is also recommended that interior partitions in storage areas be built from the slab to ceiling decking to prevent theft.

Cases of liquor are commonly kept in a separate locked portion of the dry storage area if a separate storage area by the bar is not provided. Of course, wine and beer storage requires temperature-controlled spaces. Cleaning supplies are also commonly kept in dry storage but must be separated from foodstuffs to meet health department regulations.

A variety of refrigeration units are needed. Large commercial-sized reach-in or walk-in refrigerators are used to store fresh meats, fish, produce, fruits, and dairy products. One or more commercial-sized reach-in or even walk-in refrigerators will be required. There are many options in the sizes and configurations of refrigerator units. These needs will be determined with input from the owner and chef to ensure that the right equipment is specified for current and anticipated needs. Small undercounter refrigerators are often placed in the cold foods plating areas as well as in the beverage area.

Reach-in and walk-in freezer units are the third type of storage for frozen foodstuffs. The location of the freezer units is important since, ideally, the floor will also be insulated if a walk-in freezer is used. A ramp will be needed unless the floor insulation is an integral part of the freezer unit. Walk-in refrigerators and freezers usually have galvanized steel, stainless steel, or ceramic tile walls and ceilings.

An office is necessary for the manager, head chef, and perhaps clerical staff. The manager's office is not commonly designed to be large or fancy; a minimum of 60 to 80 square feet is common. It provides the space and equipment needed to do the work and create a professional atmosphere for the occupant. It should be accessible by staff and guests. It is rare for guests to come to a manager's office, however. The manager may also require that the office have windows looking into the kitchen. Proper desk surfaces, lighting, and electrical service are needed for computer hardware. A safe is often provided in the manager's office. It is located to provide complete control and security for the handling of money and credit card receipts. In larger restaurants, an office is commonly provided for the chef as well. The chef's office should be accessible to and have visual control of the kitchen. Computers in the chef's office are standard as well to facilitate menu planning.

There is one more support space to consider in the kitchen area. Many mid-sized to large restaurants provide a separate area with employee lockers and restrooms. Too often these areas are undersized and poorly designed. Interior designers should specify employee areas that are well lighted, pleasant, and easy to maintain. Separate employee restrooms keep the staff—especially kitchen staff who may have soiled aprons—from public view.

Food preparation areas can be chaotic spaces. Anyone who spends time observing a commercial kitchen in action during the height of the dinner hour will quickly appreciate the importance of the planning required in the various food preparation areas. Each station and each staff member in the kitchen has a role to play in the preparation of food items, and these tasks and processes must be understood by the planner to ensure that the kitchen is planned for efficiency, safety, and logical work flow.

Food preparation work areas vary considerably based on the type of restaurant and the service style. Food preparation areas, or kitchens for simplicity, are generally space planned into four basic areas—pre-preparation, cold-food preparation, hot-food preparation, and the sanitary or warewashing area. Many table service establishments also include a bakery area for dessert and bread preparation. A separate salad preparation area might be needed in large restaurants. The variety of menu items, size of the dining room, and location and size of the lounge all impact the space needed for each preparation area.

All refrigerated or frozen foods begin their journey to the guest's table at the pre-preparation—or *pre-prep*—area. Preparation includes cleaning salad items, peeling potatoes, making salad dressings, or otherwise preparing hot and cold menu items before they are cooked and/or plated. Meats and fish are also pre-prepared in another section of this

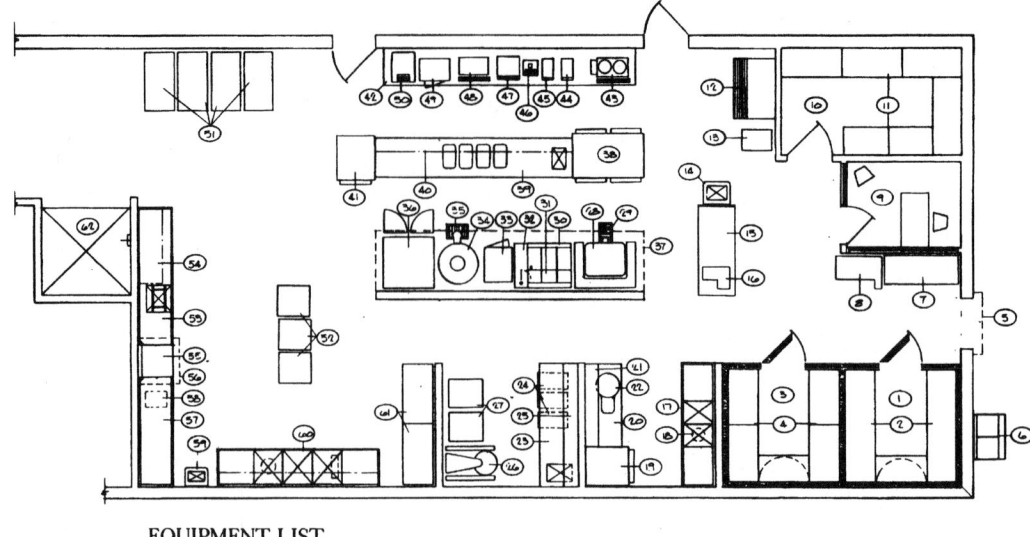

EQUIPMENT LIST

ITEM	DESCRIPTION		
1	WALK IN FREEZER	32	SPACER W/POT FILLER
2	WALK IN FREEZER SHELVING	33	STEAMER
3	WALK IN COOLER	34	40-GAL. KETTLE
4	WALK IN COOLER SHELVING	35	FLOOR GRATE
5	AIR CURTAIN FAN	36	CONVECTION OVEN
6	WALK IN COOLER/FREEZER	37	EXHAUST HOOD W/FIRE SYSTEM
	COMPRESSORS	38	PASS THRU REFRIGERATOR
7	RECEIVING TABLE	39	HOT FOOD COUNTER W/SINK
8	SCALE	40	OVERSHELF
9	OFFICE	41	FREEZER
10	STORAGE ROOM	42	BEVERAGE COUNTER
11	STORAGE ROOM SHELVING	43	COFFEE URN
12	ICE MACHINE	44	HOT CHOCOLATE DISPENSER
13	ICE CART	45	ICED TEA DISPENSER
14	HAND SINK—TABLE MOUNTED	46	WATER DISPENSER
15	WORKTABLE	47	JUICE DISPENSER
16	SLICER	48	MILK DISPENSER
17	VEGETABLE PREP SINK	49	MICROWAVE OVEN
18	DISPOSER	50	TOASTER
19	REFRIGERATOR	51	TRANSPORT CARTS
20	WORKTABLE	52	DISH CARTS
21	OVERSHELF	53	SOILED DISHTABLE
22	FOOD CUTTER	54	RACKSHELF
23	BAKE TABLE W/SINK	55	DISHWASHER
24	INGREDIENT BINS	56	EXHAUST HOOD
25	OVERSHELF	57	CLEAN DISHTABLE
26	MIXER	58	BOOSTER HEATER
27	PROOF CABINETS	59	HAND SINK
28	BRAISING PAN	60	POT & PAN SINK W/DISPOSER
29	FLOOR GRATE		SINK HEATER & OVERSHELF
30	HOT TOP RANGE W/OVEN	61	CLEAN POT STORAGE SHELVING
31	SALAMANDER BROILER	62	CART WASH

Figure 5-20 Commercial kitchen. (From *Manual of Equipment and Design for the Foodservice Industry* by Carl R. Scriven and James W. Scriven, pages 49 and 50 © 1989 by Van Nostand Reinhold. Reprinted with permission.)

area. Sinks, worktables, and food processors are some of the common pieces of equipment in this area of the kitchen. Meat saws, grinders, and slicers are also needed for meat preparation. In larger restaurants, ranges and ovens may also be included in this portion of the kitchen (Figure 5-20).

The cold-food preparation area is where salads, some appetizers, cold sandwiches, and perhaps desserts are assembled and plated. The cold-food area needs to be adjacent to refrigerators and adequate worktables for the chef to prepare and plate food items. In large full-service restaurants or other types that have a significant assortment of cold food items on the menu, a separate pickup location in the cold-food preparation area is often planned. Handwash sinks are also required in the cold-food prep area.

The largest amount of space and greatest variety of equipment are required for the hot-food production area. The arrangement of the equipment for the *hot line* will vary with the menu and cooking methods. Hot foods might be cooked by a dry method—that is, using no liquids; broiling and roasting are examples. When food is cooked using liquids, such as boiled potatoes and steamed foods, the method is considered moist cooking. The hot-food production area is where the ranges, ovens, broilers, grills, griddles, deep fryers, and other equipment for hot-food cooking are organized. Many pieces of this equipment will be required by the health department to be under venting hoods. The hot-food preparation area will also require a handwash sink.

Food flows from the hot and cold preparation area to pickup stations. Hot foods will generally be plated ready for serving to guests when placed on the pickup station counters under heat lamps or on steam tables to keep them hot until picked up by servers. Cold foods will also be passed to the pickup area if a separate pickup station in the cold prep area has not been planned. In many situations, the final plating of cold foods is done by the serving staff. For example, they may place salad dressings or condiments on the cold items prepared by the kitchen staff. Roll warmers, soup warmers, and a microwave oven are often located at the pickup station. In many upscale and large restaurants, very little of the dish preparation will be done by dining room staff, as the chef will complete the dish ready for service before it is placed on the pickup station worktable.

The pickup area should be located immediately adjacent to the exits into the dining room, though sometimes this is not possible. The better the arrangement and planning of the pickup area in relation to the kitchen and the exit into the dining areas, the better the traffic flow. If the facility is a fast food or quick service establishment, the flow from kitchen to servers must be direct. When the service expectations are more leisurely, as in upscale table service restaurants, traffic flow must be designed somewhat more indirectly so that the clanking of dishes and the noise of the kitchen are not heard in the dining room. As much as possible the flow of staff traffic and guest circulation should be separated.

The warewashing area, where dirty dishes are brought from the dining area and kitchen pots and pans are scraped and washed, is a noisy, messy area in the kitchen. It should be located relatively close to where the servers or bus persons reenter from the dining room, but should also be convenient for kitchen staff for cleaning pots and pans. The warewashing area needs a worktable adjacent to garbage bins, work space to store dishes and flatware until they are ready to be put in the dishwashers, and workspace or a place for dishware carts at the end of the dishwasher unit for stacking clean dishes and flatware. Deep sinks in a series of three units are needed to wash pots and pans and other cooking utensils. The pot-washing area can be adjacent to the dish washing area or near the hot-food preparation area, depending on the chef's and owner's preference and local code restrictions.

Materials specification for walls, floors, and ceiling in the kitchen is very important to ensure cleanliness and safety. All surfaces must be grease resistant and nonporous to allow for easy and frequent cleaning. Therefore, stainless steel, ceramic tile, and fiberglass panels designed for kitchen use are specified. Floors must be nonslippery and grease resistant. Many kitchens use sealed concrete for the floors, but nonglazed, nonporous, and slip-resistant ceramic tile is also a possibility.

Direct lighting systems are most frequently used in the kitchen. They provide good overall lightning so that chefs and kitchen staff can properly prepare foods and work in a safe environment. Thirty to 40 foot-candles are needed for most working areas and 15 to 20 foot-candles for nonwork general lighting. Good color rendition is needed in the food preparation area so that chefs and kitchen staff can ensure that only fresh food is being prepared. Light colors for walls and ceiling surfaces will aid in the overall lighting needs in the kitchen. Color-correcting fluorescent or incandescent lamps are recommended. Using incandescent lamps in the kitchen means that the food will be prepared under the same light used in the dining room. However, this will be prohibitively expensive in terms of energy use. White light fluorescent fixtures do not give the color rendition needed in the preparation areas.

Specialty Kitchens

There are two types of specialty kitchens that might be part of a restaurant concept. A popular type of kitchen in many restaurant concepts is the *display kitchen*, a cooking area in the dining room positioned so that the guest can watch the chef prepare food. The specialty kitchen was probably inspired by early diners and remains popular in many types of restaurants. Many customers feel that the best seat in the restaurant is one where they can get a good view of the chef at work in an elaborate display kitchen. In fact, some restaurants include a group dining table in the kitchen so that guests can watch all the action. In the guest's mind, there is something special in seeing his meal prepared right before his eyes. It also adds to the entertainment value of many restaurants, as guests get to watch the chef create their meals. Planning must be carefully done so that the display kitchen's location and design are well ordered and enhance the "show." Location of display kitchens must place an emphasis on seeing the faces of the chefs as they cook and keeping the messy work of cooking out of sight. This can be done more easily with half-walls topped with glass panels, an arrangement referred to as a semiopen kitchen.

Cleanliness and customer safety are as necessary in the design of the display kitchen space as in food preparation itself. Open flame grills need to be located on a back wall away from the guest or protected with heat-resistant glass. Decorative wall finishes must be selected or treated for easy cleaning. Accent lights will help dramatize the theatrical elements of the display kitchen but also need to be planned to ensure the safety and functional needs of the chefs.

Another specialty kitchen is the *marche kitchen*. "If you can walk up to a stand-alone counter, place an order, and get fresh food, cooked to order, as you wait, you are in a marche kitchen."[25] If you have gone to a sandwich shop that has very few tables or one where you stand and watch as your sandwich or other foods are prepared and then carry your own tray to a table, you have visited a marche kitchen. These are not cafeterias where the food is prepared behind kitchen doors. Marche kitchens are based on European-style shops where the kitchen equipment is in full view as the cooks prepare your food. In today's versions, plain walls and lots of simple stainless steel architectural treatments in the cooking areas are augmented by bright ceramic tiles, faux finishes, and other decorative treatments to make the cooking area more attractive. In many respects, marche kitchens are similar to some delicatessens and fast food restaurants in the United States.

Beverage Facilities

Beverage facilities, more commonly referred to as bars and lounges, are places where alcoholic beverages are served. Of course, many restaurants do not sell alcoholic beverages and do not have a bar. The location within that type of restaurant is commonly referred to as the beverage area. In this section, we discuss facilities that sell alcoholic beverages.

The vast majority of restaurants provide beverage service. People patronize bars and lounges to socialize. It is important for the designer to remember this as he or she creates an atmosphere conducive to meeting people, meeting friends for dancing, enjoying a sporting event on a wide-screen television, or even waiting for a table in the dining room.

One type of beverage service facility is the *bar*. These establishments—especially the older, more traditional ones—might also be called pubs, taverns, or saloons and can serve drinks with little or no food service. The term bar also defines the cabinet and display areas where drinks are mixed and poured by a bartender. Bars are usually smaller than spaces called lounges. A bar often provides less seating than a lounge, generally at the bar itself or at small booths or tables.

A lounge has more comfortable seating and is more often associated with higher-end restaurants, hotels, and live stage entertainment such as nightclubs and show lounges in casinos. In a lounge, the bar itself may not have seating at the bar cabinet. Seating commonly consists of small-scale lounge chairs at small tables or groups of small sofas for the

[25]Katsigris and Thomas, 2005, p. 56.

patrons. Many lounges have a dance floor with music provided by a jukebox or small band (Figure 5-21). Show lounges where various performances are offered are usually larger than lounges in restaurants, where live entertainment is less ambitious.

Many restaurants provide some kind of alcoholic beverage service even if they do not have a separate beverage area. The focus of this discussion is on a bar or lounge in a restaurant. Concepts, however, can easily be applied to beverage areas in hotels, freestanding facilities, or other types of facilities (Figure 5-22).

The beverage area in a restaurant can take many forms. It is quite common for it to be separated from the dining room so that patrons can use just the beverage service area. In a restaurant catering to families, the bar is also separate so that children do not need to go into or near the bar. Alternately, the beverage area might be a small area in a section of the dining room with no bar seating provided as shown in Figure 5-10a. In other cases, the beverage area might be as simple as a beer on tap or items served from a cooler in the kitchen.

Jurisdictional issues can impact the location of the bar and its relationship to other areas of the restaurant. An increasingly important consideration in the placement and design of the beverage area is the jurisdiction's regulations about smoking in public spaces. If smoking is allowed, most laws require that the smoking area be only in the bar. Ideally, the bar is then physically separated by full-height partition walls to contain the smoke. A jurisdiction's building code may also disallow a space plan in which patrons must go through the beverage area to reach the restrooms.

Today's upscale restaurants and bars bring exciting design possibilities to an area that many members of the

Figure 5-21 Bar and lounge, creative interpretation with fabric dividers highlighted and a combination of banquettes and stools for seating. Zen Bar. (Photograph courtesy of 3D/International. Photography by Al Rendon.)

Figure 5-22 Example of a bar area functioning separately from a dining room. (Photograph courtesy of Burke, Hogue & Mills Architects.)

post–World War II generation remember as a smoky, beer-smelling, dark place. Designers often create theatrical backdrops for the bar itself and use exciting lighting design to heighten an atmosphere that will draw crowds. Of course, not all beverage areas are theatrically designed. A beverage area in family restaurants and in many chains is designed as a pleasant accompaniment to the dining room.

The bar itself consists of the *front bar,* with or without stools for patrons, and a *back bar* for display and storage. Elaborate front and back bar millwork designs are an interesting challenge for designers. The creative display of bottles and glasses often becomes a focal point of many lounges and bars. What most people refer to as the "bar" is the guest's view of the front bar cabinet. Behind this is the back bar where bottles are displayed. Figure 5-23 provides dimensional guidelines for these items.

Bar stools at the front bar should have a seat height of 30 inches above the floor, assuming that the top of the bar is the standard 42 to 45 inches above the floor. Because of their height, bar stools should never be specified with casters. Some design concepts will specify bar stools that are fixed to the floor. This is, of course, safer but is purely a design/function decision. Design concepts sometimes use a footrest or footrail 7 to 9 inches above the floor. The footrail can help to protect the millwork from damage (Figure 5-24).

Behind the front bar are the under bar and the back bar. The *under bar* is the main working area for the bartender as he or she faces the guest. The *back bar* functions as the display area for the different liquors and for glasses, with storage space below for beer bottles, extra liquor bottles, and other accessories needed at the bar. The bar countertop should be between 18 and 24 inches deep, and the total depth of the under bar will need

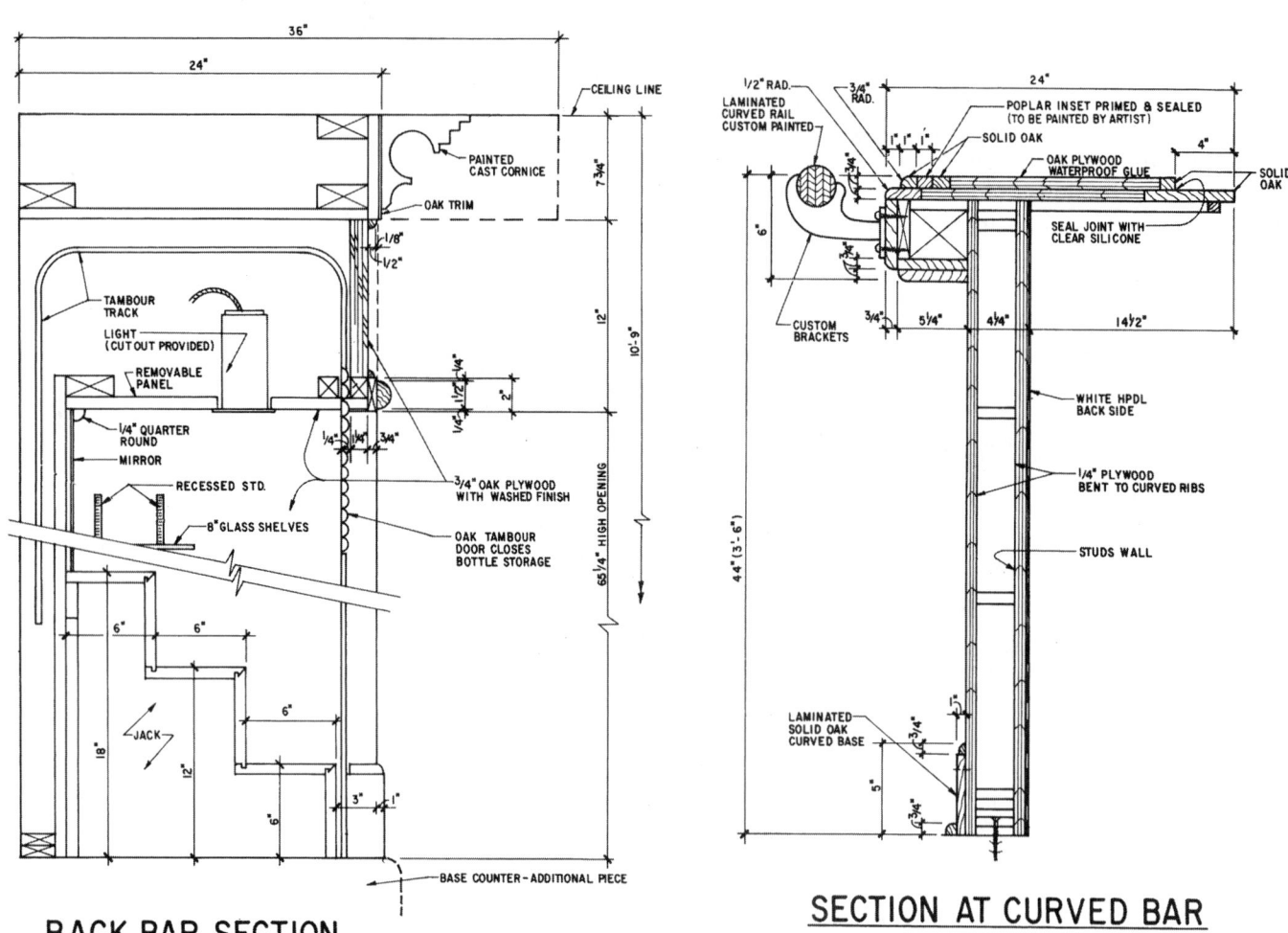

BACK BAR SECTION

SECTION AT CURVED BAR

Figure 5-23 Detailed drawing of a back bar and a curved bar. (Reprinted with permission from *Design Solutions Magazine,* published by the Architectural Woodwork Institute, Reston, VA.)

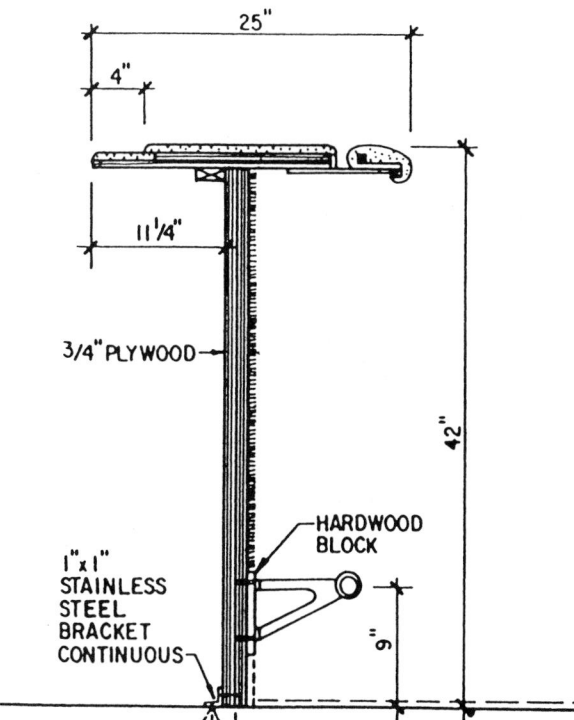

Figure 5-24 Detailed drawing of a footrail and countertop of a bar. (Reprinted with permission from *Design Solutions Magazine*, published by the Architectural Woodwork Institute, Reston, VA.)

to be 22 to 26 inches deep. The under bar includes many activity areas and has specific equipment and size needs. At the top, a *speed rail* is located to hold bottles of the house or "well" beverages so that bartenders can get to these quickly. A four-compartment sink for cleaning and sanitizing glassware, draining space for glassware, ice bins and under-counter storage, soda guns for dispensing soda, and beer taps are other equipment items of the under bar. Refrigerators may be placed here but are more likely located at the back bar.

The back bar provides display space for liquor bottles and glassware. It will be between 24 and 30 inches deep. It will be deeper if the design of the total bar has guest seating all the way around an island-shaped bar. Beverage areas need a variety of glassware, depending on the line of beverages served. Ten or more different kinds of glasses might be needed for a bar serving a full range of beverages. Bottles are displayed on tiered shelves so that the customers and bartenders can easily spot the different brands. The back bar will also have undercounter refrigerators for cold beer and wine storage and counter space for the cash register or computer. Closed storage for back stock is also common in the design.

The space between the back bar and the bar is called the activity zone. It is between 30 and 36 inches wide. This provides a comfortable space for the bartender to work between the bar and back bar without taking extra steps. Thirty-six inches allow sufficient space for one bartender to work at one of the cabinets while another bartender walks behind him or her.

Storage space in the bar area will be required for extra cases of liquor, wine, and beer. This storage space can be placed in proximity to the bar or in the kitchen. Regardless of the location, it must be planned as a secure space to prevent theft. It should also be shielded from sunlight and fluctuating temperatures. A large bar may need a separate beer cooler to hold kegs.

A service bar will be required at one end of the bar or at another appropriate location along the front bar. The *service bar* is where the wait staff orders and picks up beverages to take to the dining room. In some facilities, it is a window and shelf through the wall adjoining the dining room, with the window out of sight of dining guests. In larger facilities it may be larger, requiring compact under and back bars and a separate bartender. When a service bar is not possible, an area at the end of the bar is designed to accommodate the place where the wait staff will pick up drink orders from the bar. A POS computer would also be needed so that the wait staff can keep track of beverage orders for diners.

Generally, the furniture and finishes specified for the bar are similar to those used in the restaurant. In some cases, the design of the bar sets the tone for the dining room, and the bar will be more theatrical in design, lighting, and even furniture items than those used in the dining area (Figure 5-25).

Furniture in a beverage area generally consists of small tables and chairs, bar stools and booths, or banquettes and tables. Tables in beverage areas often are only 25 to 27 inches high to allow patrons to lounge in the more comfortable seating units often found in bars and lounges. Chair seat heights in this case will average 16 inches above the floor for these lower tables. Lounges often use more soft seating groups of loveseats and comfortable club chairs, providing the look of a living room to some of the areas in the lounge. Tables in this case are very sturdy coffee tables so that they will not break if sat upon. Fabric specification should also consider flammability standards. Understanding local code requirements concerning fabric and seating unit specification is very important in the design of beverage areas.

As an alternative to lower tables and soft seating groups, some bars use hi-top tables with tall bar stools. These tables are 42 to 45 inches high so that patrons can either sit on a stool or stand. Many of these designs include a footrail of some sort. Again, the stools should not be on casters for safety.

Lighting in the bar or lounge is usually more subdued than in the dining areas. Lower light levels are created by the use of low-wattage indirect ambient and accent fixtures. Other common accent lighting in the lounge is supplemented by candles in containers for safety. Bars designed with entertainment in mind present many lighting design challenges. One challenge is to provide sufficient light for guests seated at tables and booths engaged in conversation. Another is the lighting effects that might be needed to create the theatri-

Figure 5-25 Lounge using banquettes and low tables for a cozy atmosphere. (Photograph courtesy of 3D/International. Al Rendon, photographer.)

cal or entertainment concepts of the space. These effects are produced with a wide variety of accent lights and spotlights using colored lamps or filters. The lighting designer hired to prepare the lighting design for the restaurant is commonly retained to plan the lighting for the bar as well.

Architectural finishes will need to meet code requirements for life safety. Since smoking is more prevalent in a bar or lounge, the designer should specify flame-resistant and smolder-resistant upholstery on any seating. Local jurisdictions may have other building and safety code requirements for a lounge or bar. Accessibility regulations apply to this space as well. The plan must provide clear passage from the entry to seating areas for a patron who is physically disabled. The plan must also allow for access to all parts of the beverage area should there be sunken or raised areas. Of course, not every seat needs to be accessible.

Toilet Facilities in Restaurants

Food and beverage establishments are required by code to have toilet facilities for customers. Attractive restrooms that are well maintained and well designed help to enhance the quality of the facility. (Who hasn't visited a messy restroom, only to wonder if the kitchen is any cleaner?) Owners do not always allow a large budget for restrooms, but that is no excuse for boring all-white toilet facilities with only colored partitions to bring relief. The designer and the facility owner should recognize that the restroom facilities, along with all other public areas, help create an impression of the overall quality of the food service facility.

Toilet facilities are located either off the waiting area or toward the back of the facility adjoining the kitchen. They should be located to provide privacy for those using the facilities while others are entering and exiting the restrooms. Large restrooms will also be noisy, and locating them to the rear of the dining room will help reduce the noise of traffic to the facility. Separate restrooms will be required for men and women unless the occupancy is small enough to allow a unisex restroom. In smaller restaurants, guests and employees use the same facilities. The space allowances for public restrooms are provided in Chapter 9. This section will briefly discuss the interior design of these facilities.

As in any public restroom in a commercial property, all surfaces must be specified with durability, easy maintenance, and moisture resistance in mind. Ceramic tile, plastic laminate, and moisture-resistant vinyl wallcoverings can be used for wall treatments. High-quality sheet vinyl, linoleum, or ceramic tiles are most commonly specified for the flooring. Local codes may require specific types of materials behind the lavatories and on the walls by the water closets or urinals. The architect will also specify a floor drain in the restrooms. Baby-changing stations in both men's and women's restrooms have become quite common and may be required by local codes.

Good lighting is needed especially in the women's restroom since touching up makeup and fixing hair require good light. Over-mirror fixtures or sections of mirrors with lighting fixtures placed vertically between them to avoid glare on the mirrors provide appropriate lighting without adding significantly to the cost. It is common, though not required by code, to provide extra space and counters in the women's restroom for applying makeup, retouching hair, and conversation. Upscale restaurants provide a small amount of space in the women's restroom for a lounge to accommodate these activities. This part of the restroom is carpeted and specified with small chairs.

Coffee Shops

Coffee houses probably became popular in the West in the 17th century. Europeans used the coffee house as a social center—much like the coffee shop in the late 20th century. People gather in the early morning for their favorite coffee drink, come back after lunch, and even linger until the proprietor "throws them gently out" at closing time.

Patrons meet friends and socialize, meet new friends, hold informal business meetings, read a book, or just go to a coffee shop to get away from the house or office for a while. With so many coffee shops opening almost everywhere, congregating at a coffee shop on a regular basis has created a renaissance in this facility's construction and design. Coffee shops are commonly located in strip malls, large shopping malls, the ground floor of many high-rise office buildings, or perhaps as a freestanding facility. Coffee shops are also found in bookstores, grocery stores, and some upscale home centers or furniture stores. There are even drive-in versions so that the guest does not need to leave the car.

Most coffee shops are small, with limited indoor seating, but the trend is toward larger shops with a lot of tables and soft seating. If the shop is more for the guest "on the go," the space will likely be under 1000 square feet. If limited food service is part of the concept or if the shop is in a location where guests will stay and lounge or meet for longer time periods, the space will need to be larger. At least 50 percent of the floor space should be for seating, with about 25 percent for the preparation of coffee and other items and the remainder for the service counter.[26]

The entry should move guests easily to either the service bar/cash register or seating areas. Space is always needed in front of or along the service bar for waiting guests to order and pick up their beverages. These spaces need to be kept organized—though few customers seem to mind mingling between the cash register and pickup window. Displays of bakery goods and sandwiches next to and along the service area are common.

Since coffee consumers enjoy watching their favorite beverage prepared, the coffee and beverage preparation areas need to be visible. Espresso machines can be intricate in their design or efficiently oriented for faster service. This equipment can thus be an important design element in the interior.

Space will be needed either in the production area or in the back storage areas for dishwashing equipment. Sinks will also be needed for rinsing dishes, and a separate hand-washing sink will be required in the production area. When bakery and sandwich items are served or porcelain coffee mugs are used, these items might be located in the back area out of sight of the customer. The design of the product and service areas must carefully consider locations for the disposal of paper cups, other trash, and other dishes used by the customers.

Key to the interior design of a coffee shop is the aroma of coffee and soothing music serving as a backdrop to relaxing colors and easy-to-care-for materials and finishes. The interior design and furniture items might convey the feeling of an Old World café using simple armless chairs and 24- to 36-inch-diameter tables. Large, comfortable soft seating upholstered in durable fabrics that will handle spills, pens, and patrons' shoes is quite common. The coffee shop could also be high-tech, using finishes that appeal to the "techi" consumer. For the most part, the interior design should be both comfortable and easy to maintain.

Lighting levels are higher than in many restaurants, as most patrons are reading or working. However, as wireless connectivity for laptop computers increases, lighting should not be so intense as to create glare. Maybe this is the authors' personal wish, but extra electrical outlets to plug in laptop power cords certainly would be appreciated!

A receiving and storage area will be needed behind the visible production area and seating spaces. The business concept will drive the size of the back spaces. If food is prepared on site, a small commercial kitchen will be necessary. Less kitchen space will be needed when packaged foods (such as cookies in wrappers) are sold. Storage for supplies like disposable coffee cups, condiments, and perhaps a larger refrigerator for milk and creamers can also be accommodated in the back area. A small space for the manager's desk near the receiving and storage area is ideal to check in deliveries, place orders, and conduct other business activities.

Many coffee shops also sell coffee beans, coffee makers and cups, teas, and other items. Cabinets or display fixtures will be needed for these items. A cabinet will also be needed for condiments and straws, napkins, and possibly silverware.

Codes will require at least a men's and a women's restroom that are accessible. The size and number of fixtures will increase with the size of the facility. Designers should

---

[26]Entrepreneur Press and Lynn, 2001, p. 87.

keep accessibility regulations in mind as they design the space plan of the service area and access to tables and restrooms. Codes might affect the designer's choice of materials for architectural surfaces and upholstery. However, since most coffee shops do not use carpeting or allow smoking (avoiding the need for higher-rated fabrics on any soft seating), these code issues are less critical than in most other restaurants.

Summary

The food and beverage specialty is highly competitive and demanding. Good functional and aesthetic design supports the overall success of the establishment. Many owners who focus attention on the food and service and neglect the interior see their revenues suffer. The interior designer should diplomatically educate the owner on how good interior design adds to the overall value of the facility and enhances the success of facilities of any type or size.

Working in the food and beverage facilities design area can be an exciting and creative way to use one's skills as an interior designer. The continual updating of existing facilities, as well as those that change from one type of restaurant to another, and the construction of large numbers of new establishments means that opportunities to design food and beverage facilities will remain high. Development and operating costs are very high, and the owner will expect the interior design consultant to help create an interior facility that increases the chance of success.

This chapter began with a discussion of the importance of bringing the business concepts, theme, and menu ideas together in a unified interior design solution. It also emphasized the importance of handling functional issues of traffic flow, workplace design in the kitchen, and safety for staff and guests while meeting code requirements. A discussion of the different types of facilities set the stage for a description of the detailed planning and design criteria for a generic full-service restaurant with a beverage facility. The chapter also included a design application discussion of the very popular coffee shop.

REFERENCES

Atkin, William Wilson and Joan Alder. 1960. *Interiors Book of Restaurants.* New York: Watson-Guptill.

Baraban, Regina and Joseph F. Durocher. 2001. *Successful Restaurant Design,* 2nd ed. New York: Wiley.

Birchfield, John C. 1988. *Design and Layout of Foodservice Facilities.* New York: Van Nostrand Reinhold.

Birchfield, John C. and Raymond T. Sparrowe. 2003. *Design and Layout of Foodservice Facilities,* 2nd ed. New York: Wiley.

Brown, Douglas Robert. 2003. *The Restaurant Manager's Handbook,* 3rd ed. Oscala, FL: Atlantic Publishing Group.

Casamassima, Christy. 1999. *Bar Excellence.* New York: PBC International.

———. 2000. *Restaurant 2000.* New York: PBC International.

Cohen, Edie Lee and Sherman R. Emery. 1984. *Dining by Design.* New York: Cahners.

Colgan, Susan. 1987. *Restaurant Design: Ninety-Five Spaces That Work.* New York: Watson-Guptill.

Davies, Thomas D. and Kim A. Beasley. 1994. *Accessible Design for Hospitality,* 2nd ed. New York: McGraw-Hill.

Dittmer, Paul R. and Gerald G. Griffin. 1993. *Dimensions of the Hospitality Industry.* New York: Van Nostrand Reinhold.

Dorf, Martin. 1992. *Restaurants That Work.* New York: Watson-Guptill.

Entrepreneur Press and Jacquelyn Lynn. 2001. *Start Your Own Restaurant & Five Other Food Businesses.* Santa Monica, CA: Entrepreneur Press.

Goya, Lynn. 2004. "Destination Restaurants." *ASID ICON.* Spring, pp. 12–16.

International Code Council, Inc. 2003. *International Building Code.* Falls Church, VA: International Code Council, Inc.

Katsigris, Costas and Chris Thomas. 2005. *Design and Equipment for Restaurants and Foodservice,* 2nd ed. New York: Wiley.

Katz, Jeff B. 1997. *Restaurant Planning: Design and Construction.* New York: Wiley.

Kazarian, Edward A. 1989. *Food Service Facilities Planning,* 3rd ed. New York: Van Nostrand Reinhold.

Kliczkowski, H. 2002. *Cafés: Designers & Design.* Barcelona: Loft Publications.

Kopacz, Jeanne. 2004. *Color in Three-Dimensional Design.* New York: McGraw-Hill.

Kotschevar, Lendal H. and Mary L. Tanke. 1991. *Managing

Bar and Beverage Operations. East Lansing, MI: American Hotel and Motel Association Educational Institute.

Langdon, Philip. *The Architecture of American Chain Restaurants.* 1986. New York: Alfred A. Knopf.

Lundberg, Donald E. 1985. *The Restaurant: From Concept to Operation.* New York: Wiley.

Mahnke, Frank H. and Rudolf H. Mahnke. 1993. *Color and Light in Man-Made Environments.* New York: Van Nostrand Reinhold.

McGowan, Maryrose, and Kelsey Kruse. 2004. *Interior Graphic Standards.* Student Ed. Hoboken, NJ: Wiley.

Melaniphy, John C. 1992. *Restaurant and Fast Food Site Selection.* New York: Wiley.

Mount, Charles Morris. 1995. *The New Restaurant: Dining Design 2.* New York: Architecture and Interior Design Library (PBC International, Inc.).

Ninemeier, Jack D. 1987. *Planning and Control for Food and Beverage Operations,* 2nd ed. East Lansing, MI: American Hotel and Motel Association Educational Institute.

Ragan, Sandra L. 1995. *Interior Color by Design: Commercial.* Rockport, MA: Rockport.

Rey, Anthony M. and Ferdinand Wieland. 1985. *Managing Service in Food and Beverage Operations.* East Lansing, MI: American Hotel and Motel Association Educational Institute.

Robson, Stephani. "Strategies for Designing Effective Restaurants." *Implications.* InformDesign, Vol. 2, Issue 11.

Schlosser, Eric. 2001. *Fast Food Nation.* New York: Perennial/HarperCollins.

Scoviak, Mary. 1996. "Hotels: The Next Generation." *Interior Design.* June, pp. 150–151.

Stein, Benjamin, John S. Reynolds, and William J. McGuinness. 1986. *Mechanical and Electrical Equipment for Buildings,* 7th ed. New York: Wiley.

Stevens, James W. and Carl R. Scrinen. 2000. *Manual of Equipment and Design for the Foodservice Industry,* 2nd ed. Weimer, TX: CHIPS Books.

Stipanuk, David M. and Harold Roffmann. 1992. *Hospitality Facilities Management and Design.* East Lansing, MI: American Hotel and Motel Association Educational Institute.

Walker, John R. 1996. *Introduction to Hospitality.* Englewood Cliffs, NJ: Prentice Hall.

Walker, John R. and Donald E. Lundberg. 2005. *The Restaurant from Concept to Operation,* 4th ed. New York: Wiley.

Wallace L. Rande. 1996. *Introduction to Professional Food Service.* New York: Wiley.

Witzel, Michael Karl. 1994. *The American Drive-In.* Osceola, WI: Motorbooks International.

WEB SITES

American Institute of Wine & Food (AIWF) www.aiwf.org

Club Managers Association of America magazine www.club-mgmt.com

International Hotel & Restaurant Association www.ih-ra.com

National Restaurant Association (NRA) www.restaurant.org

Food and Drink Magazine www.fooddrink-magazine.com

Hospitality Design Magazine www.hdmag.com

InformDesign newsletter. www.informdesign.umn.edu.

Restaurant Hospitality magazine www.restaurant-hospitality.com

Note: Additional references related to material in this chapter are listed in the Appendix.

6

Retail Facilities

Working as an interior designer in the retail store specialty area is not only exciting, it also means being involved in a very large part of the U.S. economy. Retailing is the second largest industry in the United States, generating $3.8 trillion in sales annually and providing about 11.7 percent of U.S. employment. In 2004, the single largest retailer in the United States reported sales of over $250 billion per year. Grocery stores represent the single largest sector among the top 100 retailers in the United States.[1] Retail stores selling all types of merchandise are being built or remodeled. The top 10 interior design firms specializing in retail interiors among the *Interior Design* magazine "Giants" accounted for over $137 million in revenue in 2005.[2]

Retailing consists of all activities involved in the sale of goods and services to the ultimate consumer. Retail stores are established by independent owners, as franchises of

---

[1]Vargas, Melody. "Top 100 Retailers Rankings," *Your Guide to Retail Industry,* March 23, 2005. www.retailindustry.about.com
[2]Judith Davidsen, *Interior Design* Magazine, January, 2005, p. 128.

retail chains, and as store ownership groups or corporations. The interior design of a store plays a significant role in the success of that business. The layout and design of a store must provide the backdrop to best present the merchandise mix and simultaneously encourage customers to purchase the products or services offered.

Personal shopping excursions do not provide the interior design student or design professional with sufficient information and experience to understand how to create an effective and functional retail interior design solution. It is critical for the designer to understand something about the client's business and retail business in general in order to make appropriate design decisions.

This chapter provides the reader with a basic understanding of the functional considerations and design methodologies involved in retail design. It focuses on interior design issues related to *retail stores* that sell merchandise to the end user. It describes the criteria concerning the planning and design of retail spaces and provides a number of typical

TABLE 6-1 Chapter Vocabulary

- **BOUTIQUE SYSTEM:** A store planning system that arranges the sales floor into individual, semiseparate areas, each possibly built around a shopping theme that focuses on the individuality of the product.
- **CHAIN STORE:** A retail store with multiple locations that may be regional or national in scope. Can also be considered a franchise store.
- **CONVENIENCE MERCHANDISE:** Goods that are commonly used and often purchased, such as hosiery.
- **DEMAND MERCHANDISE:** A necessary item, such as a shirt or pants, that encourages the public to shop.
- **DEPARTMENT STORE:** A retail store that offers a wide variety of brands and product offerings.
- **DISPLAY FIXTURES:** A variety of cabinets and other equipment used to display a wide range of goods.
- **FREE-FLOW SYSTEM:** A store planning system that allows displays and fixtures to be moved easily.
- **GRID SYSTEM:** A store planning system that utilizes the internal layout in combination with the structural columns.
- **HARD GOODS:** Heavier merchandise that is often made of metal or wood, such as furniture, appliances, and sporting goods.
- **IMPULSE MERCHANDISE:** Unplanned purchases by the customer that depend upon good display—usually at the point of sale.
- **MAGNET STORE:** A large, well-known chain store that attracts a large number of customers. Also referred to as an *anchor store.*
- **MALL:** A large regional shopping center with many specialty stores and one or more magnet stores. It attracts customers from a large area. It might be enclosed or open.
- **MARKETING:** All the activities used to move the goods or services from the producer or seller to the consumer.
- **MERCHANDISING:** Sales promotion, which includes market research, development of new products, coordination of manufacturing and marketing, and effective advertising and selling.
- **MERCHANDISING BLEND:** Combines the retailer's merchandise with the decision the consumer uses in making selections.
- **MERCHANT:** A buyer and seller of commodities for profit.
- **NONSELLING SPACE:** Areas not allocated for the direct display or sale of merchandise, such as the stockroom and store office.
- **RETAIL:** Selling goods to the ultimate consumer or end user.
- **RETAIL SALE:** The ultimate consumer's purchase of the product.
- **RETAIL STORE:** Place of business in which merchandise is sold by a retailer primarily to the ultimate consumer. It may be owned by the retailer or by some other entity or person.
- **RETAILING:** The business activity of selling goods or services to the final consumer.
- **RETAILER:** A merchant middleman who sells goods mainly to the ultimate consumer.
- **SELLING SPACE:** All the area designated for the display of merchandise and interaction between customers and store personnel.
- **SHOPPING CENTER:** A grouping of retail stores—possibly combined with offices—often with at least one large store that attracts shoppers to the other stores.
- **SOFT GOODS:** Merchandise that is soft, such as clothing, linens, towels, and sheets. They are usually also light in weight.
- **VIGNETTE:** A display of furniture and accessories that is created to look like an actual room.
- **VISUAL MERCHANDISING:** The display of merchandise in store windows and in other locations in the selling space.

layouts for some specific areas of retail design. Two types of retail stores are emphasized: the clothing store and the furniture store. These are the kinds of stores with which students and professionals have a great deal of experience related to personal and professional needs. A brief discussion of gift stores and salons concludes the chapter.

Table 6-1 presents vocabulary used throughout the chapter.

Historical Overview

Stores or businesses for the sale of goods to consumers have existed since ancient times, each adapting to the local lifestyle, climate, and various cultures. Market squares commonly were places designated to sell goods. In Elizabethan England, shops were multistoried, with the first floor reserved for the family business and the upper stories used for family living. By the 1700s, privately owned retail specialty stores abounded in England, the Continent, and the American colonies—soon to be the United States—as consumer demands increased. By the 1800s the middle classes demanded better-quality market goods, so specialty stores increased in number. During the Industrial Revolution of the 19th century, centers of commerce developed in the central city. This was due to increased trade as the crafts and manufacturing processes developed to produce goods. The switch from open markets to actual store locations accelerated after the 1840s.

In the 1850s, the general store was the main source of trade in rural areas of the United States. Architecturally these stores featured simple construction, usually twostoried, with the shopkeeper living on the second floor. The main door was usually in the center of the front of the building, with two windows on each side and a roofed porch with steps leading up to the entry. The interior of the general store was a large, open room with a wood-burning stove and chairs encircling it. The merchandise was stored or displayed on shelves, with a large wood counter in front for the store owner. Figure 6-1 is an example of an early general store. Merchandise of all kinds was sold in this type of store, catering to as many needs as possible for rural families. Many times the general store operated as the local post office, a telephone service, and additional legal services. As cash was scarce in the rural United States, the shopkeepers developed a system of credit based on trading. Of course, specialty retail stores were also to be found in the rural town

Figure 6-1 General store circa 1900 depicting a variety of merchandise for the home. (Historic photo provided by William Berry.)

Figure 6-2 The Paris department store circa 1900 with stationary features such as display and storage cabinetry. (Photograph used by permission, Utah State Historical Society. All rights reserved.)

centers. By the 1930s, the general store began to phase out because the rural population was moving into urban areas.[3]

It is important to briefly comment on how department stores developed and how they were linked in the 19th century to the growth of large population centers. During the 1800s, general merchandise stores developed into department stores by broadening their inventory (Figure 6-2). The downtown department store evolved between the 1870s and the 1920s. These department stores provided safe places for women to shop downtown and featured ladies' lunchrooms, sitting rooms, and even baby-changing facilities. In 1872, Bloomingdale's was founded in New York City. In 1877, John Wanamaker opened a six-story building in Philadelphia, Pennsylvania, which is considered the first true department store in the United States.[4] In 1872, Montgomery Ward, located in Chicago, sent out their first mail order catalog. In 1893, Sears, Roebuck & Company was formed, and in 1896 the company published and distributed their first large general catalog.[5]

Department stores continued to evolve in the late 19th century. The invention of elevators encouraged the construction of multistoried buildings, creating more vertical square footage. During the 1920s, some department stores in the United States began opening branches. The first department stores to have branches were J. C. Penney and Sears, Roebuck. By this time, these original catalog stores as well as Montgomery Ward had grown into full-line department stores in the central cities. From 1929 to the 1950s, department stores spread into the suburbs. In the 1950s, the discount store was created. Early discount stores were designed very simply, with self-service rather than service by store personnel a key ingredient in their design.

One of the first significant shopping centers and mixed-use facilities was the Palais Royal in Paris, France, which opened 1784. It included gardens, fountains, apartments, shops, cafes, and galleries. The Palais Royal is considered the precursor of later mall developments. The Galleria Vittorio Emmanuele, which opened in Milan, Italy, in 1878, was a glass-covered four-story shopping arcade and is considered the first enclosed mall.[6]

---

[3]Murillo, 2005.
[4]Mary Bellis, "Shopping Innovations." www.retailindustry.about.com. 2005.
[5]Sears Archives, "Brief Chronology," 2005. www.searsarchives.com.
[6]American Studies, "Shopping Mall History." Eastern Connecticut State University. www.easternct.edu

The first auto-oriented shopping center in the United States is the Country Club Plaza in Kansas City, Missouri, developed in 1922 and planned with 46 percent of its space allocated for public streets and parking lots.[7] The plaza featured unified architecture and had one of the first shopping center parking garages in addition to paved and lighted parking lots.[8] The shops faced the streets, and plazas were built with fountains and statuary throughout the area. They are still maintained and used today.

As the population and popularity of the suburbs grew, so did the shopping center. In 1931, the Highland Park Shopping Village in Dallas, Texas was developed and is considered to be the first planned shopping center in the United States, as it occupied a single site and was not bisected by public streets. The majority of storefronts faced the center, with broad sidewalks providing safe transport for shoppers. During the 1930s and 1940s, large freestanding stores were built away from the city center and included parking lots specifically for consumer convenience. In the 1950s, the first two shopping centers with full-line branch stores were built; one had two strip centers face to face with a walkway in between; the other was the first two-level shopping center. In 1956, in Edina, Minnesota, the first fully enclosed two-level mall with central air conditioning and heating was built and included two department stores as anchors. This mall is considered to be the first modern regional mall. In 1976, in Boston, Massachusetts, the first "festival marketplaces" were developed. Built in downtown Boston, they centered on food and retail specialty stores. In 1976, the first urban vertical mall, Water Tower Place, opened in Chicago, Illinois. It includes high-end specialty stores, department stores, a hotel, offices, condominiums, and a parking garage and is today considered a preeminent mixed-use project.

Superregional centers, which are malls with more than 800,000 square feet, developed during the 1980s and became very popular. By the 1990s, entertainment, live shows, movies in multiplex cinemas, robotic animal displays, carousel rides, and children's playscapes, as well as facilities such as churches, schools, post office branches, municipal offices, libraries, and museums, were also included in these large malls. By the end of the 1990s, the large "brick and mortar" retailers developed their own Web sites in order to compete with other Internet sources. In the 21st century, shopping centers are evolving to fit consumer needs and interests, as well as applying new technology to the shopping experience.[9]

Overview of Retail Business Operations

The design of retail facilities depends heavily on the designer's ability to understand the retail business and the specific business of the client. Interior designers should not finalize decisions and recommendations about the design of a retail store without this background information.

The overall goals of retailing involve enticing the customer into the store and making sales. Store retailers operate fixed point-of-sale (POS) locations designed and located to appeal to high volume walk-in traffic.[10] The goal of retail design is to enhance the space so as to encourage the increased and continuous sale of merchandise. Each retailer has specific concerns in his or her area which focus on providing sufficient space allowances for the display of merchandise, preventing shoplifting and internal theft, liability, image of the facility, merchandise mix, space allocation, and growth of the business.

Although the design of the retail facility plays a significant part in the achievement of the overall goals of a retailer, marketing and merchandising play important roles as well. Let us take a brief look at key issues in marketing related to the retail industry and the interior design of retail spaces. *Marketing* is all the activities that are used to move the goods

---

[7]Historical Changes, "A Brief History of Downtowns." Eastern Michigan University, 2005. www.emich.edu
[8]International Council of Shopping Centers, "A Brief History of Shopping Centers." 2004. www.icsc.org
[9]International Council of Shopping Centers, "A Brief History of Shopping Centers." 2004. www.icsc.org
[10]U.S. Bureau of the Census, May 2002.

or services from the producer/seller to the consumer. Functions of marketing include buying, selling, storing, transporting, standardizing, financing, and supplying market information about goods. Retailers are part of what is called a *marketing channel,* a team of marketing institutions that direct a flow of goods or services from the producer to the final consumer. The marketing channel includes the producers, the wholesalers, the retailer, and the consumer. The *marketing concept* states that the goal of every business organization is to satisfy consumer needs while creating a profit. *Merchandising* is defined as sales promotion, which includes market research, development of new products, coordination of manufacturing and marketing, and effective advertising and selling. The *merchandising blend* combines the retailer's merchandise with the decision the consumer uses in making selections. The *merchant* is defined as a buyer and seller of commodities for profit. In determining which products to offer for sale, the merchant considers the benefits the consumer seeks in products, whether the products represent a functional or psychological need, whether or not the physical properties of the product satisfy consumer needs, and the advantages of supplementary services to the customer such as deliveries, installation, and alterations.

An effective *retail plan* answers the questions concerning why, what, when, where, and how specific retail business activities are to be accomplished. The right message, the right appeal, and the right services are all considerations in retail planning.[11] The retail plan also directs the conceptual interior design of the store, much like the design concept used in hospitality projects. The retailing plan is a group of activities that is crucial to the successful planning of the business operation. It is important for the interior designer to understand this underlying philosophy of retail planning for each project in order to provide an effective interior design for the facility. A retail plan includes five important stages:

1. Defining retail environments
2. Controlling financial, organizational, human, and physical resources
3. Identifying and selecting retail marketing and sites
4. Developing and managing products
5. Creating and implementing promotion strategies

The store owner's or management team's tasks and responsibilities begin with developing the merchandise blend, finding the best location, operating the store, and purchasing, pricing, controlling, and promoting the merchandise. In addition, they provide the interior designer with ideas for the design of the interior of the store. Current interior store design has changed from the earlier crowding of merchandise to a more streamlined, organized ambience with emphasis on simplicity, wider aisles, better sightlines, and the use of more flexible fixtures.[12]

In creating a retail store's environment, management must consider the physical and psychological effect that the environment will have on customers and employees. One of the initial concerns is creating a store image. This image includes store location, interior design, the actual products and their presentation, the price of items, and public relations. As the interior design is paramount to the space planning and visual impact of the store, the aforementioned areas affecting image must be considered in developing a design solution. In addition to graphics and color, the interior designer's space planning of fixed and flexible merchandising space will affect sales and the store's image. Management must consider the consumer's interest in locating shopping areas that provide safety, comfort, and attention to aesthetics.

What consumers eventually purchase is directly tied to their needs and wants. *Needs* are essential physiological and psychological requirements necessary to the physical and mental welfare of the consumer. *Wants* are conscious impulses to acquire objects that promise rewards. Simply, needs are things we must have; wants are the things we would like to have. Retailers focus on offering goods and services that satisfy consumers' wants and needs. Table 6-2 defines other terms related to consumer needs and wants.

---

[11]Lewison, 1994, pp. 31–32.
[12]Lewison, 1994, p. 269.

TABLE 6-2 Defining Needs and Wants for Motivating Buying

- **Needs:** Essential physiological and psychological requirements necessary to the physical and mental welfare of the consumer.
- **Physiological needs:** Required for survival and basic comfort such as food, clothing, and housing.
- **Safety needs:** Required for security and stability such as an alarm for the car or a cellular phone.

- **Esteem needs:** Those regarding self-respect, admiration, and achievement. The kinds of goods vary, depending on the consumer's background. Antique furniture, a new car, and designer jewelry are examples of esteem needs goods.
- **Wants:** Conscious impulses to acquire objects that promise some type of reward. Many types of goods that satisfy esteem needs can also satisfy wants.

To assist in this process, retailers have found that when the shopping experience focuses on the senses, these stimuli can create a motivation to purchase. One term associated with the focus on the senses is *atmospherics*, a conscious effort by the retailer to create a buying environment that will produce specific emotional effects on buyers. Examples of atmospherics in action are the aroma from a bakery and specific types of music in a high-fashion boutique garment store. Retailers focus on a variety of these appeal techniques to entice the consumer into the selling space. The first one is *sight appeal*. The retailer uses size, shape, and color to attract the customers, as well as harmony, contrast, and clash. Harmony is "visual agreement," and a harmonious environment is usually a more formal environment. Contrast and clash are considered "visual conflict" and are often used to create an informal shopping atmosphere. The use of paneling in a formal design in Ralph Lauren shops is an example of sight appeal using harmony. Pulsing neon lights are only one item that can be used to create the contrast and clash environment popular in stores targeting younger consumers. *Scent appeal* is also used by retailers. For example, in a bakery, the scent of baked goods is important. A cosmetics store or area in a department store may use a pleasing though not overpowering scent of perfumes to attract customers.

Stores are also designed using *theme appeal*, which involves establishing an environment related directly to the product, to holidays, or to special events.[13] Examples include Christmas decorations and displays used seasonally by most stores, and special displays tied to a local event, like a city hosting a major sporting event such as the Super Bowl or an All-Star baseball or basketball game. Stores can also combine atmospherics. A sports equipment store could combine scent appeal with sound appeal by the use of an audiovisual system playing the sound of a rushing stream or replaying sporting events.

Understanding the retail business should be a main priority for the designer wishing to work in this specialty. The designer must learn the differences between marketing and merchandising, as well as how the merchandising blend will impact the interior design of the retail store. In addition, designers must gain knowledge of the merchandising methodology of a retail store, realizing that it is critical before specific space planning and design specification activities are undertaken.

Types of Retail Facilities

As we saw at the beginning of this chapter, we stated that the retail industry has an enormous impact on the U.S. economy. Retail trade involves about 12.9 percent of all businesses established in the United States. The single-store business accounts for over 95 percent of all U.S. retailers but generates less than 50 percent of all retail store sales.[14] This means that there is a tremendous amount of opportunity for interior designers working in this specialty.

---

[13]Lewison, 1994, p. 269.
[14]Melody Vargas, "Retail Industry Profile," *Your Guide to Retail Industry*, March 20, 2005. www.retailindustry.about.com.

TABLE 6-3 Types of Retail Facilities

Types of Stores	Locations of Stores
Single-store entrepreneurial ownership	City centers
Chain or franchise store	Shopping centers—urban and suburban locations
Department store	Neighborhood
Hypermarket	Community
Discount store	Regional or malls
Warehouse store	Open-air village centers
	Superregional centers

The variety of retail stores is extensive, based on the type of merchandise that might be sold. There are only a few types of retail facilities, as shown in Table 6-3. The simplest type is the single-store entrepreneurial facility selling a specific product. Another type is the *chain* or *franchise store* that can either be independently owned or owned by the chain and managed locally. As business concepts, these are similar to the chain and franchise food and beverage facilities discussed in the previous chapter. Chain and franchise retail stores require local merchants to follow policies established by corporations, while entrepreneurs are free to explore alternative methods. The design of a chain or franchise-owned specialty store will also be mandated by the corporate owners, while the design of an independently owned entrepreneurial store is controlled by the entrepreneur.

Another type of store is the *department store*. Readers are familiar with department stores such as Nordstroms, J.C. Penney, Dillards, Bloomingdale's, Macy's and many others that offer a wide variety of brands and products. The price point for a department store is generally medium to high. Interiors are designed to create backgrounds for selling merchandise much in the way the small specialty store is designed. To compete with the sales volume and customer traffic of hypermarket and discount stores, department stores have improved personnel training and modernized their facilities, including updating their interior design. Department stores are often the anchor or largest store at a shopping center or mall.

The *hypermarket* has made a significant impact on retailing in the United States. A hypermarket is a store with at least 200,000 square feet which sells a wide variety of general merchandise and/or food. This type of retail facility is often considered a *discount store,* although not all hypermarket stores are discount stores. The biggest company developing the hypermarket location is Wal-Mart, Inc. These establishments combine a variety of merchandise in one open space. Wal-Mart Superstores add full-product-line grocery stores to the general merchandise offerings. The discount store uses very simple finishes and a minimal number of walls to subdivide the departments. Warehouse stores that are open to the public through a membership program are another subtype of the hypermarket. Companies such as Great Indoors and Design Expo are hypermarket stores that focus on home furnishings items.

The majority of retail facilities are located in either a central business district or a *shopping center.* Major investors are now focused on the redevelopment of existing properties and revitalization of high-density urban areas. Consumers are responding positively to the redevelopment of these areas as single-site places to shop, work, live, and play. These areas are generally referred to as *mixed-use lifestyle projects* or *developments.* Figure 6-3 is an example of a mixed-use facility. Urban shopping centers are being developed with a diverse collection of stores, eateries, and entertainment. Baseball stadiums, ice rinks, and entertainment facilities such as IMAX theaters are being constructed to bring more shoppers to the area in response to the public preference for shopping in one location. Landscape and hardscape areas with water features have been designed to bring families into the centers to provide fun and entertainment.[15] Additionally, access to public transportation is im-

---

[15]"2002 Leaders in Retail Architecture," *Retail Traffic Magazine,* Sept. 1, 2002. www.retailtrafficmag.com.

Figure 6-3 Mixed-use lifestyle development. Pinnacle Hills Promenade. (Drawing courtesy of Leo A Daly.)

portant in planning these shopping centers. Most of these centers have public mass transit stations located either on the property or near highways for easy personal travel.

Open-air village concepts have become popular again as a retail option. Basically, these projects are patterned on a small-town business district, with narrow roads and shops on either side and parking behind the facilities. These retail centers include pedestrian paths and often a plaza with a town square, as well as spaces planned for offices, community services, dining, and entertainment spaces.[16]

An important distinction for store owners is that a store in a shopping center will pay indirectly for the development and management of parking and overall customer amenities, while stores in a central business district will not. Retail stores in central business districts either are independently owned or are chain stores and are under no obligation to provide parking for their customers' vehicles.

There are generally three types of shopping centers. The smallest is the neighborhood shopping center with retail stores independently owned and operated. These consist of a mix of retail stores and service business offices like those of accountants or travel agents. Strip malls can be categorized as neighborhood shopping centers because the current design trend for these facilities is to emulate a town center with dining and entertainment places, as well as providing the individual stores.[17] Larger neighborhood shopping centers commonly have a grocery supermarket as a focus or magnet store. A *magnet store* (also referred to as an *anchor*) is a large, well-known chain store that attracts a large number of customers. These shopping centers will often have a magnet store in conjunction with a drugstore and a variety of retail stores, specialty stores, chain stores, and possibly small service offices.

The community shopping center has a mix of stores similar to that of the neighborhood center. However, a community shopping center often includes a medium-sized department store or hypermarket as its magnet rather than a grocery store. The community shopping center usually has some chain or franchise stores in its mix, as well as theaters and individually owned shops. Department stores are no longer considered the only

[16]"2002 Leaders in Retail Architecture," *Retail Traffic Magazine,* Sept. 1, 2002. www.retailtrafficmag.com.
[17]David Sokol, "Strip Mall Strut." April 1, 2003. www.retailtrafficmag.com

magnets for shopping centers and malls, as in the past. Examples of new magnet stores are Barnes & Noble and Linens N' Things.[18]

The regional shopping center—commonly called a *mall* today—has become extremely popular over the years. Its environment—often enclosed—and its large mix of stores and other offerings have made it a preferred destination for many shoppers. These malls offer a full range of shopping services comparable to those of small central business districts.

Regional malls usually have two or more department stores as magnet stores, along with a large variety of specialty stores which are usually chain stores rather than independently owned. Regional malls have steadily increased the scope of their services and amenities. They often include food courts, recreation areas such as movie theaters, areas for small concerts, and an area for holiday or other theme events. In addition to a mall complex, it is also common for additional stores, restaurants, hotels, and recreation facilities to be built on the fringe of the regional mall. In an attempt to increase the square footage of the mall when land expansion is not possible, developers are investing in *overbuilds*—the addition of new levels to the existing mall space.

The Mall of America in Bloomington, Minnesota, is one of the world's largest regional malls. Due to its size, it is classified as a *superregional center*. The entire mall is on 78 acres and takes up 4.2 million square feet. It contains over 520 stores including 4 major department stores, 20 sit-down restaurants, 30 fast food facilities in the two food courts, 4 nightclubs, 2 arcades, an 18-hole miniature golf course, a 14-screen movie theater, and a 7-acre amusement park with a roller coaster in the center of the mall. Plans for the updating of the Mall of America include doubling the existing space, with more than half of the space allotted for entertainment and not specifically retail stores. Hotel towers, an ice rink, a concert hall, and maybe a casino are in the planning stages. This addition will be named Mall of America II.[19]

Security has become a major concern to the consumer. Malls, open-air villages, and others feature concealed video surveillance equipment and electronic sensors, as well as security guards and dogs.[20] Architects and designers need to design retail spaces where customers are assured of safety and security.

Malls continue to be the preferred shopping facility of consumers. In an effort to appeal to younger shoppers, malls are incorporating entertainment venues as well. However, the Internet, catalogs, and cable television are changing the shopping landscape. These nontraditional shopping venues allow consumers to shop from their homes, thus avoiding traffic and saving time, which affects the use of traditional shopping centers.

Planning and Interior Design Elements

The material in this section provides the student and the design professional with a background in the basic planning and design elements that must be considered in the interior design of small retail stores. Although the discussion focuses on the small retail store, these design elements can be applied to the design of larger stores. The exact specialty of the store will affect how these elements are applied. The elements that must be considered in the interior design of the store are store merchandising, space allocation and circulation, furniture and fixtures, architectural finishes, lighting design, and codes.

The decision about what kinds of windows will be used for the storefront often depends upon the products to be sold. For example, a dress shop must have windows that display the full mannequins, thus keeping the display on the human scale. This often allows the merchant to increase the display of shoes, handbags, accessories, and hats as well as general clothing items. A jewelry store display window needs to be at eye level, which allows the eye to focus on the much smaller objects in the display window. Lighting

---

[18]David Bodamer, "The Mall Is Dead, Long Live the Mall." *Retail Traffic Magazine*, April 5, 2005. www.retailtrafficmag.com
[19]J. Mans and S. Larson, 2005. Simon Property Group, www.simon.com.
[20]J. Mans and S. Larson, 2005. Simon Property Group, www.simon.com.

BOX 6-1   **RETAIL STORE EXTERIOR DESIGN**

The exterior design of the storefront presents the first major impression of the store, whether the view is from the street or the broad corridor provided by malls. The purpose of the exterior architectural design of the store is to attract attention, create the highest level of product exposure, and maximize selling areas visible from outside. Design concepts that affect the exterior of the store include the exterior architectural design, signage, store windows, and the entrance.

A primary way the exterior design attracts customers into the store is through the storefront's configuration. Figure 6B-1 provides examples of the three basic storefront configurations: straight, angled, and arcade fronts.[21] The advantage of the *straight front* is that it does not reduce the interior selling space. The *angled front* gives the consumer a better viewing angle of the merchandise and reduces the window glare, which makes display items easier to view. The *arcade front* has several recessed windows, which increases the area of the store's window display as well as reducing glare. The interior designer will initially specify materials for display windows as part of the storefront configuration. Material specification must be made to create an appropriate backdrop for the merchandise, as well as for attracting the customer into the store. Individual retail stores prefer either closed backdrops in window displays or open views into the store. Changes in the materials used for display windows are commonly made by the visual merchandisers who create the changing window displays.

Store signage is another way of attracting customers to the store. To enhance the representation or the character of the merchandise which is offered, well-designed signage is required. *Signage,* or *shop signs,* is defined as outdoor advertisement on the premises of a store or business describing the product or services provided by the advertiser. Ideally, exterior signs should explain the name, location, and type of merchandise. Retail franchises and chains have established logos and/or signage, which are immediately recognizable by the public due to the considerable advertising investment made by these organizations. Smaller retail stores may hire graphic designers who specialize in retail signage to develop their logos and written images. Occasionally, an interior designer will be asked to develop the concept.

Windows are used to advertise merchandise. Ramped, shadow box, elevated, and island are common window types.[22] They are defined in Table 6-4. The retailer will stress the display windows since the volume of sales is influenced by the effective design of windows and displays. The majority of retailers prefer a view into the interior of the store to the window display blocking the view.

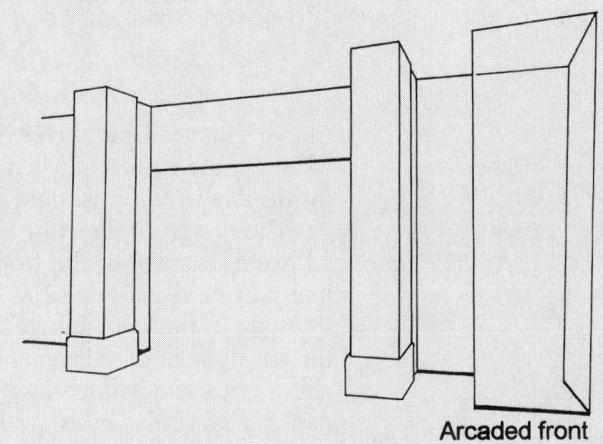

Arcaded front

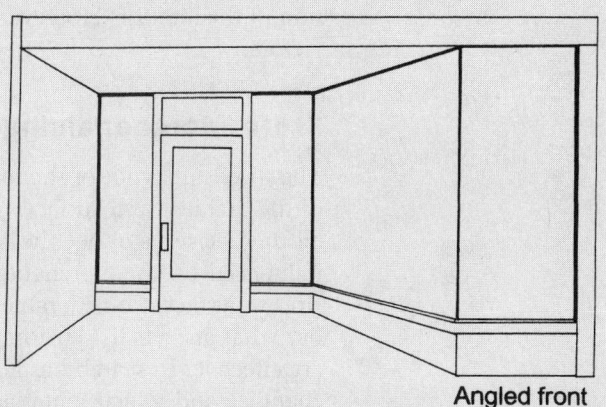

Angled front

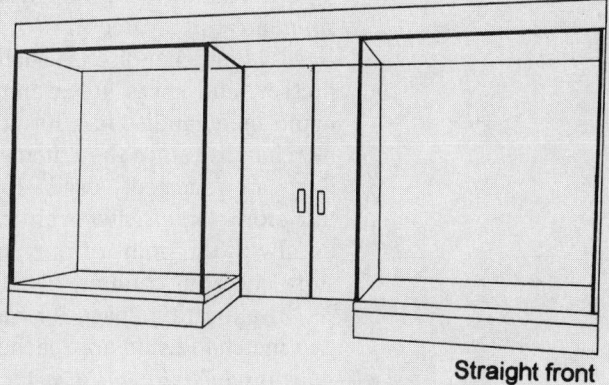

Straight front

Figure 6B-1   Three storefront configurations.

---

[21]Lewison, 1994, pp. 276–277.
[22]Lewison, 1994, pp. 278.

TABLE 6-4 Common Types of Display Windows

- **Ramped window**: Display window that has a display floor higher in back than in front, either in a wedge or tiered shape. It is often used in shoe and accessory stores.
- **Shadow box window**: Display window that is small and set at eye level. It is completely enclosed and is often used by jewelry stores.
- **Elevated window**: Display window with an elevation 12 to 36 inches above the floor.
- **Island windows**: A four-sided window used with an arcade storefront. It is commonly used in clothing stores because the product can be viewed from a variety of angles.

can be enhanced and directed within the box, creating a miniature theater effect that helps to attract the customer when a shadow box window is used. In general, lighting specified for display windows should be flexible to allow for a variety of displays.

The design of the store entrance will be included in the decisions concerning the total exterior image of the store. Many store owners view the entrance door as an important part of visual appeal as well as market recognition of the store, and will emphasize the style of the door by creating an inviting, welcome, and enticing entry. For example, the red door of the Elizabeth Arden Salons and the gold and maroon door of Cartier are important symbols for those stores. The door itself is only one part of the entrance. The designer must also consider lighting and numerous code requirements. These include no steps, the use of nonskid flooring materials, sufficiently wide doors for all traffic, and no entrance clutter.[23] Ideally, the entrance doors should allow customers to see at least a portion of the interior. However, this may be governed by location, codes, weather, and other factors.

Store Merchandising

The physical layout of the merchandise displays and fixtures, along with the specifications of the architectural surfaces and elements, is critical to the success of the store. However, all the decisions about the total planning and interior design of a retail store are heavily influenced by the merchandise to be sold and the type of customer the store owner desires to attract. Considerable marketing and merchandising research has been done to find out what attracts the customer to the store, as well as which traffic patterns within a store are effective. Research has also been conducted concerning what height for display of merchandise and which materials should be specified to attract the customer through visual, tactile, and audio appeal.

Merchandise is grouped into product-line subdivisions. Within each of these subdivisions are three categories or types of merchandise: demand, convenience, and impulse. *Demand* merchandise is usually a necessary item that encourages the public to shop. Suits, dresses, and shirts are examples in clothing stores. A bed or sofa is an example of demand merchandise in a furniture store. The retailers of small stores stock mainly demand merchandise since these items turn over faster and produce constant revenue. *Convenience* items are repeatedly used—for example, hosiery in a clothing store and lamps in a furniture store. *Impulse* items are unplanned purchases and are dependent upon good display—usually at the point of purchase. Examples include candy and gum placed at the grocery store checkout counter.

In allocating space for merchandise, the interior designer also needs to be aware of two merchandising approaches to making space decisions: the *model stock method* and the *sales/productivity ratio method*. In the model stock method, the retailer determines the amount of floor space needed to stock a desired amount of merchandise. In the sales/productivity ratio method, the retailer allocates selling space on the basis of sales per square foot for each merchandise group. The retailer/merchant will decide which method will be

---

[23]Lewison, 1994, p. 278.

used. This information directly relates to the placement and space planning of the fixed and flexible fixtures and to the proximity relationships of other merchandise, which directly affects the direction of the interior design.

Visual merchandising is another facet of merchandising goods. *Visual merchandising* is the display of merchandise in store windows and in other locations in the selling space (Figure 6-4). The objective of visual merchandising is to encourage the completion of the sale once the customer is in the store. Visual merchandisers or display designers (previously referred to as display staff or *window dressers*) are hired specifically to deal with visual merchandising for the store. A talented, creative display designer can bring customers into the store based on the reputation of the designer's show windows and other display work.

This method of visual display can create interest and expose the product to consumers, enhance the look of the product, give information, aid sales transactions, and increase sales. Many merchandising displays can also serve as storage space, as all the backup stock may be utilized in the display. Visual merchandising is considered a form of non-media advertising as it aids in creating a store image for customers.

An interior designer working as a visual merchandiser has an excellent opportunity to develop and increase portfolio work rapidly. This is a good position for an entry-level designer who needs to increase his or her work experience as well as accumulate portfolio items, especially in furniture stores.

Space Allocation and Circulation

The space in retail stores is generally categorized as selling space and nonselling space. *Selling space* is all the area designated for the display of merchandise and interaction between customers and personnel. It is as similar to the front-of-the-house spaces in hospitality facilities, though it is not referred to that way in the retail industry. *Nonselling space*

Figure 6-4 Mannequins in life-like poses are often used to display merchandise as seen in this Tommy Hilfiger showroom in New York City. (Design by and photograph courtesy of Peter Gisolfi Associates, Hastings on Hudson, NY.)

includes areas such as the stockroom, office, and any other areas not allocated for the direct display or selling of merchandise. The selling space is of major concern to the retailer. Figure 6-5 provides an example of a basic arrangement of selling and nonselling space.

When considering how the selling and nonselling spaces in stores are determined, basic guidelines are presented in Table 6-5. These guidelines must be taken into account when assisting the store owner in making decisions about space allowances for the merchandise mix, fixture types, fixture locations, architectural finishes, and internal signage.

An important goal of the retailer is to be able to place merchandise in its ideal selling location. This goal is directly related to the space plan of the store. The merchant usually discusses with the interior designer the approximate placement of the merchandise within the selling space. Exposing the customer to all the merchandise and enticing the customer to purchase additional items is the challenge for the interior designer doing space planning. For example, the bulk of demand merchandise is placed away from the entrance, forcing the customer to pass convenience and impulse items prior to reaching the intended item. Convenience items are traditionally placed somewhere in the midsection of the store. Impulse items are usually located near the sales counter/cashier or close to the entry. Other important considerations in the placement of the different types of items are the cost of the items and the concerns about theft and security. Merchandise placement is highly flexible and is dependent upon the merchant and the product mix. The final decision about

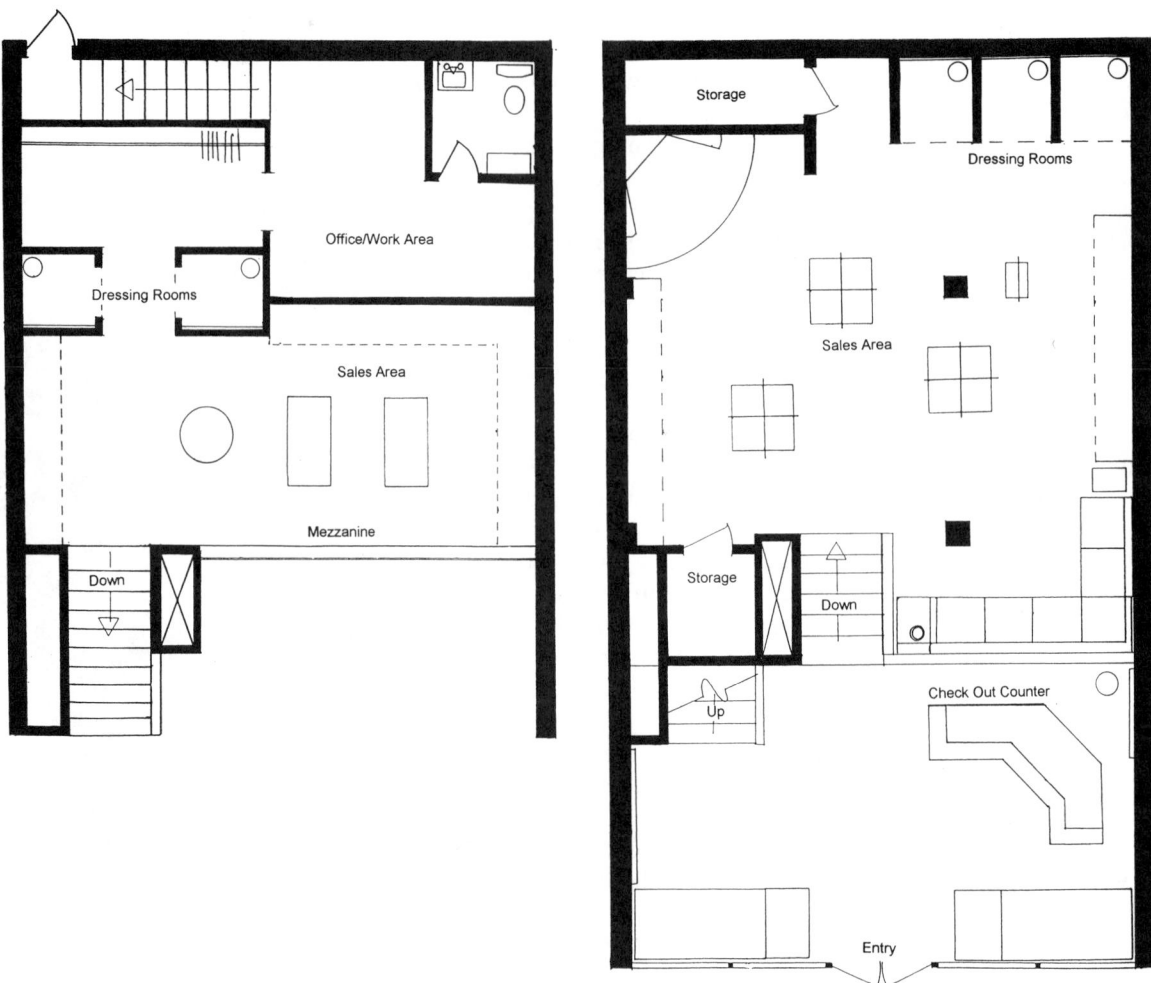

Figure 6-5 Floor plan of a tri-level free-form system showing the potential for versatility in fixtures placements. The majority of the space is devoted to selling space, with minimal nonselling space for office and storage. (Plan courtesy of SOI, Interior Design.)

where to place goods is based on two factors: the need for exposure of the merchandise, such as impulse versus convenience items, and the retailer's expected profile of customers', their age group, and their shopping frequency.

Circulation and traffic patterns establish the layout of aisles and the positioning of fixtures within the store. Merchandising research has shown that people usually turn right when entering a store. The designer needs to attract the customer to the left as well in order to reduce one-way traffic. Many retailers agree that the best placement for a product is often associated with the customer in-store traffic patterns.

Easy access from the store entrance to all sales sections is very important. Small retail stores usually use a single aisle extending the length of the store. If the store is large, minor aisles branch off from the main aisle whether that aisle is placed directly through the center of the store or as a radial main aisle creating a circular traffic pattern. In all but the smallest stores, the traffic patterns that help define the layout of the store will utilize one of the three basic patterns: grid, free flow, or boutique system.

A store that must deal with numerous columns often plans the internal layout of aisles and store fixtures using the *grid system* (Figure 6-6). The grid system makes it easier to locate fixtures and aisles within this sometimes limiting structural system. However, due to the necessity of working with the columns, the aisle pattern provides very little flexibility to the overall floor plan.

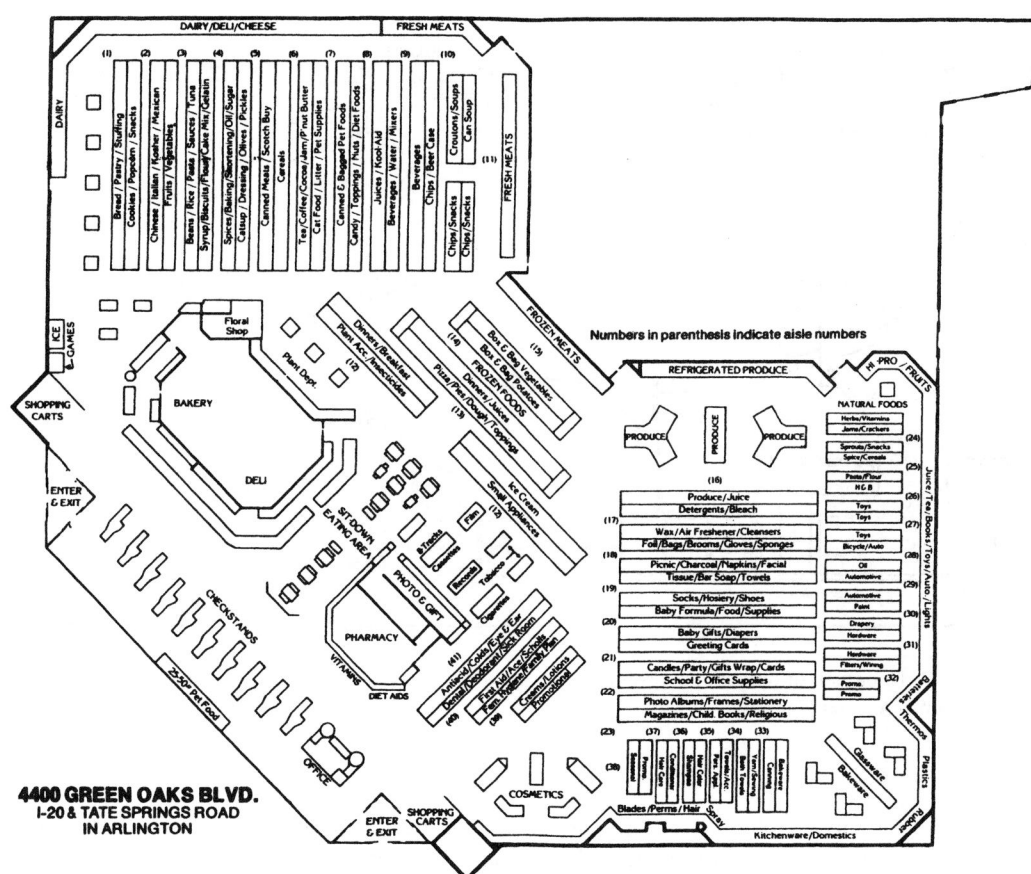

Figure 6-6 Floor plan of a grid system with fixed features such as shelving for products as typically used in a grocery store. (From Barr and Broudy, *Designing to Sell*. Copyright © 1986. Reproduced with permission of the McGraw-Hill Companies.)

Figure 6-5 is also an example of the *free-flow system*. This planning system allows displays and fixtures to be moved easily, a particular advantage to a small store. The free-flow system is recommended for the most effective use of space, especially in small stores, because the displays can be changed very easily and targeted for the volume of merchandise in stock.

The *boutique system* divides the sales floor into individual semiseparate areas, each possibly built around a shopping theme that focuses on the individuality of the product (see Figure 6-7). It is very popular in high-end stores. Personal service, uniqueness, and ambience are all considered important elements in planning and creating a boutique atmosphere.

Although these systems are all useful in small stores, they are also important planning elements in larger stores. However, stairs, escalators, and elevators add to the complexity of the planning mix in a larger store. The placement of these traffic movement elements plays an important part in attracting customers to other parts of the store as well. They must be easily accessible and meet code requirements. Escalators are usually installed in pairs and generally located in the center of the sales area. They are effective in giving the shopper an overview of the merchandise. Open stairs are often placed toward the rear of the selling space, exposing customers to more products as they proceed through the main floor to access the stairs to the upper and lower levels. Elevators are often placed on the periphery of the floor plan close to the stairways. Escalators, stairs, and elevators are placed strategically to enhance the flow of customers as they view the merchandise.

When planning nonselling space, the first considerations are the points mentioned in Table 6-5. In addition, the designer must be alert to the in-store merchandise-handling

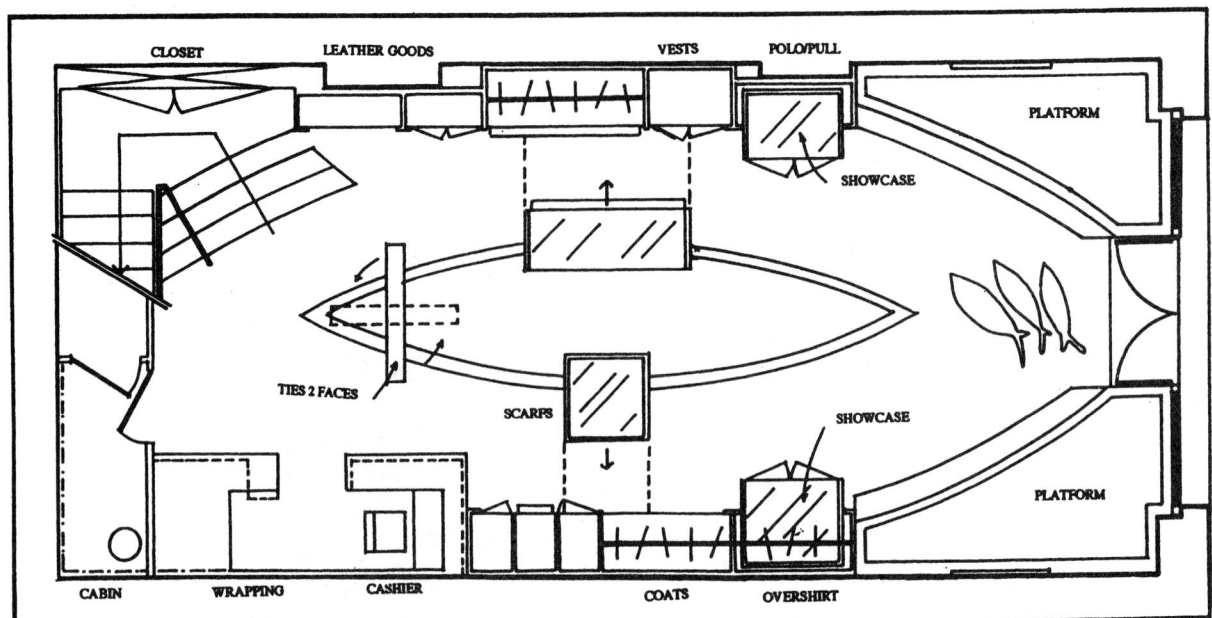

Figure 6-7 Floor plan of a boutique system displaying a creative use of space. (Plan courtesy of Jean-Pierre Heim & Associates, Paris, New York. Jean-Pierre Heim and Galad Mahmoud Architects, DPLG, Paris.)

process. After the merchandise is unloaded at the receiving dock, it should follow a traffic pattern as it is checked, marked, and then sent to storage or the sales floor. Additional storage may be needed to handle off-season stock that was not sold during the season, as well as to provide space for the layaway procedure popular in small clothing stores. Work space is necessary for service personnel to perform their duties. Depending on the type of merchandise and the focus of the store, space will also be needed for alternations and fitting rooms, inspecting merchandise, and managerial functions such as accounting and purchasing. Most stores, regardless of size, will also need some space for custodial functions, restrooms for employees (local codes will determine if a restroom for customers is required), and possibly a break room or area for employees to store personal items.

TABLE 6-5 Guidelines for Selling and Nonselling Space Allocation

Selling Space Considerations

- The most valuable space is near the front of the store.
- Space on the first floor is more valuable than basement or upper-floor space.
- The space along the aisles is more valuable than the peripheral corner space.
- Main or central aisles are more valuable than peripheral or side aisles.
- Eye-level space is more valuable than space above or below eye level, especially for new items.

Nonselling Space Considerations

- Decide initially how much reserve stock needs to be stored.

- Plan for reserve stock areas located around the perimeter of the sales floor for easy access.
- Coordinate the movement of new merchandise onto the floor with the customer traffic pattern to avoid interference.
- Make certain that outgoing merchandise is not handled in a manner that would interfere with the sales area.
- Include facilities for docking, loading, and unloading, keeping docking areas under a roof or canopy.
- In a large store, use a conveyer belt to transport items from the receiving dock to the service area, where they are marked and put into storage or stock.
- Provide space for store delivery trucks to load and keep items separate from the receiving area.

Fixtures and Furniture

Most of the furniture in a generic retail store will consist of various kinds of merchandise display fixtures. Depending on the nature of the merchandise and the store, other furniture items might be required. This section will focus on display fixtures since they are the primary furniture items.

Merchandise is displayed using a variety of counters, racks, wall systems, and platforms as well as freestanding flexible fixtures. These different types of display equipment are commonly called *display fixtures* and are also used to store and protect merchandise. A common goal of the interior designer is to provide creative design solutions in the selection and specification of merchandise display equipment. Fixtures should allow the maximum amount of merchandise to be available on the selling floor per code without appearing overcrowded. Display fixtures should also be flexible in use and easily moved. Custom cabinetry and fixtures are common in retail stores, and the interior designer will be required to produce the drawings for their manufacture (Figures 6-8a and 6-8b).

There are several common types of fixtures that are either custom millwork, installed on the wall, or freestanding units. The *island fixture* is a three-dimensional counter used for the display of a wide variety of accessories such as jewelry, scarves, and handbags, as well as cosmetics. The *slatwall fixture* is useful in displaying a variety of merchandise including apparel. Brackets of different kinds are used with the slat wall to display many kinds of merchandise. At the beginning of a season, the volume of the stocked items is up and the merchandise can be grouped close together. However, as the volume of stock is reduced, the brackets can be moved on the slatwalls to create a feeling of space and deemphasize the reduction in stock, which often is interpreted by customers as leftover merchandise.

Freestanding fixtures provide customer access from all sides. The most common freestanding fixtures are the two-way, the four-way, gondolas, spirals, and rounders. A *two-way fixture* is a floor-standing fixture that allows merchandise to be hung on hangers in two directions (Figure 6-9a). A *four-way fixture* is a floor-standing fixture that allows hanging merchandise on hangers in four directions (Figure 6-9b). Often new merchandise is displayed on two-way and four-way fixtures, especially in a clothing store. For example, a new collection of sport shirts, pants, and shorts could be displayed on the four-way. *Rounders* are usually preferred for items that are sold at a reduced price and are often positioned at the back of the store, which forces the customer to pass by the newer merchandise. A *spiral fixture* is a vertical curvilinear fixture, often metal, with hooks spaced evenly to hold clothing accessories such as belts or scarves. A *gondola* is a three-dimensional open-shelved unit with access from all sides. The average height of a gondola is 48 to 54 inches from the floor. It can be used to display many kinds of merchandise in a variety of retail stores. Additional freestanding fixtures are available as well as custom-designed fixtures, which may be required for an individual store's needs.

Stores today generally have a computerized cash register area where the customer will take merchandise to be purchased. Appropriate space will also be needed at this counter for wrapping or bagging the items. Accessibility requirements must be considered in the design of this custom cabinet. A jewelry store might include a few small stools for customers as they look at items. A few comfortable chairs should be provided in a clothing store. Of course, benches or chairs would be needed in the shoe section of a sporting goods shop. Obviously, these are only a few examples of the additional items needed in the selling spaces, depending on the merchandise mix.

Materials and Finishes

Much can be done with the interior materials and finishes in a retail store. There are numerous choices that the interior designer can orchestrate into an effective selling space. However, the choices depend upon the type of atmosphere requested by the retailer and should be discussed during the initial interview with the client. Most merchants will want their store to have up-to-date materials and color schemes. Retailers remodel and update their selling space approximately every five to seven years to create a current image and atmosphere for the products they sell.

Figure 6-8a Rendering of Schedoni, a store in Coral Gables, Florida, showing a display cabinetry planned for this high-end store. (Rendering courtesy of Pavlik Design Team, Ft. Lauderdale, Florida, 954-523-3300, www.pavlikdesign.com/info@pavlikdesign.com)

Figure 6-8b Photograph of Schedoni upon completion. Note the variety of lighting available to highlight the products, as well as the pathways and the interior architecture. (Photograph courtesy of Pavlik Design Team, Ft. Lauderdale, Florida, 954-523-3300, www.pavlikdesign.com/info@pavlikdesign.com)

The products and design elements specified for a retail store can be simple backgrounds for the merchandise or they can be created to provide a more visually active selling space. Walls in retail stores are most commonly finished in drywall with some sort of surface treatment. Design concepts, however, might include the use of masonry and wood paneling—to name just two options—to better embody the store's concept. These materials and finishes will be specified depending upon the merchandise and the concepts described by the store owner or management. For example, if the retailer desires a quiet atmosphere for shopping, then materials such as high-density, low-pile carpeting would be specified, as well as commercial-grade fabrics on the wall. If the retailer requests a high-energy environment, then more hard surfaces, such as tile or wood floors, mirrored walls, and minimal upholstery, would be appropriate. In selecting materials for architectural finishes, remember that soft, porous materials absorb sound and hard, rigid materials reflect it.

Although color selections may seem unlimited, many stores require the use of certain colors or color schemes. This is especially true for chains and franchise store owners, who must replicate store interiors based on strict corporate guidelines. In other cases, the retailer has a logo and color choices that are already established and identified with the product lines. Often the specified colors are

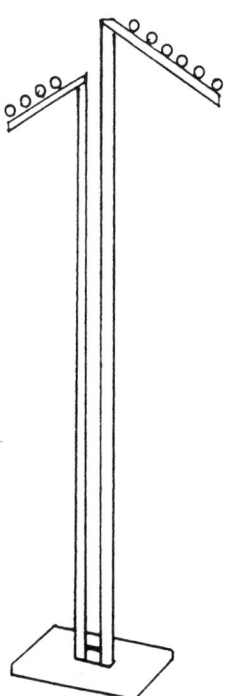

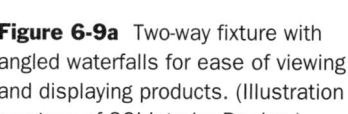

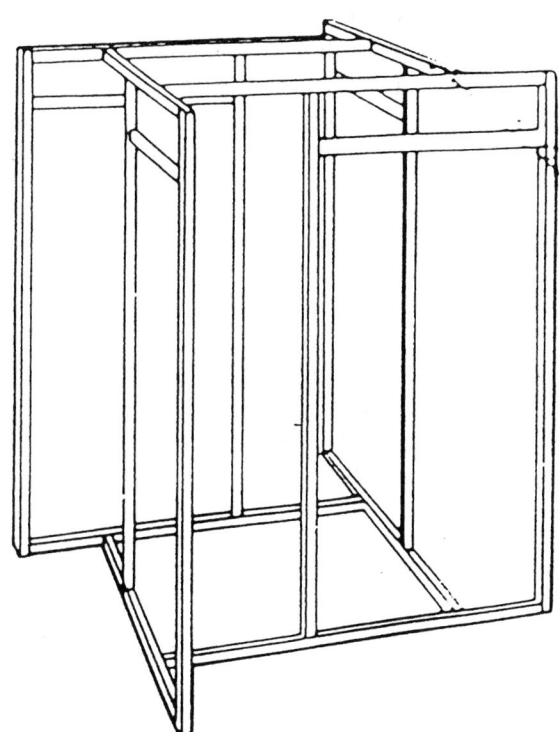

Figure 6-9a Two-way fixture with angled waterfalls for ease of viewing and displaying products. (Illustration courtesy of SOI Interior Design.)

Figure 6-9b Four-way fixture often used to display coordinates in a clothing store. (Illustration courtesy of SOI Interior Design.)

noncolors or neutral colors for the large planes that serve as a backdrop for the merchandise. Dramatic interiors can be created by using dark colors on walls, ceiling, and floors if this is a reflection of the merchandise mix and target customer. If a specific dominant color is requested by the retailer, the interior designer must make certain that it does not interact or conflict with the changing colors of the merchandise. This is especially true in clothing stores since the colors of current merchandise change more rapidly in the apparel market. Retailers recognize the value of color and color schemes in denoting certain periods or years. The majority of colors used in the interiors will reflect a tint onto the merchandise. To avoid this potential problem, noncolors and light neutrals are often used for walls and floors.

Lighting and Security Issues

The primary purpose of lighting is to improve the display of merchandise. Lighting systems can significantly increase the positive reaction of the consumer to products on display. Poor lighting or a lighting design that diminishes the visual qualities of the products will result in reduced sales of merchandise. (How often have you looked for a particular type of lighting fixture in an apparel store to be sure that the colors of garments match?) It is very important for the interior designer or lighting designer to carefully plan the types of light fixtures and lamps used throughout the store to best show off the merchandise.

In the sales area, three basic categories of lighting are used, which are directly related to the type of merchandise displayed: general, accent, and peripheral lighting. First, the store will require some type of general lighting to provide overall visibility. This can be done with a large variety of fixtures and requires lighting levels of 20 to 60 foot-candles, depending on the type of store and merchandise. The second type of lighting is very important in merchandising the goods. Accent lighting is necessary to add visual impact to displays. These lighting fixtures in particular should attract attention to the items displayed.

This is commonly achieved using track lighting since the light fixtures can easily be manipulated to highlight the changing displays. In clothing stores, be wary of placing lamping too close to the product, as it can distort color and fiber. In areas where the light fixtures will be minimally changed, recessed lights and wall washers can be used as peripheral lighting to attract attention to the wall displays and merchandise.

The recommended foot-candles needed for selling vary with the type of merchandise and the colors used. According to the Illuminating Engineering Society of North America (IESNA), between 30 and 60 foot-candles are recommended in merchandising areas.[24] In a boutique apparel store, for example, with lighting for display, the specific lighting can range from 60 to 90 foot-candles, with higher levels recommended for primary displays.[25]

Local codes may also impact lighting design in terms of energy usage. Large stores like grocery stores generally are limited in the number of watts per square foot to less than 2.0.[26] Smaller specialty stores often are allowed higher limits, depending on the merchandise. The designer must be sure that the lighting plan not only provides needed lighting levels for function but also meets any restrictions imposed by the jurisdiction for energy efficiency.

Another major concern of retailers is *security*, as they seek to deter customer theft or shoplifting, employee theft, burglary, and robbery. *Shoplifting*, the act of stealing merchandise from a store, along with other types of theft, is a major problem for the retail industry. The National Retail Security Survey reports that store theft costs U.S. retailers over $31 billion a year; 48 percent is due to unhappy employees and only 31 percent to shoplifters/customer theft.[27] Retailers attempt to prevent theft by the use of mirrors, limited-access areas, security guards, computerized cash registers, observation booths, electronic tags, television monitors, and fitting room attendants. Although 79 percent of retailers use mirrors for security, research has determined that mirrors are effective only 2 percent of the time.[28]

The most effective security measure is the electronic tag. Electronic tags are categorized under the term *radiofrequency identification*. A tag containing a circuit capable of emitting a radio signal is attached to a valuable piece of merchandise. If the tag is not removed or deactivated at the time of sale, an alarm goes off at the exit, which alerts the sales staff to theft. Another kind of electronic tag or marking device can code prices onto tickets. Still other tags are processed by optical character recognition (OCR) systems. The designer or retailer must make certain that very expensive items are not too close to the exit unless a cable wire is attached from the fixture to the product or the product is locked in a display cabinet. In addition to wrapping merchandise and taking money, personnel at the cashier/sales desk must monitor the store from this position in regard to security.

Code Requirements

The size of the store and its building type will govern the code requirements. In the International Building Code, the occupancy classification of retail stores is Mercantile. Showrooms, malls, department stores, grocery stores, and wholesale stores that are not simply warehouses are other examples of facilities classified as Mercantile. Retail stores must also meet accessibility requirements. Other codes, such as electrical and plumbing codes, are also applied to stores. Code requirements may vary somewhat when the store is located in a mixed-occupancy facility such as a hotel. The reader is urged to verify local code requirements for the particular project.

Corridors formed by full-height partitions are less common in retail stores. The traffic paths and exit accesses of a store are more likely to be aisles. Recall that an aisle is defined as an unenclosed traffic path formed by movable furniture or equipment.[29] Aisles

---

[24]Steffy, 2002, pp. 80–81.
[25]McGowan, 2003, p. 505.
[26]Karlen and Benya, 2004, p. 126.
[27]Marlene G. Albert, "Security Issues," *Retail Industry*. April 6, 2005. www.retailindustry.about.com
[28]Lewison, 1989, p. 237.
[29]Harmon and Kennon, 2005, p. 134.

can be considered exit access passageways in retail stores. When this is the case, they must be wide enough to meet the occupancy load, similar to exit access corridors. That clear width is a minimum of 36 to 44 inches. Space requirements between movable fixtures are determined by local jurisdictional codes.

Materials and finish selections will also have some restrictions related to fire and building codes. Architectural finishes for walls and ceilings must be Class A or B in almost all situations. Flooring must meet Class I or II standards for fire safety. With the large amount of combustible material in stores in the form of merchandise, the interior designer needs to use great care in the location and specification of lighting fixture so that hot lamps do not cause a fire. Decorative treatments that add interest to walls or ceilings should be carefully selected to reduce fire hazards and be specified according to local codes.

Stairs and raised floor areas must be designed for both accessibility and safety. Railings are needed for raised areas unless the local jurisdiction allows for a variance. Ramps are needed as well to ensure that the raised area is accessible. Materials on stairs leading to raised areas may need to be a different material from those on the remainder of the floor surfaces to help prevent falls and for recognition of the raised areas related to accessibility regulations. Code officials in the local jurisdiction must be consulted concerning plans for raised areas in retail stores.

Retail stores must also provide toilet facilities. A small store needs to provide only a unisex toilet facility. Larger stores must provide separate toilet facilities for men and women, with one or more fixtures for employees and the public. Mercantile occupancies are not required to have separate facilities for employees and the public. Toilet facilities must comply with accessibility standards, with a minimum of one accessible toilet facility (for each sex as necessary).

This brief discussion does not cover all the code requirements for the wide variety of retail establishments. As always, the interior designer must prepare drawings and specifications that meet existing local codes for the facility and its location.

Design Applications

There are a multitude of retail stores based on the type of merchandise sold. There are many stores that sell apparel, accessories, linens, and other soft goods. *Soft goods* are also referred to as *soft lines*. Products such as appliances, furniture, sporting goods, and the like are often referred to as *hard goods*. As noted in the section on Planning and Interior Design Elements, many elements that go into the planning of a retail store are very similar, regardless of the type of merchandise offered for sale. However, it would be impossible to discuss specific design applications for each kind of retail store in this book.

It is important to look at how the planning and design concepts discussed in the preceding section apply to particular facilities. This section on Design Application focuses on small clothing stores and furniture stores. In these types of stores, it is possible to discuss issues related to both soft lines and hard lines as the focus of the merchandise mix of specific stores. They are also familiar to students and professionals. The chapter will conclude with a brief discussion of the interior design needs of gift stores and salons.

Clothing Stores

The merchandising concept developed by the store owner is critical to the early schematic design and specification of the store. The retailer will give the interior designer information on where to group merchandise, to aid the customer in locating and selecting merchandise. In preparing drawings and specifications for the interior design of a clothing store, one of the responsibilities of the interior designer is to organize the merchandise areas into logical selling groups and allocate space and design layouts that are conducive to selling. In other words, the interior designer must make the shopping experience logical and comprehensive. The design of a small clothing store uses the same elements in space planning as many large clothing stores, including space allocation and traffic path planning, fixture specification and placement, sales area planning, location of dressing rooms and nonselling spaces, colors and material specification, and lighting.

A critical issue in a small clothing store is to maximize merchandise display and sales space, since this represents revenue-producing space just as the dining room represents revenue-producing space in a restaurant. The retailer will request that the maximum square footage be used for merchandise display and sales, while a small amount of space is allocated to nonselling functions. During the space-planning part of schematic design, the interior designer must present to the client the most flexible and functional plan. In apparel merchandising, it is important to remember that the volume of stock varies greatly, depending upon what is being sold. For this reason, the designer needs to plan space using those fixtures that will give the store owner or manager maximum flexibility in merchandise display.

In men's and women's clothing stores, the space-planning principle *in close proximity*[30] is quite effective. Because this type of store contains a wide variety of items that are used together, these items can be logically organized and displayed next to or near each other—in close proximity. For example, blouses and other tops are placed near skirts, pants, jackets, and accessories such as belts and scarves. Ties, belts, and dress pants are placed near dress shirts in men's stores. The close proximity of one product to another allows the sales clerk easy access and potential for selling more products to coordinate with the outfit. In addition, the interior designer often places three-way mirrors in close proximity to coordinating items to persuade the customer to leave the dressing room and view the outfit from one of the larger mirrors. This proximity gives the salesperson an opportunity to sell more items to complete the outfit.

Part of the overall programming information that will impact space planning is the expected volume and combination of demand, convenience, and impulse goods in the clothing store. Examples of demand merchandise in a clothing store are coats, dresses, and suits; convenience items are gloves, sweaters, ties, and socks; and impulse items are costume jewelry, scarves and handkerchiefs, and other accessories. The mix and amount of these various goods require different sizes and types of display fixtures. Obviously, the mix of these fixtures will have an impact on the overall planning of the selling space.

Clothing stores with a higher price point might have trunk shows from time to time. A *trunk show* is a merchandise demonstration by the fashion designer or manufacturer. If the trunk show is for the store's staff, then a small amount of space can be arranged around the seating placed near the dressing room. If the trunk show is for invited guests, then the movable fixtures and small seating units make it much easier for these shows to be held in the store.

Circulation and traffic paths through a clothing store are commonly achieved using the free-flow traffic pattern system, which allows flexibility, potential for creative placement of fixtures, and economical use of space. This traffic pattern system also allows for rapid changing of displays and fixtures. The majority of small retail outlets use a single, straight center aisle extending the length of the store. This aisle can vary, depending upon the placement of the fixtures. The width of the main aisle is usually 6 feet, with minor aisles ranging from 3 to 4 feet. In small clothing stores, stairs might be used to divide the selling space. Remember that accessibility requirements may impact the number of stairs and access to the raised areas. In larger clothing stores, stairs, escalators, and elevators must be easily accessible and are an important factor in determining the traffic pattern.

Flexible and fixed *display fixtures* are selected and specified once the basic merchandise zoning and the expected traffic patterns have been identified. The most commonly used flexible fixtures in clothing stores are two-ways, four-ways, spirals, and rounders. Clothing stores use mainly slat wall and modular perimeter frames as the fixed fixtures. Gondolas may also be used to display folded items such as dress shirts in a men's store or sweaters in a women's store.

Since merchandise volume changes from season to season, it is important that the clothing store fixtures be flexible in order to display the varying products to their full ad-

---

[30]Note that "in close proximity" is also used in many other types of retail stores.

vantage. One way this is done is to plan retail stores on a 4-foot module to accommodate the standard retail fixed fixtures available from fixtures suppliers. Spacing of display fixtures and counters will be impacted by jurisdictional codes and accessibility requirements. Movable fixtures are considered furniture, and there will be some flexibility in the size of aisles between fixtures. However, the interior designer should plan fixture placement for customer comfort, passage, and safety.

Clothing stores always have a few furniture items other than merchandise fixtures. The most common items are chairs, benches, or sofas placed close to the three-way mirrors or the dressing area. This seating is placed for the convenience of individuals accompanying the shopper. The scale of the chairs—the most commonly specified seating unit—should be small, and they should be constructed so that they will not tip or roll. Seating units should also be specified to accommodate persons of varying sizes. They should be specified and located so that they are not a hazard to customers walking nearby. Upholstered seats are more comfortable and more common in stores selling higher-priced and upscale merchandise. Chairs with open arms create less visual weight and can aid an older customer in using the chair. Banquettes are sometimes specified for boutiques.

An important piece of equipment in the selling space is the cash/wrap desk or counter (Figure 6-10). The designer will locate the cash register, the merchandise wrapping area, and storage required within the cash register area. The cash/wrap desk is almost always a custom cabinet designed by the interior designer to meet the requirements of the store owner. It is important that the designer have as much information from the retailer as possible about how this space will be used in order to best meet the retailer's needs.

A two-level counter is usually preferred, with the higher, outer portion used for check writing and the inside section used for the POS computer and cash drawers, the sales clerks' record keeping procedures, and gift wrapping (Figure 6-11). The higher counter top is usually at least 42 inches high, and the lower counter space reserved for the sales clerks' record keeping and package wrapping is built at a standard counter height of 36 inches. In addition, a lower, shallow outer shelf, placed appropriately for holding customers' handbags and packages, is often provided. The higher counter area allows for better security of the cash register or drawers. The accessibility standards will require that a portion of the customer's

Figure 6-10 A large custom-designed cash/wrap desk for Daniel's clothing store. Note the high-end elements such as open space, promoting luxury. (Photograph courtesy of JGA, Inc. Photography: Laszlo Regos.)

Figure 6-11 A custom-designed smaller cash/wrap desk for the Scarlet Tassel depicting the two levels: a raised outer level for check writing and an interior counter height for wrapping and receiving money. (Photograph courtesy of Moldovan Interior Design. Photographer: Chris Little.)

side of the counter be no higher than 34 to 36 inches or that an auxiliary counter be provided with a maximum height of 36 inches. Remember to include the toe kick space for the entire counter area to allow the customer and sales staff to stand flush with the space.

In the majority of stores, the cash/wrap desk will be supplied with a computerized cash register. These specialized computers will help the store owner or manager perform many management control functions. Besides printing out the receipt for the sale, the computer will keep an accurate inventory and make ordering new merchandise faster. The computer will also help the small-store owner problem bookkeeping and accounting functions. In regard to the use of the store's computer, remember that it is important to specify lighting which will prevent glare and veiling reflections on the monitor.

The selection of *colors and materials* is a little different for clothing stores than for other retail facilities. As stated earlier, it is very important that the color of the walls, floor, and ceiling not reflect a tint of a specific color onto the merchandise. It is always best to specify noncolors and neutrals for large-volume planes in the interior. Color distortion of merchandise is to be avoided. Since most of the walls are frequently covered by displayed clothing, neutral backgrounds for the walls are very common. Color punches might be appropriate as accents, such as behind the cash/wrap counter.

Materials used on floors should be specified with safety in mind as well as provide the appropriate design appeal. If the store has direct access to the outdoors, a slip-resistant mat will be needed at the door. Flooring close to the door should also be specified as slip resistant. Carpeting provides comfort and style and is a common material in many clothing stores. Carpet tiles can be used to create interesting designs on the floor surface if the space is large enough for the design to be seen effectively; however, patterned carpet can distract from the merchandise. Area rugs should be used only in locations that will not cause a customer to trip. Remember that wood floors, although warm and beautiful, also require extra maintenance.

Lighting also affects color and must be specified to allow color to read accurately as well as protect certain fibers from fading. Hiring a lighting designer who can specify the lighting requirements for the multitude of products found in a retail clothing store is important to achieve this accurate color rendition. The interior designer should be involved in the specification of the luminaries used in the store. For example, if a ceiling is white and the rim of the recessed lighting fixture is black, the contrast could create too much pattern and visual activity on the ceiling.

In creating the lighting plan and specification, the designer starts with the client's goals regarding lighting. There are standard recommended lighting levels to consider in the planning, of course. Recommended lighting levels include the following: 50 foot-candles for cashier checkouts, 100 foot-candles for merchandise feature displays, and 30 foot-candles for merchandising areas.

Usually the client wants a lighting plan that entices the customer to move from one area to another. Retail lighting needs and solutions can be very creative, leaning on theatrical lighting effects to add interest and excitement. Cold cathode (neon) lamps are used for accents, as in signage or some graphic displays, to bring excitement to the location and attract the attention of customers. Incandescent spotlights on tracks provide flexibility when moving fixtures that will be used for display or items to be the center of attention. If the store is large enough, high-intensity discharge lamps can be used for overall general lighting (Figures 6-12a and 6-12b).

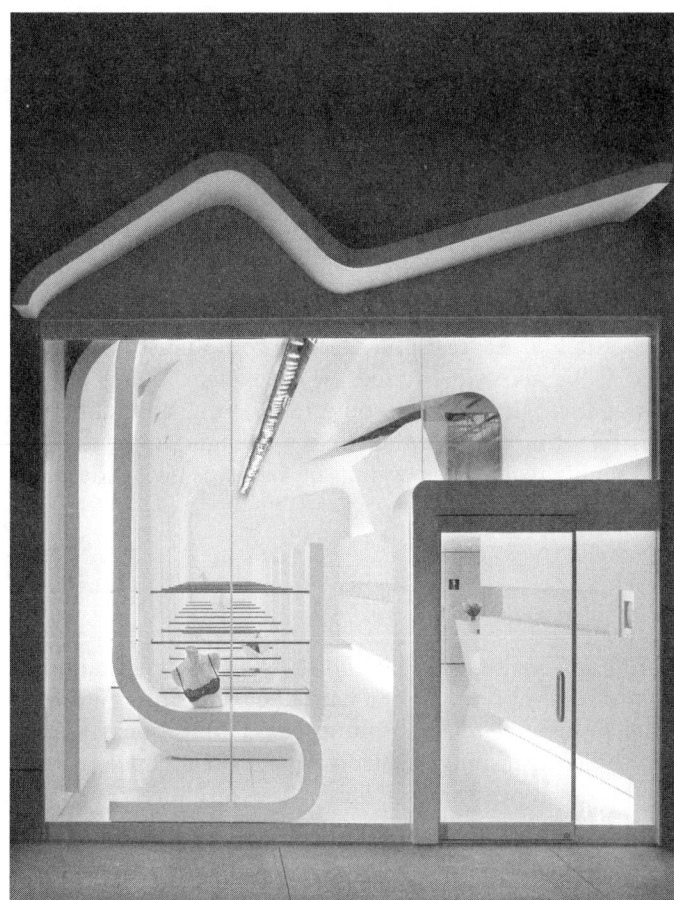

Figure 6-12a Exterior of a store prior to opening. (Randy Brown Architect and Assassi Productions.)

Figure 6-12b Interior view of the same store. Creative use of space and a white backdrop allow a focus on the product to be sold. (Randy Brown Architect and Assassi Productions.)

The last of the selling space items needing attention are the dressing rooms. Each dressing room needs to be provided with a stool, chair, or bench, a shelf for handbags or accessories, several hanging hooks, and a full-length mirror. Privacy is also an issue. In the majority of small clothing stores, the retailer prefers a three-way mirror specified at a 120 degree angle. It should be located in the selling space to allow the sales clerk to suggest additional items for purchase to enhance the outfit. At least one dressing room must meet accessibility standards.

Regardless of the size of the clothing store, a certain amount of *nonselling space* is necessary. Larger stores allot more space than small ones for nonselling functional needs. However, the larger the nonselling area, the less revenue-producing space will exist. Nonselling space must be judiciously planned to avoid wasting valuable space.

Nonselling areas in clothing stores provide facilities for receiving and signing for incoming stock, as well as unpacking and inspection of merchandise. Depending on the management concept of the store, preparation and repair work on merchandise might also be done in the back nonselling space, including ironing and/or steaming, sewing, repair work, and hanging new goods on racks before taking them to the sales areas.

Space is also required for administrative activities such as ordering, accounting, advertising, correspondence, and handling and storage of layaway items. If back stock is planned, space for storing excess stock as well as cleaning supplies, boxes, bags, bookkeeping papers, and sales receipts will be needed. Refer to Figure 6-5 for a nonselling space floor plan. Space must also be provided for the mechanical equipment that furnishes heating, cooling, light, and other utilities. Public restrooms or facilities for customers are generally provided.

Another category of clothing stores which brings in considerable revenue is children's clothing stores. Interior designers should remember that the basic concepts presented above apply to a children's clothing store; however, certain elements will be specified using smaller-scale furniture and dressing rooms which accommodate both the child and parent. Some stores include a small play area. This space must be carefully designed to ensure security and mitigate liability. An unsupervised play area where children might be injured is a potential liability.

There are a few code requirements to highlight. Remember to design aisles to meet accessibility and exit access requirements. These standards were discussed in the Code Requirements section in Planning and Interior Design Elements above. The cash/wrap desk must have accommodations for accessibility. At least one dressing room must be accessible, and additional ones may need to be accessible based on the square footage of the store. Depending on the type of door used, the dressing room needs to be a minimum of 54 by 72 inches. Less space is possible if a curtain rather than a swinging door is used. Toilet facilities must also meet accessibility regulations even if the facility is not made available to customers.

Furniture Stores

The residential retail furniture store has been selected for a discussion of design application primarily to present material on the interior design of a hard-line retail store. Although this section primarily discusses the residential retail furniture store, the principal ideas would also apply to the commercial office furnishings dealer as well as to a manufacturer's showroom. A brief discussion of the differences among these three furniture stores will address the main design considerations.

Interior design students can readily relate to the products that make up a residential furniture store. Visits and tours of furniture stores are common components of an interior design curriculum. Students also are often given the opportunity to visit manufacturers' showrooms when attending a trade show and may also visit office furnishings dealerships where commercial furniture items are displayed and sold. Interior design professionals are already familiar with furniture stores and showrooms as places to obtain goods for their clients. Furniture, appliances, hardware, equipment, and other nonapparel items are called *hard lines* or *hard-line merchandise*. The basic interior design elements utilized in the design of a furniture or hard-line store are similar to those used in the clothing store. However, because of the nature of the goods, there are several important differences in the interior design of a furniture store.

A furniture store—or generally any hard-line store—should be designed to facilitate the shoppers' recognition of the kind and quality of the merchandise. An important goal for the interior designer in planning and specifying a hard lines specialty store is to reflect the quality and nature of the product and services offered in the overall design of the facility. In addition, the layout of the store must allow for easy viewing of the generally large-scale merchandise. In a furniture store, this is done primarily by the use of *vignettes*, displays of furniture and accessories created to look like actual rooms. Many furniture stores use vignettes as window displays to entice customers into the store.

There are, of course, different qualities and styles of furniture. Some furniture stores may offer very specialized merchandise, such as a particular style of furniture (e.g., categories of antiques), while others offer a complete line of home furnishings with a variety of styles. Others may sell only a particular furniture line from one manufacturer.

Furniture stores often sell at least some items beyond the basic furniture items. Residential retail furniture stores in general offer a broad line of merchandise and usually stock many styles of furniture, area rugs, window treatments, bedding, lamps, and a wide variety of accessories from many manufacturers. In addition, a residential furniture store will offer interior design services as an impetus to further purchasing by the customer.

A furniture store almost always has large windows along portions of the exterior footprint of the store. These windows display completely furnished rooms (vignettes). Show window displays are paramount in exposing the potential customer to the products available in the store. They are also used to entice customers into the store by exposing merchandise to the passing traffic and serve to preview for potential buyers how a grouping of furniture can look in a home or commercial facility.

Furniture and other hardlines are often major purchases undertaken only occasionally. Visiting a furniture store can be exciting as well as intimidating. The architect, interior designer, and store owner must strive to make the main entrance appear to welcome the customers by allowing them to see inside, whether the doors are glass doors or solid wood doors with glass sidelights. It is important that the entrance be sufficient to provide a wide view of the interior of the store to create a welcoming feeling. It is common to place displays on each side of the door in order to expose customers to new products, to create an inviting entry, and/or to introduce the customer to a specialty item carried by the store.

The *circulation and traffic paths* within a furniture store are planned with specific goals in mind. Upon entering the store, customers are usually greeted by a receptionist or a sales clerk, depending upon the size of the facility. This "greeter" may then assist the customer or call someone to provide assistance. Of course, the customer may prefer to look through the store without assistance. Traffic paths lead the customer along the periphery of the store in order to see the window displays from another angle. These main traffic paths will also give the customer an opportunity to view the vignettes along other sides of the facility. Similar to the show windows, the internal vignettes are composed in an aesthetic, creative manner using new products or products on which the management is focusing for sales.

Depending on the size of the store, additional traffic paths may be needed at intervals to allow the customer to view many other internal sections of the sales floor. These internal traffic paths may be very flexible, meaning that they may change location from time to time as the displays of other merchandise are sold and rearranged. Some traffic paths may be fixed due to internal partitions used to create additional vignettes within the sales floor as well as column placement.

Traffic paths and aisles in a furniture store must be wide enough to move furniture as well as people. Spacing of some aisles will likely be regulated by local building codes, but generally a 4-foot aisle will be the minimum size required where code restrictions are not imposed. Often a variation in flooring materials is used for the traffic paths and the display space.

The merchandising layout of a furniture store is generally planned with categories of merchandise in mind. For example, high-end furniture lines are given visual priority and often placed toward the front, taking up perhaps a quarter of the available floor space. Depending upon the configuration of the show windows, high-end products may be placed on the right side of the store, as customers generally walk to the right upon entering a facility. This direction, however, varies with merchant preferences. Each individual store, with its own merchandise blend, will determine the focus of its products. The interior designer will rely upon the retailer for this specific information. This knowledge is critical to the interior designer, since the location of the displayed furniture in residential furniture stores plays an important part in the layout of the store.

From a merchandising standpoint, it is best to arrange the furniture into natural groupings. Such groupings are often used by higher-end and mid-priced furniture stores. Less creative approaches to display are used in stores that sell budget furniture. Many stores also group furniture items by types of rooms. In this case, the store will be planned to display several groupings of living room, dining room, and bedroom furniture—each in a separate section—so that customers can see and inspect a complete room setting. Less than full-height partitions may be constructed to create internal vignettes and to divide the sales floor in relation to the groupings. Electrical outlets placed in recessed floor boxes should be abundant for mobility in furniture placement on the main sales floor.

Depending on the size and total merchandising mix of the store, sections of the facility may be devoted to accessories, lamps, bedding, carpeting and other flooring materials, and perhaps window treatment displays. Accessories and lamps will also be used throughout the store to enhance the realism of vignettes. In addition to vignette display, lamps and accessories are often grouped together using step fixture display cabinetry.

There are some standard planning criteria for residential retail stores. If a furniture store is on more than one level, the first floor often contains living room and dining room furniture, lamps, and related accessories. The second floor may contain bedroom furniture and mattresses. Area rugs and carpets are placed toward the rear or side of the store on either the first or second floor. To some degree, this arrangement relates to the concepts of demand, convenience, and impulse merchandising. Depending on the price levels of the products and the product mix of the store, a portion of the display space may also be allotted to outdoor furniture as well as kitchen equipment. In the majority of furniture stores, sale items are placed at the back of the store or in the basement, which encourages customers to walk through the entire facility, thereby increasing their exposure to products and potential sales. Figure 6-13 is the Nebraska Furniture Mart, the largest furniture store in the United States.

Some of the nonselling areas of a furniture store will be visited by or at least visible to the customer. One of these will be the cashier's desk, which is often incorporated into the accounting or bookkeeping area at the back of the selling space with a window for receiving money and orders. Many furniture stores have an area for customer refreshments, which allows the customer and the sales clerk or interior designer to relax and discuss the products under consideration. It is important that this area be restricted, as food and drink should not be allowed on the sales floor for protection of the products sold. Since many furniture stores today have at least one interior designer on staff, an interior design studio space is often located near the periphery of the selling space. This studio will have room for the interior designers and may also accommodate a number of sample books of upholstery or other special-order catalogs. Individuals who are sales clerks rather than interior design staff are generally assigned their own desks, placed strategically throughout the selling space. These retail stores will also be required to provide restroom facilities for customers. Some very large residential retail stores also have a community room where space is set aside for informational classes for the consumer. This area is also used for staff meetings.

Figure 6-13 Interior view of the Nebraska Furniture Mart showing accessories grouped on the lower level with furniture vignettes displayed on the second level. This is the largest furniture store in the United States. (Photograph courtesy of Design Forum. Photograph by Jamie Padgett, Padgett & Co., Chicago, IL.)

Nonselling areas include storage spaces for back stock of some items, an employee lounge and employee restrooms, shipping and receiving areas, refinishing areas, and administrative offices. Since most furniture stores have either an attached warehouse or a warehouse at a remote location that is used to receive merchandise from manufacturers and store backup stock, the storage area in the main store is usually for cleaning materials, office supplies, and to hold goods that will be picked up by the customer.

The selection of *materials and finishes* for a furniture store is quite simple in comparison to that of other kinds of retail stores. It is necessary to keep the major wall surfaces predominantly neutral in order to create backgrounds that can feature many different kinds of furniture and fabrics. The majority of large wall spaces are specified as light noncolors, such as off-white or neutrals. Some vignettes displaying products that may be the mainstay of the store will use stronger colors, wallpapers, or wood paneling specifically chosen to enhance the products displayed.

Flooring materials in the main sales area need to be specified to allow for easy mobility, not only for customer access and comfort, but also for moving furniture. If vignettes are on raised platforms, some of these may have different flooring materials than those used throughout the store. This can alert customers to the change in level. In specifying carpet, the designer should stay with high-density, low-pile carpet, usually installed using the glue-down method. Many furniture stores have specified hard-surface flooring for the main traffic aisles and use carpeting for the display and minor traffic aisles. Due to the volume of fabrics on a furniture store's selling floor, the acoustical issue is not a serious problem since the fabrics and materials absorb some degree of sound.

A furniture store's *lighting* plan will consist of a combination of general and display lighting solutions. Because of the number of partition walls of various heights used to create vignette spaces, the numerous groupings of furniture, and the need to represent colors accurately, the lighting design of a furniture store requires the expertise of a lighting consultant. General lighting might be provided by fluorescent fixtures with color-correcting lamps or a mix of incandescent, halogen, and low-voltage lamps in suspended ceiling fixtures and track lighting. Track lighting using small fixtures for accent and display lighting is often needed in vignettes to highlight accessories or certain furniture items. Lighting should be planned to accommodate the accurate depiction of any color on display and to enhance the product displayed. Lighting in furniture stores can be used effectively to establish mood in the setting as well as to enhance visibility for the customer.

Furniture and other hard-line stores also have *security issues.* Small accessory items on the sales floor are common targets of customer theft and may have an electronic tag attached, much like items in clothing/gift stores. Because burglary is an issue during off hours, many furniture stores have on-site security officers or hire a security service. Employee theft also represents part of the security problem in a furniture store. For this reason, a large furniture store will have an employee checkout exit with a security guard or monitoring device in the area.

In the specification of materials and interior design, all retail stores must take care to limit potential liability. A primary consideration is floor surfaces. Slippery surfaces, uneven flooring, and exposed electrical wiring from lamps on display all create hazards that should be avoided. Placement of accessories or groupings of accessories and small items on shelves that might be tipped if handled by customers can also be a hazard. Spacing between furniture items is sometimes quite tight, and the sharp edges of tables and chairs can cause injury to customers. Of course, the store cannot completely guard against a customer tripping on furniture items; however, the spacing and layout of furniture items and vignettes to prevent such problems is very important. In other words, the interior designer must think strategically in regard to the liability factors in the design of furniture stores or in the design of any store.

A furniture store will have to meet applicable building, life safety, and accessibility codes and regulations. Furniture stores are classified as Mercantile occupancies in the International Building Code. However, since each jurisdiction or city has its own code requirements that the designer needs to address in planning a furniture store, it is the designer's responsibility to be clear on which model codes and other codes apply to the store in its intended location.

Because a furniture store is generally rather large, aisle widths and clearances in traffic paths considered exit access corridors are critical to planning. Although the occupant load of a furniture store will not be large, the distance from exit doors is usually large enough that additional exits are required. Spacing of furniture items is designed for easy flow of the customer to the items but is not generally regulated by codes.

Raised platforms for vignettes can cause problems for the interior designer. Some jurisdictions may feel that a railing is needed along the top of the riser or step so that a customer does not fall off the step. To ensure accessibility of raised platforms for vignettes, ramps might also be required. Interior designers need to check with local code officials about regulations if they wish to use raised platforms for the display of room vignettes. Raised platforms are used to call attention to specific types of products.

Architectural materials must be selected with fire and life safety codes in mind. Generally the materials on walls and floors will need to meet Class A, B, or C or Class I or II standards. The exceptions to this very general regulation for finishes are any corridors that are considered exit access corridors or those on a second or higher floor in the furniture store. Again, the designer must check with local codes for exact requirements.

Furniture stores must also be accessible. Accessible aids such as using thresholds which are flush with the floor or at least graduated; floors that are nonslip; and the use of high-density, low-pile carpet for ease of movement with walkers and wheelchairs are a few suggestions. Due to the nature of the furniture store, it is sometimes difficult for all areas to be completely accessible where the furniture is displayed, but the interior designer should do everything possible to provide sufficient space between groupings for accessible access. Public restrooms must be accessible, counters for paying bills must meet accessibility requirements, and areas with stairs or other risers must also have ramps, escalators, or elevators.

Some interior designers who specialize in retail design also specialize in the design of furniture stores and showrooms. In many cases, the interior designers working for a

---

BOX 6-2   DESIGNING COMMERCIAL DEALERSHIPS AND SHOWROOMS

In a broad sense, the space planning and interior design of a store that focus on commercial furniture products are generally not very different from those of a residential furniture store. A store that sells primarily commercial office furnishings is referred to as an *office furnishings dealership*. Commercial furniture is also sold in large office supply stores such as Staples and in some very large residential furniture stores.

Another type of store displaying and selling furniture is the manufacturer's showroom. A showroom is generally a wholesale rather than a retail store. Showrooms rarely allow customers to enter unless they are accompanied by an interior designer. That is why this type of facility is also referred to as a *trade showroom* (Figure 6B-2).

The office furnishings dealership displays, stocks, and sells only commercial quality furniture. It is called an office furnishings dealership because it sells exclusively or primarily furniture from one or more manufacturers. This furniture is usually office systems furniture. The company will also sell other furniture lines as well as case goods furniture.

The interior design of an office furniture dealership is created to show potential clients the firm's ability to design with the products they sell. Usually the selling floor will have less furniture as "display only" items. Most office furnishings dealerships combine their working areas for sales staff with display by utilizing the furniture items that they commonly sell to clients as furniture for the staff. In this way, the client sees the products in a working environment. In a sense, this is similar to the vignettes in a residential furniture store. If the company also provides interior design services, that department is often placed off the main selling floor, along with the design library of catalogs, samples, and appropriate auxiliary work spaces.

Furniture manufacturers as well as manufacturers of all types of residential and commercial products have showrooms located in or near trade marketplaces like the Merchandise Mart in Chicago and the Trade Mart in Dallas. Other manufacturers locate their showrooms near trade marts or in areas convenient to either the residential or commercial design community. A manufacturer's showroom is used mainly by interior designers for viewing actual products rather than depending on catalogs and sample books. It also contains offices for sales representatives working with the design community.

Depending on the needs of the manufacturer, the furniture items or other products might be displayed in vignettes or on specially designed display racks. Depending on the manufacturer or showroom, the majority of the floor space is allotted to furniture, with each area fully accessorized. Figure 6B-3 is an example of a showroom. In other situations, the showroom space is designed as a working office for representatives. However, the furniture shown consists of the key or primary product lines offered by the company. Nonselling space is provided for other general office functions and conference rooms as well as employee lunchrooms. Depending on the showroom, some storage space may be included. Most manufacturers' furniture showrooms do not receive merchandise at the showroom, as they sell infrequently directly to clients; this varies with the product line.

Figure 6B-2 View of furnishings displayed in the Decorator's Walk showroom. Lighting highlights various vignettes. (Photograph courtesy of Janet Schirn Design Group 2005.)

Figure 6B-3 Knoll showroom located in Houston, Texas, provides a contemporary setting for the predominantly 20th-century furniture. (Photograph courtesy of Knoll, Inc. Designer: Kenji Ito.)

particular furniture store may be responsible for the planning and design of the sales floor when the store is remodeled or they may work with the architect when a new store is designed. Manufacturers often utilize interior designers who are specialized retail designers or use staff at the product plant for the design and planning of their showrooms.

For the interior designer, furniture store layout and display can be an excellent method of design exposure to promote the designer's reputation and to secure additional clientele. A creative interior designer can develop a reputation that brings customers to the store, thus promoting the store and the designer. An excellent example is Barbara D'Arcy, whose international reputation in interior design developed through her visual merchandising of vignettes for Bloomingdale's in New York City.

Gift Stores

Gift stores are another interesting variety of retail store. Although the sizes of goods in a gift store tend to be small, the variety of goods in a gift store presents different challenges to the interior designer. The display of gifts requires varying viewing heights and an increased use of fixed-feature cabinetry in combination with specialized fixtures not commonly found in clothing and furniture stores. Otherwise, the interior design of a gift store generally involves the same design principles related to clothing stores.

As with most retail design, the merchandise mix is the starting point for the interior planning. Gift items are on average small in scale, sometimes delicate, and susceptible to breakage. Some items have a higher price point or are easily stolen if left readily accessible in the open. Gift stores also usually offer a large array of items for sale. This variety of sizes and price points will impact planning and fixture design as well as overall interior design. During programming, the interior designer discusses with the retailer the preferred zoning and product placement before planning and designing the interior space.

Effective gift store interior design starts with attention to visual merchandising at the windows of the store. Window displays should attract the customer to the window and into the selling space. Because of the small size of items in a gift store, display windows should be carefully considered and designed for better viewing of the merchandise. See Table 6-4 for information on common types of display windows; these are commonly used in gift stores. When items for sale are small, the function of the display is to initially draw attention to the window and then to the product. For example, a colored backdrop or dramatic lighting can highlight the product in the window. Using the design principles of repetition and variation in size and shape helps to create an aesthetic whole and can aid in the inclusion of several products. Often it is the harmonious arrangement of display items that entices the customer to enter the store.

Circulation and traffic patterns are established by the placement of the fixed features such as wall cabinetry and the cash/wrap counter, as well as the island fixtures and the gondolas. Depending upon the size of the store, there is usually a 6-foot-wide central aisle or main aisle, with the minor aisles being 3 to 4 feet wide. Gift store designers often use the grid system layout in jewelry stores and sometimes the boutique floor plan when developing the zoning and traffic patterns. The grid system is more conducive to fixed features such as built-in cabinetry and other display units which are not easily moved (Figure 6-14a).

An important part of the space planning of the gift store is the placement of the cash/wrap or checkout counter. The cash/wrap counter is usually placed toward the front of or at least one third of the distance into the selling space. A clear sightline should be planned for security measures. In a small shop with few employees on the sales floor, it is important that the wrapping area be situated at the cash/wrap counter. Ideally, the sales clerk should not have to turn his or her back to the customer while wrapping in order to monitor the store from this counter. The cash/wrap counter is a custom cabinet designed by the interior designer to meet the specific needs of the store owner. For example, space will be needed for the computerized cash register, as well as storage space for bags, tissue paper, and other items needed to wrap purchases. The cabinet has other design characteristics similar to those of the cabinet discussed in the section on clothing stores. The cash/wrap counter will also need to be designed to meet applicable accessibility requirements.

Display fixtures are predominantly retail cabinetry, shelving systems, and slatwall fixtures. The retail market has manufacturers of retail cabinetry which can be ready-made or custom-designed. However, interior designers may have to provide working drawings and all specifications for custom fixtures. A wide variety of gondola and open and closed shelving units can be obtained to display the many different types of items that might be sold in a gift store. The gondola fixture is popular and provides a gradation of shelving depth which allows the customer to easily view the bottom shelf. Custom-designed shelving also provides a visual break by emphasizing the end units of shelving and display cases.

With the use of slatwall fixtures and its multitude of accompanying accessories, the combination of hanging, display, and shelving seems endless. Slatwall is popular due to its versatility for display, as well as the aesthetic appeal created by the specification of custom surfaces.

An important planning consideration for gift stores or other stores selling small items is the display of goods relative to eye level. Shelving and displays are planned using average dimensions for eye level. Figure 6-14b is an example of this type of product display. Higher-priced items or new products are often placed at eye level for easy viewing by customers. Valuable products can be stored and displayed in locked glass cabinetry. Base-type cabinetry with open shelving above is often accompanied by closed and locked shelving below for storage of inventory. Due to viewing angles, the lower shelving can be more difficult to access, especially for customers with accessibility needs or senior citizens.

Establishing a harmonious interior without a feeling of clutter is a major goal of the interior designer in designing a gift store. The retailer is interested in exposing the customer to the full line of products offered, but this must be done with an organized approach to the displays. The interior designer must specify or custom design shelving which separates and highlights the individual products. With proper positioning of the fixtures, the customer can be enticed

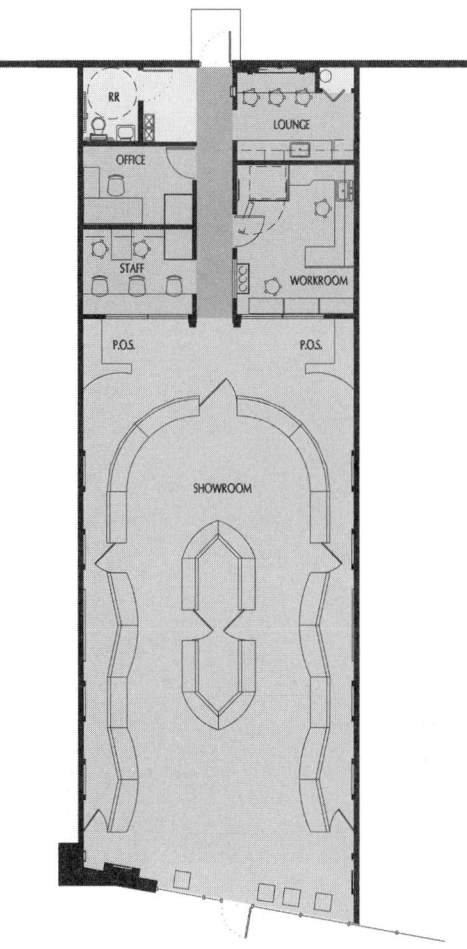

Figure 6-14a The layout of the selling space allows visibility of products and ease of movement throughout the space. (Burke, Hogue & Mills Architects.)

Figure 6-14b The fixed cabinetry allows ease of viewing and security of the product. The curvilinear design of the cabinet fronts aids in reducing the visual length of the space. (Burke, Hogue & Mills Architects.)

to walk through the space and thereby will be exposed to the majority of products for sale (Figures 6-15 and 6-16).

Gift stores will require some nonselling space, usually only a small percentage of the overall square footage of the shop. The exact needs in the nonselling areas will be clarified by the store owner. A receiving area where boxes can be opened and inspected is required. Although some of the back stock is stored in the display fixtures, additional space for stock may be needed. A few shelves to store small boxes that might be needed to wrap or ship merchandise, as well as space to hold cleaning supplies, is often required. A small desk or administrative area for the shop owner to prepare purchase orders, check in merchandise, and perform other office functions is necessary. Space for an employee restroom and a secure place for employees to store personal items are also part of the nonselling area. The store will need restrooms for customers based on the size of the store and local codes. The restroom must adhere to building and accessibility codes.

The interior *materials and finishes* used in the design of a gift store should combine function and practicality with creativity. Materials specification is varied, depending upon the items sold, the square footage, the height of the ceiling, and other factors specific to the store. A very important factor is the need to create a background which will not compete with the items for sale. The multitude of items in a gift store can create too much pattern if the architectural materials specified compete too strongly with the products. It is essential for the walls, floor, ceiling, fixtures, and all cabinetry to avoid overpowering the retail space. Noncolor or neutral background colors are usually preferred for the walls and cabinetry. Figure 6-17 is an example of an effective interior using a noncolor color scheme as a backdrop.

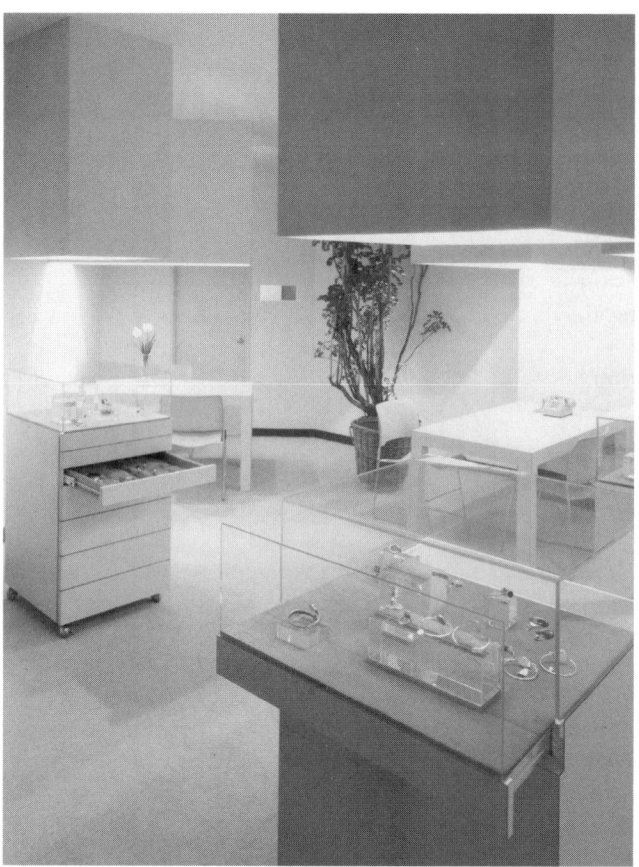

Figure 6-15 Custom-designed cabinetry for Elsco demonstrating display, storage, and lighting as well as client selling space. (Photograph courtesy of Janet Schirn Design Group 2005.)

Gift stores depend on various holidays for much of their revenue. Changing displays and utilizing temporary finish decorations help set the right mood. For each holiday, the majority of the selling space should be a compatible color or noncolor which recedes visually and allows the products to be more visible; for example, red, white, and blue for the Fourth of July, orange and black for Halloween, and pastels for Easter are generic examples of holiday color schemes that must be figured into the visual space.

High-density, low-pile carpeting is often selected when a soft floor covering is appropriate. Carpeting is the preferred flooring material in many small gift stores, especially those selling higher-end products and jewelry stores. Of course, carpet will show traffic patterns faster and will need cleaning frequently. Small to medium-sized patterns will help disguise traffic patterns. Hard-surface flooring is noisier and may require special maintenance. Some hard-surface floorings, such as marble and travertine, are often associated with a luxury interior, however.

Lighting for the selling space includes general lighting for monitoring the space and ambient lighting to attract attention to walls. Pendant lighting to designate specific areas and task lighting to highlight specific products and work surfaces are all used in planning gift stores. Track light fixtures and various pendant fixtures can be used to attract attention to specific areas or displays. Pendant fixtures at the cash/wrap counter not only provide needed task light but also help call attention to the POS area. Flexibility in the lighting design will help the store owner achieve the focused lighting needed to entice the customer. Colored lights and sparkle lighting can also be used to help create an exciting environment.

Remember that the selection of lighting fixtures also impacts the image and the design concept. Lighting fixtures can create a conservative, mysterious, luxurious, or even

Figure 6-16 The pathway created by the flooring allows customers to move easily through the space, leaving sufficient space for product display. (Photograph courtesy of Moldovan Interior Design. Photographer: Chris Little.)

Figure 6-17 White, off-white, or neutral backgrounds allow the product to be highlighted, as well as provide a backdrop for the variety of colors found in items for sale. (Photograph courtesy of Janet Schirn Design Group 2005.)

dynamic mood as they coordinate with the types of lamps used and the color scheme of the interior. The lamp families generally used in merchandise spaces are incandescent, fluorescent, high intensity discharge, and cold cathode.[31] Including a lighting consultant in the planning process is very important for interior designers who do not have experience in the lighting design of retail stores. The reader may also want to refer to the earlier discussion on lighting in the clothing store. The principles applied to clothing stores are very similar to those concerning gift stores.

Despite electronic tagging and labeling, security is an issue due to the small size of gift items. These items can be readily removed from shelving and stolen despite the presence of alarm systems. Security cameras in obscure areas of the store are effective as long as the customer's privacy is not jeopardized. Convex mirrors continue to be an inexpensive and somewhat effective monitoring device due to their visibility.

Code compliance is another concern for the interior designer hired to plan and specify a gift store. Once again, a gift store will be classified as a Mercantile occupancy in the International Building Code. If the gift store is located in another type of occupancy, such as a hotel or hospital, materials for architectural finishes may be more highly regulated than those of a gift shop in a retail store configuration. Accessibility requirements will impact the design of a gift store as well. The cash/wrap desk must meet accessibility standards and might also need to be redesigned in an existing facility space.

Salons

With the increasing interest in maintaining good health and a quality lifestyle, more dollars are being spent today than ever before on physical improvement and the multitude of subjects related to it. According to the U.S. Census Bureau, in 2001 the salon industry gained over $25 billion dollars in revenue.[32] Advertisements selling anti-aging products bombard consumers from all types of media in an attempt to promote consumer spending, flooding the market with the latest age prevention products and procedures.

One avenue for this spending is the salon or beauty salon. Those who work in a beauty salon include cosmetologists, hairstylists, shampooers, and manicurist/pedicurists. Licensing and training requirements vary for each job description. A *full-service salon* provides services that include hair cutting and styling, coloring, manicures, and pedicures. The exact mix of services obviously varies with the size of the salon and the mix of its customers. In many salons, the cosmetologists are employees. In others, a stylist or manicurist, for example, may lease a "chair" or space from the owner of the salon.

The value of an interior designer's participation in the design of a salon is multifaceted. Customers look for image and self-improvement procedures when they come to a salon. They also seek a salon with excellent services and an image of luxury and pampering. Thus, the interior designer has the opportunity to highlight his or her creative abilities more dramatically than in some other commercial installations. The interior designer needs to balance the entertainment value of the interior design with the needs of the salon owner (client) and employees. (We use the term customers or *clientele* to refer to the salon's customers. The term *client* refers to the salon owner.)

The interior designer needs to understand that salons must adhere to strict jurisdictional regulations. These regulations will impact the planning and design options. Interior designers who wish to design beauty salons and other personal enhancement facilities must become familiar with all the regulations related to the design of these spaces. Understanding the salon business is also necessary to assess the client's functional and aesthetic needs.

A *full-service salon* basically offers the following: all hair treatments, manicures, skin care, and the sale of professional salon products. Some salons also offer day spas whose services include massages, anti-aging techniques and products, facials, and nutritional counseling, among others. Knowing the service offerings mix is very important for the interior designer

---

[31]Steffy, 2002, pp. 114–115.
[32]Jenny Fulbright. "How to Start a Hair and Salon Business." April, 2005, pp. 1–2. www.powerhomebiz.com.

to plan a functional and aesthetic facility. The target market customers will also have an impact on design decisions. A shop catering to older customers will require different design specifications than one targeting a younger age group. Note that spa design concepts and elements are discussed in the section on Spas and Recreational Facilities in Chapter 4.

The interior designer needs to interview the client thoroughly to understand the aesthetic and functional needs and legal requirements of a salon. In addition to building and accessibility codes, there are health department regulations in many jurisdictions. Zoning, traffic patterns, and furniture/fixtures placement are important aspects of programming. The salon owner or franchise office will have a specific design concept related to the preferences of the clientele. A salon may have a logo, signage, and a color scheme associated with its name, and the designer should incorporate these elements into the design. This section will walk the reader through important planning elements of a generic salon to show the movement of a customer through the space. Other design tips are offered in Table 6-6.

An important element in the design of a salon is the entry. Some salons prefer large, spacious windows at the entry, while others prefer a more private, enclosed entry.

TABLE 6-6 Salon Design Tips

Reception/Waiting Areas

- The reception counter at the entry is at stand-up height for customers and at sit-down height for employees. Counter space is needed for a telephone, appointment books, and a cash register or computer.
- Provide space for customers' coats or access to a dressing room.
- A small refreshment area may be located in the waiting room or refreshments may be served by the receptionist.
- Specify appropriate display fixtures for product display and sale near the reception counter or in the waiting area.
- Pendent lighting fixtures can be excellent design features in this area.

Shampoo Area

- The number of wash basins should be at least one third of the number of styling stations.*
- At least 24 inches should be allowed between wash basins.
- Specify a shelf or shelves for products, equipment, and towels behind or within easy reach of each wash basin.

Styling Stations

- Some salons provide movable carts rather than millwork cabinets for stylists' stations with drawers or shelves to store products and equipment.
- Provide a safe place for customers to store their handbag at the styling station.
- Multiple electrical outlets are needed for trimmers and blow dryers.
- Excellent lighting for stylists is required.

Hair Drying

- Specify comfortable chairs and small tables for magazine and refreshments.
- Provide space behind chairs for floor-standing hair dryers and color lamps.
- Provide task lights so that customers can read magazines.

Manicure and Pedicure Stations

- Ideally, locate them away from the styling and waiting areas due to fumes from products.
- Provide a small counter for display of products for sale.
- Tables and chairs are specially designed units that provide ergonomic comfort for the technician and customer.
- A small sink in close proximity is desirable.

Makeup Station

- A counter at stand-up height is needed to hold products and equipment.
- Generally, the customer will be seated in a bar-height stool/chair with a back.
- Lower chairs may be used for salons that cater to older customers.
- Decorator bulbs placed on each side of the mirror at face level are commonly used.
- Full-spectrum lighting should be used to imitate daylight, nighttime, and office lighting.
- A nearby sink is desirable to clean and disinfect equipment.

*Remodeling Tips. Concession by GAMMA Arredamenti Sri, April 2005, p. 1–3. www.beautydesign.com.

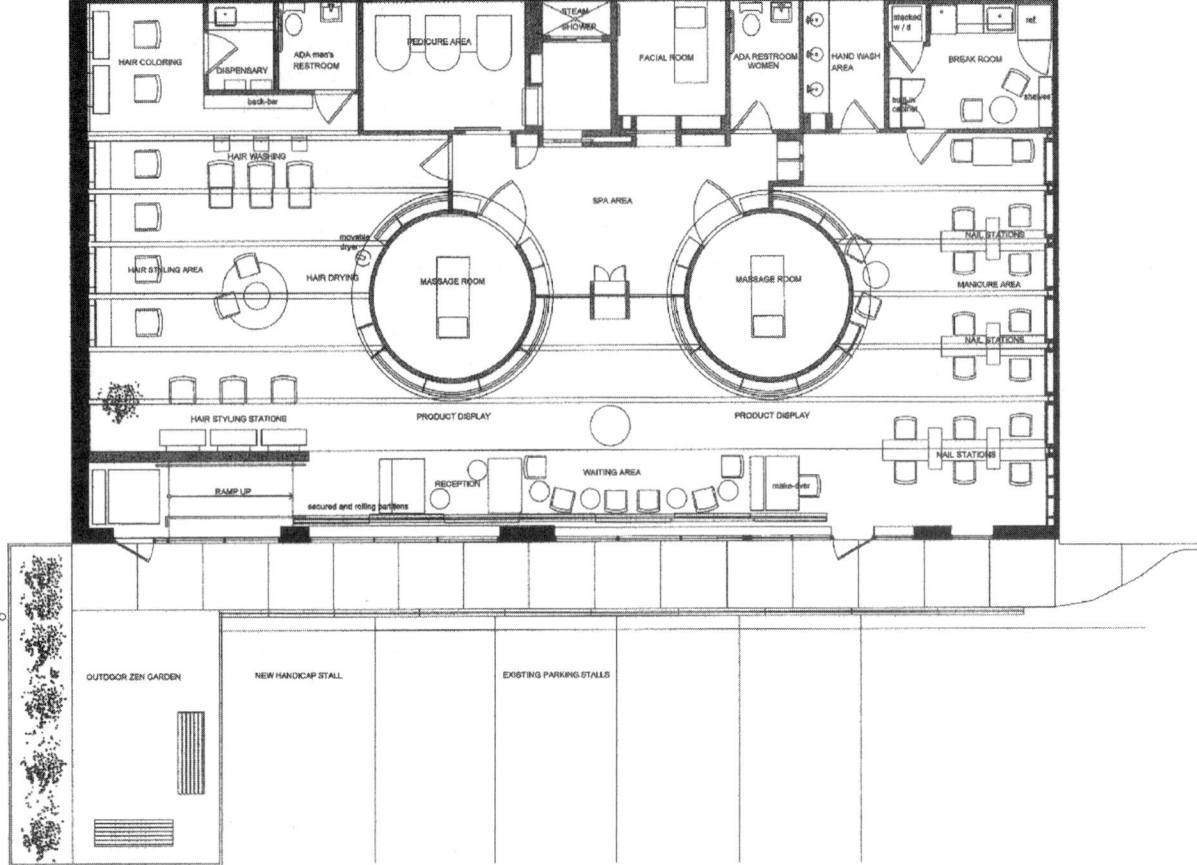

Figure 6-18 Floor plan of a salon. Note the appropriate zoning of work spaces as well as customer comfort. (Floor plan courtesy of Jim Postell, architect and designer.)

The majority of salons prefer as much natural light in the facility as possible. Figure 6-18 provides a floor plan of a salon. A reception counter where customers check in, pay for services, and make future appointments should face the entry.

After checking in, customers are directed to a nearby coatroom or dressing room if robes or salon shifts are provided. The customer then proceeds to an adjacent waiting area. The waiting area includes comfortable seating and tables with magazines. Light refreshments are generally available and may be placed in the waiting area or served from a rear mini kitchen. Displays of salon products for the hair and skin, as well as other items for impulse purchasing, are often placed on shelves or other types of display fixtures on the peripheral walls of the waiting area and reception entry.

The first service performed for the customer is a shampoo. The shampoo area generally has several washbasins with a chair that allows the customer to recline. Floor space is needed for each shampoo operator to stand and bend at the side and/or back of the basin. Storage for products and towels is needed within reach by the operator behind or beside the basin. Direct lighting on the basin is important to allow the shampoo operator to see clearly (Figure 6-19). After the shampoo the customer may be asked to wait for the stylist. Additional seating near the styling stations that provides a measure of privacy is necessary.

Styling stations can be designed in many ways. Styling cabinets can be wall-mounted or freestanding, depending upon the design and the overall traffic pattern. They can be custom made or a stock design from salon suppliers. Above the counter, a large mirror gives the customer an opportunity to watch and comment on the process. Cupboards and drawers are needed for equipment, products, and storage. Stylist chairs are special units available from salon equipment vendors.

For most customers, the hair will be blow-dried by the stylist at the main station. Others will need to spend time under a hair dryer or color lamp in a separate station. Comfortable seating is needed since customers may spend 45 to 60 minutes under the dryer. The chairs may be special designs from salon supply vendors or other seating with floor-standing dryers (Figure 6-20).

Large salons plan a separate area for hair coloring and permanents. Chemical fumes are easier to control by a ventilation system specifically designed for that space. A small room for mixing colors and other chemicals as well as recording customers' color formulas is also common.

Manicures and pedicures involve fumes and other scents from products. Thus, it is preferable to plan an area away from the styling stations or waiting areas if possible. The pedicure area is often secluded, either in a separate room, behind a partial wall, or separated by a screen for customer privacy. Manicure tables are small, generally 35 by 16 inches, but provide sufficient space for the arms and hands of the customer to rest comfortably during treatment. Storage is needed adjacent to the table for supplies and equipment. Excellent task lighting at the table is required so that the manicurist can work well.

Salons use specially designed pedicure chairs for ease of use by the operator to prevent job injuries. The chair for the customer is also specially designed. It is elevated, with the feet placed at a height that is ergonomically safe for both the pedicurist and the customer. Quality task lighting is also required. Storage and space for pedicure products, as well as equipment for other procedures, is needed.

Sanitation and cleanliness are of major importance in these areas, as infections can occur from cut skin. In fact, it is common to see manicurists and pedicurists wearing latex gloves to prevent contamination. Ergonomic issues in the use of the hand are probably more complex for the manicurist than for employees at other stations.

Salons can offer special makeup services for their customers. Customers may come to a salon for makeup before a special event. A few tips on the design of a station for the application of makeup are provided in Table 6-6.

Furniture, as discussed above, is often specified from salon specialty vendors. Furniture and fixtures in a salon need to be purchased for their ergonomic as well as aesthetic value. The client will know the exact equipment type preferred, and the interior designer will blend these preferences with all of the other elements to create a harmonious environment. In addition to ergonomic issues, more emphasis is being placed on the sculptural value of the units as the demand for more luxury in salons increases. In specifying upholstered seating for the stylists' stations, shampoo chairs, and color stations, it is imperative that the material be durable, washable, and impervious to stains and strong chemicals. Hospital-grade vinyl is often specified for these seating units.

Waiting room seating requires a sense of luxury and comfort. Therefore, designers often specify woven commercial-grade fabrics on fully upholstered chairs, benches, or sofas for this area. If the salon's target clientele is older, chairs with open arms and a seat height of at least 20 inches should be used. Be wary of specifying any type of glass-topped tables in any of the waiting areas.

There are several considerations in the selection of materials and finishes in the interior design of a salon. Carpeting is rarely used since it is difficult to maintain. Stains, chemicals, and cut hair are just some of the problems that make carpeting a difficult material for a salon. Floors should be specified with hard-surface materials that are durable and easy to clean and sanitize. Nonslip flooring is best for all treatment areas since water and other liquids can be spilled on the floor. For the comfort of the

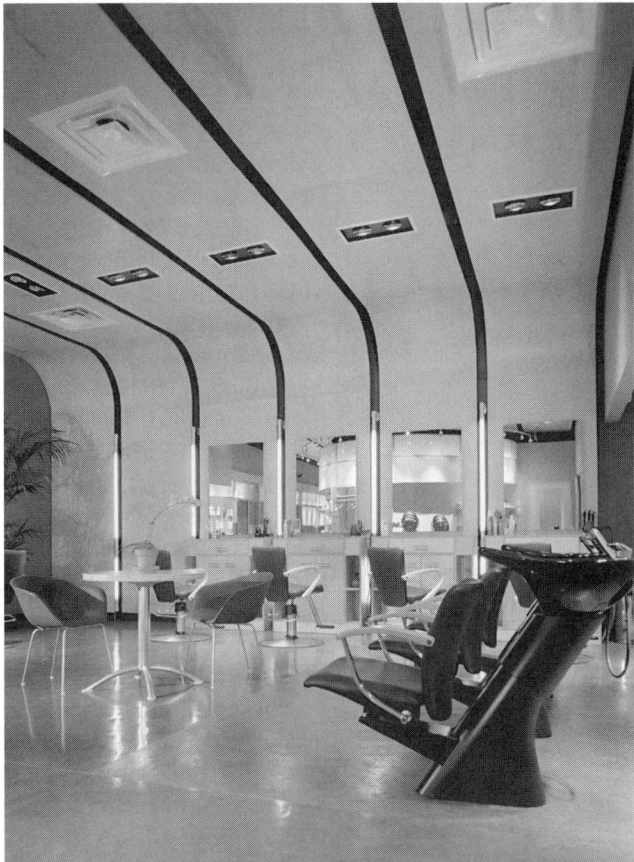

Figure 6-19 Wash basins within the salon provide attractive and comfortable stations for customer and employee use. Note the creative application of the ceiling design. (Photograph courtesy of Jim Postell, architect and designer. Photographer: Scott Hisey Photography, www.hiseyphotography.com)

Figure 6-20 Styling stations are positioned for ease of use and in close proximity to some wash basins. Note the product display within easy range. (Photograph courtesy of Jim Postell, architect and designer. Photographer: Scott Hisey Photography, www.hiseyphotography.com)

stylist, a specially designed floor pad is used in the stylist's station around the stylist's chair.

Walls can be finished in many kinds of materials. Code requirements may impact some selections. Walls near the sinks and cabinet area where chemicals are to be mixed need to be finished in materials that are easily cleaned and resist moisture. Mirrors can create the illusion of increased space in small shops. Mirrors used this way must be carefully placed to avoid the reflection of clientele in areas such as the pedicure stations.

Color schemes are created with the shop owner's desires and the target market of customers in mind. Pale tones are associated with luxury and calm, whereas more intense color schemes are associated with a more energetic clientele. It is important to remember that the color scheme may affect the customer's appearance while receiving treatment. Generally, large-volume areas such as walls are assigned high-value neutral colors or pale tones so as not to create an additional color reflection on the complexion or hair of the clientele. Many salons use accent tones in nontreatment areas to create some contrast in mood or to promote a specific color scheme associated with the salon. The color scheme must reflect current trends within the space while ensuring that dominant colors do not overwhelm the neutral color or noncolor of walls and flooring.

Designers may choose to obscure the ceiling with the use of a charcoal color or other deep-toned color if the shop has a very high ceiling—a design treatment used in many kinds of retail stores. Other treatments are also used. Remember, customers are usually, at some point, reclined so that their focus is often on the ceiling. However, the ceiling is rarely a prime design feature.

Lighting levels must be selected to ensure the proper functional levels at the many stations in a salon. In addition, the lamps selected must not inappropriately affect the color tones of customers' skin and hair. Color analysis of customers' hair and complexion, clarity in product interpretation, and ease of viewing while styling are all impacted by the lighting plan. Specify lighting which replicates natural light as much as possible. Lighting placed to the sides of the mirror will counteract any direct downward shadow, which is generally not complimentary to facial features. Lighting should appear clear and natural and reflect the customer in the most flattering light possible. Direct overhead lighting such as spotlights or canned lighting is usually avoided in this area because it is not flattering.

Careful attention to the specification of electrical outlets is very important in a salon. Most treatment areas require several outlets for equipment. After the interior designer has determined what kinds of equipment are needed in each area, an electrical engineer must be consulted to ensure that the electrical load is properly planned.

Safety in a salon is very important. With wet areas and chemicals used extensively in most salons, flooring specification is critical to prevent falls and injuries. Exposed sharp edges on cabinets and tables, as well as the privacy of the customer, are also important safety issues. Salons (and barber shops) are classified as Business occupancies in the International Building Code. Cleanliness and sanitation are major concerns for the client, as these issues affect licensing as well as clientele traffic. Because of the use of products with strong fumes from chemicals needed for some treatments, indoor air quality is a major concern. An effective ventilation system is mandatory in planning a salon. Interior designers are generally not specialists in the area of biohazardous materials, so they must be alert to the subject when selecting materials specifications and choose materials carefully. To promote good indoor air quality in salons and spas, designers should consider specifying inert hard flooring materials, paints that have a low VOC emission, and the use of biodegradable wallcoverings. As mentioned, HVAC systems need to be installed with these issues in mind.

All salons are required to have a minimum of one unisex toilet facility that is accessible. Accessibility should be considered and planned for areas such as the reception desk, and for accommodation at the shampoo station and at least one styling station. In smaller shops, employee lockers are located in this enlarged space. In larger salons, a separate employee break room with a small kitchenette is part of the space plan. A large salon often includes a small administrative office for the owner or manager, a laundry for washing and drying towels and robes, and some back storage space for extra products, towels, and maintenance supplies. Codes will require a second entry to the rear.

Summary

Designing the interiors of retail stores is exciting and challenging. It requires knowledge of space planning, extensive understanding of merchandising of goods, sensitivity to the use of color, lighting design, materials and a lot of creativity. In this specialty, the client has very specific needs in terms of space planning, fixture specification, and materials that will help set the stage to sell the products and services. And yet, the client who hires the interior designer is not the only client who must be satisfied. The store's customers and what they expect from the store must also be considered in planning and design.

This chapter has provided an overview of the business of retailing as a basis for design decisions. Basic information to help the student and professional understand how to approach the design of a retail facility provides a background that must be supplemented with further research if the reader wishes to embark upon retail design as his or her specialty in commercial interior design. The references listed below provide a great deal of information on the design of retail stores. There are also associations and organizations that the interior designer can access for appropriate and current information on trends within retail categories. A few of those organizations are listed in the Appendix.

REFERENCES

Ballast, David Kent. 1994. *Interior Construction and Detailing.* Belmont, CA: Professional Publications.

Barr, Vilma and Charles E. Broudy. 1990. *Designing to Sell,* 2nd ed. New York: McGraw-Hill.

Barr, Vilma and Katherine Field. 1997. *Stores: Retail Display and Design.* Glen Cove, NY: PBC International.

Ching, D. K. Francis and Corky Binggelli. 2004. *Interior Design Illustrated.* New York: Wiley.

Colborne, Robert. 1996. *Visual Merchandising: The Business of Merchandise Presentation.* Florence, KY: Thomson Delmar Learning.

Curtis, Eleanor. 2004. *Fashion Retail.* New York: Wiley.

Davidson, Judith. 2005. "The Top 100 Giants." *Interior Design.* January, pp. 95–128.

Deane, Corinna. 2005. *The Inspired Retail Space*. Glouchester, MA: Rockport Publishers.

De Chiara, Joseph, Julius Panero, and Martin Zelnik. 1991. *Time-Saver Standards for Interior Design and Space Planning*. New York: McGraw-Hill.

Diamond, Jay and Ellen Diamond. 2003. *Contemporary Visual Merchandising and Environmental Design,* 3rd ed. Upper Saddle River, NJ: Prentice Hall.

Fitch, Rodney and Lance Knobel. 1990. *Retail Design*. New York: Watson-Guptill.

Fulbright, Jenny. 2005. "How to Start a Hair and Salon Business." April, pp. 1–2. www.powerhomebiz.com

Green, William R. 1991. *The Retail Store: Design and Construction*. New York: Van Nostrand Reinhold.

Hall, Matthew. 2005. "VM + SD Fixture Survey 2005." *VM + SD,* June.

Harmon, Sharon Koomen and Katherine E. Kennon. 2005. *The Codes Guidebook for Interiors*, 3rd ed. New York: Wiley.

Institute of Store Planners. 2004. *Stores and Retail Spaces 5*. New York: Watson-Guptill.

Israel, Lawrence J. 1994. *Store Planning/Design*. New York: Wiley.

Karlen, Mark and James Benya. 2004. *Lighting Design Basics*. New York: Wiley.

Kliment, Stephen A., ed. 2004. *Building Type Basics for Retail and Mixed-use Facilities*. New York: Wiley.

Lee, Seung-Eun, and Kim K. P. Johnson. 2005. "Shopping Behaviors: Implications for the Design of Retail Spaces." *Implications*, Vol. 2, Issue 5. www.informedesign.umn.edu.

Lewison, Dale M. 1989. *Essentials of Retailing,* 4th ed. Columbus, OH: Merrill.

———. 1994. *Essentials of Retailing,* 5th ed. New York: Macmillan College.

Lopez, Michael J. 1995. *Retail Store Planning and Design Manual*. New York: Wiley.

———. 2000. *Retail Store Planning and Design Manual,* 2nd ed. New York: Wiley.

Mason, J. B., M. L. Mayer, and H. F. Ezell. 1991. *Retailing*. Boston: Irwin.

McGowan, Maryrose. 2003. *Interior Graphics Standards*. New York: Wiley.

McGuiness, William J., Benjamin Stein, and John S. Reynolds. 1980. *Mechanical and Electrical Equipment for Buildings,* 6th ed. New York: Wiley.

Murillo, Lourdes. 2005. "The General Store: A Hidden Treasure of the Past." El Paso Community College web site. www.epcc.edu.

National Retail Merchants Association. 1987. *The Best of Store Design 3*. New York: PBC International.

Panero, Julius and Martin Zelnik. 1980. *Human Dimension and Interior Space*. New York. Whitney Library of Design.

Piotrowski, Christine. 2004. *Becoming an Interior Designer*. New York: Wiley.

Ragan, Sandra L. 1995. *Interior Color by Design: Commercial*. Rockport, MA: Rockport.

Reznikoff, S. C. 1986. *Interior Graphic and Design Standards*. New York. Watson-Guptill.

———. 1989. *Specifications for Commercial Interiors*. New York: Watson-Guptill.

Remodeling tips. 2005. Concession by GAMMA Arredamenti Sri, April, pp. 1–3. www.beautydesign.com.

Rodeman, Patricia. 1999. *Patterns in Interior Environments: Perception, Psychology, and Practice*. New York: Wiley.

Spence, William P. 1972. *Architecture*. New York: McKnight and McKnight.

Steffy, Gary. 2002. *Architectural Lighting Design*, 2nd ed. New York: Wiley.

Tingley, Judith C. and Lee E. Robert. 1999. *Gender Sell: How to Sell to the Opposite Sex*. New York: Simon & Schuster.

Underhill, Paco. 2000. *Why We Buy: The Science of Shopping*. New York: Touchstone Books.

U.S. Bureau of the Census. May 2002. *Annual Benchmark Report for Retail Trade and Food Services*. May. Washington, D.C.: Government printing office.

Weishar, Joseph. 1992. *Design for Effective Selling Space*. New York: McGraw-Hill.

Zaltman, Gerald. 2003. *How Customers Think: Essential Insights into the Mind of the Market*. Boston: Harvard Business School Press.

WEB SITES

Institute of Store Planners (ISP) www.ispo.org

National Association of Store Fixture Manufacturers www.nasfm.org

National Retail Federation. www.nrf.com

Retail Council of Canada www.retailcouncil.org

Salon Furniture www.salonfurniture.com

Retail Industry www.retailindustry.com (a web guide for information on retail industry)

Archetype (journal of the Woodwork Institute) www.woodworkinstitute.com

Retail Construction magazine www.retailconstruction-mag.com

Retail Traffic Magazine www.retailtrafficmag.com

VM + SD magazine www.visualstore.com

Note: Additional references related to material in this chapter are listed in the Appendix.

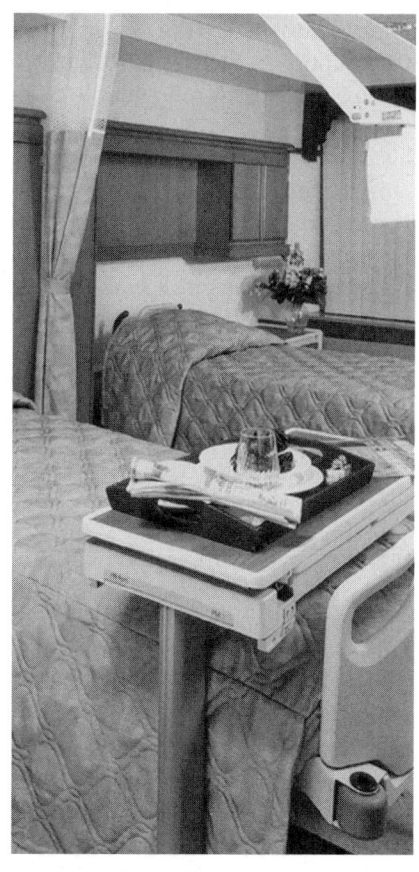

Healthcare Facilities

The current definition of the term *healthcare* states that it is the "prevention, treatment, and management of illness and the preservation of mental and physical well-being through the services offered by the medical and allied health professionals."[1] Healthcare facilities include many types of businesses that allow healthcare providers to prevent, treat, or cure diseases or ailments.

Most people have received medical treatment in one form or another. This experience begins with childhood checkups and illnesses and continues throughout adulthood. Because of these experiences, design students and professionals may have had contact with medical facilities supporting family practitioners, gynecologists, surgeons, and many other medical specialists. Additional healthcare providers such as dentists, orthodontists, optometrists, ophthalmologists, and veterinarians are most likely healthcare facilities visited by the student and the professional.

---

[1]*American Heritage Dictionary*, 1992, p. 833.

Casual exposure to healthcare facilities does not properly prepare a designer to specialize in this area of commercial interior design. For a successful outcome in designing medical facilities, the interior designer needs to have at minimum an understanding of the basic terminology associated with medical practice. The more knowledge the designer has of the healthcare field, and of the laws and regulations that apply to the design of healthcare facilities, the more effective he or she will be in creating functional and suitable project solutions.

This chapter begins with a brief discussion of the history of healthcare and continues with a general overview of organization and facilities of the healthcare industry. It describes the various types of healthcare facilities as well as general planning and design elements. Terminology for this chapter will be presented in each specialized section. Due to the broad scope of healthcare, the subject will be limited to specific discussions regarding design applications for medical office buildings and suites, hospitals, dental offices, and veterinary facilities.

Historical Overview

To provide a perspective on the evolution of medical facilities, it is important to discuss the history of medicine and patient care. As early as 3000 B.C., Egyptian records indicate the existence of physicians. Imhotep was the Egyptian god of healing. Between 1200 and 600 B.C., the Israelites practiced preventive medicine. In the 400s B.C., the Greek physician Hippocrates stated that disease had natural causes and was not caused by the gods. Ancient Egyptian and Greek temples were closely linked to healing. Historical evidence shows that places of healing existed throughout the world.

Hospitals were first associated with religious groups, with priests acting as healers. Government or public funding became more common as cultures grew more sophisticated. There are many references to Roman influence on the development of healthcare and treatment facilities. Ancient Roman institutions for the care and shelter of the sick were referred to as *valetudinaria*, referring to infirmaries, and were used for slaves and free Romans. The word *hospital* comes from the Latin word *hospitalis*, meaning an institution for guests.[2] The Romans also contributed to public health by building aqueducts which brought fresh water into Rome and a sewer system which improved health in that city.

During the Middle Ages, many contagious diseases were rampant throughout Europe. The Black Death in the 1350s is an example of devastation in that era. During the Crusades, the *hospitia* provided food, lodging, and medical care to the sick and was operated by the monks and staff in the adjacent monasteries. Religious orders operated most of the hospitals in this period and provided care not only for the sick, but also for the infirm, the poor, and travelers. The floor plan of these early hospitals was designed to look like a church structure with naves,[3] with beds lined up along the walls. The oldest hospital in Europe is the Hotel Dieu, in Paris, which was founded in the 600s A.D. During the Renaissance, the research and drawings of the human body by Leonard da Vinci aided in accelerating the study of medicine.

In the 1700s, Europe commenced the building of hospitals for the poor and those with contagious diseases. These charity hospitals were an effort to control the spread of contagious diseases. However, since they were overcrowded and unsanitary, they often contributed to disease, which spread throughout the facility.

The first hospital in the Americas was built by the Spanish government in the area now referred to as Santo Domingo, the Dominican Republic. The explorer Hernando Cortez founded the first hospital in Mexico City. In 1639, the first Canadian hospital was built in Quebec.

---

[2]*World Book Encyclopedia*, Vol. 9, 2003, p. 371.
[3]Kobus, 2000, p. 133.

In 1751, the first hospital was opened in Pennsylvania. Early hospitals in the United States were used to treat the poor. Because of their terrible reputation, the wealthy preferred to be treated in their homes or in hotels. These were considered to be more comfortable and safer in terms of protecting against infectious diseases. Physicians could bill for care delivered in a home, but it was considered unethical to bill hospital-based patients.

During the 19th century, several factors produced changes in hospital care. The first three were important developments that resulted in more widespread use of hospitals: (1) the discovery of anesthesia, (2) the introduction of antiseptic techniques, and (3) the establishment of the nursing profession. At the end of the 19th century, several innovations occurred which aided the development of more functional and efficient hospital buildings: (1) the use of long-span steel construction; (2) the development of elevators; and (3) the invention of air conditioning. Also, a variety of new floor plans were being developed, and smaller patient rooms were located off double-loaded central corridors.[4] All of these changes brought better hospital healthcare to the United States.

Hospitals also became teaching centers for doctors as well as training facilities for nurses. In the 1880s, U.S. hospitals added specialized facilities and surgical staff, which encouraged the performance of advanced surgical procedures. By 1900, the use of hospitals by physicians and patients had increased the cost of medical treatment. Private rooms for the rich and semiprivate rooms for the middle class added to the popular use of hospitals but also increased the cost of hospital care. By the 1890s, a hotel-like environment was added for affluent patients. This hotel approach resurfaced in hospital design in the 1980s. By 1929, the Blue Cross plan offered insurance to help patients pay their hospital bills.

During the Depression of the 1930s, hospital space was underutilized, as many patients could not afford hospital services due to financial stress. Hospitals turned empty patient rooms into physicians' offices. After World War II, there was an immediate increase in remodeling and expansion of hospitals as war veterans and the general population sought improved healthcare. New government programs after World War II increased the use of healthcare, which became more focused on the hospital facility. This also led to the development of the medical office building (MOB). The increasing complexity of patient care, specialization of physicians, and emphasis on ambulatory care rather than inpatient care fostered the growth of the MOB.

Newer and larger hospitals began to emerge in the 1940s due to U.S. government grants. In the 1960s, outpatient clinics for general family practice became popular. In 1965, the U.S. government established Medicare for citizens aged 65 and older. At the same time, Medicaid was established to help the poor pay for their healthcare. By the 1970s, hospitals began sharing equipment and personnel, especially in small or rural hospitals where the cost of the equipment was prohibitive. Trauma centers were established and included helicopters to transport patients. In the 1980s, the federal government developed diagnostic-related groups so that hospitals paid a fixed rate for treating Medicare patients.

New hospital designs to create healing environments continue to be important in hospital and healthcare design. The *healing environment* represents a philosophy that centers on the senses. Healing environments provide visual and acoustic comfort with design elements such as carpets to absorb noise, soothing colors, artwork, access to nature, and subdued lighting. All of these techniques aid in creating a residential atmosphere, which research has indicated aids in patient healing. The focus is on providing a more nurturing residential atmosphere with emphasis on the senses of sight, sound, touch, smell, and taste.

People have always had dental problems. In ancient cultures and into the Middle Ages, tooth extractions were often used as medical treatments for many diseases. Tooth extraction was practiced in ancient Egypt, Greece, and Rome. During the Middle Ages, dental work was performed by jewelers and barbers since there was no formal dentistry profession. Modern dentistry has continued to improve technologically, not only by developing new equipment but also through dental care, which promotes lifetime retention of teeth. Table 7-1 lists some highlights in the history of dentistry.

---

[4]Kobus, 2000 pp. 134–136.

TABLE 7-1 Milestones in Dental History

- Dental procedures were described in a French book published in 1728
- The dental profession was recognized and dentistry was practiced by the mid-1800s
- General anesthetics were used for dental treatment in 1850
- The first dental school in the United States, the Baltimore College of Dental Surgery, was founded in 1840
- X-rays were used for dental analysis in 1895
- Dental drills were broadly used by 1900
- Fluoride was added to water to reduce cavities in the 1950s

Source: World Book Encyclopedia, 2003. Chicago: World Book, Inc., Vol. 4, p. 145.

Overview of Healthcare/Medicine

Medical practice continues to change and expand as technology, knowledge, and science bring new answers and methods to treat patients. Computer databases for patient records are something to which the average reader can easily relate. Continual changes in medicine are also a challenge for the interior designer since they impact the design of any kind of healthcare facility. An interior designer wishing to specialize in healthcare design must be willing to learn about the healthcare field. Appreciation of the complexities of the field before accepting any interior design assignment leads to increased success of the project for all stakeholders and users. Learning the common terminology used by the client is critical to speeding the process and increasing success. Basic healthcare vocabulary is extensive. The designer may need to access medical dictionaries available in public libraries, in medical libraries, and on the Internet to clarify the terminology appropriate to a specific project. Table 7-2 provides a list of common terms related to information in this chapter. Additional terms are provided in other sections of the chapter.

Treatment in a hospital and other types of healthcare facilities may consist of preventive medicine, treatment for disease and/or illness, or health maintenance. The purpose is not only to save a patients' life but also to improve the patient's quality of life.

TABLE 7-2 Common Medical Terminology

- ANCILLARY DEPARTMENTS: Support functions in a hospital such as housekeeping.
- HEALTH MAINTENANCE ORGANIZATIONS (HMO): Large groups of healthcare providers offering services to member patients at either group clinics or a physician's medical office suite.
- INPATIENT: A patient who has been admitted to a hospital for medical care.
- LICENSED PRACTICAL NURSE (LPN): A nurse with a degree from a two-year nursing program.
- MEDICAL OFFICE BUILDING (MOB): Office building with one or more office suites for specialized medical practitioners.
- MEDICAL OFFICE SUITE: Various types of professional offices for practicing physicians and physician services.
- NURSE PRACTITIONER (NP): A nurse with both a bachelor's and a master's degree plus additional training in diagnosis so

- that he or she can provide some of the same care as a physician.
- OUTDATING: Many kinds of medical supplies must be used by a specific date. After that date, they are considered outdated and cannot be used.
- OUTPATIENT: A patient who does not require admittance to a hospital for medical care or treatment.
- PHYSICIAN'S ASSISTANT (PA): A nonphysician licensed to practice medicine under the supervision of a licensed physician.
- PRIMARY CARE PHYSICIAN (PCP): Usually the first physician the patient sees for treatment or another consultation.
- REDUNDANT CUEING: Sending a message to more than one sensory mode, such as with a change in floor texture.
- REGISTERED NURSE (RN): A nurse with an undergraduate degree in nursing.

TABLE 7-3 Health Maintenance Organization Models

1. Group. The physicians are partners of the group. Individual physicians are not paid directly, but rather on the basis of a group distribution decision.	3. Independent practice associations (IPA). A physician contracts with the IPA, which in turn contracts with an HMO. The physician will maintain his or her own office and see non-HMO as well as HMO patients.
2. Staff model. Physicians are salaried employees of the HMO. They physician work in the HMO's office building.	4. Network model. The HMO contracts with a group, an IPA, or individual physicians.*

*Malkin, 2002, p. 321.

The goal of healthcare design is to understand each specialized area, and the design needs of the specific assignment, and to develop appropriate design solutions and specifications.

In the field of medicine there are at least 24 accredited major specialty areas, subspecialties, and clinical disciplines. Primary care physicians (PCPs) in general practice (GP), pediatrics, family practice, and internal medicine, are those most often encountered by the public. These physicians deal with the overall health of their patients. When necessary, the PCP refers the patient to the appropriate specialist.

Physicians may work as solo practitioners, in a group practice, or as salaried physicians. A solo practitioner provides professional services to the patient and is personally responsible for that care. Solo practitioners represent the largest percentage of all practicing physicians engaged in one of the specialties or subspecialties.

Group medical practices represent the second most common form of medical practice. The American Medical Association (AMA) defines the medical group practice as

> The provision of health care services by three or more physicians who are formally organized as a legal entity in which business and clinical facilities, records, and personnel are shared. Income from medical services provided by the group are treated as receipts of the group and distributed according to some prearranged plan.[5]

A group practice can be an association of solo practitioners, a partnership, or a corporation. The members can combine their resources and expenses, which also provides more equipment and facilities as well as increasing nursing and technical staffs. Group practices often combine based on the medical specialty. Some group practices are created based on a combination of somewhat similar specialties.

Salaried physicians usually do not have private practices. These physicians have positions in hospitals or other healthcare facilities, private and commercial companies, the armed forces, and other government agencies. The majority of these positions are available in private hospitals, where physicians work in departments such as the emergency room, as consultants, as medical directors, or as department heads.

Patient care managed by a health maintenance organization (HMO) has significantly affected physicians practicing today. HMOs offer health insurance coverage under healthcare-based care guidelines. An HMO physician treats patients who utilize HMO coverage and agrees to provide services to these patients at a discount. There are now four types of HMOs, as defined in Table 7-3.

In addition to the physicians there is the nursing staff, which is generally comprised of nurses (RNs) and licensed practical nurses (LPNs). An RN has an undergraduate degree in nursing, whereas an LPN has graduated generally from a two-year nursing program. In addition to their initial training, nurses can specialize in many different areas of medicine. Nurse practitioners (NPs) generally have both bachelor's and master's degrees plus additional training in diagnosis. They can provide some of the same care as a physician and can work closely with patients on their care.

Physician's assistants (PAs) are nonphysicians licensed to practice medicine under the supervision of a licensed physician. A PA works closely with patients and can prescribe

---

[5]Havlicek, 1996, p. 1.

medications, refer patients to specialists, and provide many other services similar to those of physicians. NPs and PAs are similar in their ability to provide medical services, except that PAs are not required to have a degree in nursing since they have training as physicians.

Dentistry is an area of medicine which often hires interior designers. The dental office generally includes a dental hygienist and a dental assistant, who are both supervised by a professional dentist. The dental hygienist performs procedures such as removing deposits and stains from teeth, applying medication, and taking dental X-rays. The dental assistant may perform these same functions as well as other duties such as sterilizing instruments, mixing filling compounds, and assisting the dentist in drilling and filling teeth.

Included in this chapter is information on the rapidly growing area of veterinary medicine, especially small animal clinics and hospitals. Many of the techniques, equipment, and materials used in human medicine are similar to those used in veterinary medicine. Many veterinary specialists are on staff at veterinary school hospitals or at private animal hospitals. Veterinary hospitals located in the veterinary colleges of major universities provide medical care for large and small animals. Their specialists include neurologists, oncologists, cardiologists, and many others.

An important new regulation in the healthcare industry is the Health Insurance Portability and Accountability Act (HIPAA). This federal regulation was created to address patient privacy in the transfer of patient information from the patient to the primary physician and to consulting physicians or service groups. For the interior designer, this law impacts planning workstations for the receptionist, nurse stations, and medical records departments, as well as other patient recordkeeping departments.

A major portion of the healthcare industry is devoted to the treatment and care of patients 65 years of age and older. This patient group is experiencing rapid growth as the baby boomers started turning 60 in 2006. Chapter 8 is devoted to a discussion of the design of medical and living facilities for seniors.

The growth of healthcare has included many interdisciplinary specialties in medicine and the health professions. Sports medicine and dietetics are two that many readers have heard of. This continual growth of the healthcare industry brings unlimited opportunities to the interior designer interested in specializing in healthcare design.

The services of an interior designer can ensure the successful completion of a healthcare facility. The designer is challenged to meet specific aesthetic and medical needs while abiding by the laws governing this area of commercial design. The interior designer should be included in the initial planning of a medical facility because all of the areas are affected by the design.

Types of Healthcare Facilities

Medical office buildings (MOB) and suites, hospitals, and dental and veterinary facilities are the types of healthcare facilities most familiar to the reader. There are, of course, numerous other specialized facilities including urgent-care centers, mental health centers, and rehabilitation facilities, to mention just a few. All these facilities provide services to different groups of patients.

Although these facilities have existed in one form or another for many years, the evolution of science and technology has resulted in many changes and improvements in services requiring changes in working conditions and facility design. This section briefly discusses the different types of healthcare facilities, emphasizing MOBs and suites, hospitals, dental offices, and veterinary clinics.

The first type of medical facility is the MOB. The purpose of the *medical office building* is to provide medical practice space—or suites—for physicians. A MOB might also consist of service providers for physicians such as radiology suites, laboratories, and other special diagnostic services, as well as other medical service providers such as ophthalmologists and dermatologists. The location of an MOB can vary. Some may be built adjacent to a hospital, whereas others are freestanding units separate from the hospital campus (Figure 7-1).

Figure 7-1 Exterior view of a MOB, generally located close to a hospital. (Photograph courtesy of Architectural Design West.)

MOBs are usually owned by a healthcare corporation, a group of physicians, or an individual physician. The occupants are grouped into three categories: (1) physician tenants, (2) hospital departments and/or diagnostic services, and (3) commercial businesses such as a pharmacy. Depending on the ownership of the building, other facilities that may or may not be involved in medical services might also be tenants, such as a restaurant. Patients can take advantage of the close proximity of services within a MOB, as the facility usually groups the services together in an efficient manner to facilitate outpatient use.

Medical office suites are another type of medical facility. They are the business locations of physician provider practices. The suite is a group of spaces including exam or treatment rooms in combination with appropriate nonmedical spaces. There is a wide variety of design requirements for a medical suite based on the specialty and the number of physicians included in the practice. Although a general practitioner working with only one other physician in a small town will have space needs similar to those of a large multiphysician practitioner in a big city, each may need space for additional services beyond the basic exam and treatment room. This chapter deals extensively with the general design needs of a medical office suite.

The *hospital* is another type of medical facility familiar to the reader. The American Hospital Association (AHA) defines a hospital as a "healthcare institution with an organized medical and professional staff with in-patient beds available round the clock, whose primary function is to provide in-patient medical, nursing, and other health related services to patients for both surgical and non-surgical conditions, and that usually provides some outpatient services particularly emergency care; for licenser purposes, each state has its own definition of hospital."[6] A hospital can be a center for research, technology, and education as well as patient care. Physicians can treat their patients in a hospital on both an inpatient and outpatient basis. Table 7-4 lists several specialty types of hospitals.

The *general hospital* is the best-known type of hospital. It deals with a wide variety of diseases and injuries and contains numerous medical departments A very large general hospital is often called a *medical center*. The most common medical departments in a hospital include emergency, surgery, obstetrics, pediatrics, acute care medical units, diagnostic imaging, pathology, rehabilitation therapy, oncology, and clinical services. There are also nonmedical departments that support the medical departments. A few key departments are purchasing, housekeeping, dietary services, and all admittance and recordkeeping areas. The criteria used to classify hospitals are presented in Table 7-5.

---

[6]Kiger, 1986, p. 27.

TABLE 7-4 Types of Hospitals

- Cancer center
- Chemical dependency recovery center
- Children's hospital
- Clinic
- Freestanding birthing center
- General hospital
- Medical center
- Psychiatric hospital
- Rehabilitation center
- Teaching and research-based
- Trauma center

A hospital can be owned by private interests or a government agency. It is managed by a governing board such as a hospital board of trustees composed of a president and the trustees or board members. When the hospital is owned by the city, board members are elected by the citizens. The board of trustees of a hospital is responsible for establishing and reviewing the policies of the hospital, as well as selecting a hospital administrator who will actually manage the facility.

The hospital administrator is responsible for overall management of the hospital and all departments and divisions within the hospital. There are administrative heads for these departments, such as the administrative head of the surgical department. There are also department heads or supervisors, such as a nursing supervisor. This structure is much like that of a corporate office.

Some physicians at the hospital have private practices and treat their patients while hospitalized. These physicians are not employed by the hospital; rather they are granted the privilege of practicing and treat their patients in the hospital facility. Other physicians and medical staff such as nurses are employed by the hospital. This type of management is commonly used in a voluntary hospital.

Nursing services usually represent the largest component of hospital personnel, and the efficient organization of the nursing department is critical to the operation of the hospital. The department of nursing has a director with several supervisors in charge of a patient unit or ward. A nursing supervisor is in charge of a group of patient units and supervises the overall operations as it relates to nursing care. Each nursing department is on a ward or unit and has a head nurse, often referred to as a charge nurse, who functions as the administrator of that particular area. RNs, LPNs, student nurses, aides, and volunteers all report to the head nurse. Included in a nursing unit are the operating rooms, recovery rooms, intensive care units, and emergency rooms.

Another type of healthcare facility is a *dental office* or dental clinic. Dental offices can be located in a multistory commercial building, a freestanding medical center or MOB composed of physicians' offices, a hospital, or a separate building devoted to dental practice. The locations vary in terms of the size of the dental practice, demographics, and the need for a dental facility in the area. A dental practice may be a general practice or one of the dental specialties such as oral surgery, orthodontics, periodontics, or endodontics. Many dental practices consist of one dentist with a staff of assistants. Dental practice groups also are formed by several professionals in larger cities or to combine dental specialties in one practice.

The interior designer needs to make certain that the design solution not only is functional but also provides a calm and reassuring environment to ease patient discomfort and fear of dental treatment. Materials specification, acoustics, lighting design, and planning

TABLE 7-5 Criteria Used to Classify Hospitals

General or specialized medicine	Size
Types of medical problems	Ownership
Short-term or long-term patient stay	Teaching or nonteaching facility

TABLE 7-6 Other Types of Healthcare Facilities

- Burn treatment centers
- Cardiac rehabilitation centers
- Diagnostic imaging centers
- Laboratories
- Medical spas
- Oncology treatment centers
- Pharmacies
- Physical therapy centers
- Sports medicine treatment centers
- Surgi-centers

of the office environment all play a role in creating that functional and reassuring environment. Dental facilities require specific information pertinent to the profession, and the interior designer needs to access that data through research about the profession and from client interviews. Many issues specific to dental practice will impact the design and specification of an office suite and must be addressed by the designer.

A variety of *other healthcare facilities* may be part of a hospital campus or are freestanding, privately owned facilities. One that has become increasingly common is the *urgent care center*, sometimes called an *emergi-center*. These neighborhood healthcare centers provide noncritical emergency care much like hospital outpatient clinics, acting as an alternative to hospital emergency room use at a lower cost. They are located in neighborhood environments, often near medical office buildings and somewhat remote from hospitals.

Rehabilitation centers provide care for patients recovering from strokes, paralysis, amputations, surgical procedures, and cardiac complications. In this type of facility, 24-hour nursing care is available. The patient in a rehabilitation center is usually medically stable, and the physician has prescribed some form of rehabilitation therapy. The physician, who is usually not located at that facility, visits his or her patients there.

Hospice care centers are another type of medical facility. Hospice patients are generally dying of an incurable disease. The purpose of the hospice is to ease the patient's pain and discomfort, provide caring emotional support, and assist families in this transitional stage. Grief counseling is also provided to family members who request assistance. Hospice care can be provided either on an inpatient basis at a hospital or at a freestanding healthcare facility specifically for these patients. Hospice care is also available in the patient's home.

Veterinary hospitals and clinics for small and large animals are a very popular type of medical facility in the United States. The design and type of veterinary clinics and hospitals vary. For example, universities with a college of veterinary medicine have large facilities for the treatment of both large and small animals. Veterinary clinics in urban areas are usually located close to a veterinary hospital. Emergency veterinary centers are often open only during the clinic's off hours, typically 6:00 P.M. to 8:00 A.M.

There are other types of freestanding medical facilities. Table 7-6 provides a short list of some of them.

Planning and Interior Design Elements

The previous section briefly described different types of medical facilities. Each type of facility has distinct planning, materials, code, and aesthetic requirements and guidelines. For example, a hospital is considered by the International Building Code to be an Institutional Occupancy. A medical or dental office suite is considered a Business Occupancy. Spaces within a hospital can include retail space and food service—a public cafeteria—creating a potential mixed occupancy for code consideration.

The majority of medical facilities have similar design considerations. For example, the size of an exam room in a hospital clinic is similar to that in a medical office suite. Hospitals have more extensive code restrictions and more limitations on materials specifications due to state health department regulations. Design restrictions for medical office suites are based on the size of the medical office building and whether it is attached to a hospital or is freestanding.

Creating a professional appearance for each of these facilities is a major goal of the interior designer. In designing medical facilities, the interior designer must work with an architect, contractor, or other consulting professional. The designer will also coordinate design decisions with the building's owner or with a representative of the owner. Design responsibility may involve space planning, materials specification, lighting design, signage design, color coordination, and mechanical interface with building and medical equipment. Space planning and specification are also impacted by building, life safety, and accessibility codes.

This section focuses on the similarities of space planning and specification requirements in the interior design of healthcare facilities. A discussion of design applications in specific facilities will follow.

Feasibility Studies

A feasibility study of a proposed healthcare facility usually takes considerable time, as it involves not only research but also funding issues, codes, and many government regulations in regard to the building type. It should contain information on existing facilities, site evaluation, availability of utilities and support services, and a study of the possibility of either demolishing the existing facility or considering adaptive use.

In the construction of a major facility such as a new hospital, the feasibility study will often be conducted prior to the in-depth departmental programming needed to proceed to schematic design. Architectural issues and projected costs of future development are based on this research and initial planning. The feasibility study needs to be developed as part of the overall planning process and should include older facilities as well as new ones. This study should be conducted especially when there are significant changes and additions.

The group conducting the feasibility study is responsible for including applicable codes and specific criteria related to the project. Some of the codes and regulations research for healthcare facilities involve the use of certain documents such as:

1. *Americans with Disabilities Act (ADA)* or other accessibility requirements
2. *Guidelines for Construction & Equipment of Hospitals and Medical Facilities*
3. *International Building Code* and/or other applicable building and mechanical systems model codes
4. *NFPA 101 Life Safety Code* from the National Fire Protection Association

The feasibility study involves a variety of consulting services, which will develop an assessment of existing facilities as well as address potential expansion. The feasibility study should include not only a written report on the healthcare facilities but also exhibits such as photographs, drawings, and floor plans of existing buildings, as well as information on security and the ability to expand, to mention only a few key issues. Additional drawings of the developed alternatives for the facility, charts on gross floor areas, and a budget cost estimate for the rebuild and/or expansion should also be included.

The reader should be aware that the feasibility study elements discussed above infrequently relate to the design of medical office or dental office space. However, if a large medical office building is being considered, the feasibility of the project can be studied by a developer wishing to focus on tenants in the medical professions or a group of physicians who develop an office building for their own use and for investment opportunities. They will require the architect or other consultant to conduct a feasibility study before full programming tasks begin to ensure the economic possibilities of the new property. Obviously, an MOB will not be as complex as a hospital project. However, depending on the mix of expected or desired tenants, special design research and planning will be needed in preparing the feasibility study. For example, if one of the tenants will be a diagnostic imaging office, special design considerations are needed for shielding the X-ray procedures.

Space Allocation and Circulation

Space allocation and circulation planning is an extensive and complex task for any size or type of medical facility. Well-organized space planning is a prime responsibility of an interior designer contracted to design any medical facility. Planning efficiency is vital to many of the overall goals physician clients will discuss for their projects. In a hospital, there are dozens of interrelated services that must be provided, and the efficient design of space to accommodate these services is critical to effective patient care and the hospital as a business.

In the programming phase, charts and graphics are developed to help clarify relationships and needs. Specific graphic tools that are often created are relationship diagrams, an adjacency matrix, an interrelationship matrix, and bubble diagrams. These tools are critical in developing and assessing information from the client in order to provide for an efficient, functional, and collaborative use of the overall facility and specific medical spaces. Especially in a hospital or another very large medical facility, workload analysis is performed to be sure that the space relationships within areas help create effective facilities. For example, a functional program is developed which identifies the relationships between departments, staff requirements, design issues, and traffic flow.

Programming for space allocation identifies the specific needs of each area or department within the healthcare facility. Issues which are identified include room requirements and dimensions, the function of the department, and departmental adjacency issues related to the flow within the operation.[7] Net square footage per room and per department is important information included in the initial planning.

Space allocation is critical to planning an efficient medical suite in a MOB or another office building. Most spaces are similar in size with some notable exceptions. According to Malkin, "suites can be laid out on either a 4-foot or a 4-foot 6-inch planning grid . . . with a 28 foot bay depth for a small suite."[8] This helps create an efficient double-loaded corridor for a small suite. Larger suites will require larger bay depths to accommodate a larger number of exam rooms and ancillary spaces. Treatment rooms are often larger than exam rooms and impact the planning grid.

Window placement also impacts the grid and the layout of a medical suite. Unfortunately, too many office buildings are designed from the outside so that windows do not always relate to the planning grid for medical suites within them. In general, a MOB will have window placement better planned for the interior space allocation requirements of suites than a nonspecific office building. Additional detailed information on space allocation, traffic flow, and the sizes of spaces in a medical suite is provided in the Design Application section of this chapter.

Space adjacencies directly affect patient care as well as the overall operations of the medical facility. In a hospital, space allocation will include public and administrative spaces such as the information desk and admitting desks located off the main entrance and the emergency room entrance. Space and circulation planning for additional administrative spaces also considers public and administrative departments such as the business office, medical records office, data processing center, resource center, public services, and communications center. Ancillary to inpatient care are the diagnostic, interventional, and therapy departments such as diagnostic imaging, which are important in providing good patient care. Finally, logistical support departments manage the systems including elevators, pneumatic tubes, and automated carts. A familiar example is the removal of waste and used linens (see Table 7-7).

In a hospital, wide corridors—often 6 to 10 feet, depending on code requirements—are needed to move traffic and medical equipment such as patient gurneys. Due to the complexity of the plan of a hospital, way-finding and signage play very important parts in the overall circulation planning undertaken by the architect and the design team.

Nursing units are designed and planned around circulation patterns emphasizing shorter distances from the nurse station to the patient room clusters. Circular towers and compact square units are common arrangements used to keep nurse stations close to as many patient rooms in a unit as possible. In a hospital inpatient area, planning theory today involves a reduced number of patient beds per hospital. This is mainly due to the increased number of outpatient clinics and treatments available to the public, thus reducing

---

[7]Kobus, 2000, p. 171.
[8]Malkin, 2002, p. 12.

TABLE 7-7 Space Adjacencies

According to Bobrow/Thomas & Associates, hospital rooms should include at least some of the following applications: 1. A patient floor consisting of 60 to 72 beds could be divided into standard patient care units of 20 to 24 beds, which can be further divided into a cluster of 10 to 12 beds. 2. Seventy-five percent of hospital rooms should be single-patient rooms and 24 percent should be isolation rooms.	3. Each patient care unit should have two to three patient bed clusters, each containing a nurses' station, staff support areas, and storage areas. 4. Each patient floor should have two to three patients units. 5. Patient floor support areas should include a waiting/reception area, staff work areas, staff support areas, storage space, a multipurpose room for patient care, and a small kitchen.

Source: Bobrow/Thomas & Associates, *Building Type Basics for Healthcare Facilities.* Hoboken, New Jersey: John Wiley & Sons, 2000, pp. 174–175.

the need for inpatient care. In addition, HMOs and Medicare dictate the amount of time the patient stays in a hospital, mainly based on a cost factor, which is also factored into the reduction in inpatient stays.

As a result of the reduction of inpatient care, hospital patient rooms are being converted to private rooms and new hospitals are being designed with more private rooms than semiprivate rooms. These private rooms are designed to accommodate in-room treatments, which requires appropriate electrical equipment for monitoring patients, siting patient rooms in a position easily visible to the nursing staff, and placing toilets on the exterior wall of the patient rooms.[9]

Materials, Finishes, and Color Usage

Materials specification is the one factor common to the various types of healthcare facilities. Selection of architectural finishes is based on codes, sanitation, cleanability, allergens, and bacterial growth as well as on aesthetic issues. The comments in this section are general in nature and can be applied—depending on local jurisdictional health department and building code restrictions—to any type of medical facility.

Paint and wallcoverings are the most common wall treatments used in a medical facility. Paint is considered the most versatile material due to the broad range of colors and finishes offered. A problem with painted walls is that they can be easily marred by carts, chairs, and equipment. Semigloss and enamel paints are used rather than flat ones in most cases. It is desirable that the paints used be low-VOC products. There are wallcoverings that are acceptable by the majority of codes for medical interiors. Textured, cleanable wallcoverings are often preferred, as they not only facilitate acoustical control but also diminish glare. In walls which encounter wheelchairs, a more textured, woven wallcovering may need to be used below the chair rail to protect the wall. Acoustical cloth can be specified for this dado area. Always remember that codes must be verified before applying any type of textiles to walls. Although it may be allowed in a medical office suite (since it is a business occupancy), a textile wallcovering will be more restricted in a hospital or nursing facility since these facilities are considered institutional occupancies.

The majority of window treatments specified for medical interiors are usually neutral-colored or noncolored blinds which meet the applicable codes and give a consistent exterior appearance. Depending on the situation, the client may be able to add window treatments in some spaces to enhance the interiors. For example, adding draperies or panels in the exam rooms in a medical suite may make the space appear less clinical and more friendly. Any fabric hanging in a medical facility must meet applicable codes. Textiles that are not Class A cannot be used unless treated with fire-retardant chemicals.

---

[9]Kobus, 2000, pp. 167–170.

A major architectural surface that must be treated with special consideration in a medical facility is the floor. Hospitals, MOBs and medical office suites, and other medical facilities generally use a combination of resilient and hard flooring materials. Durability and maintenance are major factors in this specification, with emphasis on antimicrobial products for exam rooms, treatment areas, and inpatient rooms.

Depending on the use of the space, the designer may be able to specify any of the hard or resilient surfaces or carpeting. As treatment areas and inpatient rooms need daily cleaning, flooring such as a heavy-duty hospital-grade floor vinyl is often specified. Corridors which experience heavy cart traffic use vinyl flooring as well as tightly woven carpeting or carpet tiles. Vinyl flooring for corridors would be used in the preoperative and postoperative areas, whereas carpeting would be specified in the nursing unit corridors to reduce noise. Inpatient rooms would be specified using vinyl flooring for a variety of reasons, including the need for daily scrubbing, durability, and antimicrobial properties. Vinyl flooring materials are available in a wide variety of colors.

A medical suite has more flexibility in material specification for the floors due to its occupancy type. Resilient materials are preferred in areas such as the laboratory or in minor surgery spaces. Commercial-grade vinyl sheet goods or vinyl tile flooring can be used in the majority of medical interiors because they meet the standards for cleanability and durability and do not encourage bacterial growth. Hard-surface flooring should be specified with caution, as slippage could be an issue, depending upon the material selected and its placement within the facility. For example, in cold and wet climates and in sites where the majority of patients have difficulty walking, hard surfaces can easily cause slippage.

The use of carpeting in medical facilities varies greatly with the type of facility, the function of the space, and the code requirements. Hospitals use carpeting mainly in public spaces and offices. A medical office suite may have carpeting in the waiting room, the business office, and sometimes the exam rooms. Carpeting has certain characteristics that make it desirable for medical facilities, including acoustical control, static control properties, antimicrobial factors, and the ability to act as a buffer against injuries. When specifying carpet, use a low-pile, high-density carpet to ease the movement of wheelchairs and wheeled carts or equipment. Finding a tight weave that provides ease of movement for wheelchairs and carts but is not so tight as to cause friction or bruising if a patient falls is always a concern in selecting the appropriate flooring.

Color can play an important part in the healing of patients in healthcare environments. According to Mahnke and Mahnke, "A correct color environment contributes to the welfare of the patient and the efficiency and competence of the staff."[10] Color choices can range from subdued, pale, grayed, or dull tones to saturated color, depending upon the type of medical facility and the use of the space. Examples of color effects include soft yellows, which promote healing; blues, which can help reduce blood pressure, and shades and tints of many colors, which create a healing environment. Generally, the physician and the staff are aware of the color range that will work for their specialty, their staff, and their patients.

Many colors used in healthcare design today emphasize creating a warm, inviting, and secure environment. Color research continues to provide information directly related to its application in healthcare facilities. General commercial color schemes change based on the market. Hospitals and medical offices cannot afford to change every 7 to 10 years, as do other commercial businesses. The designer must present color schemes which are appropriate to the architectural style, have proven use for medical care, and are somewhat time-honored to avoid an outdated appearance.

One of the major improvements in interior hospital design is the effort to bring in more natural light with the addition of courtyards and the use of basements/lower levels opening into healing gardens. If natural light is not possible, there are many lighting fixtures which replicate it.

Excellent resources for the design of medical facilities include *Guidelines for Design and Construction of Hospital and Healthcare Facilities* by the American Institute of Architects Academy of Architecture for Health, *Medical and Dental Space Planning* by Malkin,

---

[10]Mahnke and Mahnke, 1993, p. 85.

and *Building Type Basics for Health Care Facilities* by Kobus, Skaggs, Bobrow, Thomas, and Payette. The References this chapter include numerous other important books that the reader may wish to consult regarding healthcare design.

Mechanical Systems

For the most part, the mechanical systems planning of a medical facility will be the responsibility of the architect. An interior designer will often, however, plan locations for electrical outlets and other minor systems. A few comments on mechanical systems are therefore in order.

Medical facilities are monitored closely by a variety of government agencies to ensure that the facility and all of its mechanical systems are operating efficiently and are adhering to all of the rules and regulations set by federal, state, and local codes. For example, to control infectious diseases, there are airborne infection isolation rooms, requiring that all air in the area be exhausted directly to the outdoors after being filtered. Another example is the nursery, which requires a quiet environment. HVAC systems should provide patients with comfort and safety and the medical facility with an energy-efficient system. In a hospital, the air handling system must control the distribution of air as well as exhaust and filtration.

For patients with compromised immune systems and/or contagious diseases, specialized areas including protective environment rooms and airborne infection isolation rooms are provided. This is one reason many medical office suites are designed with a waiting area for healthy and sick patients. In a hospital setting, the problem is more serious. In an airborne infection isolation room, the air pressure to adjacent rooms is negative and the air is exhausted to the outdoors. To protect other areas of the hospital from this infectious area, an anteroom is provided to function as an airlock.[11]

Vertical transportation is a major design consideration for the hospital or MOB. In a hospital, oversized elevators are often needed for gurneys, surgical carts, and other equipment. There are also "clean" elevators designated for only sterile supplies. Elevators should be grouped in building cores. As appropriate to the facility, they should separate visitor, patient, and staff circulation.

Telephones, intercoms, and data networks are part of the communications systems in a hospital. Patient information is collected electronically. In many hospitals, electronic charting of patient procedures and progress is used predominantly. This is also becoming the norm in medical office suites as well as other types of medical facilities.

An important point in the design of medical facilities is privacy. Walls between most medical services rooms such as exam, patient, and treatment rooms should have acoustical privacy. This can be achieved by installing partitions between the walls with a sound transmission class (STC) of 45.[12]

Codes

Strict regulations for healthcare facilities are imposed by the various applicable codes and local health departments. Hospitals, infirmaries, and limited care facilities—to name only a few—are considered institutional occupancies by the International Building Code. Medical offices, physicians' and dental offices, and some ambulatory outpatient clinics are all considered business occupancies by the International Building Code unless they are attached to an institutional facility. Interior designers must be alert to these regulations and specify appropriately for the type of facility.

Corridor architectural treatments are of the highest importance for fire safety and must be selected carefully. Usually materials in corridors must be Class I, while those in smaller spaces can be Class II. Textiles used for curtains in exam, inpatient, and treatment rooms need to be fire retardant. Usually the manufacturer or the furniture representative can provide information about the fire and life safety measures regarding their particular product.

---

[11]Kobus, 2000, p. 184.
[12]Kobus, 2000, p. 188.

They should give the designer written information verifying the flame retardancy of textiles and other architectural materials used in the project. If the fabric is not fire retardant, it can be sent to a company that specializes in applying fire-retardant chemicals. Designers should remember to test a yard of the fabric prior to the chemical application of all yardage because the chemical can change the appearance of the material. In addition, in states that have adopted CAL 133 or TB 133 regarding seating units, fabric and seating unit specification will be carefully monitored by the local fire marshal.

A hospital and all of its public areas must be accessible and designed in accordance with the ADA guidelines or other accessibility guidelines in effect. At present, 10 percent of patient hospital rooms and toilets must meet the ADA guidelines as well. Accessible patient rooms must have a turning space 60 inches in diameter for wheelchairs. Many other code regulations also apply to hospitals and MOBs. The interior designer should carefully consult these guidelines while developing and planning commercial design projects.

Design Applications

This section will focus on the design and planning elements of healthcare facilities including MOBs and medical suites, certain areas of a hospital, dental clinics, and veterinary facilities. These are the types of healthcare facilities that interior designers and students usually encounter.

In designing these healthcare facilities, it is quite common for the interior designer to work with an architect, a contractor, and the client. The client may be the building's owner or the medical personnel leasing the space. The responsibilities of the interior designer may include space planning, materials specification, lighting design, color coordination, and mechanical interface planning. Space planning and specification work also involves the application of building, life safety, and accessibility codes.

The majority of all medical facilities have similar design elements. For example, an exam room in a hospital clinic is similar in size to an exam room in a medical office suite. Patient safety is paramount, since many patients have limited mobility and depend on the facility's staff for assistance in an emergency. Sanitation, cleanability, allergens, and bacterial growth on materials and finishes in any type of medical facility are critical issues to consider in making specification decisions. Considerable research has been done not only on the functional and practical application of materials but also on the psychological effects of color and pattern selections. Code restrictions will vary somewhat since a hospital is an institutional occupancy under the building and fire safety codes, while most medical office suites are considered business occupancies unless attached to a hospital. The hospital facility will be heavily regulated by the state health department as well.

This section will focus on planning and specification concepts for a general practice medical office suite, beginning with a brief discussion of design consideration of a MOB. It then considers planning and specification for the lobby, inpatient rooms, and nurses' stations in a hospital. The design of a general practice dental office follows, and the chapter concludes with a brief discussion of a veterinarian's clinic.

Medical Office Building

A MOB can be either a single-story or multistory building or a group of buildings designed to provide medical care. MOBs are often located next to or near a hospital campus. Many include other related businesses such as pharmacies, optometry offices, copy centers, coffee shops, gift stores, and medical spas, to mention only a few.

It is common for one or more practice suites to be located on a floor of a multistory MOB. The complex includes a variety of medical specialties. For example, it is not unusual to find a suite for a family practitioner, pediatric specialist, and cardiologist on the same floor or in the same building. To some extent, it might be necessary for the interior designer to consider this mix of specialties when designing any of the suites since all patients will use common areas to reach a specific physician's suite. Multistory MOBs will

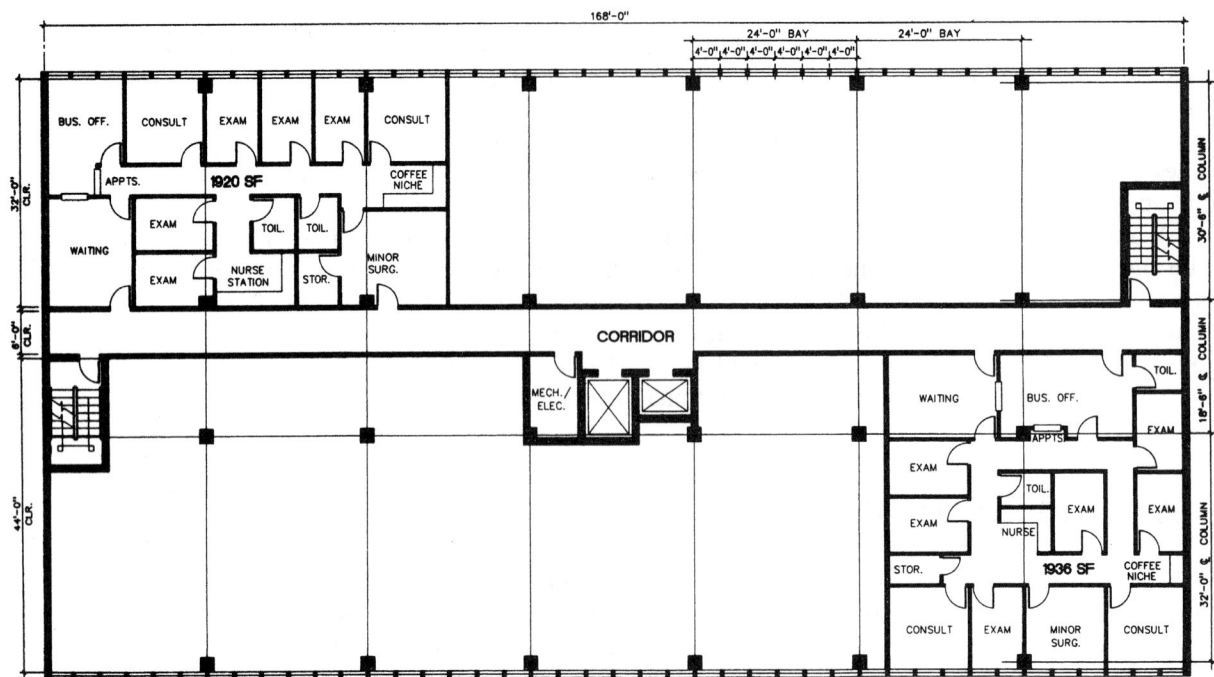

Figure 7-2 Floor plan of an upper level in a multistory MOB showing two layouts for medical office suites. (From Malkin, *Medical and Dental Space Planning for the 90's.* Copyright © 1990. Reprinted by permission of John Wiley & Sons, Inc.)

have a service core with the elevators, stairs, mechanical equipment, and public restrooms in the center of the building. Depending on the design of the building, this service core can be located at the end of a double-loaded public corridor (Figure 7-2).

Single-story MOBs often have direct access to each medical suite from either an exterior courtyard or a parking lot. The layout of the basic public corridors and the specification of architectural finishes for these areas are the responsibility of the architect. If the space is leased, the physician client can designate the placement of walls and the selection of materials. The interior designer provides this space layout and materials specification after detailed consultation with the physician and staff. If a load-bearing wall is impacted, the interior designer must hire a structural engineer or an architect to provide the solution with appropriate drawings and instructions. Non-load-bearing walls have fewer restrictions regarding placement.

Typically, the interior designer will be involved with the materials and furniture specification for the MOB as well as the medical suites. Ideally, if the MOB is a new building, an interior designer is part of the initial planning team, providing pertinent information regarding the layout and specification of the suite. The HVAC, lighting, electrical, and plumbing systems require professionals in their fields. However, many times these issues have been resolved prior to the interior designer's introduction to the project.

With medical facilities, the interior designer also works with representatives of medical equipment and supply manufacturers. If the cabinetry, exam tables, and seating are provided by a medical supply vendor, the interior designer's obligation includes the specification of materials and colors for the medical equipment using the manufacturers' selections or possibly custom specifications. The interior designer will also have to coordinate with the architect and general contractor.

Entrance planning for the MOB is important so that the patient can easily access the medical suites within. To provide this access, comprehensive signage at the entry to the building, in the lobby, and on each floor is mandatory. In large MOBs, as with hospitals, way-finding graphics using color and shape aid the patient in locating specific services within the building. Information should be available at each elevator site, and suite numbers should be posted on each floor.

In a large MOB, an information booth or security desk will have a map of the building to assist patients in locating the specific medical suite. "You-are-here" maps in the main entry, as well as in other areas of the facility, aid the patient in way-finding. Patients as consumers are familiar with this method, as all large shopping malls use way-finding maps.

The style of the entry doors to the medical office suites is generally specified by the architect, contractor, or corporation owning the facility. Generally, it cannot be changed due to the desire for consistency within the corridors in order to give the space a consistent design image. Codes and other building regulations will also dictate the specification of the main entry doors into the suites. Door security is very important as well due to the cost of equipment, the security of medical records, and the storage of medical drugs within some offices. With today's technology, many of these corridors are supplied with security cameras which monitor the space.

Medical Office Suites

Each medical specialty has specific needs and concerns that may or may not be shared by other specialties. The interior designer who specializes in medical design is not required to be proficient in every medical specialty. However, the designer should have an overall understanding of the field of medicine, the various entities, and the function that interior design plays within these facilities. For each project, the interior designer must research the specialty as well as interview the physician and staff to understand in detail the daily functioning of the practice (Figure 7-3). This section will focus on the interior design needs of a general practitioner's medical office, with additional comments regarding medical specialties where appropriate. Although the singular term physician is used, it is assumed that other physicians in the practice would also be consulted on request.

The interior designer of a medical suite located in a MOB is responsible for providing an aesthetically attractive and welcoming environment which reflects the medical functions of the practice. This design responsibility begins with the planning and design of the reception area. This initial introduction to the medical office can give the patient a feeling of comfort and confidence in the facility. For example, if a physician's office is extremely outdated, the patient may wonder if his or her medical skills are outdated as well.

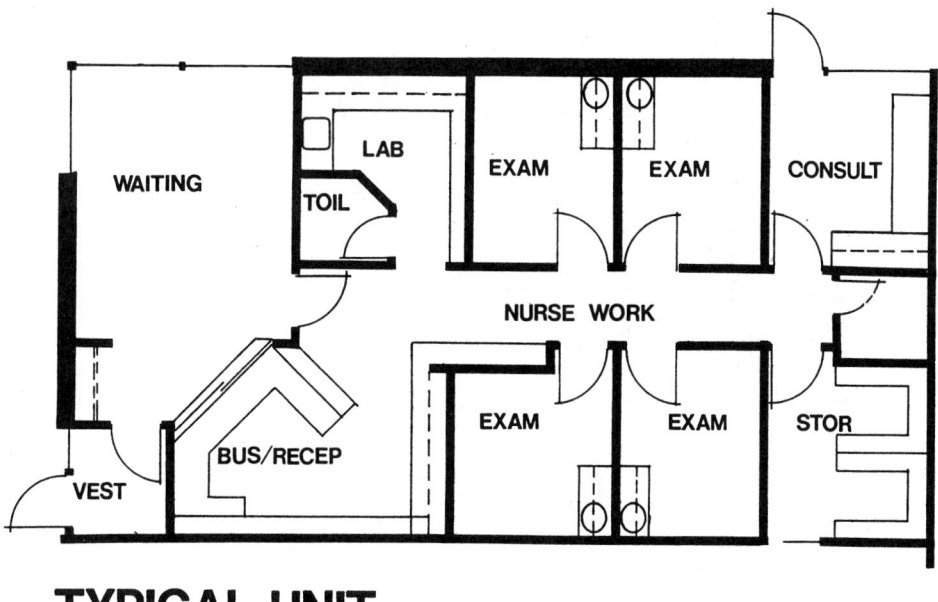

TYPICAL UNIT

Figure 7-3 Floor plan of a medical office designed for a solo practitioner. (Plan courtesy of Architectural Design West.)

It is common for the interior designer to be responsible for space planning within the medical suite, assuming that this planning does not involve the design of load-bearing walls. The pertinent information in planning this space is obtained during the programming phase, initially from the physician and the staff. The interior designer may need to consult with medical equipment and supply manufacturers, depending on the designer's contract. Building, fire safety, and accessibility codes will impact the space allocation and planning of the suite. Medical office suites are generally considered business occupancies by the building codes and must meet the prevailing jurisdictional accessibility guidelines for a medical care facility unless other local codes or conditions apply (Figure 7-4).

The typical medical office suite can be divided into two general spaces: medical and support functions. The medical areas include one or more nurses' stations, examination rooms, laboratory space, and medical storage. Depending on the specialty, other medical areas could include cardiac testing, physical rehabilitation, or an outpatient surgical room. Support function spaces include the waiting room, receptionist's and secretarial areas, business office, medical records storage area, offices for physicians, restrooms, office supply storage area, break room, and often a small conference room.

Traffic flow and circulation planning are very important in a medical suite. Generally, the space is planned to keep the patients in the medical areas and restrict their movement through nonmedical spaces. Clustering the nurse station and exam rooms together makes it easier for the nurses to control patient traffic flow. Patients are escorted by nurses to the exam or treatment rooms. In many cases, the patient is not escorted out after the consultation with the physician. Good signage is needed so that the patient can easily find the exit. Ideally, the corridors and directions will take the patient to the business office window prior to leaving the enclosed medical treatment areas. In this way, appointments are made and payment is handled efficiently.

A private entrance for the physicians and staff is common so that the physician can enter the suite without going through the waiting area. Preferably, this secondary entrance—assuming that it is not out through the physician's private office—is where supplies can be delivered. This can also be accomplished by locating the second exit in the employee lounge or break room. However, this might not be feasible in a large suite if it is considered the second exit required by code.

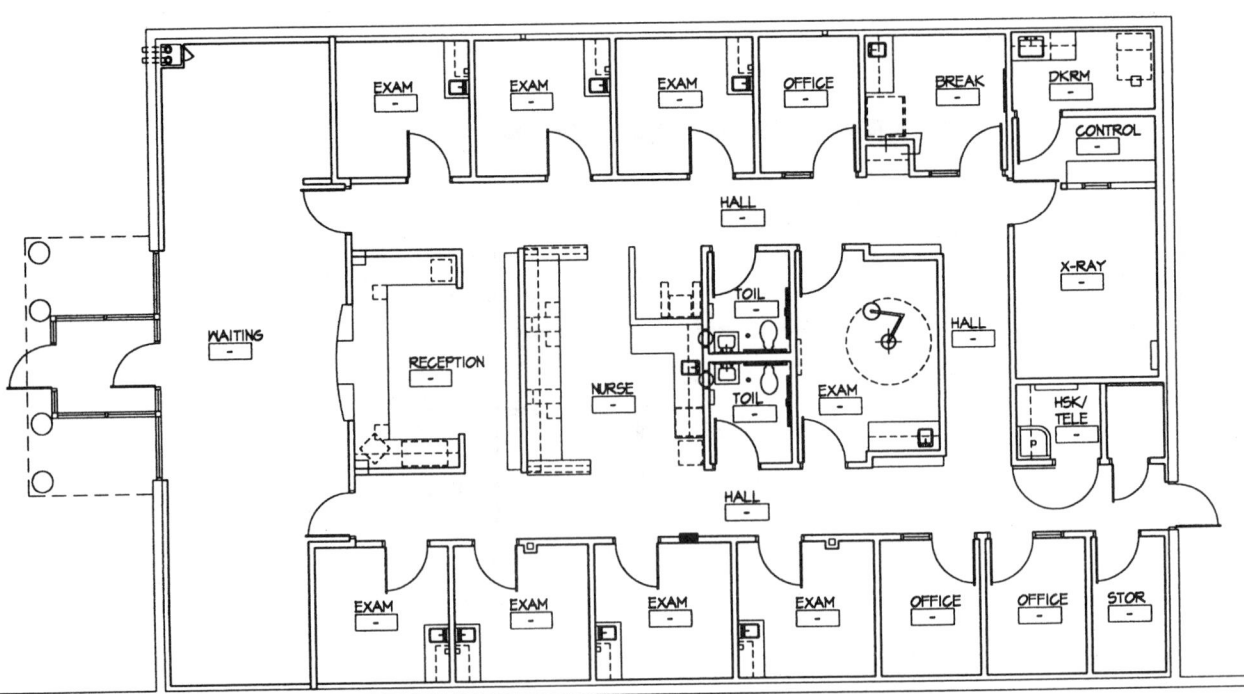

Figure 7-4 Floor plan of medical offices designed for a group medical practice. Note the traffic flow created by the corridor placement. (Plan courtesy of Architectural Design West.)

Reception Area and Waiting Room

The patient's introduction to the physician is the entry into the waiting room of the medical suite. The waiting room and reception area is where the patient will check in for appointments and wait until it is time for the examination. The design of this introductory space can aid the patient by reducing stress, as well as helping to create comfort and confidence in the medical expertise of the physician. A harmonious, pleasing waiting area can affect the patient's opinion, consciously or subconsciously, on the physician's sensibilities concerning patient care.

The clinical-looking medical suites of the past have given way to designs that are user friendly and create an ambience of warmth, comfort, and welcome. Technology has supplied designers with surfaces and textiles which are antimicrobial, allergy resistant, and durable as well as aesthetically pleasing. Thus, the overall atmosphere of a medical suite produced by textures, colors, sometimes small patterns, lighting, and accessories can contribute to creating an appealing space.

In planning the layout of the waiting room and reception area, sufficient space at the entry door is required for both ambulatory and nonambulatory patients. A clear traffic path should be provided to ensure easy access to the receptionist's area and to the door into the medical part of the suite.

The majority of medical suites have some form of divided space between the waiting room and the receptionist. In order to monitor the waiting room, the receptionist must be able to see all areas of the room as well as be visible to patients entering, waiting, and exiting the office. The receptionist, who often doubles as a secretary, can be separated by a window in a wall or by a custom-built receptionist's counter, which also acts as a divider between the waiting room and the main medical area. This is done to provide privacy and security of patient records as well as to control patient traffic. The design of the receptionist's window and area should provide an inviting focal point. In addition to greeting patients, the receptionist's duties often involve secretarial chores, receiving payments, recording medical record information, monitoring the telephone, filing, and assisting the physician to obtain patient information. These functions may be the responsibilities of several people in a large practice.

A door leading to the exam rooms and the major medical treatment spaces is often locked from the waiting room side and is controlled by the nursing staff. This plan provides acoustical and visual privacy as well as security. The door is generally adjacent to the receptionist's area or window and leads patients into the corridor that will take them to an exam room.

The physician and staff have a general idea about their seating preferences in the reception/waiting area. Some physicians may want to encourage interaction with other patients. With this request, the interior designer will place the seating units in the waiting room together, facing inward to promote conversation. This arrangement is termed *sociopetal spacing*, according to Dr. Edward T. Hall. Other physicians may prefer spacing that does not promote interaction and is achieved by *sociofugal* spacing, in which seating units are lined up and the distances between rows do not promote conversation. Medical research indicates that the human ear cannot clearly discern conversation if the seating units are over 8 to 10 feet apart. Seating placement should be adjusted according to the degree of interaction requested.

There are no code requirements on the spacing of traffic aisles around the seating units. Typically, 36 inches minimum is provided for circulation behind a group of chairs,[13] which allows for mobility of a wheelchair, and 32 inches in front of the chairs, which allows for ambulatory movement. This varies considerably, depending upon the size of the space and the placement of the furnishings. Remember, 36 inches should be allowed for wheelchair clearance and 5 feet should be provided for wheelchair turnaround.

The majority of physicians' waiting rooms are designed using chairs as the main seating unit. Chairs provide versatility in furniture placement, as well as a psychological and physical barriers between patients. Chairs should meet the requirement of the type of patient to be seen by the physician. For example, they should accommodate a variety of body sizes. The seat height needs to be 20 to 22 inches and should be sufficient to aid the patient in arising from the chair. Open arms that are the length of the side of the chair are important for the

[13]Panero and Zelnik, 1979, pp. 268, 269.

elderly and those patients with bodily weakness. It is also important to avoid sharp corners and edges on the chair's design. Another important detail is the need to avoid splayed legs which extend beyond the perimeter of the chair, as these might cause the patient to trip and fall. Above all, the chair should be sturdy and easy to use for the majority of patients.

The fabric specified for the chairs often depends upon the medical focus. For example, a pediatrician's office may request hospital-grade vinyl fabrics or prefer plastic seating units for easier maintenance. The materials specified for a dermatologist's office should be easily cleanable, use antimicrobial fibers, and avoid heavy woven textures that might suggest a repository for bacteria. A psychiatrist might request a woven texture with emphasis on a tactile effect, which may give the patient a sense of warmth and security.

Preferred patterns in fabrics are usually small and visually nonvibrating. Some medical offices request solid fabrics. With the current technology in fibers, there is now less concern about solid fabrics showing spotting and soiling. However, designers often prefer to specify small patterns, which can inject an interesting design element into the space. Pediatricians are more likely to accept contrast in pattern than other physicians due to the higher metabolic response of their younger patients. Whatever the specialty, consider maintenance, soiling, and spilling in the selection of textiles for seating in the waiting room.

Settees or sofas are specified when it is required or requested that family members or other persons sit together to monitor children or to provide close contact with a family member. Settees can also be used for patients who are oversized and require a broader width than a typical armchair provides. Manufacturers of seating units for healthcare facilities can provide extra-width chair seating for the obese patient. In specifying a settee for a waiting room, the designer should remember that the arm height and seat height must operate as aids in arising from the seat. The seat needs to be at least 20 inches high and the arms at least 24 to 26 inches high. These specifications are similar to those for seating used in assisted living facilities, as discussed in Chapter 8.

Lighting specification in a waiting room is very important not only from a life safety point of view but also for effect and comfort within the space. Waiting rooms generally have a combination of lighting fixtures, with overhead fluorescent lights being the primary light sources. Lighting in the waiting room can also involve ambient lighting provided by wall sconces, spotlights, or track lights around the perimeter of the space. Wall sconces provide uplighting as well as warmth to the area, balancing the harsher light from ceiling fixtures. Incandescent or halogen table lamps might also be used to aid reading, as well as to create pockets of warmth within the space.

The medical specialty can impact the amount and type of lighting. For example, a psychiatrist's office will prefer warm lighting to create an inviting, personal, secure environment. Lighting in a dermatologist's waiting room must be carefully planned so that it does not emphasize skin ailments. Researching lighting effects is very important in specifying for medical offices.

The patient may spend up to 30 to 45 minutes in the waiting room prior to the exam. For this reason, the accessories should not only enhance the space but also operate as a viewing opportunity or distraction for the patient. Accessories include artwork appropriate to the space and subject matter, magazine racks, and displays of medical information the physician provides for patient education. Many offices today provide a closed circuit television showing programs of medical information. The designer needs to provide racks and end tables for storage of periodicals. Coffee tables are generally not used since they can impede accessibility.

Research on cardiac patients has determined that observing fish in an aquarium can help reduce stress. In a pediatrician's office, the aquarium distracts and entertains the young patient and is a point of interest and activity. However, prior to the specification of an aquarium, it is important to assess the availability of staff to care for it.

Receptionist Area and Business Office

It is the responsibility of the receptionist to greet patients, make appointments, answer the phone, and perform the other support duties previously discussed. Depending upon the size and space plan of the medical suite, the business office may be adjacent to the receptionist's area or in a separate location. Generally, larger medical practices will have separate rooms for reception and the business office, while smaller ones will have a space with combined functions.

The workstation for the receptionist is generally custom-designed millwork to enhance the ambience of the waiting room. This cabinetry must be inviting and consistent in design as viewed from the waiting room. It must also be secure and not encourage patient invasion of the space. Patient privacy is important today. The design of the receptionist's area must take this issue very seriously (Figures 7-5a and 7-5b).

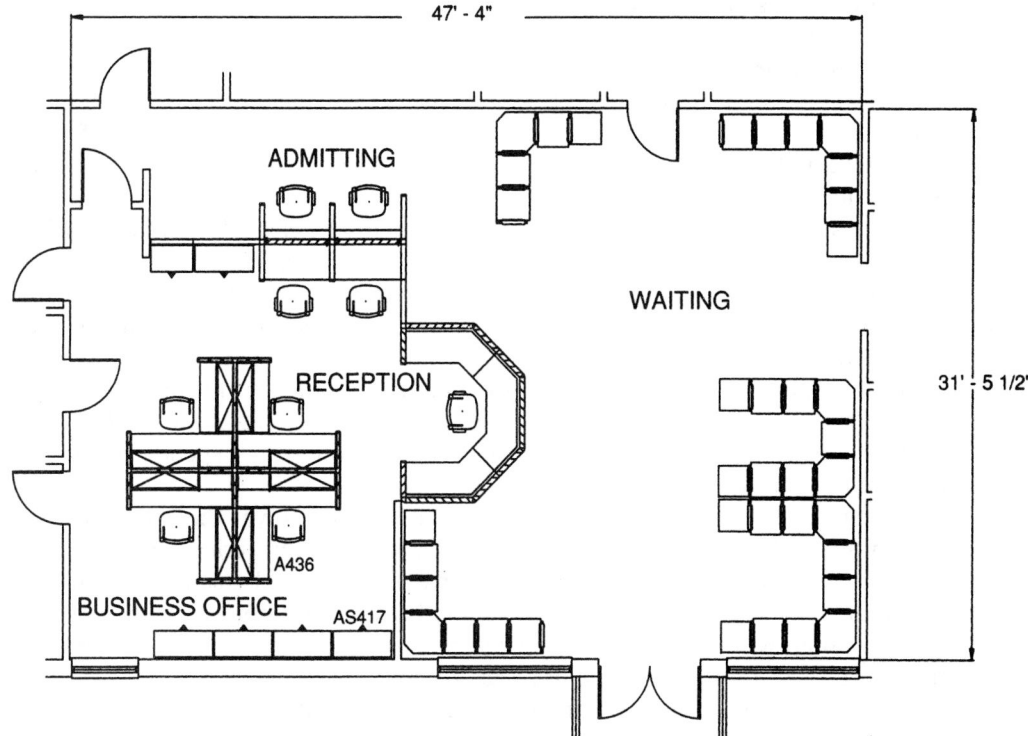

Figure 7-5a The floor plan displays the relationship between the reception area and business office as well as placement of patient seating. Admitting cubicles are used in larger or specific types of facilities. (Drawings courtesy of Milcare, Inc.)

Figure 7-5b Chairs designed for healthcare reception areas must be stable, comfortable, and devoid of sharp edges. (Photograph courtesy of Carolina Business Furniture.)

Security when moving into the medical space where the exam rooms are located is usually provided by a door located close to the reception desk. The interior designer and/or architect are responsible for designing the receptionist's work station and for providing appropriate working drawings. Versatility of design and creativity, as well as an organized, efficient workstation, is the goal. To provide the best solution, the interior designer must interview the client and staff to determine the various functions of the space.

Due to the advances in technology, medical records and other pertinent data are stored on the computer. For this reason, some physicians prefer an open reception area using millwork or a partial-height wall rather than a full-height wall and window separating the staff from the waiting patient. The receptionist's area is often custom millwork designed to suit the needs of the practice. Many doctors choose to use systems furniture for this area due to its flexibility and adaptability. Other administrative functions in the business office might require systems furniture, millwork or movable desks.

Specifications for the reception space must include durable, cleanable surfaces such as laminates, sealed wood, solid surfaces, and some stones such as granite. If stones are specified for countertops, it is imperative that they be sealed with an appropriate sealer for medical use. It is important to remember that countertop surfaces throughout the medical suite must be smooth and sturdy for the staff to produce legible patient notes and records. Based on recommendations from the field of ophthalmology, the interior designer should specify light-toned work surfaces, as dark surfaces can cause eyestrain as the worker's eyes shift from white or light paper to a dark surface. This, of course, is dependent upon the predominant use of the surface.

Furniture for the receptionist and the business office also involves the specification of appropriate posture chairs and task chairs that are adaptable for varied employee sizes and uses. Fabric for these chairs should be attractive, durable, and cleanable, as well as antimicrobial and nonallergenic. Patterned and solid textiles are both appropriate selections for this seating. Refer to Chapter 3 for information regarding ergonomic chairs for the workplace. In a medical office, it is especially important that seating be selected for the health and well-being of the user. In addition, ergonomically designed furniture will increase worker productivity.

Medical offices are highly computerized today. The computers in the business office are linked to terminals in the exam rooms, physicians' offices, laboratory, and other areas of the medical suite. These computers may also be linked to a hospital and to other medical providers in order to obtain and transmit appointment schedules and possibly medical information online. Use of technology means that the interior designer must specify millwork or furniture that can accommodate the depth of the computer monitor and keyboard as well as other peripherals. The use of computers also impacts the lighting specified in the business office to help reduce glare.

To provide a productive work area, effective lighting in the receptionist's area and business office is mandatory. Overhead fluorescent lighting, which may be part of the build-out allowance, is usually provided. The interior designer, along with the lighting engineer or consultant, can be contracted to determine the appropriate overhead lighting requirements for the medical suite. Task lighting will be required in most situations. The Illuminating Engineers Society recommends 150 foot-candles for these office areas.

Architectural finishes in the waiting area and business office areas can be specified similarly to those in any business office setting. The key to selecting materials in these areas is to create a pleasing environment that reflects the desires of the physicians and staff. In selecting flooring for these spaces, remember that the task chairs have casters and the flooring must adapt to their use. Different casters will be required for carpet versus hard-surface flooring. Tufted, low-pile carpets are preferable in the business office areas, although other resilient and hard-surface materials might be selected by the client. Additional information on architectural finishes is provided in the Planning and Interior Design Elements section of this chapter.

The storage of medical records in this area can vary, depending upon the degree of technology used. The designer must remember that many state medical laws require that the medical office maintain paper medical records for a certain number of years. In addition, the large majority of physicians are slow in adapting to electronic medical records.[14] This is important, as it impacts the recordkeeping storage capabilities of the office. Primary care physicians will maintain more detailed patient records than specialists who see patients on referral. The primary care physician has records of the patient's visits, as well as copies of visits to specialists and other related medical facilities. It is obvious that the standard vertical filing unit or the lateral file cabinet would not provide sufficient storage for these medical records.

Open filing and mobile filing units have been designed and developed for medical office record keeping. Open filing units are open shelves that allow storage of side-tab file folders, with the tabs often identifying the name and possibly the type of treatment or diagnosis of the patient. The shelves can be stacked six or seven high, providing more filing than the standard lateral file and a less expensive solution for the small practice (see Figures 3-8 and 3-9). Mobile filing units that move on floor tracks can be an efficient space saver for larger medical practices. Depending upon the style of the cabinet, these units can move from side to side or from back to front to allow more filing in less floor space.

Examination Rooms

When it is time for the appointment, the patient is escorted, generally by a nurse, from the waiting room into the main medical area. The basic examination room for the majority of practices is fairly standard in size, either rectangular, approximately 12 by 8 feet, or 96 to 110 square feet. The door into the exam room is hinged on the jam opposite that of a typical door opening, which ensures more privacy for the patient on the exam table. After entering the exam room, the patient is allowed privacy to change into a hospital gown, if needed. This privacy is provided by a cubicle curtain within the space, as well as by hooks and/or clothes hangers, a mirror, and a stool or chair for aid in removing shoes. The patient usually is seated on the exam table while awaiting the arrival of the physician. To reduce the patient's stress, magazines, medical literature, and artwork are provided (Figure 7-6).

In planning the interior of the exam room, the designer must allow sufficient space for the physician and nurse to stand on either side of the exam table. The standard size of the exam table is 27 inches wide by 54 inches long, with a pull-out extension and possibly stirrups at one end.[15] These typical exam tables are also supplied with a built-in step to allow the patient to easily access the reclining space. Exam tables are designed with a height of 29 to 36 inches, which allows the physician and nurse to examine the patient easily without placing undue stress on the back when leaning over the patient. With the increasing treatment of obese patients, exam tables are wider and some are designed with pneumatic lifts.

The physician, upon entering the exam room, must be able to easily access the sink in order to wash his or her hands prior to the exam. Hand sanitizers can also be available for use. With the establishment of health protocols, physicians, staff, and patients have become even more alert to the washing of hands and the use of gloves in patient care. The physician should be provided with a mobile armless stool with casters and an adjustable seating height. The physician must be able to easily access the cabinetry countertop, the cabinets, and the sink without rising from the mobile stool. This arrangement also improves interaction with the patient (Figure 7-7).

In addition to the sink, the sink counter provides a pull-out space for recording medical information or, with today's technology, space for a computer monitor and keyboard for recording patient information and even creating prescriptions. The counter surface should be smooth, stable, and durable to provide sanitation and accurate recording of notes and writing of prescriptions if computers are not used for these purposes.

Furniture in the exam room should be functional, easy to use, and easy to maintain. As Figures 7-6, 7-7, and 7-8 indicate, furniture in an exam room is minimal. The small armless stool for the physician is usually covered in a hospital-grade vinyl. Guest and

---

[14]Malkin, 2002, p. 49.
[15]Malkin, 2002, p. 58.

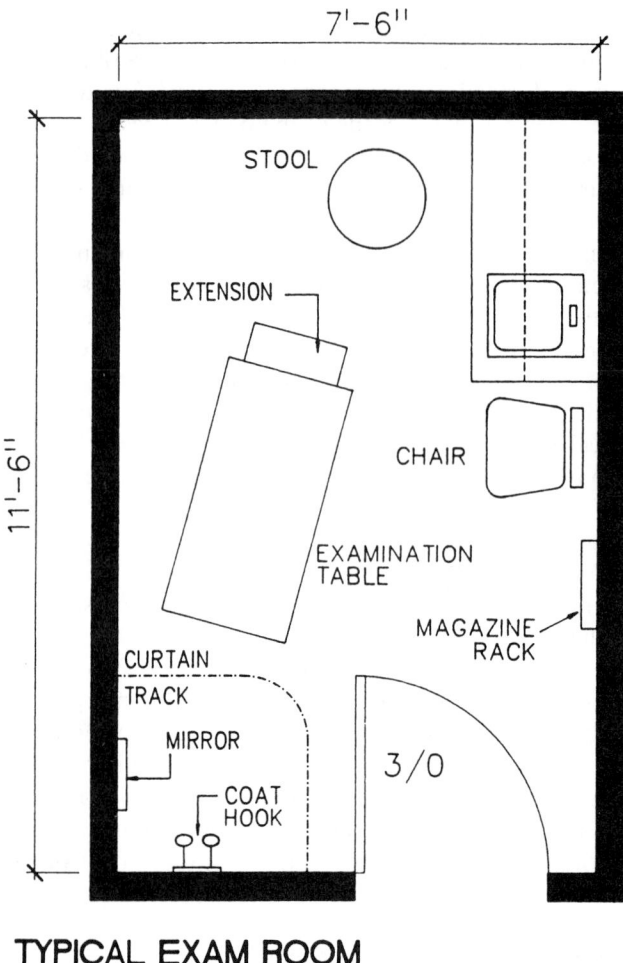

7'-6"

11'-6"

STOOL

EXTENSION

CHAIR

EXAMINATION
TABLE

MAGAZINE
RACK

CURTAIN

TRACK

MIRROR

3/0

COAT
HOOK

TYPICAL EXAM ROOM

Figure 7-6 Floor plan of a typical examination room. (From Malkin, *Medical and Dental Space Planning for the 90's.* Copyright © 1990. Reprinted with permission of John Wiley & Sons, Inc.)

patient chairs are usually provided with or without open arms, commonly covered in hospital-grade vinyl or a tightly woven commercial fabric. Cabinets can be either stock or custom-built, with smooth worksurfaces and a variety of doors and drawers for storage. Remember to allow for some knee space under the countertop so that the physician can access the surface for recording information. Two work heights can be provided for this purpose: a 36-inch-high counter for standing and a 29- to 30-inch-high counter/desk space for recording information while seated.

Note the position of the exam table in the typical room seen in Figure 7-6. It is placed this way so that the physician and staff have access to the patient from all sides. Exam tables in specialty rooms may be placed in a different arrangement. The exam table is usually purchased by the physician through a medical equipment and supply representative. The interior designer will specify the hospital-grade vinyl to be upholstered on the exam table from a selection of fabrics available from the manufacturer. It might also be possible for the interior designer to request a COM vinyl. However, this will be more expensive, and the manufacturer may not allow custom material. Exam tables are usually made of stainless steel or wood.

Colors and architectural finishes are very important, as they directly impact the patient's response to the exam space. If the patient and the medical specialty are not considered in the specification of materials, the choices may increase patient anxiety or affect certain aspects of diagnosis. For example, a saturated red color should not be used, as it will raise blood pressure, especially in adults, for approximately 45 minutes. Interestingly, children's overall higher metabolisms are not as impacted by saturated colors.

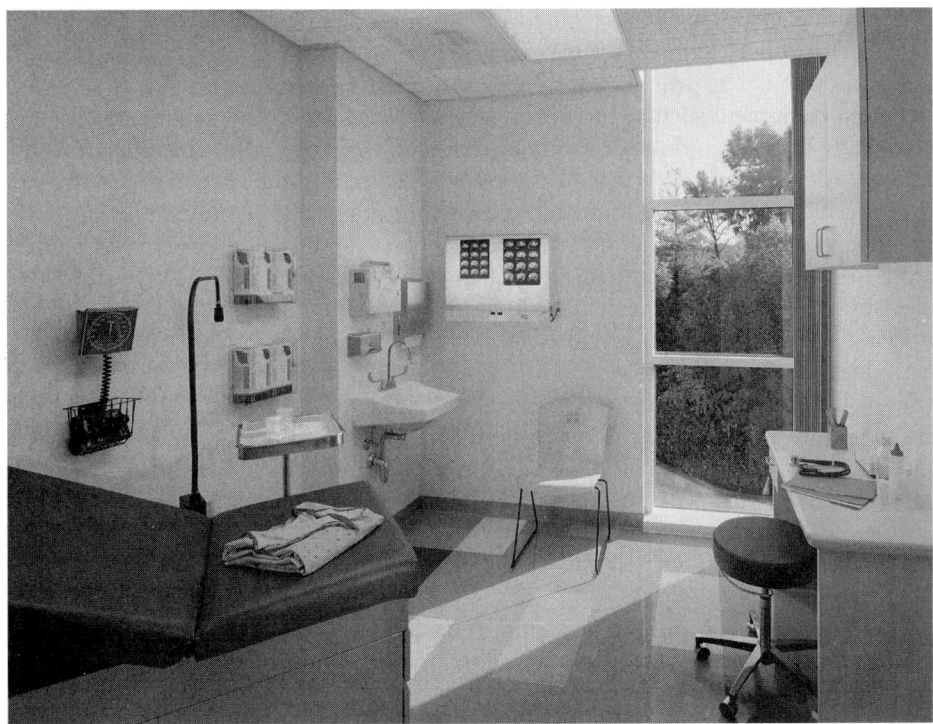

Figure 7-7 Examination room in the Contra Costa Regional Ambulatory Care Center. Note the efficienct use of space and cleanability of materials. The full window view aids in promoting a healing environment. (Photograph courtesy of Anshen + Allen. Photographer: Robert Canfield.)

There are some general guidelines for color choices in medical offices. Color schemes replicating nature provide a feeling of familiarity and warmth. Light colors aid the elderly patient in viewing the facility. Saturated colors should be avoided in exam rooms because they can influence the diagnosis. Pastel tints in pediatric offices can aid in calming children. Most importantly, the physician and the staff must have good visual acuity in the exam room, and the colors specified can make a difference. Also, if the room has darker colors, the patient may question how sanitary the room is.

Architectural wall finishes in an exam room are important, as they affect the patient's care and response. Paint is an economical and versatile finish that provides many choices and is easy to clean and maintain when the semigloss variety is specified. Flat latex paint has a tendency to absorb oils as well as show handprints, which would be offensive to a patient. Programming repainting into the future maintenance of painted walls should be discussed.

If a wallcovering is specified for the exam room, check the manufacturers' specs for cleanability, scrubbable, durability, and code classifications. Realize that heavily textured wall surfaces could cause abrasion and are more difficult to clean. Depending on the type, texture, style, and pattern, the wallcovering could be applied to one or two walls of the exam room or to all four walls. If borders are included, use them wisely, as they tend to reduce the visual space. These techniques will provide for an interesting treatment of a small space, and the options are infinite.

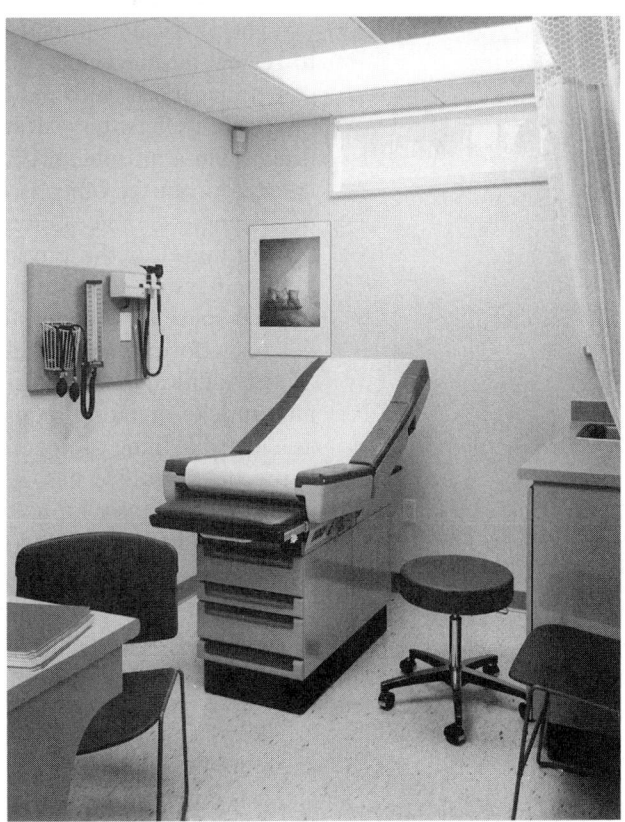

Figure 7-8 View of an examination room with a full view of the exam table. (Photograph courtesy of Architecture for Health Science and Commerce, PC.)

Flooring in an exam room is most often a resilient hard surface such as a commercial-grade vinyl tile. A low-pile, loop carpet with antimicrobial features, usually manufactured in nylon, is also an option. The primary consideration in flooring specification is ease of movement for wheeled equipment such as the doctor's stool, wheelchairs, and examination equipment that might be brought into the exam room. Sanitation and ease of maintenance are also important factors determined by the medical specialty, codes, and the client's preference.

Lighting specification is a very important element in the design of an exam room. Obviously, the physician and staff require visual acuity when examining the patient, for recording findings, for writing prescriptions, and when using equipment. Approximately 100 foot-candles should be provided as general lighting, supplemented by task lights per area and per specialty. Task lights are provided by mobile examination fixtures as well as undercounter lighting focused on the countertop. For example, in an ophthalmologist's exam room, some of the lighting is built into the exam chair.

No matter what medical exam is being performed, the lighting needs to be planned so that the physician and/or the nurse can control it during the examination. As most medical suites are provided with fluorescent ceiling fixtures for general illumination, the designer will need to suggest the specification of lamps that do not change the color of skin tones. Options in fluorescent lamps have increased dramatically and provide more natural lighting effects.

Accessories in an exam room are very important for reducing patient stress as well as providing some form of education and entertainment while waiting. Accessory areas are kept to a minimum and often include a small bookshelf or rack for magazines or patient education literature. A small end table could be placed by the patient's/visitor's chair to hold magazines. Photos, prints, drawings, and other appropriate accessories can enhance the space; however, subjects that can produce anxiety should be avoided. Using live plants requires extra care. Silk plants are a better option.

Physician's Private Office

The physician's private office—also called the consultation room—is a retreat for study, to review business matters, or to relax and rest. It is also the place where the physician sometimes meets with patients for special consultations. Depending on the specialty, the physician prefers this private office for consultation with patients since it is less clinical in design and atmosphere. Private offices are generally 10 by 10 or 12 by 12 feet. A private entrance from the office is often requested, although a private entrance in a private corridor is an acceptable option.

Furniture for the physician's private office includes an executive desk, whether case goods or systems furniture, an ergonomically designed desk chair, a credenza, and a designated space for a computer and printer. After office hours, the physician will use the office to perform much of the research on patient illnesses and treatments via the Internet.

In addition to the furniture listed above, two chairs for patients, bookshelves for the multitude of literature required for the profession, cabinetry or additional shelving, as well as a lockable filing cabinet for private information, is typical. Sometimes a safe is requested. If the private office has ample space, a small conference table with four chairs can be added. Physicians who use their office outside of standard office hours, such as surgeons, need a sofa in their office to rest and possibly sleep. A private restroom, often with a small shower, is also preferred by many physicians (Figure 7-9).

Natural light is preferable; thus, physicians' offices are generally located on an exterior wall. Ceiling fluorescent lighting can be softened with special reflectors. Task lights at the desk and sofa (if one is included) help to create needed light for work and a more comfortable atmosphere.

As with other executive offices, the finishes and accessories in a physician's private office can mirror those in the rest of the suite or vary in color scheme, texture, and materials. It is common to upgrade wall treatments and flooring specifications in private offices. The office should have an atmosphere similar to that of an executive office. Many physicians will display not only their academic degrees and accomplishments but also specific works of art reflecting their own taste. The physician's office can provide a view of his or her personal life.

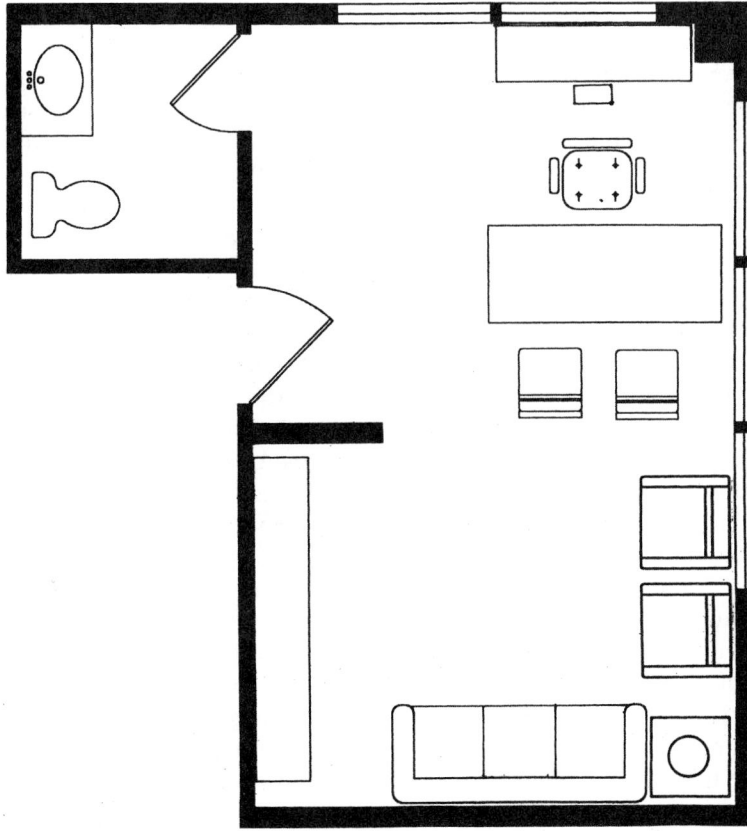

Figure 7-9 Floor plan of a physician's private office. Zoning provides the physician with areas for rest and work. (Drawing courtesy of Pei-Hsi Feng.)

Nurse Station and Laboratory

One of the major responsibilities of the nurse station is to monitor patient traffic anywhere beyond the waiting room and business office. The placement of the station in the main part of the medical suite is important to the overall functioning of the space. Ideally, it should be close to the reception area, the exam rooms, and the laboratory. The interior designer must plan the space with these adjacencies in mind. If the size of the medical practice warrants, more than one station can be provided. The space planning must include research and information from the staff obtained during programming in order to produce a well-functioning, related space.

The size of the nurse station will vary with the size of the practice and the number of physicians and exam rooms in the medical suite. A station in a small practice could be simply a length of counter space with attached cabinetry. Physicians as well as other medical personnel use the station, so it must be planned accordingly. Adjacent to the nurse station, or in close proximity, is the laboratory.

The tasks conducted at a nurse station are many, and it is considered the core of the medical practice floor plan. Exactly which tasks are conducted there depend on the size of the practice. The following tasks are common: preparing or dispensing medications, recording test results, weighing patients, consulting with physicians and staff, and giving injections, as well as many routine office tasks vital to the operation of the medical practice. Depending on the size of the practice, blood samples from patients might be drawn here; instrument sterilization can also occur. In a larger practice, these two tasks will be done in the laboratory.

The major furniture items required at the nurse station are countertops, ergonomically designed seating, and cabinetry for storage. The cabinetry generally consists of two different counter heights. The upper counter, 40 to 42 inches high, provides a standing-height surface for recording patient information. It also can operate as a partial wall to protect records from patients' view. The nurse station also generally must accommodate at least one sink and an undercounter refrigerator (Figure 7-10).

Higher stools at an average height of 30 to 32 inches can also be used in conjunction with these higher countertops. On the inner side of the nurse station, a desk surface 29 to 30 inches high is provided for longer-term seating for recording patient information as well as other duties. These workstations are often systems furniture, although they are sometimes specified as millwork. Nurses should also be provided with ergonomically designed task chairs with versatile adjustments for seating height, depth, and back (Figure 7-11).

In some large medical practices, small foldup units are installed on the walls of the corridors to provide temporary work space for nurses and physicians. These individual charting stations with computers can also be designed as walk-up alcoves so that patient information can be recorded and printouts of prescriptions and other information for patients can be obtained by the physician near the exam rooms. Portable or alcove charting stations are common in hospitals today as well as in some MOB offices.

Laboratory areas in MOBs are highly regulated by the Occupational Safety and Health Administration (OSHA) and other federal and state health agencies. Due to stringent requirements, laboratories in medical office suites are often small and capable of performing only basic blood, urine, and other minor tests. However, larger medical practices may have a separate laboratory conducting a greater number of tests. This is an important issue to discuss with the physician in order to space plan and specify appropriate laboratory facilities that meet health department regulations and codes in the jurisdiction.

A laboratory in a medical office requires countertops, cabinets, one or more double-compartment sinks, a refrigerator for medical supplies, and electrical outlets to accommodate equipment. Counters in a laboratory may be at stand-up or seated height or a combination of both. The use of antimicrobial materials, as well as attention to cleanliness and sanitation, is important. It is very important to remember that any refrigerator in a nurse station or laboratory—or any other area considered medical—cannot be used to store food items. In a small facility, it might be possible to specify two refrigerators in the nurses' station if a break room is not included in the overall plan.

Ideally, one toilet facility adjacent to the laboratory provides an expedient transfer of patient specimens from the toilet facility to the lab via a pass-through compartment. This toilet must be accessible and large enough to accommodate a wheelchair with turnaround space, a grab bar and a wall-hung sink to allow someone in a wheelchair to access the sink, a help light, an automatic light switch, and other facilities that federal and jurisdictional codes may require. Additional guidelines for accessible toilet facilities are presented in Chapter 9.

Color specifications for the laboratory generally include white or off-white, with possible color accents provided by hospital-grade vinyl or hard surfaces for seating. The laboratory needs to be pattern free and contrast free. The predominant use of a noncolor allows the technicians to focus on the test results. If vinyl upholstery is used, materials containing any VOC must be avoided in this compact space. The laboratory must have special venting and air quality control required by OSHA or other health department standards.

Lighting in the laboratory is paramount to proper testing. Overhead ceiling lighting is usually provided, as well as task lighting for specific areas. Ideally, the laboratory will have no windows, preventing light admittance. If the laboratory is located on an exterior wall, a very durable blackout window treatment could be used. Depending on the tests conducted in the laboratory, exhaust fans may be required. The nature of the laboratory is such that the interior designer must thoroughly research regulations and codes related to this space.

Other Support Spaces

Support spaces within a medical office suite include specialized treatment rooms, storage spaces, a staff lounge, and restrooms. An example of a specialized treatment room is a room in a cardiologist's medical suite to conduct cardiac stress tests using a treadmill, a treatment table, and other testing equipment. Another example is a small X-ray room in a general practitioner's office where chest X-rays and other simple radiographic exams can be conducted. Many general practitioners and internists have a small surgery room for simple outpatient surgical procedures. Any of these specialized rooms may involve specialized equipment, storage capabilities and construction guidelines.

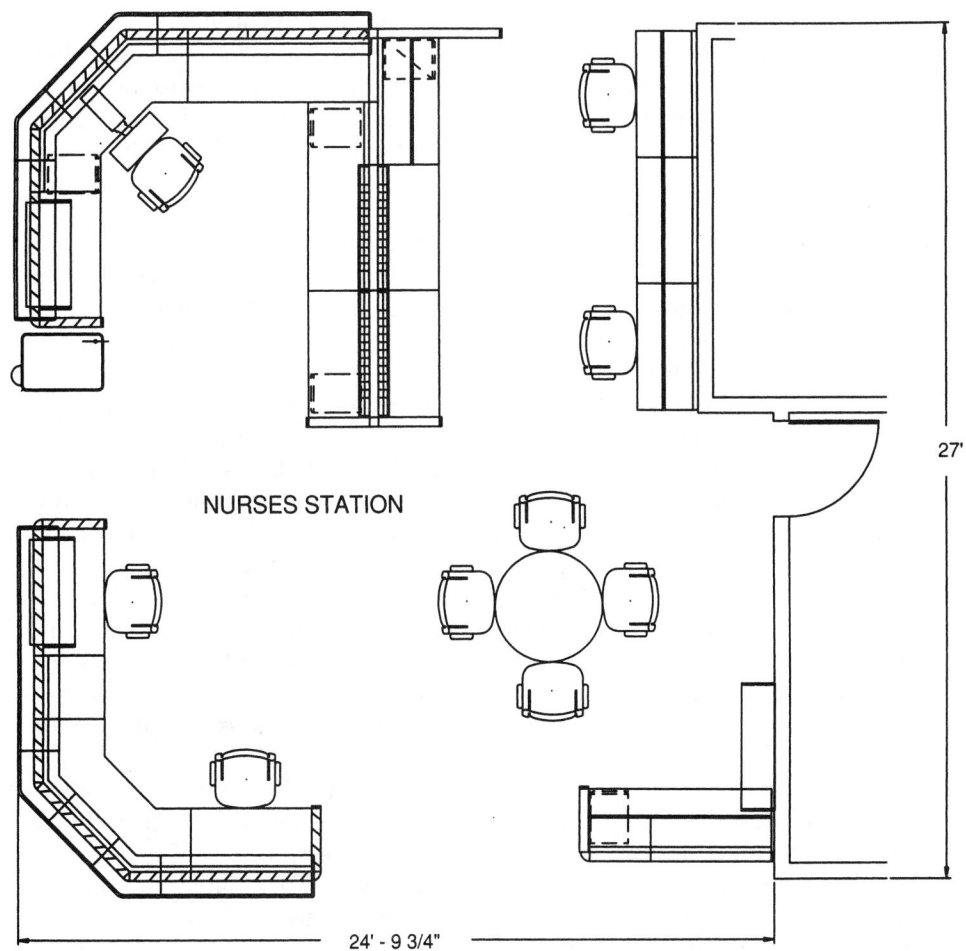

NURSES STATION

27'

24' - 9 3/4"

Figure 7-10 Floor plan of a nurses' station. Note the indication for higher countertops on the periphery of the cabinetry. (Drawings courtesy of Milcare, Inc., Zeeland, MI.)

Figure 7-11 Drawing of a nurses' station, a combination of systems furniture with custom specified cabinetry. See the floor plan in Figure 7-10. (Drawing courtesy of Milcare, Inc., Zeeland, MI.)

Multiple well-functioning storage spaces are necessary in a medical suite. The office will need to store quantities of gloves, patient gowns, sterile supplies, blankets and sheets, office supplies, medical forms, and pharmaceutical items. Housekeeping storage requires space for paper towels, cleaning disinfectants, toilet paper, and mops, which need to be readily available. Many leased spaces have a central cleaning crew provided by the owner(s) of the building. Storage of medical supplies and pharmaceuticals needs special consideration to prevent theft and outdating.

The lunchroom or break room needs to be a functional, relaxing, and inviting space for staff use and can provide a creative assignment. This area requires basically kitchen cabinetry with space for a refrigerator, sink, microwave oven, possibly a small dishwasher, recycle bins, tables and chairs, a telephone, Internet access, and a magazine rack. Careful placement of the microwave oven is necessary since it may affect cardiac patients. Often a television with a DVD player is provided to view educational materials. In a large practice, an employee locker room with secure lockers is provided for the staff. Sometimes lockers are included in the break room. This space could also hold a small washer/dryer.

It is important for the designer to consider the placement of the kitchen in relation to the medical treatment space. The microwave oven could cause cooking odors to seep into the treatment spaces if the kitchen is not properly vented. Compact planning could include refrigerator drawers as well as a small dishwasher with a quiet motor. The lunchroom is often placed at a distance from the treatment area. In fact, some medical offices have planned the lunchroom to be accessible from the building corridor. Materials specification for lunchrooms could include easily cleanable surfaces, fibers for acoustical control, and wallcovering for sound absorption. The material selected must not absorb cooking odors.

Patient and staff toilets are necessary. A large practice often locates toilet facilities off the waiting room, while a smaller practice will place it within the medical space. A large practice will also have toilet facilities within the medical space for the staff and possibly for patient use once the patient is escorted to an exam room. The number of toilet facilities depends on the number of occupants and on code requirements. The majority of medical suites today have separate toilets for males and females. A toilet space may be a single-user space with only one water closet and lavatory or a larger space to meet code requirements. The toilet facility must be accessible. Finishes must be specified for easy maintenance and meet code requirements.

Hospitals

Hospitals are complex facilities regardless of the type of medical care provided. It is important, however, to discuss specific areas of a generic hospital facility in this chapter. Hospital design is multifaceted, involving many technical and functional considerations along with appropriate aesthetic specifications. An interior designer who wishes to focus on hospital design must do considerable research on hospital functional areas and practices. Since many projects involve systems and structural design, an interior designer with this interest area should affiliate with an architectural firm specializing in hospital design.

A hospital provides medical treatment and care in spaces appropriately planned for those purposes. In addition to providing medical treatment spaces, hospitals are office complexes housing admitting, billing, medical records, and other office functions. Hospitals also provide meals to patients and public or semipublic food services facilities for visitors and employees. Gift shops, floral shops, and the receiving and distribution of supplies are also part of the overall operation of a hospital. Referring to a hospital as a complex design problem is an understatement.

Understanding the administrative structure, the chain of command, and the financial responsibilities of the hospital and how these impact the process of design is important for a successful hospital project. For example, if a project does not involve new construction or a major renovation, the interior designer can work directly with the purchasing department and the physical plant supervisor. The department head of the area to be redesigned will also be involved. Constructive, efficient working relationships with these various entities affect the design process, delivery, installation, financing, and client satisfaction.

TABLE 7-8 Hospital Terminology

- **Acute care patients:** Those requiring immediate or ongoing medical attention for a short period of time.
- **Administrator:** The overall manager of the hospital or healthcare facility.
- **Ambulatory care patients:** Those able to walk around.
- **Attending physician:** A hospital physician responsible for the diagnosis and treatment of the patient.
- **Crash cart:** A small mobile cart equipped with medications and equipment to handle extreme emergencies within the nursing unit.
- **Critical care units:** Inpatient units for patients requiring intensive care.
- **Healing environment:** Planning and design that create a hospital setting blending technology with humanism to provide soothing, efficient surroundings and quality medical care.
- **Intern:** A medical school graduate who is working to gain practical experience in the hospital.
- **Medical treatment spaces:** Spaces within a hospital where treatment of a patient occurs.
- **Nursing unit:** A cluster of patient rooms.
- **Resident:** A physician who has finished an internship and is receiving extended training in a particular specialty.
- **Salaried physician:** An attending and/or consulting physician who is an employee of the hospital.
- **Way-finding:** Techniques which help the patient and visitor to easily locate various areas of the hospital.

Hospital design has evolved over the years. Previously, many hospitals created a cold, antiseptic, sterile institutional environment lacking warmth. Since the 1980s, hospital design has focused on a less sterile, nonclinical approach using concepts familiar to hotel design and yet maintaining the strict guidelines for sanitation and extreme cleanliness required for patient care. Adherence to codes is mandatory and has been applied with scrupulous attention to today's hospital design. A healing environment is evident in the design of these hospitals. Even medical spas have been added to enhance the healing concept and environment. The modern hospital is a more comfortable place to be as a patient, employee, or family member (Table 7-8).

Medical areas such as surgery areas and intensive care units continue to require a sterile appearance for maintaining sterile conditions. Other medical areas, such as maternity, diagnostic imaging, and physical therapy departments, emphasize design elements such as color and texture, making them more patient friendly.

Part of what has made a hospital less stress-inducing is the changes in the design of inpatient areas. Hospital design has not duplicated residential design in patient rooms but rather has added some familiar elements to create a more inviting environment for the patient.

In collaboration with an architect or hired directly by the hospital administration, an interior designer might be involved in the design planning and specification of virtually any area of a hospital. The planning and design of many clinical areas requires greater knowledge than all but the most experienced healthcare designers will have. Thus, this section will focus on the main lobby, patient rooms, and the nurse stations—spaces that will more commonly be the interior designer's responsibility.

The healing environment approach to planning a hospital became an important trend in the late 20th century. Such an environment comforts patients and staff. In providing a healing environment within a hospital, the interior designer blends technology with humanism by providing soothing, efficient surroundings with quality medical care. Healing environments combine gardens for use when outside as well as for viewing from inside the hospital. Ideally, the garden will be visible from every patient room. Unfortunately, considering some of the views from patient rooms, this is not always done by the architect, designers, and hospital administration.

A healing hospital environment also incorporates family support space within the patient room and/or ward area, larger windows in the patient rooms, and both natural and artificial light to increase the patient's sense of well-being. The Center for Health Design has extensive information on healing environments and new trends in hospital design. Their Web site is listed in the References.

Main Lobby

The patient's first encounter with the hospital is the exterior view, with expectations of the interior based on exterior architectural elements. Patients and family members usually enter a hospital facility either through the main lobby or through a parking garage into an elevator, which often leads to the main lobby. Emergency patients, of course, are admitted through the emergency room, which is not adjacent to the main entry but rather placed in an area that provides expedient access and space for emergency vehicles.

The hospital's main lobby should be a warm, inviting, welcoming space and encourage ease of movement through it. It is a hub for visitor, staff, and patient traffic. Incoming patients and family members are met by greeters who aid them in locating the appropriate departments, such as admission or surgery. These same greeters assist visitors in finding their way to a family member or friend who has already been admitted.

Finding one's way in a large general hospital or medical center is a challenge to everyone. Way-finding and cue-searching techniques which aid the patient and visitor to easily locate various areas are very important parts of the design of the lobby and throughout the hospital. Building maps and signage—including signage with braille—close to the main entry are very important. Maps, signage, and graphic symbols at each elevator lobby are also necessary (Figure 7-12). Another form of way-finding involves the use of color for the various departments. Interior landmarks also aid in way-finding, as does the use of natural light, which helps the visitor to determine direction.

The hospital's main lobby often has design elements found in hotel lobby planning. It has to accommodate a large number of people and traffic patterns since it is one of the hubs of the hospital. Like many hotel lobbies, the hospital lobby has groupings of furniture placed throughout the space and coordinated with the overall traffic patterns. These furniture groupings allow families to gather, relax, and have a conversation. Designers need to address acoustical issues that impact these conversation areas. For example, the use of textiles, fibers, and materials which absorb sound in an attempt to create a cozier space within a large area can be effective. These spaces are designed using plants, sculpture or other artwork, fireplaces, sometimes fountains, low-wattage lighting, and comfortable seating units in an effort to alleviate anxiety (Figure 7-13).

Hospital lobbies are often designed with large windows to admit as much natural light as possible and thereby help to create a healing environment (Figure 7-14). Often, a healing garden is accessible through the main lobby or on a lower floor. Healing gardens include not only plant life aesthetically placed but also fountains, as well as places to sit. They focus on the senses of sound, sight, smell, and touch. The healing garden is also effective if the patient can view it, or parts of it, from his or her room.

Besides being a place for quiet visiting or waiting, a lobby includes other spaces and functions. The admitting area in the lobby is the place where nonemergency patients check in. Gift and floral shops are usually located within or adjacent to the lobby. The public cafeteria or lunch area should be close to the entrance and easily accessed by visitors.

An incoming patient will be directed by a greeter or signage to the admitting area. To reduce patient anxiety, the organization and communication between the lobby and the admissions area need to function effectively. The configuration of the admitting area will vary with the operational needs of the hospital. Some hospitals register patients by phone prior to arrival, thereby reducing much of the initial exchange of personal information. If this is not the case, privacy should be maintained as the patient checks in and gives

Figure 7-12 Signage at the entrance to a medical facility aids patients and visitors in the way-finding process. (Photograph courtesy of APCO Graphics, Inc., Atlanta, GA.)

personal information to the admitting staff. Desks with side panels or counters with half-height walls creating booths provide privacy for this exchange of information (Figure 7-15).

Additional lobbies in the hospital are positioned near the individual diagnostic and treatment areas. For example, the surgical suite has an admitting desk for the patient, as well as a small lobby and waiting room for family and friends. Patient nursing units are planned with a small lobby by the elevators, as well as a lobby or visiting room where patients and visitors can meet outside the patient's room. These areas are usually furnished with chairs, end tables, televisions, refreshment areas, and perhaps even a fireplace, as well as accessories such as art, plants, and periodicals.

Another type of employee located at the main entrance and lobby is a security officer. Sometimes this professional is visible and sometimes not, depending on the hospital's approach to security. Security cameras monitor not only the parking lots but also the main entrance, lobby, and elevator banks.

Inpatient Rooms

When the admittance procedures are complete, the patient is taken to an assigned room on a nursing unit prior to or after treatment, such as with most surgeries. It is important to note that the hospital corridor is required to be a minimum of 8 feet wide. This corridor often has a tightly woven, uncut carpet, whether broadloom or carpet tile, which reduces the noise of carts, wheelchairs, and gurneys rolling by.

Prior to entering the assigned room, the patient will encounter the nurse station monitoring that particular unit.

Figure 7-13 Reception area in an emergency room at a children's medical center. Note scale of the furniture for adults as well as children. (Design by The Hillier Group and Karlsberger Companies. Photograph © Robert Benson.)

Figure 7-14 Gardens are programmed into healthcare facilities to aid in creating the overall healing environment. (Contra Costa Regional Ambulatory Care Center. Photograph courtesy of Anshen + Allen. Photographer: Robert Canfield.)

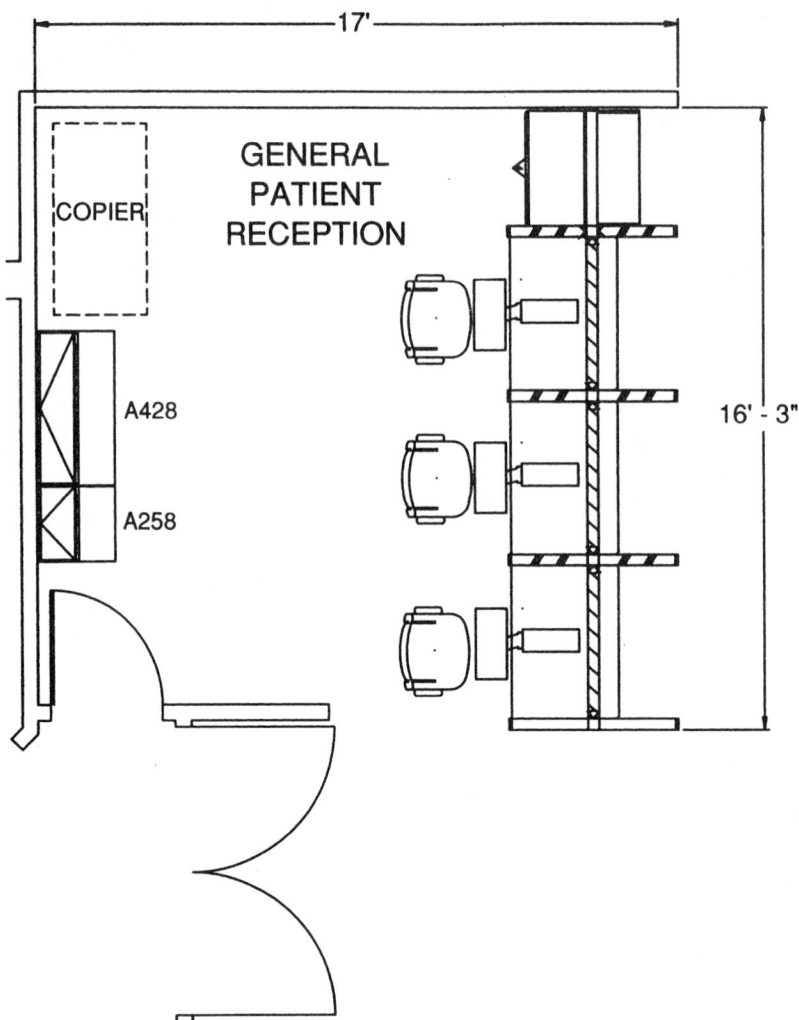

Figure 7-15 General patient reception and admitting area. Note the panels placed between each admitting station to allow privacy for patient records. (Drawing courtesy of Milcare, Inc., Zeeland, MI.)

These can be general units which provide acute nursing care to all hospital patients. Some units are specialized, such as the intensive care unit for patients needing extra attention. A typical nursing unit consists of a nurse station, several inpatient rooms, one or more treatment rooms, and other ancillary spaces, depending on the nature of the nursing unit. The planning and design of the nursing station is discussed in the next section.

Hospital inpatient stays are shorter and fewer due to regulations set by Medicare and some HMOs. This has led to an increase in outpatient treatment. It also means that the inpatient needs more observation and care. This directly impacts the size of and planning of the nursing units.

Hospitals offer both private and semiprivate patient rooms. In today's hospital design, more facilities are planned and built using all private patient rooms. From a medical standpoint, these individual rooms assist the nursing staff since there are no incompatibility issues, as in semiprivate rooms. Another advantage is that infection and disease control is limited to one patient. Many more patient treatments can be conducted in the private room, which is cost effective. Finally, private rooms provide more space for family members. HIPAA regulations are vigorously enforced for private rooms.

The door to the patient's room is extra wide to allow a gurney to be moved in and out—usually 4 feet. The door must swing into the room, not outward into the corridor per code requirements. Space allowances must be planned to permit considerable room around the sides and at the foot of the bed so that staff may treat the patient. Doors into private bathrooms must be 3 feet wide or wider.

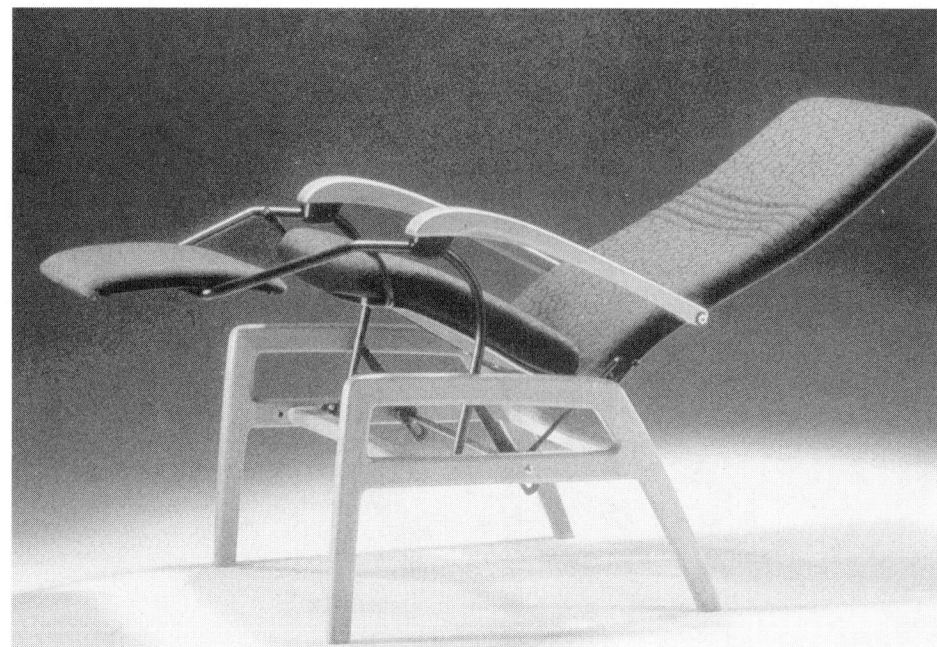

Figure 7-16a Care Chair, a specialty reclining chair used for patient comfort and mobility. (Photograph courtesy of Kusch + Co.)

Patients prefer a private room for many reasons, including privacy, control of the lights and television, room for visitors, and a private restroom. Other amenities in the private room include a desk and chair with a phone, task lighting, Internet access, a flat-screen television, a bulletin board for the patient's use, a sofa bed for family members, and a recliner. The medical furnishings include, of course, the hospital bed, a nightstand, a movable food tray, a headboard with medical equipment capabilities such as oxygen and plug-ins for monitors built in, a cubicle curtain for additional privacy, and a built-in cabinet with a sink and storage space for biohazardous supplies. At the entry to the room, nurses have a dispenser for antibacterial lotion, which they use prior to treating the patient. A clock within easy sight of the patient is a very important amenity to specify (Figures 7-16a and 7-16b).

The private patient room will also include storage space for personal items and a private bathroom. Closed closet space and a locked drawer for personal items are often provided as a built-in unit, as well as a desk and a television viewing area. The door of the private bathroom opens into the patient room and is positioned per the architect's preference. The bathroom includes an accessible water closet with a high seat, grab bars, a nurse's alarm button, a sink, and a shower with a seat. Accessories such as towel racks and hooks, as well as a paper towel dispenser and soap dispenser, are also included. Lighting, which includes overhead and vanity lighting and a night light, will be specified (Figure 7-17).

Standard acute care inpatient rooms can also be semiprivate. The typical semiprivate room has two beds separated by a cubicle curtain for privacy. Each bed is provided with a headwall that can contain lighting fixtures and connections for medical gases such as oxygen. The headwall may have a self-contained nightstand with drawer space or, more commonly, a freestanding nightstand on casters for mobility. This latter specification allows the nursing staff to access the patient more readily (Figures 7-18a and 7-18b).

Figure 7-16b QC Chair used in hospital patient rooms for patient and visitor use. Note the casters, footstool, and reclining mechanism. (Photograph courtesy of La-Z-Boy Inc., Monroe, MI, 313-241-4700.)

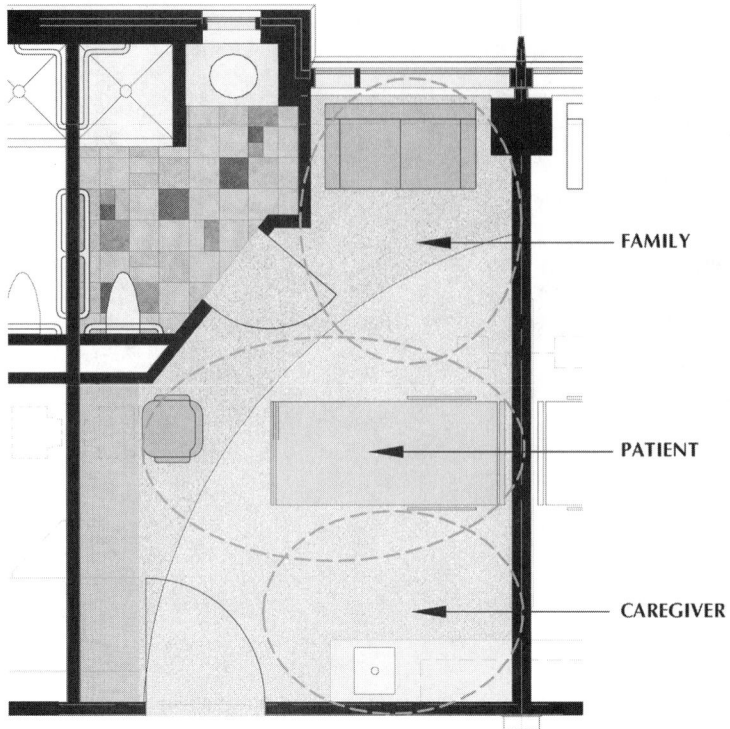

TYPICAL PATIENT ROOM
LAKESIDE HOSPITAL, OMAHA, NE

Figure 7-17 Floor plan of a private patient room in Alegent Lakeside Hospital. Note the zoning of spaces for the caregiver, patient, and family, as well as space provided for storage and a desk. (Floor plan courtesy of Leo A Daly.)

Each patient will have at least one chair, an individual television with volume control, light controls, and a closet. Both patients share the same bathroom; therefore, sanitation, virus, and bacteria control need to be doubly addressed in order to prevent the spreading or sharing of disease. Infection control in semiprivate rooms takes additional time to address by the nurses and other staff. Emergency power systems are required for all inpatient areas, although electrical codes do not require that all areas be on emergency power.

The same materials are specified for both private and semiprivate patient rooms. Materials specification creating a noninstitutional appearance while still abiding by all hospital codes is important in providing a healing environment. Color selection for patient rooms can vary, focusing on creating a restful, positive environment. Color schemes that create a secure, cheerful ambience are used today, in contrast to the earlier white and pale green, which were considered calming, antiseptic colors in the early 20th century.

It is important that the architect and designer plan spaces for family members and other visitors. A visitors' waiting area centrally located on each patient floor is typical. A lounge on each floor and a small kitchenette for family use give families a place to congregate without disturbing or stressing the patients (Figures 7-19a and 7-19b).

The overall space planning of inpatient rooms is primarily the responsibility of the architect. Interior designers provide input on architectural finishes, movable furniture specification, and some planning processes. HVAC and other mechanical systems are designed by the architect and by specialists in those areas. However, it is important for the interior designer to research all systems and architectural concerns in order to better understand the total process.

Nurse Stations
The nurse station is the hub of each nursing unit and needs to be designed with attention to detail. Standard acute care inpatient rooms are divided into units which include

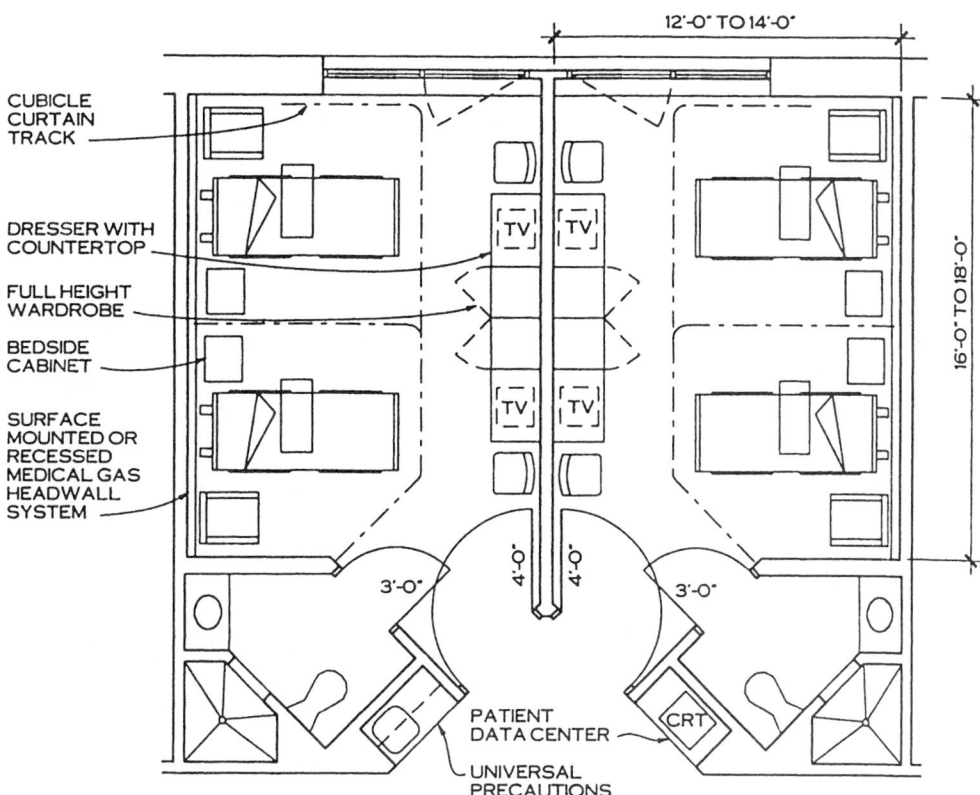

Figure 7-18a Floor plan of a semiprivate patient room in a hospital indicating two beds separated by a cubicle curtain in the space between the beds. Minimal space for storage and visitors is provided. (Drawing from Ramsey, *Architectural Graphic Standards,* 9th ed. Copyright © 1988. Reprinted by permission of John Wiley & Sons, Inc.)

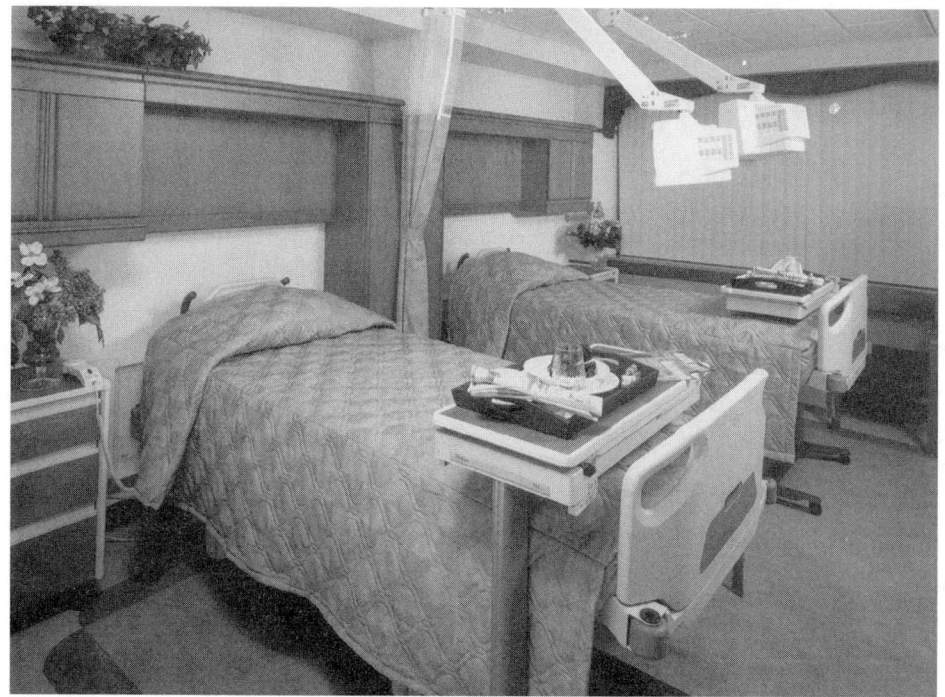

Figure 7-18b Semiprivate patient room in a hospital. Note the cubicle curtain, individual televisions, storage area, night stands, and light bridge for patient use. (Photograph courtesy of Elissa Packard, ASID; Vintage Archonics, Inc., Photographer: Lisa Tyner.)

Figure 7-19a Custom-designed space for parents' use in the pediatric intensive care area of New York University Medical Center. Note the lockers and shower space for parents' use while they stay in the hospital near their critically ill children. (Photograph courtesy of Interior Design Solutions, Susan Aiello, ASID, New York State Certified. Photographer: Paul Whicheloe.)

Figure 7-19b Space for family use in the pediatric intensive care area of New York University Medical Center. The lounge chairs are medical recliners, which convert into beds when fully reclined. (Photograph courtesy of Interior Design Solutions, Susan Aiello, ASID, New York State Certified. Photographer: Paul Whicheloe.)

a nurse station and a variety of support spaces which serve a group of patient rooms. The tasks at a nursing station include recording all medical information on patients; providing communication between physicians, nurses, and other medical personnel; and preparings medications. It is also an area for filling out forms, scheduling staff shifts and staff meetings, and communicating with members of the patient's family. From this list of tasks, it is clear that a variety of medical personnel use this space. Consequently, the architect and the designer need to allow sufficient working space for all these activities.

The design and layout of the nurse station is important in enhancing nursing efficiency and patient–nurse interaction. Since nursing units today are designed to be more compact—with the nurse station in the center, surrounded by patient rooms—the nurse station is located to reduce the time needed for the nurse to move from the station to the patient's room. This planning is very important in patient care (Figure 7-20).

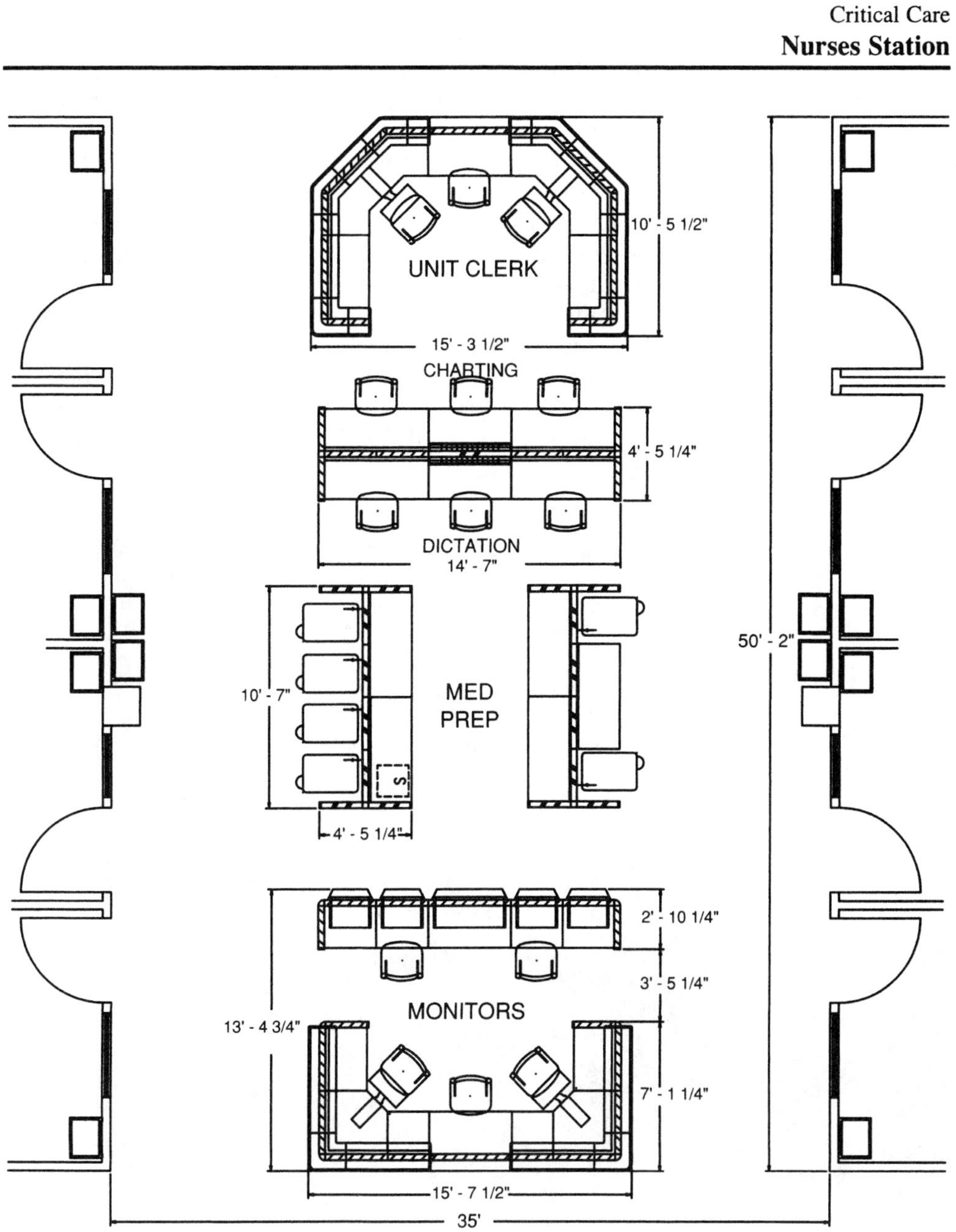

Critical Care
Nurses Station

Figure 7-20 Nurses' station in the critical care unit of a hospital. (Drawing courtesy of Milcare, Inc., Zeeland, MI.)

Depending upon the design and layout of the patient/nursing floors, nurse stations vary in placement and size. Refer to Table 7-7 for unit sizes. One approach to planning nurse stations suggests that patient care units should be divided into smaller areas, with nursing stations monitoring patient rooms as well as adjacent spaces.

Today's nursing station combines two working heights: one 40 to 42 inches high, and used for recording while standing, and one 29 to 30 inches high for standard desk height. Given the concept of visual monitoring in use today, nurse stations are commonly designed with a 36- to 40-inch panel on the exterior, which allows for visual monitoring of patient rooms while seated at the lower desk height. If the nurse station has sufficient floor space, a higher counter placed in the center can also be used for recording patient information as well as being a monitoring area with a raised viewing height (Figure 7-21).

Computers, patient call buttons, patient monitoring equipment, and crash carts need to be incorporated into the nurse station. *Crash carts* are small, mobile carts equipped with medications and equipment to handle extreme emergencies within the nursing unit. Computerized charting stations for patient records can be rolled into the patient room and then placed in the nurse station.

Materials specification for all nursing units and the nursing station should be consistent. The aesthetic design concept for the corridor, elevator bank, nurse station and visitors' waiting area should also coordinate with the design of patient rooms. Some common areas that often have different materials than those used in regular acute care nursing units are the children's floor in a hospital, which requires a more playful appearance, and the maternity ward, which might have materials and colors associated with babies.

Obvious concerns in the nursing station area are sanitation, ease of cleaning, and ease of maintenance. This area requires materials that can take the abuse and traffic of various carts, chairs on casters, and foot traffic. Although high-density, antimicrobial carpet tiles might be appropriate for corridors, the area near and around the nursing station is often finished in a commercial-grade vinyl tile. Seating units on casters that are very stable at desk height are also to be specified. Nontextured surfaces for all workstation surfaces are important. The outside face of the nurse station cabinets can be of other materials, depending on the hospital's preference and state codes.

Figure 7-21 Nurses' station position in a corridor. Note the shorter length of the corridor, which aids the nurse in accessing patient rooms more readily from the station. (Photograph courtesy of Elissa Packard, ASID, interior designer. Vintage Archonics, Inc. Photographer: Lisa Tyner.)

TABLE 7-9 Dental Practice Vocabulary

- **Asepsis:** The methods used to prevent infection.
- **Endodontics:** The branch of dentistry that treats disorders of the pulp, as in root canal therapy.*
- **Malocclusions:** improper meeting of the upper and lower teeth.†
- **Operatory:** Dental treatment area.

- **Orthodontics:** The branch of dentistry concerned with diagnosing, correcting, and preventing irregularities of the teeth and poor occlusion.‡
- **Pedodontics:** The branch of dentistry concerned with the treatment and care of children's teeth.

*Webster's Dictionary, 4th ed. 2002, p. 469.
†Ibid., p. 386.
‡Ibid., p. 1016.

Many codes and restrictions will impact the design of the nursing unit as a whole and the nurse station specifically. Accessibility is a must, and adherence to fire safety codes is required. These regulations are adopted and enforced by city, state, and federal governments, and it is the interior designer's responsibility to research and understand the codes that apply to hospital design. Additional information applicable to the nursing unit and the nurse station is presented in the Planning and Interior Design Elements section of the chapter. The reader should also consult the works listed at the end of this chapter for additional information.

Dental Facilities

The interior designer who specializes in healthcare facilities may include the design of dental practices. The field of dentistry is detail oriented and is governed by national, state, and local codes. The knowledge required for the planning and specification of all the spaces within a dental practice suite goes beyond creating an aesthetically pleasing environment. Coordination with the dentist, staff, equipment suppliers, and other consultants is critical, as inaccurate planning can affect service in the treatment rooms.

The majority of dental practices focus on general dentistry or a specialty such as pedodontics, endodontics, or orthodontics. *Webster's New College Dictionary* defines a dentist as a "person whose profession is the care of teeth and the surrounding soft tissues, including the prevention and elimination of decay, the replacement of missing teeth with artificial ones, the correction of malocclusions."[16] The field of dentistry involves diagnosis, treatment, communication, and management (Table 7-9).

The largest dental organization in the United States is the American Dental Association (ADA), which has a publishing division that informs dental professionals about the latest scientific, socioeconomic, and political issues affecting the practice of dentistry. Readers should not confuse the acronym of the ADA applied to the dentistry association and the Americans with Disabilities Act.

Dentists recognize the value of sales and marketing in their specialty and will discuss these issues with the designer in relation to the interior design of the practice space. This emphasis on marketing translates into a heightened concern by the client for the interior design and aesthetic environment of the dental facility. According to Malkin, "dentists were among the first to advertise; use color coordinated uniforms; open offices in shopping malls; and attend seminars on office design, stress reduction, and the psychology of dealing with patients."[17] Creating an environment that helps reduce patient stress is thus very important in the design of dental facilities.

In programming and planning the dental practice, the interior designer needs to understand the dental community's emphasis on infection control. In 1988, OSHA commenced

[16]*Webster's Dictionary,* 2002, p. 386.
[17]Malkin, 2002, p. 401.

compliance with the Centers for Disease Control's and the ADA's methods used to prevent and control infection, referred to as asepsis. The purpose was to protect the dentist, staff, and patients from contracting any type of infection or virus from cross-contamination. Practitioners must use stringent safety and control measures to protect the patients and staff. Many of these environmental controls will impact the materials that can be specified in the dental office. This design application section will focus on the interior design of the general dentistry practice. Many of the design elements and concepts discussed apply to a dental specialty practice.

Space allocation is relatively simple. A patient enters a waiting room and moves to a reception window similar to that in any medical office. An assistant generally escorts the patient to a treatment room, also called an *operatory,* to wait for the dentist. In a general dental practice there are usually one or more dentists and one or more dental assistants and dental hygienists, depending on the size of the practice and the number of treatment rooms. Ideally, a dental practice will have three treatment chairs per dentist within the operatory space. In addition to this major area, a room or area specifically for the dental hygienist is often planned into the overall space, and sometimes treatment chairs for pedodontic and orthodontic uses as well (Figure 7-22).

Other spaces needed in the suite will depend on the specialty and the size of the practice but might include a business office, private offices for the dentists, a laboratory, X-ray facilities, a prep area, a staff lounge, and, of course, storage space and toilet facilities. In some practices, the dentists may wish to add a consultation room to confer with patients.

The overall layout of the dental office will vary considerably based on the needs and number of operatories in the treatment area. The size of the space can be as small as $8^1/_2$ feet by $8^1/_2$ feet but is generally 100 square feet. It is very important that the operatory be functionally designed so that the dentist has easy access to a sink within the space. Work counters hold instruments and supplies needed for both the dentist and the dental assistant. Drawers in the cabinetry are available for storage. However, pull-out trays and counter space are needed to hold sterilized tray setups for antiseptic practice. Ergonomic issues are a major part of this planning, as it involves not only the movements of the dentist within a very small work space, the mouth, but also reach factors, standing height based on pneumatic lift capabilities, and traffic patterns.

A critical concern in the design of the operatory rooms is the dentist's preferred delivery system, that is, the way the dentist works with the patient. This is a significant issue in planning a dental clinic, and the interior designer must discuss it with the dentist and staff. Based on the selection of the delivery system layout, the placement of instruments determines the room's layout (see Figure 7-23). There are pros and cons for each delivery system, and the dentist may prefer to install one type or two different delivery systems based on the dental style preferred, the type of treatment, or the square footage of the suite. The advantages of the rear delivery system and the over-the-head delivery system are that it allows the assistant to circulate within the space and the central instruments are outside of the patients' view. The disadvantage of the rear delivery system is the inability to reach all supplies while in this position. The side delivery system can require a smaller room. The disadvantage of this system is that the supplies are not all within easy reach. For a more detailed discussion of the functional design of operatory and dental treatment rooms, the reader should review *Medical and Dental Space Planning* by Jan Malkin or other works listed at the end of this chapter.

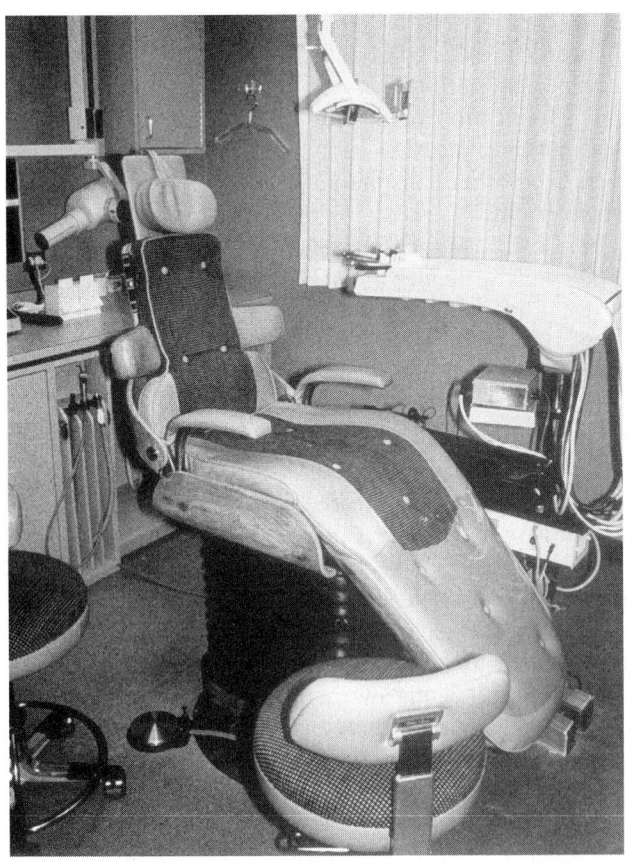

Figure 7-22 Dental operatory. The materials specified for the chair, walls, cabinetry and floor all meet code requirements for healthcare and cleanability. (Photograph courtesy of SOI, Interior Design. Bettie B. Anderson, photographer.)

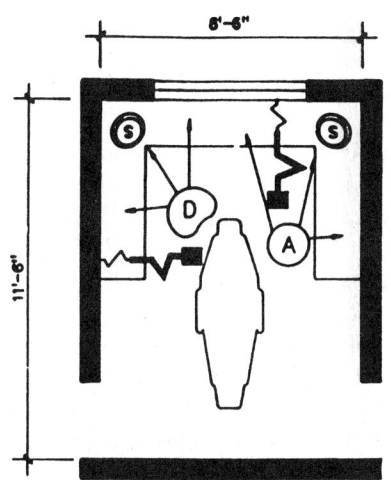

PLAN A · SIDE DELIVERY

"U" DESIGN OPERATORY DENTIST AND
ASSISTANT WORK OFF OF FIXED CABINETS.
CABINET MOUNTED INSTRUMENTATION PULLS
OUT ON A FLEXIBLE ARM.

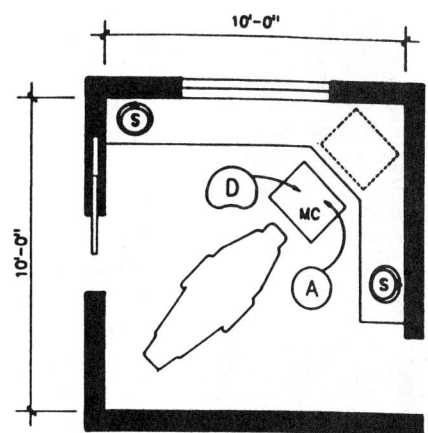

PLAN B · REAR DELIVERY

DIAGONAL CHAIR PLACEMENT WITH SINGLE
DUAL-PURPOSE MOBILE CART BEHIND PATIENT'S
HEAD. DENTIST AND ASSISTANT WORK OFF THE
SAME CART.

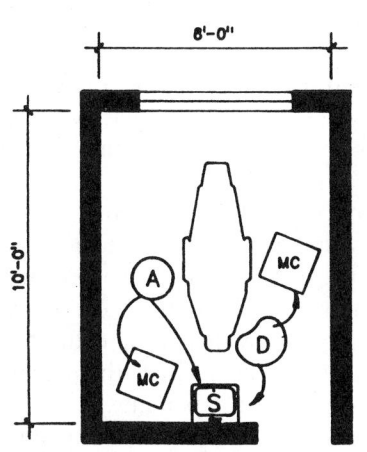

PLAN C · SIDE DELIVERY

ASSISTANT AND DENTIST WORK OFF
OF SPLIT (SEPARATE) MOBILE CARTS.
NO FIXED CABINETRY IN ROOM.

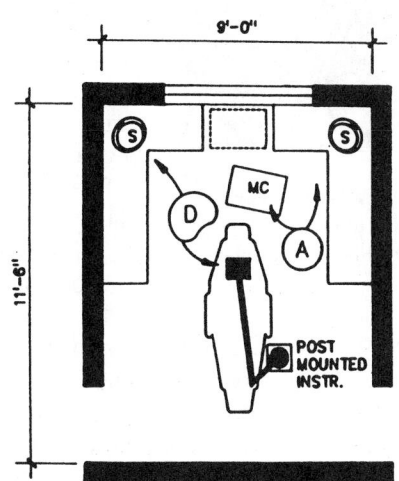

PLAN D · OVER-THE-PATIENT

MODIFIED "U" ARRANGEMENT FOR STORAGE OF
MOBILE CART. ASSISTANT WORKS OFF OF
MOBILE CART BEHIND PATIENT AND DENTIST
RECEIVES DYNAMIC INSTRUMENTS OVER THE
PATIENT'S CHEST (INSTRUMENTS ARE POST
MOUNTED).

Figure 7-23 Four plans for dental operatories. (From Malkin, *Medical and Dental Space Planning for the 90's.* Copyright © 1990. Reprinted by permission of John Wiley & Sons, Inc.)

The operatory is the place where the patient spends the most time. Creating functional, pleasant surroundings for the patient, as well as for the dentist and staff, is very important. Depending upon the view, access to windows is usually a positive feature within an operatory (Figure 7-24). Natural light is also important for color matching of crowns and caps, which need to match the existing teeth in color and texture. If the dental office is located on the main level of the building, some dentists prefer a design with a walled garden surrounding the operatories so that patients have a beautiful natural setting to view during dental procedures. Remember, reducing patients' fear and anxiety regarding

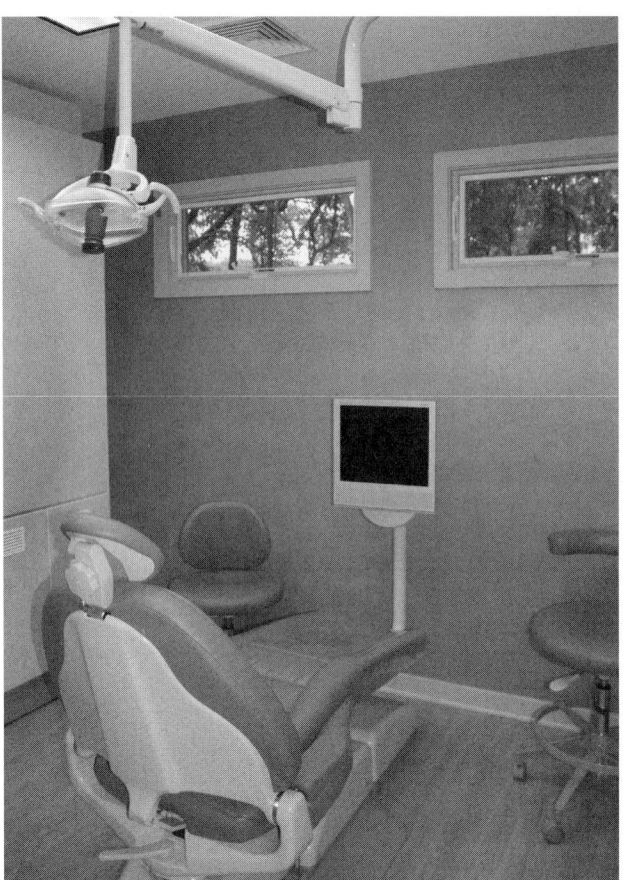

Figure 7-24 Contemporary operatory. High windows allow for natural light and some view without violating the patient's privacy. (Photograph courtesy of Designs by Ria, Ria E. Gulian, ASID. Photographer: Danelle Stukas.)

dental procedures is part of the designer's goal. If windows are not present, landscape prints, murals, or other artwork on the walls, and sometimes on the ceiling, help to relieve stress.

Wall treatments in these areas are often commercial grade-vinyl wallcoverings with miimal texture, which are easily cleanable. If specifying vinyl wallcoverings, the designer must research their composition to avoid VOCs and other pollutants. Some dentists prefer painted walls, which provide great flexibility in color choices. If paint is specified, use one that is washable and scrubbable. Semigloss paint is considered an acceptable choice. However, the designer must specify a wall surface with few imperfections that might be magnified by the sheen of semigloss paint.

Intense colors and large patterns on the walls should be avoided, since these rooms are small. Neutrals and soft pastels are preferred. The interior designer can add a splash of brighter color on the stools used by the dentist and the dental assistant. The dentist may even agree to a stronger color on the operatory chair.

The dental profession uses a combination of lighting in the operatories in addition to natural light. Overhead lighting using fluorescent ceiling fixtures is often provided in leased spaces. Lamps which best replicate natural light— full-spectrum lamps—should be specified by the interior designer. Task lighting for the dentist is part of the dental equipment purchased through medical equipment and supply houses. The lighting design should ensure that the space is free of shadows. Dentists use halogen light where greater clarity is required.

Let us now return to the waiting area, reception area, and business office. The furniture and finish specifications in these areas are similar to those used in a physician's medical suite. The waiting room should be warm and welcoming, with emphasis on the reduction of patient stress. As dental treatment is often associated with pain and discomfort, it is important to create an environment which relaxes as well as distracts the patient. This is especially true in the pedodontic office, where children are the patients.

The majority of waiting rooms are smaller than those in a medical office suite since there are fewer patients. They are furnished with chairs using the same principles discussed for medical suites. Small armless or open-arm chairs are the most common seating solution. As most dental waiting rooms are small due to less waiting time, sofas or settees are not generally specified unless intended for use by family members such as a mother and child. Accessories such as a magazine rack, artwork, plants, and a television monitor for educational videos often are placed in the dental waiting room (Figure 7-25).

The reception area in the dental office can be either closed off by a reception window or, most likely, separated by a counter and work space for the office staff. A counter 40 to 42 inches high can be provided for patients to write checks or record dental information while also providing some privacy for the staff. The staff usually works at a 29- to 30-inch-high workstation, which can be custom built or specified with systems furniture. This configuration is similar to that of the waiting area depicted in Figure 7-5a. The section on materials specification for medical office suites is a good starting point for the designer of the dental clinic as well. Many dentists prefer a residential look to the waiting area to help alleviate patient stress.

A dentist's private office can be specified with furniture and finishes similar to those of any business office. Furniture items should allow the dentist to work on the computer, do paperwork, read, and possibly consult with staff or patients. Materials and colors should appeal to the dentist while retaining the principles used throughout the clinic.

Acoustical control is important in the dental office. There is usually a door between the waiting room and the corridor leading to the operatories. However, because the operatories themselves rarely have doors, hearing ambient noise can be a problem for patients. A good sound-masking system throughout the suite, sound-absorbing carpet, and acoustical wallcoverings can help reduce ambient noise. In addition to control acoustics, do not locate the operatories adjacent to the waiting room. Separation of the waiting room from the operatories can be planned by placing the dentist's office, the conference room, or storage closets adjacent to the waiting room wall, thus reducing the noise.

In planning the installation of FF&E, make certain that all architectural finishes and general lighting fixtures are in place prior to the installation of the dental chairs and all other large pieces of medical equipment. This will ease the final installation of large pieces of equipment and create a cleaner interior installation.

The designer will have additional planning and specification issues in a dental office. The proper design and shielding of X-ray equipment and the location and layout of the darkroom must be carefully addressed. A central location of the laboratory for sterilization of instruments and preparation of some compounds will increase the effectiveness of the staff. Sinks are necessary, and special ventilation may be needed in the lab and the prep room. Public and staff restrooms, as well as the location of support spaces such as storage areas and staff lounges, are all important to the general dental practice.

Today's dentists are interested in maximizing technology, which can, if planned, allow maximum use of the space. Twenty-five percent of all general dentists in the United States now use computers in the treatment rooms.[18]

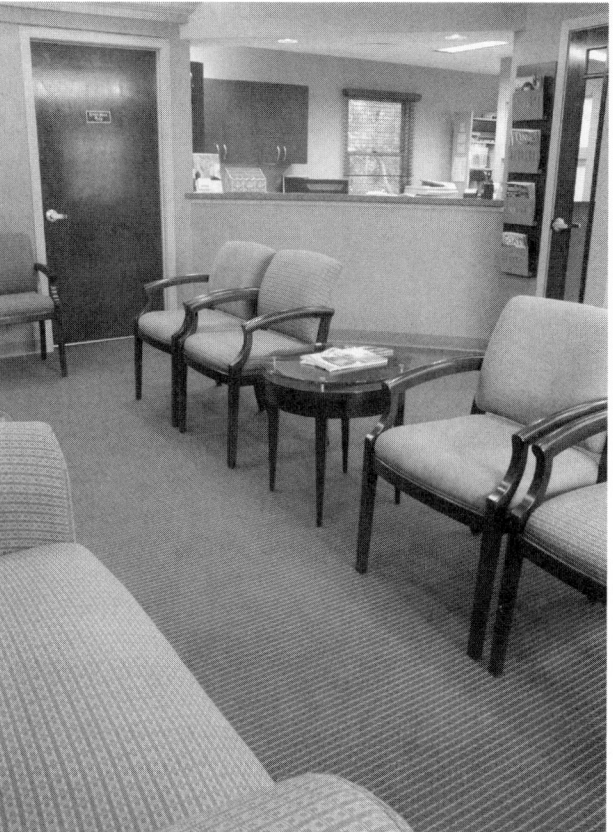

Figure 7-25 Waiting room in a dental reception area. Note the chairs with open arms to aid patient mobility. (Photograph courtesy of Designs by Ria, Ria E. Gulian, ASID. Photographer: Danelle Stukas.)

Computer use requires ergonomic work stations to improve employee productivity and for proper charting of patients' records. The computer allows dentists and staff to record and chart progress notes; to use digital radiology, whose images can be viewed on a monitor; and to use intraoral and digital cameras for greater magnification. The Internet allows dentists greater and more expedient access to research, dental schools, colleagues, and laboratories, thus reducing the wait time for pertinent information. The computer also accelerates data management, as well as record practice management and business applications.[19]

Dental offices are considered business occupancies by the International Building Code and as mercantile occupancies by fire safety codes. Exact requirements will vary based on the number of occupants, though most dental practices will have an occupant load under 50. Architectural finishes in corridors and exits must be Class A or I, while those in operatories and most other areas may be Class B or II materials. Corridor and doorway sizes must meet the accessibility and building code requirements for business occupancies.

At least one public restroom must be accessible, and at least one operatory must be ADA accessible. All other ADA requirements for commercial public spaces will also need to be applied especially to new construction and major remodeling projects. The interior designer should consult with the local building official with jurisdiction to ensure proper code compliance.

The interior design of dental facilities involves intricate planning not only for the efficient use of the space but to deal with ergonomic issues as well. Creating a stress-free, warm environment for the patient is important as well.

---

[18]Levato, 2004, p. 30S.
[19]Lavato, 2004, p. 36S.

TABLE 7-10 Terminology for Veterinary Facility Design

- **Boarding:** Space within a veterinary clinic where an animal can be kept overnight, whether it is healthy or needs medical care.
- **Large animals:** Horses, cows, pigs, and others of significant size.
- **Runs:** Enclosed areas where animals such as dogs can run free.

- **Small animals:** Dogs, cats, rabbits, and others of a small size.
- **Solace room:** Place at a veterinary clinic or hospital where the pet/animal owner may have privacy after an animal has died.
- **Veterinarian:** Medical professional trained to treat small and large animals.

Veterinary Facilities

In the United States today, there are approximately 50,000 veterinarians providing a variety of services. They are located in small and/or large animal private practices, clinics and hospitals, and group practices. Veterinarians also work in research settings, in zoos, and as teachers, as well as for federal or state government. This design application section will concentrate on the small animal clinic, which is the most prevalent type of veterinary facility. The "client" here refers to the veterinarian's client: the owner or caretaker of the pet.

According to *Veterinary Economics* magazine, a major publication for veterinarians, 63 percent of U.S. households have a pet. This publication also reported that in 2004, pet owners spent $34.4 billion on their pets.[20] Due to the popularity of pets, small animal veterinary clinics and hospitals are abundant.

The majority of large animal veterinary clinics are located in or near rural areas, with a focus on livestock. The rural large animal owner focuses on the care of the animal as an investment. Some large animal practices focus on the horse. These clinics can be near racetracks or breeding farms; others are located in cities like Denver, Colorado, and Phoenix, Arizona, where horse properties exist within the city limits.

The most common type of veterinary facility is the clinic that specializes in small animals and some large animals. More than one veterinarian may be involved in the practice as an owner or staff member. In addition, the small animal veterinarian employs veterinary technicians and assistants as well as office staff. Staff members have multiple duties and are important to the successful operation of the facility. Staff members may work full-time or part-time. Others, such as professional pet groomers providing grooming services at the veterinary clinic, work on a contract.

In addition to healthcare services for pets, a veterinary clinic can provide boarding services. This is of particular interest to city dwellers who would like to leave their pets with a trusted service. A new service offered by some clinics is "doggie day care." This is a daytime service that operates from 8:30 A.M. to 4:30 P.M. to accommodate working people who own dogs (Table 7-10).

The interior design of a veterinary clinic involves conditions that, although not unique, challenge the interior designer unfamiliar with this type of facility. Nervous and sick animals create "accidents," and the resulting odors must be dealt with regularly. This means that all architectural and equipment surfaces must be easy to sanitize and clean, requiring materials to withstand considerable scrubbing of surfaces in order to stay clean and odor free. This excessive but necessary cleaning schedule can result in some remodeling or replacement of materials.

A typical small animal clinic includes the reception area and waiting room, business office, client education room, exam rooms, and treatment areas. A *solace room*, or area for the grieving or mourning client whose pet has died, is often provided in today's plans for clients. Back office areas are the veterinarian's office, employee area, storage area, kennel runs, boarding area, surgery suite, laboratory, food preparation area within the boarding compound, pharmacy, and corridors to link these areas (see Figure 7-26).

---

[20]"Pet Spending in America and Abroad," 2005, p. 24.

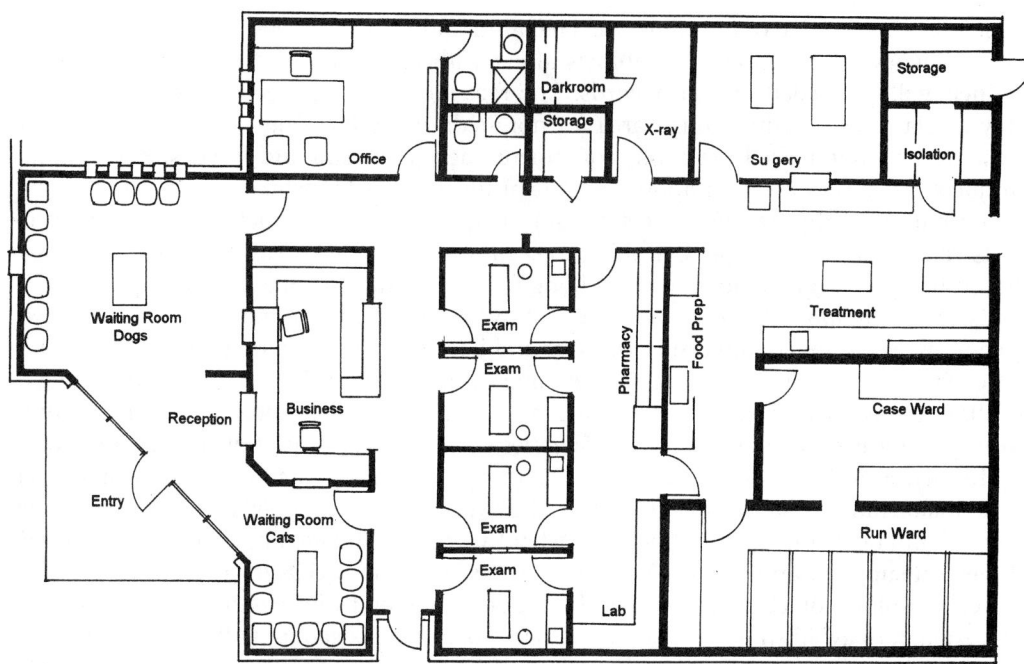

Figure 7-26 Floor plan of a veterinary hospital. Note the division of spaces planned for cats and dogs in the reception area. (Floor plan courtesy of Spencer Animal Hospital, Inc., Dennis Mangum, D.V.M.)

Ideally, upon entering through the main entry, the client will find a waiting area for dogs and a separate waiting area for cats, with the reception area separating these two spaces (see Figure 7-27). The client will proceed to the reception desk to check in for an appointment, as in a medical office building.

The reception area is also grouped with the business area, which provides bookkeeping, appointment scheduling, billing, filing, and recording patient medical information.

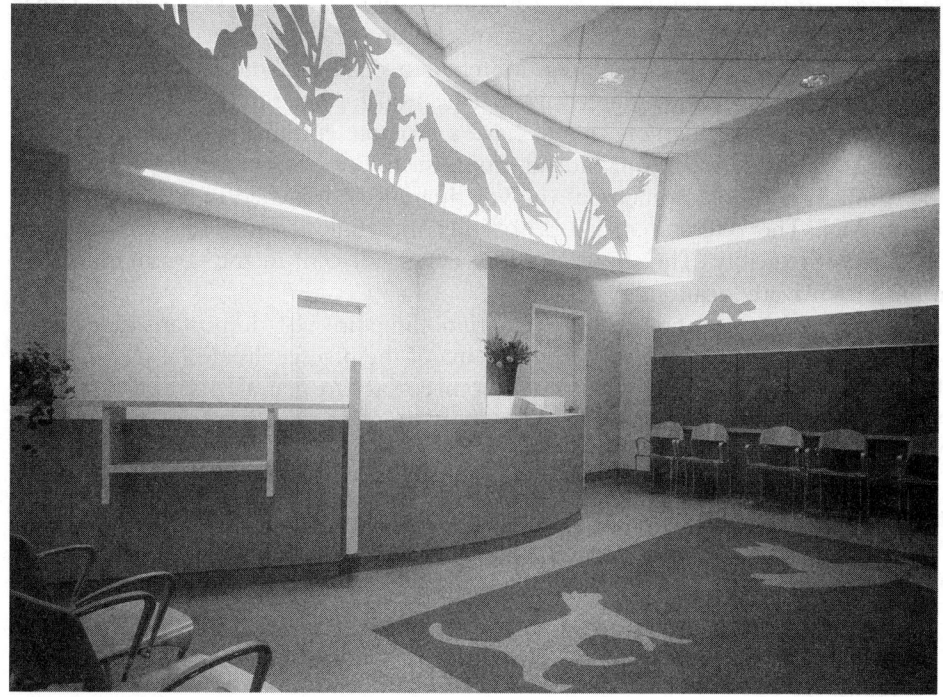

Figure 7-27 Creatively designed reception area in a veterinary clinic. The design on the floor designates the areas for cats and dogs. (Photograph courtesy of Hugh A. Boyd Architects, Montclair, NJ.)

Depending on the size of the clinic, the reception and business areas are usually furnished with millwork workstations and cabinets along with or instead of desks. Appropriate file cabinets will be needed to hold records. The reception area will require storage and possibly display space in the waiting area for nonmedical product sales. It is not unusual for a veterinary clinic to sell pet food, equipment such as collars and leashes, and bathing products. This sales area is important, as it produces further income for the clinic.

Furniture for the waiting rooms should be specified with cleanable surfaces, as accidents can occur while the pet is waiting to see the veterinarian. Chairs in the waiting area should be open-legged tandem or wall hung for ease of maintenance. Molded plastic seating is quite common in the waiting area. Woven textiles for seating should be avoided, as they are easily soiled and can collect dirt and bacteria. Some veterinarians prefer a built-in bench. If a bench is specified, make certain that the height is between 20 and 22 inches to allow for ease in rising without the use of chair arms. The interior designer should avoid placing live plants in veterinary facilities, as some plants are poisonous to animals.

Ideally, a facility should include two exam rooms per veterinarian, as the exam room is the major funding source for the clinic. The average exam room is 11 by 10 feet on average. Equipment consists of a treatment island with a pneumatic lift, cabinetry for storage of medical supplies, and a sink. Wall space to review X-rays needs to be provided, as well as LCD displays for client education. The countertops and the treatment island must be high enough to avoid straining the veterinarian's back when examining the pet. It is mandatory that all surfaces in the exam rooms be specified as antimicrobial and easily cleaned.

When a new clinic is being designed and built, a solace room or area is often provided. In older facilities, an exam room can be used or remodeled for this purpose. It is usually the size of an exam room. A solace room should include three or four chairs and perhaps cabinets so that it can be converted into another exam room.

The pharmacy, laboratory, treatment area, and surgical suite are usually specified with specialized equipment similar to that used in a hospital or MOB. Large animal clinics will require additional special equipment for treatment and surgical areas. The architect and interior designer will work closely with the veterinarian for space planning and equipment specification of these specialized medical areas.

All clinics include boarding space for animals that must be kept overnight after procedures. Others offer boarding for healthy animals. Ideally, cats and dogs are boarded separately. Dogs are larger and more vocal and can stress the cats. Dogs require larger cages and need a run for exercise. Provision for cleaning the dog cages is another important consideration in the boarding area. Materials needed for boarding and dog runs will be discussed in the section on materials specification for veterinary facilities.

The employees and veterinarians should have a separate entrance into the clinic. Employees may take dogs for walks out on the grounds, and not leaving through the main entrance is ideal. In addition, sometimes the veterinarian is drenched in mud after treating a large animal. The veterinarian needs to enter the clinic without observation, and proceed to a shower facility. The shower can be either adjacent to the veterinarian's office or in another private location.

Architectural finishes specified in a veterinarian clinic are very important due to the nature of the facility. The overall design and scheme of the project should be pleasing but also withstand the constant cleaning that will be necessary to maintain sanitary requirements. As much as possible, nonabsorbent materials should be specified to limit residual odors. As for materials specification, in general all the clinical areas and reception areas require very durable, scrubbable surfaces, and antimicrobial products with low or no VOCs. The materials should be light in color.

The flooring must be not only visually appealing but also durable, slip-resistant, antimicrobial, easily cleanable, and impermeable to liquids and odors. The flooring materials used in veterinary facilities include vinyl composition tile, heavy-grade sheet vinyl, ceramic tile, stained and sealed concrete, and terrazzo, to mention only a few of the most widely recommended materials. Porcelain tile sealed with epoxy for the exam rooms is sometimes used as well. Continuous cove or flash cove base is recommended to avoid seams, which can collect bacteria and dust.

There are several good options for wall finishes. Paint offers versatile finishes and types and many color schemes. For example, washable latex semigloss enamel paint is acceptable for use in the waiting room, reception area, and business areas as well as the exam rooms. Epoxy paint is good for ward and run areas, and epoxy coatings are best used for dog runs. A medium-duty Type II vinyl wallcovering with a vinyl coating can also be used in these areas. Stain Resistant Type II is effective. Ceramic tile for wall surfaces can be used for wainscoting, backsplashes, and shower enclosures. Plastic laminates are also effective as a wainscot; however, this product needs to be mounted on plywood rather than drywall.[21]

Sound-absorbing materials and noise control are factors that the design team must address. The goal is to contain noise and prevent it from spreading throughout the facility. This begins with the specification of ceiling treatments. The ceiling in a veterinary facility is usually suspended acoustic tile; painted drywall is also common. If acoustic tile is used in the entry and the waiting/reception areas, designer tiles, usually 2 by 2 feet, should be specified. In the dog runs and boarding areas, a water-felted panel is considered more durable, as it is sag-proof. The surgical areas need clean-room ceilings using specialized ceiling tiles with sealed edges and back coatings to meet code requirements.

Acoustical control is important in all the clinical areas, runs, kennels. To reduce noise in the exam rooms, two layers of glass separated by a 2-inch air space should be used. In addition, a solid-core wood or hollow metal door is needed, as well as stripping around the door to seal in the sound. Dog runs can be very noisy. Sound-absorbing materials such as free-hanging sound baffles, solid walls, and solid doors block sound in this area. Ideally, the ceiling should be at least 10 feet high and the walls should go from floor to ceiling in the dog run space.[22]

Odor in a veterinary clinic is a major concern, and clients will know if it is not controlled. Exam rooms, bathrooms, and darkrooms require exhaust fans. A specialized hood should be placed over the sink in the laboratory. Frequent cleaning of exam rooms, cages, dog runs, and all flooring aids in reducing odor. Runs require frequent cleaning, which includes the installation of a floor drain for waste removal. Part of the solution for reducing odors is a high-quality HVAC system. Architects often specify a separate HVAC unit for the ward, kennel, grooming area, and bathing area, with another HVAC unit for the veterinarian's office, reception area, and exam rooms. Other technical HVAC specification would rest with the architect.

The veterinarian generally has preferences for colors and materials, which can be based on demographics. Color preferences generally include white, off-white, ivory, cream, and pale tones for the walls and floors. These color choices vary slightly, depending upon the clinic's regional location. Light colors, of course, have advantages in that light is reflected, spots are easily detected, and moods can be directly affected by the degree of light on the surfaces used. Colors associated with nature such as forest green, brown, and rust tones are some of the preferred accent colors. Treatment, surgical, and acute care areas usually have off-white walls. Research indicates that client preferences include vinyl flooring and nonporous furniture surfaces. Kennel walls are kept in a light tone as well.[23]

Both general lighting and task lighting such as a surgical light in a treatment/surgery room will be needed. Incandescent lighting is preferred in the waiting room. Fluorescent lighting is used in the exam rooms, business office, and most other areas. Special surgical lighting fixtures will be needed in the surgery space and possibly the treatment rooms.

A veterinary clinic is classified as a business occupancy by the International Building Code. Depending on the size of the clinic, and on the specific animals treated and the procedures performed, some areas of the facility may need to meet higher code standards for fire protection. In general, the veterinary clinic will also need to be designed with awareness of the accessibility guidelines of the jurisdiction.

This design subspecialty of medical facility design is challenging and interesting. The interior designer must meet the design requirements of the veterinarian, as well as the

[21]Hafen, 2004, p. 5.
[22]Hafen, 2000, p. 2.
[23]Rogers, 1991, p. 5.

preferences of the pet owners or caretakers. At the same time, the designer must create an interior that soothes and calms nervous pets—the nonspeaking users of the space!

Summary

Interior design of healthcare facilities is a complex and extensive subject which requires considerable research and preparation by the professionals involved. Interior designers who engage in any area of healthcare facility design become familiar with medical terminology and understand the business of healthcare. Specialized knowledge of medical practice is critical to produce a successful project that meets the needs of the client, the project's stakeholders, and the patients who will utilize these spaces.

Interior design impacts humans both physically and psychologically. In healthcare facilities, these issues become intensified due to the treatment and healing processes involved. Considering the complexities of healthcare design, it is imperative that the designer use this chapter as a guideline only and do considerable research by reading additional works focusing on the specific area of the healthcare design project. The works at the end of this chapter are a good starting point for further reading.

To provide the reader with a comprehensive overview of healthcare facilities, this chapter has presented a very brief description of the history of healthcare and an overview of the field of medicine, including the typical facilities an interior designer might encounter in a design project. It has also provided specific guidelines on the design of the most common healthcare facilities for the professional and the student who may have a healthcare assignment.

REFERENCES

American Heritage Dictionary of the English Language, 3rd ed. 1992. Boston: Houghton Mifflin.

American Institute of Architects Academy of Architecture for Health. 1996. *Guidelines for Design and Construction of Hospital and Healthcare Facilities.* Washington, DC: American Institute of Architects Press.

Anderson, Kenneth N., ed. 1994. *Mosby's Medical, Nursing and Allied Health Dictionary,* 4th ed. St. Louis: Mosby.

Berger, William N. and William Pomeranz. 1985. *Nursing Home Development.* New York: Van Nostrand Reinhold.

Burt, Brian A. and Stephen A. Eklund. 1992. *Dentistry, Dental Practice and the Community,* 4th ed. Philadelphia: W. B. Saunders.

Bush-Brown, Albert and Dianne Davis. 1992. *Hospitable Design for Healthcare and Senior Communities.* New York: Van Nostrand Reinhold.

Christenson, Margaret A. and Ellen D. Taira, eds. 1990. *Aged in the Designed Environment.* New York: Haworth.

Cox, Anthony and Philip Grover. 1990. *Hospitals and Health-Care Facilities.* London: Butterworth.

De Chiara, Jospeh, Julius Panero, and Martin Zelnick. 2001. *Time-Saver Standards for Interior Design and Space Planning.* New York: McGraw-Hill.

Doble, Henry P. 1982. *Medical Office Design.* St. Louis: Warren H. Green, Inc.

Dorland's Illustrated Medical Dictionary, 28th ed. 1994. Philadelphia: W. B. Saunders.

Farr, Cheryl. 1996. *High-Tech Practice: Thriving in Dentistry's Computer Age.* Tulsa, OK: PennWell.

Field, Marilyn J., ed. 1995. *Dental Education at the Crossroads.* Washington, DC: National Academy Press.

Foner, Nancy. 1994. *The Caregiving Dilemma.* Berkeley: University of California Press.

Friedman, JoAnn. 1987. *Home Health Care.* New York: Fawcett Columbine.

Hafen, Mark. 2000. "Minimize Noise and Odor." *Veterinary Economics Magazine.* August, pp. 1–3, www.hospitaldesign.net.

———. 2004. "Building Materials and Finishes." *Veterinary Economics Magazine.* December, pp. 1–8, www.hospitaldesign.net.

Haggard, Liz and Sarah Hosking. 1999. *Healing the Hospital Environment: Design, Maintenance and Management of Healthcare Premises.* New York: Routledge.

Hall, Edward T. 1966. *The Hidden Dimension.* Garden City, NY: Doubleday.

Havlicek, Penny L. 1996. *Medical Groups in the U.S.: A Survey of Practice Characteristics.* Chicago: American Medical Association.

James, Paul and Tony Noakes. 1994. *Hospital Architecture.* Singapore: Longman Group.

Johnston, Ivan and Andrew Hunter. 1984. *The Design and Utilization of Operating Theaters.* London: Edward Arnold.

Kiger, Anne Fox, compiler. 1986. *Hospital Administration Terminology.* Chicago: AHA Resource Center.

Klein, Burton and Albert Platt. 1989. *Health Care Facility Planning and Construction.* New York: Van Nostrand Reinhold.

Knapp, John. 1996. *The Floor Plan Book: Veterinary Hospital and Boarding Kennel Planning and Design,* 2nd ed. Lenexa, KS: Veterinary Healthcare Communications.

Kobus, Richard L., Ronald L. Skaggs, Michael Bobrow, Julia Thomas, and Tomas M. Payette. 2000. *Building Type Basics for Healthcare Facilities.* New York: Wiley.

Kovner, Anthony, ed. 1995. *Jonas's Health Care Delivery in the United States,* 5th ed. New York: Springer.

"Laminates Imbue Dental Offices with Personality," 2005. *W & WP Magazine.* April, pp. 1–4, www.iswonline.com.

Laughman, Harold, ed. 1981. *Hospital Special-Care Facilities.* New York: Academic Press.

Lebovich, William L. 1993. *Design for Dignity.* New York: Wiley.

Levato, Claudio M. 2004. "Putting Technology in Place Successfully." *Journal of the American Dental Association.* October, Vol. 135, pp. 30S–31S.

Liebrock, Cynthia. 1993. *Beautiful and Barrier-Free.* New York: Van Nostrand Reinhold.

———. 2000. *Design Details for Health: Making the Most of Interior Design's Healing Potential.* New York: Wiley.

Mahnke, Frank H. and Rudolf H. Mahnke. 1993. *Color and Light in Man-Made Environments.* New York: Van Nostrand Reinhold.

Malkin, Jain. 1992. *Hospital Interior Architecture.* New York: Van Nostrand Reinhold.

———. 2002. *Medical and Dental Space Planning,* 3rd ed. New York: Wiley.

Marberry, Sara. 1995. *Innovations in Healthcare Design.* New York: Van Nostrand Reinhold.

———, ed. 1997. *Healthcare Design.* New York: Wiley.

Marberry, Sara and Laurie Zagon. 1995. *The Power of Color: Creating Healthy Interior Spaces.* New York: Wiley.

Martensen, Robert R. 1996. "Hospital, Hotels and the Care of the 'Worthy Rich.'" *Journal of the American Medical Association.* January.

Merriam-Webster's Collegiate Dictionary, 10th ed. 1994. Springfield, MA: Merriam-Webster.

Merriam-Webster's Medical Desk Dictionary. 1993. Springfield, MA: Merriam-Webster.

Miller, Richard L. and Earl S. Swensson. 1995. *New Directions in Hospital and Healthcare Facility Design.* New York: McGraw-Hill.

Panero, Julius and Martin Zelnik. 1979. *Human Dimension and Interior Space.* New York: Watson-Guptill Publications.

"Pet Spending in America and Abroad." 2005. *Veterinary Economics Magazine.* August, pp. 24–26.

Ragan, Sandra L. 1995. *Interior Color by Design: Commercial.* Rockport, MA: Rockport.

Rakich, Jonathon S., Beaufort B. Longest, Jr., and Kurt Darr. 1992. *Managing Health Services Organizations,* 3rd ed. Baltimore: Health Professions Press.

Rogers, Elizabeth. 1991. "Interior Design of Veterinary Facilities." Utah State University. Research report.

Sacks, Terence J. 1993. *Careers in Medicine.* Lincolnwood, IL: NTC Publishing Group.

Schmidt, Duanne Arthur. 1996. *Schmidt's Anatomy of a Successful Dental Practice.* Tulsa, OK: PennWell.

Snook, I. Donald, Jr. 1981. *Hospitals: What They Are and How They Work.* Rockville, MD: Aspen Systems Corp.

Spivak, Mayer and Joanna Tamer, eds. 1984. *Institutional Settings.* New York: Human Sciences Press.

Stedman's Medical Dictionary, 26th ed. 1995. Baltimore: Williams and Willkins.

Toland, Drexel and Susan Strong. 1981. *Hospital-Based Medical Office Buildings.* Chicago: American Hospital Association.

Webster's New College Dictionary, 4th ed. 2002. New York: Wiley.

Weinhold, Virginia. 1988. *Interior Finish Materials for Healthcare Facilities.* Springfield, IL: Charles C. Thomas.

Wilde, John A. 1994. *Bringing Your Practice into Focus.* Tulsa, OK: PennWell.

World Book Encyclopedia, Vols. 4 and 9. 2003. Chicago: World Book, Inc.

WEB SITES

Allergy Buyers Club www.allergybuyersclub.com

American Dental Association (ADA), www.ada.org

American Medical Association (AMA) www.ama-assn.org

AIA Academy of Architecture for Health, www.e-architect.com/pia/health/mission.asp

American Hospital Association (AHA), www.aha.org

American Medical Association (AMA), www.ama-assn.org

Center for Health Design, www.healthdesign.org

Centers for Disease Control (CDC) www.cdc.org

Design Ergonomics, www.design-ergonomics.com

Gates Hafen Cochrane Architects, ghc@ghcarch.com

Occupational Safety and Health Administration (OSHA) www.osha.gov

Joint Commission on the Accreditation of Healthcare Organizations (JCAHO) www.jointcommission.org

Medical Specialties Guide, www.medicalresourcesusa.com/specialties.htm

National Hospice Organization, www.nho.org

Veterinary Hospital Design, www.hospitaldesign.net

ASID *ICON* www.asid.org

Dental Economics www.de.pennet.com

Healthcare Design magazine www.healthcaredesignmagazine. com

Journal of the American Dental Association, www.ada.org

Journal of the American Medical Association www.ama-assn.org

Medical Economics Magazine www.pdr.net/memag/index. htm

New England Journal of Medicine www.content.nejm.org

Veterinary Economics Magazine, www.vetecon.com

Design Ergonomics, www.design-ergonomic.com/learning/ learning_ergo.htm

Veterinary Hospital Design, www.hospitaldesign.net

Note: Additional references related to material in this chapter are listed in the Appendix.

8

Senior Living Facilities

The term *senior citizen* generally refers to a person 65 years of age and older. According to the 2000 U.S. census, 35 million Americans are 65 years of age or older, with women on average living longer than men. In the year 2000, 4.3 million Americans were over the age of 85; by 2040, it is projected that 23.3 million citizens will be over that age.[1] More seniors are living alone in various types of senior housing categories. In 2006, the baby boomers began turning 60. Although they might not be considered senior citizens, and although many do not want to think of themselves as seniors, this large group of people will place huge demands on all types of facilities for senior-age generations. The issues in planning these facilities range from age to health issues and from physical abilities to mental clarity.

The increased focus on healthcare, wellness, and physical fitness has provided senior citizens with opportunities to extend their life span with better-quality health and a comfortable, relaxing lifestyle. Even though most have officially retired, many continue to work

[1]Regnier, 2002, p. 7.

TABLE 8-1 Chapter Vocabulary

- ACTIVE ADULT COMMUNITIES: Residences for older persons—usually 55 years of age and older—who are physically active. The community also provides active recreation, entertainment, and educational opportunities.
- ADULT DAY CARE: Provides an individual plan of care during the daytime hours.
- AGING IN PLACE: The ability to remain in one's home as one ages.
- ALZHEIMER'S DISEASE: One of the most commonly diagnosed forms of dementia.
- ASSISTED LIVING RESIDENCES: Provide housing and activities of daily living (ADLs) for those who do not need 24-hour nursing care but require some daily care.
- CONGREGATE HOUSING: Housing for the elderly that includes one meal a day, housekeeping, and some activities.
- CONTINUING CARE RETIREMENT COMMUNITY (CCRC): Provides housing for assisted living through skilled nursing homes.
- DEMENTIA: A disease that leads to the gradual deterioration in mental capacity and functioning due to disease or damage to the brain beyond normal aging.

- GERIATRIC OUTPATIENT CLINIC: Clinic that focuses on medical needs of the elderly.
- INDEPENDENT LIVING: Living in a housing unit without health service.
- INSTRUMENTAL ACTIVITIES OF DAILY LIVING (IADLs): Activities such as housekeeping and preparing meals.
- LONG-TERM UNITS: Twenty-four-hour housing and skilled nursing care for elderly persons who are medically ill. Also referred to as *nursing homes* or *skilled nursing facilities*.
- NATURALLY OCCURRING RETIREMENT COMMUNITY (NORC): Senior living facility that is created when an apartment building or condominium is converted to a retirement living facility.
- REHABILITATION CENTERS: Facilities that provide recovery care for patients who have had surgery or an accident which prevents them from staying at home.
- RESPITE CARE: Care provided to give the primary caregiver temporary relief from caring for the senior. It is often provided by an adult day care center.
- SENIOR CITIZEN: Generally refers to people 65 years of age and older.

for several years at their old jobs or at new part-time jobs. Of course, this state of well-being is not characteristic of all seniors. Many will need special care that cannot easily be provided in the home environment. Unlike earlier generations, it is also harder for families to provide care for grandparents once they cannot live independently.

This chapter uses the term *housing* from time to time in the discussion of senior living facilities. It is important to note that this is not a discussion of residential design in a textbook about commercial interior design. The senior living facilities discussed in this chapter are not single-family dwellings or even apartments used by senior citizens living among persons in various age groups. This chapter focuses on facilities specifically for the person approximately 60 years of age or older. The discussion will range from the most able to the least able person and the facilities appropriate for the various stages of aging.

In many ways, designing facilities for seniors is like designing a residence, a healthcare facility or even hospitality spaces for any age group. However, there are many factors that impact the design planning and specification of facilities specifically for seniors. To provide a successful design for senior housing, the interior designer must study senior living concepts and learn about products, codes, and other issues of the interior environment that apply to these types of facilities.

This chapter begins with a very brief introduction to the history of senior housing followed by an overview of the industry and a brief discussion of the many different types of facilities offered. General interior design issues are covered, as well as specific design applications of assisted living and dementia facilities. A brief description of geriatric medicine will be included as it impacts seniors and their choice of facilities.

Table 8-1 presents vocabulary used throughout the chapter.

Historical Overview

Throughout history, families provided home care for their aging members. Some persons did not have family support, and society provided minimal housing through the efforts of religious organizations, governments, and charity groups. For many decades, the quality of the accommodations and care for seniors provided by many of these groups was extremely poor.

The majority of senior housing history in the Western world occurred in England, where hundreds of shelters were provided for the aged from the 12th to the 15th centuries. Housed in these facilities were people who did not have the ability to support themselves and were in need of long-term care due to various stages of illness or disability. Most of these facilities were supported by Roman Catholic monasteries and administered by persons appointed by the king and the bishops. However, in 1536, King Henry VIII, in his struggle with the Roman Catholic church, closed all of the Roman Catholic monasteries and these long-term care facilities. He later appointed a board of local citizens to supervise the management of long-term care facilities. Queen Elizabeth I required each community to take care of the elderly in their own homes and to provide for their care in some form of senior housing. Much later, in the 18th century, England enacted the Poor Law to provide care for the elderly and sick in institutions throughout England.

The American colonies largely copied the English method of caring for the sick and elderly, providing homes for the aged. For example, in 1722, Philadelphia created an institution for the poor, followed by New York City in 1734 and Charleston, South Carolina, in 1735.[2] In the 18th and 19th centuries in the United States, care was provided by families or governmental and religious institutions in cities and rural areas.

Industrialization of the United States during the late 19th and early 20th centuries changed the profile of urban life and the ability of city dwellers to provide elder care. Urban dwellers had less money, less room in their homes, and fewer children to care for aging parents. As there was no federal assistance at this time, the majority of local and state governments sent their needy citizens to "poor farms" or "almshouses," which did not provide adequate care or appropriate housing. In an effort to avoid these government facilities, some immigrant communities established organizations that aided the aging by providing better long-term care.

Many benchmarks in the history of senior living facilities in the United States are derived from legislation enacted in the 20th century. In the 1930s, the New Deal promoted the concept that the aging should receive federal support based on individual need. The first legislation enacted to promote this concept was the Social Security Act of 1935, signed by President Franklin D. Roosevelt. This act provided matching grants to each state for Old Age Assistance (OAA) to retired workers. People living in "poor houses" were not eligible to receive OAA. Thus, privately owned old-age homes became available so that the elderly could collect OAA payments. This was the start of the nursing home industry as it is known today.

In 1939, the Federal Security Agency (FSA) was established to administer major programs in the field of social security, job placement, education, and public health. The Social Security program and the Public Health Service were two of the agencies under this umbrella. The FSA is now essentially part of the Department of Homeland Security, although some agencies have been moved to other departments. Part of the original FSA provided funds through Social Security checks to the elderly, allowing them to purchase care in private homes referred to as the "Mom and Pops" homes during the 1940s, 1950s, and 1960s.

Hospitals and elder care had a poor reputation in the early 20th century. As you will recall from the discussion in Chapter 7, hospitals were considered places only for the poor. After World War II, almost every community needed modern healthcare facilities. In 1946, the Hospital Survey and Construction Act (Hill-Burton Act) provided funding for the construction of superior hospitals. Federal legislation in the 1950s offered subsidies to construct nursing homes, resulting in a large increase in the number of these facilities. Amendments to the Social Security Act required states to license nursing homes. At this time, the federal government also declared that federal funding could be provided to residents of nursing homes.

Medical care in nursing homes began to improve significantly in the 1950s when the federal government provided grants to build nursing homes closer to hospitals. This proximity improved care in these facilities, and their design became more similar to that of

---

[2]"History of Long Term Care Industry," 2005, p. 1 www.longtermcareeducation.com/A1/g.asp.

hospitals. This also meant that a nursing home was now thought of as part of the health-care system rather than the welfare system.

Nursing homes remained largely unregulated in the 1960s, creating many variations in care and conditions within the facilities. Congress developed policies referred to as "Conditions of Participation" to ensure that senior citizens collecting Medicare payments received quality care. In 1968, Congress passed the Moss Amendments, which legislated improved nursing homes and higher institutional standards. Additional provisions outlined the educational and experiential backgrounds required for individuals to become licensed nursing home administrators.

Regulations for increased standards of care and facility conditions continued to affect the nursing home and the senior care industry. In 1971, the Miller Amendment established a new standard known as *intermediate-care facilities.* This classification meant that some nursing homes qualified for federal reimbursement when the amount of skilled care was lowered, reducing costs to the government but also lowering standards of care. Then in 1972, Public Law 92-603 was passed, which contained reforms for nursing homes including Medicaid reimbursement on a "reasonable cost-related basis."[3]

Changes in Medicare, Social Security, and federal regulations of nursing and other senior care facilities continued in the late 20th and early 21st centuries. Developments in care of the elderly and disabled (who are also covered under Medicare and Social Security) continues to challenge the senior living facilities industry and healthcare providers. One significant change occurred in 1995, when the Social Security Administration was separated from the Department of Health and Human Services and became an independent federal agency.

This brief review of the history of healthcare facilities and care for the senior population, as well as the disabled and impoverished, provides only a snapshot of the changes that have occurred. While early facilities focused on care provided for seniors by the government, seniors today are living longer, requiring new methods and types of care facilities. Senior living facilities since the 1980s have increasingly provided more versatility and luxury, focusing on particular categories of age and degrees of wellness.

Overview of Senior Living Facilities

With the exception of facilities for independent living and for younger seniors, the interior design of senior living facilities is diverse and complex. It is not simply a matter of designing a residence with grab bars in the bathroom or lever handles on the kitchen and bathroom sinks. To specialize in this area, the interior designer should be educated and experienced in the design of medical facilities and other areas of commercial design such as hospitality, food and beverages, and entertainment, as well as residential interior design. Because the design of senior living involves more than housing issues, it is also impacted by the medical needs of the aging population. The designer also needs to understand the senior and health issues of seniors.

Senior citizens represent a rapidly growing segment of the population. In 1900, only 4 percent of the U.S. population was over 65 years of age.[4] In the year 2000, over 100,000 persons were over the age of 100. By the year 2020, 17 percent of the U.S. population is projected to be over 65 years old. According to the U.S. census, more people are living longer due to better medical treatment and research, as well as an emphasis on wellness and quality of life in the senior years. A large percentage of these older citizens are women who often elect to live alone. They are remaining in their own homes and also residing in single units provided by various types of senior housing. Five percent of the senior population lives in nursing homes of some sort, and one eighth of the senior population lives with family members. Politicians know that a high percentage of seniors vote, and they are listened to by state and federal representatives. Seniors are also represented

---

[3]From "The Evolution of Nursing Home Care in the United States," 2006, www.pbs.org
[4]*World Book Encyclopedia,* 2003, Vol. 14, p. 738.

TABLE 8-2 Organizations Associated with Seniors and Senior Living

- National Council of Senior Citizens
- American Association of Retired Persons (AARP)
- Gray Panthers
- Service Corps of Retired Executives (SCORE)
- Retired Senior Volunteer Program (RSVP)
- Foster Grandparent Program (FGP)

by agencies and organizations that advocate for their interests. Table 8-2 presents a short list of senior organizations.

The growing population of senior citizens has fueled the need for senior living facilities and influences the design of other facilities, such as shopping and restaurants, to accommodate seniors. As this growing population has had the opportunity to plan financially for their retirement, and as they are accustomed to certain daily amenities, they are demanding attractive senior living facilities with some luxury appointments or increased services. Many seniors have Social Security payments, pensions from their employers, savings, stock investments, and real estate, which allow them to be more discriminating in the type of housing they choose.

Aging in place is a concept that has resulted in an unprecedented amount of research and opportunities to disseminate information on the design challenges faced when seniors wish to remain in their homes as long as possible. According to a research study by the American Society of Interior Designers, to age in place means "to remain in one's current home rather than relocate to new quarters, a senior community or, if need be, a care facility."[5] Many seniors strive to remain in a private residence, whether it is in the original family home or a new location like a retirement community, as long as possible. Interior designers can do much to help seniors make small modifications to their homes to allow that to happen and keep the aging resident safe.

For many seniors, a time comes when living alone in a private residence is no longer an option or even a desire. Many move to one of the various types of senior living facilities that provide companionship, ease of home maintenance, and needed medical or nursing care. Housing needs for the senior citizen vary in type, degree, quality, and configuration. Some types of facilities include active adult communities such as retirement resorts, assisted living facilities, and long-term or skilled nursing care units for the frail and infirm. Very specialized care is also provided in Alzheimer and dementia units when an individual faces the loss of mental capacity.

Moving a senior to a facility that provides any type of services and care can be quite expensive. Most seniors living in senior facilities are retired and have reduced incomes supplied by Social Security, pensions, and/or savings. For the majority of seniors, healthcare is provided and paid for to some degree by Medicare, a federal program associated with the Social Security system.

Medicare is administered by the federal government and pays for part of the medical care of persons aged 65 years or older. Medicare Part A covers hospital expenses, and Part B covers medical expenses such as visits to the doctor's office. The senior citizen is required to pay a monthly premium to Medicare, which covers expenses from Part B. In addition to Medicare, the senior is encouraged to have a supplemental insurance policy to cover any medical costs not covered by Parts A and B. As of January 2006, Medicare has offered senior citizens a Part D prescription program, which will provide financial aid to help pay for medications through an insurance policy with premiums paid by the senior. Prescription medicines are a major cost in medical care, especially for those living in senior housing.

Long-term care insurance is offered by many insurance companies to aid persons in paying for housing in a skilled nursing care facility or another type of medical-related senior housing. However, not all seniors elect to carry long-term care insurance. Lack of this type of insurance can cause undue financial stress and bankruptcy if an extended stay in a nursing facility is required.

---

[5]ASID. 2001, p. 2.

BOX 8-1 GERIATRICS

The aging process involves biological and social changes as well as environmental challenges.* Part of these changes can be related to health-care needs due to aging. *Geriatrics* is a branch of medicine that specifically treats the aging population and deals with the diseases of old age. A *geriatrician* is a physician who specializes in the diseases of the senior citizen. The field of medicine known as *gerontology* focuses on the aging process beginning with 40- and 50-year-olds.[†]

Gerontology is the scientific study of the process of aging and the problems of seniors,[‡] as well as the study of the social passage that occurs over time. *Senescence* refers to the aging process[§] and is studied by biologists who focus on the aging body's processes. Other persons involved in the geriatric area include psychiatrists and psychologists, who study the mental processes of aging, and sociologists, who study the impact on the elderly of the modern world.

The term *senility* refers to the deterioration of mental capabilities characterized by memory loss, confusion, and an inability to perform basic skills such as reading. This term is no longer used. The two most common brain disorders which affect the aging population are *infarct dementia,* in which blockage of the arteries causes small strokes, and *Alzheimer's disease,* which destroys brain cells.

*Perkins, 2004, p. 8.
[†]*World Book Encyclopedia,* 2003, Vol. 17, p. 300.
[‡]*Webster's Dictionary,* 4th ed., p. 595.
[§]*World Book Encyclopedia,* 2003, Vol 8, p. 137.

To provide a successful design solution, the interior designer needs to become acquainted with all factors relating to the needs of senior citizens. This chapter will focus on the typical types of facilities and some of their needs. Knowledge of general medical facility design is also important to the designer wishing to design the interior of senior living facilities. A review of Chapter 7 is important, as is the study of materials such as those suggested at the end of this chapter. *Building Type Basics for Senior Living,* by Perkins, provides a very good overview of interior design and planning of the many different types of senior living facilities.

The designer is challenged to produce an aesthetic environment while applying all codes related to the specific type of facility. The interior design of senior living facilities is rewarding in ways that go beyond the expectations of many in the field.

Types of Senior Living Facilities

Several different types of senior housing are available, providing the variety of options. Many of these options exist for those who need to make changes in their living conditions for health reasons or to reduce their single-family home responsibilities. One group of senior living facilities is for those who are healthy or essentially healthy and require little nursing care. These are active adult communities, retirement communities, and congregate housing, characterized by independent living situations. The second group of senior living facilities is for people who require more continuous nursing care, including 24-hour skilled nursing units. These include: assisted living residences, adult day care, continuing care retirement communities, long-term care/skilled nursing facilities, and dementia units.

Independent living basically refers to the absence of health services in the housing unit. Adult communities that impose age restrictions offer many social activities and increased security, which appeals to many seniors. Sun City, Arizona, is an example of an independent living area with over 100,000 persons aged 55 years or older. It offers a variety of social activities in large recreational facilities. The *skilled nursing facility,* which provides 24-hour nursing care, is the extreme opposite of this active retirement community.

An *active adult community or retirement community* provides a relaxed lifestyle within a residence, whether a single-family dwelling, duplex, or condominium. Some of these communities are also considered retirement resorts where higher-quality amenities may be offered. Usually a combination of lifestyle housing types are available. In a retirement community, housing is usually restricted by age—commonly to persons 55 and over—and many residents are retirees. In a retirement community, the resident is expected to be generally healthy and self-sufficient. Recreational and social activities are very important to these communities. Residents pay fees to use the recreational facilities, which are often restricted to members.

Often these communities are developed as self-contained communities providing health care and even hospital facilities, fitness centers, and community services such as grocery stores, retail stores, and professional offices. These adult communities also provide active recreation facilities such as golf, swimming, and tennis, entertainment at the activities centers or country clubs, and opportunities for continuing education. Many well-known active adult communities are located in Arizona, Nevada, California, and Florida, where the weather is conducive to an active lifestyle. Active adult communities are also being developed in other states.

A subtype of the active adult community is the *naturally occurring retirement community* (NORC). This might occur when an apartment building or condominium is converted to a retirement facility or age-restricted facility. Usually these facilities are located in urban settings and situated in any residential area. Services are those that are normally in any neighborhood, not specifically for the NORC. In fact the age-restricted apartment building may be adjacent to non-age-restricted single family homes.

Another category of senior facilities is *congregate care retirement communities* or *congregate living facilities* (CCFs). Congregate care living refers to independent living in a group setting, most commonly apartments. Nursing services are not part of the normal needs of the residents; however, health service assistance is available on a limited basis. Another term used to describe congregate housing is independent living apartments. Residents are usually older than those in active adult communities.

The resident unit apartments or cottages vary in size and bedroom numbers from the one bedroom, full kitchen, living room, bedroom, and bathroom of 700 square feet, to the larger units with two bedrooms with den, two full bathrooms at 950 square feet, and more. Congregate living facilities can be rental or owned by residents. Monthly maintenance fees are often assessed to these units. Congregate housing is not licensed as are other types of senior housing; however, it does have to meet consumer protection laws.

Often these facilities provide one or two meals a day, as well as housekeeping services and the activities for facilities residents. Transportation for shopping and doctor's appointments and other services are provided to maintain the independence of residents who no longer wish to drive. Congregate care facilities can assist residents with *instrumental activities of daily living* (IADLs) such as providing housekeeping. Security is another factor that appeals to seniors living in this type of facility, since someone is available to help in an emergency such as a fall or other injury, unlike in most independent living arrangements. Many congregate housing facilities are associated with assisted living and long-term care facilities on the property or within the complex.

Continuing care retirement communities (CCRC) are another category of housing offered to seniors. CCRC facilities provide housing along with varying levels of health services, depending on residents' needs. They provide a continuum of care from independence for older healthy residents to assisted living and long-term/skilled nursing care for those requiring greater degrees of health care. The residents are elderly, with some requiring personal care in bathing and dressing. Residents may, depending on the services offered, receive physician care, laboratory tests, and other minimal medical procedures on site.

The CCRCs focus on promoting health by providing good nutrition, exercise, and social interaction. Use of common dining rooms assists in creating socialization. A CCRC often provides recreational and social activities for residents. Activity rooms, common areas for activities, and transportation to services and activities are common. Though similar in some ways to the resident of the congregate living facility, the typical resident of the CCRC is older and needs more assistance on a daily basis. The philosophy of aging in place is a keystone of the CCRC.

Each resident of a CCRC is assessed to determine his or her health status and ability to pay. An initial entry fee may be charged to join the community, as well as a monthly fee for the remainder of the stay. These fees vary considerably, depending upon the size of the facility and the range of services offered.

Assisted living residences have a philosophy of service that focuses on each resident's goal of independence and dignity. These facilities are also sometimes called assisted-care communities or *personal-care homes.* Residents generally do not require constant care, as in a nursing home facility, but are no longer able to live safely on their own. Assisted living thus emphasizes flexibility in individual support services and health care. The Assisted Living Federation of America defines assisted living as a "combining of housing, personalized supportive services and health care designed to meet the individual needs of persons who need help with the activities of daily living, but do not need the skilled medical care provided in a nursing home"[6]

Residents of assisted living facilities are generally elderly, although some are younger adults who have suffered life-altering injuries or illnesses. Seventy-eight percent of the residents are women, with an average age of 84.3 years, and need assistance with at least three *activities of daily living* (*ADLs*). The average man living in assisted living facilities is 82.5 years of age.[7]

Assisted living facilities vary in size and services and are very important in providing care for the aging population. All meals are served by the staff in common dining rooms. Residents most often have their own apartments or rooms, and staff members are there to meet scheduled and unscheduled residents' needs as they occur.

Adult day care is a daily program in a freestanding or attached facility that provides social and medical support to the client during daytime hours. It is defined as "a community-based group program designed to meet the needs of functionally impaired adults through an individual plan of care. It is a structured, comprehensive program that provides a variety of health, social, and related support services in a protective setting during any part of a day but less than 24-hour care. Individuals who participate in adult day care attend on a planned basis during specified hours. Adult day care assists its participants to remain in the community, enabling families and other caregivers to continue caring for an impaired member at home."[8] Many of these programs are offered by nonprofit or public entities, and many are associated with an assisted living facility, a skilled nursing facility, sometimes medical centers or complexes such as a MOB, and a rehabilitation center. Adult day care began in 1933 in Moscow, Russia, as a day hospital program to reduce the bed shortages in psychiatric facilities. In 1943, Great Britain adopted the concept to aid war veterans.[9]

The adult day care facility provides services and a place for seniors with special health needs to stay during the day, allowing a respite for the family member who acts as a caretaker. Often, it allows the family caretaker to maintain a day job as well. The advantage of an adult day care facility is that it allows the senior to remain at home with family members instead of being housed in a senior residence.

The adult day care staff provides activities throughout the day geared to the patient/client's interests. Other services include meals and snacks, as well as assistance in using the bathroom. Some facilities provide beauty salons and barber shops as added amenities. Movies as well as music therapy, artwork, and activities such as communal games or small-team activities such as puzzles, crafts, or shuffleboard are also provided (Figure 8-1).

Nursing staff and other medical personnel are available to assist the clients, depending upon the size and scope of the facility. As some clients with dementia attend the adult day care program, a fenced yard is provided for outdoor wandering. Licensing of adult day care facilities is required in each state; licensure agencies vary by state and affiliation.

The frail elderly and others with serious illnesses or traumatic injuries cannot live independently and require skilled nursing care for extended periods. A *long-term care facility* (also called a *skilled nursing facility*) usually provides 24-hour medically based care by nursing professionals and other trained personnel. Long-term care facilities have four major program components: (1) resident rooms, (2) a nursing unit, (3) common areas, and (4) support spaces.[10] These facilities are most commonly called *nursing homes,* a term that

---

[6]Definition of assisted living, copyright 1999–2005, Long Term Care Education, www.longtermcaraeducation.com, p. 1.
[7]Regnier, 2002, pp. 15–16.
[8]Perkins, 2004 p. 20.
[9]Perkins, 2004, p. 26.
[10]Perkins, 2004, p. 28.

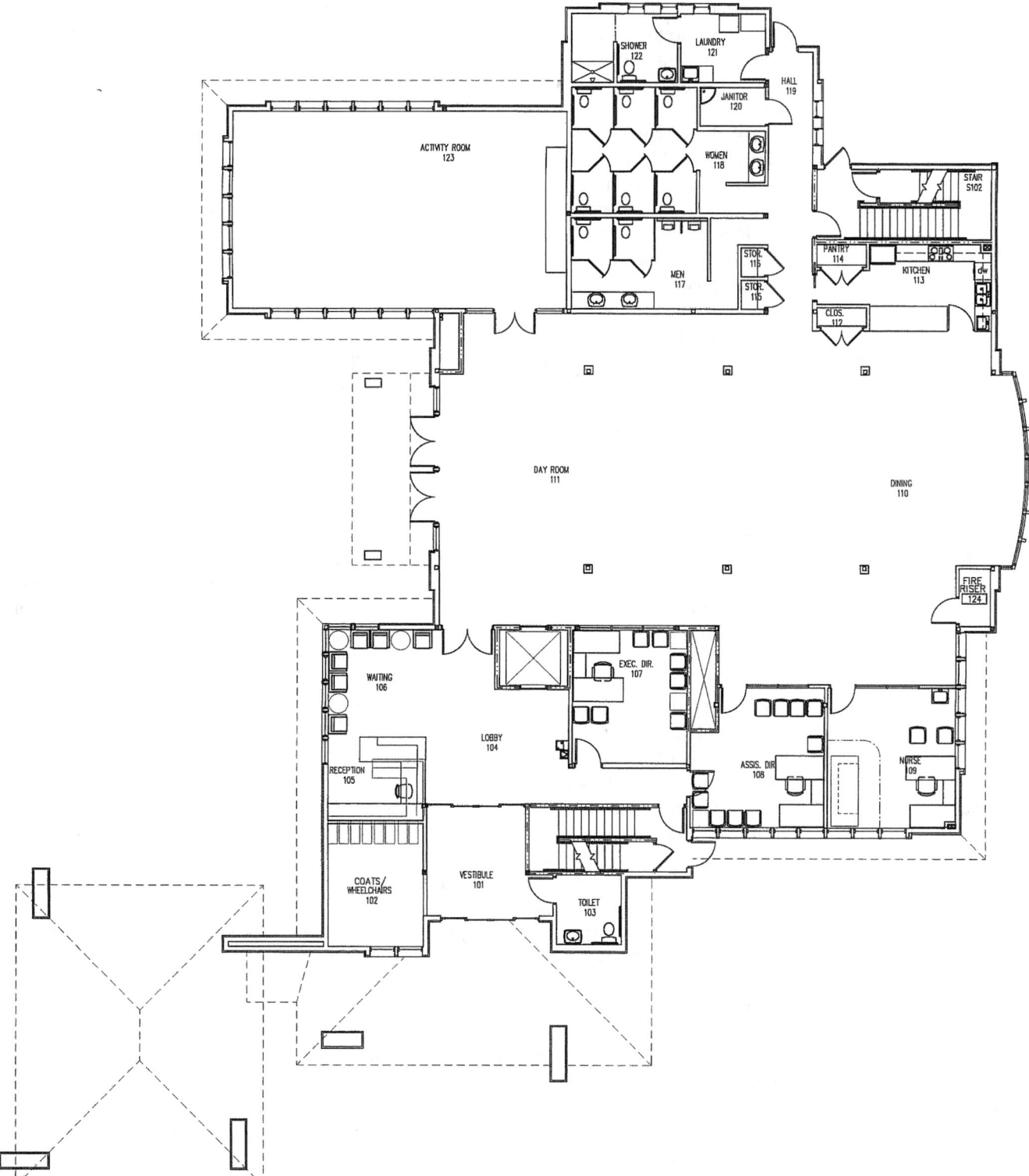

Figure 8-1 Floor plan of the main level of the K. C. Wanlass Adult Day Center. Note the large day room, the fenced patio and garden space, and the overall zoning of spaces. (Plan courtesy of Architectural Nexus, Inc.)

has been used for decades. Some nursing homes also provide subacute programs or short-term rehabilitative stays if a resident is recovering from an illness or serious injury.

The typical patient in the long-term care facility is over 85 years of age, and 70 percent use wheelchairs. Over half are diagnosed with some form of dementia, thus requiring 24-hour nursing care. Others who are in the last stage of life may be in a hospice section of the facility. *Rehabilitation centers* provide recovery care for patients who have had surgery or an accident which prevents them from staying at home. Patients recovering from illnesses and injuries such as strokes, amputations, and paralysis may stay in a rehabilitation center for several weeks or longer. The difference is that the patient in a rehabilitation center is typically medically stable and is ready to begin rehabilitation therapy.

All these types of patients need a great deal of care and have less independent mobility, if any. Meals may be served in the patient's room or in group dining areas in the nursing units. The trend is toward private rooms with more space for personal possessions and a more residential appearance. Activities are planned both for daytime and evenings for those who can leave their rooms. Moving residents out of their rooms for short periods can be a supportive part of a resident's life.

Long-term care facilities are highly regulated due to the needs of the residents. Long-term care is typically paid for by the resident's insurance policy, personal funds, health insurance, or Medicaid for those who qualify. Due to increased government-funded reimbursements, governments are targeting continuing cost through reduced reimbursements.

Owners of these facilities include nonprofit, public, and for-profit organizations as well as individuals. Nonprofit organizations are usually foundations, religious groups, or other national groups. The for-profit facilities are owned by large national or smaller regional chains. County and state governments and the federal government also own many public long-term care facilities such as those owned by the Veterans Administration.

Another type of senior living facility is *special care units* (SCUs) for the care of patients with dementia and Alzheimer's disease. *Dementia* is a disease that leads to a gradual deterioration in mental capacity and functioning due to disease or damage to the brain beyond normal aging. *Alzheimer's disease* is one of the most commonly diagnosed forms of dementia. This disease gradually destroys reason, judgment, language, and memory. Patients in the first stages of Alzheimer's disease are usually ambulatory and healthy. Over time, the disease erodes their independence through the loss of memory, confusion, and inability to perform basic mental skills. Thus, the design of the facility for these patients aims at avoiding an institutional appearance and plan.

Special care units were first organized in the 1980s to deal with patients with Alzheimer's disease and other forms of dementia. Usually these units are housed in long-term care or assisted living facilities and operate as a separate unit or wing. Other facilities are freestanding units dealing solely with the dementia patient. SCUs provide an environment that to some extent replicates the home in that the overall facility is planned with a living room or lounge space, a dining area, and patient bedrooms with toilet facilities. Space plans include a continual corridor for engaged wandering by the patient. Figure 8-2 shows the wandering loop part of an Alzheimer unit floor plan. Other functional areas such as nurses' stations, the dining room, and common areas designed to provide a measure of normal life are included in the plan.

Alzheimer's disease has received national attention due to famous Americans who have suffered from it. These high profile cases have helped in the creation of foundations and fund-raising programs to study the cause, treatment, and possible cure for Alzheimer disease. In many ways, they have been responsible for innovations in the planning and design of these facilities.

The *geriatric clinic* is the last major type of facility for the care of seniors. These clinics provide health care services to seniors with problems such as limited physical mobility and mental challenges. Specialty psychiatry, neurology, many forms of therapy, and social work to aid in daily living are all part of geriatric medicine.

In the 1990s, geriatric clinics and outpatient facilities were developed to treat and house the increasing number of senior citizens. These clinics treat patients with physical problems, incontinence, hearing loss, vision problems, depression, and reduced cognition. Geriatric clinics may be located within a senior housing facility or campus and provide general exams as well as other medical services such as ophthalmologic and dental exams. Included in the geriatric medical clinic are therapy services which aid the infirm residents.

The geriatric medical clinic has more visitors than average due to the family members or staff members needed to accompany the patient to the exam. The patient will pay for

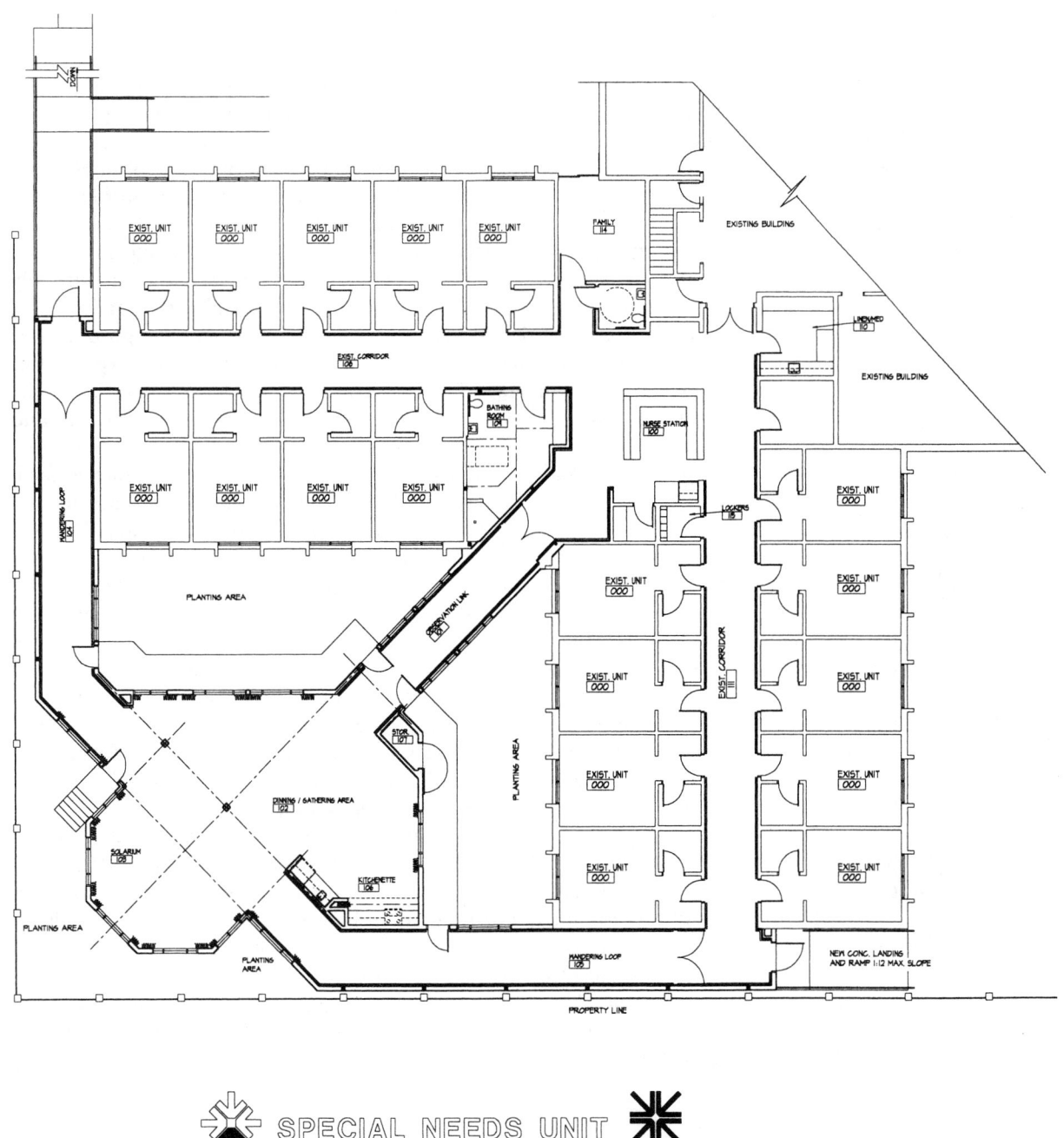

Figure 8-2 Floor plan of an Alzheimer unit showing a corridor that provides continuous mobility for the restless patient. (Plan courtesy of Architectural Design West.)

services through a variety of resources including Medicare, Medicaid, supplemental insurance, and personal funds. If the clinic is associated with some form of senior housing, it may cover the cost of the medical treatment as part of the fees already paid by the resident.

Geriatric clinics are licensed in most states through the state department of health services. Licensed clinics must meet local and state requirements in order to receive reimbursement for services. If the facility is associated with a hospital program, it has to meet high standards for monitoring patients. If the clinic is located in a MOB, it may be classified as a business and therefore is not as highly regulated as clinics affiliated with a hospital.

Planning and Interior Design Elements

This portion of the chapter will focus on the overall similarities in space planning, design, and specification needs of senior living facilities. Here we will address some important issues that apply to the majority of senior living facilities, with specific discussion of selected types later in the chapter. The material in this section provides an overview of interior design elements common to most of these facilities. In the specification of furniture and finishes, the designer needs to address problems encountered by many seniors, such as loss of muscle strength, hearing impairment, decreased visual acuity, loss of balance, increased sensitivity to cold and direct sunlight, and some mental disparities. These issues strongly impact what can be specified in senior living facilities. Remember also that active adult communities will typically have housing similar to the housing for any age group, since the majority of these residents are generally healthy and can care for themselves. Active adult community housing styles will have few restrictions except those imposed by the local jurisdiction regarding basic residential construction or specially imposed codes and restrictions.

An interior designer may be part of a design team creating a new or remodeled facility or may be hired by the owner or family members to design the living space for the senior resident. The interior designer's responsibilities will vary, depending on the facility. When involved in new construction, the designer works not only with the person who will be living in a specific unit, but also with the manager or the facility owner's representative. Design treatments for apartments or patient spaces will be limited in most situations except for the active adult and retirement communities. Space planning and materials specification are strongly impacted by building, life safety, and accessibility codes.

As with any new commercial facility, the design and construction of a new or remodeled senior living facility or development begins with a feasibility study. It is important for the developer and owner of the property to study the practicality and prospects of a new facility in order to determine whether or not the project is financially sound. One of the goals of this study is to determine the project's long-term viability.

Specialists and design professionals will be hired to provide appropriate information. Such things as a program and objective, a time line, a budget, and a market and financial feasibility report will be included in the study. Financial and market analysis is critical to obtain necessary funding for the project. Information on site evaluation, availability of utilities, and support services is also needed. For an existing facility, the study will look at remodeling, some form of adaptive use, or the possibility of demolishing the facility and building a new one. The feasibility study will include a written report as well as exhibits providing information that will help the design team in the planning and interior design of the facility.

Space Allocation and Circulation

Space allocation and circulation are especially pertinent to the planning of these facilities, as seniors may have limited mobility for walking or otherwise transporting themselves throughout the facility. Appropriate space allocation and planning is also important for the resident's way-finding. Discussions during programming with the owners and staff of the facility aid the design team in assessing the functional and collaborative use of the overall spaces. As with hospital design, workload analysis is very important, considering the number of employees required in the various types of senior housing.

Programming activities identify the specific needs of each area or department for space allocation. Room functions and dimensions and adjacency impact the overall plan. The configurations and length of corridors impact the layout of the building and are critical in providing proper resident care and allowing residents to move easily within the facility. Space adjacencies directly affect resident care as well as the overall operation of each type of senior facility. A functional program should be developed which focuses on relationships between residents, departments/areas, staff requirements, and design issues.

Space allocation varies considerably among the types of senior facilities. Nurses' stations are placed throughout these facilities at strategic points based on residents' nursing needs; however, nurses' stations in an Alzheimer's facility are designed to be less obtrusive and institutional-looking. Assisted living and long-term care facilities need similar amounts of space for patients/residents, but an active adult community residence can be much larger, since it can be a single-family dwelling. Sociopetal spacing is important in planning, as it causes residents to interact and increases their socialization. Cluster spaces are positioned to encourage more resident interaction as well.

Although space requirements vary, there are some dimensions which apply to all but active adult community housing. For example, corridors need to be 6 to 8 feet wide. Seating should be placed at various points to allow the resident to rest or wait for family members and friends. Dining room resident spaces should be allocated 25 to 30 square feet per resident for assisted living, whereas 25 to 35 square feet should be figured in an Alzheimer's unit.[11]

Corridors naturally demark circulation and access to spaces in the facility. Considering the lack of muscle strength of the senior citizens in some of these facilities, it is important to reduce the length of the corridors to avoid fatigue and falls caused by too lengthy a walk back to the unit. Circulation paths need to lead to common areas and areas which create more socialization for the resident. Figure 8-3 shows the varying widths of corridors to aid visual reduction of the lengthy corridor space. These varying widths can accommodate additional seating groups for residents. Of course, the seating units need to still allow a 5-foot-wide passage for residents walking in the corridor.

Furniture

Furniture specifications for senior living facilities can vary considerably depending on the type of facility. For example, in active adult retirement communities, residents generally provide their own furniture, whereas in an Alzheimer unit, the basic furniture is in place. This discussion will concentrate on furniture items specified for units where it is less likely that residents/patients will bring their own furniture.

Spaces in senior facilities often have specific requirements for types and sizes of furniture. Furniture should be of commercial quality, and manufacturers specialize in healthcare furniture. The designer must carefully discuss this with the management during programming to ensure that the right piece of furniture is specified for each application. Ease of maintenance, safety, and ease of residents' use of furniture items are critical in these seemingly residential environments. A fabric that looks wonderful on a dining room chair may not work when residents are incontinent. Coffee tables can cause tripping and falls. Chairs with arms are necessary to help residents arise. These are just a few examples.

In the common areas such as living rooms in group facilities, furniture groupings are similar to those found in personal residences. They are placed to encourage interaction of residents. Common areas are designed to entertain guests if residents do not want to use their own units. Groupings might also be needed for watching television or movies, as some types of facilities will not have televisions in the residents' rooms.

Seating specification requires careful consideration. The height and depth of sofas and chairs in the living room are important for comfort and use. Seating for seniors must be higher than average because of the loss of muscle tone in the thighs. A greater seat height makes it easier to sit and rise from chairs and sofas. Arms on sofas and chairs should be full length from the front edge of the seat to the back to provide more support. In addition to seat height and arm height, seniors require less depth in seating than average. Therefore, seating height should be 20 to 22 inches, seating depth 20 to 22 inches, and arm height 24 to 26 inches. In specifying sofas, the designer must make certain that the seat cushions are not too soft. A firm foam cushion with a Dacron wrap is sufficient to provide comfort and maintain the seating height. These same principles apply to the selection of dining chairs.

In the dining room, space planning should include tables of various sizes, such as those for two, four, or six persons. Some facilities include booth seating for four in the dining

---

[11]Perkins, 2004, p. 82.

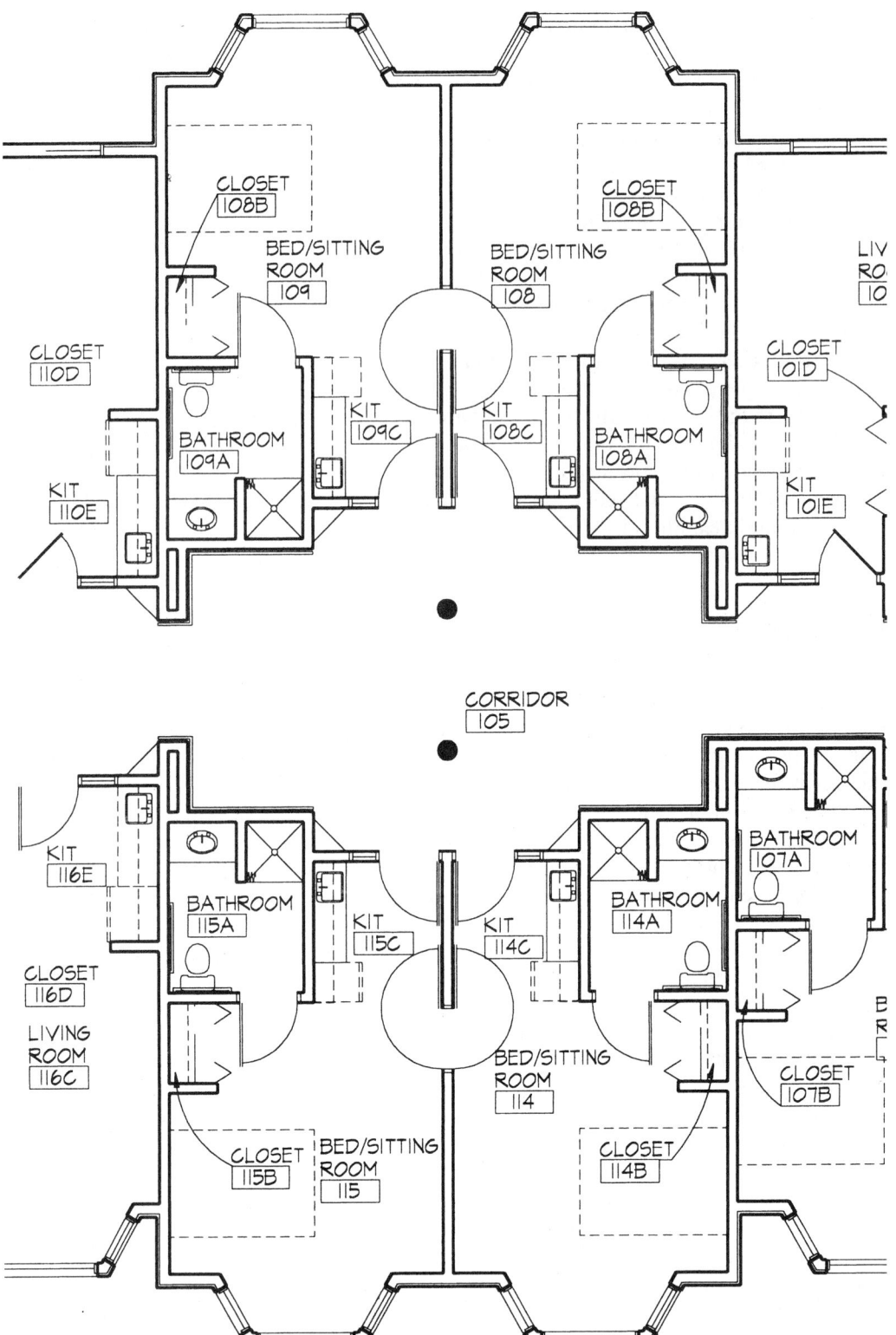

Figure 8-3 Along the lengthy corridor, wider areas are provided not only to break up the visual space but to allow for furniture placement and social interaction. (Plan courtesy of Architectural Design West.)

room for those with fewer mobility problems. If meals are served on trays, a 48-inch-square table is recommended. If meals are served by wait staff, a 42-inch square table will accommodate four residents. As with any dining facility, arrangements should be made for grouping tables together when a resident has a family gathering or a group of residents wish to sit together for a special occasion. Thus, square or rectangular tabletops are most

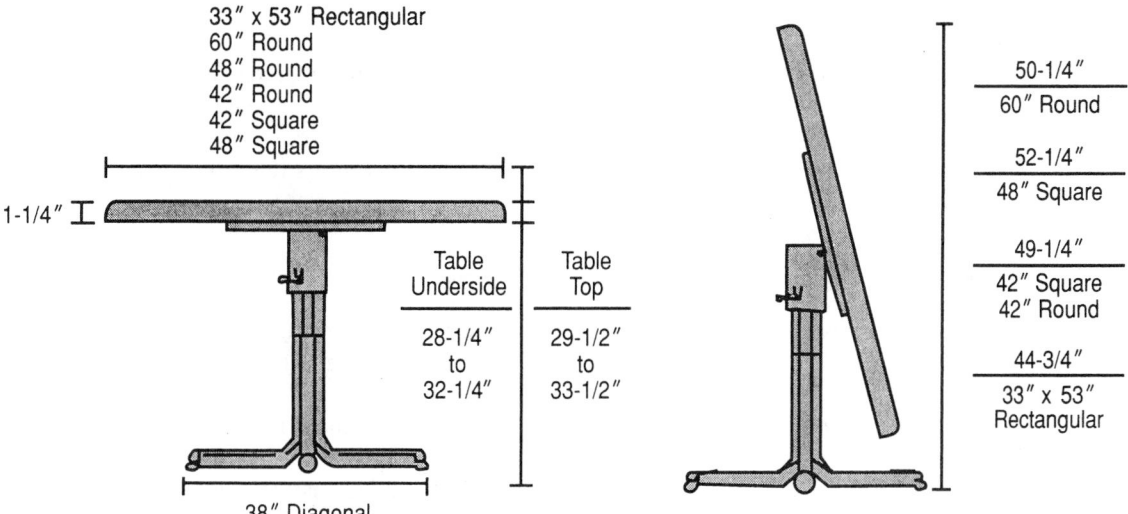

33" x 53" Rectangular
60" Round
48" Round
42" Round
42" Square
48" Square

1-1/4"

Table
Underside

28-1/4"
to
32-1/4"

Table
Top

29-1/2"
to
33-1/2"

38" Diagonal

50-1/4"
60" Round

52-1/4"
48" Square

49-1/4"
42" Square
42" Round

44-3/4"
33" x 53"
Rectangular

Figure 8-4 Tilt-top table allows for nesting, storing, easy movement, and easy cleaning. The base has casters that can be retracted. All these features are important for a dining room in senior housing. (Drawing courtesy of Sunrise Medical Continuing Community Care Group, Stevens Point, WI.)

often specified. Round tables are considered more friendly and are preferred by some facilities because of the lack of corners. Some tables have adjustable-height tops (Figure 8-4).

Apply the dimensional conditions noted above for sofas to dining room chairs and remember to specify chairs with arms, either open arms or fully upholstered units. Upholstered seating and backing of dining room chairs will provide some acoustical control.

Dining chairs need to be very stable and durable. Manufacturers produce these chairs from hard woods, some with stretchers for more support. Chairs are manufactured with handles on the backrest to aid the staff in pulling the chair for the resident in facilities providing nursing assistance. If casters are used on the dining chairs to assist senior residents in moving them, make certain that the casters are used only on the front legs.

Chairs and all other furniture should not tip but be designed to be stable for senior use. Avoid furniture with sharp edges and movable parts such as folding chairs. Although senior citizens like rocking chairs, this type of furniture can be a hazard in that a resident could trip over the back rockers and some rockers can easily tip. Additional information on chairs in medical facilities can be found in Chapter 7.

Key issues in specifying upholstery in common areas and residents' rooms in many senior living facilities are maintenance and cleanability. Many fabrics that are appropriate in a residence are harder to maintain in high-use areas or resident spaces due to possible illnesses. Crypton is a very popular upholstery material for these areas, as it is washable, scrubbable, and antimicrobial. This is important where incontinence is a problem. Some hospital-grade vinyl fabrics are also used for seating units (Figure 8-5).

Depending on the type of facility, more personalization and personal furnishings are used in the resident's room or apartment. In many assisted living facilities, residents bring their own furniture and furnishings. However, in long-term care facilities, most of the furnishings in the resident's room will be supplied by the facility since the bed will likely be some

Figure 8-5 The "It Rocks" Chair for Alzheimer and dementia patients is a special type of chair designed for senior housing and use. (Photograph courtesy of Primarily Seating, New York, NY, 212-838-2588.)

type of hospital bed. In an Alzheimer unit, a few pieces of furniture belonging to the resident are included to assist memory identification.

It is very important to specify furniture items that seem more residential than institutional. Maintaining a home environment, regardless of the type of facility, has been shown to improve residents' disposition, mental health, and recovery from illness. Naturally, maintenance, safety, and code restrictions always influence decisions regarding items provided in the interiors.

Materials, Finishes, and Color Usage

Architectural finish specifications and color schemes are important tasks for the interior designer in completing a senior living facility. Because of the nature of these facilities other than active adult community housing, there are many codes and regulations that must be considered and applied in the specification of architectural materials and finishes. In specifying these materials, the interior designer must avoid a sterile, institutional appearance while providing materials required for commercial installations. The goal is to produce a safe place which will help senior residents live comfortably while maintaining their independence and dignity within the parameters of the facility.

At the same time, the designer needs to create an environment that does not appear to be institutional but is pleasing and comforting. The environment of senior housing should be a safe, comfortable space that is somewhat reminiscent of the atmosphere of a home. The designer needs to incorporate into the design all of the safety measures, like grab bars and handrails, yet make certain that their installation is not obtrusive.

Floor covering specification is important for safety of the residents, as well as for providing important aesthetic enhancement. Code restrictions apply especially to the common areas and corridors rather than residents' apartments or units. However, adherence to codes and sensitivity to the safety of residents in their living units are important parts of the interior designer's responsibility.

Carpeting is the most popular flooring material specified for the common areas and any other areas which benefit from acoustical materials. Carpeting is also common in dry areas of the residents' rooms or apartments. Broadloom is generally used rather than carpet tile since its installation is less expensive. However, carpet tiles can be used effectively in areas where spillage is a major problem, as they can be removed for cleaning and reinstalled or replaced. The designer should select a carpet that is durable and safe. This is accomplished by using a moisture-barrier carpet and a backing system which is helpful in dealing with spills and incontinence. It is important to avoid all materials which produce off-gassing if possible since these odors can cause problems for residents with respiratory illnesses.

Carpeting has been developed which is appropriate for the problems of senior living, including walking, slipping, cleaning, and wheelchair use. A loop carpet of 28 to 32 ounces is often used, as its density and low pile allow wheelchairs and walkers to move smoothly over it. This smooth surface is easier on the legs, creates a minimal buffer when falling, and provides a softer, nonglare surface. Make sure that the surface is nonabrasive.

Many seniors walk gazing on the floor rather than looking ahead. Thus, it is important to avoid busy flooring patterns, as these might confuse the resident as depth perception changes with age. Also avoid dark colors and contrasting patterns and colors, which can produce not only visual problems but confusion in regard to the pattern. Some residents might interpret the pattern as an object on the floor and attempt to step over it, causing them to fall. Because residents generally have some loss of visual acuity, contrast between the wall and the floor should be present to draw attention to the change of planes and the boundaries. Borders are not recommended because they create one more pattern which might be interpreted as a step. Nonglare lighting should be evenly distributed on the floor to avoid pockets of light. There should be flush transitions from one flooring material to another to prevent falls.

Hard-surface flooring is specified in areas where frequent cleaning or water is used, such as the bathrooms, kitchens, and utility areas. Vinyl sheet flooring is popular because it can be installed to the baseboard (referred to as *flash-coved base*) as well, thus eliminating any seams between floor and wall. This is especially helpful with the mopping of floors. In specifying sheet vinyl, avoid a finish with a high sheen and use a low-luster product instead.

If ceramic tile is specified for flooring, make certain that it has a nonslip, nonglare surface. Vinyl tile and sheet goods are preferred for flooring in bathing rooms and bathrooms since they have softer surfaces. When ceramic tile is used, remember that grout can be porous. An epoxy grout or a grout with additives which can retard porosity should be used.[12] There are many sizes, colors, and styles of ceramic tile to choose from.

A large variety of wall finishes can be used. The designer must be sure that the wall finish specified meets code requirements for the particular use of space and the type of space. Paint is one of the most popular materials used on walls in senior housing and allows interior designers a great deal of flexibility. Painted walls, depending upon the finish selected, can be durable and require very low maintenance when latex semigloss paint is specified. It is important to select the proper finish in order to avoid chipping, fading, and cleaning problems. If possible, the designer should use paint that is VOC free.

Paint can be used to highlight certain areas or activities, as well as present a nonobtrusive background. One area where accenting with paint is very effective is in the resident's bathroom. The designer could place an accent color around certain fixtures to focus attention. This, of course, is dependent upon the type of facility and the resident's health issues. Many assisted living facilities use paint more often than wallcoverings due to its versatility and the ability to change colors readily.

Fabric-backed vinyl wallcoverings which are stain resistant are often preferred for certain areas of the facility due to their durability. If wallcoverings are common in each unit, plan the space so that no two adjacent rooms have identical wallcoverings. This will aid residents in identifying the rooms as well as providing individuality for these separate spaces. Specification of vinyl wallcoverings with antimicrobial properties is important since it protects the residents from mold, bacteria, and fungi, all threatening to their diminished health. Vinyl wallcoverings are durable and affordable and can provide interior ambience. When specifying these wallcoverings, check the building codes to make certain that the proper weight is selected. For example, Type I vinyl wallcovering is light duty, 7 to 13 ounces per square yard, and can be installed above a chair rail. Type II vinyl wallcovering is medium duty, 13 to 22 ounces per square yard, and can be used where wheelchair traffic is more prevalent. Type III vinyl wallcovering is heavy duty, 22 or more ounces per square yard, and can be used in public spaces and food service areas.[13] Crash rails are commonly specified in senior housing where there is abuse of the wall area below the chair rail due to wheelchair collisions and cart abuse.[14] Remember that Type II and III vinyl wallcoverings may be required by code for corridors. Table 8-3 provides a few tips on specifications of corridor wall surface amenities.

Regarding the *application of color*, remember that senior citizens experience many vision problems that affect their ability to discern color. Chief among them is yellowing of the cornea from cataracts. This disease causes white tones to appear yellow and blue colors to appear gray. Colors with warm undertones are easier for the senior eye to see, and incandescent lighting produces more warm tones than fluorescent lightning.

Interior designers should always check the light reflectance of any color they specify for senior facilities, as it directly impacts the residents' comfort. A very light color causes considerable glare, whereas a very dark one reduces the ability to see clearly. Using a light reflectance between 50 and 60 percent, depending upon the color, is a safe range in which to specify color for the walls. Floors can be darker than walls, and the materials used for the wall and the floor should have some contrast to indicate the change in planes. Color and pattern can be used on fabrics specified for the dining room chairs, and the colors of seating units in the common living room areas can create interesting spaces. Color is also an excellent tool for enhancing way-finding throughout a facility. Remember to use light-colored letters on a darker background to assist the resident in reading the signage.

---

[12]Perkins, 2004, p. 207.
[13]Perkins, 2004, p. 208.
[14]Perkins, 2004, p. 208.

TABLE 8-3 Guidelines on Wall Treatment Amenities

- Provide a shelf outside each unit door for placement of packages to assist the resident.
- In an Alzheimer unit, memory boxes at the entry doors for residents' rooms can help in identifying their space.
- Doors should be installed with accessible hardware such as levers and loops, which are easier for the senior to operate.
- Handrails along the corridors must be comfortable for the resident to grasp, must be easily cleanable and durable, and

must be able to sustain the use of anti-bacterial cleaning agents.
- The dado area between the baseboard and the handrail is a good place to specify acoustical cloth or a wallcovering that provides sound absorption as well as durability.
- Wood trim can be used on walls, which creates a residential environment.
- Corner guards should be used because of the heavy use of wheelchairs and carts in the corridors.

Lighting

Seniors generally have reduced visual acuity. They need three times more light than younger persons in order to see clearly. Also, their eyes take longer to focus on an object. The majority of seniors have cataracts, reducing the ability to see full color as well as the degree of light on a surface. Thus, the designer needs to find the right balance, as too bright a light can cause vision difficulty.

Lighting design is very important. No bare bulbs should be used, and the light source must not produce glare. Bright spots of light must be avoided especially at floor level. Fluorescent lighting is usually preferred for senior facilities, although this may diminish visual color rendition for seniors with cataracts. Use decorative wall sconces as accent lights rather than spotlights or down lights to produce good low lighting without glare. It is best to use 20 to 30 FC in corridors and to avoid shadows and dark pockets. Keep lighting as consistent as possible in the hallways. Indirect lighting systems produce less glare and fewer shadows. Another area of concern is the light source which reflects on the flooring. Make certain that the light has an even distribution to avoid shadows and spots, which might cause some seniors confusion. A good rule of thumb in senior housing is to increase the foot-candle level by 15 to 20 percent.[15] The dining room should have 50 foot-candles to aid in seeing the food. Indirect lighting is used in activity rooms because it provides an even distribution of light on the worksurfaces. Remember to include task lighting where appropriate.

Window coverings are important in controlling light levels and glare. It is important to balance natural and artificial light within a room. For example, on a sunny day, the windows and glass doors could produce bright light spots and glare if the interior light is not sufficient to balance the exterior light.

The type of lighting specified varies with the type of facility. In long-term care facilities, ceiling fixtures are commonly used, as well as a table lamp at the bedside. A night light to aid the resident in locating the toilet is mandatory. Over-the-bed lighting is helpful when a medical examination is required for a bedridden patient. In assisted living units, no ceiling fixtures are installed in the living rooms; table lamps are preferred, as in most homes. The bedrooms in an assisted living facility need a bedside lamp and night lights, and some have overhead lighting. The bathroom lighting needs to be evenly distributed to provide good acuity for reading medicine labels and performing activities.

Other Systems

Since seniors are more sensitive to temperature changes, than younger persons, the temperature in the common areas is usually higher than in a facility planned for younger persons. Medications and thinning of muscle and skin can affect the senior citizen's reactions to temperature. Color selections can be helpful. Wall colors can enhance the feeling of

---

[15]Perkins, 2004, p. 221.

warmth without overly stimulating the residents. Residents' rooms or apartments should have individual temperature controls so that each resident can be as comfortable as possible. Of course, this is generally not possible in Alzheimer units, which do not allow resident control of room temperature.

Apartments and rooms for residents are all provided with safety systems such as nurse call and emergency call systems, telephones, and a fire alarm. Since seniors have visual acuity problems, the numbers on the telephone should be enlarged with contrasting or lit buttons. The phone can be set with a higher volume to aid hearing. Depending on the type of facility, Internet use with computers in the rooms or located at various areas in the facility, cable television, security, voice-to-voice communication between the nurses/staff and the residents, and other systems may also be included in the planning. Residents like the ability to communicate with the staff, as it makes them feel more secure. Nurses and staff in facilities with 24-hour nursing care now use pocket pager systems, which are quieter than speaker systems and provide the staff with mobility without constant monitoring at the nurse station.

A security alarm system, referred to as an *elopement-prevention system,* is very effective in an Alzheimer unit to alert staff when security has been breached. Security systems also bring a sense of well-being and safety to the patients' families. The fire alarm is part of this security system and is required by law.

The National Institute on Aging states that one third of persons between the ages of 65 and 74 have hearing problems; this prevalence increases to one half by age 84. Some of these hearing problems involve excessive noise, lack of privacy in the resident units, transmission of noise from one area to another (e.g., from kitchen to dining room), and the difficulty of hearing conversation due to background noise. The design team should eliminate as much background noise as possible. Architects should plan the facility with attention to the way sound travels through it to reduce noise. The interior designer can help by specifying acoustically absorbent materials.

Since the dining room is the one area where seniors gather on a frequent and regular basis, a brief discussion of the acoustics of this area is appropriate. The dining area has a tendency to produce more noise than other areas. Conversations during meals, chair legs scraping, walking with canes or walkers, and the use of carts and wheelchairs all contribute to producing noise in this area. Dining rooms are usually large open spaces and have many hard surfaces. These surfaces cause more noise due to their inability to absorb sound. Solutions to reducing sound in this area include the use of carpeting, resilient vinyl flooring where requested, curtains and/or draperies at the windows, upholstered seating, linens, and possibly acoustical cloth on portions of the wall. Another solution is to create separate dining spaces within the larger room by introducing partial walls, much as in restaurant planning. It is important to remember that senior residents with diminished hearing talk louder than younger persons. This in itself contributes to a noisier dining space. Finally, dining areas and other areas of interaction should not be impacted by a noisy heating and air conditioning system, which is distracting and confusing.

Way-finding is mandatory in these types of facilities. It aids residents in locating certain areas easily and adds to their sense of security. Way-finding can be improved with sensitivity to lighting, placement of artwork, floor covering and finish specifications, and utilization of special architectural features. For example, in an Alzheimer unit, Dutch doors at the residents' rooms assist residents with room recognition and provide some privacy. Visual cues are important in way-finding. The use of the same flooring in common areas rather than the flooring material used in the residents' units is helpful. Half-wall partitions or interior windows help the senior to see into the next room or space, which aids in identifying spaces. These are just a few examples of techniques that can be used to aid in way-finding in senior living facilities.

Codes

In general, senior living facilities are considered institutional occupancies in the International Building Code. In addition, interior designers should consult the National Conference of States on Building Codes and Standards, Inc. (NCSBCS), which publishes the

Directory of Building Codes and Regulations[16] for specific code requirements of each state for every facility type. Many code books can be obtained at their web site, www.ncsbcs.org. Each state has written regulations governing senior housing, and state licensing agencies are often more strict than the building codes. For example, nursing homes have to comply with legislative acts and obtain certificates of need (CONs). There are also licensure regulations, department of health standards, building codes, and other testing procedures.

This highly regulated occupancy requires careful attention to building code requirements as well as life safety and fire safety standards. Smoke and heat detectors, fire alarms, emergency call systems, and architectural systems must be installed to protect lives. NFPA 101 of the National Fire Protection Association is the source for fire protection system design.

Accessibility codes are very important in senior housing. The ADA applies to all senior facilities with the exception of single-family dwellings in active adult communities. Planning for the aging requires adjustment of some code minimums. For example, seniors lose upper body strength, and not all codes take this into consideration. Grab bars are helpful, as seniors need a different placement than younger persons who are disabled. The aging need two grab bars, one behind the toilet and one to the side, with the water closet located at least 24 inches from the side wall for staff assistance. In planning senior housing, ramps should be avoided where possible. Flooring material should be consistent in level from one area to another, and higher light levels should be applied appropriately to aid the senior in seeing.

Currently, green design is applied to senior housing projects as well as sustainable design. Unfortunately, not enough facilities embrace green design and utilize green products even though they create healthier environments for seniors. Environmental issues also cover indoor air quality standards as well as elimination of asbestos and lead paint.

It is suggested that the design team add 6 to 18 months for the planning, design, and construction of senior housing in order to research, plan, apply, and adjust the codes and the many regulations. All of this takes considerable time.

Design Applications

Many seniors no longer find it feasible to live on their own. Perhaps they need medications daily or the routines of cooking meals and caring for themselves have become too great a challenge. Relocating to an assisted living facility or a long-term care facility is a viable option when additional supervised care is needed. This section provides interior design elements for three major types of senior living facilities: assisted living, long-term care, and facilities for Alzheimer's and dementia patients.

Assisted Living Facilities

The Assisted Living Federation of America (ALFA) defines assisted living as "a special combination of housing, supportive services, personalized assistance and healthcare designed to respond to the individual needs of those who require help with activities of daily living (ADL) and instrumental activities of daily living (IADL). Supportive services are available 24 hours a day, to meet scheduled and unscheduled needs, in a way that promotes maximum dignity and independence for each resident and involves the resident's family, neighbors and friends" (ALFA, 2000).[17]

Fewer senior citizens are housed in long-term care facilities today, mainly because they are in better physical shape due to the focus on wellness and the advances in medicine. However, assisted living facilities have increased in number throughout the United States in the past 10 to 15 years. These residents do not need 24-hour nursing care and opt for an assisted living facility, which aids them in retaining some independence and creates a social environment. In addition, assisted living is less costly than a long-term skilled nursing facility. Residents of assisted living facilities are on average 82 to 87 years old. Many

[16]National Conference of States on Building Codes and Standards. www.ncsbcs.org.
[17]Regnier, 2002, p. 3.

TABLE 8-4 Criteria for Identifying an Effective Assisted Living Facility

1. The building should have some residential features and blend with the neighborhood.

2. The majority of the facility needs to have living units containing from 40 to 60 resident units in order to make the service affordable.

3. Each resident room or apartment should replicate some of residential features such as a kitchenette, a living room, bedroom, and a fully accessible bathroom.

4. Spaces for walking and activity areas for developing upper and lower body strength are paramount to maintaining good health for the seniors.

5. Common spaces where the resident and family members can spend time together outside of the resident's room or apartment should be planned.

6. Multipurpose rooms or a small chapel could function for religious services throughout the week.

Source: Victor Regnier, 2002, p. 4.

of them have special needs or problems; 30 percent are incontinent, 40 percent use wheelchairs or walkers, 50 percent have some form of memory loss, 60 percent need assistance in bathing, and 25 percent need toileting assistance.[18] The average length of stay in an assisted living facility is 24.5 months. The majority of these residents are women, who represent 75 to 80 percent of the assisted living population in the United States.

A large number of assisted living facilities are owned by nonprofit organizations which offer affordable housing to seniors who need assistance in paying for the service. Others are publicly owned facilities which are formed because there is a need to offer the service in their community. And, of course, there are many for-profit corporations that focus on upper-income residents in wealthy areas who can pay for their care.

Assisted living facilities have four components: (1) residents' units much like small apartments; (2) common areas such as clusters of space for socialization; (3) common facilities such as the dining room, which is shared by all residents; and (4) support spaces which house the offices, nurses' stations, and all other areas necessary to support the facility.[19] See Figure 8-6 for a floor plan of an assisted living facility.

Many basic services are provided to assisted living residents. All meals, housekeeping of their units, laundry, medication assistance, and bathing assistance are provided. Facilities often have a beauty salon and barber shop, transportation, and exercise equipment. An emergency call system is provided for safety. Other health services, such as weekly checkups and physical therapy, are also common.

Common areas like the dining room, living room, multipurpose room, and library are shared by all the residents. They provide a place for meeting with family members and gathering as a group for social interaction. The residents report that their favorite social activities are talking and visiting with other residents and visitors, as well as watching television, listening to music, and reading. In good weather, patios and healing gardens are enjoyed by the residents.

The assisted living building should be attractive and welcoming on the exterior, with attention to landscaping. The structure should project a residential ambience, since it represents the resident's new home. Many assisted living buildings are luxurious in appearance, often looking like expensive condominiums and apartment houses. A porte-cochere at the entrance is necessary to provide shelter for the resident when entering and leaving the building. Patios at the entry extend living spaces for the residents and should provide seating, shade, and a view for relaxing (Table 8-4).

Off the entry, there is usually a lobby with a living room or a gathering space much like a country club or hotel. Residents like to sit near the entry to watch visitors come and go or to wait for family to arrive, so some seating is specified in this area. A receptionist or greeter is generally positioned in the lobby to assist visitors and to monitor the door. Staff offices are adjacent to the entry so that they are easily accessible to the residents and visitors.

---

[18]Regnier, 2002, p. 4.
[19]Perkins, 2004, p. 28.

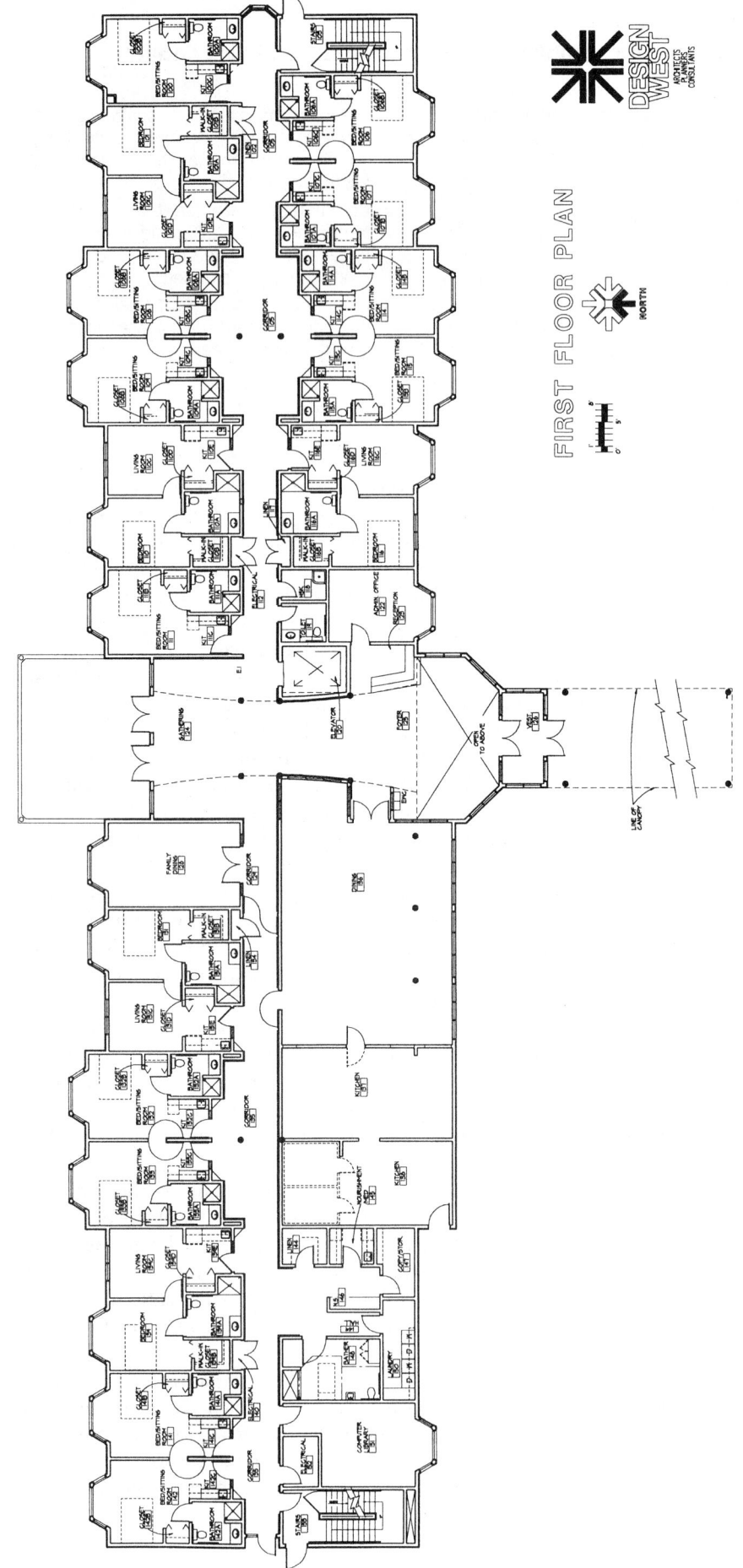

Figure 8-6 Main floor plan of an assisted living facility. Note the close proximity of the lobby, dining, and gathering (living room) areas. (Plan courtesy of Architectural Design West.)

The living room needs to be inviting and furnished with seating groups to encourage interaction with other residents. Groupings consisting of a sofa with two to four chairs are appropriate. Sociopetal spacing is considered the most appropriate placement of seating in this area. Coffee tables are generally avoided, as they can block the spaces leading to the seating and can be a hazard. Table luminaries and artwork are included in these spaces. Artwork is often of a type familiar to the residents, possibly with subjects that spark memories or motivate conversation. Ambient general lighting supplements the table fixtures, helping to create cozy pockets of light for the residents. Senior citizens do not like overhead lighting directed down onto their faces. Non-wood-burning fireplaces help create a welcoming, warm, and cozy space. The use of the fireplace also is a reminder of the home environment, and appeals to many residents and families (Figure 8-7).

The dining room is often located close to the lobby and is somewhat visible from that space. It is probably the most social area of the facility, where residents can share meals with other residents, family members, and other guests. An effort should be made to provide smaller dining areas within the large space to aid in acoustical control. Partial walls or low partitions, perhaps between booths, are helpful. Round tabletops are friendly but can be a problem when larger groups wish to sit together. Square and rectangular tables seating two, four, or six are most common. Usually tables 42 to 48 inches in depth and a height of 29 to 30 inches are specified. Some tables to have an adjustable height, as seen in Figure 8-5.

The selection of chairs for the dining room is extremely important aesthetically but also for the safety and security of the residents. Test these chairs for strength, weight, and inability to tip over. Chair height for senior dining needs to be 20 inches, with open arms the full depth of the chair. Chairs with an upholstered seat and back aid in controlling the acoustics of the space. Designers often use Crypton fabric on the seating and another vinyl or commercial fabric on the back. In selecting the chair style, check to make certain that the back legs do not project out beyond the back profile to avoid tripping. Spacing between tables should allow for passage of wheelchairs and people using walkers.

A wide variety of architectural finishes can be used to create a pleasing residential atmosphere in the dining room. Wallcoverings need to be durable and cleanable, with subtle patterns and soft colors. Some commercial textile wallcoverings can be used if they meet code requirements. Avoid dark colors and high-contrast colors on the walls. Strong contrasting colors and bold prints may also cause dizziness in some people.

Ideally, the dining room is sited to provide the residents with a view of the exterior through large windows. Flame-retardant fabrics are required for window coverings. Other

Figure 8-7 View of the dining room in an assisted living facility from the gathering (living room) area. Chairs directly outside the dining space provide seating while waiting. (Photograph courtesy of SOI, Interior Design.)

TABLE 8-5 Ten Typical Types of Assisted Living Units

1. Semiprivate unit which is usually reserved for residents with dementia if offered by the facility
2. Small studio much like a hotel room
3. Alcove studio which has a separate sleeping area but is not as large as a bedroom
4. Small one-bedroom unit similar to a small apartment with a living room and a bedroom
5. Large-one bedroom unit which provides more closet space
6. Two-bedroom, one-bathroom unit with the second bedroom used as a guest bedroom
7. Double master unit for higher-income residents with two bedrooms and two full bathrooms
8. Small hotel unit patterned on a hotel suite with two bedrooms and one bathroom
9. Share suite unit with separate bedrooms and bathrooms and shared living room and kitchen
10. Bedroom unit where 8 to 10 residents in clusters share the common space

Source: Perkins, 2004, pp. 43–45.

window treatments include shutters or blinds. Make certain that these window treatments can be opened or closed, depending on the time of day.

Carpet for the dining room floor is commonly specified; however, due to spillage problems, some facilities opt for vinyl tile. Color is an issue with this specification, as the floor represents a large volume of space. Avoid dark colors and contrasting patterns for carpeting as well as wall treatments.

Activity rooms are very important to the resident. This area can provide occupational therapy as well as general activities such as crafts, games, and educational presentations. Religious services can be planned in a special chapel, or in the activity rooms or recreational areas. These areas need to be attractive to make them appealing to the residents. Resilient flooring or loop carpet can be used there. Often exercises are planned with the use of a chair so that the resident is seated for safety reasons. In this area, allow spaces for serving refreshments and make certain that no steps are used. A bathroom should be in close proximity to this area. Other service or recreational areas also might be included, depending on the facility.

Corridors in assisted living facilities should not be more than 150 feet long from an elevator or dining room to the resident room farthest from these areas. Corridor distances should also be limited between the common areas and the resident units due to the diminished strength of the senior citizen. Consider placing some form of seating every 35 to 40 feet of corridor space to allow residents to rest while returning to their units. Make certain that the corridor is wide enough for the furniture placement to meet code requirements for passageways.[20] Provide all corridors with handrails 32 inches above floor level. Artwork and accessories can be placed in corridors for aesthetic reasons and as a method of way-finding for the resident. Keep the walls in the corridors light with approximately 60 percent light reflectance. Make certain that light reflecting on the floors is evenly distributed and creates no dark pockets, which might be confusing to the resident (Figure 8-8).

Resident living units vary in size and amenities, depending on the facility. Although there are options, the majority of assisted living spaces consist of one bedroom, with a few two-bedroom or shared units. Developers of these facilities usually include a mix of unit sizes to appeal to a broad spectrum of potential residents. Generally, these rooms or apartments are smaller than those found in an independent living facility (Table 8-5).

Let's discuss a typical one-bedroom unit. It may or may not have an entry into the living room space, a small kitchen—sometimes called a tea kitchen—and an accessible bathroom. Residents generally furnish the living room with their own furniture, creating a seating group for watching television and visiting with family and friends. A recliner, sofa, side tables, lamps, and accessories are most common, and other items may also be

_____

[20]Perkins, 2004, p. 70.

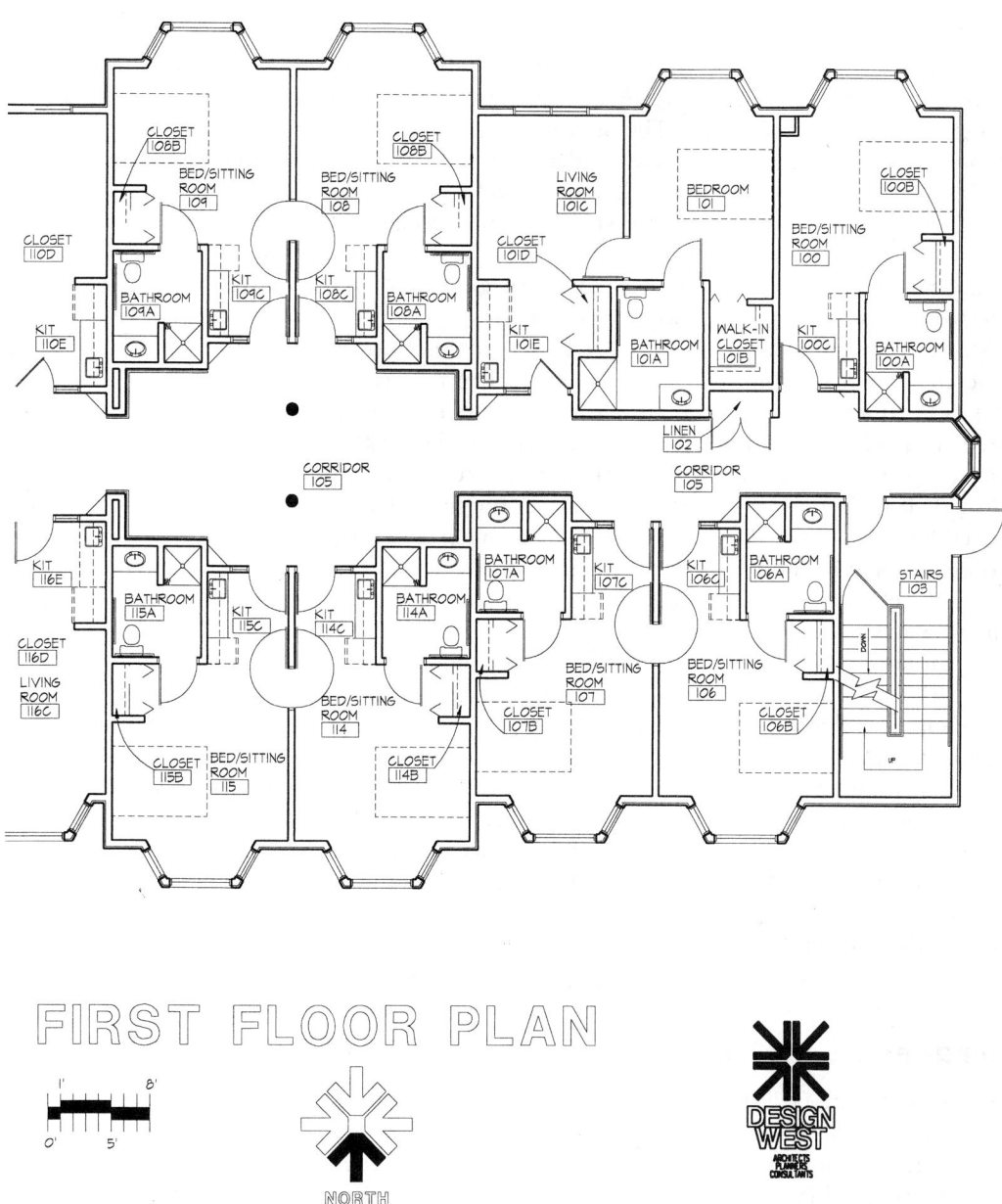

FIRST FLOOR PLAN

NORTH

DESIGN WEST
ARCHITECTS
PLANNERS
CONSULTANTS

Figure 8-8 A variety of unit floor plan configurations are offered, depending upon the residents' needs. (Plan courtesy of Architectural Design West.)

brought in. Carefully plan the furniture layout in the event that the resident uses a wheel-chair or walker.

The kitchen is generally placed toward the entry into the unit and is composed of a sink, small refrigerator, microwave oven, and cabinets with a countertop. The refrigerator may be raised off the floor to give the older resident a comfortable height for reaching into the appliance. An undercounter light provides task lighting for simple food preparation.[21] Modifications in cabinet design may be needed for a resident confined to a wheelchair.

Windows are very important, as they provide a view of the exterior. Facilities are being built with lower window sills approximately 24 inches above floor level. They give the resident a feeling of spaciousness and allow easier viewing. The window treatments are provided by the facility and are consistent throughout the building.

---

[21]Perkins, 2004, p. 48.

In the bedroom, beds and other furniture are normally provided by the resident. However, some facilities provide the bed. A bedside table, a lamp, and a comfortable chair are typical furnishings for this space. A walk-in closet with the hanging rod at a height within the senior's reach is common. The bathroom is located beside the bedroom. The designer should plan the space so that the resident can see the bathroom from the bed and have a clear path to it. A night light will assist in aiding the resident walking to the bathroom.

Depending on the resident's wishes and condition, the accessible bathroom will have a shower with a seat or perhaps a tub. Make certain that the shower controls and the shower wand are within easy reach. Vertical grab bars are necessary at the entry to the shower as well as in the shower for safety. If the resident is in a wheelchair, the threshold should be minimal to allow a wheelchair to roll into the shower. The bathroom will also have an accessible sink and a lavatory. The medicine cabinet should not be placed behind and above the sink because it may require too much of a stretch for the senior citizen. Instead, it should be placed to the side of the sink on a wall. A mirror, however, can be placed above the sink. An accessibly sized toilet with the seat 18 inches high is provided, with grab bars to the side and to the back. Not all of the bathrooms in an assisted living facility need to be accessible. Management may require the design of the bathrooms to be adaptable so that they can be converted to an accessible arrangement.

Ensure that the door openings into all spaces are 3 feet wide, that the locations of light switches are at an appropriate height, and that an emergency call button and a 5-foot turnaround space for a wheelchair are provided.

Although resident rooms or apartments have bathrooms with showers or tubs, not all residents are able to bathe themselves. Bathing rooms are areas shared by some of the residents when this is the case. The current approach to the design of this area is to replicate a spa ambience. Aromatherapy is included with the use of scented lotions, and music can be piped into this area to create a pleasing environment. Surfaces need to be easily cleaned and are most often ceramic tile that is nonskid for the floors. Ceramic tiles offer a variety of sizes, colors, and surface finishes. Avoid any surface finish which might be abrasive, as the skin of seniors tears easily. Lighting should be provided above the tub and in the shower. Make certain that the placement of the bathing rooms does not intersect with the common areas.

Long-term Care Facilities

A long-term care facility can be referred to by several names. The most common ones include *nursing home, skilled nursing facility,* and *comprehensive-care facility.* This discussion will use the term *long-term care facility* in considering the common design elements in these types of facilities. Long-term care facilities have been created for the resident who needs 24-hour nursing care but not acute care, which would require hospitalization. Three typical subgroups of a long-term care facility are the hospice, where residents are in the last stages of life; dementia units, which include Alzheimer patients; and rehabilitation units, where patients stay for a period of time after an injury, surgery, or some illnesses such as a stroke.

The long-term care facility has evolved over time and is now highly regulated by federal, state, and local laws. In fact, these facilities are the most strictly regulated of all the senior housing types discussed in this chapter. They are licensed by the state department of health. The average age of residents is 85 years, with mobility and medical needs. Over half of these residents have some form of dementia. Most long-term care facilities are freestanding, although some are part of CCRCs or other types of senior housing. This section will focus on the design of the resident rooms and nurse stations for the nursing units. Other areas will also be briefly discussed.

Generally, the resident rooms in long-term care facilities are arranged around a nursing unit. Areas for dining, bathing, lounging, and some support spaces are also planned. A typical nursing unit contains 40 beds due to licensing regulations. This means that the nurses station needs to be designed for the appropriate number of staff at all times; in addition, residents require more nursing staff during the day, when more activities occur. Code requirements mandate that the farthest residents room cannot be more than

120 feet from the nurses station.[22] Newer and renovated long-term care facilities are grouping these nursing units into "neighborhoods" called clusters, making resident group areas less populated and smaller. For example, a typical nursing unit of 40 beds could have two areas with 20 beds each, which are divided into clusters of 5 to 10 residents.

The nurse stations require equipment similar to that found in hospital nurse stations. The interior designer must also remember that the space is used to greet guests, and thus should be welcoming as well as obvious to the visitor. Computers are used for record keeping, to expedite ordering, and for some communications. Counter space is needed for paperwork and patient charting, and storage space is needed for electronic monitoring equipment and supplies. Privacy for discussion of residents' health issues is also required. As with other medical facilities, some states require that hard-copy medical records of residents be retained. The recommended space allowance for a nurse station is 250 to 500 square feet (Figures 8-9a and 8-9b).

Residents in long-term care facilities usually share a room. The size of the rooms or the square footage per person within that space is regulated by codes. Approximately 100 to 144 square feet per person is recommended. More nursing homes today are building rooms that are either semiprivate or private to meet families' demands (Figure 8-10). Other improvements include larger windows, a variety of light sources, and in-room cable television. In semiprivate rooms, it is important to design spaces to provide for individual televisions without acoustical interference. Beds in these facilities are hospital bed styles with pneumatic controls. The room is also designed with a small closet, drawers for clothing, and a nightstand with a locking drawer. A hospital-style chair with arms for arising and a high back for a head rest is also required. Some recliners built specifically for healthcare are good in these situations. Meals are served in a dining area or in the resident's room, depending upon the degree of illness. The room has a private bathroom designed with all the normal accessible features. The bathroom also includes a vanity cabinet and a lavatory with space below to allow for wheelchair access. Showers are not typical in long-term care residents' bathrooms, as it is generally not safe for the resident to shower without assistance. Remember that the door into the bathroom must have an opening 32 to 42 inches wide.

Most residents in long-term care units are assisted in bathing by staff members. Today bathing rooms are being designed for more comfort and less stress for the patient. Hard surfaces, the sound of water, and drafts all create an unpleasant bathing experience for the resident. Privacy is very important even though staff members serve only one resident at a time. The minimum size for bathing rooms is 48 inches square. In addition to the shower and tub, a hand-wash sink for the staff, storage for bathing products, shower curtains and cubicle curtains, and an accessible toilet are common. The bathing room must be designed so that it is easy to roll in wheelchairs or shower chairs (Figure 8-11). This size also allows the staff member to be in the space with the resident. Some bathing rooms contain larger fixtures such as jetted tubs. These special tubs are designed for easy access by the infirm. They are somewhat noisy when the water is running, and can confuse and frighten the dementia resident. Additionally, increased warmth from heat lamps could increase the resident's comfort. These bathing areas should be planned so that residents do not have to go through public spaces to return to their rooms.

The facility will also have dining facilities for those residents who can take meals away from their rooms. The majority of facilities are now providing smaller dining spaces in the units rather than one large dining room, as in the assisted living facility. Ideally, these dining areas will limit the number of diners to 15 to 20 residents. Many facilities have a private dining room which can be used by families, as well as function as a meeting room for staff and administrators.

There are several other kinds of function spaces in the long-term care facility. The activity room and/or living room should provide some social activity for residents. Generally, this area is located near the nursing stations to provide monitoring of the space. These activity spaces are very important, providing social interaction, games, shared viewing of television programs or movies, and a place for parties. Medical spaces for exams

[22]Perkins, 2004, p. 33.

Figure 8-9a Nurses' station in a geriatric psychiatric facility. Note that the design has incorporated residential features. Use of indirect nonglare lighting, nonslip, nonshiny flooring, and colors easy on the aging eye have been applied to this patient area. (Photograph courtesy of Elissa Packard, ASID, interior designer. Vintage Archonics, Inc. Photographer: Lisa Tyner.)

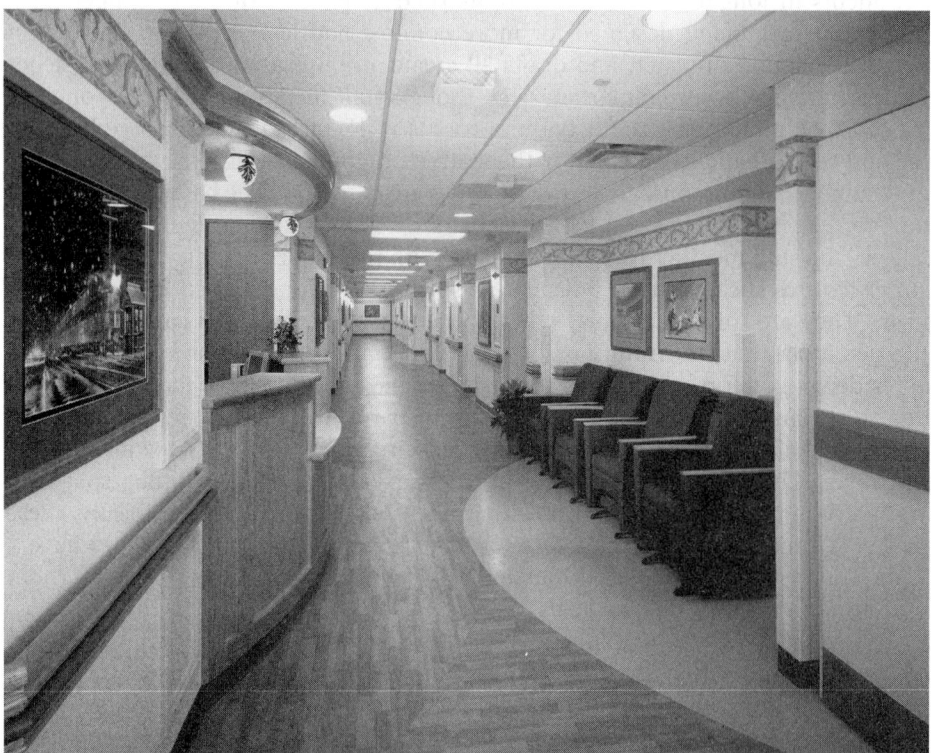

Figure 8-9b Corridor in a geriatric psychiatric facility showing chairs placed opposite a nurses' station. The curve in cabinetry and flooring aids in visual shortening of the corridor. (Photograph courtesy of Elissa Packard, ASID, interior designer. Vintage Archonics, Inc. Photographer: Lisa Tyner.)

Figure 8-10 Room in a long-term care facility using traditionally styled furniture, which gives the space a residential atmosphere. (Photograph courtesy of Sunrise Medical Continuing Community Care Group, Stevens Point, WI.)

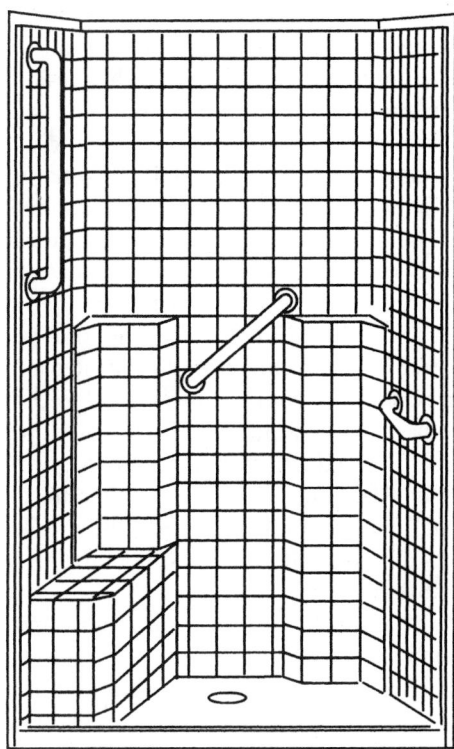

Shown here as Right Hand model with optional grab bars

Figure 8-11 Accessible shower which is a barrier-free design. (Courtesy of Best Bath Systems, www.best-bath.com)

and some treatments are included. A physical therapy space is often included in a long-term care unit to help residents recover from illness. A small coffee shop, gift shop, and library are also often included in the overall planning. Patios, often enclosed, within the configuration of the building allow residents to be outdoors in good weather.

Designers should apply many of the principles used in assisted living to the common areas of the long-term care facility, with further attention to the residents' diminished health. In long-term care, holistic functioning of physical, mental, and spiritual health is pursued.[23]

Dementia and Alzheimer Facilities

Included in the long-term care category is dementia, specifically Alzheimer's disease—the most common form of dementia. Statistics show that there are about 4.5 million persons with this disease in the United States and that every five years, the percentage of Alzheimer's disease patients doubles. An early symptom of Alzheimer's disease is noticeable memory loss beyond the simple loss that comes from normal aging. Sometimes violent behavior and disorientation accompany the memory loss. Some risk factors for Alzheimer's disease include age, family history, head trauma, and mutations of certain genes. Protective factors against Alzheimer's disease include estrogen, anti-inflammatory medications, statins, a low-fat diet, exercise, and mental activity.[24] The Alzheimer unit requires special attention, and it cannot be assumed that it will be designed like the typical assisted living facility or long-term care facility.

In searching for an appropriate Alzheimer unit, families need to visit a facility to assess the overall design and the services offered. The Alzheimer's disease facility must be fully licensed, including the administrators, the nursing staff, and some therapists, as well as the dietitian. Areas of concern for families in regard to facility design are safety and security, wandering spaces, secure doors, friendly staff, noise and temperature control, sturdy furniture, and a warm, welcoming environment.[25]

In dementia and Alzheimer units there is a higher percentage of semiprivate rooms; however, this situation is changing since more families are requesting private rooms. Some Alzheimer residents' health is improved by having another resident share their room. For this reason, some semiprivate rooms will remain on these nursing units.

In designing an Alzheimer unit, attention should be given to exit control, walking paths, and residential features. It is also important to provide personal spaces, as well as familiar sights and smells. Interior designers and staff can create a stimulating environment through color, contrast, and pattern. The interior should be attractive, residential in appearance, and yet in keeping with the regulations which govern these facilities (Figure 8-12).

Alzheimer units are usually located in a wing of a long-term care facility or assisted living facility and represent about 25 to 35 percent of the total resident population.[26] The interior designer needs to create an environment that replicates a residence with bedrooms, kitchen, living room, dining room, and some activity areas to promote the comfort of the Alzheimer resident. Part of this comfort is attained through reference to the senses; for example, the sense of smell can be triggered by baking cookies in the kitchen on the wing.

The rooms of residents in Alzheimer units are similar to other long-term care bedrooms. Bedrooms have a small bathroom including a sink, a toilet, and usually a shower. Special factors must be considered in the design of bedrooms for Alzheimer residents. These are summarized in Table 8-6.

The kitchen, entry, living room, activity rooms, dining room, and even the staff workroom are considered the common areas of the wing. The kitchen and dining room are very important spaces for the Alzheimer resident. They are often located close to the wandering loop (see Figure 8-2). The kitchen needs to be residential, with all the normal kitchen appliances and cabinetry plus a hand-wash sink for staff. There should be key

---

[23]*Terrace Talk*, 2005, p. 5.
[24]Bennett, 2005, p. 4.
[25]Mace and Rabins, 1999, p. 383.
[26]Regnier, 2002, p. 147.

Figure 8-12 Elements used in planning healing environments are evident in this photo of an Alzheimer care facility. Note the use of chairs with rounded edges. (Design by Taliesin Architects, Elizabeth Rosensteel, Principal. Photograph © 1997 by Robert Reck.)

switches for the appliances and outlets for residents' safety. Appliances should be on kill switches behind a locked door and controlled by the staff. Round tables are often used in these areas to avoid sharp edges. Chairs with open arms, sturdy bases, and upholstered seats with moisture-barrier fabric should be specified. Chairs with a handle or opening on the crest rail are ideal for nursing assistance. As with most areas of the unit, there should also be an area designated for staff record keeping in this space.

The living room functions as a seating area and can include shared activities such as watching television or a movie. Dementia residents like to be with each other rather than in their bedrooms. For this reason, sufficient space needs to be planned for shared activities and groupings. Activities should be planned away from exits, especially the main entry. Staff offices are placed near the exits to monitor them. It is recommended that the exit doors be somewhat disguised to divert the residents' attention. One method is to paint the exit door the same color as the wall.

TABLE 8-6 Design Considerations for Bedrooms of Residents with Alzheimer's Disease

- Wallcoverings should not have identifiable images, as residents may try to pick at the patterns.
- Wallcovering or paint should be light in tone and color, without high contrasts except around the toilet.
- Wallcovering especially in bathrooms should be antimicrobial and scrubbable.
- Flooring in residents' rooms is often vinyl due to the need for daily scrubbing.
- High-contrast patterns and dark colors should be avoided on the floor since the resident might confuse a pattern on the floor with an object to be stepped over.
- No area rugs or small rugs should be used.
- Bedrooms should not be placed so that they open directly onto living room. Use Dutch doors to provide privacy.
- Keep activity areas away from the bedrooms, as they are too stimulating.
- Provide windows with a view in the residents' bedrooms.

It is important for Alzheimer and dementia residents to have corridor space for walking. In Figure 8-2, a continual path or wandering loop allows the resident to walk continuously. However, plans should avoid dead-end hallways because Alzheimer residents may come to the end of a corridor and be unable to turn around, thereby adding to their confusion.

It is desirable to provide a secure outdoor space for dementia patients to help reduce their agitation. This area will be accessed from the corridor of the unit. It will be obvious in design and provide some cueing of its function. The outside area, or healing garden, will require a solid fence 6 to 8 feet high with a pathway which loops around the garden and ends back at the garden's entry. Benches and shaded areas provide comfort if residents remain outside for a while. Nontoxic plants are mandatory in this space.[27]

Alzheimer and dementia residents need way-finding cues which are more obvious than those in other senior housing facilities. As mentioned, odors from the kitchen and coats beside the garden door are forms of way-finding for Alzheimer unit residents.

The interior design of an Alzheimer and dementia senior living facility is a challenging project. The designer must learn about these diseases to understand appropriate design product specification. Careful attention must be paid to the information provided by the administration and the nursing staff concerning the needs of the residents, their problems, and the solutions.

Summary

In designing senior housing, the interior designer needs to research the various types of facilities, of which each is dependent upon the residents' physical and mental health. Senior housing, especially long-term care and dementia units, is highly regulated by federal, state, and local codes. Designers must abide by these rules and regulations in regard to space planning and materials specifications. They must also create a harmonious and attractive environment which enhances the physical and mental well-being of the residents.

These types of facilities are rapidly increasing in number throughout the United States, and interior designers who are interested in this area of healthcare must be prepared to design these projects appropriately. By the year 2030, almost 70 million people in the United States will be over the age of 65. By 2050, the number of people over the age of 100 is expected to be about 1 million. Due to the increased emphasis on wellness, developments in medical treatments, and the advances in medication, U.S. senior citizens will be living longer. The emphasis in designing these facilities is on deinstitutionalization and a focus on the individual resident. The interior designer can aid in providing code-compliant, attractive, and appropriate facilities for senior housing.

---

[27]Regnier, 2002, p. 148.

REFERENCES

Aging in Place: Aging and the Impact of Interior Design. 2001. Research study. Washington, DC: American Society of Interior Designers.

Anderson, Kenneth N., ed. 1994. *Mosby's Medical, Nursing and Allied Health Dictionary,* 4th ed. St. Louis: Mosby.

Bennett, Mary. 2005. "Kathryn Caine Wanlass Adult Day Center." *Terrace Talk.* Summer, pp. 4ff.

Berger, William N. and William Pomeranz. 1985. *Nursing Home Development.* New York: Van Nostrand Reinhold.

Bunker-Hellmich, Lou. "Aging and the Designed Environment." *Implications,* Vol. 1, Issue 1.

Bush-Brown, Albert and Dianne Davis. 1992. *Hospitable Design for Healthcare and Senior Communities.* New York: Van Nostrand Reinhold.

Caron, Wayne. 2005. "Living with Alzheimer's." *Implications,* Vol. 3, Issue 11.

Christenson, Margaret A. and Ellen D. Taira, eds. 1990. *Aged in the Designed Environment.* New York: Haworth.

Cox, Anthony and Philip Grover. 1990. *Hospitals and Health-Care Facilities.* London: Butterworth.

Dorland's Illustrated Medical Dictionary, 28th ed. 1994. Philadelphia: W.B. Saunders.

Dvorsky, Tamara and Joseph Pittipas. "Elder-Friendly Design Interventions." *Implications,* Vol. 2, Issue 7.

Foner, Nancy. 1994. *The Caregiving Dilemna.* Berkeley: University of California Press.

Friedman, JoAnn. 1987. *Home Health Care.* New York: Fawcett Columbine.

Goodman, Raymond J., Jr. and Douglas G. Smith. 1992. *Retirement Facilities.* New York: Watson-Guptill.

Hall, Edward T. 1966. *The Hidden Dimension.* Garden City, NY: Doubleday.

Klein, Burton and Albert Platt. 1989. *Health Care Facility Planning and Construction.* New York: Van Nostrand Reinhold.

Kobus, Richard L., Ronald L. Skaggs, Michael Bobrow, Julie Thomas, and Tomas M. Payette. 2000. *Building Type Basics for Healthcare Facilities.* New York: Wiley.

Kovner, Anthony, ed. 1995. *Jonas's Health Care Delivery in the United States,* 5th ed. New York: Springer.

Laughman, Harold, ed. 1981. *Hospital Special-care Facilities.* New York: Academic Press.

Lebovich, William L. 1993. *Design for Dignity.* New York: Wiley.

Liebrock, Cynthia. 1993. *Beautiful and Barrier-Free.* New York: Van Nostrand Reinhold.

Long Term Care Education Web site. 2005. "History of Long Term Care Industry." www.longtermcareeducation.com/A1/g.asp

Mace, Nancy L., and Peter V. Rabins. 1999. *The 36-Hour Day.* New York and Boston: Warner Books.

Marberry, Sara and Laurie Zagon. 1995. *The Power of Color: Creating Healthy Interior Spaces.* New York: Wiley.

Merriam-Webster's Medical Desk Dictionary. 1993. Springfield, MA: Merriam-Webster.

Panero, Julius and Martin Zelnik. 1979. *Human Dimension and Interior Space.* New York: Watson-Guptill.

Perkins, Bradford with J. David Hoglund, Douglas King, and Eric Cohen. 2004. *Building Type Basics for Senior Living.* New York: Wiley.

Public Broadcasting Service Web site. 2006. "The Evolution of Nursing Home Care in the United States. "Today's Nursing Homes." www.pbs.org/newshour/health/nursinghomes

Ragan, Sandra L. 1995. *Interior Color by Design: Commercial.* Rockport, MA: Rockport.

Regnier, Victor. 2002. *Design for Assisted Living.* Hoboken, NJ: Wiley.

Sacks, Terrence J. 1993. *Careers in Medicine.* Lincolnwood, IL: NTC Publishing Group.

Spivak, Mayer and Joanna Tamer, eds. 1984. *Institutional Settings.* New York: Human Sciences Press.

Stedman's Medical Dictionary, 26th ed. 1995. Baltimore: Williams and Wilkins.

Steffy, Gary. 2002. *Architectural Lighting Design.* New York: Wiley.

Terrace Talk. 2005. "The Sunshine Terrace Foundation's Vision for Long Term Care." Summer, p. 5.

Webster's Dictionary, 4th ed. 2002. New York: Wiley.

World Book Encyclopedia, Vols. 8 and 17. 2003. Chicago: World Book, Inc.

Weinhold, Virginia. 1988. *Interior Finish Materials for Healthcare Facilities.* Springfield, IL: Thomas.

WEB SITES

American Association of Retired Persons, www.aarp.org

Care Scout www.carescout.com

Eldernet, www.eldernet.com

Live Oak Institute, www.liveoakinstitute.org

Long Term Care Education, www.longtermcareeducation.com

National Conference of States on Building Codes and Standards, Inc., www.ncsbcs.org

Online Newshour, Public Broadcasting Service, www.pbs.org/newshour

Pioneer Network, www.pioneernetwork.com

Retirement Resorts, www.retirementresorts.com

Sunshine Terrace Foundation www.sunshineterrace.com

Wikipedia Encyclopedia Foundation, Inc., www.en.wikipedia.org

Center for Health Design magazine, www.healthdesign.org

Design for Senior Environments magazine, www.nursinghomesmagazine.com

Healthcare Design Magazine, www.hcdmagazine.com

Implications, www.informdesign.umn.edu

CHAPTER
9

Institutional Facilities

Institutional facilities represent a wide variety of business types, varying to some degree with personal opinion or experience. Basically, there is no one definition of institutional facilities in the interior design literature. In a workable definition, an *institution* is defined as an "established organization or corporation, dedicated to education, culture, and especially of a public character".[1]

Most interior designers agree that institutional facilities design is primarily the design of publicly funded facilities. Generally, these include educational facilities, government and public buildings such as post offices and courthouses, libraries, museums, theaters, religious facilities, and recreational facilities such as sporting arenas. We have included banks in this category because they are controlled by the government even though they are generally owned privately. Most types of institutional facilities are owned by a government agency rather than privately. There are, of course, many types of institutions that are privately owned, such as private schools.

---

[1]*Merriam Webster's Collegiate Dictionary*, 1994, p. 606.

The facilities discussed in this chapter and the next are essentially public spaces used by large numbers of people. Some are owned by governments, and others are privately owned and receive little or no public funding. The types of institutional facilities discussed in these two chapters were selected since they are more likely to be the ones encountered in interior design programs.

In this edition, we have decided to divide the material on institutional facilities into two chapters. Chapter 9 provides functional and design information on the types of facilities that are primarily government owned or regulated. These include banks, courthouses, libraries, and educational facilities. Chapter 10 discusses institutional facilities that are more cultural in nature, including museums, theaters, places of worship, and recreational facilities.

One additional type of space remains in this chapter: multifixture toilet facilities found in the large installations discussed throughout this textbook. Comments pertinent to accessible toilet facilities are also presented in this chapter.

Overview of Institutional Design

The design needs and requirements of institutional facilities vary greatly. These facilities often have a diverse group of client stakeholders involved in the design process. For example, there is the client who has initiated the project and is probably the primary authority or user of the space. A second stakeholder is the person or group that funds the project. Most agencies have a facilities department that oversees all physical plant elements of the organization. Staff members who work at the existing facility can contribute input to the project or portions of the project. Benefactors who donate large sums to the facility may want or expect input. The public that will use the facility will express approval or disapproval. The designer must understand and apply all the needs, interests, and preferences of these stakeholders to the project—which is not an easy task.

Institutional facilities are often financed with public funds and are open for review and criticism from the public. The designer must recognize the public's input and needs even though the direct client is the director, manager, or owner of the facility. The public, including the taxpayer, benefactor, or contributor, might consider spending money on unnecessarily expensive design treatments or FF&E in institutional facilities as irresponsible spending. As architects and designers can attest, complaints are often expressed after construction of any government building, as many taxpayers will believe that the agency has misspent public funds. The designer must walk a very fine line when designing and specifying institutional facilities, satisfying those who actually work in the space, taxpayers who use the space, and those who fund the space.

It is important for the interior designer to recognize the emotional content and response of the public, both positive and negative, regarding institutional facilities, what can affect the acceptance or rejection of a facility. For example, a neighborhood library provides a place for study, research, or to obtain the latest novel or DVD. For some, this library is a quiet retreat such as might be experienced by a senior citizen. For a young child, the library can be an exciting place to find "so many books" compared to what is at home, opening a new world to the child.

An interior designer who elects to specialize in one or more types of institutional interiors must be prepared to encounter these diverse interests, to facilitate and coordinate them into a completed project that accomplishes diverse goals and satisfies varying interests. The interior designer must research and study each specialty area and the many specific requirements that are common to any of these types of interior spaces. Institutional designers also need to be superior project managers, have excellent organizational and communication skills, and have a deep regard for the functional concerns of the client over and above personal aesthetic expression. Knowledge of codes and local regulations is mandatory, as is the ability to work successfully with a team that will often consist of consultants outside the designer's own firm.

This chapter presents information about selected types of institutional facilities in a format similar to that of previous chapters. However, the design planning and elements sections provided in other chapters are presented in a limited manner. Each type of facility is treated independently and includes a short historical overview, an overview of the specific subject matter, and types of facilities, ending with a brief discussion of planning and design concepts. Note that elements labeled "Chapter Vocabulary" in the preceding chapters are incorporated by facility type in this chapter since these terms are facility specific.

Banks

The design of a banking facility must offer customers a sense of security. Readers understand that a *bank* is an institutional facility that provides for the depositing, lending, and protection of money and other financial assets. We deposit funds in a particular bank for many reasons. Whatever this reason, the bank customer needs to know that the banking operation is stable, that the bank management operates in the best interests of the depositors and other investors, and that the deposits and other transactions made there are secure. Contributing to this sense of security is the appropriate application of the interior and exterior design of the facility.

The commercial bank is the type of banking facility with which the public has most experience. It offers many services such as savings and other forms of deposit, checking accounts, safe deposit boxes, loans, credit and guarantee cards, and trust management. More specialized commercial banks may emphasize business loans and services, large real estate development loans, commercial paper transactions, investment counseling, or other services. This section focuses on the basic commercial bank providing standard consumer services, although other types of banking facilities will be discussed briefly.

Table 9-1 presents vocabulary used throughout this section.

Historical Overview

Banks have been in existence since ancient times. Banking emerged as a specific entity in the Renaissance, when commercial families like the Medici took on functions of deposit and credit. The term *bank* comes from the word *banca*, an Italian word meaning "bench" because early Italian banking was conducted on a bench. Merchant bankers who dealt in

TABLE 9-1 Banking Vocabulary

- **BRANCH BANK:** Satellite of a main bank such as a branch of a commercial bank. Branch banking is allowed in most states.
- **COMMERCIAL BANKS:** Provide a wide variety of services such as checking and savings accounts, and consumer and small business loans. They may be chartered by a state or the federal government.
- **CREDIT UNION:** Financial institution with a member cooperative that receives funds from depositors. Savings and checking accounts and small personal loans are common services.
- **FEDERAL DEPOSIT INSURANCE CORPORATION (FDIC):** Federally operated institution that guarantees the deposits held by FDIC-insured banks.
- **FEDERAL RESERVE SYSTEM:** The central banking system of the United States. Its primary responsibility is to control the nation's money supply. The Federal Reserve System is made up of 12 Federal Reserve Banks and other centers.
- **PLATFORM:** Term for the location in a bank of loan officers and managers.
- **SAVINGS AND LOAN ASSOCIATIONS:** Financial institution that specializes in holding savings of depositors and making mortgage loans.
- **SOURCE DOCUMENT:** The original version of a document and/or the first page of a multipage document or form.
- **UNIT BANK:** Another name for the main bank (or individual bank) when a banking facility has more than one location.
- **VIRTUAL BANKING:** Banking from home or other locations via computer.

Figure 9-1 Exterior view of a traditional bank façade with classical motifs. (From Whiffen, *American Architecture Since 1780*. Copyright © 1969. Reprinted with permission of The MIT Press.)

goods and coins developed due to the economic strength of the guilds. By the 1600s, England was a leader in banking institutions where the practice of deposit banking accelerated. Of note, during this period written drafts on bank balances began to be popular.[2]

Banking in the United States grew rapidly due to the country's expanding economy and growing need for a repository of exchange. The first bank was opened in 1792 in Philadelphia[3] and established the design concept of banks using classical motifs, which was imitated for many years. As government regulation stabilized banking practices, new services were added to attract customers. The first savings bank was established in the early 1800s, and the first trust company was formed in 1822. In 1863, Congress passed the National Bank Act, which provided for uniform bank notes. The Federal Reserve System was created in 1913 to regulate bank credit and the money supply. The Banking Act of 1933 created the Federal Deposit Insurance Corporation (FDIC). The first drive-in bank was built in Chicago in 1946.[4] As the U.S. economy increased after World War II, banking institutions continued to upgrade.

The architectural and interior design of banking facilities in the United States has been impacted by changes in both banking practices and construction advances. The first banks relied heavily on the classical styles of ancient Greece and Rome. Classical motifs suggest longevity and stability, qualities believed important to attract customers (Figure 9-1). The monolithic appearance of these buildings created a sense of security for depositors. Interiors with high ceilings, tall ornate columns, and cage-like teller areas projected a sense of security, continuity, and importance (Figure 9-2).

At the turn of the 20th century, architects like Louis Sullivan ignored the conventions of the classical era and developed modern construction methods which admitted more natural light into the facility and exposed the customer to new methods, materials, and design elements. Continual development of new construction methods allowed the construction of high-rise buildings with glass-curtained exterior walls influenced by architects such as Mies Van Der Rohe. Banks were often located on the street level of a high-rise building, housed in open spaces, which allowed the pedestrian to see into the banking facility. Designers were then faced with the need to find ways to keep the open feeling while still providing the security desired by the customer.

Branch banking allowed for smaller facilities, and the design of the bank could directly reflect the customer's regional architectural styles. Today's branch banks are designed in many styles to fit into their neighborhoods. The reader should not forget that branch banking has also entered the supermarket. Many banks rent space from a supermarket so that customers can take care of most bank business near home when they shop for groceries.

Bank management and interior designers involved with banking facility design face many new challenges. These challenges are listed in Table 9-2.

An Overview of Banking

Banks derive their profits from fees applied to various transactions and the interest required on loans. At the same time, banks must pay depositors interest on the money they

[2]*World Book Encyclopedia*, Vol. 2, 2003, p. 88.
[3]Wilkes and Packard, 1988, Vol. 1, p. 388.
[4]Packard and Korab, 1995, p. 36.

Figure 9-2 Interior of a bank building circa 1900. Note the high teller cages and barred windows. (Photograph used by permission, Utah State Historical Society. All rights reserved.)

leave in the bank. The type of bank most readers are familiar with is the retail commercial bank that deals with individuals and small businesses.

Banks must be chartered either by the states or by the federal government. More prestige is associated with those banks chartered by the federal government because those charters are more difficult to obtain. Federally chartered banks are required to join the FDIC, to have funds on deposit at the federal reserve district bank, to purchase stock in the district reserve bank, and to meet other conditions. State-chartered banks must join the FDIC if they want to be a member of the Federal Reserve System.

The design of banking facilities has always reflected the function and activities of the business. For example, in early banks, classical motifs and cashier cages were used to give the impression of security and stability. Today, security cameras, modern designs, and advertising campaigns inform the public not only of the services offered by a specific bank, but of the safety and security of the institution as well.

The interior designer must study the business of banking in order to create and execute a successful design. A commercial bank is structured like any major corporation, with a board of directors headed by a chairman of the board who oversees the operations of the bank. A CEO or president and vice presidents will work at the main unit bank and supervise all branch managers. Corporate officers at the main branch may be in charge of loan committees, trust committees, public relations, personnel, and other corporate services. Branch managers are in charge of the daily operations of a branch and supervise a

TABLE 9-2 New Challenges in Banking

- The expanding utilization of technology in the bank and for banking services
- Implementation of Americans with Disabilities Act (ADA) guidelines in the design of public spaces in a bank
- Reductions in the number of tellers and bank employees as services are provided electronically
- Growing concern with the security of employees and customers
- Movement of banking facilities to different branch sites such as grocery stores and automatic teller machines in shopping centers

group of loan officers, tellers, secretarial staff, accounting staff, and others with specific job functions at the branch.

A design project may be started by the bank's facility office at its corporate headquarters or sometimes by a branch manager. In most situations, the decision maker for the bank will be someone from the corporate office who collaborates with the branch manager. This is an important distinction, as the designer must satisfy the demands of both the corporate decision maker and the local branch manager who may have hired the interior designer directly.

Many large banks with branch offices have a specific design image and guidelines that they prefer, and they have invested considerable capital in creating that image. This information is obtained from the branch manager or corporate facilities planner during the programming stage. The interior designer must recognize the design image, the logos, and the chain of command in regard to decision making.

Types of Banking Facilities

Banks, credit unions, savings and loan associations, and other similar banking facilities are part of the financial services industry. Credit card companies, insurance companies, and stock brokerage firms are other examples of businesses within this industry. The most typical part of the financial services industry is the commercial bank. *Commercial banks* are subdivided into unit banks, which are the main bank facility, and branch banks, which operate at satellite locations. Commercial banks offer credit, debit, and check guarantee cards in addition to savings accounts, various investment accounts, safe deposit boxes, and various types of loans. Automatic teller machines, banking services on the Internet such as virtual banking, and other electronic banking services have changed the design of banking facilities and the way customers interact with their banker.

The credit union and the savings and loan association are also familiar to most readers. *Credit unions* are member cooperatives that receive funds from depositors. *Savings and loan associations* are financial institutions in which deposits are obtained from customers and loaned to members or other customers. Credit unions and savings and loan associations generally offer fewer services than commercial banks and are limited by law as to the services they can offer.

These three types of banking facilities are the ones with which the interior designer will likely become involved. Table 9-3 defines some additional types of banking facilities which may be designed by an interior designer specializing in banking and financial services facilities.

Gaining a clear understanding of the differences in the types of banking facilities is necessary to create viable and effective design solutions. The space planning, functional needs, and design specification of a federally chartered central bank will be different from those of a neighborhood state-chartered branch bank. These differences must be recognized and understood for the design project to succeed.

TABLE 9-3 Other Types of Banking Facilities

- **Central banks:** Operated by the federal government such as the Federal Reserve System banks.
- **Clearinghouses:** Maintained by banks for settling claims and accounts.
- **Investment banks:** Serve as middlemen in the buying and selling of securities such as stocks and bonds.
- **Offshore banks:** Private banks located outside the United States.
- **Private banks:** Banks serving very wealthy individuals.
- **Savings banks:** Services emphasize savings and thrift to customers.
- **Trust companies:** Banking facilities that specialize in the administration and control of large amounts of funds held in trust. Trust banks also make loans.

Planning and Interior Design Elements

In the planning and design of a banking facility, the interior designer generally is part of a team that includes the architect, facilities personnel from the bank, and members of the bank staff. The design concept is strongly influenced by the need to convey the impression of security and stability, as well as specific design images associated with the bank. Design challenges involve space allocation, furniture and materials specifications, code compliance, and security issues. The last is the responsibility of the architect, although interior designers are part of the process.

Where a bank is located can have a significant influence on the design of its interior and exterior. Banks located in the central business district may require a different image and design appearance than branch banks located in the suburbs or rural areas. A bank branch in an affluent suburb can also be quite different from a branch of the same bank in a less affluent neighborhood. These location and customer differences are important for the interior designer to understand. For example, the bank management may think that architectural finishes that are appropriate in an affluent neighborhood should not be used in a less affluent one. That choice is driven by the bank's management decisions regarding the design of their facilities.

The design of the architecture and interiors of a bank needs to project a feeling of power, stability, and security—qualities critical to banks seeking customers in all neighborhoods. The exterior design should project an image with which the customer can identify. Some customers may prefer traditional, classical designs that give the impression of longevity. An image of conservative policies and safe, reliable management is often conveyed by the use of brick, stone, and classical columns. Other customers prefer modern designs that use large windows and open planning. Contemporary designs give the impression that the bank is on the cutting edge of technology and thinking, which may appeal to many customers.

Bank design in the 21st century requires a balance between a stable, secure look and an open, honest appearance. The floor plan and layout must provide the privacy that customers want when discussing financial issues and that the bank needs to ensure security and safety. Space planning must make the bank comfortable and safe so that customers can make their way around the public spaces easily and quickly. Employees must be given the functional work spaces to conduct banking activity accurately and securely. The following discussion focuses on the public areas of the typical commercial bank.

The first considerations in the design of a bank facility are space allocation and circulation. A typical bank can be divided into two basic spaces. The first is the public spaces that the customer will use to make deposits and withdrawals and conduct other banking business. These areas must include a small waiting area, the teller line and queuing space before the tellers, and the desks or cubicles for loan officers. The second group of spaces is the operations area, which includes the vault where safety deposit boxes are located, counting rooms, storage, lunchrooms, employee restrooms, conference or meeting rooms, and records rooms. Figure 9-3 is a floor plan of a typical small bank. For a main unit bank, other spaces will be needed for the corporate officers, specialty functions like securities work, and other spaces common to a corporate office.

Upon entering the banking facility, the customer should experience a sense of welcome and friendliness combined with an equal feeling of safety and security. These needs are often provided by finishes and furniture pieces similar to those found in many offices and hotels. Depending on the size of the bank facility, a receptionist may be present to direct the customer to the right area of the bank. Security guards still exist in the largest banks. The vast majority of smaller branch facilities depend upon security cameras and other hidden security systems in place of guards. The lobby or entry area may also serve as the location of the automatic teller machines (ATMs). A small counter for writing, adequate lighting for after-hours banking, and placement of security cameras are necessary to allow the customer to use ATMs in safety.

A small seating near the entry is needed for customers who must wait to see a bank employee or for family members accompanying a customer. Depending on the size of the bank, this waiting area may consist of a few small armchairs or a comfortable group of

Floor plan

A. Covered parking
B. Foyer
C. Lobby
D. Waiting room
E. Check counter
F. Conference room
G. Private office
H. Break room
I. Tech center
J. Commercial lane
K. Drive-thru

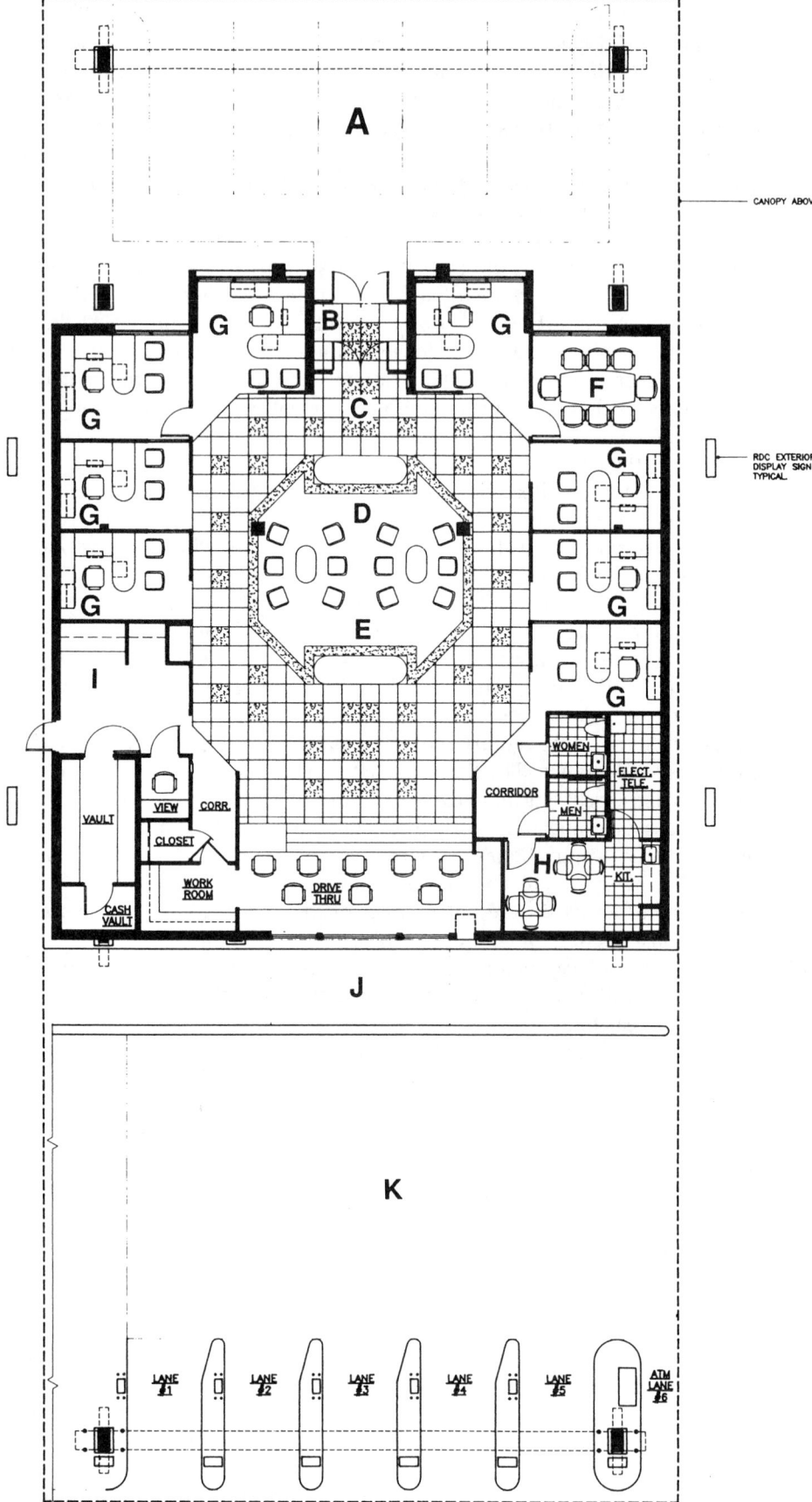

Figure 9-3 Floor plan of a commercial bank with drive-through lanes. (Plan courtesy of Stephen L. Morrill, AIA, Principal, SLM & Associates, Architects.)

soft seating units such as a sofa, love seat, or settee and individual club chairs. The specification of individual chairs rather than multiple seating units is more common. These seating pieces are usually covered in a commercial-grade woven textile in small patterns to help break up the monotony of the large quantities of basic finishes commonly used in the public areas.

The essentially large, open public area of a bank draws the customer to the teller line. The customer usually proceeds to a standing-height counter, called a *check stand*, to fill out the required transaction forms. Check stands are usually custom millwork and require a smooth surface for the top and numerous pigeonholes or slots for the storage of transaction forms. The exact design of the check stand will be guided by the bank's requirements. Banks should provide a sit-down 29-inch-high check stand or other accommodation to meet accessibility requirements.

Upon completion of the forms, the customer moves to a *teller window (or cage)* or stands in the line for the tellers. Space must be allowed to accommodate a line of customers waiting to approach one of the teller windows without blocking the flow of customer traffic. The teller area is also created by the use of custom millwork. Figure 9-4 is an example of some design criteria for the teller station.

Teller areas are rather standardized in design. Individual banking companies may have special needs that differ from these standards. Generally, the teller counter is designed so that a stand-up countertop at least 42 inches above the floor is provided. Each teller window should have an opening of at least 24 inches. Modern banks seldom use grilles at the teller windows, but banks with a traditional design scheme may ask for a grille as part of the cabinet design. Small teller openings provide privacy for the customer as money is deposited and especially when it is counted out for withdrawals. Material specification for writing surfaces at the teller line (and check-writing desk) is important for security. Interior designers like to use wood because of its warm appearance. However, it is not a good surface for writing or for security. Hard surfaces such as marble and granite make it easier for the police to lift fingerprints if the bank is robbed.[5]

Designers often have the opportunity to design exciting cabinet faces on the customer's side of the teller cabinet. The inside working area of the teller cabinet must be designed using the strict size and need parameters of the bank. It must contain room for adding machines, computer monitors, storage for forms of various kinds, and locking drawers for cash and coins. Tellers should be provided with ergonomically designed high stools with a back.

There are a few other work areas related to the teller line. One is employee access to the drive-in window. At least one section of the teller line is placed along an exterior wall to accommodate this function. A second is a separate teller window or desk for customers who seek to enter the vault, where customer safety deposit boxes are located.

Accessibility guidelines are met by providing sit-down versions of the teller cabinet. These accessible stations generally have a larger window opening or an open desk for the convenience of those in wheelchairs or with other accessibility needs. The stations should be placed alongside or adjacent to the teller windows. Guest seating that can easily be moved is provided only at sit-down teller stations.

Generally, the majority of customers exit the bank after conducting business with the teller. However, some customers come to the bank for other reasons. The area where these other services are provided is often called the *platform*. In the platform area, a new customer can open an account, apply for a credit or debit card, seek personal or small business loans, or discuss other services that require meetings with new accounts employees, loan officers, or personnel other than tellers.

The platform area is designed using workstations of freestanding desks, systems stations, or millwork with partial-height walls dividing the stations. The bank branch manager is usually located at the only workstation in the platform with full-height walls. Of course, in an older bank being remodeled, private offices will be more prevalent. Privacy for customers who visit the platform is very important because customers are discussing personal financial information and demand acoustical privacy. Since this area is open,

---

[5]Clay, 2005. p. 38.

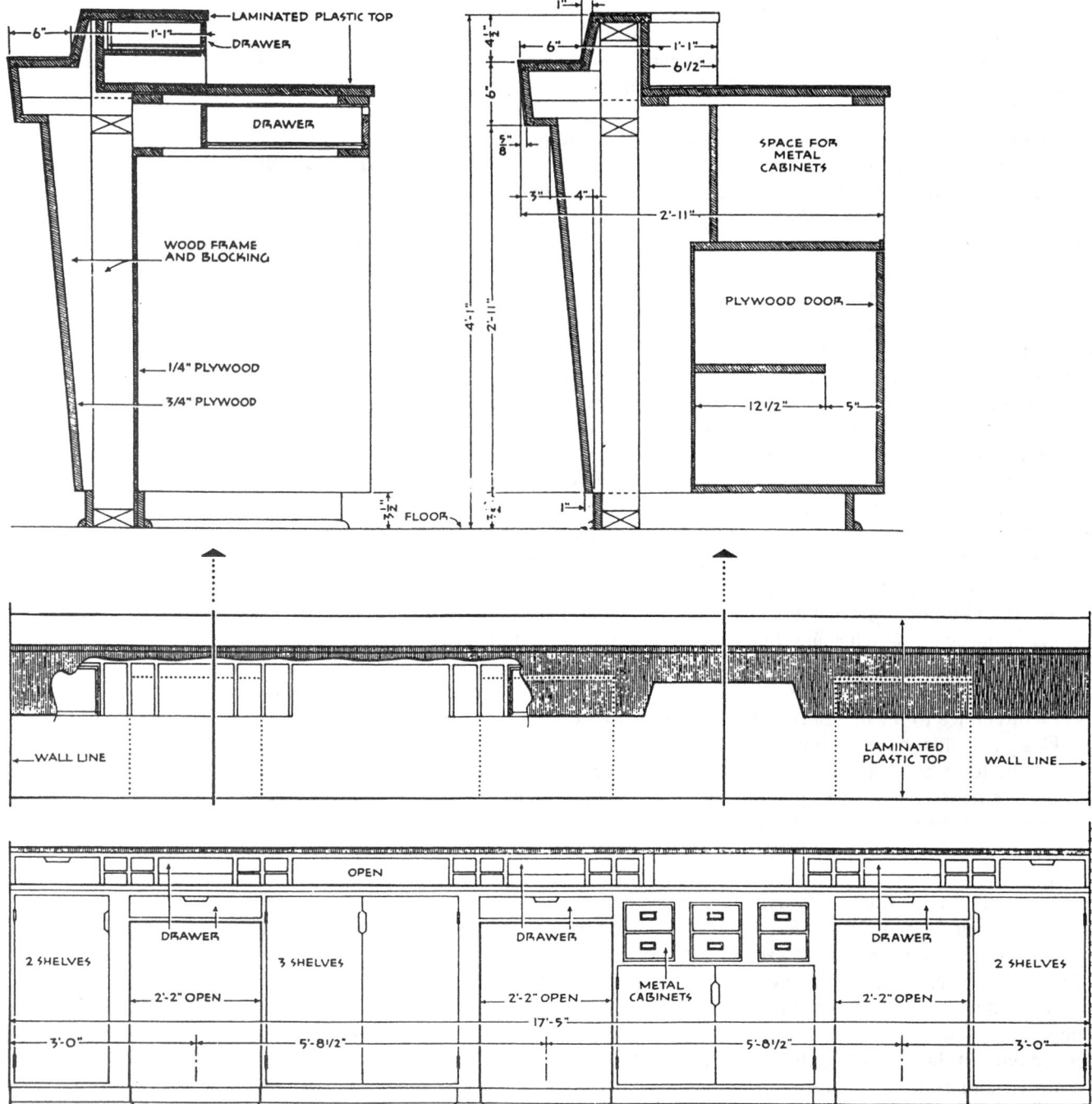

Figure 9-4 Detailed drawing of custom millwork for a tellers' area in a bank. (Reprinted with permission from *Design Solutions Magazine*, published by the Architectural Woodwork Institute, Reston, VA.)

privacy is achieved by the use of upholstered panels, credenzas with overhead storage units, or plants placed between desks. Privacy is important for the interior designer to provide (Figure 9-5).

Appropriate furniture items must be selected for all the activities conducted on the platform. Standard desks can be used for all these tasks, though some banks prefer systems furniture. Banks often use desks of different sizes to indicate the status of these employees. For example, a loan officer has higher status than a new accounts representative. Therefore, the loan officer might be given a 36 by 72-inch desk, while the new accounts representative might be given a 30 by 60-inch desk. Chair size and type is another way of indicating status. A desk chair with a higher back and upholstered arms is usually

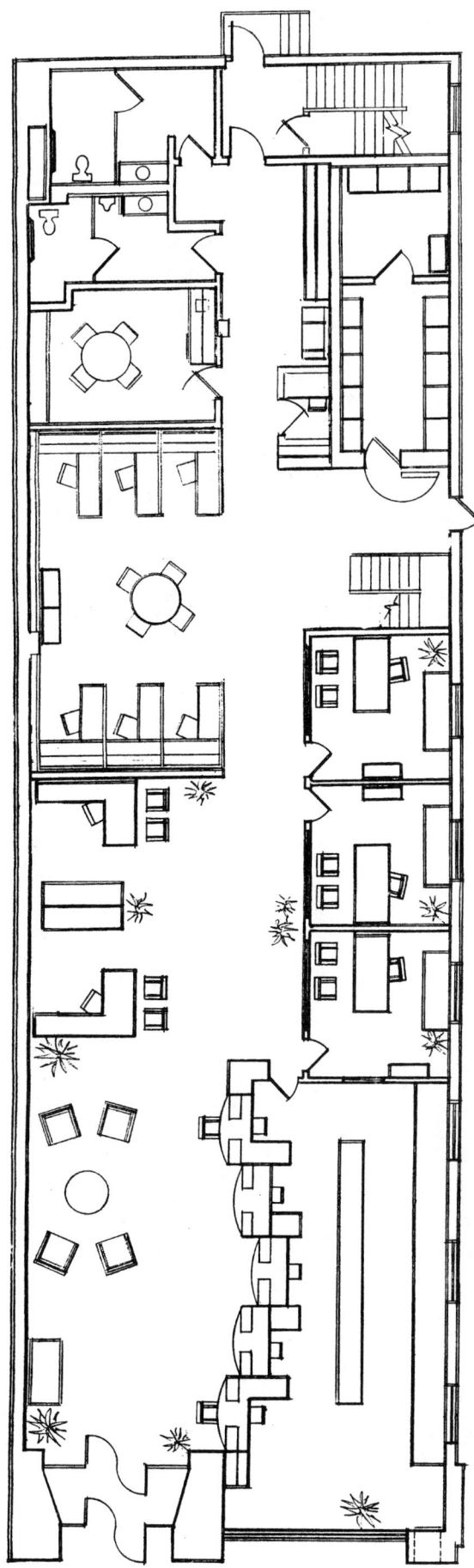

Figure 9-5 Floor plan for the first floor of a bank showing the entry, tellers' area, lobby, and new accounts, and officers' area. (National Bank of Arizona, Flagstaff, AZ. Design by and plan courtesy of Carl E. Clark, FASID, Design Source, Flagstaff, AZ.)

Figure 9-6 Reception desk in an upscale bank. (Photography courtesy of Burke, Hogue and Mills Architects.)

Figure 9-7 Conference room for the Bank of New York. Note the luxury of space and the use of light. (Photograph courtesy of Burke, Hogue and Mills Architects.)

specified for the loan officer, while a smaller secretarial or task chair is commonly specified for the new accounts station. The guest chairs used on the platforms are usually easy to move and have arms for client ease.

Sometimes the receptionist is located at a workstation with a high counter, usually at bar height, for customer service. Guest chairs are not usually included at the reception desk since customers will be directed to the waiting area or a particular work area after stopping for information. Figure 9-6 is an example of a reception room in an upscale bank.

It is not uncommon for larger bank branches and main banking facilities to provide meeting places where customers can gather to hear a presentation by a bank employee. These spaces may be a simple room with small side chairs, a conference room similar to those discussed in Chapter 2, or spaces that are almost lounges, with soft seating and even a small coffee bar (Figure 9-7).

Architectural finishes for floors, walls, windows, and ceilings in the main public banking spaces are limited to some degree by building and fire codes. Banks are considered business occupancies by the International Building Code and the Life Safety Code. Flooring materials should be specified with consideration for safety, noise, and ease of maintenance. Depending upon the location and the region, it may be necessary to use slip-resistant hard-surface materials at the entry. If other materials are used at the entry, the designer must also provide floor mats.

Flooring materials are an important design element in the large, open area of the main public banking space. This area experiences heavy customer traffic, so maintenance is a key factor in material specification. Many hard and resilient surface materials are used in the public area. High-density, low-pile tufted carpet that is installed by the glue-down method is commonly used in the public areas and behind the teller line. This type of carpet is easy to clean, allows for movement of chairs and carts, and provides safety for customers of all ages. Small, conservative patterns are often used for carpeting in banking, though larger patterns help to hide traffic paths. Ease of maintenance and elimination of static charges that could damage sensitive equipment are key issues in the selection of carpeting.

Walls and windows need to be specified with fire safety and acoustics in mind. Walls can be treated with many kinds of materials. For example, wood paneling is often preferred when a traditional atmosphere is required. The many different styles of textured vinyl wallcoverings provide aesthetic statements. Textile wallcoverings provide a certain level of acoustical control but must be treated for fire retardance, which can reduce acoustical efficiency. Large window walls are commonly left without any window treatments unless the windows face the west or south. Vertical or horizontal blinds are often the preferred window treatment for large areas of glass. In a traditional interior, overdraperies or swags can be added over the blinds. In the majority of locations when textiles are used, fire-retardant fabrics are required by code.

The color scheme for a bank interior can be based on a corporate color scheme or one specifically targeted for a certain region. Traditional-style banks rely heavily on wood tones and the traditional hues of the colonial period, whereas contemporary-style banks use a variety of color schemes to establish a modern ambience (Figure 9-8). To prevent a newly designed bank from appearing outdated in a few years, the designer should avoid trendy color schemes. Many times, architectural surfaces provide the background in the large, open spaces of a bank. Subdued patterns or

Figure 9-8 The interior of this credit union creates a utilitarian, contemporary atmosphere with the use of saturated colors and contrast. Credit Union 1 – Fairbanks Branch. (Photograph courtesy of RIM Design. Chris Arend © Photography.)

solid colors or finishes are normal on these surfaces, with patterns and bolder colors used for seating fabrics and accessories.

Lighting is important since many employees are not working on original documents, also called *source documents*. Good lightning is needed to ensure that errors are not made by employees or customers as banking business is transacted. Most banks are designed with general lighting levels identical to those in offices, approximately 70 to 150 foot-candles, and with task lighting at work stations requiring additional illumination. An assortment of sconces, spotlights, and track lights can be used to wash walls with ambient light and to highlight artwork or otherwise create visual interest. High ceilings offer the opportunity to use high intensity discharge lighting fixtures for overall lighting.

The computer has supplanted paperwork in banks. Tellers, loan officers, and other personnel use computers for almost all record keeping and other functions. Furniture specification and millwork design must accommodate the computer. Ergonomically designed seating is critical for employees who sit at a computer all day. Mechanical interface and power specification must be coordinated with the interior designer's furniture specification. The public also uses the computer for many bank transactions. *Virtual banking,* in which bank customers can transact business from their home computer, has to some degree changed the size and design of financial institutions.

The interior design of a bank should produce a feeling of stability, safety, and quality. Accessories provide the final touch in creating this atmosphere and should reflect quality design. Functional accessories such as trash receptacles at check stands, as well as plants, artwork, and sculpture, should all be of excellent quality and in keeping with the theme of the bank.

Courthouses and Courtrooms

All levels of government own or lease buildings to house agencies and facilities necessary for conducting the business of the jurisdiction. One type of facility that can be found at any level of government is a courthouse and the courtrooms within. Naturally, it is not possible to discuss each type of courtroom for each level of legal jurisdiction. To present information about designing for the client who will be the most critical, this section will focus on the design of federal courthouses and courtrooms.

Courthouse design is a challenging part of commercial interior design practice. Planning and specifications for the interior design of a courthouse is heavily influenced by security, accessibility, and sustainable design issues. Design decisions to accommodate the functions within a courthouse are arguably more important than the aesthetic decisions. At the same time, new courthouses—especially on the federal level—are designed by leading architects and designers. They are encouraged to create interesting attractive as well as functional facilities.

This section begins with a brief historical overview and an explanation of the court system. It is important for the reader to review Box 9-1, as the U.S. General Services Administration (GSA) plays a critical part in the design of all federal facilities.

Historical Overview

The first courts were probably tribal councils based on the codes of a particular society. Artifacts from the Mesopotamian culture reveal evidence of written legal codes and laws. Many are aware of the Hebrew court, the Sanhedrin, whose purpose was to interpret the Hebrew laws of the time. The first refined legal codes were developed by the ancient Romans, who also created a modern court system. After the fall of the Roman Empire, feudal courts run by local lords became the predominant justice system in Europe. In the 1100s, Italian universities commenced the training of lawyers/attorneys using ancient Roman law as a base. Eventually this written law replaced the laws of the feudal courts.

In the 13th century in England, the king's courts developed an unwritten set of customs, or *common law*. It was so called because it applied to everyone in the land. Common law

| BOX 9-1 | U.S. GENERAL SERVICES ADMINISTRATION |

The mission of the U.S. General Services Administration (GSA) is to "help federal agencies better serve the public by offering, at best value, superior workplaces, expert solutions, acquisition services and management policies."* The GSA provides procurement services—as well as many other services—to federal agencies. It also helps develop policies to improve the services federal agencies provide to the public. Some examples of the other services the GSA provides, as noted on their web site are renovation of existing facilities; operating child-care centers for federal employees; encouraging and practicing energy conservation and green building; and preserving and maintaining historic properties owned by the federal government.

A key group within the GSA germane to the planning and design of federal facilities is the Public Building Service (PBS). The PBS is concerned with the real estate and buildings owned by the government. It is the landlord for the civilian federal government. Over 340 million square feet of work space for the over 1 million federal employees are managed by the PBS and GSA. The PBS also directs the federal government's building program, including construction, renovation, alternation, and repair of federal office buildings, courthouses, and other civilian facilities. Through the PBS, the GSA has instituted the Design Excellence Program. This program includes a two-step architect-engineer selection process and the use of private sector peers to provide feedback through the use of review panels of well-known architects. The program stresses creativity and provides greater efficiency in the methods the GSA uses to hire architects and engineers.

The majority of this agency's work is done in alliance with architects and engineers from the private sector. Design professionals who specialize in the design of federal facilities do so knowing that while excellent design is encouraged, their designs will be scrutinized in relation to design guidelines different from those of clients in the private sector. Critical to these standards are design specifications regarding sustainability, accessibility, and security.

The federal government has committed to utilizing sustainable design principles in building projects. The GSA is charged with integrating sustainable design as seamlessly as possible while remaining vigilant to concerns about cost effectiveness. According to the GSA, sustainable design principles including the use of environmentally preferred products, enhancement of indoor environmental quality, protection and conservation of water, and minimization of nonrenewable energy consumption[†] are all important to reduce negative impacts on the environment and the health of the federal workers.

The GSA uses the LEED rating system to aid in applying principles of sustainable design in federal facilities projects. As of 2003, all new GSA building projects must meet the criteria for LEED certification. An example of a GSA facility addressing sustainable design is the newly constructed Social Security Administration building in New Bedford, Massachusetts, where a green roof was included in the design.

Accessibility to federal facilities is critical, and the GSA requires that federal facilities be accessible to all citizens. The design of public buildings must meet accessibility standards as designated by the Architectural Barriers Act (ABA) enacted in 1968. The ABA applies to all federal buildings and requires that facilities designed, built, altered, or leased with certain federal funds be accessible to persons with disabilities. The Americans with Disabilities Act (ADA)—first enacted in 1990 and under review in 2006—expanded accessibility requirements for all buildings, including federal buildings. Projects involving any federally owned or leased buildings must comply with the ADA guidelines. There are penalties for noncompliance.

Design planning and specification for security has become a critical issue in the design and ongoing retrofitting of federal facilities. Screening devices and metal detectors at entrances, careful traffic segregation to restrict nonemployee passage through secured spaces, and even planning locations of mailrooms and storage facilities to minimize potential blast effects are just a few of the security concerns that impact the design of all federal buildings today.

There are many other resources and agencies through the GSA and PBS that provide the designer with information in the design of federal facilities. One very useful resource is the publication *Facilities Standards for the Public Buildings Service* by the PBS. This document establishes design standards and criteria for new buildings and alterations, as well as for repair and reconstruction work in existing and historic structures for the PBS. It includes policy and technical criteria to be used in programming, design, and documentation of federal buildings. Information about ordering or downloading this document can be found on the GSA Web site.

*GSA Web site, www.gsa.gov as of February 7, 2006.
†GSA website, www.gsa.gov as of February 7, 2006.

courts used traditional legal principles based mainly on precedents, as practiced today. English common law evolved into the court system used in the United States and Canada and remains part of the law in these countries today. In the early 1800s, Napoleon established the Napoleonic Code (also known as the Code Napoleon) based on Roman laws. The Code Napoleon evolved into the court system used by European and Latin American countries.

The early courts of the American colonies were patterned on the English common law system. After independence, the American colonial courts became state courts. In 1789, the U.S. Congress passed the Judiciary Act creating the U.S. federal court system.[6]

State and local jurisdictional courts in the United States developed over time as legal practice became more complex. In the early years, judges often traveled from township to township to try legal cases. Due to the need to travel, the terms *circuit court* and *circuit judge* evolved. In 1912 the term *circuit court* was replaced with *court of appeals,* although it is still referred to informally as the circuit court. Today, each of these circuits has one court of appeals.

The U.S. Supreme Court was founded under Article III of the U.S. Constitution. All other federal courts are created by an act of Congress. The Supreme Court is the highest court in the United States, and while it is generally thought of as the final court of appeal, it can also hear cases of original jurisdiction. A decision by the Supreme Court cannot be appealed. Justices are nominated by the President of the United States and confirmed by the Senate. Along with other duties, a Supreme Court justice is now assigned to each judicial circuit.

Overview of Courthouses and Courtrooms

People come to a courthouse for many different reasons. Members of the public might come to a courthouse to register to vote or secure a business name. They might come to become a citizen of this country or obtain a marriage license. And, of course, they might enter a courthouse to take part in a legal proceeding.

A *court* is a governmental institution presided over by a judge or another member of the judiciary where cases, trials, or hearings are conducted under prevailing law. A *trial court* is the place where most civil and criminal trials occur and evidence is first considered. A trial court may exist at the municipal, county, state, or federal level. At the municipal level and up to the state court level, cases are heard that impact municipal laws such as those concerning traffic violations. The state court hears cases concerning a robbery or assault. Federal courts deal with criminal and civil cases that involve federal laws and matters related to the U.S. Constitution.

Depending on the level and type of case, officials associated with the courts include the judge, jury, district attorney or prosecuting attorney, defense attorney, or public defender. Additional court staff includes the clerk of the court, marshal, and bailiff. Court officials also include the chief justice and justices of a state supreme court or the U.S. Supreme Court and the justice of the peace at the municipal level.

When a new federal courthouse facility or a major remodeling of an existing facility is considered, a court facility planning committee is formed. Federal courthouse design projects usually require a team composed of one or more members of the judiciary, the GSA, the U.S. Marshals Service (USMS), and additional federal agency representatives. It is also common for an architect and possibly interior designers who serve as employees of the GSA to be part of the planning team. They can be involved in selecting the private sector design team that will be responsible for the project plans and documents. Similar types of design committees will be formed at the state and local levels for a new court at those levels.

Types of Courts

Because of the complexity of the court system, a brief discussion of the state and federal court system is presented here. The reader should be aware that this information focuses

---

[6]*World Book Encyclopedia,* Vol. 4, 2003, p. 1104.

TABLE 9-4 Courts and Courthouse Terminology

- **Appeal:** A proceeding that occurs when a defendant in a criminal case or either party to a civil case does not feel that the decision of the trial court was correct.
- **Appellate courts** (also called *appeals courts*): A court that reviews cases after conclusion by the trial courts if requested.
- **Bailiff:** A court official common in U.S. courts. He or she assists the judge and helps ensure security in the courtroom.
- **Bar:** A railing that separates the area for spectators from the area for the judge, jury, and other parties to the case. It is also a term for the legal profession.
- **Bench:** The place where the judge sits in a courtroom.
- **Court:** a government institution that settles legal disputes and applies the law to cases brought. All courts are presided over by a judge. The term *court* can refer to a judge or to a judge and jury. It also refers to a location for settling disputes.
- **Court of general jurisdiction:** This court hears any kind of civil or criminal case except those sent to a special court such as a bankruptcy court.
- **Court of limited jurisdiction** (also called a *court of special jurisdiction*). This court hears and tries only special types of cases such as small-claims cases.
- **Court of original jurisdiction:** The court where a case or hearing is first heard and action is initiated.
- **Court of special jurisdiction:** This court hears cases such as those involving juvenile problems or traffic violations.
- **Civil case/court:** A civil court that settles disputes involving noncriminal cases such as those involving negligence, breach of contracts, and disputes of will.
- **Courtrooms:** Spaces used to conduct formal judicial proceedings. Courtrooms are the central facility within the courthouse.
- **Criminal case/court:** A criminal court that deals with offenses against state and/or federal laws.
- **District court:** A local or other level of jurisdiction that has trial court responsibilities within a prescribed district or area.
- ***En banc* court:** A type of courtroom used in an appeals court. *En banc* is a Latin term used to refer to an entire appellate court hearing a case. The most common *en banc* hearings take place in the U.S. Supreme Court and state supreme courts. An *en banc* courtroom may have the judges' bench either in a horseshoe shape or a long bench for the 9 to 11 members.
- **Prosecution:** An official of the court who represents the state or federal government in criminal cases.
- **Supreme court:** The highest court in either the state or federal judicial system.
- **Trial court:** The court where most civil and criminal trials occur. It is also called the *court of original jurisdiction*.
- **Well:** The area in a courtroom consisting of the spaces for the litigants, jury, judge, and court staff in front of the bar.

on the higher levels of court proceedings and is not intended to be a complete and detailed description of the court system at all levels. Courthouses are found most often at the county, state, and federal levels. Also note that the discussion of state courts in general also applies to the District of Columbia (Table 9-4).

State courts handle cases that affect state constitutions and laws. States use various names for their trial courts, including *district court, circuit court,* and *superior court.* Other names particular to a state may also be used. A case usually starts in a *court of original*

TABLE 9-5 Types of Courts

■ Appellate	■ District	■ Probate
■ Bankruptcy	■ Domestic	■ Small-claims
■ Business	■ Family	■ State
■ Circuit	■ Federal	■ Superior
■ Civil	■ Justice	■ Supreme court
■ Constitutional	■ Juvenile	■ Tax
■ County	■ Magistrate	■ Traffic
■ Criminal	■ Municipal	■ Trial

jurisdiction in which the case is first heard. State trial courts are considered *courts of general jurisdiction,* as they can try any kind of criminal or civil case related to their jurisdiction. Civil or criminal cases go to a state court of general jurisdiction, where a ruling or jury decision is made. The states also have courts of special jurisdiction (sometimes called *courts of limited jurisdiction*) that try certain kinds of cases, such as family and municipal courts (Table 9-5).

An *appeal* can be made to the state court of appeals if one of the litigants (except the prosecution in a criminal matter) does not agree with the decision of the trial court. The case is heard by a panel of three judges. They can affirm the lower court decision or disagree and set aside or modify the decision of the lower court. An appeal can also be made to the supreme court of the state if desired after the appeal court decision is handed down. Some states do not have an appeal court process, so a case can move from the lower court directly to the state supreme court. The decision of the state supreme court is final. For the most part, trials held in a state court will not be appealed to a federal court, though there might be exceptions. Of course, some state court proceedings might be heard at the U.S. Supreme Court if constitutional or federal law is involved.

Federal courts deal with both civil and criminal cases involving the U.S. government, federal laws, and the Constitution. The federal courts include district courts, courts of appeal, and the U.S. Supreme Court. Federal courts can review cases between groups or individuals involving a civil or criminal matter from more than one state.

The first courts to hear the majority of cases involving federal law violations are the U.S. district courts. There are general jurisdiction courts mostly represented by the district courts throughout the United States, with at least one district court per state and the District of Columbia. Federal district courts are the trial courts on the federal level. An appeal of a district court matter is made to the next general jurisdiction court, the U.S. Court of Appeals. A proceeding at a court of appeals often operates as a reviewing body, like state courts of appeal. Should the litigants not be satisfied with the appeals court's decision, the case might be heard by the U.S. Supreme Court, the highest court in the United States. The Supreme Court does not have to hear an appeal after proceedings at a U.S. court of appeals.

There are also federal courts that are considered subject matter courts. Examples are the U.S. bankruptcy courts and the U.S. tax courts. The U.S. Court of Appeals also hears other cases, such as those from the subject matter courts—for example, a case concerning taxes.

Planning and Interior Design Elements

All courts have design guidelines and elements peculiar to the level and type of court. Federal courts have the most stringent design guidelines; thus, this discussion will focus briefly on design guidelines for federal courthouses. Courtroom design will also vary with the court. This section will discuss key design guidelines for planning and specification of a generic federal district courtroom.

It is not uncommon for a federal building project to take seven years to reach completion.[7] Becoming involved in a federal project is a huge responsibility in time and accountability, and the decision should not be made lightly. The design for a courthouse and its interior spaces follows the process used for any type of commercial interior. There are several critical requirements for a federal courthouse project that impact the design process and final design solutions.

During programming, the design committee, consisting of court employees and a GSA architect, will use *a Facilities Assessment Survey* as part of the long-range planning assessment for the facility. In addition, the GSA's Courthouse Management Group (CMG), which is responsible for the management of federal courthouse projects, will review materials developed during the programming phase. Once all the preliminary programming documentation is prepared in the GSA-prescribed manner, funding requests are sent to the U.S. Congress, which must authorize the project and appropriate the funding. The de-

---

[7]Security and Facilities Committee, 1997, p. 2–17.

sign phase begins once the funding has been appropriated. Final selection of the project architect and the design team is made by the GSA and court personnel after funding has been appropriated.[8]

The architecture of federal courthouses must reflect stability, integrity, and justice while contributing to the architecture of the region or community. An orderly appearance must be evident in the design of the building and the interiors. The materials used throughout must be durable, natural, and regional in origin and must give a sense of permanence. Even so, the design of a federal facility must follow the strict guidelines in the *Facilities Standards for the Public Buildings Service*.

The design architect must provide a plan to the courts which addresses projected 30-year needs of that particular structure/courthouse. Value engineering is utilized to determine the value received for the money spent over the lifetime of a building. The construction cost per square foot is considered, as well as the life-cycle cost. The courts also consider the fact that the construction costs for a new courthouse are usually higher than those of the typical federal office building due to the specific needs of a courthouse, such as overall security and security of courtrooms and judges' secure chambers.[9]

Security planning is a paramount concern to the GSA and must be thoroughly addressed by the design team. Security issues include not only the interior but the exterior as well. Traffic flow within the courthouse is complicated by the need to keep various groups of people coming to a courthouse separated. Other concerns are secure parking and security checkpoints at public access entrances. It is easy for the reader to understand that security concerns have added considerably to the cost of new courthouse building construction following the terrorist attacks of September 11, 2001.

Courthouses are considered to be Business Occupancies in the International Building Code since they are civic buildings. A courthouse will contain offices, cafeteria/food service spaces, and assembly spaces, as well as smaller spaces for holding prisoners. Courtrooms are considered Assembly Occupancies, and the layout of these very functional spaces is tightly controlled and must meet code requirements. This mixture of occupancies creates an interesting challenge for the architect and interior designer, who must be sure that the plans and specifications meet local code requirements, as well as those of the federal government.

Designing Courthouses

Although this section will focus on the interior design of courtrooms, a short discussion on key issues in courthouse design is provided as background. There are many specific concerns in the design of courthouses and courtrooms, including the following:

- Separate circulation patterns for the public, attorneys, judges, court personnel, and prisoners
- Barrier-free access
- Overall security
- Special attention to acoustic and lighting levels
- Balancing information technology and audiovisual systems design with the need for highly aesthetic spaces

Certain spaces are common to most courthouses, including the entryways, lobbies, public corridors and elevators, clerks' offices, judicial chambers, courtrooms, and private/judicial corridors and elevators. Other common areas include the cafeteria, service areas, central court libraries, secure prisoner-holding areas, and secure parking areas. A courthouse will also have spaces where attorneys may meet with their clients and rooms for jury assembly and deliberation. This discussion focuses on a typical U.S. district courthouse.

There are many critical planning guidelines for the design of a courthouse. One of the most important concerns circulation patterns. Three separate circulation systems are required: (1) public circulation, which requires a single entry through a security desk;

---

[8]Security and Facilities Committee, 1997, p. 2–6.
[9]Security and Facilities Committee, 1997, p. 2–9.

(2) restricted circulation with controlled entry for judges, court personnel, and official visitors; and (3) secure circulation for prisoners controlled by the USMS.[10]

The public must enter the courthouse through a security screening point located at the main entrance. Some of the courthouse employees and attorneys will also enter through the main entrance. Public access is generally limited to the lobby and some spaces on the main floor, as well as the public elevators and corridors outside courtrooms. Jury assembly room(s)—where prospective jurors meet before being escorted to the courtrooms before being *empaneled* to serve on a jury—must be located on the main public entry level and must have a controlled entry. The cafeteria is considered a heavy-traffic area and must be located close to the main public entry. It is less common for a courtroom to be located on the ground floor. Most courtrooms are located on mid-level floors in the courthouse.

Judges have a controlled entry that is separate from the public entry. This is most often from a secured parking garage in the basement and a private elevator. Private corridors are provided for judges and other court staff. Judicial chambers are frequently located on upper floors away from courtrooms. Depending on the design of the building, the judges' chambers can be located close to a specific courtroom or within a grouping of judges' chambers. The clerks' must have easy access to the courtrooms, the judges' chambers, and the public circulation. The central court libraries are important to all the legal staff, including judges, and a restricted staff corridor is required to access them.

Prisoners are brought through another secure entry in the basement or rear of the building, and another elevator is used to escort them to holding rooms and then the courtrooms. The USMS is responsible for all security in federal courthouses. The USMS office and central cell block have a public counter and controlled access to the office. The central cell block, located within the USMS area, requires secure access using a vehicular sally port for the prisoners through a secure parking area. Prisoners will be placed in holding cells in the lower level before they are escorted to holding cells located next to the trial courtrooms by the USMS.[11]

Good signage is very important in the courthouse. It is designed to keep human traffic where it is supposed to be while allowing members of the public to find their way easily. People will need to move easily from the entrance lobby to places like the juror assembly rooms, public elevators to courtrooms, or the offices of clerks and other courthouse personnel that they may need to see.

The U.S. district court conducts both criminal and civil trials. The courtroom is the focus of this type of courthouse and this discussion. Attorney and witness rooms next to or near courtrooms will be accessed from the public corridors. Jury deliberation rooms, prisoner holding spaces, and staff spaces are generally planned adjacent to or near the courtrooms. If the judges' chambers are on a different floor, small judicial robing rooms may also need to be planned near the courtrooms. The grand jury rooms are usually located near the office of the U.S. Attorney. All grand jurors enter through a restricted corridor. The public will access other offices within the courthouse through these public corridors. The other types of federal courts will have different space requirements. However, these circulation corridors are typical.

The design of federal court buildings and interiors must meet ADA accessibility requirements and the Uniform Federal Accessibility Standards (UFAS). When courtrooms within a courthouse are planned, the ADA requires that the area be adaptable, that is, easily convertible to meet accessibility needs.

There are several key elements to the accessibility requirements for a courthouse and courtrooms. Ramps and lifts are needed to accommodate those in wheelchairs. Wheelchair accommodation must be provided where seating is included, such as in the courtroom, cafeteria, lobby, and waiting areas in corridors. Videotext displays and braille alternatives can be incorporated into signage. These are just a few of the necessary accessibility accommodations.

Today, courthouse security has become a major design issue. It should be part of the earliest planning and research for the eventual design team. Security design solutions should

---

[10]Phillips and Griebel, 2003, p. 78–79.
[11]Security and Facilities Committee, 1997, p. 14–7.

TABLE 9-6 Courthouse and Courtroom Security Issues

- Separate entrances and traffic corridors are needed with appropriate security screening devices.
- Security cameras should be placed in appropriate locations for continual screening by the USMS.
- Most seats in courtrooms are bolted to the floor rather than movable.
- Spectators may need to be screened again when entering specific courtrooms.
- Windows in judges' chambers are not to be exposed to the street level.
- Landscaping and outdoor furniture may be used to keep certain vehicles away from the building.
- Emergency lighting on battery backup power should be provided for courtrooms, courtroom holding cells, judicial chambers, controlled circulation areas, and prisoner-attorney interview rooms.

be comprehensive but unobtrusive if possible. Although most of these issues will be the architect's responsibility, the interior designer should be aware of them. There are specific guidelines for meeting security design requirements that must be incorporated into the overall design. The *U.S. Courts Design Guide* clarifies many of these requirements. Some of the security planning issues that must be considered are listed in Table 9-6.

Acoustical control in a courthouse is mandatory due to the need for privacy and confidentiality. Speech intelligibility and privacy are the two critical design factors concerning acoustics within a courthouse. It is critical for speech to be intelligible to all parties within a courtroom but not outside the courtroom. This is one of the reasons that a buffer sound lock vestibule is placed between the public corridors outside courtrooms and the courtrooms themselves. Privacy is also a major concern in attorneys' facilities, judges' chambers, and jury spaces. These spaces must be designed to ensure complete acoustical privacy.

Designing the courthouse to accommodate constantly upgraded computer technology and other electronic devices is another critical issue. Court reporting equipment and court computer services and other electronic presentation equipment has significantly changed courthouse and courtroom design. All courtrooms and offices are supplied with desktop computers. Electronic evidence display equipment in the courtroom creates new challenges for the architect and interior designer. Satellite video broadcasts will provide educational programs and administrative information to the courts. In planning these systems, regular electrical service and computer networks require a separately zoned space with a dedicated ground and an uninterrupted power supply.

To reduce the cost of lighting systems, the GSA encourages the specification of standardized rather than custom lighting fixtures. The GSA also promotes the use of efficient, compact fluorescent lamps which provide various light levels. The *U.S. Courts Design Guide* also encourages the use of indirect fluorescent fixtures or wall washers to highlight architectural features.

The interior designer must be aware of the many goals and regulations of the GSA in regard to finishes. The GSA requests that finishes for the interior of federal courthouses be practical and reflect the importance and dignity of the judicial system. They also must be appropriate for the space and the design concept, be durable, and require little care. Finally, they must be within the budget. A limited palette of finishes that meets code, functional, durability, and cost requirements is preferred by the federal government for courthouse projects. Higher-grade and aesthetically interesting materials are common in the lower-level public areas as well as the courtroom facilities, where custom millwork is common. Detailed information to help the designer specify interior finishes and materials is found in the *Facilities Standards for the Public Buildings Service*.

Designing Courtrooms

The exact nature and type of the court will impact the configuration of areas within the courtroom and the placement of FF&E. Because of space limitations, this discussion focuses on a generic trial courtroom that might be designed for a federal district court.

Our generic courtroom will be a column-free space so that everyone, but especially the judge and marshals, can view the entire space. A district court's standard courtroom

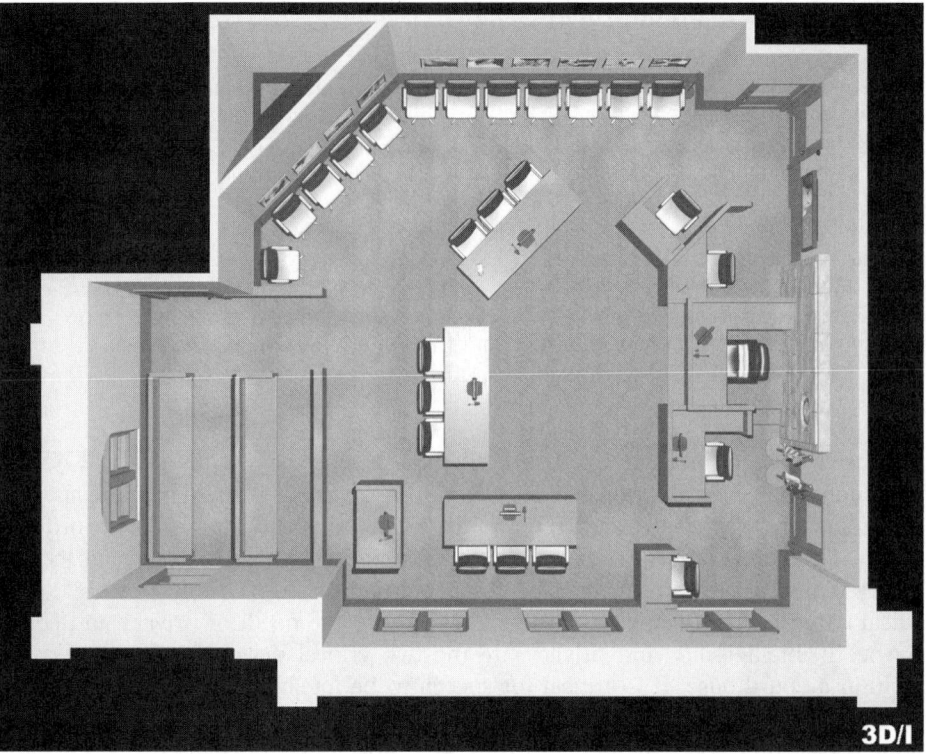

Figure 9-9 Aerial view of a county courthouse courtroom. (Computer rendering courtesy of 3D/International.)

includes a judge's bench, witness stand, law clerk, courtroom deputy clerk, and court reporter/recorder at the front of the courtroom. Generally flanking these areas is the jury box and space for an interpreter. Counsel tables for the two sides face the judge's bench. The area containing the participants to the proceeding is commonly called the *well*. Figure 9-9 is an aerial view of a typical courtroom.

Public seating for spectators is behind the counsel tables and the railing sometimes called the *bar*. Space for witnesses is generally provided in small rooms between the courtroom and the public corridor by the rear or public entry to the courtroom. A sound lock vestibule prevents noise penetration between the corridor and the courtroom.

An *en banc* courtroom for an appeals court will have a slightly different arrangement. Since appeal cases are heard by more than one judge, the bench will be wider to accommodate the appropriate number of judges hearing the case. It might, in some cases, include a semicircular bench for 9 to 11 judges. It is curved or angled so that all the judges can see each other.

There are several key design elements for the judge's bench. In our generic trial courtroom, the judge's bench is usually elevated three or four steps above the courtroom floor and placed either in the center of the room or in a corner of the room. Space must be provided for a computer without obstructing the judge's view of the courtroom. The bench should have a raised cap around the periphery to hide the computer and other paperwork on the bench's worksurface. Storage for office supplies and books should also be provided at the bench. The judge's chair will usually have a high back and enclosed arms like a large executive office chair. Footstools can be provided as well. The judge should be able to alert the USMS Control and Command Center with an alarm button placed at his bench. Judges' benches are now lined with ballistic materials[12] (Figure 9-10).

The courtroom's deputy clerk station must be adjacent to the bench, or nearly so, since the judge and the deputy clerk must be able to communicate with each other dur-

---

[12]Security and Facilities Committee, 1997, p. 4–48.

Figure 9-10 Interior of a county courthouse courtroom as depicted in Figure 9-9. Note the raised cap at the judge's bench. (Photograph courtesy of 3D/International.)

ing the proceedings. The deputy clerk must also be able to see all persons involved in the process within the courtroom. This work area must be designed so that it is also raised above the main floor but below the level of the judge's bench. Often a second staff member will be seated there. A computer should be placed at the station in such a way that it does not block the view of the court. The top of the worksurface requires a 4-inch rail around the periphery to help contain papers. A swivel desk chair should be provided. Space is also required to hold files, evidence exhibits, and a court recording machine. The station is provided with an alarm system connected to the USMC Control and Command Center.

The witness box presents an interesting design challenge. Depending on the court, it is located next to the bench—often seemingly attached to one side of the bench. Some courtrooms are designed with the witness box directly across from the jury box. The witness box will usually be designed to house one witness and possibly an interpreter. It should be raised approximately 12 inches above the court's floor level. Witnesses, as well as the court, must be able to see and be seen. A deep fixed shelf along the top front of the witness box must be included to allow witnesses to examine exhibits used as evidence. The witness box chair is usually fixed to the floor. However, since the witness box must be accessible, a fixed chair should be easily removable by court personnel for someone in a wheelchair. Sometimes a wheelchair lift or ramp is used. Interpreters at the witness box must be seated beside or slightly behind the witness. The interpreter's chair is not a permanent fixture in the witness box.[13]

The jury box is positioned at right angles to the bench in most courtroom designs. If the bench is in a corner, the jury box will be located to one side of the bench, across from the witness box, which will be on the other side of the bench. During a trial, the jurors are required to hear, see, and be seen by the court. The jurors should be able to see the attorneys', clients', and witnesses' full faces, so the placement of the jury box is very important. Jurors should be separated from the attorneys' space to prevent them from hearing conversations between attorneys and clients. At least 6 feet of space from the jury box to the spectator area should be provided.

[13]Security and Facilities Committee, 1997, p. 4–50.

Figure 9-11 Courthouse hearing room where jurors convene. Note the utilitarian approach to this space. (Photograph courtesy of 3D/International.)

Seating in the jury box is usually in two rows. The higher tier of the jury box must be 6 inches lower than the judge's bench. Generally, the front row of the jury box is raised 6 inches or one step and the second row is 12 inches above floor level.[14] The jury box usually has a modesty panel in front. Each juror is supplied with a comfortable, fixed-base, swivel/rocking armchair. The term *jury-based chairs* comes from the design of the base used to secure the chairs in the jury box. Juror chairs should be 33 inches apart and side by side, with 42 inches between back-to-back positioning of the chairs.[15] Figure 9-11 is an example of a hearing room.

In a district court and in most generic trial courts, there will be work areas for a law clerk and the court reporter. The law clerk's station is positioned so that the clerk and judge can see each other and converse. It is also raised, but below the bench. The front of the station has a raised rail like the deputy clerk's station. Movable swivel chairs are provided for each position. The storage area should house files, office supplies, and a phone connected to the USMS Command and Control Center.

The court reporter produces the transcript of the trial proceedings. Thus, he or she must be able to hear every comment, as well as be able to see the facial expressions of witnesses, attorneys, and the judge. The court reporter needs to be located near the witness box. The station should be provided with a small desktop for paperwork and open space to accommodate mobile stenographic equipment. This station needs to be somewhat mobile.

The positions of counsel tables for the defense and prosecution in a criminal matter, for example, are not predetermined within the court well even though they are usually placed within a certain area of the courtroom, generally facing the judge's bench. This placement is dependent upon the type of court. For example, in trial courts, the counsel tables will be placed with a walkway between them. This is done so that the attorneys can confer with clients and each other without being overheard.

The counsel table is generally just that—a table fixed to the floor. There are usually two to three movable swivel chairs at each counsel table. With permission from the judge, the attorney may use a portable computer at the counsel table. In some courtrooms, computers are provided as part of the equipment.

An additional item that may be specified, depending on the type of court, is a movable lectern. Some court proceedings require the attorneys to stand at a lectern and not approach the witnesses. In an appeals case, attorneys must stand at a lectern provided with a clock to time their presentation. The lectern should have task lighting and a microphone.

There is one more functional area in the well. Space must exist for the display of evidence. Visual displays are important in presenting evidence and other information pertinent to the case.[16] One suggestion is a wall-mounted screen or other surface which can be used for writing or projection. It must be easily viewed by the court and the spectators. Litigants often use slide projectors, movie projectors, video monitors, recorders, and computers with PowerPoint capability. The interior designer should consult with the court to determine the type of equipment used and should investigate future equipment needs.

Dividing the courtroom well from the spectators is a spectator rail or a paneled divider often thought of as the bar. The rail must have a handicap wide gate for admittance

---

[14]Thacker, 2005, p. 1.

[15]Security and Facilities Committee, 1997, p. 4–52.

[16]Security and Facilities Committee, 1997, p. 4–56.

into the well area. Benches or fixed seating are provided in the spectator area. Spacing between rows of benches is determined by code. Wheelchair space and assisted listening devices are required by accessibility guidelines such as the ADA guidelines.

One of the many kinds of special courtrooms is for juvenile cases and other cases involving children. Figures 9-12a and 9-12b show courtroom facilities specifically designed for children.

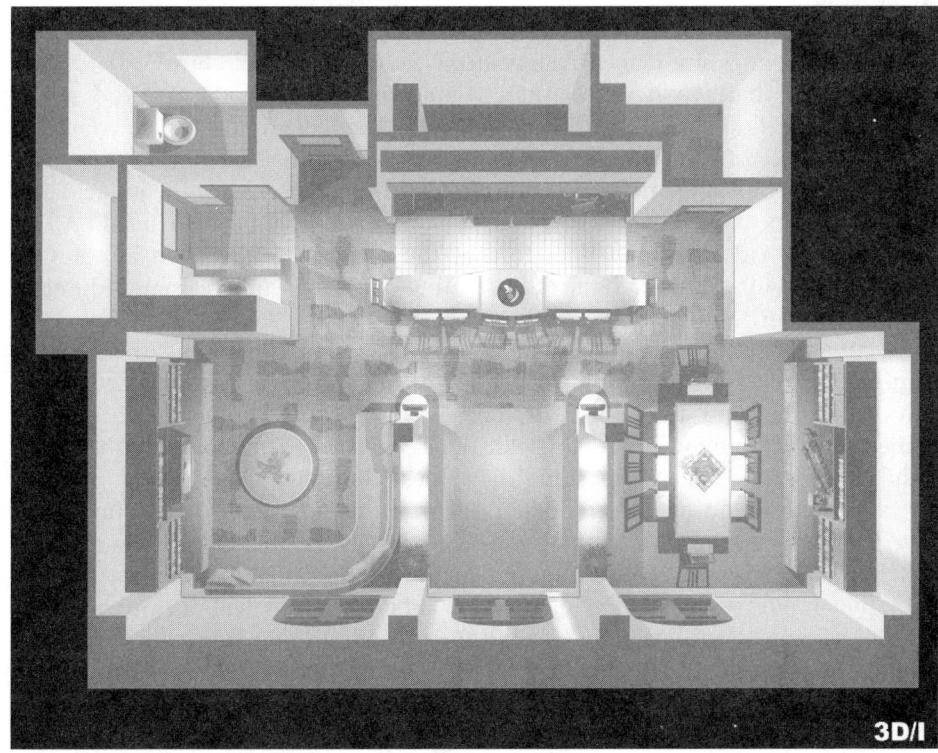

Figure 9-12a Aerial view depicting a specialty area designed for a children's court. (Computer rendering courtesy of 3D/International.)

Figure 9-12b Photograph of the completed project shown in Figure 9-12(a). Note the lower scale of the furniture provided for this children's court facility. (Photograph courtesy of 3D/International.)

Finishes for a courtroom should emphasize the dignity of the court and be in keeping with the overall design of the building. "Issues of real consequence to people should not be handled in a shabby space."[17] The GSA has specific requirements and guidelines for finishes in federal courthouses and courtrooms. Wall finishes need to be durable and require little care. Good light reflectance and acoustic control are also important. The preferred floor covering is a high-quality, dense carpet with static control such as nylon carpet. Carpet padding under the commercial-grade carpet will help absorb sound. When specifying carpet and padding, realize that carts may be used within the well.

All the custom millwork items in a courtroom, such as the judge's bench, jury and witness boxes, and railings must meet American Woodworking Institute (AWI) requirements. Premium-grade hardwood veneer materials and solid hardwoods are the design standard for millwork, doors, trims, and wall paneling. The federal government standard does not permit the use of exotic or nonsustainable wood materials.[18]

There are very few movable furniture items in a courtroom. Seating for the judge, court staff, and attorneys most often consists of chairs on casters rather than fixed. All of these items should provide reasonable comfort, as the participants are often in court all day. Fabrics selected for fixed and movable seating must be stain-resistant, durable, commercial-grade materials that will resist wear.

In the design and specification of millwork and furniture for courtrooms, the designer must remember that all participants in the court process must be able to see and hear each other. With this fact in mind, the interior designer has to consider the height of furniture and the dimensions of the worksurfaces. Clear, open views of all participants should be provided and not impeded by a desk railing that blocks the view.

In new construction and major remodeling, courtrooms are placed in the middle of the building, eliminating windows. If there are windows within the space, they must be clerestory windows to provide security from outside intrusion. The building must be carefully sited by the architect so that surveillance from other buildings will not provide a visual or security advantage to outsiders. Ground floor windows and courtroom windows above ground level must be designed with ballistic-resistant materials. If a courtroom has an exterior window, the designer will need to provide for room-darkening coverings when media presentations are made.

The ceilings in courtrooms are higher than those in most rooms, creating a challenge for lighting design. The lighting in a courtroom must achieve the recommended lighting levels and allow for possible video recording, evidence display, and use of personal computers. Lighting designs focus higher quantities and qualities of lighting on the bench, on the front of the courtroom, and for highlighting the U.S. flag and the well area. This requires adjustable lighting solutions. There should be a difference in lighting levels between the court well and the spectator area, with more versatile lighting capabilities focusing on the well.

The general lighting level in a courtroom should range from about 40 to 75 footcandles,[19] and lights must be dimmable when needed. Many courtrooms combine incandescent and fluorescent lighting fixtures. Soffits, coves, recesses, and reveals can be used to house HVAC, lighting, and sound systems, which aids in incorporating the equipment into the overall design. In large courtrooms, pendent fixtures might also be used. The use of suspended acoustical tiles or gypsum wallboard finishes is suggested, depending upon the building's design. Courtroom lighting must provide emergency lighting capabilities in case of a power outage.[20] Interestingly, the judge's bench must not have an emergency light which might highlight his or her position when the lights are dimmed.

Interior designers have a resource from the federal government: the *U.S. Courts Design Guide* (4th ed.), a publication prepared for and by judges, architects, engineers, designers, and court administrators to assist in the planning of federal court construction projects. The *Guide* focuses on court facilities including space planning, security, acoustics, mechanical and electrical systems, and necessary automation.

---

[17]Phillips, Griebel, 2003, p. 110.
[18]Thacker, 2005, p. 1
[19]Security and Facilities Committee, 1997, p. 4–64.
[20]Security and Facilities Committee, p. 4–65.

Libraries

Libraries collect, preserve, and make available for use a wide variety of information and materials. The word *library* evolved from the Latin word *liber,* which means "book." The term *library* is accepted to mean a collection of books as well as the building that houses them. A library is also a repository for microfilm, CDs and DVDs, manuscripts, audiovisual materials, videotapes, films, maps, and even artifacts. Patrons can also use computers for research, attend educational seminars, and view art displays, to mention only a few activities. Libraries now are basically multimedia resource centers as well as depositories for books.

For a child, visiting and borrowing books from a community library for the first time is a thrilling experience. Although the majority of elementary schools have their own libraries, their collections are usually smaller than those in public libraries. Library visits become more frequent as children grow older. Preparing book reports not only helps teach children to read, but introduces them to the wonders of the enormous amount of information that a library contains. Secondary school students find library resources useful in making career choices and deciding what college or postsecondary training to take, as well as pursuing research projects for secondary school. Despite the age of the user, the need to use the resources of a library never seems to end.

Whether the library is a tiny community library in a rural area or as large and extensive as the Library of Congress, it helps people shape their lives through information. Library design contributes to this enhancement of knowledge, and it is an interesting and rewarding specialty area of institutional interior design.

Historical Overview

Records from ancient civilizations indicate that as early as 5000 B.C., Sumerians were using clay tablets as a method of record keeping. Other ancient civilizations, such as those of the Babylonians and Assyrians, also maintained records in tablets. The Egyptians developed papyrus around 500 B.C., allowing the use of scrolls to record historical records using their writing form of hieroglyphics. The library at Alexandria in Egypt had the largest collection of scrolls in the ancient world until the structure and all of its contents were burned. The ancient Greeks had libraries housed in some temples. The ancient Romans encouraged the building of libraries and allowed more public access to the materials. Most ancient libraries had very restricted use.

Much of the ancient world wrote on leather—for example, the Dead Sea Scrolls in the Middle East. Parchment, made from thin layers of animal skins, promoted the development of books because the size of parchment could not compete with the length of papyrus scrolls. By 400 A.D., parchment had replaced the more fragile papyrus. The Chinese invented paper in 1 A.D. and were known for their extensive libraries. By 1500 in Europe, paper had replaced parchment.

During the Middle Ages, books were created and preserved in the monasteries and made available to certain persons. A *scriptorium* was a place for copying books, mainly of religious content, within a monastic community. Due to the value and rarity of books, many of the collections were chained to shelves for security purposes. With the Renaissance came a broader emphasis on reading, writing, and learning. At this time, not only were books collected by monasteries, universities, and monarchs, but merchants had private libraries as well. In 1571, the collection of Lorenzo de Medici was opened as a public library; simultaneously, the Vatican developed its extensive library, which still exists. France developed a national library as early as 1367 A.D., and London opened its first public library in 1425.[21]

Johann Gutenburg's invention of movable type in 1450 helped create the need for libraries, since it was now easier to produce printed works rather than handwritten manuscripts. The increase in the number of books helped to eliminate the need to secure books to shelves, allowing them to be taken to early reading rooms. Books were stored on shelves by the 1600s—the precursor of the stack system for book storage in libraries that remains

---

[21]*World Book Encyclopedia,* vol. 12, 2003, pp. 258–59.

the standard today. Libraries continued to grow in size and stature over the following centuries as education increased in importance, and the public took advantage of the information contained in university, national, and religious libraries.

Early libraries in the United States were private, housed in the residences of scholars, ministers, and wealthy merchants. Early circulating libraries were privately owned and operated for a profit. The first public library in the United States was founded in Boston in 1653, and Harvard University has had a library since 1638.[22] In 1731, Benjamin Franklin developed a subscription library which allowed citizens to use it if they paid prescribed dues to become members. By the end of the 1700s, the public need for the circulation of books was being met through book lending clubs.

The Library of Congress in Washington, D.C., was established in 1800 by Congress. Thomas Jefferson's private library was purchased by Congress after the War of 1812 to replace the materials burned by the British in that war. The Library of Congress is considered the greatest research library in the United States. Around 1850, libraries open to the public were being organized. In 1876, the Dewey Decimal Classification system and the first library school were founded. Later in the 19th century and into the early 20th, the industrialist Andrew Carnegie donated millions of dollars for the construction of community libraries, many of them still in use today.

Libraries in the United States were designed predominantly with a traditional or classic theme up to the 1940s. Veterans of World War II were given the opportunity to attend college under the GI Bill of Rights. This large influx of students caused new libraries (and colleges) to be constructed throughout the country starting in the 1950s. New construction methods allowed for larger interior open spaces, providing enhanced comfort and flexibility to the library environment. Library architecture and interior design, as well as library services, continue to change as technology provides new methods of storing and making materials available. The library has expanded to include not only books in print but also microfilm, videos, computer facilities, the Internet, and periodicals of all sorts. One of the early uses of the Internet was for scientists and scholars to exchange information and make library resources available to remote locations.

Overview of Library Facilities

Like any commercial interior project, a library has an administrative structure and a group of decision makers who will be involved. A library may be owned and administered by a private entity such as a religious group or by local, state, and federal authorities, which construct and control public libraries.

There are library collections in many kinds of facilities. The federal government maintains libraries in many agency office buildings. Law libraries are indispensable to legal offices. State historical archives provide invaluable research material on the state and on local areas. The Vatican Library is indispensable to religious scholars. Museums make their library collections available to students and scholars. Interior design students find their resource libraries necessary to complete projects. Universities have extensive libraries of current and archival materials (Table 9-7).

Modern libraries provide other archival functions and offer many other services for users. Libraries archive historical documents donated by individuals or groups, providing researchers with opportunities to examine original documents, manuscripts, and rare photographs of their community. Many libraries have audiobooks on tape and braille books to assist the blind. Libraries also sponsor exhibits of historical artifacts or the works of local artists and craftsmen. Educational opportunities such as lectures, seminars, and community programs are available, generally free of charge to community members.

The reader's community library is one example of a public library. A public library in most U.S. cities and towns is administered by a library board and a head librarian. Several librarians, secretarial staff, and volunteers are responsible to the head librarian and the board. The most distinguished federal library is the Library of Congress in Washington,

---

[22]Packard and Korab, 1995, p. 382.

D.C. First established as a library for Congress in 1800, it was rebuilt after the War of 1812 and is the largest library collection in the United States. Copies of all published books and copyright registered materials are stored and cataloged at the Library of Congress.

A library in an elementary or secondary school operates with a head librarian, assistants, and perhaps adult as well as student volunteers. The head librarian reports directly to the school principal and indirectly to the superintendent of schools and the local board of education. The board of education is an elected body, so that the board changes on a regular basis. This often creates an interesting challenge concerning decision-making authority during many school library projects.

A special collections or archival library has a head curator, much like a museum. The curator administers, researches, makes presentations, and monitors the collection, as well as determining the direction it will take. Assistants, secretarial staff, and volunteers report to the curator. The assistant is often the primary contact for members of the public using the special collections.

The administrative structure of college and university libraries is complex and varying, dependent upon the type of educational facility. Student workers and secretarial staff are commonly the first contact with a student patron. Librarians and assistant librarians report to the university librarian or head librarian and work in such areas as multimedia, reference, cataloging, periodicals, documents, information systems, materials acquisition, serials and binding, special collections, computer services, and instructional laboratories. Sometimes the university's head librarian is on the same administrative level as a college dean who reports to a provost or academic vice-president. Universities and colleges also have outside governing boards. These are state-appointed or elected boards of regents as well as boards of trustees specifically assigned to one university. There are also specialized libraries on many campuses, as well as in some college buildings within the university—for example, a library specifically organized for interior design and architecture students.

All types of libraries have a chain of decision making and planning in the design of an addition, major remodeling, or renovation. The process usually begins with the head librarian making a request to the city manager for a public library in a small city, to the principal for an elementary or secondary school library, or to the provost for a university or college library. It is not unusual for the client to form a design committee to work with the architect and interior designer. In larger facilities, a representative from the facilities department will also commonly be involved. Smaller duties such as paint specifications ares less likely to go through an extensive chain of command and may be handled directly by the head librarian or those appointed to the project.

Types of Library Facilities

The various types of libraries differ essentially in the ownership and focus of the collection. Ownership of a library collection will influence who is able to use the library. For

TABLE 9-7 Library Vocabulary

- **Carnegie libraries:** Facilities funded by the Carnegie Foundation, founded in 1911, to aid community libraries and schools.
- **Carrel tables:** Small enclosures, usually freestanding, for individual study.
- **Catalog systems:** Methods used to catalog all the materials in a library into categories to make it easier for a patron to find needed materials. The two systems used are the Dewey Decimal system and the Library of Congress system.
- **Closed stacks:** Materials available only by request from the library staff. They must be used within the library or the closed stacks reading room.
- **Interlibrary loan:** A user's request for a book from another library.
- **Open stacks:** Materials open to the public to freely access and use.
- **Special collections:** Documents with historical or archival value that require special care to protect them from damage. Most materials in special collections are in closed stacks.
- **Stacks:** The open shelves containing the library materials.

TABLE 9-8 Types of Specialty Libraries

- **Archival libraries:** Facilities whose collections focus on documents of historical value. The National Archives in Washington, D.C., is the best-known archival library.
- **Private libraries:** Facilities owned by individuals and businesses.
- **Research libraries:** Libraries containing new and old materials of unusual subject

or worth. For example, the Folger Shakespeare Library in Washington, D.C., focuses on the Elizabethan period.

- **Special libraries:** Facilities that focus on a certain subject matter. They can be privately owned or supported by a government or a university. An example is the Daughters of the American Revolution (DAR) genealogical facility in Washington, D.C.

example, a library owned by a city or town is open to the residents but might not allow nonresidents to check out materials. The law library in a private law firm will be restricted to employees of the firm. Interior design firms rarely allow outside designers to use the resources of the firm's library. The collection of materials also defines libraries today. Table 9-8 lists many of the types of library facilities not discussed in this section.

National libraries are owned by the federal government. The most familiar example is the Library of Congress, which is open to public use on a limited basis. In addition, there is the National Library of Medicine, the National Archives, and the National Agricultural Library.

Public libraries are owned by communities and exist for the benefit of their residents. This facility may be a small public facility with a few thousand books or a large city library with millions of items in its collection. Small public libraries often emphasize children's books since some elementary schools have only small libraries, if any. A public library often provides multimedia services, educational programs, or community use of

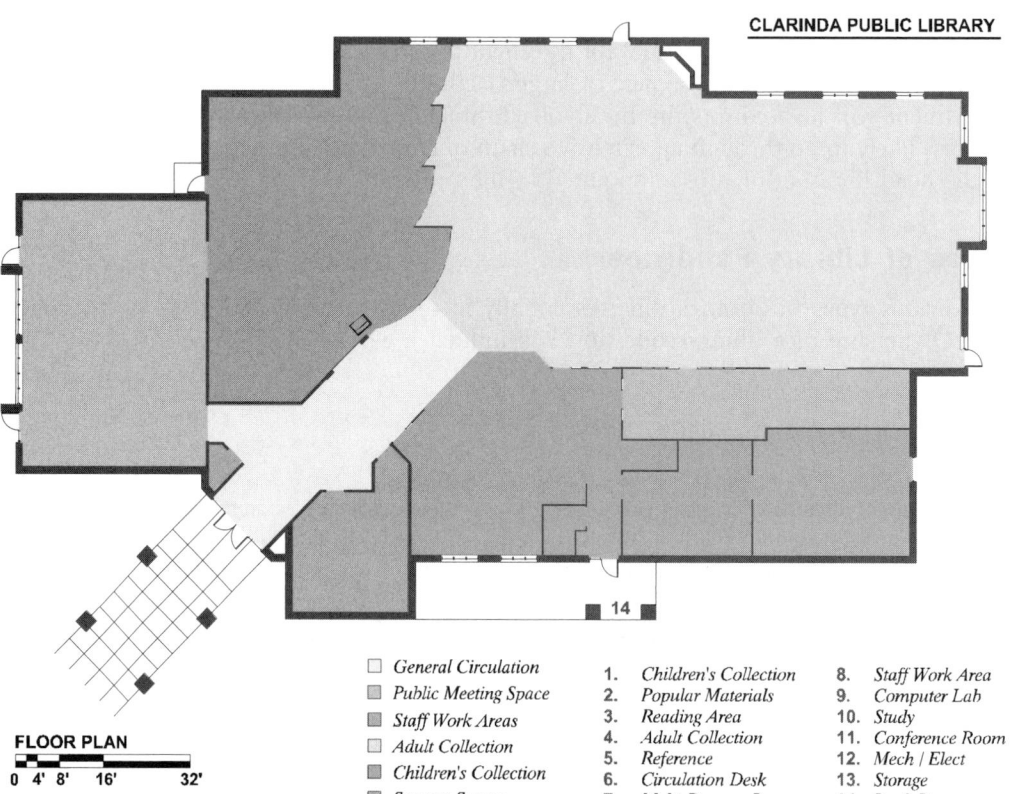

CLARINDA PUBLIC LIBRARY

FLOOR PLAN
0 4' 8'   16'   32'

- ☐ General Circulation
- ▨ Public Meeting Space
- ▨ Staff Work Areas
- ☐ Adult Collection
- ▨ Children's Collection
- ▨ Support Spaces

1. Children's Collection
2. Popular Materials
3. Reading Area
4. Adult Collection
5. Reference
6. Circulation Desk
7. Multi-Purpose Room

8. Staff Work Area
9. Computer Lab
10. Study
11. Conference Room
12. Mech / Elect
13. Storage
14. Book Drop

Figure 9-13a Floor plan of the Lied Public Library designed for use in a small town. (Plan courtesy of FEH Asociates, architects.)

assembly spaces. The New York Public Library is a prime example of a public library on a grand scale (Figures 9-13a, 9-13b, and 9-14).

The *school library* is the third type of library. Today, a school library might be called a *library media center, learning resource center,* or *instructional materials center.* Elementary and secondary schools have libraries for the use of students. Their collections are generally not very large and generally smaller than those of many city libraries. A school library provides a convenient place for students to research material for class assignments, use computers to do research on the Internet, and have a quiet place to study.

Academic or *university libraries* are the fourth type of library. University library collections expanded and new services were instituted after World War II. Undergraduate, graduate, and specialized libraries grew to meet the needs of specific colleges. Library users are primarily students and faculty, but the public can also be granted certain library privileges. Academic libraries provide many services to users including media centers, copy centers, and computer areas for research and Internet use. Harvard University houses the world's largest university library system. Most academic libraries have extensive collections of books, magazines, government documents, and other materials. The majority of university libraries also have a special collections section where items of historical significance to the university and the surrounding community can be preserved and studied safely (Figure 9-15).

The first goal of any library is to assemble a collection that meets the needs of the patrons. Some people go to

Figure 9-13b Interior view of the Lied Public Library shown in Figure 9-13a. Note the application of lighting in this high eye use facility. (Photograph courtesy of FEH Associates, Architects.)

Figure 9-14 A children's library in an elementary school requires furnishings on a smaller scale than the average library. (Architect: Dekker, Perich, Albuquerque, NM. Photograph copyright © Kirk Gittings.)

Figure 9-15 Exterior view of the main entrance to a university library designed by Edward Larabee Barnes. (Photograph copyright © Utah State University Photography Services.)

libraries simply to get away from home for a few hours, to read newspapers and periodicals, or to find a quiet environment in which to study. Libraries also must have as a goal the creation of a pleasant, comfortable atmosphere that allows patrons' needs to be met. The interior designer, the architect, and the rest of the design team should help the library accomplish that goal.

Planning and Interior Design Elements

The planning and design elements are similar for all library projects, yet extensive in content. Space limitations prevent a detailed discussion of each type of library facility. The remainder of this section focuses on the main floor of a generic public library. Offices, back work areas, public restrooms, and meeting rooms will not be discussed.

Due to the increased use of library services, many facilities have pursued renovation, expansion, adaptive use, or new construction. The interior designer will work with the head librarian, the primary library staff, and possibly the library board in the design or redesign of a public library. Generally, a representative from the city government will also be involved, probably from the city planning or engineer's office. The interior designer will be part of a design team led by an architect and will likely include one or more specialty consultants, depending upon the scope of the project.

Aside from funding, the library client will be concerned with space planning to ensure that the layout of the functional areas is efficient and easy for the patron to use. The design team, with the approval of the head librarian, will provide specifications for furniture items, architectural finishes such as flooring, and other required items. Specifications for acoustics, lighting design, and mechanical systems are critical to ensure an interior climate that will protect the collection.

The public is also considered the client. Perhaps a member of the public will be on the design committee. If not, the public using the library will eventually judge its quality based on ease of use of the facility, the presence of comfortable chairs and tables, accessibility, and user-friendly computer access. The public will also judge the library based on the texts, references, and periodicals that the library staff makes available.

Let us begin our review with space planning considerations. Libraries are divided into distinct function areas, the most common one being the book stacks. Patrons enter a lobby area and approach the checkout, book returns, and information desk. Beyond this point is the main library space where the user will find book stacks, current periodicals, special reference materials, and media materials. Adjacent to this main area might be the children's library, special collections if available, computer rooms, browsing areas, conference rooms, restrooms and adult reading rooms. There are also spaces for the library staff including offices, cataloging space, workrooms, possibly a boardroom or staff lunchroom, and storage and custodial space.

A library patron might go to a bank of computer terminals to research the location of a particular book or other material. The computer has made card catalogs—specially designed 3 by 5 inch cards—extinct in most libraries. These computers are often placed near the checkout or information desk. Some of them may only contain the collection catalog, while others may allow a patron to use the computer for Internet searches. This is where other devices for microforms, microfilm, and microfiche are housed. These devices use special films on which newspapers, magazines, catalogs, and dozens of other types of documents are retained.

Once the book's (for simplicity) identification number has been found, the patron moves to the stacks (Figure 9-16). The aisles between the rows of stacks, called *range aisles,* are 36 to 44 inches wide, depending on the specific application of the building and/or accessibility codes for the facility. Large aisles between book stacks or aisles that allow for various other combinations of library storage equipment might also be needed.

There is an important functional difference between open and closed stacks. If a patron can personally enter the book stacks to retrieve the book of his or her choice, the stacks are known as *open stacks*. If the patron must request a book (or other material) from a library staff member, the stacks are known as *closed stacks*. A closed stack does not mean that patrons may not use the materials, but that only staff members have actual access to them. Closed stacks are common in archival areas of many libraries and where a special collection is housed. A closed stack area is most often located in a separate space

Figure 9-16 Book stacks in a library require continuous and sufficient lighting. (Photograph copyright © Utah State University Photography Services.)

Figure 9-17 University library circulation desk. The curve is repeated on the floor, desk, and ceiling. (Photograph courtesy of RIM Design. Chris Arend © Photography.)

in the library. These areas also require special mechanical systems planning due to the delicate nature of the materials.

Bookshelves for the stacks are open shelves with a nominal depth of 8 to 12 inches on one side.[23] These bookshelves, as well as many cabinets to hold documents and to store specialized collections like videotapes or records, are selected from manufacturers that specialize in library equipment. The names of many of these vendors are listed in source guides published by the interior design trade magazines as well as in the Web sites provided by the vendors. The location and planning of the stacks and other materials storage must be done very carefully since the weight of the book stacks is significant. If an interior designer is planning a library floor, he or she must consult with an architect or structural engineer concerning floor loads.

Books and other materials are checked out at the entry desk. Generally, users will exit through some sort of security device to ensure that books and other materials are not leaving the library without having been properly recorded and checked out. Figure 9-17 shows a typical circulation desk where books and other literature are checked out.

Typical furniture specification in libraries involves library tables with small, easy-to-move chairs and carrel tables and chairs. Library tables can be specified for four or eight patrons. A depth of 42 to 48 inches allows study space at each position with a table height of 29 to 30 inches. Tables are usually wood frames and tops or wood frames with laminate tops. Light to medium-colored surfaces for tabletops help prevent eyestrain, which occurs when there is too much contrast between dark surfaces and light surfaces such as paper.

Carrel tables have become prevalent as more and more patrons use libraries for study and research. A carrel is also a convenient place to work with a personal laptop computer. A study carrel is double-faced and surrounded on threesides by partial panels to provide privacy. The standard floor footprint of a double-faced carrel is 35 inches wide by 48 inches deep plus space for the chairs. It is important that the designer specify light-colored surfaces for carrels, as the light can easily be blocked by the high side panels and the overhead shelf. Small tables or carrels with reduced-height backs and sides are often specified for media equipment such as microfiche viewers and computer terminals.

Seating at study tables and carrels usually consists of small armless chairs made of wood, with unupholstered seats and backs. This type of chair is selected because of its ease of maintenance, resistance to abuse, historic style, and sometimes low cost. Ergonomically designed chairs would be ideal should the budget allow. The basic library chair has a seat height of 16 to 18 inches and a seat depth of 20 to 22 inches. Figure 9-18 shows a style of chair typically used with carrels.

Another area in a library is a reading room or reading area. These spaces are often designed with comfortable, fully upholstered chairs and comfortable commercial-grade fabric or leather. The chairs can be placed in either a sociofugal or sociopetal arrangement. Sociopetal placement might have four big upholstered chairs placed in a circle facing a

---

[23]McGowan, 2004, p. 392.

Figure 9-18 Carrel at the left. Note the curved rockers on chairs and the repeated curve on the carrels, study table, and chair backs. (Photograph courtesy of RIM Design. Chris Arend © Photography.)

central low table with magazines or periodicals. Though the arrangement of the chairs encourages interaction, the table creates a slight psychological barrier. The sociofugal arrangement might have the large reading chairs in a back-to-back configuration with possibly a sofa table between them. Fabrics can be specified as solid colors, patterns, or textures as long as they are commercial-grade materials that can take the heavy use and abuse expected in libraries (Figure 9-19).

Unique and appropriate custom millwork for the checkout and information desk and other areas can be created by the interior designer. Functional needs are paramount, and the designs must be approved by the client and the library staff to ensure that these needs are met. Smooth countertop material for ease of writing, light surfaces to reduce eye fatigue, and sufficient work space for the librarians are all important. The checkout desk in particular should have a lowered counter section to meet accessibility guidelines. The reference and information desks must also be accessible.

Materials specifications for a library involve mainly architectural finishes and furniture or millwork items. A wide range of color schemes can be specified that enhance the overall design and meet the needs of the library decision makers. Depending upon the function of the space, lighter values or muted tones are commonly used to reduce eyestrain and eye fatigue and to increase light reflectance. Computer stations often require darker surfaces to reduce contrast between the monitor and the surrounding surfaces. Walls can be painted or covered with a textured commercial-grade wallcovering. Textured wallcoverings are used to help reduce noise within the facility and to add interest. Floors are usually covered with a high-density, low-pile, tightly tufted carpet installed using the glue-down method. This aids patrons in wheelchairs and allows mobility for book carts. Carpets are usually tweeds or small patterns to hide traffic paths and soil and to reduce problems for people with limited vision.

It is important to make the children's section of the library a pleasant, user-friendly space. Child-sized tables and chairs are necessary, along with a few adult-size tables and chairs. The larger tables are provided so that parents and preteen children will have

Figure 9-19 Reading area in a library with comfortable upholstered chairs grouped around a fireplace. (Interior design by Globus Design Associates. Susan L. Quick, ASID, project designer.)

furniture that is comfortable for their body size. Book stacks should be lower since it would be unsafe for a child to try to reach books on shelves over 4 feet high without assistance. If the library is in a large city, a separate information desk is often placed in the children's library. Murals and bright colors help create an enjoyable atmosphere, encouraging children to come back to the library (Figure 9-20). Libraries also are providing specific areas for teenage patrons, including computer stations and meeting rooms (Figure 9-21).

Good lighting design is critical. Book stacks eliminate much of the daylight from windows and block direct ceiling lights. It is not always easy to achieve the lighting levels recommended by the Illuminating Engineering Society, which suggests 30 foot-candles/FTC in the stacks and 70 foot-candles/FTC in most other areas. In the book stacks, light fixtures can be mounted as indirect sources at the top of the stack or positioned between the stacks. Task lights are often provided on the study tables and carrels in older libraries or those with very high ceilings, since these areas are difficult to light with ceiling fixtures. Light values of colors increase light reflection and reduce eye fatigue. High contrast in colors and finishes should be avoided, as the movement of the eye from light to dark surfaces causes eyestrain.

The design of computer workstations throughout the library is also important. Ergonomically designed computer workstations at the checkout and information desks for the staff are necessary in a library since comfort and healthy work areas are important for library employees. Employee work areas behind the scenes in offices should be specified with ergonomic seating and workstations as well. Ideally, ergonomically designed computer areas or rooms for patron use should also be specified to accommodate a variety of body sizes and capabilities, including accessible workstations. Adult, child, and teenage computer stations should be in separate areas, with the furniture scaled to the appropriate age. Figure 9-22 shows children's computer stations in a library. Note the small scale of the furnishings.

Artwork is often used to enhance the facility. Sometimes the artwork is on loan from local artists. Artwork accessories are most likely to be used in the reading rooms. Pieces that

Figure 9-20 Creative and inviting entry to a children's library. Note the smaller scale of the openings and furnishings. Bright colors and fantasy invite the children into the space. (Photograph courtesy and property of Creative Arts Unlimited, Inc.)

Figure 9-21 A teen room located in the West St. Petersburg Public Library. Note the individual banquettes and computer spaces. (Photograph courtesy and property of Creative Arts Unlimited, Inc.)

Figure 9-22 Computer stations in a children's library using smaller-scale furnishings. (Photograph courtesy and property of Creative Arts Unlimited, Inc.)

represent the city or geographic area are popular subjects. A library will often have an art loan program in which framed prints can be checked out to patrons for a period of time.

Codes related to libraries can be extensive, requiring research and study by the designer. The International Building Code classifies libraries (as a general class) as A-3 Assembly, and the Life Safety Code also classifies libraries as assembly occupancies. Decisions about exits, aisles, corridors, finishes, and so on should comply with these codes.

In addition to the standard accessibility guidelines for an assembly occupancy, libraries must meet other ADA guidelines. These apply to all the areas that the public may use. If fixed seating is used at study tables, at least 5 percent of these units must be accessible and clearances between fixed accessible tables must adhere to the dimension guidelines in Section 4.3 of the ADA. Checkout desks must have a lowered counter or another acceptable provision for an individual in a wheelchair. Security gates must also allow sufficient clearance for a wheelchair. The space between stacks and any cabinets must be at least 36 inches, and 42 inches is preferable. The designer should research the appropriate guidelines and codes to ensure that the library design meets all applicable state and local regulations.

The cost of replacing stolen library materials is quite high. Thus, a major security issue is the prevention of loss due to theft. Security devices at the building's exits exist in almost all libraries today. These devices work with electronic security identification tags placed on library materials. More intense scrutiny of patrons and even employees entering many facilities—notably government-owned libraries such as the Library of Congress—involves metal detectors and hand screening similar to that used at an airport. Security issues must be discussed with library staff during programming so that the appropriate measures are incorporated into the space plans and specifications of the facility.

The design of a library facility involves recognizing the needs and desires of a large group of stakeholders. Each stakeholder group often has a slightly different set of needs. Thus, a library is an interesting design challenge for commercial interior designers. The emphasis in library design will always be on the collection of materials available to the public, with the building and interiors providing a background, creating an inviting and harmonious space for public use. Whether the project is a small public library or a new academic library, the designer must research the administrative structure, the type of facility, and all of its needs to ensure that a professional solution is provided.

Educational Facilities

Teaching and learning can take place in many environments. It is always easy to recognize our school system as our primary educational facilities. As adults, we also teach and learn in other environments—corporate training rooms, hotel conference centers, outpatient training at a rehabilitation center, association seminars at trade conferences, and countless other settings. Children also find educational opportunities outside the classroom, such as at bookstores where readings are given and attending museum programs with their parents. In many cases, the teaching and learning environments of these alternate locations have been discussed in other chapters of this book. This chapter will focus on facilities that offer structured, publicly funded educational programs at elementary and secondary schools and at colleges or universities.

The student and the teacher represent the core of education and the success of the process. The teacher must provide methods and guidance to help each student comprehend information until recognition and learning take place. It is the school district's or other governing body's responsibility to provide an environment that encourages and assists the learning process within a budget acceptable to the taxpayers or others who fund the facility. Creating that environment is the role of the interior designer and other designers who specialize in educational facilities.

This section focuses on the elementary school, although some comments concerning design elements specific to the secondary school are included. University, college, and specialized postsecondary school facilities are not discussed in depth.

Historical Overview

Learning and formal education are used to promote the survival and prosperity of society. Education started as storytelling since few had the ability to read and write. In fact, as we saw in the section on libraries, there were not many opportunities to write and few who had the chance to learn these skills until the early modern era. Learning grew throughout recorded history and gradually formalized and expanded, becoming a lifelong process.

Education in ancient cultures had many focuses. In ancient Egypt, the priests controlled education and promoted homogeneity within the culture. Children studied reading and writing from age five until their teen years, when they were guided into a more targeted form of training. In ancient Israel, the mother taught the young child and the father directed his son's study of religious, social, and moral laws. Early Greek education centered on democracy, civil life, and cultural activities. Roman mothers and fathers were the educators of the child until the age of 16. The Romans adopted Hellenistic methods of education such as oratory, the Greek language, and the musical arts. When the Roman Empire became Christian, classical education in the liberal arts expanded.

Education continued to change during the Middle Ages. At this time the church took over much of the responsibility for education, and studies had a definite religious emphasis. Generally, only the clergy and the nobility were formally educated. Renaissance and Reformation education emphasized the importance of the individual and centered on the classics and new ideas. Universities were founded in the 17th century, which helped lead the way to the formal training of teachers and the further expansion of secular knowledge.

The first schools in the New England colonies were founded in Boston in 1635. The first secondary school in America was Boston Latin, and the first university in America was Harvard, which was founded in 1636. Most formal education was for the wealthy in the early years of the United States and did not become available for the other social classes until the 18th century. Strict discipline in many one-room schoolhouses was the educational philosophy in the 18th and early 19th centuries. In this schoolhouse, one teacher was responsible for teaching all the elementary grades. Secondary school was uncommon except for the wealthy until the late 19th century, when compulsory public education for all students began.

Schools in the United States went through many changes in the 20th century, not the least of these being the construction of separate facilities for elementary and secondary classes, as well as individual classrooms for each grade and even each subject matter. In the early 1900s, the middle school was separated to provide vocational and secondary education for students who would not study beyond ninth grade. Today, the middle school provides a transition from the elementary school to the more compartmentalized high school.

One-room schoolhouses existed in many rural communities until shortly after World War II. As the country gradually changed from an agricultural to an industrial society, education became increasingly important for all classes and at all levels. Universities developed in part due to the increase in population and affluence, advanced technology, and the desire for better jobs. The Morrill/Land Grant Act of 1862 provided for the development of state universities in many states.[24] The intensive expansion of technology to meet the needs of World War II production and leadership heightened the need for better education and facilities. Higher education exploded after World War II as the GI Bill of Rights gave veterans the opportunity to attend the college of their choice.

For centuries, children were educated at home in the ways of the world and to the extent that their parents had any formal education. Lessons in reading, writing, and mathematics were reserved for the ruling classes. As this very brief overview indicates, gradually parents came to appreciate the value of formal education. Educational opportunity should be and is a privilege and a right of all students.

Overview of Educational Facilities

Formal education is based on a standard curriculum. Basic formal education today includes those subjects considered necessary to function in society. The majority of states require that students under 16 receive an education that meets certain minimal requirements. Some parents elect to home school their children; however, most children receive their basic education in public or privately funded formal schools. A few terms that will clarify our discussion are presented in Table 9-9.

The administrative network of educational facilities is very important for the interior designer to understand. As with many commercial interior design projects, the client is a group of stakeholders. That group starts with the superintendent or the principal and faculty at the facility. Other stakeholders are the administration of the facility, the students and other users, and the public. The public's interest is based to some degree on the spending of tax dollars, as well as on concern for the quality of the education, and the safety and comfort of the students.

The type of school determines its administrative structure. Primary and secondary public schools are usually governed by a board of education and a superintendent of schools. Members of the board are elected. The changing composition of the board can and does affect the profile of the school over time. The superintendent of schools is hired by the board of education to oversee all the educational programs and employees of a school district. Below the superintendent of schools and board of education, each school in the district will have a principal, vice-principals, teachers, specialists, support staff, and professional staff such as librarians, a nurse, and a psychologist.

Privately funded schools have a similar administrative structure. A governing board or board of directors serves the same basic function as the board of education and superintendent of schools. Below them are a principal or headmaster or headmistress along with assistants, teachers, support staff, and professional staff. If the school is funded or supported by a specific outside group, such as a religious denomination, its administration

---

[24]*World Book Encyclopedia*, Vol. 6, 2003, p. 103.

TABLE 9-9 Educational Facility Vocabulary

- **Chancellor:** A title given to the head of a university. The chancellor (or president) may be responsible for one school or several schools.
- **K-6-3-3:** An educational plan calling for one year of kindergarten, six years of elementary school, three years of junior high school, and three years of high school. This division may vary with the school system.
- **Multipurpose rooms:** Classrooms or activity spaces that can accommodate more than one kind of educational or social experience.
- **Parochial school:** A school owned by a religious denomination.
- **Provost:** The title given to the faculty member who has overall responsibility for academic programs at a university or college. The provost reports directly to the president or chancellor, and the deans of the colleges report to the provost.

and policies will also be under the scrutiny and judgment of the advisers or representatives of that group.

Universities and four-year colleges have a more complex administrative structure. Generally, there is a state board of regents at the top. These boards often have responsibility for a group of colleges and universities within a state. Depending on state law, the board of regents must report to the state legislature, which appropriates and determines the apportioning of funding for the various universities and colleges. There may also be a division within the state government or a support group of the board of regents that handles facilities management, influencing the design and construction of the schools.

A university may have its own board of trustees or an executive council consisting of the university president or chancellor, provost, several vice-presidents, and the deans of the colleges. The president is the head of the university, the provost is second in command, and the deans are the heads of academic college programs needing instructional space, as the reader is no doubt aware. Each college has a dean, several department chairs or heads, a faculty, and support staff. There are also staff departments for campus planning and facilities management, physical plant managers and staff, and staff for maintenance, dormitories and student services, food services, and purchasing, to mention a few. All of these stakeholders may be involved in the design of new facilities because they are responsible either for the budget or for the management of the facility.

Now let us take a brief look at how design projects might be administered, starting with elementary and secondary schools. Priorities, needs, and concerns in the design of a publicly funded elementary or secondary school include a multitude of issues. A major concern is the cost of the structure. The board of education and the superintendent confer on methods to finance the project, which usually involves a bond issue on which the citizens will vote in an election. With a new school building, the board of education, the superintendent, and usually the principal of the building are involved directly in the planning process. Always of critical importance is to determine the need for sufficient space for all the required educational activities, as well as those projected for the future.

As was discussed earlier, there are other stakeholders who will also voice needs and concerns. Important to the users will be the ability of the structure to offer quality education to the students and provide the appropriate functionality. Once these basic concerns and needs are identified and a funding strategy is developed, a request for proposal (RFP) is issued, presentations by several architects are made to a selection committee, and a contract for the work is then awarded.

Many other issues are raised in planning a new elementary or secondary school. The educational philosophy of the school will impact the space plan and perhaps the design elements as well. A school that practices team teaching may use more multipurpose spaces for classrooms than a school with one teacher per classroom. The use of computers in all grades and the design of computer classrooms are paramount design issues. The interior designer also must understand how the environment, through lighting and color, can affect learning. Education journals have published reports on lighting, color, surface materials, acoustics, climate control, and seating as they impact student learning and behavior.

Projects for public colleges, universities, and community colleges, as well as private universities and professional schools, will be similar to those described above. No project actually begins until approval for funding is obtained from the institution's administration or governing body. Because of the complex administrative structure of the university or college, it is important that the architect and interior designer, whether hired directly by the facility or by the architectural firm contracted by the university, be aware of the chain of command and the identity of the ultimate decision makers.

Almost all schools, regardless of the type of student or school, have facilities departments that oversee construction and renovation projects. It is important for architects and designers to work well with the facilities managers and to develop rapport. Smaller remodeling projects might be funded by a college or department through a dean's office but still need to be approved by the facility's planning office. When approval occurs, all but the smallest projects must go through an RFP process before design work begins. The actual construction and purchase of goods will involve competitive bidding for the majority of projects.

Types of Educational Facilities

Education and learning take place in a variety of locations. The most typical educational facilities are elementary school, secondary school, and undergraduate and graduate advanced education in colleges and universities. In addition, there are preschools and nursery schools for young children, boarding schools, and special schools, such as those for the blind.

Formal education begins for most children in elementary school. Middle school generally includes grades 6 to 8 in the United States. Education in middle schools links the educational experiences of elementary and secondary school (or high school). Elementary schools provide children of ages 5 to 10 or 11 with the basics of a formal education and begin the learning process. The earliest forms of education focus on mathematics, reading, and writing. Today's elementary education includes many other subjects as well. Figure 9-23 shows a decorative corridor in an elementary school.

The high school years provide greater freedom for students in the choice of subjects. For example, various learning tracks are provided, such as college preparatory courses or courses geared to vocational education. After graduation from high school, teens may elect to attend an academic college or university, a community college, or some other form of formal education such as a technical or trade school. Figure 9-24 shows a large classroom in a technical school. Industrial, technical, and trade/vocational schools provide specialized training in a variety of areas. Advanced education in such areas as law, medicine, dentistry, and veterinary science is another familiar setting.

Publicly funded elementary and secondary schools receive all or most of their operating and building funds from local school districts through taxes. Most community colleges receive funding from local taxes, and most universities and four-year colleges are funded by state legislatures. Private schools are

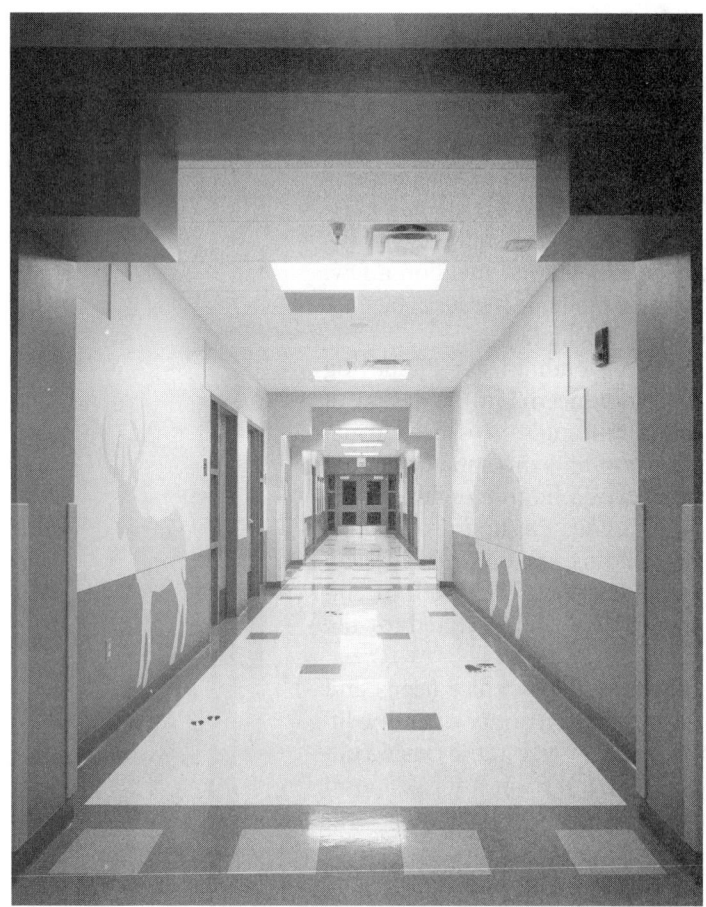

Figure 9-23 Corridor in an elementary school. Design elements such as the wall graphics, step arch, and floor tiles aid in visually reducing the length of the corridor. (Architect: Dekker/Perich, Albuquerque, NM. Photograph copyright © Kirk Gittings.)

Figure 9-24 Unique classroom design specific to a particular subject matter showing the auto bay at the New England Institute of Technology. (Photograph courtesy of Sharon Oleksiak, ASID, WG Ltd. Interiors; Robert Stillings, architect; Ahlborg and Sons, contractor.)

funded by endowments, donations, and supervising bodies such as religious denominations, as well as annually through tuition and fees. Some private trade or professional schools are for profit, and may obtain initial funding like any other business and continued funding through tuition and fees.

Important in the educational process is the need to provide for social, cultural, and athletic activities as well as classrooms and laboratories. Figure 9-25 is an example of a

Figure 9-25 Student lounge and food service area. Note the use of the automobile as sculpture in this space. (Photograph courtesy of Sharon Oleksiak, ASID, WG Ltd. Interiors; Dennis Leonard Builders, Inc., contractors.)

Figure 9-26 Champ Hall reception room. The traditional elements are used to enhance the atmosphere of longevity and stability, features that aid in recruiting students. (Architects: Architectural Design West, Scott Theobald, AIA, principal. (Photograph © Utah State University Photo Services.)

student lounge. A campus will have classroom buildings, offices for the administration and the faculty, a cafeteria, gymnasium, auditorium, library, and vocational education classrooms. Depending on the type of school and the educational focus, other spaces may be provided to meet specific needs.

Open classrooms, closed classrooms, programmed instruction, individualized instruction, and distance learning involving television and the Internet are just some of the ways students are educated. Educators continue to explore all methods of instruction to improve the learning process.

Colleges and universities have had to meet many challenges. Many have become more market-minded, with some of the recruiting emphasis placed on the appearance of the campus (Figure 9-26). Funding from state legislatures or private benefactors varies with the changing economy, causing colleges and universities to create new ways to fund and administer education. Budget crunches have forced many universities to look for new funding sources. For example, business schools at major universities have provided residential conference centers on campus for executive seminars. The Wharton School of Business at the University of Pennsylvania is well known for this activity.

A major factor changing traditional education at all levels is the widespread use of computers. Students in all age groups use the computer to learn, to obtain information, and to work better and faster. The computer aids teachers and professors in their academic activities, as well as providing an effective teaching tool in the classroom. Internet use for research and course work is changing the way education is delivered, as well as reshaping the facilities in which education takes place.

Planning and Interior Design Elements

It is not possible to discuss specific planning and design elements for all types of educational facilities. There are many special issues at each level, such as space needs and classroom requirements and environmental specification to suit the school population. An elementary school includes general classrooms, administrative offices and spaces for the faculty, special-purpose classrooms such as a music room, indoor activity spaces such as a gymnasium and cafeteria, and other spaces that might be unique to a particular school. This section focuses on the planning and design elements of the public elementary school general classroom.

Elementary schools typically include a kindergarten and grades 1 to 5 or 6. Floor plans for basic elementary classrooms have changed dramatically from the one-room schoolhouse of the 19th and early 20th centuries, where all grades were taught in the same room. In the 20th century, it was common for a school plan to have one classroom per grade. However, students might have to move from classroom to classroom, depending upon the subject. Depending on state law, a general classroom was designed to accommodate up to 28 students.[25]

Until approximately the 1960s, traditional classrooms were furnished with student desks in rows facing the front of the classroom, where the teacher's desk was placed. Students remained in this one classroom with the same teacher for the full day unless they went to a special class such as art or music. In the 1960s, the open classroom model was developed to meet changes in educational philosophy. Classrooms were built without interior walls, and students were grouped by interest and subject matter. However, this plan was eliminated due to many philosophical and practical problems, and walls returned. Later, large open classrooms were subdivided with movable partitions.

Another plan involved classrooms without windows, in the belief that they help students concentrate on their studies without outside distractions. Still another is classrooms designed to be flexible and adaptable. For example, a classroom might serve as a math classroom in the morning, individual study pods for history in the afternoon, and community studies in the evening.

In today's classrooms, students generally sit at individual desks or tables that can easily be moved or at group tables. General classrooms also need space to accommodate wall displays, appropriate-height shelves, and storage of supplies. Storage space is also needed for children's coats and backpacks or book bags, since elementary schools usually do not have lockers for the lower grades in a hallway. Classrooms must also be designed to accommodate computers. Regardless of grade level, computer learning is very important in today's technology-savvy environment. A few details on computer learning stations are provided later in this section.

Furniture in the elementary school will be specified at a scale to fit the different age groups. Elimination of sharp edges on tables, desks, and cabinets is very important. Chairs should be designed to resist tipping. To resolve some safety issues, many school districts use student chairs and desks that are one unit and can be bolted to the floor. Naturally, this limits the multiple furniture placement concepts, and its use would be based on the school administration's directives. Classroom furniture for the elementary grades generally consists of specialized products available from educational product vendors. Trade magazines, resource books, and Web sites provide information on suppliers of classroom and laboratory furniture.

Color schemes for educational facilities have changed over the past 50 years. Research studies have shown that children are not adversely affected when bright colors are used as accessory items in classrooms. Walls and floors should be specified in light values and neutral colors. Neutral background colors allow flexibility in the choice of colors for the environment. For example, neutral, lighter tones do not compete with artwork and other projects created by the student. A major advantage of light neutral colors is that they create higher light reflectance than medium-value colors, which improves overall lighting.

Ease of maintenance, resistance to abuse, and safety are all factors to consider in specifying materials for the elementary classroom. Finishes on cabinets and desktops must be easy to clean or refinish inexpensively. Semigloss and gloss paints for walls are good choices since they are easy to clean. Textured wallcoverings can be useful for acoustical control, though they may be harder to clean. Window treatments are primarily vertical or

---

[25]McGowan and Kruse, 2004, p. 406.

horizontal blinds in a neutral color, which aids in maintaining focus within the given space. Window treatments are needed when the teacher wishes to show a movie, slides, or other projected visual materials.

Floor treatments must be specified with safety in mind. High-density, low-pile, tightly tufted commercial carpets can be used in classrooms where spillage of ink or other liquids is expected to be minimal. In many classrooms, teachers have requested that the reading area be carpeted, while the desk areas or other activity areas have vinyl flooring. Hard-surface and resilient materials are frequently specified because of their lower cost and ease of maintenance. Safety can be an issue with these materials, since it is easier for children to slip and fall on these types of flooring.

An important influence on classroom design is the computer. Classrooms with computers require special furniture, lighting, and climate control. The elementary classroom will require computer desks that are suitable for students of various age groups who will be using the computers. There is considerable information on the specification of computer furnishings for elementary students. Table 9-10 lists several ways of avoiding computer-related problems.

In planning computer stations in elementary facilities, the designer must consider the specific tasks for the computer, the age of the children, and the size of the class or group using the facility. Generally, a computer work station for children will need a desk surface 29 to 30 inches deep by 45 inches wide. The top should only be 23 inches high. Ideally, ergonomic chairs with castors should be specified and have an adjustable pneumatic seat 15.5 to 20.5 inches high to adjust to the student's needs. The back height should be a minimum of 13 inches from the top of the seat, with a seat pan 18 inches wide by 17 inches deep.

Elementary and secondary schools are considered education occupancies by the building and fire codes. College and university classrooms are considered assembly and business occupancies, depending on the occupant load. A brief discussion of code issues follows.

Since an elementary school also has spaces such as a cafeteria and a gymnasium, it might also be considered a mixed occupancy. Careful review of local code requirements is necessary for appropriate planning, design, and specifications. Code-specified exit and egress design in educational occupancies is vital. Exits and exit access corridors generally require Class A or B and I or II materials. Classrooms may be finished with Class A, B, or C materials. Accessibility guidelines must also be applied to the design of the classrooms and other spaces in an elementary school.

Classrooms such as laboratories, shops, and other areas that may involve hazardous materials will have additional code requirements, regardless of the type of school. Figure 9-27a shows a plan view of science classrooms. The designer must study and understand the purpose of each space and the teaching methods used there in order to meet the planning and specification challenge. Special classrooms such as those for music and art, science laboratories, sports, and vocational education will have other needs that must be addressed. Figure 9-27b shows a science classroom.

TABLE 9-10 Children's Computer Stations: Design Guidelines

Preventing computer-related problems in the elementary classroom involves education and the application of certain principles. These principles include:

- Use ambient and task lighting to avoid glare on the monitor's screen.
- Use an adjustable keyboard to keep hands and wrists in a neutral position.
- Position the computer screen so that the child does not have to tilt the head up.
- Use computer hardware geared to a child's smaller hands.
- Provide the computer station with furniture that is appropriate in scale to the age of the student.
- Position the chair so that the child can sit with the feet on the floor, with the knees no higher than the hip.
- Place the keyboard so that the keys are directly under the fingers.

Source: "Ergonomic Seating for Children." The Back Shop, 2005, pp. 1–3.

In developing the plans and specifications for a new school, the design team should work closely with the school administration to incorporate as many sustainable design criteria defined by the U.S. Green Building Council (USGBC) as possible. (See Chapter 1 for a discussion of sustainable design.) Although it is more difficult to incorporate sustainable design criteria in the renovation of an existing educational facility, the design team should try to specify interior finish materials and furnishings that can follow USGBC recommendations.

Designers who specialize in educational facilities find it to be a challenging area. Whether the design project involves an elementary or secondary school, a university, or

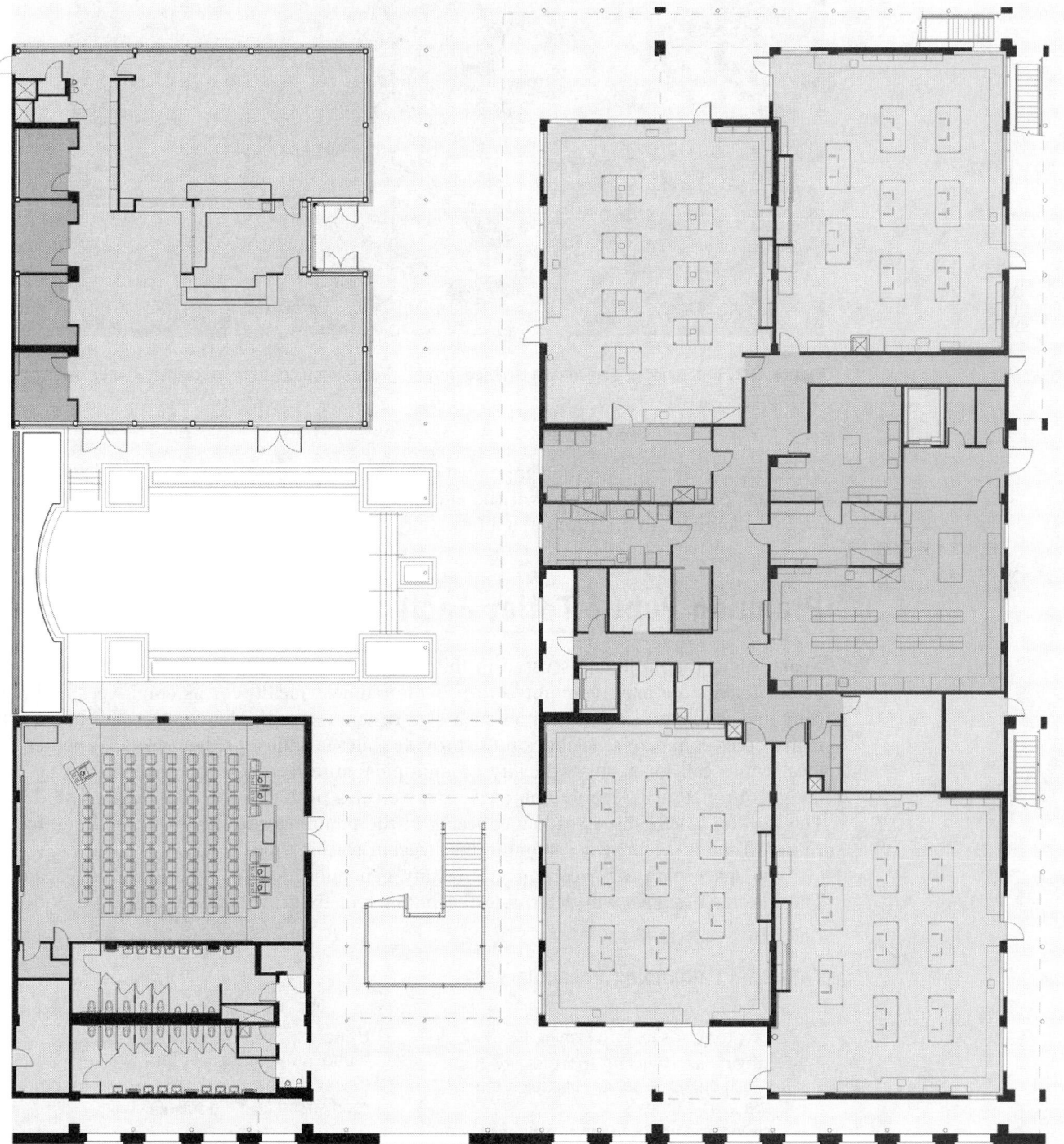

Figure 9-27a Floor plan of the DeAnza Science Center. (Plan courtesy of Anshen + Allen, architects.)

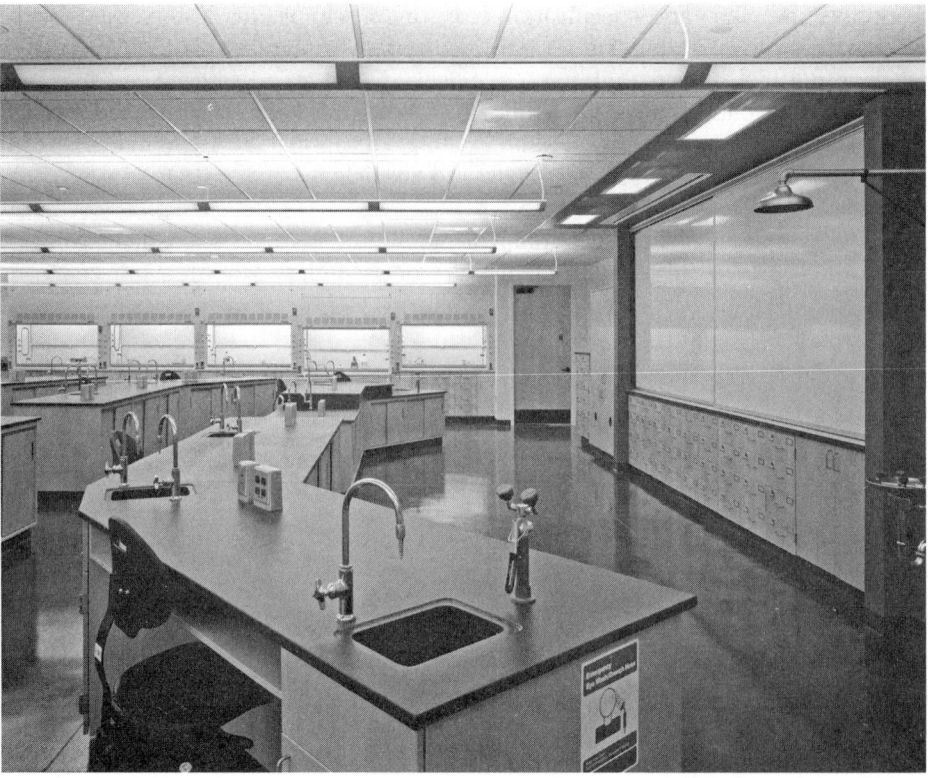

Figure 9-27b Interior of the DeAnza Science Center. (Photograph courtesy of Anshen + Allen, architects. Photographer: David Wakely.)

specialized facility, it requires a great deal of knowledge about the facility's particular needs and functions. Resources listed at the end of this chapter provide additional information on the planning of educational facilities.

Planning Public Toilet Facilities

Nearly all of the projects discussed in this book require public toilet facilities. A small office or retail store may be required to provide a unisex facility for its employees and possibly its customers. Larger facilities such as a restaurant, the public spaces of a hotel, and many other commercial facilities must provide toilet facilities for their users. Whether the local codes call for a unisex facility or multiple-fixture facilities, the space planning and design of toilet facilities in commercial areas creates problems for many design students. This section briefly discusses key concepts in the planning and design of public toilet facilities. Table 9-11 provides some terms relevant to this topic.

The space plan for a commercial facility generally includes required toilet facilities. The interior designer will determine the number of fixtures required, based on code re-

TABLE 9-11 Plumbing Vocabulary

- **Lavatory:** A sink for washing the hands.
- **Single-user toilet:** A toilet facility in which only one person occupies the space at a time.
- **Sink:** The term used for all other sinks, such as service, janitor's, and kitchen sinks.

- **Urinal:** Specialty water closet typically found in a men's toilet facility.
- **Water closet:** A plumbing fixture in restrooms also called a *toilet.*

quirements and occupancy characteristics, and locate the facilities. The designer will also specify architectural surfaces, fixtures, partitions, and other treatments. Plumbing diagrams for commercial interiors are rarely if ever completed by the interior designer. Plumbing locations are generally checked with the architect, who may also have to have the locations approved by a plumbing engineer. The location of toilet facilities must be coordinated with a building core and any wet columns for high-rise buildings.

The number of water closets and lavatories required for any type of commercial interior space is regulated by the building and plumbing codes. The occupancy type and the number of occupants of a space also affect the number of fixtures required. Local building authorities may have requirements that supersede the model codes. Accessibility and building regulations in other countries may be different from those in the United States.

The remainder of this discussion focuses on toilet facility requirements for business occupancies. However, much of this information applies to all types of commercial facilities. It is generally necessary to provide separate facilities for men and women when the occupancy contains both sexes and has more than four employees. However, some jurisdictions will allow a unisex restroom for businesses that have a small number of employees. At least one water closet must be provided for the building or portions of the building. There must be one lavatory for every two water closets. Other requirements for the numbers of fixtures can be found in an appropriate table in the building code or the plumbing code adopted by a jurisdiction.

In a multistory building, each floor must provide toilet facilities. When a floor is divided for two or more occupants, these facilities will probably be provided on each floor. When the office is a leased space as part of a series of office suites in a one-story building, each suite will likely require its own restroom. Some one-story and low-rise office buildings are designed (with prior approval) with toilet facilities in a common area. Remember to provide baby changing stations in both men's and women's toilet facilities.

When a unisex facility is allowed, it must meet accessibility guidelines. A layout similar to that shown in Figure 9-28 is generally appropriate. Some other sizes and arrangements

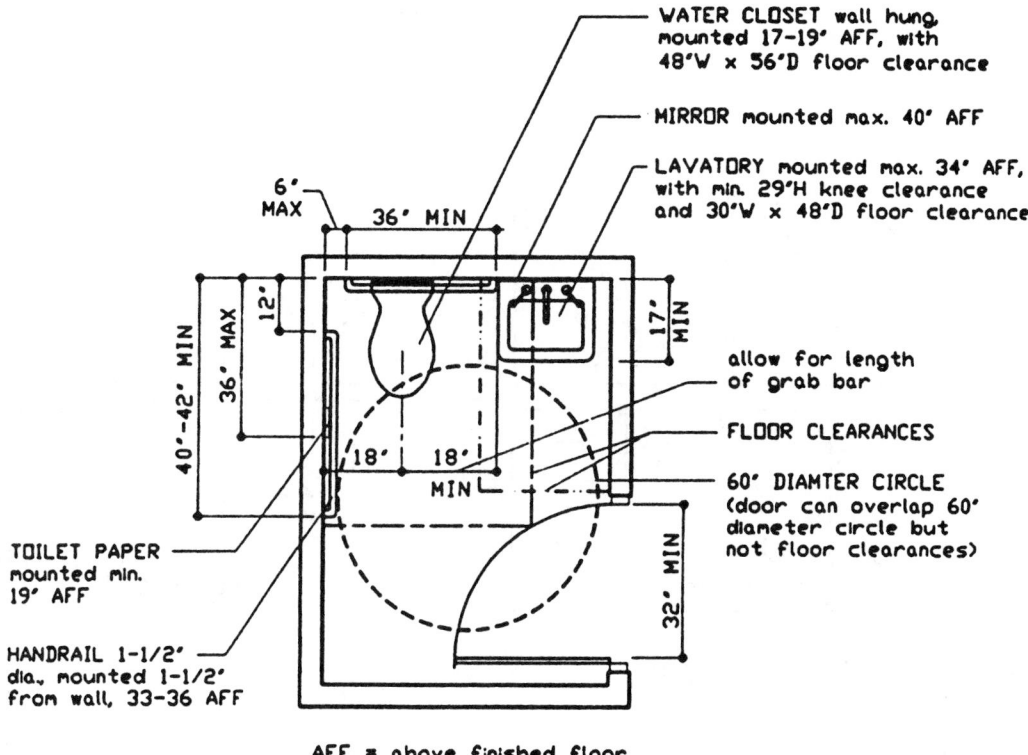

Figure 9-28 Single-user restroom. (From Harmon, *The Codes Guidebook for Interiors,* third edition. Copyright © 2005. Reprinted by permission of John Wiley & Sons, Inc.)

are possible. No partitions to separate the water closet from the lavatory are necessary in a unisex toilet facility. In some cases, a toilet room will be required for both sexes. The layout of fixtures in this case will be similar to that shown in Figure 9-29. In a single-user restroom for men, a urinal need not be provided in addition to a water closet unless local codes require both fixtures. Figure 9-29 shows a typical floor plan for a multifixture facility.

Privacy is important in the location and planning of toilet facilities. With a single-user restroom, the door should not be in a direct line with a corridor or aisle so that someone walking in the corridor can see directly into the facility. When a multifixture facility is called for, it is common to have a set of double doors to enter the space or at least a full-height wall as a screen at the entry. Either of these fixtures provides sufficient privacy for those who have entered the toilet facility.

Most projects use prefabricated partitions between fixtures obtained from specialty vendors. The scope and needs of some projects allow interior designers to custom design the stalls along with the other cabinetry for lavatories. Custom-designed partitions can create an exciting space in an area often considered to be utilitarian. Local code restrictions and the project's budget are limiting factors in the design of custom stall partitions. Specialty vendors also supply paper towel dispensers, built-in trash receptacles, soap dispensers, and other similar items.

Location of mirrors and specification of lighting are other concerns. Mirrors are generally located over the lavatories. If additional mirrors are used, they should not be placed so that someone walking past an open restroom door can see a reflection of those inside. General lighting is provided with ceiling fluorescent fixtures or a combination of spotlights, accent lights on the walls by the mirrors, and ceiling fixtures.

Toilet facilities in public buildings must be easy to maintain and keep sanitary. Moisture resistance and deliberate user damage are key factors in determining the architectural finishes for walls. Vinyl wallcoverings and high-gloss paints are economical and easier to repair. Ceramic tiles and materials such as marble and travertine are the easiest to maintain and the hardest to damage. However, their added expense prevents their use in many facilities.

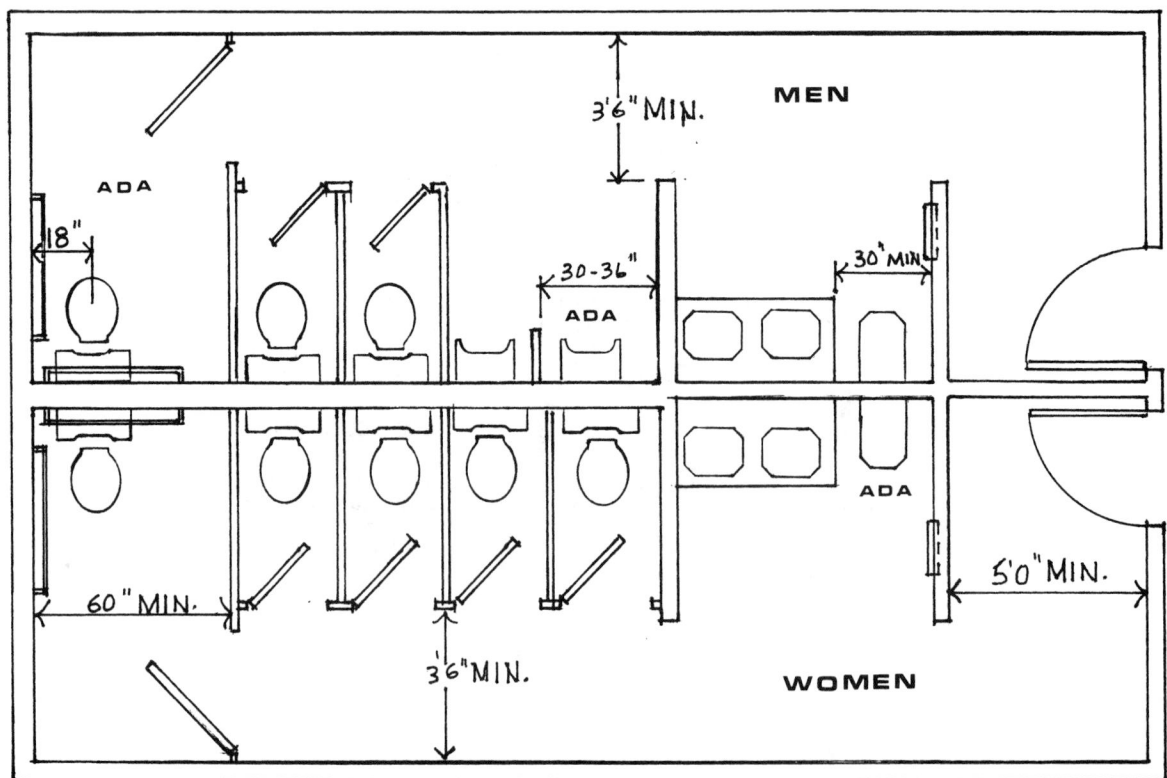

Figure 9-29 A multifixture restroom.

Floors are generally finished in a nonslip ceramic tile, which is easy to clean and lasts a long time. Some small single-user facilities may take a commercial-grade vinyl tile. Carpeting is rarely used where the water closet and sinks are located due to the difficulty of maintenance and potential bacterial growth.

Hotels, large restaurants, department stores, and large corporate office facilities may provide a ladies lounge along with the toilet facility. This is planned so that the patron walks through the lounge before entering the toilet facility. A few chairs or a sofa may be placed in the lounge. Some facilities provide a separate makeup counter with low stools or chairs in the lounge. In this case, a mirror and lighting appropriate for putting on makeup are necessary.

The design of toilet facilities can be made an interesting part of the project or can be a disappointment in the total design. Beautiful lounges and restrooms were the norm in high-rise and specialty business spaces in the early and mid-20th centuries. Unfortunately, many businesses do not allow designers to make the restrooms as interesting in design as the rest of the space. Although function is very important, aesthetic design of the toilet facility can be an interesting challenge to any interior designer.

Summary

Institutional facilities include many specialized commercial interiors. This chapter has discussed some of the key issues in the design of just a few of the many types of institutional commercial interiors. Designers responsible for the interior design of such facilities will be challenged to create interesting spaces that meet the varied needs of the clients and users.

The interior designer must research the institution and its characteristics prior to the initial interview with the potential client. Understanding the client and the client's needs is of paramount importance. The needs and goals of the owners or managers of the project must be combined with the designer's skills in preparing program statements, space planning decisions, and all the necessary design documents. Research on and application of applicable codes, security issues, and environmental considerations are critical to developing a successful institutional project.

This chapter has briefly discussed the key elements in the planning and design of banks, courthouses, libraries, and educational facilities. It has also briefly discussed the planning and design of public restrooms. The references listed below provide more detailed information on the planning of these interiors and assist the designer in gaining a fuller understanding of the functional concerns of institutional facility design.

REFERENCES

Bennett, Corwin. 1977. *Spaces for People.* Englewood Cliffs, NJ: Prentice Hall.

Brubaker, C. William. 1998. *Planning and Designing Schools.* New York: McGraw-Hill.

Clay, Rebecca A. 2005. "Integrating Security and Design." ASID ICON. Spring, pp. 36–41.

Copplestone, Trewin, ed. 1963. *World Architecture.* London: Hamlyn.

Dober, Richard P. 1992. *Campus Design.* New York: Wiley.

"Ergonomic Seating for Children." 2005. The Back Shop. www.thebackshop.co.uk

Fisher, Bobbi. 1995. *Thinking and Learning Together.* Portsmouth, NH: Heinemann.

Fraser, Barry J. and Herbert J. Walberg. 1991. *Educational Environments.* New York: Oxford University Press.

Garner, Bryan A., ed. 2004. *Black's Law Dictionary,* 11th ed. St. Paul, MN: Thomson Group.

Green, Edward E. 1996. "Fitting New Technologies into Traditional Classrooms: Two Case Studies in the Design of Improved Learning Facilities." *Educational-Technology.* July–August.

Harmon, Sharon Koomen and Katherine E. Kennon. 2005. *The Codes Guidebook for Interiors,* 3rd ed. New York: Wiley.

Harrigan, J. E. 1987. *Human Factors Research.* New York: Elsevier Dutton.

Harvey, Tom. 1996. *The Banking Revolution.* Chicago: Irwin Professional.

Jackson, Philip W. 1991. *Life in Classrooms.* New York: Teachers College Press.

Jankowski, Wanda. 1987. *The Best of Lighting Design.* New York: PBC International.

Klein, Judy Graf. 1982. *The Office Book.* New York: Facts on File.

Lake, Sheri. 1997. "Government/Institutional Design Specialty." *ASID Professional Designer.* May/June, pp. 24–.

Lord, Peter and Duncan Templeton. 1986. *The Architecture of Sound.* London: Architectural Press.

Mahnke, Frank H. and Rudolph H. Mahnke. 1987. *Color and Light in Man-Made Environments.* New York: Van Nostrand Reinhold.

McGahey, Richard, Mary Malloy, Katherine Kazanas, and Michael P. Jacobs. 1990. *Financial Services, Financial Centers.* Boulder, CO: Westview Press.

McGowan, Maryrose. 2005. *Specifying Interiors: A Guide to Construction and FF&E for Residential and Commercial Interiors Projects,* 2nd ed. New York: Wiley.

McGowan, Maryrose and Kelsey Kruse. 2004. *Interior Graphic Standards: Student Edition.* New York: Wiley.

Merriam-Webster's Collegiate Dictionary, 10th ed. 1994. Springfield, MA: Merriam-Webster.

Miller, Roger LeRoy and Gaylord A. Jentz. 2006. *Business Law Today,* 7th ed. Mason, OH: Thomson.

Munn, Glenn G., F. L. Garcia, and Charles J. Woelfel. 1991. *The St. James Encyclopedia of Banking and Finance,* 9th ed. Chicago: St. James Press.

Museum of Fine Arts (Houston, TX) and Parnassus Foundation. 1990. *Money Matters: A Critical Look at Bank Architecture.* New York: McGraw-Hill.

New Encyclopedia Britannica, 15th ed. 1981. Chicago: Benton.

Packard, Robert and Balthazar Korab. 1995. *Encyclopedia of American Architecture,* 2nd ed. New York: McGraw-Hill.

Perkins, Bradford. 2001. *Building Type Basics for Elementary and Secondary Schools.* New York: Wiley.

Pevsner, Nicholas. 1976. *A History of Building Types.* Princeton, NJ: Princeton University Press.

Phillips, Todd S. and Michael A. Griebel. 2003. *Building Type Basics for Justice Facilities.* New York: Wiley.

Pile, John. 1990. *Dictionary of 20th Century Design.* New York: Facts on File.

———. 1995. *Interior Design,* 2nd ed. Englewood Cliffs, NJ: Prentice Hall.

Propst, Robert. n.d. *High School: The Process and the Place.* Report. New York: Educational Facilities Laboratories, Inc.

Raschko, B. B. 1982. *Housing Interiors for the Disabled and Elderly.* New York: Van Nostrand Reinhold.

Reznikoff, S. C. 1979. *Specifications for Commercial Interiors.* New York: Watson-Guptill.

———. 1986. *Interior Graphic and Design Standards.* New York: Watson-Guptill.

Security and Facilities Committee of the Judicial Conference of the United States, General Services Administration. 1997. *U.S. Courts Design Guide.* 4th edition. Washington, DC: U.S. Government Printing Office.

Steffy, Gary. 2002. *Architectural Lighting Design.* New York: Wiley.

Thacker, Gerald. 2005. "Federal Courthouse." Whole Building Design Guide. www.wbdg.org

Tillman, Peggy and Barry Tillman. 1991. *Human Factors Essentials: An Ergonomics Guide for Designers, Engineers, Scientists, and Managers.* New York: McGraw-Hill.

Violan, Michael and Shimon-Craig Van Collie. 1992. *Retail Banking Technology.* New York: Wiley.

Wheeler, J. L. 1941. *The American Public Library Building: Planning and Design with Special Reference to Its Administration and Service.* New York: Scribner.

Wilkes, Joseph A., ed. in chief, and Robert T. Packard, associate editor. 1988. *Encyclopedia of Architecture, Design, Engineering, and Construction,* Vols. 1–5. New York: Wiley.

World Book Encyclopedia. 2003. Vols. 2, 4, 6, and 12. Chicago: Work Book.

Yee, Roger. 2005. *Educational Environments: No. 2.* New York: Visual Reference Publications.

WEB SITES

American Banker Online, www.americanbanker.com

American Institute of Architects, www.aia.org/caj_art_securitydesign

Discovering Justice, www.discoveringustice.org/courthouse/gsa.shtml

Federal Deposit Insurance Corporation, www.fdic.gov/bank/individual/bank/index.html

Federal Reserve Board, www.federalreserve.gov/otherfrb.htm

Library of Congress, www.loc.gov

National Center on Accessibility, www.ncaonline.org

National Clearinghouse for Educational Facilities (NCEF) www.edfacilities.org

Public Libraries Com, www.publiclibraries.com

Sage Publications, http://ann.sagepub.com/cgi/content/abstract/576/1/118

School Library Journal, www.schoollibraryournal.com/index.asp

The Back Shop, www.thebackshop.co.uk/ergonomic_seating_children.html

Whole Building Design Group, www.wbdg.org

Architectural Record www.archrecord.construction.com

Architectural Review www.arplus.com

Building Design and Construction www.bdcnetwork.com

Design-Build (Design-Build Institute) www.dbia.org

Journal of the American Planning Association (APA) www.planning.org/Japa

Note: Additional references related to material in this chapter are listed in the Appendix.

CHAPTER

10

Cultural and Recreational Facilities

We go to the places discussed in this chapter to learn, become satisfied, to participate with and enjoy the company around us, and in some way to escape our everyday lives. *Culture* is a term that includes the knowledge, beliefs, customs, and morals of a group. Recreation is an opportunity to participate in many kinds of activities to refresh our bodies and minds. There are many kinds of places where we can go to achieve an understanding of other cultures and better understand our own.

There are many recreational activities that we can engage in as a participant or enjoy as a spectator. We go to museums to view artifacts of cultures other than our own, learning how people lived in other times and places, or to see representations of our own way of life and interests. Theaters of many kinds offer us a place to relax and break away from our own lives and watch live performances or, more often, movies that let us escape. A place of worship can bring comfort, contemplation, or solace in difficult times. Regardless of one's denomination, attending a place of worship enriches life. Sports is big business, with almost everyone involved in some sort of sport or cheering on favorite teams.

Facilities of these kinds can be considered institutional since the term *institution* is defined as an organization predominantly for the promotion of art, science, religion, and education. Institutional facilities in general are both publicly and privately funded. The facilities discussed in this chapter fall into both of those categories.

This chapter will present information on the basic operations and governing of museums, theaters, religious facilities, and sports facilities. As with each of the other types of commercial facilities discussed in this book, there will be brief discussions on planning and design elements to be considered when designing one of these facilities.

Overview

Like any commercial facility, a design project for any type of facility considered in this chapter includes a diverse group of clients and other stakeholders. The client might be a federal agency responsible for a museum complex such as the Smithsonian Museum in Washington, D.C., or a city council involved in the renovation of a community concert hall. The client might be a private entity working to develop a new tournament-quality golf course and housing development or the building committee of a place of worship preparing to construct a new sanctuary.

The stakeholders in the decision-making process are often many and varied. Some of these stakeholders have never been involved in the design and construction of a major structure or know anything about the design process. Not only must these parties be satisfied, but also their constituents, members, and eventual users of the facilities as well. Designers must be sensitive to and, hopefully, understand and include all the needs, interests, and preferences of the stakeholders in the design. This is not always an easy task. However, it is one of the challenges that draw interior designers to projects involving cultural and recreational facilities.

Funding is often a critical issue in the development of these facilities. Publicly funded projects take many years, since the local residents must often vote for the needed tax increases or tax incentives. Some publicly owned facilities may receive private funding as well. For example, a new sports arena involves some funding from the primary team who will use the complex. It is also becoming common for commercial entities to "brand" the facility with their name—a funding technique referred to as *naming rights*. This means that a commercial entity such as a bank has paid a lot of money for the construction or promotion of the facility and has thus secured the right to name it.

Privately owned museums, for example, obtain funding by a fund drive to raise matching dollars for a grant or federal assistance. Individual members and benefactors contribute generously to provide matching funds. An individual benefactor can contribute the majority of funding, perhaps through a trust. Religious facilities usually receive private donations through fund drives from members of the denomination.

When public funds for any of these facilities for public use are involved, the design team must recognize that the project is open to public criticism. Readers have probably read in their local papers about citizens' reactions to new courthouses or sports stadiums which seem overpriced, since tax dollars were used. For this reason, designers often have to respond to comments and complaints from the public regarding certain design selections.

Commercial projects such as those discussed in this chapter provide architects and interior designers with opportunities to showcase their abilities to a wide audience. In addition, designing for a private institution which is open to public attendance is challenging and exciting. It is important to understand the goals of these specialized clients with their varied constituencies. And, as with any type of commercial facility, understanding the business of the entity is critical to developing plans and specifications that meet the diverse functional needs and the needs of the users.

TABLE 10-1 Museum Vocabulary

- ACQUISITION: A new object added to a museum collection.
- CONSERVATION: Specialized work performed on items in a museum's collection in order to stabilize and save them.
- CURATOR: Individual in charge of a portion of a museum, such as the curator of decorative arts.
- DOCENTS: Volunteers who provide tours and educational presentations, as well as assist in fund-raising and other support services.
- EXHIBIT HALL (and called *hall*): A term sometimes used for the spaces for exhibits.

- GALLERY: A room or series of rooms for the display of works of art, objects, and antiquities. A gallery can also be a free-standing commercial facility for the display and sale of art objects.
- GUILD MEMBERS: Member volunteers who often perform tasks similar to those undertaken by docents. They sometimes focus on fund-raising and museum event planning.
- MUSEOLOGY: A program of advanced study that prepares an individual to work in the administration of museums.
- REGISTRAR: Museum staff member responsible for cataloging objects that belong to or are loaned to a museum.

Museums

Museums provide visitors an opportunity to pursue a variety of interests. Tours of a local museum are highlights for many elementary schools. An outing to a local museum gives children an opportunity to see the things they read about in their classrooms. Parents enjoy taking their children to museums, where they too can learn about history or historical objects. Scholars use museums and their archives to further study areas of interest.

A *museum* is "an institution, building, or room for preserving and exhibiting artistic, historical, or scientific objects."[1] A museum generally concentrates on one area, such as an art museum, natural science museum, or sports museum. Museum collections vary, including the fine and decorative arts, historic documents, and furniture such as that found at the Metropolitan Museum of Art in New York City.

A museum is sometimes referred to as a gallery or institute, such as the National Gallery of Art in Washington, D.C., or the Art Institute of Chicago. Generally, a museum contains a permanent collection, while a *gallery* is usually associated with the sale of art and identified in the retail category. A gallery also refers to exhibit spaces within museums, although these spaces might also be called *halls* (Table 10-1).

Museums offer members, special interest groups, and the general public an opportunity to attend exhibits, performances, lectures, and other events and support funding projects. In most cases, the visitor is not allowed to touch the displayed artifacts. Interactive displays, where visitors are encouraged to become involved with selected exhibit items or reproductions, give the visitor of any age a chance to pursue deeper learning (Figures 10-1a and 10-1b).

Whether the museum is a large facility located in a major city or a small, privately owned museum in a suburb or rural area, the collection is a major draw. Education is a major focus of all museums and is provided through the display and study of the objects and holdings within the collections. Visiting the museum to study an object is a far more exciting educational experience than viewing the same object as a photograph in a book.

Museums usually want a unique facility to showcase their collections, which include both the exterior and interior of the structure as art. Thus, nationally and internationally recognized architects are involved in large projects. Since the interior design of museums involves many technical considerations, the interior designer generally works with an architectural firm experienced in the design of museum and exhibit facilities. Of course, interior design professionals will be retained to design a small art gallery or a small

---

[1]*Webster's New World College Dictionary,* 2002, p. 949.

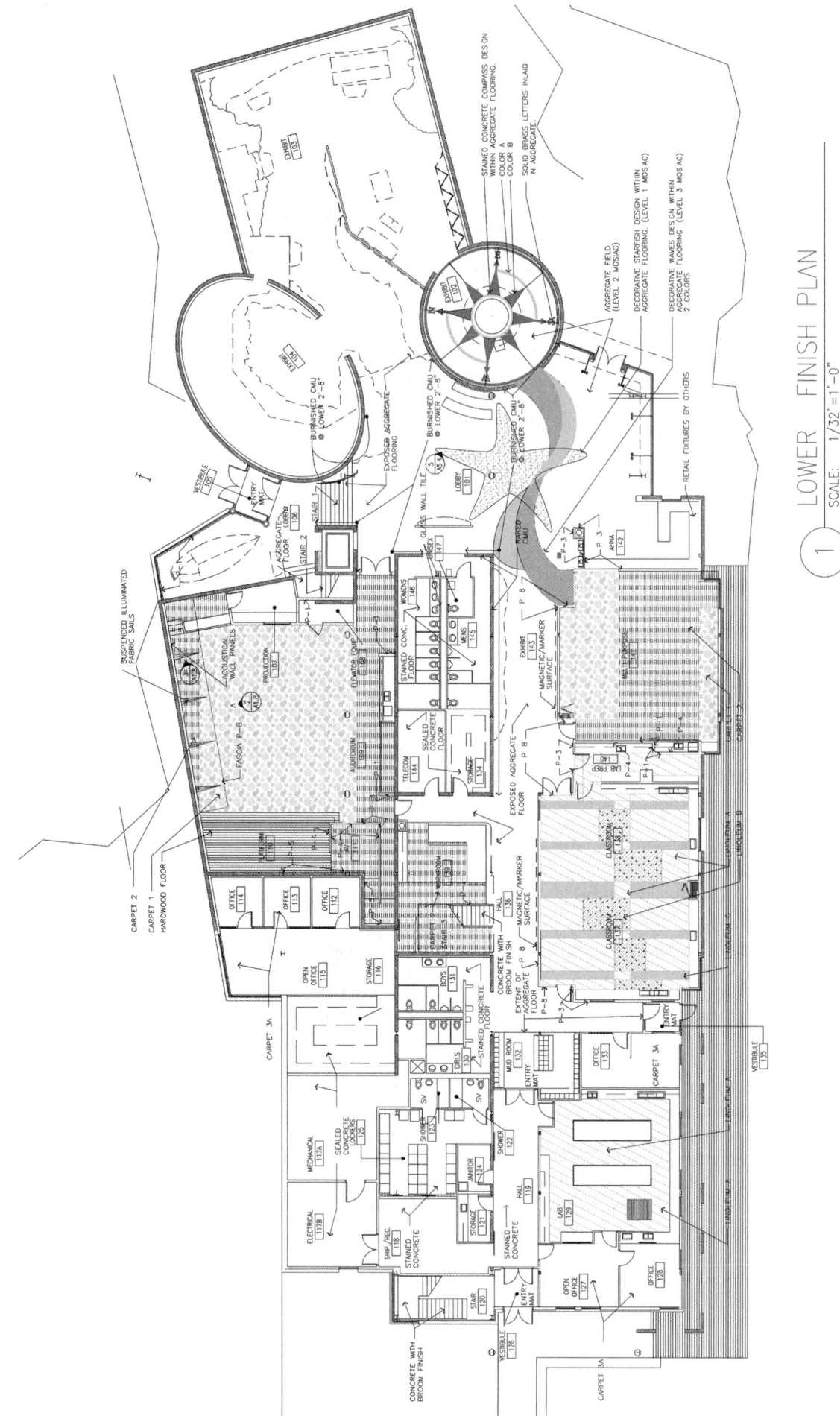

Figure 10-1a Floor plan of the Alaska Islands visitor center and museum. (Floor plan courtesy of RIM Design.)

Figure 10-1b Interior entry to the Alaska Island museum exhibits. (Photograph courtesy of RIM Design. Chris Arend Copyright © Photography.)

community museum. However, only designers who are educated or specialized in museum design or have worked in a museum would be retained to participate in the design of a major museum or gallery space.

This section provides an overview of considerations in the design of a museum facility. A brief history and description of the types of museum facilities is included. Important design planning issues and design elements that affect the interior design of a small museum are also presented.

Historical Overview

The term *museum* evolved from the Greek word *mouseion,* which was originally the temple of the Muses, the goddesses of the arts and sciences. The word *mouseion* is also found in ancient Egypt in reference to a library and a research area.[2] The museum as we know it today originated in Renaissance Italy when objects of antiquity were collected by the monarchs, the Vatican, and wealthy families. Simultaneously, European explorers created the need for display spaces when they returned home with their findings. At this time, collectors placed their acquisitions in cabinets which were positioned in long, narrow rooms called *galleries.* Galleries to display artworks were incorporated into palaces such as the Louvre in Paris, which later became public museums.

There was a great expansion in the development of museums and galleries to house antiquities and art objects in the 1600s. One of the first official museums was opened at Oxford University in 1683.[3] As many ancient artifacts were discovered in the 1700s due to excavation and exploration, collections at public museums grew. In 1759, the British Museum in London opened, and the Louvre, became a public museum in 1793. The word *museum* became popular at this point in describing a place housing a collection. Churches have also functioned as museums due to the elaborate architecture, sculpture, and paintings included in these structures.

In 1773, Charleston, South Carolina opened the first museum in the American colonies. It focused on the natural history of the region.[4] One of the first museums in the new

---

[2]*World Book Encyclopedia,* 2003, Vol. 13, p. 939.
[3]Wilkes and Packard, 1988, Vol. 3, p. 502.
[4]*World Book Encyclopedia,* 2003, Vol. 13, p. 940.

United States was founded in 1786 in Philadelphia, where the painter Charles Wilson Peale displayed a collection of paintings and other items.[5] The Smithsonian Institution in Washington, D.C., began as a bequest from James Smithson in 1835. It is now the largest museum and research complex in the world. Most other early museums did not open in the United States until the late 19th and early 20th centuries.

In the 20th century, U.S. museums became larger, requiring more space for their collections, as well as for preservation and conservation. At this time, museums also became more focused on specific types of collections. A museum of the history of fire, for example, might only display antique fire equipment.

The public's interest in ancient artifacts was also reflected in the architectural styles preferred for museums, especially from the 1850s on. These styles included Neo-Classical and the Renaissance Revival. Architectural styles of the past were challenged by contemporary designs created by new construction techniques of the 20th century. After World War II, the architecture of new museums was more contemporary in style. Museums such as the Guggenheim Museum in New York City, designed by Frank Lloyd Wright, and even smaller museums such as the Des Moines Fine Art Museum in Iowa, designed at three separate times by Eliel Saarinen, I. M. Pei, and Richard Meier, are museum structures characteristic of the 20th century. Museums today reflect not only traditional or contemporary architectural styles but also a combination of both. Typical examples include the Houston Museum of Fine Arts's original traditional building with the north addition designed by Mies van der Rohe. Mario Botta's San Francisco Museum of Art and Robert Venturi/Denise Scott Brown's Museum of Contemporary Art in San Diego, California, are other examples of architecture blending with art in the creation of museum facilities.

The retail gallery for the display and sales of works by artists and craftsmen started in the late 1700s, when craftsmen and artists needed a venue for sales other than commissions from wealthy patrons. Museums are not categorized as retail facilities, although they usually have a museum shop or gift shop providing educational literature and objects for public purchase. The retail gallery remains the typical outlet for art by established and emerging artists and craftsmen. These facilities may be more appropriately categorized as part of retail store design. However, there are concepts of museum design that can also be applied to the design of a gallery, hence their inclusion in this chapter.

An Overview of Museums

A museum has three basic functions: to acquire new materials, to exhibit and preserve the collection, and to provide special services for the public. In a way, a museum can be compared to a retail store in that it must display art or artifacts for public viewing—although the museum collection is not for sale. In addition, museums receive, store, and restore objects in the back areas of the facility, similar to the concept of retail store planning. Office areas for curators and the staff need to be accommodated. As public structures, many museums provide food service for the public and the employees as well as a museum shop. A museum may also have auditorium or conference space for educational activities or performances.

Museum funding is obtained from federal and state grants, foundations, and private donations. These donations can be either monetary or desirable items for a museum collection. Both privately owned and publicly owned museums seek funding from federal and state agencies such as the National Endowment for the Arts and the Institutes of Museum and Library Services. Additional funding sources include foundations, which give annual grants to museums. Other funds come from donations, membership dues, food service, and museum shop sales to cover daily operating expenses as well as expansion plans. Government funds and grants allow expansion and remodeling of the museum. Matching funds through grants is another way of funding new projects for the facility. How the museum is funded will impact what can be done in remodeling an existing facility or building a new one.

The majority of museums are administered by a museum director, one or more *curators*, an advisory board, salaried staff, volunteers called *docents*, and other volunteers called

---

[5]Wilkes and Packard, 1988, Vol. 3, p. 507.

guild members. The museum director oversees the supervision of the facility, its organizational structure, staff, meetings, and exhibits.

Education is an important function of museums. Staff and volunteers offer gallery talks as well as tours throughout the facility. Auditoriums for public lectures and media presentations, as well as conference rooms for benefactors' use and advisory board meetings, are all important spaces in many museums. Larger museums have archival research areas where scholars may study documents or articles from the collection not on display. Naturally, a high priority in the design of any museum is the galleries in which the collection is displayed. Most galleries house parts of the museum's permanent collection, so these spaces are not changed very often. Special spaces are set aside for rotating and special exhibits.

A museum has other important spaces besides the galleries. Patrons like to purchase gift items and educational materials from museum shops. Larger museums such as the Metropolitan Museum of Art in New York City or the Boston Museum of Fine Arts have museum shops which bring in additional revenue. Food service is another means of providing patron comfort as well as more revenue for the museum. Sufficient and appropriate storage of the collection and items on loan for exhibits is also a major concern. These are examples of the many details addressed by the design program to ensure a quality project solution.

Security of the museum, including the building, the entire collection, all employees, and the public in attendance, is a concern that needs to be addressed in depth in planning a museum. Security consultants are usually hired by the architect or the museum director to present the best security measures for the facility.

These concerns and requirements are part of the programming and design considerations the interior designer, the architect, and other team members will need to address. The size and complexity of the project, the funding available, and the experience of the project team members all impact the final project solution.

Types of Museum Facilities

It is important to realize that the type of museum is dictated by the core collection more than by any other factor. Another way of categorizing types of museums is by ownership. Still other museums are dedicated to the preservation of historically significant structures and land sites. Museums can also be classified as botanical gardens, zoos, planetariums, and nature centers. Table 10-2 lists several types of museum facilities.

There are four very common types of museums: art museums, history museums, science museums, and natural history museums.[6] *Art museums* display and preserve sculpture, paintings, fine art, and items of additional areas of interest to the collection. The breadth and depth of the collection depend upon its focus. *History museums* are dedicated to the collection of artifacts and information dealing with the past of a particular culture or many cultures. History museums are very popular with the public, as many are identified with an individual's ancestry. History museums are also used as educational facilities for students, encouraged by both parents and teachers. Large history museums in major cities often deal with a broad range of historical topics, such as the American History Museum in Washington, D.C. State-owned and locally owned history museums will cover topics of local interest, such as a state historical society museum. History museums can include many subcategories based on the specialization of the collection. A few examples include automobiles, railroads, baseball, aviation, music, American Indians, the American West, and broadcasting.

History museums can also be sites of major historical significance or sites of local historical import donated to the federal, state, or local government. The Old Statehouse in Boston, Massachusetts; Mount Vernon, the home of George Washington; and Sutter's Mill in Sacramento, California, are examples of important historic sites.

The third primary type of museum is the *science museum,* where exhibits of natural science and technology are displayed. Science museums originally included displays of artifacts that are also considered natural history artifacts, such as geological objects. Today,

---

[6]*World Book Encyclopedia,* 2003, Vol. 13, p. 938.

TABLE 10-2 Types of Museums

Collections	Specialties
■ Anthropology	■ Aviation history
■ Children's	■ Entertainment industry
■ Crafts	■ Historical sites, where land, architectural and artifacts within buildings are preserved
■ Cultural history	
■ Decorative arts	■ Large or important private homes or mansions that have been donated to the state, the federal government, or a foundation for preservation
■ Fine arts	
■ History	
■ Military history	■ Local history
■ Natural history	■ Maritime history
■ Science and technology	■ Museums of modern art or photography
	■ Sports

the science museum is more interactive than static and involves the visitor in many of its exhibits. In Chicago, the Museum of Science and Industry is popular with both the public and educators. This museum is also the only building remaining from the World's Columbian Exhibition of 1893. The Reuben H. Fleet Science Center in San Diego, California, is an example of an interactive science museum. A visit to this type of museum is exciting for school-age students and provides a ready source of knowledge.

The collections of museums of *natural history* exhibit items from geology, paleontology, biology, and astronomy, to name a few. These museums have many kinds of exhibits, such as dinosaur bones or replicas, preserved mammals and animals, butterflies, and a variety of other natural objects which seem to fascinate elementary school students—and people of all ages. The Smithsonian Institution's Museum of Natural History is very popular, as is the American Museum of Natural History in New York City. Interior designers who wish to pursue museum design should visit the various types of museums open to the public in order to expand their knowledge base.

Planning and Interior Design Elements

In developing a plan for a museum, the interior designer will be part of a team and/or committee which consists usually of an architect, an advisory board, a museum director or curator, and usually a benefactor. This team will initiate and develop a plan based on the focus of the collection and the interpretation of the design needs. Included in this planning stage will be attention to such things as materials specification, color schemes, and display methods or other items that might be needed in the scope of the project.

There are many factors that impact the designer's involvement in any kind of museum or gallery project. Initial detailed programming is vital to understanding the needs of the museum, the focus and mission of the museum, and the makeup of the collection. The degree of public use, the physical plant, the staff, and general needs are also important in dealing with the design of museum or gallery spaces.

Museum collections and exhibits are available to the public. They affect public opinion and provide learning beyond the classroom or what might be gained from reading books. The public's preferences in terms of what it might go to see in a museum certainly impact the goals of the facility. The designer's mission is to create an environment that provides a suitable background for a variety of exhibits, as well as comfort for the public and security for the collection. This section will focus on the design needs for a fine arts and a decorative arts museum.

The space plan and interior design of a museum are highly dependent on the focus of the collection. Interior spaces may be designed in keeping with the exterior architectural style or may vary to best display the items in each gallery.

Off or adjacent to the main entrance, the common areas or zones for fine arts and the decorative arts museums include the entry and reception area, the security guard station, and the museum shop. Leading off these areas will be all the exhibit galleries and possibly the cafeteria and the public restrooms. Conference rooms, an auditorium, office spaces, a library, storage spaces for the collection, conservation areas, loading docks, and other support spaces are required and are generally less available to the public.

Museum gift shops, restrooms, visitor orientation spaces, and usually food services are often positioned off the lobby and within easy access for public use. Generally, security guards are positioned near the main entry as well as at other locations throughout the facility. In many museums today, visitors may have to go through a security screening device or allow their bags to be hand checked before entering the museum. Signage helps the visitor locate auxiliary space or provides directions to the galleries. For accessibility, signage with high-contrast, large print is required for the visually challenged.

The architect and designer need to address traffic flow, materials specification, fire codes, and all other safety issues, as well as the design of any millwork or furniture pieces that will be placed in the entrance lobby due to the large number of activities in this area. Benches provide visitors with places to sit, especially for those who find it difficult to stand for a period of time. Adequate turnaround space for wheelchairs is a necessity.

The overall floor plan for the majority of museums must provide a certain amount of flexibility to allow for changes in various exhibits. Often items from the museum's permanent collection are on permanent exhibit in galleries that infrequently change. Other galleries and exhibit spaces will be designated for changing special exhibits showing items on loan from collectors or other museums. A museum's permanent collection is often partially in storage due to the lack of exhibit space for the entire collection, and the designer must plan storage spaces for this permanent collection. To provide the needed flexibility for exhibit spaces, large, open galleries may be subdivided by movable partition walls for some of the exhibits. Storage for movable partitions is generally planned in the back of the museum near the loading dock, although some museums may store smaller partitions in storage areas near galleries.

The design of exhibit galleries is often guided by a specialist in exhibition design. This specialist is included in the initial programming discussions. The interior designer and architect base some decisions for the design of the galleries on the advice of this specialist. With the specialist's input, space planning of the various galleries should be done by the designer to move the visitor through the exhibit space easily. In a large museum, it is not difficult for the visitor to become somewhat lost.

Each gallery needs an appropriate backdrop for the specific exhibits. These backgrounds must be as easy to modify and adapt as possible so that gallery space is not closed longer than necessary when exhibits are changed. Interior designers must remember to specify wall treatments in the galleries that can be easily changed, will readily hide holes due to hanging methods, and are easily cleanable. Textured wallcoverings and paint are common wall treatments. Neutral and noncolor backgrounds are traditionally used for museum displays. Museums are also experimenting with nontraditional backgrounds, using bolder colors and a variety of materials as the backdrop for certain exhibits. Bold colors are used to attract the attention of the viewer, to focus on certain items on display, and to create some variance from the traditional approach.

An assortment of display methods must be provided and correlated to the items in the collection or those on loan for special exhibits. A museum staff member or a custom cabinet maker will design and build display fixtures for the various exhibits. Museums usually have a shop within the facility where displays can be fabricated. Display cases are generally constructed of metal, wood, and/or glass with attention to the need for appropriate conservation materials and methods. Display cases often require lighting fixtures or have other power needs. A museum lighting consultant can provide guidance on the types of fixtures needed to safely illuminate items in the collection.

Display cases allow visitors a close-up view of the objects while protecting them within locked cabinets. Some locked display fixtures used in retail stores can also be adapted to museum exhibits. Lighting design, color schemes, architectural finishes, security locks, and space planning for proper traffic patterns for viewing of exhibits are all critical decisions related to the design of gallery spaces.

The design of the galleries often includes places for the public to sit and study significant pieces or simply to rest. Benches allow the visitor to view any area of the exhibit room. They also bring relief to a patron who has difficulty standing for a long time. Since benches are not as comfortable as chairs, they do not encourage long-term lounging or dozing, which would be discouraged by the security guards. A broad bench is considered safer and more versatile for use in an exhibit because of the absence of a back. Benches aid security monitoring as well, since there is no place to hide behind a bench.

A sturdy upholstered or nonupholstered, open-legged broad bench is preferred for galleries. Some galleries use furniture items by significant designers, such as Marcel Breuer's Wassily chair. Leather, vinyl, and tightly woven commercial-grade fabrics are preferred when upholstered benches are used. Rarely are other kinds of furniture specified for visitors' use in the exhibit spaces.

The specification of flooring for the museum is another responsibility of the interior designer and the architect. This specification depends on the space. For example, it is common for the lobby and major traffic corridors to be specified with a hard-surface, nonslip flooring, which is easy to maintain. Stone or hardwood flooring can also be specified in these areas. Inset floor mats at entry doors help prevent slipping on hard-surface floors in inclement weather.

In the galleries and exhibit spaces, flooring specification must consider some important functional factors. For example, a gallery with hardwood flooring and wallboard walls could be quite noisy. Carts for exhibits moving across the floor could also produce noise due to the flooring material. Obviously, carpeting is a quieter surface than hardwood flooring. It is also more comfortable to walk on for both visitors and staff. When carpeting is specified in the galleries, it is best to use a commercial-grade, high-density, low-pile carpet which will allow wheelchairs, carts, walkers, and baby strollers to operate effectively. Solid or tone-on-tone carpets in a neutral color or noncolor, or medium-value or muted colors, are most often used. High contrast and large patterns can detract from the exhibits. The designer should keep in mind the light reflectance of color, the ability of color to reflect on another surface, and the volume of space represented by the floor as it affects color choices. Carpet borders should be avoided in galleries, as they limit the versatility of exhibit placement.

To ensure the preservation of art objects and antiquities, museums must consider the mechanical system of the building. It is important for specialists in conservation to be consulted in planning a new museum or renovating an existing one. A conservation consultant will work with the design team to ensure that the interior and HVAC systems preserve the works displayed. The HVAC system for air quality and temperature control directly affects the preservation of the collection. Understandably, one of the most important issues in the HVAC operations of a museum is climate control; relative humidity is the most important climate control factor in the planning and design of museums. The desirable level of relative humidity for most museums is 50 percent.[7] Art and artifacts can be harmed by too much humidity, and climate control is vital in protecting the collection.

Lighting in the exhibit spaces is a major concern for the museum and staff, as it directly impacts some of the conservation issues encountered in maintaining a collection. In museum building design, more emphasis is being placed on the control of natural light rather than allowing the symmetry of the exterior to dictate the light sources. Lighting highlights objects on display. However, if not correctly specified, it can also damage items such as textiles, watercolor paintings, and other valuable collections. Lighting engineers and designers trained in exhibit lighting should be consulted when new or remodeled spaces are developed. The museum director has usually had some lighting education as well.

The intensity of all forms of light should be controlled in a museum or exhibit space. A general rule for lighting is to use uniform lighting for all vertical surfaces where the art will be displayed. Nonuniform lighting should focus on individual art objects. A track lighting system works well in museums and galleries because it allows versatility of placement and focus. It is important to consider the distance from the object to the light source

[7]McGowan, 2004, p. 359.

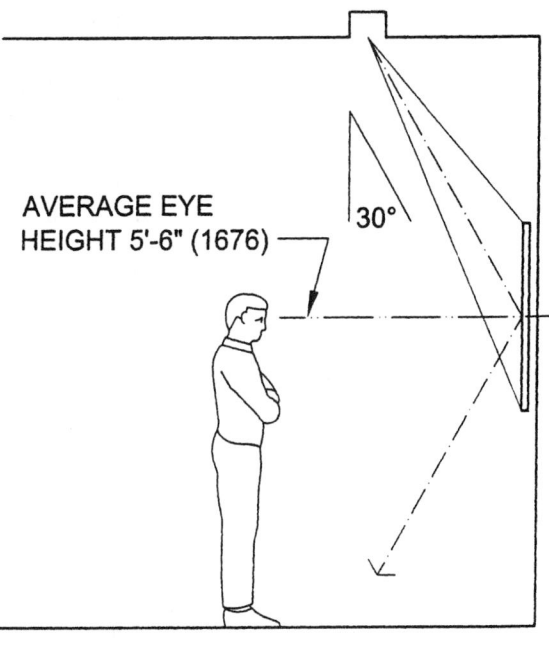

OPTIMUM AIMING ANGLES

Figure 10-2 Drawing of a viewing angle in a museum. (From Maryrose McGowan, *Interior Graphic Standards.* 2004. Reproduced with permission from John Wiley & Sons.)

so that damage is minimized. Recessed lighting with an adjustable lens is used in art galleries for paintings. A "continuous spectrum, high color-rendering source allows the art to be viewed under spectral distribution conditions similar to those under which it was created."[8] It is recommended that the general display lighting level for paintings such as watercolors be maintained at 5 FTC or less. Fluorescent lighting needs to be provided with UV shields. Figure 10-2 provides examples of viewing angles in a museum.

Interactive education and integration of the computer as a research and information tool helps scholars and students to learn more about the museum's collection. As visits to the museum can require extensive travel, use of the computer to obtain information and facilitate research exposes the public to the museum's collection. Larger museums have established learning centers adjacent to selected galleries where visitors may utilize computers to search for information on items in the collection. One such learning center is in the American Wing of the Metropolitan Museum of Art.

Security is one of the most important issues in the design of all museums. A museum security consultant will be involved during programming to evaluate and make recommendations. As part of security planning, nongallery spaces such as the museum shop should not be accessible through exhibit space. Storerooms and conservation areas need to be tightly monitored. To avoid theft, there should be no access to ductwork in these storage spaces.

In addition to supplying specifications for the exhibit spaces, interior designers will be involved in the space planning and specification of several kinds of support spaces. Most museums offer food services to the patrons and the public in general. The food service facility can entice the public into the space by the atmosphere and comfort created by the interior design. The aesthetics of the cafeteria or restaurant cannot be ignored, as it represents another opportunity to present design as art. Interior designers need to select tables, chairs, and banquettes that are easily cleanable, comfortable, and space efficient as well as appealing. Multiple food service options are available in larger museums, such as a food court near the front entry and a full-service restaurant within the facility for more formal dining such as at the Dallas Museum of Fine Arts. Location, ventilation, and

---

[8]McGowan, 2004, p. 358.

acoustical control are all issues that need to be addressed in order to maintain the separation between food services and exhibit spaces.

Another source of revenue for museums, both large and small, is the museum shop and bookstore. Sometimes a museum will establish an ancillary shop in shopping malls as a retail facility. Another purpose of the museum gift shop is to educate the people viewing the exhibits as well as provide items for sale which represent the collections on exhibit. Custom millwork is needed for the storage and display of the items for sale. Refer to Chapter 6 for further guidelines on planning gift stores (Figure 10-3).

Other spaces include auditoriums, libraries, and staff offices. Many museums provide auditoriums for lectures and large group meetings. The majority of museums have a lecture series for educational purposes. These lectures are presented in the auditorium, the design of which is similar to theater design. Guest lecturers usually require projection capabilities to support their PowerPoint, or other presentation methods. Visibility, acoustics, and comfort are all important. Museums usually have a boardroom where the advisory board meets on a regular basis. Its size and layout depend upon other factors, but its design should be based on the principles used for corporate boardrooms. Libraries are often located in museums and are available to the public for research. Documents, texts, original manuscripts, and other significant literature are open to scholars and the public. Staff offices are often located in the back of the museum. They require security as well, since items from the collection or items to be acquired might be kept there for short periods of time. Previous chapters and the section on libraries in this chapter should be reviewed regarding the design of these support spaces.

A museum is classified as a Group A or assembly occupancy by the building and fire safety codes. This classification is based on the number of visitors. There are strict guidelines concerning egress, door sizes, corridor sizes, and materials specification that must be applied. These guidelines exist to protect the public using the facility.

Since a museum is a mixed occupancy, other building code requirements apply to the gift store, food services area, auditorium, library, office spaces, and other areas that affect

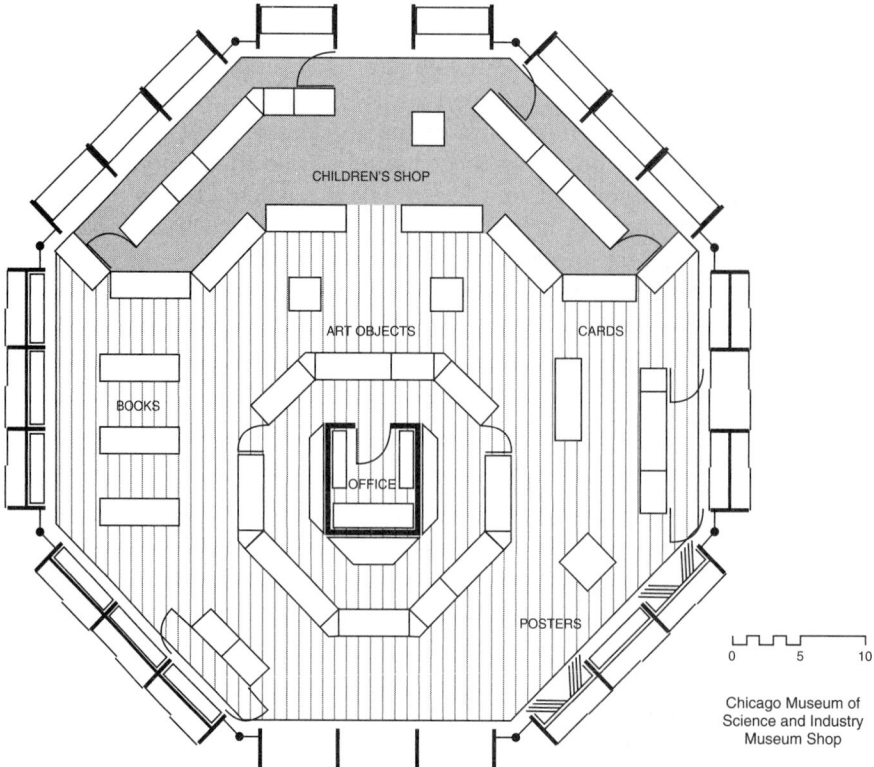

Figure 10-3 Floor plan of a gift shop in a museum. (From Barr and Broudy, *Designing to Sell*. Copyright © 1986. Reproduced with permission of the McGraw-Hill Companies.)

the public. Accessibility requirements must be met for new construction, and existing structures must meet guidelines to allow access for physically challenged visitors. These requirements include an accessible-height counter area at the information desk, ticket counters, food services, and the museum shop. Space needs to be provided for wheelchairs in the auditorium and assisted listening devices or interpreters for the hearing impaired. Appropriately sized corridors, elevators, passageways, doorways, floor surface specifications, ramps, and signage must be provided.

A successful museum project requires planning that provides adequate exhibit spaces, materials that aid in creating a multiuse backdrop, and specialized lighting, as well as the numerous issues mentioned in this section. Interior designers and architects need to be educated and experienced in museum planning and building, as well as being willing to research and update their knowledge before engaging in a museum project, regardless of its size. Students interested in specializing in museum design should take courses in arts management, museum studies, history, and lighting design, as well as contacting museum personnel for suggestions about additional education.

Theaters

A theater is a building or outdoor structure where performances such as plays, operas, or films are presented. Theater does not refer to the building alone but also defines where the performance takes place. The most familiar types of theater performances include acting, dance, opera, musical, oratory, movies, and other visual and audio-oriented productions. The term *theater* comes from the Greek verb *theatai,* meaning to "see, watch, look at, or behold."[9] It also refers to the script, the stage, the production company, and the audience (Table 10-3).

Identifying the types of performances is very important because it impacts especially the overall design of the theater's interior. Interior designers must study theater design and needs, as there are many technical challenges to be met and practical decisions to be made. For example, seating must be comfortable for extended periods of time, architectural elements must reflect the types of performances presented, and the design and specification of architectural elements must be compatible with varying lighting requirements. Meeting code requirements is mandatory since a theater will always include a large number of patrons. Acoustics must be optimal to allow the audience to hear comfortably and accurately.

Theaters can be designed for one purpose, such as presenting dramatic plays, or can be multifunctional, producing a musical comedy one month, a drama another month, or even showing movies at other times. Multiple-use theaters challenge designers to meet the requirements for each type of production.

Theater design is rarely undertaken by an interior designer alone. The following section provides an overview of this challenging commercial space. Given the technical issues involved in theater production, further research and study are required.

Historical Overview

Theaters existed in ancient Sumeria, Egypt, and Athens and were usually associated with religious festivals. Ancient Greek theater was performed outside a temple or sometimes in a marketplace. The *orchestra* appeared at this time and referred to a large, circular, flat area in the center of the theater used for dancing during the performances. Tragedies were the first productions. Comic satyrs and later comedy, which made fun of politicians, became popular. These productions were performed in the amphitheater, which consisted of the orchestra at the lower level and stone seating placed on the hillside for the audience. These amphitheaters housed 10,000 to 20,000 people. A modern example of this configuration is the Hollywood Bowl in Los Angles, California.

---

[9]Wilkes and Packard, 1988, Vol. 3, p. 52.

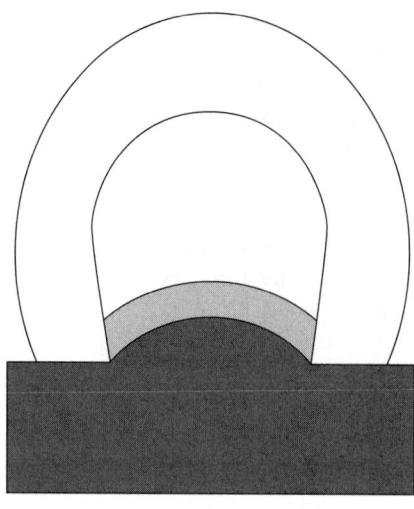

HORSESHOE-SHAPED
AUDITORIUM
PROSCENIUM STAGE

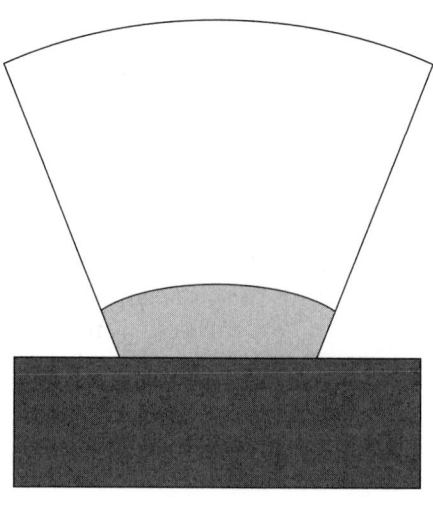

FAN-SHAPED
AUDITORIUM
PROSCENIUM STAGE

Figure 10-4 Drawing of a theater horseshoe floor plan. (Reprint: George C. Izenour, *Theater Design.* 2nd ed. 1996. New Haven, CT: Yale University Press.)

Figure 10-5 Drawing of a theater fan-shaped auditorium. (Reprint: George C. Izenour, *Theater Design.* 2nd ed. 1996. New Haven, CT: Yale University Press.)

The ancient Romans copied the Greek theater style, but Roman dramatic productions were less popular than the gladiator sports. It was the Romans who first built theaters on flat land with raised seating, rather than building into the hillsides, as in Greece. Later, the Byzantine emperor Justinian closed all theaters, having decided that the subject matter of many productions was offensive to early Christianity. After the fall of the Roman Empire, theater reemerged and by the 900s, the church used theater to present biblical stories and religious ceremonies. These productions were performed outdoors. In 1420 in Paris, theater productions were moved indoors. During the 1400s, morality plays became popular in England as well as Europe, focusing on problems of the individual as influenced by the Italian Renaissance. The Baroque theater produced the horseshoe proscenium stage. From this point on, the orchestra diminished in size and the seating increased.

In the late 1500s, theaters in London were constructed using a circular floor plan with galleries for the audience. This was not theater-in-the-round because there was space for the stage, wings, and backdrop. In 1599 the Globe Theater, where William Shakespeare's plays were commonly performed, was built in the shape of an octagon and was galleried for audience use. The theater charged admission, which provided the main financial support for the theater company. Visitors to Washington, D.C., will find a replica of the Globe Theater at the Folger Library.

In the 1600s, *masques*—dances or ballets—became popular with the European nobility. Later, during theater productions, an *intermezzi,* or intermission, was added to allow time for scene changes. The intermezzi provided entertainment consisting of songs and dances which later evolved into ballet and opera productions. The Western world's oldest state theater, founded in 1680, is the Comedie-Française in Paris.[10]

Productions focused on middle-class interests by the 1700s, as this group attended performances in increasing numbers, resulting in larger numbers of theaters. Vaudeville shows at theaters and dance halls where variety performances were held added to the interest of theatrical performances. Sufficient lighting on the stage continued to be a problem until the 1800s, when gaslighting provided enough light on the stage to view the actors behind the proscenium arch.

In the United States, the first theater was built in the mid-1700s in Philadelphia. By the 1800s, theater as an entertainment form was popular throughout the country, including

[10]*World Book Encyclopedia,* 2003, Vol. 19, p. 248.

TABLE 10-3 Theater Vocabulary

- AUDITORIUM: That part of a theater where patrons sit to watch the performance. It can also be a room in a building such as a school used for performances, meetings, or educational programs.
- BACKSTAGE: The production and storage spaces in a theater. The stage is the major component of the backstage area.
- BALCONY: A projecting area of seating in the upper areas of the theater.
- GREENROOM: A room where benefactors are met and performers relax.
- HOUSE: The part of the theater occupied by the audience.
- LEGITIMATE THEATER: A performance by members of Actors Equity or other professional performance unions.
- MEZZANINE: The lowest balcony in a theater.

- ORCHESTRA: In Greek theater, a circular space used by the chorus in front of the proscenium. The term has additional meanings today.
- PROPERTY OR PROPS: The small accessory pieces used to finish the design of a set or supplement scenery.
- PROSCENIUM: The part of a stage in front of the curtain.
- REPERTORY THEATER: A theater that presents several different productions each year.
- STAGE: The part of the theater where the performance takes place.
- STAGING OR STAGED: Terms that means putting on the performance.
- SUMMER THEATER: A repertory theater organized for the summer season.

frontier towns. Large and small towns had opera houses, and traveling production companies or local performers entertained. During the Victorian period, theater performances focused on pantomimes, melodramas, dramatization of novels, and costume dramas. Increased use of mechanical devices for staging effects entertained and enhanced the theatrical experience. Initially, in England, seating for the audience consisted of benches covered in green baize. In the late 1800s, elegant theaters with formal dress codes were built with luxurious appointments, box seats, and comfortable seating for the audience, which encouraged the attendance of the wealthy and their patronage of this art form.

Advances in theater design and architecture in general continued to impact the theater. The horseshoe floor plan (Figure 10-4) continued to be used until the late 1800s, when Adler and Sullivan, Chicago architects, produced a fan-shaped auditorium which provided better sightlines for the audience (Figure 10-5).

By the 20th century, U.S. theater was moving away from the melodrama of the Victorian period and showing a preference for realism. Major developments in stage machinery, lighting with electricity, and other technological advances enhanced the realism on stage. As in Europe, operettas and musical comedies continued to be popular.

Entertainment venue options changed in the early 20th century with the introduction of movies and movie theaters. Competition from radio and movies further impacted theater attendance. In the 1930s, theatergoing declined due to the Depression. With the introduction of television, which brought the theater on a small scale into the public's living room, theater attendance was further challenged.

New York City is probably the best-known theater center in the United States. Beginning in the 1950s, performances were staged in off-Broadway theaters away from the central theater district as an alternative to Broadway plays. These usually involved unique scripts and productions considered to be a major force in experimental theater.[11]

An Overview of Theater Facilities

Theater designers must consider the many technical issues involved in staging a performance. Theater design also places emphasis on creating an environment filled with comfort and amenities, as evidenced by the changes in the design of movie theaters.

The ownership of a performing arts facility varies, depending upon its classification. Theaters owned by local governments can be large enough to house a resident company

---

[11]*World Book Encyclopedia*, 2003, Vol. 19, p. 245.

TABLE 10-4 Theater Management Structure

- Owner of the facility or primary user of the spaces
- Benefactors
- The funding authority
- Administrative staff, who is responsible for such activities as public relations and financial issues

- The house manager and others who work with the public
- Artistic and events management staff
- Performance staff such as directors and stage hands
- Building maintenance staff

such as a symphony or might be small community theaters. Commercially owned theaters are built for profit, such as movie theaters. Educational institutions such as colleges and universities usually own one or more theaters, and the majority have a variety of auditorium spaces. These theaters provide a platform for performances of students who are majoring in theater. The universities also provide the community with traveling productions. Sometimes these facilities are rented to outside promoters or production companies. Private theaters may be owned by individuals, amateur dramatic companies, organizations, religious groups, or even art galleries.

Depending upon its ownership, the uses, concerns, goals, funding, and needs of the facility will vary. Different administrative structures to manage the facility and the performances that are staged also impact design decisions. Table 10-4 presents the typical management structure.

In the design of a theater, the client consists of several different groups. One client is the organization or individual donor who initiates the project—for example, the theater department in a university. A second client is the person or organization that authorizes spending for the project—in this example, the university administration and governing body. The conductor of a major company will have a role in the design or remodeling of the theater for a resident symphony. Technical and house staff who may operate lighting, adjust scenery, and provide customer service are also likely to be involved in the design process. Still other clients are the public and other users of the facility.

The clients' needs and concerns are many and varied. Of major importance is the need to design and build the best-quality building and production systems for the expected types of performances. Performance needs include an adequate-sized stage, storage spaces, dressing rooms, and costume areas. As an additional revenue-producing area, the lobby usually sells refreshments and often items such as brochures and CDs or DVDs related to the production or the history of the theater. Sufficient comfortable seating with a good sightline to the stage is vital. The design team must plan and specify the theater building and its interior to meet building and fire codes, adhere to accessibility guidelines, and address practical and legal factors in order to avoid any liability issues that might threaten the client.

Types of Theaters

The theater can be designed for musical or dramatic performances. Some theaters are designed for specific types of productions, such as the Helen Hayes Theater and the Schubert Theater in New York City, which focus on theatrical productions. Others are multiuse, housing a variety of production types. Lincoln Center for the Performing Arts in New York City stages many kinds of performances from opera to ballets and plays.

Theaters are also categorized by the floor plan used to develop the auditorium, stage, and backstage areas. The major schools of stage design include the proscenium style and the open stage style. However, there are four basic types of stages. The *proscenium stage floor plan* is the most common and is designed to be viewed only from the front. The proscenium floor plan has a heavy curtain or wall that frames the stage and is referred to as the *proscenium arch*. The curtain is closed when it is necessary to change scenery or move from one act to another. Sometimes there is an orchestra pit between the stage and the audience (Figure 10-6). Theater types are defined in Table 10-5.

TABLE 10-5 Types of Theaters

- **Amphitheater:** Generally an outdoor theater.
- **Arena theater:** A theater with the stage in the middle of the auditorium surrounded by seating. It is often referred to as *theater in the round*.
- **Black box:** A simple performance space with minimal scenery and amenities. Seating often consists of folding chairs to help production crews create a variety of performances.

- **Concert hall:** Primarily presents musical performances, especially for orchestras and singers.
- **Environmental theater:** A theater where the performers and the audience share the same space.
- **Movie theater:** A place where motion pictures are shown.
- **Opera house:** Primarily presents operas and other musical performances.

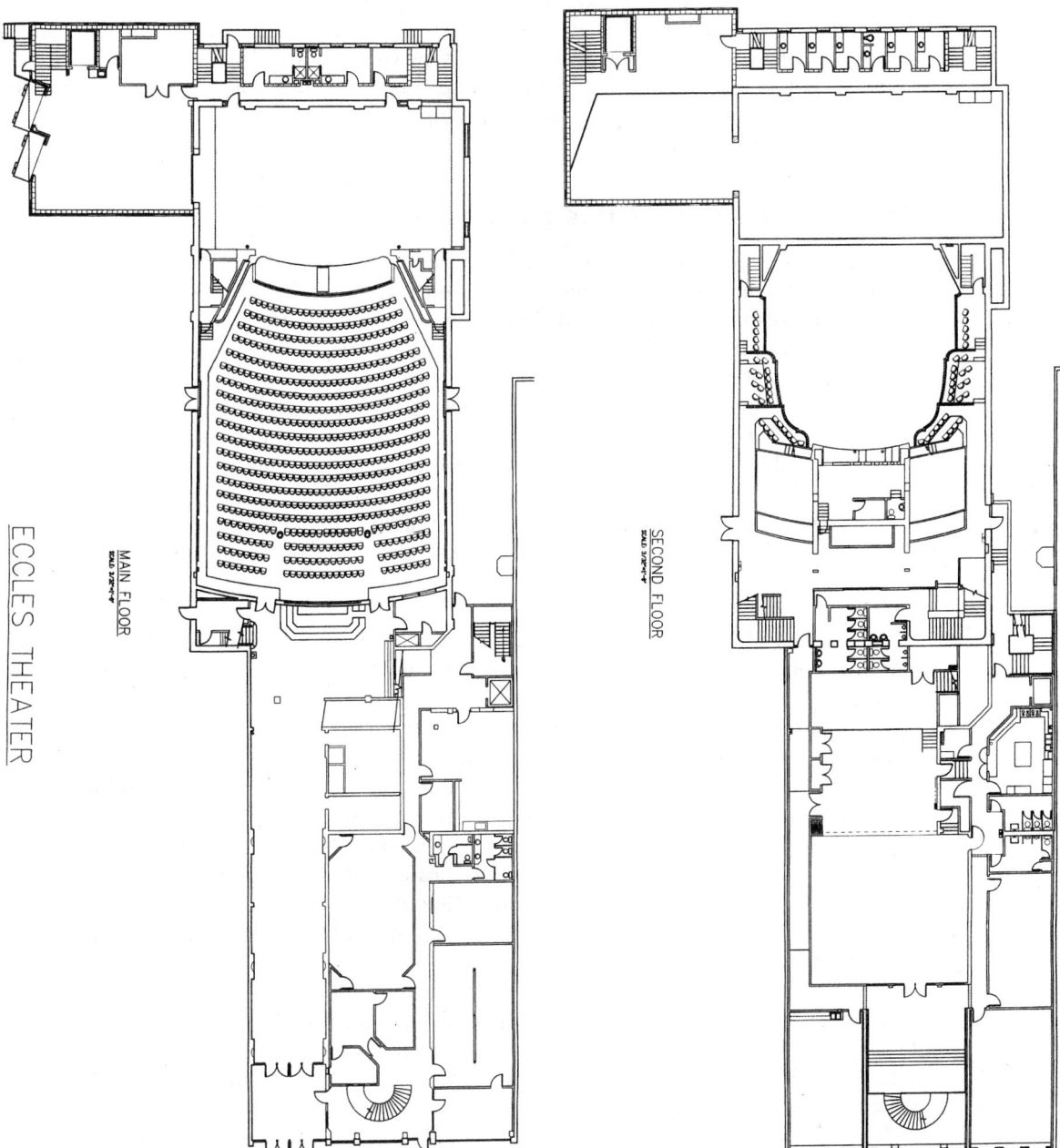

Figure 10-6 Proscenium-style floor plan depicting the main floor auditorium and the box seat area on the upper level. (Plan courtesy of Jensen Haslem Architects PC. Project architect and designer: Lanny Herron.)

The *open stage floor plan* projects a portion of the stage into the audience so that the audience sits partially on three sides of the stage, with only a curtain between the stage and the audience. In the design of this type of stage, it is important that all members of the audience have a good view. The *theater in the round* is often called the *arena stage*, as members of the audience sit on four sides of the stage. The entire production must address all four sides of the audience. The *flexible stage* (also called *modular*) theater provides the ability to rearrange the audience seating and the performance area based on the production. The Walt Disney Modular Theater in Valencia, California, is one of the few examples.

Behind the proscenium and the open stage floor plans, out of sight, are the sides of the stage called the *wings*. This is where the actors wait in preparation for their entrance onto the stage. Although most scenery and accessories are stored in backstage or in property and scenery rooms, a small amount of scenery important to the production can be stored in the wings.

The placement of audience seating in the auditorium is affected by the type of theater. Main floor seating may be designed with aisles along the walls and intermediary aisles providing easier access to central seats. This type of plan is called the *American* or *conventional seating plan.* When the main floor seating is planned with aisles only along the walls, the plan is called the *Continental seating plan.* The house will also often have mezzanine and balcony seating.

Planning and Interior Design Elements

Each theater design project has different issues and concerns specific to the type of theater and the productions to be staged. The overall planning and design concepts are similar. The discussion of planning and design elements in a theater must be limited. To simplify this necessarily brief discussion, this section will focus on the proscenium layout for dramatic productions.

Depending upon its location, a theater may be a freestanding building or contiguous with other buildings, such as in a downtown setting. The architect will focus on the entrance to the theater, which provides the initial impression as well as the invitation into the facility. Theater entrance design varies from the traditional styles familiar in New York City theaters to more contemporary designs in many theaters built today. The entrance to contemporary theaters often has large windows, such as in the Jesse Jones Hall in Houston, Texas. These windows create a spacious feeling and can be advantageous especially if the exterior view enhances the space.

The design of the entry is a further challenge since a large number of doors are required by codes. Architects can emphasize the exterior doors and surroundings as an introduction to the design of the facility. Older theaters often have ornate entrances inviting the patron to enter; these doors may have to be adapted to modern codes. Contemporary theaters generally use less ornate entries.

Architectural finishes for lobbies must be durable, easy to clean, withstand the abuse of crowds, and meet code requirements. In the entry, nonslip hard-surface flooring with floor mats is common. Commercial floor mats can be designed with the theater logo to make these utilitarian items attractive. Some theaters prefer heavy-duty commercial-grade carpeting at the entry. Heavy-duty commercial-grade wall treatments in the entry lobbies can vary, helping to create design interest. Other entry/lobby wallcoverings include stone, wood paneling, and paint.

Patrons should be able to move easily from the lobby to the monitored coat check area, restrooms, water fountains, refreshment area, and then the entrance to the main auditorium. Public restrooms in a theater must meet accessibility guidelines and code requirements. A monitored checkroom should be placed off the main traffic paths but convenient to the front entrance.

Refreshments in legitimate theaters are usually sold by the theater or subcontracted to a vendor who provides limited quality items such as beverages and packaged goods. The goal of providing refreshments is to bring in additional revenue, as well as providing a social environment or break for the audience during intermission. In some theaters, a private buffet is offered to benefactors and donors who have contributed to the production or theater. The area designated for refreshments is limited since food and beverages are not allowed in the auditorium. If liquor is served, the location of the refreshment area will need to be coordinated with the delivery of liquor cases and lockable storage after hours.

Architectural finishes are specified with functionality in mind. When carpeting is specified for these high-traffic lobby areas, a high-quality commercial-grade carpet should be used. Designers often specify patterned carpet in the lobby since it shows less soiling and hides traffic patterns. Small patterns with little contrast or tweeds should be used on stairways to the auditorium, mezzanine, and balcony, since larger patterns can be visually confusing to some patrons. Due to the large crowds gathering in the lobby areas, acoustical issues must be addressed to provide more comfort for the patrons. Acoustical panels, acoustical wallcoverings, and baffles can all assist in reducing the noise level in these areas. Wallcoverings must be Class I and are available in a variety of materials.

Lighting solutions may be designed or selected by the architect, interior designer, lighting designer, and/or theater lighting specialist. Typical lighting solutions for the lobby area include wall sconces, chandeliers, strip lighting along soffits, or other subdued indirect lighting which enhances the space.

There are patrons who cannot stand for a long time in the lobby area and need minimal seating. Often this seating consists of narrow benches placed along a wall. Interior designers should check with the fire and building codes to see if benches or other furniture can be specified in the corridors. Egress code requirements at an emergency exit may impact the use of furniture in these areas.

Beyond the entrance lobby, most theaters have three basic sections: the auditorium, the stage, and behind-the-scenes spaces. The auditorium, also referred to as the *house*, is where the audience sits during the performance. Sometimes the term *auditorium* includes the lobby, entrance, and comfort areas. In the following discussion, *auditorium* will refer to audience seating.

With the proscenium stage, there are many challenges in designing the auditorium portion of the theater. The stage and the main auditorium require that the design be the background and not in competition with the production. The audience's attention should be drawn to the stage unless the production design itself creates a peripheral attention area (Figure 10-7).

The color selected for the auditorium walls must emphasize the stage. Interior designers must research colors to make certain that light is absorbed and not reflected back into the auditorium space. For example, do not specify colors which contain yellow tints, as they reflect light and draw attention. Theater designers usually prefer pale grays, dusky purples, or any tone that absorbs light during the performance. When the lights are dimmed during the performance, the auditorium walls should not call attention but rather blend into the space. Reflective surfaces are generally avoided in the peripheral spaces. In historic theaters and those designed with a traditional feeling in the interior, gold foil can be used.

In the design of an auditorium, the layout of the seating and the floor configuration are major concerns. The design of the audience seating must ensure that each theater patron can see the stage without undue straining to see or hear the performance. Seating for the main floor is generally arranged at a pitch calculated to provide for proper sightlines to the stage. The size of the theater and the configuration of the stage will determine whether a continuous pitch from the back of the auditorium to the stage is feasible or if stairs will be required. Ideally, the

Figure 10-7 Interior view of the American Conservatory auditorium, San Francisco. (Photograph courtesy of Gensler. Photograph by Marco Lorenzetti/Hedrich-Blessing.)

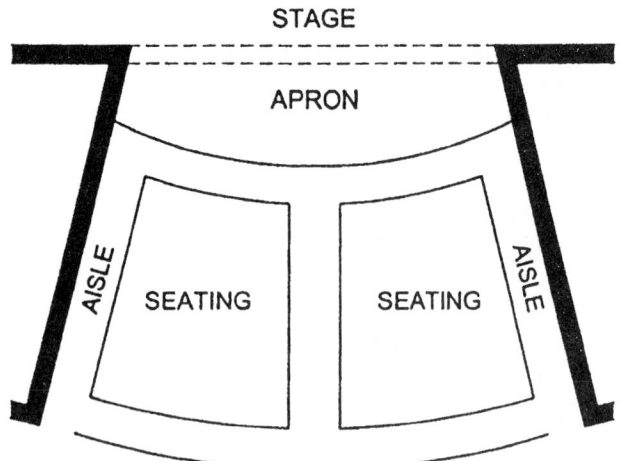

Figure 10-8a American seating plan. (Reprint: J. Michael Gillette. *Theatrical Design and Production.* 2nd ed. 1992. McGraw-Hill.)

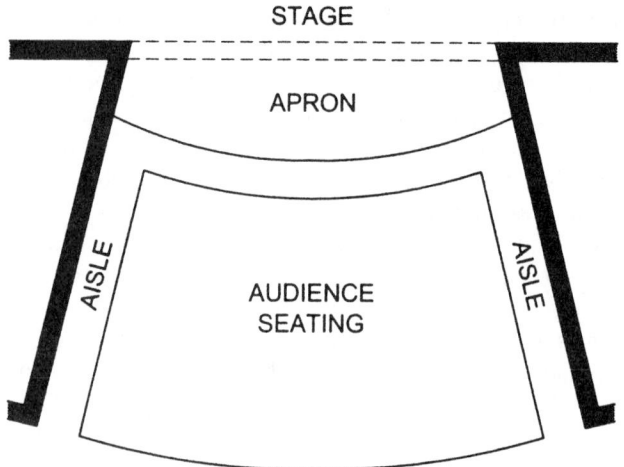

Figure 10-8b Continental seating plan. (Reprint: J. Michael Gillette. *Theatrical Design and Production.* 2nd ed. 1992. McGraw-Hill.)

main floor will have a continuous pitch, while the mezzanine and balcony are usually stepped.

To provide good viewing from any seat, the rows are arranged in a slight curve. Depending upon the design of the auditorium, box seats are usually located above the main floor facing and flanking the stage on either side. These box seats are often sold to benefactors for use or sold to patrons at a higher price than the average auditorium seats. The balcony and mezzanine spaces are elevated at the rear of the house, with balcony seating being farthest from the stage. Railings must meet a specific height requirement for the safety of patrons sitting in the front rows of the mezzanine, balcony, and box seats.

Theater design requires strict adherence to building and fire safety codes, including the amount of space required between rows. In the American seating plan, rows can be closer together, as intervening aisles are provided for a quick exit. The Continental seating plan requires more spacing between rows because there are no intervening aisles, only those on each side. Therefore, a patron sitting in the middle of the row would have farther to travel to get to an aisle and, in an emergency, to get to the exit (Figures 10-8a and 10-8b). A percentage of spaces must be provided for wheelchairs, and a percentage of seats are required to provide assisted listening devices. The amount of accessible seating depends upon the size of the auditorium and its seating capacity, as well as the seating plan and the floor layout.

The design team, which may include theater specialists, will work together to select the auditorium seating. Comfort, leg space, and the passage of other patrons are factors in determining chair sizes and row widths. It is important that the client and the design team sit in a variety of theater seats prior to purchasing. Theater seating frames are usually constructed of cast iron or steel and are either riser mounted or floor mounted. Pedestal-mounted and cantilevered standards can also be considered. Tandem seating is most common in theater seating except in the box seats, which often provide individual chairs. Seats on the main floor, mezzanine, and balcony are usually bolted to the floor, while the box seats are usually freestanding. Seating is selected on the basis of comfort, stability, versatility in regard to patron size and height, durability, code compliance, and aesthetics.

The Continental seating plan allows more space between the seat and the back of the seating in front of the patron. Minimum measurements for this type of seating are 38 to 42 inches. Ideal spacing for maximum comfort when seated is 36 inches between the seat and the back of the seating in front. If 40 inches are allowed, passage in front of a seated patron is possible. Spacing between rows in the American seating plan is tighter (32 to 33 inches) since there are more aisles for exiting.[12]

---

[12]MaGowen, 2004 (student edition), p. 364.

Fabrics selected for the seats need to be very durable, with ease of maintenance. Fire-retardant textiles are required in most situations. Commercial-grade tightly woven wools and nylons are commonly specified. Fabrics for the box seats can be COM but also must meet fire codes requirements. Because box seats are often designed for benefactors, more luxurious fabrics are used. These chairs are generally attractive, comfortable, and geared for a variety of body shapes and sizes. Also important to remember is that the largest sound-absorbing surface in an auditorium is the seating.

An important part of the project for the interior designer and other members of the design team is the specification of flooring for the auditorium. High-density, low-pile, tufted carpeting is often chosen for noise control and ease in walking. If hard-surface flooring is used in the seating area, carpeting is often specified for the aisles to provide ease of walking, reduce noise when patrons are using the aisles, and avoid slipping. The designer must avoid high-contrast patterns in the auditorium, as they can be visually distracting. In selecting colors and patterns for an auditorium, the designer must also remember that patrons' clothing also creates a large volume of pattern and color.

The architect, theater lighting specialist, and interior designer will determine the most effective lighting design for the auditorium and other areas of the theater. Once those decisions are made, the interior designer selects lighting fixtures such as chandeliers and wall sconces, as well as finishes for all lighting used in the public spaces. The size of the chandelier is usually determined by the lighting engineer, using a formula which considers the volume of the space and the degree of lighted surface required.

Lighting for the stage is general, specific, and with special effects. The theater lighting specialist will be consulted for this installation. There is also a lighting control booth which controls all lighting for the production. This booth is often placed at the back of the theater, above the auditorium and sometimes behind the balcony, depending upon the configuration of the theater. With today's computer technology, much of the lighting can be programmed.

To provide easy movement throughout the public spaces, good signage is required. Signs directing patrons from the lobby to the auditorium should be visible, legible, and informative. Ushers often assist patrons in locating their seats when they enter the auditorium. Other necessary signs indicate restrooms, refreshment areas, and ticket booths. Easily viewed egress signage is mandatory for safety in the auditorium, especially in an emergency.

Acoustics are a major concern for the architect. The designer should be aware of the issues of materials specification and how these can affect the noise and listening level within the theater. The architect should plan the auditorium space so that no noise enters from the lobby once the doors are closed. In the auditorium, the walls and ceilings need to be hard surfaces in order to reflect sound. This reflection determines the clarity of sound. The walls near the performer(s) should be angled to enhance projection and prevent echoes at the stage. The design factor that affects reverberation time in theaters is ceiling height, and this needs to be addressed by the architect.[13]

Backstage is the area behind the proscenium, including the wings, set storage, and preparation area. Other areas considered part of the backstage area are the dressing rooms, costume storage and maintenance areas, restrooms for staff, the performers' lounge, possibly a greenroom, and the loading docks. Some of these areas, such as dressing rooms, may be located in the basement below the stage. In the stage area, in the wings, and near the stage openings, walls are painted black or charcoal to be unobtrusive.

Other backstage areas are specified with a neutral tone in varying values, depending upon their function. Small kitchen facilities are usually included in the greenroom to provide refreshments for benefactors, directors, actors, and special guests. Receptions for benefactors after the performance can be planned for the greenroom, depending upon the size and quality of the design.

Space for the performers' dressing rooms varies in size and configuration. Major stars and featured actors usually are assigned individual dressing rooms, while the rest of the cast use a larger shared space. The design team should allow a minimum of 16 square

---

[13]MaGowen, 2004 (student edition), p. 365.

feet per performer for dressing room space. When the space is shared, the room must be very functional, providing space for makeup, costumes, dressing, and minimal storage. A dressing table with special lighting requirements is provided for the actors for the application of theater makeup. In private dressing rooms for individual performers, the space should allow for a makeup area with a lavatory, chairs, a sofa or chaise for reclining, tables, lamps, full-length mirrors, space to hang costumes, a dressing space, and preferably individual restrooms.

The majority of the office spaces for the theater are located toward the front of the facility. The size and placement of these offices depend upon the type of facility. If the theater houses a resident company, more office space will be needed than in a theater for touring productions. Ideally, these offices should have a views of the lobby, good lighting, and sufficient square footage to function effectively. Windows opening to the lobby or ticket area are designed to aid the staff in monitoring the space during nonproduction hours. Systems furniture and case goods are very effective.

As discussed above, theater design requires detailed programming, which includes a variety of professionals on the design team as well as the professionals and client(s) associated with the theater and the construction of the project. The interior designer is an important member of the team. His or her materials specification directly affects the safety, comfort, ambience, aesthetics, and general environment of the facility.

Religious Facilities

A religious facility is defined as "a building, or group of buildings, such as a church, a synagogue, sometimes called a temple, or a mosque, in which people worship, or other buildings used for religious or secular purposes by the worshippers."[14] Considering the variety of religions and religious practices throughout the world, a specific project requires considerable research and preparation by the design team in order to interpret its requirements correctly. Maintaining objectivity is important, as the religion may differ from that of the designer.

Religious structures are facilities where group considerations are mainly based on the philosophy of the denomination. Sensitivity to the belief system of the denomination, building committee contributions, membership input, and liturgical requirements are all important in developing a successful project. So too is an understanding of the administrative hierarchy involved in decision making and spending and the size of the congregation.

Throughout history, religious spaces have allowed persons who share common beliefs to gather as a community to practice and study the precepts of the denomination. The building of sacred spaces has influenced architectural and design styles of secular buildings as well. For example, throughout the Gothic period the focus was on cathedral building, which influenced housing styles as well as furniture forms. These forms returned during the Victorian period of the last half of the 1800s, with motifs and concepts applied to structures and furniture.

Today's religious structures reflect not only past architectural styles but also new forms as building systems have advanced and denominations have required different building formats to meet their individual needs. A wonderful example of a church built in the Gothic style is the National Cathedral in Washington, D.C., begun in 1907 and completed 85 years later. There are also many impressive contemporary structures; readers may be familiar with the Crystal Cathedral in Garden Grove, California, which is often televised.

An in-depth discussion of the many religious structures existing today is beyond the scope of this section. The following discussion will focus on the floor plans and facilities which are currently typical of the church and the synagogue. In no way does this intend to deny the importance of the facilities of other religions not covered in this section (Table 10-6).

---

[14]Packard and Korab, 1995, p. 531.

Historical Overview

A place of worship and the practice of religion can occur anywhere, either indoors or outdoors. Religious facilities, like religious practice, have existed for millennia. Judaism is one of the world's oldest religions. Elements of the modern temple come from the designs of the earliest temples, where an outer court, open to women, led to an inner court where only men were allowed.

The word *church* comes from the Greek word *ecclesia* and refers to an assembly of Christians. An earlier definition of the word referred to a political assembly of citizens.[15] The word *ecclesiastical* is in common use in today's churches and generally refers to the organization of the church or clergy. Terms for the places of worship of other religions include the Jewish *synagogue*, Muslim *mosque*, Shinto *shrine*, and Buddhist *temple*.

The floor plan of the traditional Christian church, which includes the transept and the nave, is identified as the Latin cross or *cruciform* floor plan. This floor plan has its origins in ancient Egypt as the hypostyle hall. The ancient Romans adapted the floor plan and structure of the hypostyle hall for use as government buildings referred to as *basilicas*. After the fall of the Roman Empire, the Christian population remaining in these territories used the abandoned basilicas as churches. The ancient Romans developed the dome as well as the cross barrel vault, which allowed the transept to be widened, creating the Latin cruciform floor plan. High barrel vaults were not always structurally sound, and it was not until the Gothic period that the high vaulted ceilings were stabilized.

Culture and religious practice continued to evolve according to the needs of specific groups. The Byzantine culture in Constantinople flourished and was responsible for building churches and promoting the sciences and the arts. The floor plan associated with the early Greek culture and the Orthodox Church is the Greek cross floor plan designed in the shape of a square generally topped with one large central dome and several smaller ones. During the Gothic period in Europe, massive cathedrals were built, often requiring more than a century for completion. The pointed arch and vaulted ceilings with flying buttresses on the exterior provided for more stability and higher ceilings. The Italian Renaissance brought a return to the classical architecture of the ancient Greek and Roman cultures. A prime example is the Basilica of St. Peter's in Vatican City.

The Reformation movement in Europe in the 1500s witnessed a change in church floor plan based on the new philosophy. The design of church architecture was somewhat varied, depending upon the type of worship. For example, in England in the early 1500s, Henry VIII dissolved the Roman Catholic churches and monasteries and used the church structures for what was to be the Church of England (Anglican). Methodist churches today still reflect the influence of the Anglican floor plan. Many other denominations built meeting houses rather than churches so that both religious services and community meetings could be held in the same building. Many churches became smaller and simpler in detail as well.

The first church in America was probably built in Jamestown, Virginia, in the early 1600s. The Pilgrims in Plymouth, Massachusetts, several years later built meeting houses for their Puritan denomination. Later, Anglican churches were built throughout the New England colonies as well as in the middle Atlantic and southern colonies. The first synagogue in America was built in Newport, Rhode Island, in the mid-1700s. Roman Catholic churches existed in the southwestern part of America (colonial Spain) as early as the 1500s. These churches were built of materials available in the region, such as adobe bricks made of clay, straw, and water.

The architectural styles of churches in the American colonies were influenced by the denomination and the geographic area. For example, Protestant New England congregations used readily available wood as a common building material. If the church was small, the interior had a central aisle leading to the pulpit or altar, with pews flanking each side. In the middle Atlantic and southern colonies, the Church of England predominated and maintained the cruciform floor plan for the majority of the church buildings. After 1714, southern structures were made of brick and often constructed in a Georgian style. After

---

[15] *Webster's New World College Dictionary,* 2002, p. 449.

TABLE 10-6 Religious Facility Vocabulary

- ALTAR: A raised platform where ceremonial activities occur in religious facilities.
- *BALDOCHINO*: An ornamental canopy over an altar or seat of honor.
- CANTOR: A synagogue official who sings or chants religious music.
- CHANCEL: The space around the altar of a church for the clergy and sometimes the choir, often enclosed by a railing.
- DIOCESE: The district of churches governed by a bishop.
- MEGACHURCH: A congregation with regular attendance of 2,000 persons or more.
- NAVE: The long. narrow part of a cruciform or Latin cross floor plan. It is where the congregation stands or sits during the service.
- PASTOR: The head of a Protestant or Catholic church parish.
- PHYLACTERY: A small box with scriptures worn on the left arm or the head.
- PRIEST: An ordained clergyman in an Anglican, Eastern Orthodox, or Roman Catholic church.
- RABBI: The ordained teacher of Jewish law and the head of a local synagogue.
- RECTOR: The head of an Anglican church parish.
- ROOD SCREEN: Screen separating the chancel from the nave in some types of churches.
- SACRISTY: A room attached to the church where the vestments and sacred utensils are stored.
- SANCTUARY: The most sacred part of a religious facility. It is where the altar, if one is used, is placed.
- SYNAGOGUE: A house of worship for a Jewish congregation.
- *TALLITH*: A shawl with fringed ends worn over the head or shoulders during morning prayer.
- *TEFILLIN*: A phylactery worn by a member of the Jewish religion.
- TRANSEPT: The transverse segment of a cruciform floor plan, which crosses over the nave at the chancel end. Additional seating can be placed here, and small chapels may be located at the ends.
- VESTIBULE: A passage or small room between the entrance and the interior of a building.

the Revolutionary War, there was even more freedom in the layout and construction of religious buildings. As the U.S. population increased and moved west, various designs of religious facilities flourished.

Overview of Religious Facilities

The client of a religious facility includes a variety of stakeholders. Clergy as well as congregation members form building committees to work with the architect and interior designer. Denominations vary in their administrative structure, and this needs to be understood by the design team. For example, in the Episcopal Church, a bishop governs a diocese, which is composed of districts containing established congregations as well as mission churches. The Presbyterian Church's governing system consists of boards referred to as *sessions,* which include the minister and lay elders. In the Roman Catholic Church, each parish has a priest. In the Jewish faith, the rabbi is the leader of the local synagogue. Naturally, all these religious groups have additional higher authorities who may be involved in some of the decision-making related to the design of any type of religious facility.

Whatever the actual complexity of the project, the design team will address funding, budget constraints, and time allotted for the renovation or new construction; these are crucial factors for nonprofit religious facilities. Unique to the design of places of worship is the impact that the building project has on members' lives, as it represents their spiritual home. They may express strong opinions on design, sometimes based on personal taste and sometimes on past practices and the appearance of the religious building. Individual members may respond emotionally to the use, change, or application of design elements even though the design must represent the consensus of members, the administration, and the religious doctrines.

The design team needs to recognize that religious governing bodies vary, congregational profiles are infinite, and their needs and differences must be respected above all. Each congregation has specific needs and requirements, and design principles effective for one house of worship, may not apply to another. A detailed discussion of the sanctuary and ancillary spaces will be included in the section on Planning and Interior Design Elements.

Types of Religious Facilities

The primary types of religious facilities are the churches, synagogues, temples, and mosques that are constructed for the purpose of practicing religious ceremonies and holding meetings. Their designs vary, based on the denomination practicing there more than any other factor. Twentieth- and 21st-century religious architecture expresses the changes in religious philosophy and practice. Structures built today must meet the needs of contemporary congregations, whether they wish to retain traditional floor plans or adopt newer concepts.

The most important area in a religious building is the sanctuary. The sanctuary is the focal point in the worship service, and its layout and design should express that focus, depending upon the denomination. When a congregation decides to build a new facility, this is the space usually built first. The traditional Christian church floor plan, which includes the transept and the nave, is identified as the Latin cross or *cruciform floor plan.*

Although the design of the sanctuary is most critical to the congregation, a variety of support spaces for the congregation also identify its activities and interests. Examples include social spaces like parish halls, assembly rooms, perhaps a small library. Administrative offices for the clergy, as well as office staff nurseries and sometimes residences for the clergy, are also provided. Several denominations provide extensive classroom and other educational spaces as part of the church campus, creating parochial schools (Figure 10-9).

A Jewish congregation gathers for worship and study in the synagogue or temple. The synagogue has schools within the facility that educate the congregation in the Hebrew language, Jewish history, and the scriptures. There are Orthodox, Reform, and Conservative Jewish congregations, each having specific building needs.

A mosque is the place of worship for the Islamic religion. Architectural styles of mosques vary from country to country. The worshippers face east during the religious service, where the pulpit called a *minbar* is located.

One of the fastest-growing denominations in the United States is that of the evangelical/pentecostal churches. It is within this category that *megachurches* are found. The term *megachurch* basically refers to the size of the congregation and the church facility itself. The belief system and especially the needs of these churches have influenced religious facility floor plans and layouts dramatically. For the first time in centuries, church construction and design on a large scale no longer relies predominantly on the Latin cross floor plan or a modified version of it. The auditorium in a megachurch is the main worship space, which can be considered the sanctuary.

There are a few other kinds of religious facilities. Private schools and universities for lay education are familiar to most readers. Seminaries, convents, and yeshivas—to name just a few—provide religious education in preparation for a religious career.

To specialize in the interior design of religious facilities, a designer needs to study and to develop an understanding of the various types of religious groups and their philosophies. Architects and designers specializing in religious architecture and facilities are taking note of the trend toward megachurchs, multiuse buildings, and larger campuses. The size and scope of these huge projects require a full range of commercial experience, research, and regulations.

Planning and Interior Design Elements

The floor plan of a religious facility directly impacts the worship space, which influences the interaction between the congregation and the clergy. The floor plan for religious structures has evolved over millennia. For example, the traditional cruciform plan has changed to new floor plans based on a different focal point within the service. One illustration is a church in the round, which provides seating for the congregation totally surrounding the altar or pulpit area. The purpose is to avoid a two-dimensional effect by providing a three-dimensional approach which creates the potential for greater participation by the

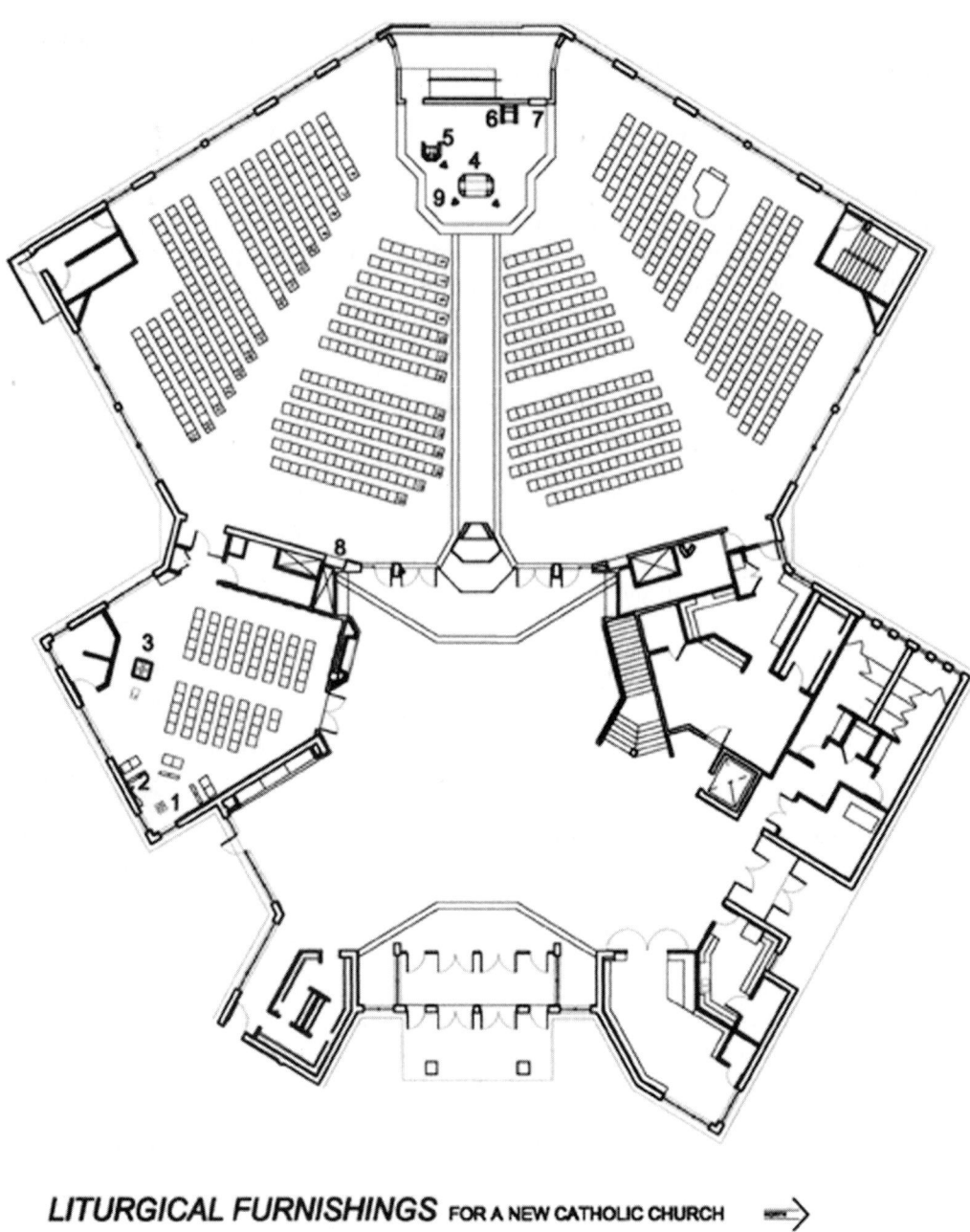

LITURGICAL FURNISHINGS FOR A NEW CATHOLIC CHURCH ➡

1 TABERNACLE	4 MAIN ALTAR	7 PROCESSIONAL CROSS
2 SANCTUARY LAMP	5 AMBO	8 AMBRY
3 DAY CHAPEL ALTAR	6 PRESIDER'S CHAIR	9 LITURGICAL CANDLE HOLDERS

Figure 10-9 Contemporary floor plan of a church which, in the past, traditionally used the nave and transept. The central nave/main aisle is evident in this floor plan. (Plan courtesy of Jim Postell, interior design and furniture design.)

congregation. Not all denominations embrace these new concepts, of course. Contemporary religious buildings generally require an open, inviting atmosphere in an attempt to be all-inclusive. The design team should achieve this goal.

This section will concentrate on background planning and design elements for the Christian church and the Jewish synagogue. A brief discussion of some of the different configurations of floor plans for Christian and Jewish facilities will help the student understand the various practices. In the Roman Catholic church, the layout of the nave usually involves rows of pews facing the altar in the sanctuary. A cross may be hung behind,

Figure 10-10 Traditional ceiling and traditional lancet-shaped stained glass windows blend well with the layout and fixtures in this contemporary application. (Photograph courtesy of Jim Postell, interior design and furniture design. Lance Lew Photographer.)

above, or on the altar, which is located on the elevated level of the sanctuary. In the Roman Catholic and Episcopal churches, a tabernacle holding the communion wafer is on the wall behind the altar. The sanctuary is where the priest will conduct the service, called a *mass.* Usually the sanctuary is on a raised floor level, which allows the congregation to view it. The sanctuary may be divided from the nave by a railing called a *communion rail* and often by some type of *rood screen.*

The priest can stand in front of the altar or at the pulpit to deliver the sermon. The centrally located altar in most Christian churches is approximately 6 by 4 feet, whereas in a cathedral, the altar is approximately 10 by 8 feet. As the priest or minister is standing at the altar, the altar should be 39 to 40 inches high.[16] The pulpit should provide the clergy with some mechanism to aid in delivering the sermon, such as an adjustable-height reading surface to allow for clergy and lay readers of varying heights. Other useful aids are a reading light and a microphone. Some clergy prefer to have some sort of lighting control at this post (Figure 10-10).

The majority of Protestant churches vary in floor plan based on their religious philosophy and the denomination. Church architecture may be very elaborate, such as in the National Cathedral in Washington, D.C., or very simple, as in a Friends meeting house. The megachurches are using some principles of theater design to produce an auditorium using the fan seating plan. Traditional church pews have used this layout to some degree for many years. There are generally two main elements that divide the Protestant worship space: the nave, where the congregation sits, and the sanctuary, or chancel, where the minister or others, such as the choir, may sit. The sanctuary includes the altar, pulpit, lectern, seats for ministers and priests, and space for communion generally. In some denominations, the word *sanctuary* refers to the sanctuary space as well as the nave where the congregation is seated (Figures 10-11a and 10-11b).

---

[16]Roberts, 2004, p. 224.

Figure 10-11a The sanctuary area designated for the minister and the choir. First Baptist Church in San Antonio, Texas. (Photograph courtesy of 3D/International.)

Figure 10-11b The gathering space within the church campus where parishioners gather for receptions and proceed to the sanctuary or other areas. First Baptist Church in San Antonio, Texas. (Photograph courtesy of 3D/International.)

A pulpit and a lectern are provided on either side of the sanctuary. The lectern is where some of the scriptures are read, church announcements are given, and other church activities are presented to the congregation. Solo music performances may also use this space. The pulpit is where the minister reads the gospel and/or gives the sermon. This space requires the amenities mentioned earlier. A communion rail, depending upon the communion practice, is placed between the nave and the sanctuary. In some Protestant churches, a full immersion tub is positioned behind the altar area, with a drapery covering the space.

There are additional spaces in most Protestant churches as well. A sacristy can be provided either in a room off the back of the church or close to the sanctuary for vesting by the minister. An altar guild room provides storage for altar linens, as well as some floral preparation space and storage. Baptism rites vary in the Protestant churches from sprinkling to full immersion, from babies to adults, so the location of the baptismal font or tank can vary greatly. Protestant churches have vestibules or lobbies which also provide a transition from the exterior to the nave. Community spaces include a fellowship hall or large reception room that provides informal seating. A kitchen, classrooms, a nursery, and storage space for the services are likewise needed for the church campus.

The Jewish synagogue is built in a contemporary architectural style, usually rectangular in shape, with the sanctuary designed so that the congregation faces the eastern wall. In Judaism, there are rules for the building of synagogues and the interior treatment of the worship spaces. The sanctuary can vary, depending upon which form of Judaism is practiced: Orthodox, Reform, or Conservative. The focal point is always the ark, where

Figure 10-12 The focal point in a Jewish synagogue is the ark. Note the creative and attractive use of materials and lighting. (Jim Postell, interior design and furniture design.)

the Torah, the scrolls that contain the first five books of the Bible, is kept (Figure 10-12). The ark is located on the eastern wall of the sanctuary and is covered either by two small doors or a curtain called a *paroche*. On either side of the ark are plaques of the Ten Commandments. In front of the ark is a table called a *bimah (bema)* where up to five people can gather on three sides of this reading area (Figure 10-13). Seating for the rabbi and the cantor is placed on either side of the ark; each seat has a box. The rabbi will remove the Torah from the ark and place it on the table to read to the congregation. Seating for the congregation is provided in rows, usually with a central aisle and side aisles. Each seat should contain a lockable box for the Torah, prayer book, prayer shawl, *tallith*, and *tefellin*. Seating in a synagogue could include individual upholstered chairs, portable or stackable chairs, and/or tandem seating. Orthodox congregations may have separate seating for men and women.

A vestibule or lobby is located in the back of the Jewish sanctuary, much like Christian churches. The social area of a synagogue needs to be adjacent to the worship space to allow members easy access after the services. This social space, or community room, can be used for special services and rituals as well as dances, theatricals, or games. The design team needs to analyze and assess this area to create flexibility and function. The community rooms are used for special services, such as at Passover, and will require a kitchen. If the synagogue is Orthodox, two kitchens are required: one for dairy products and one for meat products. Offices for the synagogue include the administrative offices, which are placed adjacent to the main entrance. The rabbi's office is more secluded to allow study and consultation.

Figure 10-13 The *bimah* (*bema*), which is placed in front of the ark and where readings are shared with the congregation. (Photograph courtesy of Jim Postell, interior design and furniture design.)

If the project involves restoration of a facility listed on the National Register of Historic Places, the design team must do extensive research to make certain that all guidelines are followed. The national organization Partners for Sacred Places is an excellent resource for this type of project. Its purpose is to educate, aid, and assist religious facilities and members to locate resources and funding, and to provide information through publications as well as conferences.

The major furniture in a Christian and Jewish worship space is the seating for the congregation. Pews have been the preferred seating choice in churches for many years, as they provide efficient seating. They are usually constructed of oak, maple, or any wood which can stand up to constant use. Many churches use pews with cushions, which require durable, easily cleanable fabrics. Pews should be stable and often are fastened to the floor for safety. Roman Catholic and Episcopal churches use kneelers attached to the back of each pew. Ideally, the kneeler is padded and covered with a vinyl or contract-grade fabric. It is important to note that pews with kneelers require approximately 39 inches between the back of the pew and the seat of the pew behind it to pull the kneeler down as well as provide space for the parishioner to kneel. Pews are also designed with book racks on the back which house the hymnals and prayer books. Pews in the back of the congregation should not be more than 75 feet from the altar in order to provide good viewing.[17]

Many religious facilities continue to use chairs instead of pews for seating. The chairs can have rush or cushioned seats and kneelers attached to the back of each chair. The use of chairs in the worship space allow for a flexible seating layout and is preferred by contemporary as well as some traditional church floor plans. One problem with chairs is that they can be easily damaged when moved and stacked for storage. Chairs also require extra storage rooms when they are removed from the worship space. When specifying chairs, avoid sled bases and always consider the movement of chairs on the flooring selected. In some areas, fire code compliance requires chairs to be ganged together. While the spacing between pews and the sizes of the aisles are regulated by codes, the central aisles in many churches are wider than required to better accommodate processions such as those in a wedding or religious ceremonial event. Megachurches install theater seating in their auditoriums, which adapts well to the pitched or stepped floors in their worship spaces. These seats are usually tandem seating and fixed to the floor. This type of seating is not recommended for kneelers.

There are vendors which specialize in liturgical and religious products for the interior designer. These items may be purchased by the architectural or design firm, or by the church or the liturgical designer. Other items, such as the altar, can be custom made.

In determining the materials specification for religious facilities, considerable research on the denomination and the liturgical response and use of materials is important. For example, each group has a specific response to product needs, materials, and colors in relation to the congregation, the philosophy, and the structure.

Flooring specification is a major decision. The vestibule or lobby may require hard-surface flooring such as wood, marble, limestone, or granite, although care must be taken to use a nonslip surface near the entries. More economical hard flooring selections include terrazzo.

Carpeting specified for a sanctuary and nave area should be tufted, high-density, low-pile carpet installed using the glue-down method, which will provide better wear and show fewer traffic paths. Dense, low-pile carpet is helpful to church members who use wheelchairs and walkers because it creates an even surface without the drag created by a higher pile. The flooring material should be specified with maintenance, durability, acoustical, and aesthetic issues in mind.

Carpeting in the sanctuary is preferred by many congregations due to its ability to absorb sound. If musical performances are part of the services, carpeting can be used for the aisles only with hard flooring in the pew areas, much as in theater design. This application will promote good acoustics and clarity in hearing the sermons and the music. Traditional churches have hard flooring such as stone in the sanctuary. The National Cathe-

---

[17]Roberts, 2004, p. 42

dral in Washington, D.C., is a typical example of a stone floor used in a traditional placement.

Color is an important design element in the interior specification of religious facilities. It is also a design element associated with the Christian calendar and used by a variety of denominations. For example, purple is used for the Lenten season and green for the Epiphany/Ordinary Times observances. Other churches may have specific color requests based not on the church calendar but on the philosophy of the denomination. Black or dark colors are often avoided, as they may be inconsistent with the concept of "light as opposed to darkness." The majority of churches have a neutral color scheme for the walls and ceilings, with color accents in clergy vestments, choir robes, pew cushions, and wall hangings. A large volume of space in the sanctuary/auditorium is the flooring, which is often carpeted in a color representative of the church calendar. Two traditional carpet colors for worship spaces in a Christian church are red and green.

The window treatment most commonly associated with church architecture is the stained glass window. These windows have been popular since the Gothic period. Traditional stained glass windows depicted images and stories from the Bible, which helped to educate the illiterate masses in church doctrine. Today's stained glass windows are less concerned with depicting biblical stories. Often this is funded by a benefactor who dedicates it to a family member or religious figure. Stained glass windows are important design elements in religious facilities. Vendors that specialize in their production and restoration work with the denomination building committee and the design team to produce these windows and install them properly. Some church buildings prefer heavy fabric such as draperies to hang over the windows and darken the sanctuary space. Any fabric used at the windows must be fire retardant.

The HVAC system planned by the architect needs to provide for the comfort and safety of the congregation. Some congregations use candles and incense during the service, and their fumes need to be ventilated out. Most mechanical systems for churches and synagogues are planned and designed for high occupancy levels when in use.[18] Lighting systems should be easy to use and designed to meet the various needs of the sanctuary space. The types of fixtures specified will be dictated by the layout of the space and the denomination's worship needs. A lighting designer or engineer is often included in the design team to provide the special lighting required in a religious facility. Sufficient light is needed to read the hymnals and scripture, as well as to highlight important signage such as that of exits. Certain areas of the sanctuary require more light due to the importance placed on the altar or ark area. It is important to avoid contrasts of brightness in order to prevent eyestrain. Light sources can include incandescent lamps, fluorescent lamps, and high intensity discharge lamps, to mention a few.[19] The Illuminating Engineer Society recommends a medium to high level of visibility for reading in the worship spaces. In traditional churches, pendant chandeliers provide light for the pews. In selecting chandeliers, consider the scale of the lighting in relation to the overall volume of the space.

The acoustics of a worship space are impacted by the architectural style, the materials specified, and the number of parishioners present. Carpeting and pew cushions or upholstered seats absorb sound and provide a quieter atmosphere. However, in situations where musical performances are primary, hard surfaces such as the wall and floor aid in projecting the sound. In order to enhance the musical component, a long reverberation time is required, whereas a short reverberation time is preferred for clarity of speech.[20]

Building codes and accessibility requirements need to be strictly adhered to in new construction and major remodeling of religious structures. Worship spaces are classified as assembly occupancies in the International Building Code and other model codes, and these codes will impact the design. For example, building and fire codes dictate the number of exits and the seating layout, as well as the width and placement of aisles and the exits. Codes will also impact the materials that can be used on the architectural interior surfaces in the sanctuary as well as in other spaces in the building. The fire safety codes

[18]Roberts, 2004, p. 137.
[19]Roberts, 2004, p. 214.
[20]Roberts, 2004, p. 189.

address exit location, exit signage, flame-retardant finishes, and sprinkler systems.[21] The National Electric Code governs the design and installation of the electrical system.

Accessibility design guidelines applicable to other commercial spaces are more flexible in religious facilities. A religious facility is considered a private organization, much like a private club, and is thus exempt from strictly enforced ADA guidelines. However, state and local building codes require that all assembly buildings comply with the American National Standard A117.1, published by the Council of American Building Officials. These accessibility guidelines must be applied to avoid legal action due to accessibility problems. Such design issues as the width of aisles, pew spacing, reserving a percentage of pew space for persons in wheelchairs, and providing assisted listening devices in some pews are part of these requirements. If a religious facility is listed on the National Register of Historic Places, the structure is exempt from certain ADA guidelines.

Since many religious facilities provide child care for the congregation and the community, the spaces for these services must be code compliant in regard to the number of children per teacher, the restrooms, and the floor area per child.

Recreational Facilities—Golf Clubhouses

Sports are played throughout the world, whether as an organized athletic event or as unorganized sports activities in a neighborhood among friends. Amateur sports have impacted millions of citizens as participants, and spectators follow their favorite team or sports star. Televised sporting events provide sports fans with an opportunity to support their favorite teams and bring interest to a large variety of sports activities. Regardless of the season, there is some sort of sports activity for persons with every interest.

Cities build community recreational facilities of all kinds for those who wish to participate in amateur sports. Cities and corporate sponsors, along with team owners, build massive stadiums for sports like football and baseball. At the stadiums, people are spectators rather than participants. *Spectator sports* refers to the audience as observers of either an individual player or a team. Spectator sports are big business, involving billions of dollars. Many of these dollars are used to build stadiums and facilities. These stadiums, both open and enclosed, bring thousands of spectators to the event.

Some types of sports do not require massive stadiums, yet they have large numbers of spectators for professional events or facilities. Golf is one of these sports. Golf is one of the most popular sports in the United States and throughout the world. It is categorized as a spectator sport, with thousands attending tournaments and millions watching on television and the Internet. Golf is also one of the most popular amateur sports, with over 26 million Americans participating. There are more than 16,000 golf courses in the United States. About one third of them are private clubs, either country clubs or golf clubs, each with a clubhouse facility.

Historical Overview of Golf

The game of golf has a long history. It emerged in Scotland in 1744, when the Honorable Company of Edinburgh Golfers organized the first golf club. This golf club later provided the first written rules of the game. In 1754, the Society of St. Andrew's Golfers was formed and became the leader in establishing the game's rules and standards. Golf was popular throughout the British Isles and eventually spread to Europe and North America, being introduced in the United States in the late 1700s.

Golf became firmly established in the United States around 1900. At that time, there were approximately 1,000 golf courses in the country. One of the oldest is St. Andrew's Golf Club in Hastings-on-Hudson, New York, established around 1880. The United States Golf Association was founded in 1894 and serves as a governing body for the game of golf in the United States. In 1916, the Professional Golf Association (PGA) was formed.

---

[21]Roberts, 2004, p. 95.

TABLE 10-7 Golf Club Vocabulary

- FAIRWAY: the portion of the course that extends from the tee to the green for each hole.
- GREEN: The area at the end of the fairway with the hole.
- HOLE: A hole is positioned on each green. The goal of the golf game is to get the ball into the hole with as few strokes as possible.
- MATCH PLAY: A type of golf game when golfer or a team of golfers play against another golfer or team. The best score for each team at each hole wins the hole.
- PRO SHOP: a retail store selling clothing and golf (and/or other) sports equipment.
- ROUND OF GOLF: Playing all 9 or 18 holes, depending on the length of the course.
- STROKE: each swing of the golf club.
- STROKE PLAY: Golf game involving individual golfer keeping track of each stroke.The fewest number of strokes wins the round.
- TEE: flat area of land where the golfer takes the first swing.

The U.S. PGA tour, established in the 1930s, is the largest tour program, overseeing approximately 50 tournaments.

Golf has grown steadily since the turn of the 20th century. Of the approximately 16,000 golf courses in the United States today, approximately 2,500 are owned by the public, and over 11,000 are open to the public for a fee.[22] One third of all golf courses are private clubs. Approximately 26 million people play golf annually in the United States and many more around the world. During the late 1990s, almost 500 new golf courses were built worldwide annually.

An Overview of Golf Facilities

Webster's New World College Dictionary defines a club, such as a golf club, as "a group of people associated for a common purpose or mutual advantage," while a clubhouse is a "building occupied by or used by a club."[23] A private club is "not open to or intended for public use."[24] A golf course includes a practice area, driving ranges, and the course itself. Generally, there is a clubhouse that contains a pro shop, food service, restrooms, locker rooms, offices, and storage areas. Additional buildings are also needed to maintain the golf course. A public course owned by a community may not be very elegant, but it provides an inexpensive opportunity for individuals and their guests to play golf. A private club is a different matter altogether, with extensive clubhouse facilities primarily for use by members, but it may also be open to the public (Table 10-7).

The business of a golf club is to provide a course to challenge amateur and/or professional players. The design of a new course includes many stakeholders with various responsibilities: developing feasibility studies, performing environmental assessments, and meeting regulatory requirements. Planners who specialize in golf course design will be joined by landscape architects and the facility's architect and design team. Architects and interior designers are naturally involved in planning the design for the clubhouse and other structures that are part of the facility. Some projects hire a club operational specialist (COS) for the planning phase, as this professional can influence marketing, technology, and image, as well as the successful operation of the facility.[25]

Golf courses have 9 or 18 holes and sometimes as many as 27. Obviously, this means that the golf course requires a great deal of open land. In fact, the earliest courses in Scotland were on grazing land or land that was otherwise unusable for crop tillage due to its rolling nature. Potential developers of a golf facility begin the process by using an economic study to see if the golf facility is viable for a particular community. Site analysis and environmental limitations and impacts are included in the planning and design

[22]*World Book Encyclopedia*, 2003, Vol. 8, p. 260.
[23]*Webster's New World College Dictionary*, 2002, p. 278.
[24]*Webster's New World College Dictionary*, 2002, p. 1142.
[25]"Effective Clubhouse Design," 2001, p. 51.

documents prepared by consultants. Since there are no rigid specifications for golf course layout and design, the golf course design consultant studies the land site and develops a routing plan for the course. Premier professional golfers like Jack Nicklaus, Greg Norman, and Arnold Palmer help design new golf courses.

Golf clubs almost always have a clubhouse facility where members and players can converge to relax before and after play. The clubhouse provides not only practical services such as lockers, showers, and toilet facilities but also pro shops, which sell golf equipment, and food and beverage services. Depending upon the size and type of clubhouse and the organization, the facility may also include a spa, a fitness center, and banquet rooms, as well as overnight accommodations.

With so many choices in clubs, today's golf complexes and country clubs must offer amenities to entice the public or members to use the facility. Beautifully appointed interiors are part of the formula in designing a successful clubhouse, whether it is formal or casual, traditional or contemporary. Members are increasingly using their clubhouse for entertaining guests. As a result, clubhouse design is becoming more residential in character.

Types of Golf Club Facilities

There are three types of golf clubs. All have basically the same components: a clubhouse and course. They vary greatly in amenities and design and in other offerings such as tennis courts. Variations in ownership also exist; golf clubs are typically owned by a municipality, a group of members, a corporation, a golf organization, and/or a resort hotel.

The *public club* is open to the general public, with access to the golf course and clubhouse. It is often owned by a municipality and thus is sometimes referred to as a *municipal club* or *course*. Some offer memberships, although most do not require membership fees. For the most part, the public club is also considered a *daily-fee course*. This means that a membership fee generally is not required, and players pay a fee only for the day. Public courses usually have a small clubhouse with minimal amenities. A golf shop, restrooms and locker rooms, and a small food service facility like a simple grill for light sandwiches are common. The Silverbell Golf course in Tucson, Arizona, and the Three Crowns Golf Club owned by the city of Casper, Wyoming, are two examples. The latter sits on land previously occupied by one of the largest oil refineries in the world; the land was donated to the city.[26]

Private clubs and clubhouses are abundant in the United States and include some of the most luxurious facilities. Members of the public are not permitted to play at the club or use its facilities except at the invitation of a member. Private clubs are owned by the members or by a corporation. Initiation and ongoing membership fees for private golf clubs produce the revenue to maintain the facilities. The Isleworth Country Club in Windermere, Florida, has an 82,000-square-foot clubhouse which includes 11 plasma televisions, table tennis and pool tables, a golf simulator and swing analyzer, a basketball hoop and a half court, and an indoor putting green. In addition, the dining room, entertainment, locker rooms, and fitness center are luxurious.[27]

A *resort club* is the third primary type of golf club and course. Many resorts are built with a focus on the golf course and other recreational amenities on the property. Guests of the hotel use the course while it is also open to the public. Fees to play the course may be included in room "packages" for guests, while the public would pay a higher fee than a hotel guest. Resort clubs have many amenities and luxuries since the expenses of the facilities are offset by the room rental rates (see Chapter 4 for more information on resorts). The Arizona Biltmore Resort and Spa in Phoenix is one of the many premier golf resorts in the world. A major focus of the resort clubhouse will be the pro shop. Players and visitors like to acquire the logo ware of the resort; thus, the retail area of the pro shop will be larger than that at other types of golf courses.

Although these are the main types of golf courses, there are some additional types. A *semiprivate club* is one where memberships can be purchased but play is also open to the general public. Depending on club rules, day use by the general public may be restricted

---

[26]Better. Nov./Dec. 2005. p. 80.
[27]Better. May/June 2005. p. 54.

TABLE 10-8 Types of Golf Club Facilities

- *Country club*: A social and recreational club that is usually private or semiprivate; the golf course is open only to members or guests of members. Restaurants, tennis and swimming can also be available.
- *Day-use club*: A fee is paid for the day, and no membership fee is involved. The club can be public or private.
- *Municipal*: Owned by a tax-supported city, county, or state and open to the public.

- *Private*: Owned privately. The organization varies greatly, depending upon the club's size, ownership, and location. Initiation fees and annual dues are required.
- *Public*: Open to the public, with access to the golf course and clubhouse.
- *Semiprivate*: Offers membership but allows the public to play at specific times.

in terms of which facilities other than the locker room, pro shop, and perhaps the restaurant the public may use.

A *golf and country club* is a more family-oriented club with amenities and facilities that appeal to a family. Many country clubs are private, although the golf course might be open to the public. Country clubs have dining facilities, swimming, tennis, and fitness centers, among the possible other facilities and activities (Table 10-8).

Planning and Interior Design Elements

The clubhouse is a very popular place to gather with friends, colleagues, and family. Clubhouses today are much more extensive than formerly. For example, in addition to the traditional dining facilities, bar area, and golf-related areas, clubhouses now also include weight rooms, spas, and beauty salons. Many golf facilities are private clubs with the dining facilities open to the public.

Golfer demographics have changed over the years, with increasing numbers of women and children involved in the sport. Although the golf and country club has long been a family-oriented recreational facility, other types of golf clubs have had to make adjustments to the clubhouse and other amenities offered to attract these new members. This has meant larger locker rooms and toilet facilities for women, and child-care programs and spaces for children's activities. Some clubs have added a mother's room for nursing and a parent-child restroom where mothers can change the baby's diapers. In addition, many of today's clubhouses are casual in design, with informal dining rooms, sports bars, and grills. Spaces are more family-oriented, which means larger informal areas and open lounges.[28] At the same time, generous spaces in the layouts promote a feeling of luxury.

Clubhouses are designed to function for the golfer and other guests. The floor plan can vary, depending upon the type of ownership and bylaws as well as the variety of services offered. Clubhouses can be very simple in design and function or luxurious, with elaborate facilities supporting many functions. Of course, all the buildings of the club will be designed by an architect to achieve a cohesive style using indigenous materials. The clubhouse is sited close to the first tee and the 9th and 18th greens (Figure 10-14).

Clubs and clubhouses may include a wide variety of functions. This section will focus on the most important private and public areas of a generic clubhouse. The discussion of planning and design elements highlights the main building, including the lobby and lounge, a generic restaurant, locker rooms, and the pro shop.

It is not unusual for there to be three entrances to the clubhouse: a private entrance for members, one for the public, and one directly to the pro shop from the parking area. The entrance lobby is a large space which allows users to easily find their way, although many facilities include signage to help direct members and guests. Spaces which are commonly accessed off the entrance lobby are the lounge, the dining room(s), and the corridor to functional spaces such as the locker room, fitness center, and spa. The administrative offices

---

[28]Wilder, 2001, p. 2.

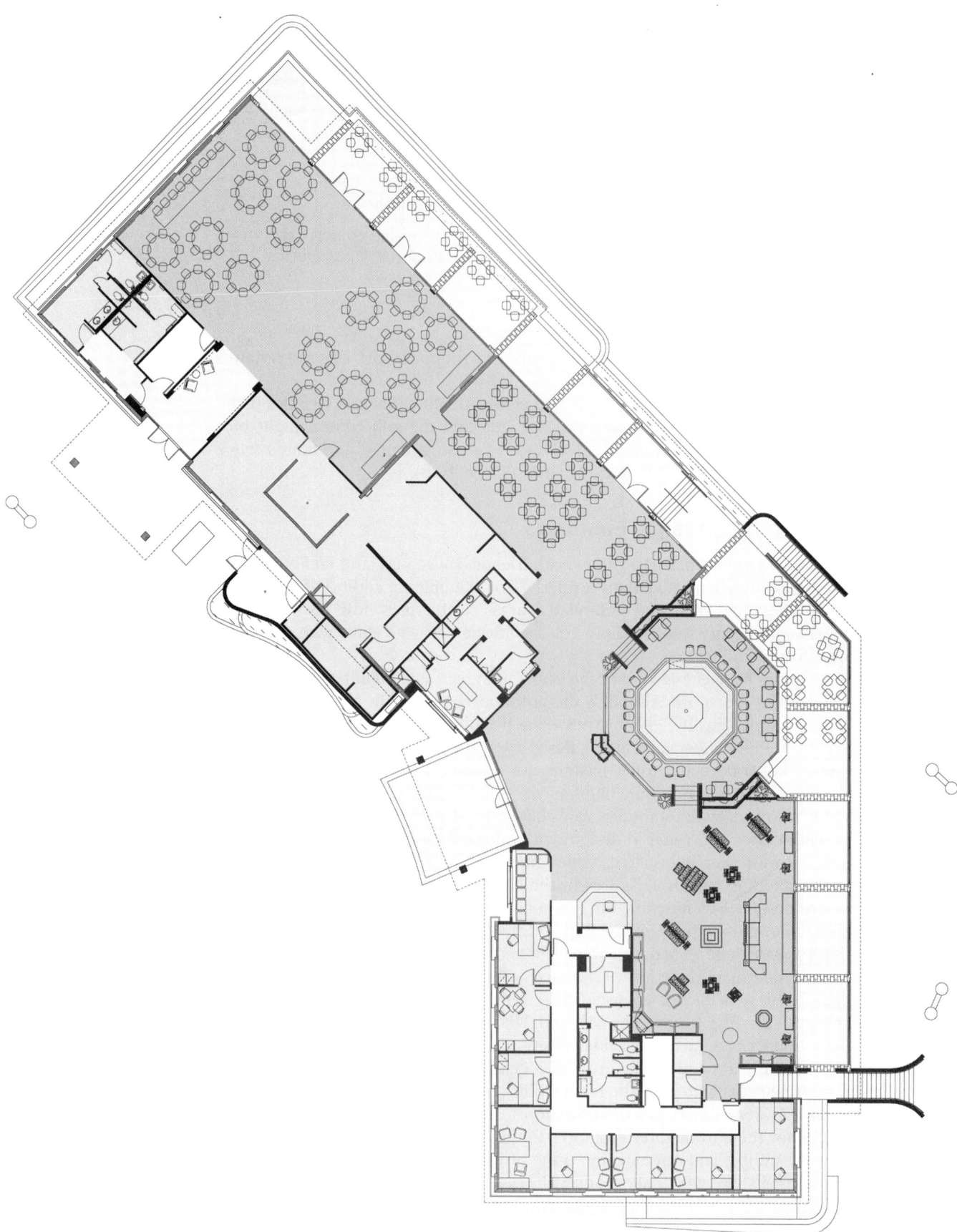

Figure 10-14 Floor plan of a golf clubhouse. Note the volume of space allotted to the central kitchen and the dining spaces. Champions Gate clubhouse. (Drawing courtesy of Burke, Hogue & Mills Architects.)

Figure 10-15 Dining room in the Champions Gate clubhouse. Note the emphasis on the exterior view. (Photography courtesy of Burke, Hogue & Mills Architects.)

might be located off the main entrance, where they are available to the members but also discreetly placed for privacy.

The lounge or living room generally has conversation groupings including sofas, chairs, end tables, lamps, and coffee tables. Fireplaces are often situated in this space, and at least one of the groupings should focus on the fireplace. As clubhouse design emphasizes a residential appearance, interior designers need to present a plan which reinforces this concept.

The dining room in a large clubhouse would be located off the main entrance, with a lounge and a casual bar in this vicinity (Figure 10-15). Smaller, more casual eating areas such as a sandwich grill with outside service near the pro shop are common. Large dining spaces can be very flexible if divided by panels. The dining area can also be planned with half-height walls to divide the large space into more intimate dining spaces. Dining areas and the kitchen often become the hub of operations for a clubhouse. Making the kitchen services unobtrusive is one of the keys in clubhouse design.[29]

The bar is one of the more popular areas of the clubhouse and an important source of revenue for a golf facility. It can be placed adjacent to the dining room. Smaller bars are often located on the patios near the pro shop and locker rooms. Depending on the club, the bar can be a casual sports bar with seating at the bar as well as at small tables. Broadcasts of sporting events are popular in the bar, as well as live entertainment on the weekends (Figure 10-16). A more traditional club might have a more formal bar lounge where the "entertainment" is really the camaraderie of the members. Furniture in this case might be sofas, club chairs, and even tables where card games may occur.

Locker rooms are generally close to the exterior door leading to the first tee but accessible from the main clubhouse as well. They are planned for both interaction and privacy. The interior designer and the architect must create locker rooms which are functional and efficient as well as providing privacy. Space allocation for expanded locker rooms and fitness centers has also become necessary.

For the golfer, the locker room is one of the most important facilities provided by the club. Today's members want larger locker rooms with more amenities. The pro shop is usually located near the locker rooms and close to the first tee. The bag and cart storage areas are adjacent to the pro shop and locker rooms for easy access before and after the golf game. Pro shops function as a retail facility, selling golf equipment, supplies, clothing,

---

[29]Wilder, 2001, p. 4.

Figure 10-16 Bar area in a golf clubhouse. Televisions and an exterior view are popular elements in this area. (Photography courtesy of Burke, Hogue & Mills Architects.)

and memorabilia. An entrance from the parking lot is beneficial both for members and for nonmembers who do not need to enter the clubhouse. Access to the locker rooms from the pro shop is also common in clubhouse planning (Figure 10-17).

Besides controlling players' access to the course, the pro shop is a retail store. It must be planned using the same good techniques and concepts as for any retail store. A cash/wrap counter and merchandise displays are planned to encourage shopping by players and nonplayers alike. At many golf course facilities, logo ware is very popular, and the display of clothing and other items with the club's logo is an important planning issue.

Figure 10-17 The pro shop provides products for sale, such as sports equipment and clothing. (Photography courtesy of Burke, Hogue & Mills Architects.)

Patios, terraces, and balconies are important design elements for any clubhouse. Players and guests enjoy relaxing outdoors before or after playing golf. Some people simply enjoy the view of the course from the patios outside the clubhouse. The interior designer will be responsible for specifying furniture and furnishings for these areas. Food and beverage services are always part of the allure of outdoor seating at this facility. In the summer and in warmer climates, outdoor exhibition kitchens can become exciting secondary focal points on the patios.

The interior designer is generally responsible for much of the furniture, furnishings, and materials specification of the clubhouse. Naturally, this work is done in concert with the architect, the client, and possibly other design team members. The furniture selections for social areas like the lounge and dining room focus on styling, comfort, and often casual elegance, with placement which encourages interaction as well as a certain level of privacy.

Furniture specification and placement for the social areas is very important in that it must lead to effective, comfortable, and inviting spaces for the member or guest. Conversational groupings with no more than 10 feet between seating units are ideal for comfortable interaction. Clubs with older members will look for seating units that make it easier to stand. Given the growing number of women members, seating should also be comfortable for women. Textile specification for seating units should include comfort and durability. Since drinks are often served in the social areas, the fabrics must be easy to clean, although not everything should be vinyl or leather. The fabrics also need to be appropriate in scale and design. Other furniture in the lounge will include end tables and coffee tables so that the member or guest has a place for a drink. It is important to consider the reach distances when planning the use of coffee tables in the lounge. Buffets, console tables, and display cabinets can also be included in this area.

The dining room will be planned for a variety of group sizes, from single diners to large groups. A variety of tabletop sizes that can be combined to accommodate these different groups is necessary in planning the space. Refer to the discussion in Chapter 5 on food and beverage facilities for information on space planning, furniture planning, and specification in these areas of the clubhouse.

Furniture for the locker room needs to be functional and smaller in scale. This is true of both men's and women's locker rooms. First, of course, are the lockers. They can be full-length or tiered at 42 inches high, depending on the club management's wishes. They are most likely made of wood or wood laminates. Benches are placed in the locker area so that a member can sit in front of his or her locker. Benches are usually 16 inches high and 18 inches deep. The length of the bench is dictated by the overall design but should be 4 to 6 feet to facilitate movement. Televisions are positioned throughout the locker room to allow for continued viewing of many sports events.

A locker room lounge is quite common in private clubs as well as others. A small lounge attached to the men's and women's locker rooms provides a place for members to relax while in casual clothes that might not be allowed in the main lounge. Chairs usually have fabrics which are easily cleanable, durable, and antimicrobial, yet comfortable to the skin. In the casual seating areas, small end tables for lighting, literature, and drinks are provided. It is not unusual to place a chaise lounge somewhere in the locker room in case someone feels ill. Card tables in the men's locker room suites are also common in the larger clubs. Women members generally prefer to have a card room off the main lounge. Chairs with casters are preferred by most members for this activity. Women's locker rooms will also need small bench seating or stools in front of the makeup mirrors.

The pro shop's furnishings will be quite simple. Counters, and display cabinets and cases are required for merchandise display and storage. Specialized display racks are needed for the display of golf clubs, bags, and perhaps other sporting equipment that might be sold in the pro shop. A cash/wrap counter that is large enough to accommodate both the register for sales of goods and space for booking and checking in for tee times or court times is also needed. Chapter 6 on retail design should be reviewed if the designer is contracted to design the pro shop since the concepts are very similar.

Many of the finishes and architectural materials in a clubhouse will be those suitable for the hospitality industry. There are, however, many products designed specifically for the fitness center industry that will be appropriate to areas of the clubhouse. As today's clubhouses are also used for entertaining guests, requests by members to create a more comfortable, residential atmosphere on a larger scale are common. Due to the multiple uses of a golf facility clubhouse, an interior designer needs to keep in mind the various needs of the areas in the facility. Concerning finishes, one important issue is where golf shoes with cleats, even soft cleats, can be worn in the interior. Some clubhouse bylaws do not allow golf shoes with cleats or dirty shoes in the clubhouse lounge and dining areas.

Carpet is a very popular choice for flooring in many areas. The carpet used in golf clubs will need to be replaced approximately every three to five years due to the heavy use and abuse. There are specific yarn systems and carpet construction which are more effective for the golfer's use. Where golf shoes are allowed, such as in the pro shop, the interior designer should specify a high-density, low-cut pile carpet because an uncut pile would cause pulling from cleats. A 60 oz per square yard pile density for traditional spikes on golf shoes and a 42 oz per square yard pile density for soft spikes on golf shoes are standard. It is also suggested that solution-dyed fibers be used because they provide fade resistance and color fastness, which are especially important with patterned carpets in this type of facility. Nylon yarn is preferred due to its resistance to wear and its rebound from crushing.[30]

The installation of hard or resilient flooring depends on its use. For example, it is critical to specify nonslip surfaces in the locker room and in other areas where slippage may occur. Textured surfaces of the resilient floor material add to the comfort and safety of the user. Hard-surface flooring in the entry and lobby could be stone, in the dining room carpeting to aid in acoustical control, and in the locker room antimicrobial carpeting.

Materials for walls can vary greatly. The interior designer must carefully review the uses of the spaces in order to make specification decisions on wall finishes which consider function, acoustics control, fire safety, and code compliance. Dining rooms and lounge spaces are often designed with large windows facing the course to take advantage of the wonderful view a course creates. At the same time, these hard surfaces can cause sound to bounce off the surface, creating more noise within the space and hindering comfortable conversation. The designer must use other architectural finish materials to absorb that additional sound. Such materials include cleanable acoustical cloth on the walls, dense carpeting, and fabric on the chairs. In some club dining rooms, draperies are allowed to increase sound absorption.

A wide variety of materials can be used as wall finishes. Wood paneling, wallpapers or textiles, tile, stone, and, of course, paint all may be used on interior walls, assuming that they meet appropriate building and fire safety codes. A traditional interior might include extensive millwork and wood paneling, including French doors and windows. A contemporary interior might include large, open windows, stone, glass block, and stainless steel. Paint is a versatile and economical wall finish that allows for numerous themes and concepts. The location of painted surfaces should be specified with care since some areas will receive more wear and tear than others.

When specifying paint, the interior designer should test the paint, and the paint finishes, at various times of the day. Color choices are greatly impacted by daylight, the types of artificial light sources used, and the use of the space. For example, a luxurious restaurant at the clubhouse with the majority of business in the evening and at night may require a quieter, cozier, more elegant color scheme and atmosphere. The grill might need the opposite type of color scheme. Whatever the color scheme, the interior designer must make certain that the colors selected are appropriate to the use of the space, as well as enhancing the space and creating a harmonious environment.

Acoustical concerns create interesting design challenges for the interior designer and architect. The high ceilings in the entry lobby, lounge, and reception area create a grand effect but also create acoustical problems, especially where hard flooring is installed. Noise from the locker room and activity rooms should be contained as much as possible in those

---

[30]"Effective Clubhouse Design," 2001. p. 20.

areas so that the lounge and dining rooms maintain a lower level of controlled ambient noise for conversations. Floor and wall treatment specifications are key factors in controlling acoustics once the zoning of spaces has been determined.

Lighting poses other design problems for the designer. Large windows that allow for wonderful daylighting effects create challenges regarding artificial lighting of spaces at night. High ceilings often mean that the designer must integrate wall sconces or wall-washing fixtures with spotlights or even pendent lights and chandeliers to illuminate the lounge and entry. Functional spaces like the locker rooms and the pro shop require functional lighting that does not become too glaring against the hard surfaces of walls and cabinetry. The reader should refer to Chapters 4, 5, and 6 for discussions of lighting design issues related to hospitality, food service, and retail spaces similar to those found in the clubhouse.

A clubhouse is a mixed-use occupancy, and in planning and specifying the interior, the designer will have to be very careful to meet multiple-occupancy regulations. When spaces with different occupancy classifications cannot be separated, the other spaces must meet the most stringent code requirements. In the generic golf clubhouse described here, there could well be spaces designated as Assembly occupancies—dining areas, the bar, locker rooms, fitness rooms, and community rooms; Business occupancies are spaces such as club offices and perhaps a beauty shop or barber shop; the pro shop is a Mercantile occupancy; and the building where golf carts are stored and serviced will be considered a Hazardous occupancy. The cart storage building is usually not connected to the main clubhouse, so this does not impact the code restrictions. However, all these occupancies in one place emphasize the care needed in specifying products and materials, as well as in planning the space.

It is not unusual for smoking to be allowed in some areas of the clubhouse. Newer clubs may have a separate bar or a cigar bar for smokers, with nonsmoking areas predominating. If smoking areas are allowed within the clubhouse, an air filtration or ventilation system that will adequately replace the room's air will be specified by the architect.

In general, accessibility guidelines must be met in the clubhouse unless the facility is a private club. There are exemptions for private clubs regarding the ADA guidelines. Other state and local code compliance may make accessibility design necessary for the convenience of members. Any club open to the public must meet federal accessibility requirements.

The interior design of clubhouses is an interesting commercial design specialty with potential involvement in many kinds of commercial spaces. Becoming involved in the interior design of any type of recreational space is an enjoyable way to engage in the profession. It does, however, require research as well as experience in hospitality and retail design.

Summary

Cultural and recreational facilities are exciting, creative, and challenging commercial interior design specialties. The design of these interiors requires specialized knowledge, and interior designers must gain experience by working as assistants until they become knowledgeable about the business and its planning needs. The ability to work with consultants who are often outside of the designer's firm is critical. It is difficult for any designer to gain all the specialized knowledge required to undertake the interior design of any of the facilities discussed in this chapter.

Given the breadth of business and design issues relevant to the successful design of cultural and recreational facilities, this chapter has presented key elements to aid the reader in developing an understanding of these facilities. Unfortunately, many kinds of facilities that would also fall into these categories could not be included. The reader is encouraged to review some of the sources listed below and to seek out other references. Only in gaining a complete understanding of the business of the client is it possible to design a facility that satisfies the many stakeholders involved in any of these projects.

REFERENCES

American Association of Museums. 1998. *The Official Museum Directory*, 28th ed. Washington, D.C.: National Register Publishing.

Appleton, Ian. 1996. *Buildings for the Performing Arts: A Design and Development Guide*. Oxford: Butterworth Architecture.

Architectural Record. 1977. "The Getty Center." November, pp. 72–105.

Barrie, Thomas. 1996. *Spiritual Path, Sacred Place: Myth, Ritual and Meaning in Architecture*. Boston: Shambhala.

Bennett, Corwin. 1977. *Spaces for People*. Englewood Cliffs, NJ: Prentice-Hall.

Better, Craig. 2005. "New Course Review." *Travel + Leisure Golf*. November/December. pp. 80–82.

Better, Craig. 2005. "New Course Review." *Travel + Leisure Golf*. May/June. pp. 54, 60–62.

Brawne, Michael. 1982. *The Museum Interior*. New York: Architecture Books.

Brockett, Oscar E. and F. J. Hildy. 1999. *History of the Theatre*, 8th ed. Boston: Allyn & Bacon.

Brown, Catherine R., William B. Fleissig, and William R. Morrish. 1984. *Building for the Arts: A Guidebook for the Planning and Design of Cultural Facilities*. Santa Fe, NM: Western States Arts Foundation.

Clawney, Paul. 1982. *Exploring Churches*. Grand Rapids, MI: W. B. Eerdmans.

Clements, Patrick L. 2002. *Proven Concepts of Church Building and Finance*. Grand Rapids, MI: Kregel.

Copplestone, Trewin, ed. 1963. *World Architecture*. London: Hamlyn.

Deiss, William A. 1984. *Museum Archives*. Chicago: The Society of American Archivists.

Diedrich, Richard J. 2005. *Building Type Basics for Recreational Facilities*. New York: Wiley.

Dillon, Joan and David Naylor. 1997. *American Theaters: Performance Halls of the Nineteenth Century*. New York: Preservation Press.

"Effective Clubhouse Design, Using a Club Operational Specialist." 2001. In *Clubhouse Design & Renovation*, 3rd ed. Jupiter, FL: National Golf Foundation.

Forsyth, M. 1987. *Auditoria: Designing for the Performing Arts*. London: Bartsford.

Gillette, J. Michael. 2004. *Theatrical Design and Production*, 5th ed. New York: McGraw-Hill.

Harrigan, J. E. 1987. *Human Factors Research*. New York: Elsevier Dutton.

Holly, Henry Hudson. 1971. *Church Architecture*. Hartford, CT: Mallory.

Hourston, Laura. 2004. *Museum Builders II*. New York: Wiley.

Izenour, George C. 1997. *Theatre Design*, 2nd ed. New York: McGraw-Hill.

Jankowski, Wanda. 1987. *The Best of Lighting Design*. New York: PBC International.

Klein, Judy Graf. 1982. *The Office Book*. New York: Facts on File.

Lake, Sheri. 1997. "Government/Institutional Design Specialty." *ASID Professional Designer*. May–June, pp. 24.

Lord, Gail Dexter. 1999. *The Manual of Museum Planning*, 2nd ed. Walnut Creek, CA: Altamira Press.

Lord, Peter and Duncan Templeton. 1986. *The Architecture of Sound*. London: Architectural Press.

Loveland, Anne C. and Otis B. Wheeler. 2003. *From Meetinghouse to Megachurch*. Columbia: University of Missouri Press.

Maguire, Robert Alfred. 1965. *Modern Churches of the World*. New York: Dutton.

Mahnke, Frank H. and Rudolph H. Mahnke. 1987. *Color and Light in Man-Made Environments*. New York: Van Nostrand Reinhold.

McCarty, L. B. 2001. *Best Golf Course Management Practices*. New York: Prentice Hall.

McGowan, Maryrose. 2004. *Interior Graphics Standards*. New York: Wiley.

Merriam-Webster's Collegiate Dictionary, 10th ed. 1994. Springfield, MA: Merriam-Webster.

Moore, Kevin. 1997. *Museums and Popular Culture*. London: Cassel.

New Encyclopedia Britannica, 15th ed. 1981. Chicago: Benton.

Newhouse, Victoria. 1998. *Towards a New Museum*. New York: Monacelli Press.

Packard, Robert and Balthazar Korab. 1995. *Encyclopedia of American Architecture*, 2nd ed. New York: McGraw-Hill.

Patterson, W. M. 1975. *A Manual of Architecture for Churches*. Nashville, TN: Methodist Publishing House.

Pevsner, Nicholas. 1976. *A History of Building Types*. Princeton, NJ: Princeton University Press.

Pile, John. 1990. *Dictionary of 20th Century Design*. New York: Facts on File.

———. 1995. *Interior Design*, 2nd ed. Englewood Cliffs, NJ: Prentice Hall.

Roberts, Nicholas W. 1986. *Interior Graphic and Design Standards*. New York: Watson-Guptill.

———. 2004. *Building Type Basics for Places of Worship*. New York: Wiley.

Rosenblatt, Arthur. 2001. *Building Type Basics for Museums*. New York: Wiley.

Solinger, Janet W. 1990. *Museums and Universities*. New York: Macmillan.

Steele, James. 1996. *Theatre Buildings*. London: Academy Editors.

Tillman, Peggy and Barry Tillman. 1991. *Human Factors Essentials: An Ergonomics Guide for Designers, Engineers, Scientists, and Managers*. New York: McGraw-Hill.

Walsh, John, Deborah Gribbon, and the J. Paul Getty Museum. 1997. *The J. Paul Getty Museum and Its Collections*. Lost Angeles: Getty Trust Publications.

Webster's New World College Dictionary, 4th ed. 2002. Cleveland: Wiley Publications.

Wilkes, Joseph A., ed. in chief, and Robert T. Packard, associate ed. 1988. *Encyclopedia of Architecture, Design, Engineering, and Construction*, Vols. 1 to 5. New York: Wiley.

Williams, Peter W. 1997. *Houses of God: Architecture in the US*. Urbana: University of Illinois Press.

World Book Encyclopedia. 2003. Vols. 8, 13, and 19. Chicago: World Book, Inc.

Web Sites

Adherents www.adherents.com

American Conservatory Theater www.act-sfbay.org

American Jewish Congress www.ajcongress.org

Chicago Art Institute www.artic.edu

Church Resource Guide www.churchresourceguide.com

Crystal Cathedral www.crystalcathedral.org

Cybergolf www.cybergolf.com

Estes Net www.estesnet.com/ComDev

Getty Center www.getty.edu

Golf Club Finder www.golfclubfinder.com

International Council for Christians and Jews www.iccj.org

John F. Kennedy Center for the Performing Arts www.kennedy-center.org

Lincoln Center for the Performing Arts www.lincolncenter.org

Metropolitan Museum of Art www.metmuseum.org

Museum of Fine Arts, Houston www.mfah.org

Museum of Modern Art www.moma.org

National Golf Foundation www.ngf.org

National Park Service www.nps.gov

Partners for Sacred Places www.sacredplaces.org

Smithsonian Institution www.si.edu

St. Patrick's Cathedral www.ny-archdiocese.org

Washington National Cathedral www.cathedral.org

Club Management Association of America www.cmaa.org

InformeDesign at the University of Minnesota, www.informedesign.umn.edu

Official Museum Directory www.officialmuseumdir.com

Retail Focus: Publication of the National Sporting Goods Association www.nsga.org

Travel + Leisure Golf Magazine www.travelandleisure.com

Note: Additional references related to material in this chapter are listed in the Appendix.

Appendix

General References

The references listed in this appendix are those that might be used in the design of a variety of commercial facilities. Readers are advised to check with local jurisdictions for the code books applicable in their area of interior design practice.

Allen, Edward and Joseph Iano. 2004. *Fundamentals of Building Construction,* 4th ed. New York: Wiley.

American Institute of Architects. 2003. *Security Planning and Design.* New York: Wiley.

———. 2005. *Security Design: Achieving Transparency in Civic Architecture.* Washington, DC: AIA.

Arthur, Paul and Romedi Passini. 1992. *Wayfinding.* New York: McGraw-Hill.

Ballast, David Kent. 2005. *Interior Construction and Detailing for Designers and Architects,* 3rd ed. Belmont, CA: Professional Publications.

Binggeli, Corky. 2003. *Building Systems for Interior Designers.* New York: Wiley.

Birren, Faber. 1988. *Light, Color & Environment,* 2nd rev. ed. West Chester, PA: Schiffer.

Bisharat, Keith A. 2004. *Construction Graphics.* New York: Wiley.

Bradshaw, Vaughn. 2006. *Building Control Systems,* 3rd ed. New York: Wiley.

Brawley, Elizabeth C. 2005. *Design Innovations for Aging and Alzheimer's.* New York: Wiley.

Callender, John Hancock, ed. 1986. *Time-Saver Standards for Architectural Design Data,* 6th ed. New York: McGraw-Hill.

Cavanaugh, William J. and Joseph A. Wilkes, eds. 1998. *Architectural Acoustics.* New York: Wiley.

Ching, Francis D. K. and Cassandra Adams. 2001. *Building Construction Illustrated,* 3rd ed. New York: Wiley.

Ching, Francis D. K. and Steven R. Winkel. 2003. *Building Codes Illustrated.* New York: Wiley.

Deasy, C. M. 1990. *Designing Places for People.* New York: Watson-Guptill.

De Chiara, Joseph, Julius Panero, and Martin Zelnik. 2001, 1991. *Time-Saver Standards for Interior Design and Space Planning.* New York: McGraw-Hill.

Early, Mark W., ed. in chief, Jeffrey S. Sargent, Joseph V. Sheehan, and John M. Caloggero. 2005. *National Electrical Code Handbook,* 10th ed. Quincy, MA: National Fire Protection Association.

Egan, M. David. 1988. *Architectural Acoustics.* New York: McGraw-Hill.

Faga, Barbara. 2006. *Designing Public Consensus.* New York: Wiley.

Farren, Carol E. 1999. *Planning and Managing Interior Projects,* 2nd ed. Kingston, MA: R. S. Means.

Garner, Bryan A., ed. 2004. *Blacks Law Dictionary,* 11th ed., St. Paul, MN: Thomson Group.

Garrison, Elena M.S., ed. *The Graphic Standards Guide to Architectural Finishes.* New York: Wiley.

Gordon, Gary and James L. Nicholls. 1995. *Interior Lighting for Designers,* 3rd ed. New York: Wiley.

Haines, Roger W. and C. Lewis Wilson. 1994. *HVAC Systems Design Handbook,* 2nd ed. New York: McGraw-Hill.

Hall, Edward T. 1969. *The Hidden Dimension.* New York: Doubleday-Anchor Books.

Hall, William R. 1993. *Contract Interior Finishes.* New York: Watson-Guptill.

Harmon, Sharon Koomen. 2005. *The Codes Guidebook for Interiors,* 3rd ed. New York: Wiley.

International Code Council. 2003. *International Building Code.* Falls Church, VA: International Code Council.

Jackman, Dianne R. and Mary K. Dixon. 1983. *The Guide to Textiles for Interior Designers.* Winnipeg, Manitoba, Canada: Peguis.

Karlen, Mark and James Benya. 2004. *Lighting Design Basics.* New York: Wiley.

Kearney, Deborah. 1993. *The New ADA: Compliance and Costs.* Kingston, MA: R. S. Means.

Kilmer, Rosemary and W. Otie Kilmer. 1992. *Designing Interiors.* Fort Worth, TX: Haracourt Brace Jovanovich.

Kopacz, Jeanne. 2004. *Color in Three-Dimensional Design.* New York: McGraw-Hill.

Leibrock, Cynthia. 1992. *Beautiful Barrier Free: A Visual Guide to Accessibility.* New York: Van Nostrand Reinhold.

Mahnke, Frank H. and Rudolph H. Mahnke. 1987. *Color and Light in Man-Made Environments.* New York: Van Nostrand Reinhold.

McGowan, Maryrose. 1996. Specifying Interiors. *A Guide to Construction and FF&E for Commercial Interiors Projects.* New York: Wiley.

———. 2004a. *Interior Graphic Standards*. New York: Wiley.

———. 2004b, ed. *Interior Graphic Standards. Student Edition*. New York: Wiley.

McGowan, Maryrose. 2005. *Specifying Interiors: A Guide to Construction and FF&E for Residential and Commercial Interiors Projects,* 2nd ed. New York: Wiley.

McGuinness, William J., Benjamin Stein, and John S. Reynolds. 1980. *Mechanical and Electrical Equipment for Buildings,* 6th ed. New York: McGraw-Hill.

McPartland, J. F. and Brian J. McPartland. 1996. *National Electrical Code Handbook,* 22nd ed. New York: McGraw-Hill.

Mendler, Sandra F. and William Odell. 2000. *The HOK Guidebook to Sustainable Design*. New York: Wiley.

Miller, Mary C. 1997. *Color for Interior Architecture*. New York: Wiley.

Nadal, Barbara A. 2004. *Building Security*. New York: McGraw-Hill.

National Fire Protection Association (NFPA). 2003. *NFPA 101: Life Safety Code*. Quincy, MA: NFPA.

Null, Roberta with Kenneth F. Cherry. 1998. *Universal Design*. Belmont, CA: Professional Publications.

Panero, Julius and Martin Zelnick. 1979. *Human Dimension and Interior Space*. New York: Watson-Guptill.

Pile, John. 1997. *Color in Interior Design*. New York: McGraw-Hill.

———. 2005. *A History of Interior Design*. New York: Wiley.

Piotrowski, Christine M. 2002. *Professional Practice for Interior Designers*. 3rd ed. New York: Wiley.

Preiser, Wolfgang and Elaine Ostroff. 2001. *Universal Design Handbook*. New York: McGraw-Hill.

Ramsey, Charles G., Harold R. Sleeper, and John Ray Hoke, Jr., eds. 2000. *Architectural Graphic Standards*, 10th ed. New York: Wiley.

Reznikoff, S. C. 1986. *Interior Graphic and Design Standards*. New York: Watson-Guptill.

———. 1989. *Specifications for Commercial Interiors*, rev. ed. New York: Watson-Guptill.

Riggs, J. Rosemary. 1989. *Materials and Components for Interior Design*, 2nd ed. Reston, VA: Reston Publishing (Prentice Hall).

Rosen, Harold J. and John Regener. 2004. *Construction Specifications Writing: Principles and Procedures,* 5th ed. New York: Wiley.

Seffy, Gary. 2002. *Architectural Lighting Design,* 2nd ed. New York: Wiley.

Sewell, Bill. 2006. *Building Security Technology*. New York: McGraw-Hill.

Simmons, H. Leslie. 1989. *The Architect's Remodeling, Renovation, and Restoration Handbook*. New York: Van Nostrand Reinhold.

Sommer, Robert. 1983. *Social Design*. San Francisco: Rinehart Press.

Sorcar, Pratulla C. 1987. *Architectural Lighting for Commercial Interiors*. New York: Wiley.

Specifications for Making Buildings and Facilities Accessible to and Usable by Physically Handicapped People. Standard A117.1-1980. New York: American National Standards Institute.

Spiegel, Ross and Dru Meadows. *Green Building Materials*. New York: Wiley.

Stewart, Thomas A. 1993. "Welcome to the Revolution." *Fortune*. December 13, pp. 66ff.

Templeton, Duncan and David Saunders. 1987. *Acoustic Design*. New York: Van Nostrand Reinhold.

Terry, Evan, Associates. 1993. *Americans with Disabilities Act Facilities Compliance: A Practical Guide*. New York: Wiley.

Wakita, Osamu A. and Richard M. Linde. 2002. *The Professional Practice of Architectural Working Drawings*. New York: Wiley.

Watson, Lee. 1990. *Lighting Design Handbook*. New York: McGraw-Hill.

Weaver, Martin E. *Conserving Buildings: A Manual of Techniques and Materials*, rev. ed. New York: Wiley.

Wilkes, Joseph A., senior ed., and Robert Packard, associate ed. 1988. *Encyclopedia of Architecture, Design, Engineering and Construction*. New York: Wiley.

Magazine Resources

Many magazines are listed with Web site addresses at the end of each chapter. Readers may also want to search *Ulrich's International Periodicals Directory* for other magazine titles of interest. This directory is published annually and can generally be found at the reference desk of public and university libraries.

Trade Associations

The reader may also wish to refer to the *Encyclopedia of Associations*, published annually and available at the reference desk of most libraries. Addresses and Web site addresses are accurate as of this printing, but contact information might have changed. Other associations pertinent to particular types of commercial spaces are listed at the end of each chapter.

American Animal Hospital Association
P.O. Box 15089
Denver, CO 80215
www.aahanet.org

American Association of Museums
1225 I St., N.W.
Washington, DC 20005
www.aam-us.org

American Association of School Administrators
801 W. Quincy Street, Suite 700
Arlington, VA 22203
www.aasa.org

American Dental Association
211 E. Chicago Ave.
Chicago, IL 60611
www.ada.org

American Furniture Manufacturers Association
P.O. Box HP7
High Point, NC 27261
www.afma4u.org

American Hospital Association
1 N. Franklin Street
Chicago, IL 60606
www.aha.org

American Hotel and Lodging Association
1201 New York Avenue, N.W.
Washington, DC 20005-3931
www.ahla.com

American Institute of Architects (AIA)
1735 New York Avenue, N.W.
Washington, DC 20006
www.aia.org

American Library Association
50 E. Huron St.
Chicago, IL 60611
www.ala.org

American Lighting Association
P.O. Box 420288
Dallas, TX 75342
www.americanlightingassoc.com

American National Standards Institute (ANSI)
25 W. 43rd Street
New York, NY 10036
www.ansi.org

American Society of Furniture Designers
P.O. Box 2688
2101 W. Green Drive
High Point, NC 27261
www.asfd.com

American Society for Testing and Materials (ASTM)
100 Barr Harbor Drive
West Conshohocken, PA 19428
www.astm.org

American Society of Interior Designers (ASID)
608 Massachusetts Avenue, N.E.
Washington, DC 20002-2302
www.asid.org

Architectural Woodwork Institute
1952 Isaac Newton Square West
Reston, VA 20190
www.awinet.org

Association for Project Managers
1227 W. Wrightwood Avenue
Chicago, IL 60614
ww.constructioneducation.com

Association for Women in Architecture
2550 Beverly Boulevard
Los Angeles, CA 90057
www.awa-la.org

Association of Registered Interior Designers of Ontario (ARIDO)
717 Church Street
Toronto, ON M4W 2M5 Canada
www.arido.ca

British Contract Furnishing Association
25 West Wycombe Road High Wycombe
Buckinghamshire, UK HP 112LQ, London
www.thebcfa.com

Building Owners and Managers Association (BOMA)
1201 New York Avenue, N.W.
Washington, DC 20005
www.boma.org

Business and Institutional Furniture Manufacturers Association (BIFMA)
2680 Horizon, S.E.
Grand Rapids, MI 49546
www.bifma.org

Center for Health Design, Inc.
1850 Gateway Boulevard, Suite 1083
Concord, CA 94520
www.healthdesign.org

Center for Universal Design, The Center for Accessible Housing
North Carolina State University
P.O. Box 8613
Raleigh, NC 27695-8613
www.designNncsu.edu/cud

The Color Association of the United States
315 West 39th Street, Suite 507
New York, NY 10018
www.colorassociation.com

Color Marketing Group
5845 Richmond Highway, Suite 410
Alexandria, VA 22303
www.colormarketing.org

Construction Specifications Institute (CSI)
99 Canal Center Plaza
Alexandria, VA 22314
www.csinet.org

Council for Interior Design Accreditation
(Formally Foundation for Interior Design Education Research)
146 Monroe Center, N.W., Suite 1318
Grand Rapids, MI 49503
www.accredit-id.org

Illuminating Engineering Society of North America
120 Wall Street, 17th floor
New York, NY 10005
www.iesna.org

Institute of Store Planners (ISP)
25 N. Broadway
Tarrytown, NY 10591
www.ispo.org

Interior Design Educators Council (IDEC)
7150 Winton Drive, Suite 300
Indianapolis, IN 46268
www.idec.org

Interior Designers of Canada (IDC)
Ontario Design Center, 260 King St. E., Suite 414
Toronto
Ontario, Canada M54A 1K3
www.interiordesigncanada.org

International Association of Lighting Designers
Merchandise Mart, #9, 104
200 World Trade Center
Chicago, IL 60654
www.iald.org

International Code Council (ICC)
5203 Leesburg Pike, Suite 600
Falls Church, VA 22041
www.iccsafe.org

International Facility Management Association (IFMA)
1 E. Greenway Plaza, Suite 1100
Houston, TX 77046
www.ifma.org

International Furnishings and Design Association (IFDA)
191 Clarksville Road
Princeton Junction, NJ 08550
www.ifda.com

International Interior Design Association (IIDA)
13-500 Merchandise Mart
Chicago, IL 60654
www.iida.org

Merchandise Mart Properties, Inc.
Suite 470, The Merchandise Mart
200 World Trade Center
Chicago, IL 60654
www.mmart.com

National Association of Store Fixture Manufacturers
3595 Sheridan Street, Suite 200
Hollywood, FL 33021
www.nasfm.org

National Council for Interior Design Qualification (NCIDQ)
1200 18th Street NW, Suite 1001
Washington, DC 20036
www.ncidq.org

National Endowment for the Arts
1100 Pennsylvania Avenue, N.W.
Washington, DC 20506
www.nea.gov

National Fire Protection Agency (NFPA)
1 Batterymarch Park
P.O. Box 9101
Quincy, MA 02269
www.nfpa.org

National Kitchen and Bath Association
687 Willow Grove Street
Hackettstown, NJ 07840
www.nkba.org

National Restaurant Association
1200 17th Street, N.W.
Washington, DC 20036
www.restaurant.org

National Trust for Historic Preservation
1785 Massachusetts Avenue, N.W.
Washington, DC 20036
www.nationaltrust.org

Organization of Black Designers (OBD)
300 M Street, S.W.
Washington, DC 20024
www.core77.com/obd/info.html

Partners for Sacred Places
1616 Walnut Street
Philadelphia, PA 19103
www.sacredplaces.org

Underwriters' Laboratories, Inc.
333 Pfingsten Road
Northbrook, IL 60062
www.ul.com

U.S. Department of Justice (DOJ)
Office of Americans with Disabilities Act
950 Pennsylvania Avenue, N.W.
Washington, DC 20530-0001
www.usdoj.gov

U.S. Environmental Protection Agency (EPA)
Ariel Rios Building
1200 Pennsylvania Avenue, N.W.
Washington, DC 20460
www.epa.gov

U.S. Green Building Council (USGBC)
1015 18th Street, N.W. Suite 508
Washington, D.C. 20036
www.usgbc.org

Glossary

Accent lighting: Lighting used to call attention to specific areas or elements of a space.

Access floors: A raised floor added over a floor slab. The space houses electrical, telephone, and data cables and HVAC ducts. Also called **raised floors.**

Acquisition: A new object added to a museum collection.

Active adult community: A totally planned senior community where people live in homes, duplexes, or apartments.

Acute care patient: A patient requiring immediate or ongoing medical attention.

Adaptive use: The process of redesigning and converting a building to a use other than that for which it was originally designed.

Adult day care: A daily program in a freestanding or attached facility that provides social and medical support to the client during daytime hours.

Aging in place: The opportunity for seniors to remain in their homes as long as possible rather than move to a nursing facility.

Aisle: An unenclosed path of travel that occupies space between furniture items and/or pieces of equipment.

Altar: A raised platform where ceremonial activities occur in religious facilities.

Alternative officing: Strategies that provide office space other than permanently assigned traditional offices.

Alzheimer's disease: One of the most commonly diagnosed forms of dementia.

Ambient lighting: Provides a uniform level of illumination sufficient so that individuals in the space can safely move about the area. Also referred to as **general lighting**.

Ambulatory care: Usually indicates that the patient does not require admittance to a hospital for treatment.

Amenities: Services or items that are provided to make the guest's stay at a lodging facility more convenient or pleasant.

American (or conventional) seating plan: An arrangement of rows of seats in an assembly space, such as a theater, with a central aisle and perimeter aisles.

Amperage: The amount of electrical current required to operate any kind of electrical device.

Amphitheater: Generally considered to be an outdoor theater.

Anchor store: A large, well-known chain store that attracts many customers to a shopping center. It is a focal feature of the shopping center. Sometimes called a **magnet store.**

Ancillary departments: Functional departments in a hospital that support the medical services and units. Ancillary departments can also be found in other types of commercial facilities.

Ancillary space: A support space in an office facility. Common ancillary or support spaces include conference rooms, storage areas, file rooms and mailrooms, employee cafeterias, and copy centers.

Angled front: Storefront design that gives the consumer a better viewing angle of the merchandise.

Appeal: A proceeding that occurs when a defendant in a criminal case or either party to a civil case does not believe that the decision was correct.

Appellate court (also called *appeals court*): Reviews cases after conclusion by the trial court if requested.

Arcade front: Storefront design that has several recessed windows.

Archival library: A facility that has focused its collection on documents of historic value.

Archives: Documents, photos, drawings, or any other kinds of public or private papers or materials that are preserved for their historical value.

Arena theater: A theater in which the stage is in the middle of the auditorium with seating surrounding the stage.

Armored or BX cable: Two or more insulated wires and a ground wire all covered by a flexible wound metal wrapping. Sometimes called *flexible cable.*

Asepsis: The methods used to prevent infection in dental procedures.

"As is": Space is rented by the tenant without any changes to the interior.

Assisted living facility (ALF): Semi-independent living

facility for those who require minimal nursing or other care. Also called **personal-care homes.**

Atmospherics: A conscious effort by the retailer to create a buying environment to produce specific emotional effects on buyers.

Attending physician: The physician in a hospital responsible for the diagnosis and treatment of the patient.

Auditorium: The part of a theater where the patrons sit to watch a performance. It can also be a part of a building, such as a school, used for performances, meetings, or educational programs.

Back bar: The display area for the different liquors and glasses, as well as storage space for beer, extra liquor, and other items needed at the bar.

Back of the house: Those areas in a commercial facility such as a hotel or restaurant where employees have minimal contact with the customer or public.

Backstage: The production and storage spaces in a theater.

Balcony: A projecting area of seating in the upper parts of the theater.

Baldochino: An ornamental canopy over an altar or seat of honor.

Bailiff: Court official common in U.S. Court of Appeals Courts. Assists the judge and helps ensure security in the courtroom. Staff member in other level courts as well.

Bank: An institutional facility that provides for deposits, lending, and protection of money and other financial assets.

Banquette: An upholstered bench along the wall commonly fronted by a table.

Bar: A railing that separates the area for spectators from the area for the judge, jury, and other parties to the case. It is also a term for the legal profession.

Bar: A small beverage facility providing a small amount of seating and little food service.

Bar chart: A type of schedule that shows a list of activities in one column and uses horizontal bars to indicate the expected length of time it will take to complete each activity. Sometimes called a **Gantt chart.**

Base building: The shell of the building including the building's core, such as elevators and restrooms.

Base feed: A trough that runs along the base of divider panels and contains separate channels for electrical conduit and telecommunications cables.

Basilica: Ancient Roman government buildings that later became churches. It is a specific size and type of church today.

Bearing walls: Walls that support the loads of floors and/or ceilings from above.

Bed and breakfast inn: A lodging facility that provides sleeping and breakfast service.

Belt-line electrical service: System furniture setup with the outlets and electrical channels located 24 or 30 inches above the base of the panel

Bench: The place where the judge sits in a courtroom.

Beverage facility: A business, either as a section of a restaurant or as a freestanding facility, that serves primarily alcoholic beverages for on-site consumption.

Bimah (or *bema*): A table in the area in front of the ark where up to five people can gather on three sides of this reading area in a synagogue.

Black box: A simple performance space with minimal scenery and audience amenities. Seating often consists of folding chairs to help production crews create a variety of performances.

Boarding: Space within a veterinary clinic where animals can be kept overnight, whether they are healthy or need overnight medical care.

Board of directors: Individuals elected by shareholders to run a company. The board is legally responsible for such things as selecting the president and other chief officers, delegating operational power, and setting policy on matters concerning stocks, financing, and executive pay levels.

Board of regents: A voluntary group of individuals usually appointed by a state governor to oversee a university system.

Boutique hotel: A hotel designed using trendy, high-fashion appointments in its design and amenities. Many are smaller than nonboutique hotels.

Boutique system: A store planning system that divides the sales floor into individual, semiseparate areas, each possibly built around a shopping theme that focuses on the individuality of the product.

Branch bank: A satellite of a main bank such as a commercial bank. Branch banking is allowed in most states.

Brownfields: Industrial or commercial buildings/sites that have been abandoned or underutilized due to some sort of environmental contamination.

Build to suit: An arrangement whereby the landlord will build the interior of the commercial space to suit the needs of the tenant.

Building permitting privileges: A jurisdiction grants design professionals the authority to submit their sealed or stamped construction drawings to the jurisdictional building code official to obtain a building permit to proceed with actual construction.

Building standards: Predetermined architectural finishes and other details the tenant can use with no extra charge.

Built-out allowance: A dollar amount per square foot provided by the landlord to the tenant to pay the cost of building partitions, providing basic mechanical features, and adding architectural finishes for leased commercial space.

Bull pen: A large number of employees doing essentially the same kind of work in a large, open area divided by low systems panels or a large group of desks.

Business of the business: Gaining an understanding of the business goals and purposes of a commercial client before or during execution of the design.

Cantor: A synagogue official who sings or chants religious music.

Capital assets: An accounting term generally meaning property, buildings, and equipment that a firm requires to conduct its business.

Capital improvement: Permanent changes to the building's interior that cannot be removed without damaging the structure, such as wood floors. They increase the value of the space.

Carnegie library: A facility funded by the Carnegie Foundation, which was founded in 1911 to aid community libraries and schools.

Carpel tunnel syndrome: A musculoskeletal disorder that usually affects the arms, wrists, and fingers. It is associated with repetitive tasks like computer keyboarding.

Carrel table: A small enclosure, usually freestanding, for individual study.

Case goods: Furniture items made of "cases" like desks, credenzas, bookcases, file cabinets, and so on.

Catalog system: Any of the methods used to catalog library materials to make it easier for a patron to find needed materials.

Cathode ray tube (CRT): The computer screen or monitor.

Central bank: A bank operated by the federal government and functioning as a depository for other banks.

Central processing unit (CPU): The hardware or "brain" of a computer where computations and data manipulation take place.

Certificate of appropriateness (COA): A document given by the architectural review board allowing the proposed alteration or new construction related to a project of historic value or adaptive use.

Certificate of need: A document that regulates the construction of new healthcare facilities.

Chain: Multiple locations of one restaurant or lodging facility type. A term also applied to stores and other kinds of commercial facilities.

Chancel: The name usually given to the sanctuary in most Protestant churches.

Chancellor: A title given to the head of a university. The chancellor may be responsible for one school or, in some states, several schools.

Check stand: A stand-up-height cabinet in a bank where depositors fill out forms to add or withdraw funds from their accounts.

Chief executive officer (CEO): The highest-ranking individual in a business. Sometimes called the *president* or *principal*.

Civil case/court: Civil courts settle disputes involving noncriminal cases such as those involving negligence, breach of contracts, and disputes over wills.

Clearinghouse: An establishment maintained by banks for settling mutual claims and accounts.

Clientele: A common term for consumer's of salon services.

Closed office plan: A floor plan in which the office is planned around the private office with full-height walls for use by one individual. Also called a *conventional office plan.*

Closed stacks: Shelves of library materials available only by checking them out from library staff.

Club floor: A floor or area of a hotel that has restricted access to the guests on that floor or area. It usually has a small lounge where special amenities or extra services are provided.

Coaxial: A data cable with a central core conductor surrounded by insulation material covered by a metal sheath that acts as a second insulator. This cable is finished with an outer coating.

Commercial bank: A facility offering common banking services such as savings and checking accounts, safe deposit boxes, loans, and possibly trust administration.

Commercial hotel: A facility that caters to the business traveler and is located in urban centers or near central business district.

Commercial interior: The interior of any facility that serves business purposes.

Common law: Law that applies to everyone in the land. Common law courts used traditional legal principles based mainly on precedents.

Component: One of the items, such as a shelf, drawer unit, or work surface, that is used with a divider panel for an open office systems station.

Concept: An overall idea that unifies all parts of the design of a facility and provides a specific direction for all aspects of the design.

Concert hall: A type of theater that primarily presents musical performances for orchestras and singers.

Concierge: A hotel staff member who provides information and assistance to guests. The term is also associated with alternative office arrangements in which one office or workstation may be used by several people. The reservation to use the office space is made through the concierge at the office.

Conditional Use Permit (CUP): A permit given to a property owner by the municipality allowing a building's use in a zoned area that normally does not allow that use.

Conference center: A type of hotel specially designed for smaller meetings and conferences than would be held at a convention hotel.

Connector: The hardware used to connect panels together in open office systems projects.

Conservation: Specialized work performed on items in a museum's collection in order to stabilize and save pieces of artwork or antiquities. This term also means preventing loss of resources or other material items from harm, waste, or depletion and is applied to restoration or adaptive use.

Continental seating plan: Main floor seating of an assembly occupancy such as a theater in which aisles are located only on the perimeter sides of the space.

Continuing care retirement community (CCRC): A planned community providing rented or purchased living facilities for seniors whose needs may range from no assistance up to and including skilled nursing care.

Continuing education unit (CEU): Credit given for attendance at approved seminars, workshops, and training sessions that provide updating and information on the practice of interior design. Other professions also provide CEU credits.

Congregate housing: Housing for the elderly that includes one meal a day, housekeeping, and some activities.

Convenience goods: Items that are much used and often purchased, such as hosiery in a clothing store.

Convention hotel: One that caters to large business, professional, or other organizational groups where the emphasis is on meetings or related activities.

Conventional furniture: Desks, credenzas, file cabinets, and bookcases.

Core drilling: A hole is drilled in a concrete floor in a high-rise building in order to bring electrical and other cable services from below.

Corporate culture: A combination of policies, employee behavior, company values, company image, and assumptions about the world of work at a company.

Corridor: Any circulation space set off by partitions, rails, or dividers over 69 inches in height.

Court: A government institution that settles legal disputes and applies the law to legal cases. The term can refer to a judge or to a judge and jury. It also refers to a location for settling disputes.

Court of general jurisdiction: A court that hears any kind of civil or criminal case except those sent to a special court such as bankruptcy court.

Court of limited jurisdiction: Also called a *court of special jurisdiction*. These courts hear and try only special types of cases such as small-claims cases.

Court of original jurisdiction: The court where a case or hearing is first heard and action is initiated.

Court of special jurisdiction: A court that hears cases such as juvenile or traffic violation cases.

Courtrooms: Spaces used to conduct formal judicial proceedings. Courtrooms are the central facilities within the courthouse.

Cradle-to-cradle: Products that can either be reused or recycled or that will decompose when sent to a landfill.

Cradle-to-grave: Products that are used for a period of time and are not reused, recycled, or otherwise discarded before their useful life is complete.

Crash cart: A small, mobile cart equipped with medications and equipment to handle extreme emergencies within the nursing unit.

Credenza: A storage unit, usually 30 inches in height, that holds files and supplies. It is usually placed behind a desk in an office.

Credit union: A member cooperative type of bank.

Criminal case/court: A court that deals with offenses against state and/or federal laws.

Critical care unit (CCU): An inpatient unit for persons requiring intensive care, especially for cardiac conditions.

Critical Path Method (CPM): A scheduling method that shows a variety of tasks, using symbols and lines or other means to connect the tasks that must be accomplished in a certain order before the next set of tasks can be started.

Cruciform floor plan: The traditional Christian church floor plan, which includes the transept and the nave.

Cue-searching: Another term for way-finding. See **way-finding**.

Culture: Includes the knowledge, beliefs, customs, and morals of a group.

Curator: The individual in charge of a portion of a museum, such as the curator of decorative arts.

Curtain wall: An exterior wall that supports no weight except itself and is attached to structural members of the building.

Customer's own material (COM): Textiles selected by the designer that come from a source other than the furniture manufacturer.

Dead load: Permanent structural elements of the building such as partition walls.

Dealership: A retail sales and design office that is primarily associated with one or more manufacturers of commercial furniture.

Decibel (dB): The scale of measurement of sound.

Dedicated circuit: A separate circuit with its own hot, neutral, and ground wires, none of which are shared with any other circuit.

Delayering: A change in business structure that eliminates layers of management.

Deliverable: A tangible design product such as a construction drawing, a furniture plan, a specification, or a sample board.

Demand merchandise: A necessary item that encourages the public to shop. A bed in a furniture store is an example.

Dementia: A disease that leads to gradual deterioration in mental capacity and functioning due to disease or damage to the brain beyond normal aging. **Alzheimer's disease** is one of the most commonly diagnosed forms of dementia.

Demising wall: Any partition used to separate one tenant space from another. Each tenant is responsible for one-half of the thickness of all demising walls.

Demountable wall: A floor-to-ceiling partition that is held in place by tension and can generally be relocated easily with little demolition and new construction. Also called **movable wall**.

Dentist: A health care professional who treats a patient's teeth, gums, and related tissues.

Department manager: Commonly a third-level manager responsible for specific work activities.

Department store: A retail facility selling a wide variety of goods to the end user.

Design-build: One contract is given to a single entity for both the design of the facility and the construction of the building.

Design guidelines: Criteria developed by preservation commissions to help property owners rehabilitate existing structures in conformity with any new construction. This term also has other meanings, depending on the type of commercial project.

Design review: The process of ascertaining whether modifications to historic structures or settings meet standards of appropriateness established by a review board. This term also has other meanings, depending on the type of commercial project.

Deuce: A table for two in a restaurant.

Diocese: The district of churches governed by a bishop.

Direct glare: Glare coming from a light source.

Discount store: A retail facility selling a wide variety of goods to consumers at prices generally less than those found at department or specialty stores.

Display fixture: Equipment used to display products for sale in a variety of retail stores.

Display kitchen: A cooking area in the dining room of a restaurant positioned so that the guest can watch the chef prepare food.

District court: A local or other level of jurisdiction that has trial court responsibilities within a prescribed district or area.

Divider panel: A vertical support unit that, combined with others, forms the stations in open office systems projects.

Docent: A volunteer who provides tours and educational presentations, assists in fund-raising, and performs other support services at a museum.

Downsizing: A reduction in the number of employees in a business with the goal of being more responsive to customers and becoming more cost-effective.

Elopement-prevention system: A security system that seeks to stop patients in an Alzheimers facility from secretly leaving the facility.

Emergi-center: A freestanding facility that provides treatment comparable to that in a hospital emergency room for nonurgent conditions.

Employee churn: Turnover in the office staff.

Empaneled: Individuals selected to serve on a jury.

Empowerment: Allowing the employee to make certain decisions rather than requiring him or her to go through layers of managers.

En banc court: The type of courtroom used in an appeals court. It also refers to the entire appellate court hearing a case.

Energy efficient: Products that use less energy and perform as well as products that are not energy efficient.

Ergonomics: The scientific study of the physical functioning of humans in the environment.

Esteem need: The need for self-respect, admiration, and achievement.

Ethical behavior: Conduct that is considered right by and for those practicing the interior design profession.

Environmental theater: A theater where the performers and the audience share the same space.

Exhibit hall (or hall): A term used by some museums to refer to the spaces used for exhibits.

Extended use: Any process that increases the useful life of an old building. An extended use of a building might also be considered an adaptive use.

Facility management: The total nonfinancial asset management of a business.

Facility planning: The programming and space planning of offices and other areas of a commercial business.

Fairway: The portion of the course that extends from the tee to the green for each hole.

False-face preservation. The retention of only the façade of a historic building during conversion and rebuilding. Can also be called *façadism*.

Fast food restaurant: A quick-service restaurant that rarely provides wait staff service.

Fast track: Design projects that proceed from concept to completion very quickly. Often plans for one part of the project are being completed while other parts are already under construction to ensure early occupancy.

Feasibility study: An analysis of economic, demographic, and other criteria along with project goals and needs to determine if the project is possible and potentially profitable. It is generally conducted before design begins. It can be applied to any kind of commercial project.

Federal Deposit Insurance Corporation (FDIC): A federally operated institution that guarantees the deposits held within FDIC banks.

Federal Reserve System: The central banking system of the United States. A primary responsibility is to control the U.S. money supply.

FF&E: Acronym that stands for furniture, fixtures, and equipment.

Fiberoptics: A data cable utilizing a thin glass filament wire for the transmission of signals.

Fixture: The housing of the luminaire without the lamp. Many items used to display merchandise in stores are also referred to as fixtures.

Flash-coved base: Flooring and base material is monolithic.

Food service facility: Any retail space devoted to providing cooked or prepared food to consumers, whether that food is consumed on the premises or not.

Four pair: Four sets of two copper wires twisted together and covered by an insulating material. The most common type of voice and data cabling used today.

Franchise restaurant: One in which the owners purchase a license to operate the restaurant under the guidance and requirements of the company that holds the rights to the original concept. A franchise might also be associated with other types of commercial facilities such as retail stores and lodging facilities.

Free address: A system of unassigned work spaces that

is available to any employee of the firm on a first-come, first-served basis.

Free-flow system: A store planning system that allows displays and fixtures to be moved easily.

Front bar: That part of the bar in a beverage facility where customers may sit.

Front of the house: Those areas in a commercial facility such as a hotel or restaurant where employees have the most contact with the customer or public.

Full-service restaurant: A restaurant offering a large selection of menu items and a wait staff to take orders and serve the food.

Full-service salon: Provides hair cutting and styling, coloring, manicures, and pedicures.

Function space: One of the areas used in a lodging facility for conferences, meetings, trade shows, banquets, seminars, and other activities requiring space for large numbers of guests.

Gallery: A room or series of rooms for the display of works of art, objects, and antiquities. A gallery can also be a museum facility without a permanent collection of objects. In addition, a gallery can be a commercial facility for the display and sale of art, objects, and antiquities.

Gantt chart: See **bar chart**.

General contractor: A firm that has overall responsibility for actually building a building/project.

General lighting: Usually an overall level of illumination needed for general traffic movement and safety within any interior space.

General-use furniture: Conventional case goods made of wood or steel, such as desks, credenzas, and file cabinets.

Geriatrician: A physician who specializes in the diseases of senior citizens.

Geriatric outpatient clinic: Medical clinic that focuses on medical needs of the elderly.

Geriatrics: A branch of medicine that treats the aging senior population and deals with the diseases of old age.

Gerontology: Studies the aging process beginning with persons in their 40s and 50s.

Glare: Uncomfortably bright or reflected light that makes it difficult for an individual to see properly.

Graywater: Water from sinks, showers, and the laundry that is collected and lightly treated for reuse for watering lawns and other places where potable water is not required.

Green: The area at the end of the fairway with the hole.

Greenroom: The room backstage in a theater where benefactors are met and performers relax.

Greyfields: Obsolete retail and commercial sites located in cities, suburbs, and small towns that are now commonly targeted for sustainable uses.

Grid system: A store planning system that utilizes the internal layout in combination with the structural columns.

Group medical practice: A group of physicians who provide medical care to patients in a group office facility such as a medical office building.

Guesting: An assigned or unassigned work space provided to a visiting worker from another company.

Guestroom bay: The amount of space required to house a single standard guest room in a lodging facility.

Guest service: Any of the various services provided to enhance a guest's stay at a lodging facility, such as room service or valet and bell service.

Guild member: A volunteer at a museum who provides a variety of services such as educational presentations and tours.

Hard goods: Heavy merchandise that is often made of wood and metal and has substantial weight, such as large appliances and furniture.

Haute cuisine: "High food." Generally connotes very expensive food.

Healing environment: An environment providing patient-centered health care through environmental and design elements that are comforting and soothing.

Healthcare: The science and art of dealing with the maintenance of health and the prevention, alleviation, or cure of disease.

Health maintenance organization (HMO): A large group of multispecialty healthcare providers offering services to member patients at either group clinics or a physician's office suite.

Historic district: An area within a community that has been determined to be of specific historic significance to the community.

Historic district ordinance: A local law that identifies historic areas within the community and helps to preserve them. An ordinance might also establish a historic commission to oversee restoration efforts such as identifying historic properties and providing education.

Hole: A hole positioned on each green. The goal of the game of golf is to get the ball into the hole with as few strokes as possible.

Hospice: A facility or program designed to provide a caring environment for the terminally ill.

Hospital: A healthcare facility for the treatment, care, and housing of patients with illnesses, injuries, diseases, or other medical conditions.

Hostel: A lodging facility that often caters to students and budget-minded travelers who are looking for a clean room and few other services.

Hot desk: An unassigned work space. It gets its name from the concept that the chair may be "hot" from the previous user.

Hotel: A large lodging facility that offers guest rooms ranging from standard rooms to luxurious suites, along with a variety of food and beverage services and other amenities.

Hoteling: A system of unassigned work spaces available to workers by reservation.

Hotel management company: A group of individuals or a company which has made an agreement with the hotel owners to operate the hotel facility.

House: A term used to refer to the part of the theater occupied by the audience.

Hypermarket: A retail store with at least 200,000 square feet which sells a wide variety of general merchandise and/or food.

Impulse items: Items purchased spontaneously by the customer, dependent upon good display, usually at or near the point of sale.

In close proximity: A space-planning principle by which items used together (as in a retail store) are displayed next to or near each other.

Independent living: The absence of health services in the housing unit.

Independent restaurant: A restaurant owned and managed by an individual or a partnership, created from the individual's or partners' own imagination and creativity.

Infill building: Structures built to replace buildings that have been torn down or otherwise are missing from a street.

Inn: A small to medium-sized lodging facility that conveys the feeling of a small, comfortable home.

Inpatient: A patient who has been admitted to a hospital for medical care.

Instrumental activities of daily living (IADLs): Activities such as housekeeping and preparing meals.

Intensive care unit (ICU): Hospital inpatient unit for persons requiring specific types of intensive care due to the serious nature of their illness or injury.

Interior landmark: An interior that is at least 30 years old and has historic value.

Interlibrary loan: A system whereby a library user can request a book not available at a local library.

Intermediate-care facilities: A nursing home with a lower level of skilled care required.

Intern: A medical school graduate who is working to gain practical experience in the hospital.

Island window: A four-sided display window used with an arcade-style storefront. Most commonly used in clothing stores.

Investment bank: A banking facility that serves as a middleman in the buying and selling of securities such as stocks and bonds.

Jury-base chair: Many styles of chairs that use a leg flange, which allows the chair to be bolted to the floor.

Just-in-time work station: An unassigned work space where a worker or group of workers can congregate.

K-6-3-3: An educational plan calling for one year of kindergarten, six years of elementary school, three years of junior high school, and three years of high school.

Key: A renewable unit in a lodging facility.

Lamp: The glass bulb or tube that, with its inner workings, creates light.

Landing site: An unassigned work space where the employee "lands" rather than selects through a reservation.

Large animals: Animals such as horses, cows, pigs, and others of significant size.

Lateral file cabinet: Space-efficient file unit that is generally 18 inches deep and has a variety of widths.

Lavatory: A sink used for washing the hands.

Lease-hold improvement: Architectural finishes and other construction items installed by the tenant, not by the landlord. Also called *Tenant improvements.*

LEED certification: Leadership in Energy and Environmental Design (LEED) is a voluntary green rating system that helps define buildings that are healthy, profitable, and environmentally responsible.

Legitimate theater: A professional performance by members of Actors Equity or other professional performance unions.

Library: A collection of books and the building that houses the collection.

Licensed practical nurse (LPN): A nurse with a degree from a two-year nursing program.

Life cycle assessment (LCA): Studies materials, finished products, and buildings to evaluate their environmental and health impacts over their life.

Life cycle costing (LCC): A method of combining the actual cost of the products used in a project with the cost of maintenance and periodic replacement and the residual value of the items.

Line manager: An individual responsible for the activities directly related to a company's production of goods or services.

Live load: Such things as the weight of people, furniture, and equipment added to a building.

Local Area Network (LAN): A telecommunications network designed to eliminate the possibility of crossing signals that would interrupt the network.

Lodge: A lodging facility commonly associated with some kind of recreational activity such as skiing or fishing.

Lodging facilities: Facilities that provide sleeping accommodations for individuals away from their permanent home. Sometimes called a *lodging property* or *transient living facility.*

Long-term care: 24-hour housing and skilled nursing care for elderly persons who are medically ill. Also referred to as *nursing homes* or *skilled nursing facilities.*

Lounge: A beverage facility providing more seating than a bar, with more emphasis placed on some type of entertainment. A lounge may serve food.

Magnet store: A large, well-known chain store that attracts many customers to a shopping center. Also called an **anchor store.**

Maitre d': The head waiter in a restaurant.

Mall: A regional shopping center that has a large number of stores. Usually the largest shopping center in a community, offering retail stores, food and beverage facilities, and even entertainment facilities such as movie theaters.

Manager: An individual at any level whose responsibilities are to plan, control, organize, provide leadership, and make decisions concerning his or her employees.

Marche kitchen: A kitchen style in restaurants where customers walk up to a counter, place an order, and obtain freshly cooked food as they wait.

Marketing: Activity that occurs whenever goods change hand before being used. Selling, transporting, and supplying goods and services to consumers are part of marketing.

Marketing channel: A team of marketing institutions that direct a flow of goods or services from the producer to the final consumer.

Marketing concept: The comprehensive goal of every business organization—to satisfy consumers' needs while creating a profit.

Match play: A type of golf game in which a golfer or a team of golfers play against another golfer or team. The one with the best score at each hole wins the game.

Medical office building (MOB): An office building containing one or more office suites for specialized medical practitioners.

Medical treatment spaces: Spaces within a hospital where patients are treated. Also called *exam rooms.*

Megachurch: A church with regular attendance of 2000 persons or more.

Merchandising: A group of activities including market research, development of new products, coordination of manufacturing, and effective advertising and selling.

Merchandising blend: Combines the contents of the retail merchandise with the decision the consumer uses in making selections.

Merchant: A buyer or seller of commodities for profit.

Mezzanine: The lower balcony in a theater.

Milestone chart: A scheduling method that lists tasks in a column on the left and other information, such as target finishing dates, in a column on the right.

Mixed-use lifestyle project: In this context, it refers to a shopping center with stores, offices, and housing.

Model stock method: A system whereby the retailer determines the amount of floor space needed to stock a desired amount of merchandise.

Modified open plan: The plan of an office that combines some number of private closed offices with modular systems furniture workstations.

Motel: A lodging facility that caters to the traveler using an automobile.

Movable wall: See **demountable wall**.

Movie theater: A place where motion pictures are shown.

Multipurpose room: A classroom or activity space that can accommodate more than one kind of educational or social activity.

Museology: A program of advanced study that prepares an individual in the administration of museums.

Museum: An institution that collects art objects, antiquities, and/or other objects, for the purposes of preservation, display, study, and education.

National library: A library owned by the federal government.

Naturally occurring retirement community (NORC): Occurs when an apartment building or condominium is converted to a retirement facility or age-restricted facility.

Nave: The long, narrow part of a cruciform or Latin cross floor plan. This is where the congregation stands or sits during the service.

Need: An essential physiological or psychological requirement for the physical and mental welfare of the client or consumer.

Net area required: The square footage comprising of office spaces and support areas but excluding circulation spaces and architectural features such as columns and wall thicknesses.

Nonconforming use: A building or use of a building that is not in keeping with the area's zoning regulations or other structures in the area.

Nonselling space: A store's square footage allocated to storage, offices, restrooms, stockrooms, and other spaces not directly related to the sale of merchandise.

Nurse practitioner: A nurse with both bachelor's and master's degrees plus additional training in diagnosis who can provide some of the same care as a physician.

Nursing home: A healthcare facility where nursing and assisted care is given to patients unable to care for themselves.

Nursing unit: A cluster of patient rooms.

Office furnishings dealership: A retail store that sells commercial office furniture.

Office landscape: A design methodology developed in the 1950s using conventional furniture and plants but few if any wall partitions.

Offshore bank: A private bank located outside the United States.

Open plan: Planning methodology using movable wall panels and/or furniture items to divide the office space and create the work areas.

Open stacks: Shelves of library materials open to the public.

Open stage floor plan: A theater space plan where the stage projects into a portion of the audience so that the audience sits partially on three sides of the stage.

Opera house: A theater that primarily presents operas and other musical performances.

Operatory: A dental office treatment room.

Orchestra: In Greek theater, a circular space used by the chorus in front of the proscenium. Today, it is the section of seats in front of the stage and/or a group of musicians.

Organizational chart: A graphic representation of a business's formal organizational structure.

Outdated: A date after which medical products are no longer safely usable.

Outpatient: A patient who does not require admittance to a hospital for medical care or treatment.

Overbuilds: A way for developers to add selling or other space to an existing shopping center or mall.

Owner's representative: A person or firm hired by the client to act on behalf of the client with the designer.

Paroche: Two small doors or a curtain covering the sanctuary of a synagogue where the ark, holding the Torah, is located.

Parochial school: A school owned by a religious denomination.

Pastor: The head of a Catholic church parish.

Pedestal: A configuration of drawers 15 to 18 inches wide below a desktop or work surface.

Performance lighting: Lighting systems such as spot lights or track lights to permit illumination on speakers or performers.

Physical plant: A term usually associated with a building and the equipment within it in any kind of commercial facility.

Physician's assistant (PA): A nonphysician licensed to practice medicine under the supervision of a licensed physician.

Physiological need: Needs required for survival and basic human comfort, such as food, clothing, and shelter.

Platform: The area in many banks where loan officers and other account representatives have desks.

Plenum: An air space between the ceiling tiles and the structural ceiling in commercial buildings.

Point of sale (POS): The cash register or sales area of any kind of business where the purchase is made by a customer or entered on behalf of a customer.

Poke-through system: A method of providing electrical and telecommunications services to office panels by drilling holes through the floor deck and accessing wiring from the ceiling plenum below the floor deck.

Porte cochere: A canopy located over the driveway by the main entrance of a building, used to protect individuals from bad weather and call attention to the main entrance.

Postoccupancy evaluation (POE): A review of the completed project obtained some time after client move-in to obtain feedback on the successes and problems encountered in the project.

Posture chair: Desk chair that has a design providing improved posture and comfort.

Potable: Water that can be used for drinking and cooking.

Power entry: The point at which the building's electrical service is wired to a special vertical panel in open office furniture planning projects.

Power pole: A metal or wood box that is attached to the ceiling and can carry electrical, telephone, and data cables to systems panels or millwork cabinets.

Practice acts: Legislation that limits who may practice a profession.

Prefunction space: A secondary lobby outside a ballroom or other function spaces providing gathering space.

Premises: The space described to be rented.

Preservation: The utilization of methods to keep buildings and other objects and sites safe from harm or destruction.

Preservation commission: A municipal agency that designates and regulates historic districts and landmarks. It can also be called a *historic district review board*, *landmarks commission*, or *design review board*.

Priest: An ordained clergyman in the Anglican, Eastern Orthodox, or Catholic Church.

Primary care physician (PCP): A physician who deals with the overall health of the patient and is usually the first physician a patient sees.

Private library: A library owned by an individual or a business.

Private bank: A bank designed to provide services to very wealthy individuals.

Programming: The first phase of any project, in which information about the project is obtained by the interior designer.

Project management: A systematic process used to coordinate and control a design project from inception to completion.

Property: Another term for a lodging facility, including the building and all the land owned by the facility. May be applied to other commercial facilities.

Property or prop: An accessory piece used to finish the design of a set or supplementary scenery. Props are also used by actors.

Proposal: A marketing tool that outlines what will be done and how, who will do the work, and other information requested or provided.

Prosecution: An official of the court who represents the state or federal government in criminal cases.

Proscenium: The part of a stage in front of the curtain.

Proscenium-style floor plan: A theater design in which a heavy curtain or wall frames the stage.

Provost: A title given to the faculty member who has overall responsibility for the academic programs of a university.

Public library: A library open to the public and generally financed by the government.

Queuing space: Space provided for people to wait in line to be served, such as at a restaurant, hotel registration desk, or retail store cash/wrap desk.

Rabbi: The ordained teacher of Jewish law and the head of a local synagogue.

Radiofrequency identification: A type of electronic tag placed on valuable merchandise in a store.

Ramped window: Display window with a display floor higher in back than in front, either in a wedge or a tiered display shape.

Reconstruction: Rebuilding damaged buildings or creating structures and sites in the condition in which they originally existed.

Rector: The head of some denominations of Protestant churches.

Redundant cueing: Sending a message to more than one sensory mode.

Reengineering: A method of reorganizing a business and its way of operating to achieve improved overall performance.

Reflected glare: Glare coming from surrounding equipment.

Registered nurse (RN): A nurse with an undergraduate degree in nursing.

Registrar: Museum staff member responsible for cataloging objects that belong to or are loaned to a museum.

Rehabilitation: To return a building or an interior to its former use or to create a new use through alteration or refurbishment while retaining some of its original historic appearance.

Rehabilitation center: A medical center that provides care for patients who have had surgery or are recovering from such conditions as strokes, amputations, or paralysis.

Remodeling: The process of changing the appearance of a building's exterior or interior.

Renewable energy: Energy sources that are not depleted when used, such as solar energy.

Renovation: Altering an existing building using contemporary materials to extend its useful life and function. Renovations are rarely of an historic nature.

Rentable area: The total amount of square footage required for office and support spaces, including allowances for demising walls, and interior architectural features such as columns, mechanical chases, or closets, and even a portion of the exterior walls.

Repertory theater: A theater that presents several different productions each year.

Request for proposal (RFP): A document prepared by the client to request information from the designer regarding a potential design project.

Request for qualification (RFQ): A document prepared by the client to request information that focuses on the design staff's experience and qualifications related to a proposed project.

Research library: Library containing new and old materials of unusual subject or worth.

Resident: A physician who has finished an internship and is receiving extended training in a particular specialty of interest.

Residential hotel: The majority of guest accommodations are for long-term stays, perhaps months or even years.

Respite care: Temporary relief given to the primary caregiver caring for the senior or others. Care often provided by an adult day care center.

Restoration: Carefully returning a structure to its original appearance and integrity, thereby bringing the structure back to a former condition which now has historic significance.

Retail: Selling merchandise or services directly to the end user (final consumer).

Retail plan: Answers the questions concerning why, what, where, and how specific retail business activities are to be accomplished.

Retailer: A merchant who sells goods to the final consumer.

Retailing: The business activity of selling goods or services to the final consumer.

Retail store: A place of business in which merchandise is sold to the consumer.

Retirement resort: Another name for an active adult community.

Return: An additional desk unit that creates an L- or U-shaped desk. The return is only 25 inches high.

Rigid conduit: Heavy steel tube through which insulated wires are fed to carry electrical wiring.

Rood screen: A screen separating the chancel from the nave in a church.

Room: A separate unit, whether rentable or not, in a lodging facility.

Room mix: The configuration of different types of rooms required, based primarily on the size and number of beds in the facility.

Rounder: A type of store display fixture that is round.

Round of golf: Playing all 9 or 18 holes, depending on the length of the course.

Runs: Enclosed areas where animals such as dogs can run free.

Sacristy: A room attached to the church where the vestments and sacred utensils are stored.

Safety need: Human needs related to security and stability.

Salaried physician: A physician who works as an employee of a hospital, a government agency, or another organization rather than in private practice.

Sale: When merchandise and money change hands between the retailer and the consumer.

Sales/productivity ratio method: The retailer's allocation of selling space on the basis of sales per square foot for each merchandise group.

Sanctuary: The most sacred part of a religious facility. It is where the altar, if one is used, is placed.

Satellite office: A work center established away from the main office but convenient to the territory of outside workers. It is not generally a branch office.

Savings and loan association: A financial institution in which deposits are obtained from member customers and loaned out to members or other customers.

Savings bank: A type of bank that emphasizes savings and thrift to customers. Services focus on customer savings accounts. It can also be called a *mutual savings bank.*

Scent appeal: A retail merchandising technique that attempts to entice the consumer to buy through the introduction of aromas that are associated with products.

School library: A library housed in a K-12 school.

Scoping statement: A document detailing what will be done and possibly the estimated fee for the project.

Scriptorium: A place for copying books, mainly with religious content, within a monastic community

Sealed drawing: A drawing to which an architect has affixed his or her seal, which signifies that the architect is licensed by the state.

Seat turnover rate: The estimated number of times a table in a restaurant will be used in any one day.

Selection committee: A group of client representatives that will decide which firm gets the contract for a project.

Selling space: The amount of square footage in a store allocated to the display and sale of merchandise.

Senescence: The aging process.

Senior citizen: Generally refers to people 65 years of age and older.

Service bar: The area where the wait staff orders and picks up beverages for restaurant service.

Service counter: The area in a coffee shop (or other food service facility) where the customer orders and may wait for the order.

Service station: A work area located in the dining room of a restaurant to provide space for storing clean and dirty dishes, glasses, and coffee services.

Shadow box window: A small, completely enclosed display window at eye level.

Shared assigned work area: An office or station shared by two or more persons, perhaps by two part-time workers.

Shop signs: Store signage that acts more like outdoor advertising.

Shoplifting: The act of pilfering merchandise from a store.

Shopping center: A group of specialty retail stores and possibly service businesses.

Short list: A list of three to five design firms selected by the client to provide more detailed presentations on a pending project.

Sick building syndrome (SBS): An unhealthy condition caused by poor indoor air quality, poor lighting, and bad acoustics in the work environment.

Sight appeal: A retailing technique to entice the customer to buy using elements such as size, shape, contrast, or harmony.

Signage: Advertisement signs outside the premises of a store or other business describing the products or services provided by the business. Signage also refers to any kind of sign used inside a business facility to direct or inform customers.

Single pedestal desk: A desk with only one drawer pedestal.

Single-phase electrical service: The former standard for electrical service in most commercial buildings. It provides 240/120 volt service.

Single source of contact: The one person at the design firm or the client's place of business who has the authority to make decisions or provide information concerning the project.

Single-unit restaurant: A restaurant that exists only in one location. Usually independently owned.

Single-user toilet: A toilet facility that is used by only one person at a time.

Sink: All sinks other than lavatories, such as service, janitors', and kitchen sinks.

Skilled nursing facility (SNF): A state-licensed health-care facility providing 24-hour nursing care to patients.

Small animals: Dogs, cats, and rabbits are considered small animals.

Sociofugal: Furniture spacing that does not promote social interaction.

Sociopetal: Furniture spacing that promotes social interaction.

Soft goods: Merchandise that is considered to be soft and light in weight, such as apparel and linens.

Solace room: Place at a veterinary clinic or hospital where the pet/animal owner may have privacy after the animal has died.

Solo practitioner: A medical practitioner who is personally responsible for the medical care provided to patients.

Sommelier: A wine waiter.

Source document: The original document.

Sparkle lighting: A type of lighting produced by a variety of light sources that creates special effects and gives atmosphere to a space. Commonly used in restaurants and lodging facilities.

"Spec" or speculation: Developers of commercial property often build a building before it has any tenants in the hope that someone will lease it before or after construction is completed.

Special care units: Nursing facilities for the care of patients with dementia, Alzheimer's disease, and other critical or special needs.

Special collection: A library or museum collection, usually of historical or special archival materials, that requires special care to protect it from damage.

Special library: A facility that focuses on a certain subject matter. It may be privately owned or supported by a government agency or a university.

Specialty restaurant: One that serves a certain type of food, features a particular theme, or offers a certain style of service.

Spectator sports: Any type of sporting event in which the audience observes either an individual player or a team.

Speed rail: A place that holds bottles of the house beverages along the inside edge of the main bar cabinet so that bartenders can find them quickly.

Spiral fixture: A verticle curvilinear store fixture with hooks spaced evenly to hold clothing accessories such as belts.

Stacks: Shelves containing library materials.

Staff manager: An individual who provides support, advice, and expertise to line managers.

Stage: The part of the theater where the performance takes place.

Staging: Putting on a performance.

Stakeholder: An individual or group with a vested interest in the project, such as a member of the design team, the client, the architect, and a vendor.

Station: An individual work area set up using open office systems furniture.

"Stick built": A slang term for construction of partitions and other parts of a building on site.

Stick furniture: A term designers use to refer to wood office furniture and seating.

Stroke: Each swing of the golf club.

Stroke play: A golf game involving individual golfers keeping track of each stroke. The person with the fewest number of strokes wins the round.

Subs: An industry term for subcontractors.

Summer theater: Repertory theater organized for the summer season.

Sunset: A term related to legislation that includes automatic termination of the program or law unless it is reauthorized by the jurisdiction's legislature.

Supervisor: Commonly the lowest-level managers in a business, who are generally responsible for the employees who actually perform most of the work.

Supreme court: The highest court in either the state or federal judicial system.

Surgi-center: A freestanding healthcare facility where ambulatory outpatient surgery can be performed.

Sustainable design: Design that is done to meet the present needs of the project while considering the needs of future generations. Sometimes referred to as *green* design.

Synagogue: A house of worship for a Jewish congregation.

Systems creep: Every time a panel run makes a turn, an allowance must be made in the drawings for the thickness of the panel and hardware.

Systems furniture: Divider panels and components used to provide work areas for open office projects.

Tallith: A shawl with fringed ends worn over the head or shoulders during morning prayer in the Jewish religion.

Task lights: Luminaries that are sold to fit under shelf units (for systems furniture) or on a table or desk. They provide light to a particular area for the task.

Tee: Flat area of land where the golfer takes the first swing.

Tefillin: A phylactery worn by a member of the Jewish religion.

Telecommunication center: An executive office center where the main office has leased space where employees work. More than one corporation may have offices in the executive office center.

Telecommuting: A work arrangement in which workers spend most of their workday away from the main office and accomplish tasks using computers and modems or possibly telephones.

Teller cage: The former name for the teller window in a banking-type facility.

Tenant work letter: A contract used to supplement the lease describing the interior construction and finishing of a leased space. It specifies what the landlord will provide and what the tenant is responsible for.

Theater: A building, part of a building, or an outdoor venue in which performances of some kind are presented to an audience.

Theme appeal: In retail design, a technique establishing an environment directly related to a product, holiday, or special event.

Third-party project manager: An individual hired by the client to act as the client's agent during the project. This person differs from the project manager representing the interior design or architectural firm. Also can be called *owner's representative.*

Three-phase electrical service: The present standard in electrical service to commercial buildings. It provides 208 Y/120 volt service.

Title act: Legislation that limits the use of a specific title such as *interior designer, certified interior designer,* or *registered interior designer* to those who meet the requirements established by the jurisdiction.

Torah: The scrolls that contain the first five books of the Bible.

Trade fixtures: Materials or equipment attached to the building that was paid for by the tenant. When removed, they cannot damage the structure and are not an integral part of the structure.

Trade showroom: A wholesale store that displays furniture and other merchandise for those in the interior design or other trades. It is not open to the general public.

Transept: The transverse segment of a cruciform floor plan that crosses over the nave at the chancel end.

Transient living facility: A term sometimes applied to lodging properties.

Trial court: The place where most civil and criminal trials occur. It is also called the *court of original jurisdiction.*

Trunk showing: A presentation of merchandise by a designer or manufacturer at a retail store.

Trust company: A bank facility that specializes in the administration and control of large amounts of funds held in trust.

Twenty-five pair cable: A telecommunications cable that has 25 pairs of copper strands. Used in older commercial buildings and rarely installed in new buildings today.

Twisted pair: Two copper wires twisted together and shielded by an insulator. It is the simplest type of data and voice communication cable.

Unassigned office space: An office station or private office not assigned to any one individual. It can be used by a variety of individuals.

Under bar: The main working area of the bartender as he or she faces the guest.

Urgent care center: Neighborhood healthcare center providing noncritical emergency care.

Urinal: A special water closet found typically in a men's restroom.

Usable square footage: The amount of space that can be used for an office or other facility. It excludes demising and exterior walls, structural columns, chases, and electrical closets within the space.

Value engineering: A system for budgetary decision making that considers both the initial capital costs of the design or product specified and the life cycle costs of maintenance and replacement.

Veiling reflection: Reflection that occurs when a light source is reflected onto a worksurface or computer monitor, making it difficult to see paperwork or the images on the monitor.

Vertical file cabinet: The traditional filing unit, which is usually 15 to 18 inches wide by 28 inches deep.

Vestibule: A passage or small room between the entrance and the interior of a building.

Veterinarian: A professional who treats and cares for animals.

Vice president: A member of the second highest layer of management in large businesses. A vice president is generally responsible for a specific department or division in a corporation or other type of business.

Vignette: A display of furniture and accessories that is created to look like a real room.

Virtual banking: Transacting business from home or other locations via computer.

Virtual office: A setup where the worker has everything needed to do the job in a briefcase so that he or she does not report to a permanent office at a commercial facility.

Visual display terminal (VDT): A device that displays the data generated in the central processing unit. Sometimes called a *visual display unit* or *monitor*.

Visual merchandising: The art of displaying merchandise in store windows and other locations in the selling space. Previously referred to as *window dressers*.

Volatile organic compounds (VOCs): Toxic fumes emitted from carpeting, paints, the glues used to make composite woods in furniture, and many other common materials and products used in commercial and residential interiors.

Wait staff: Persons who provide service to customers in restaurants.

Want: A conscious impulse to acquire an object that promises a reward. In this book, it is discussed in the context of retail store design.

Water closet: A plumbing fixture in restrooms. Also called a *toilet*.

Waterfall front: A chair designed so that the seat pan is rounded and soft at the knee edge.

Way-finding: The use of signs, graphics, and directional arrows to help individuals find their way around complex properties and building interiors.

Well: The area in a courtroom consisting of the spaces for the litigants, jury, judge, and court staff in front of the bar.

What-if analysis: A method of forecasting what might happen to a schedule (or other processes) if a new element or situation occurs.

Wing: One of the sides of the stage behind the proscenium and the open stage out of sight of the audience.

WLAN: Wireless version of a Local Area Network.

Work plan: A document defining all the tasks needed to take a project from inception to completion.

Workstation: The space that represents an office in an open plan project.

Work surface: The product that serves as the desktop in an open plan project.

Index